Psychoanalytic Versions of
the Human Condition

Psychoanalytic Versions of the Human Condition

Philosophies of Life and Their Impact on Practice

EDITED BY

Paul Marcus and Alan Rosenberg

New York University Press

NEW YORK AND LONDON

NEW YORK UNIVERSITY PRESS
New York and London

Library of Congress Cataloging-in-Publication Data
Psychoanalytic versions of the human condition : philosophies
of life and their impact on practice / edited by Paul Marcus and
Alan Rosenberg.
p.   cm.
Includes bibliographical references and index.
ISBN 0-8147-5501-1 (hardcover : alk. paper). —
ISBN 0-8147-5608-5 (pbk.   )
1. Psychoanalysis. I. Marcus. Paul, 1953–   . II. Rosenberg,
Alan, 1939–   .
BF173.P7764   1998
150.19'5—dc21   96-6852
                          CIP

New York University Press books

Manufactured in the United States of America

10 9 8 7 6 5 4 3 2 1

To Irene
—PM

To discover a light of holiness in all the languages and wisdoms of the world.

—Rabbi Abraham Isaac Kook

Contents

Acknowledgments

I (Paul Marcus) would like to thank my colleagues at the Center for the Psychoanalytic Study of Social Trauma of the National Psychological Association for Psychoanalysis for their interest and encouragement in the development of this book. I am also grateful to my wife, Irene, a child and adult psychoanalyst, for her helpful editorial suggestions. Most of all, however, I am grateful to her for her cheerful willingness to give me the time to work on this book while she saw her patients and took care of just about everything else that needed to be done in our busy household. To my children, Raphael and Gabriela, I ask them to forgive me for sometimes not being as available to them as I would have liked because of book matters. I promise to make it up to them.

Alan Rosenberg would like to thank Morris Rabinowitz for his continued support and invaluable assistance throughout the preparation of this anthology.

Introduction

Paul Marcus and Alan Rosenberg

> It would be folly to attempt to define psychoanalysis on
> the basis of technique or practice. Techniques change
> over time and the essence of psychoanalysis lies in its
> ideas concerning the nature of its inquiry and its views
> of man, not its technical procedures.
> —Arnold M. Cooper

What is psychoanalysis? Considering the question carefully, one realizes
that the answer is neither straightforward nor simple. Psychoanalysis has
meant different things to different people, in different places and at different times in its history. How one defines psychoanalysis and who one
considers a psychoanalyst will differ greatly depending on the assumptions that one starts with and where one is culturally, geographically, and
linguistically situated. Psychoanalysis is best understood as a "floating
signifier," a term that is historically contingent. In a certain sense, then,
the question What is psychoanalysis? can be answered only in a context-
dependent and open-ended manner. The situation is made more complicated by those who consider themselves part of the psychoanalytic community yet are prone to intense conflicts, fierce loyalties, rivalries, and
even hatreds concerning what they believe constitutes the "fundamentals" of psychoanalysis. Psychoanalysis has also generated its share of
heretics and dissident thinkers who have been excommunicated by the
psychoanalytic establishment. One has only to remember the Freud-
Klein controversies and the Lacanian episode to see how the psychoanalytic establishment tries to silence dissent. Tolerance for difference does

not seem to be one of the qualities that institutional psychoanalysts have in abundance.

In the most general sense, then, this volume provides a forum for psychoanalytic scholars from a wide range of theoretical perspectives to answer the question What is psychoanalysis?[1] Contemporary psychoanalysis, says historian Fred Weinstein, "far from being a monolithic entity that can compel loyalty to a single perspective, as critics still sometimes describe it, is too fragmented to be constituted as a unified discipline." There was a time in the United States, he writes, "even rather recently, when proponents of 'mainstream psychoanalysis' could insist on the primacy of Freud's drive theory and the version of the world associated with it, man as pleasure seeking" in an erotically tinged universe (1990, p. 26). All this has changed. Today there are competing psychoanalytic versions of the world, markedly different ways of understanding the human condition. As Jay R. Greenberg and Stephen A. Mitchell point out, "Psychoanalytic models rest upon . . . irreconcilable claims concerning the human condition" (1983, p. 404).

Some examples: Kohut's theory of the self has transcended the classical boundaries of drive theory and the compartmentalization of the mind into agencies of continuing combat. Kohut suggests that classical psychoanalytic theory views the individual as "Guilty Man," who continuously struggles toward fulfillment of his drives. He lives under the sovereignty of the pleasure principle, endeavoring to reconcile inner conflict, and he is often frustrated in his goal of tension reduction by his own deficits or those of the people who brought him up. By dramatic contrast, Kohut's self theory formulates the concept of "Tragic Man," who struggles to fulfill the aims of his nuclear self. That is, Tragic Man is attempting to express the pattern of his very being, the ideals, ambitions, and self-expressive goals that transcend the pleasure principle (Monte 1980, p. 217). A second example: the British psychoanalytic tradition established by Melanie Klein, W. R. D. Fairbairn, D. W. Winnicott, Wilfred Bion, and others tends to characterize man as fundamentally object seeking. Relationships provide the primary data of psychoanalytic inquiry, for "psychology may be said to resolve itself into a study of the relationships of the individual to his objects" (Fairbairn, 1943, p. 60). Object relations theorists thus view the central human problematic not in terms of pleasure seeking, but in terms of establishing and maintaining gratifying and lasting relationships to one's objects.

In contrast, the hermeneutic critique of psychoanalysis advocated by such thinkers as Paul Ricoeur, Donald P. Spence, and Roy Schafer fostered still another psychoanalytic version of the world, and posited man as meaning-seeking. Psychoanalysis, they argue, is not a biological science as the classical model assumes, it is essentially an interpretive discipline. Thus, psychoanalysis must fundamentally address the meaning with which people endow their daily experience. From this perspective, the central problem for the person is to create a coherent narrative of self-identity.

To make matters more complicated, though all three versions of man—as pleasure seeking, object seeking, and meaning-seeking—have their advocates, there are important differences within each perspective. For example, Klein, Fairbairn, Bion and Winnicott are all, broadly speaking, object relations theorists in the British tradition, but they diverge from each other in many respects. As Weinstein notes, throughout the many acrid experiences that Freudian psychoanalysis had with C. G. Jung, Alfred Adler, Wilhelm Reich, Melanie Klein, Otto Rank, Karen Horney, Harry Stack Sullivan, and Erich Fromm, there was something that could still be called "mainstream psychoanalysis." But that situation no longer exists: the different theories are not "translatable"; the different perspectives share little more than concepts of unconscious mental processes, repression, and transference (1990, p. 27). Moreover, these different traditions are markedly divergent in the way they understand these basic concepts (e.g., Schafer's conceptualization of the unconscious differs from the Kleinian or object relations conceptualization and even more from a Jungian one). In other words, psychoanalysis today lacks the kind of unifying, authoritative core that proponents of the drive theory always provided. In Thomas Kuhn's terms, it lacks a disciplinary matrix for its activities as a science. The absence of any agreed on way to assess all the different psychoanalytic versions of the world is one important criterion of this deficiency (Weinstein, 1990, p. 27).

This situation has not gone unnoticed within the discipline: Schafer writes that "psychoanalysis emerges as an array of master narratives that dictate specific and incommensurable storylines for the interpretive work of analysis" (1992, p. xvii). Marshall Edelson notes with dismay the discipline's "preoccupation with new psychoanalytic theories" that in part reflects a "theory in crisis" characterized by "profound malaise" (1988, p. xiv). And Nathan G. Hale in his widely acclaimed book *The Rise and Crisis of Psychoanalysis in the United States* describes the "psychoanalytic crisis of the last decade" as "a crisis of clashing theories, competing modes of therapy, and uncertainties of professional identity" (1995, p. 360). Indeed, there may be much truth to Edith Kurzweil's claim that "the fragmentation of psychoanalytic theory proves . . . that the Freudians primarily are united by their profession rather than by their ideas" (1989, p. 283).

Given this proliferation of theories, each one clashing with the other as it tries to assert the supremacy of its "truths," the crucial question to ask is How does the reader decide which theory is "true"? We want to make clear where we stand on this important question. We also hope that our comments will help the reader avoid becoming overwhelmed or demoralized in the face of the "veritable Babel of theories," as the current psychoanalytic landscape has been characterized (Kurzweil, 1989, p. 256).

We believe that there are no facts that can be established outside a given theory; that is, all facts are theory laden. Rival ways of narrating facts within a language cannot be evaluated from a theory-neutral perspective, since the theory that generates them may be incommensurate. As Jane Flax has pointed out, we must be aware of the constructed nature of all narratives (1993, pp. 3–4). As there are no theory-neutral, uncontested methods for making a determination about which theory is "true," readers will have to make their own judgments about this issue. Says Flax,

> truth is discourse specific, the rules that determine what counts as truth in one domain may not apply in another . . . a discourse as a whole cannot be true or false, because truth is always contextual and rule dependent. No master rules or decision procedures are available that could govern all discourses or resolve conflicts among choices between them. Hence, truth claims may be incommensurate across discourse. (p. 40)

It should be emphasized that this way of conceptualizing truth has the support of many in the philosophical community. For example, the well-known analytic philosopher Donald Davidson emphasized the same point when he indicated that justificatory factors are always internal to discourse, are always intralinguistic: "[n]othing . . . no thing, makes sentences and theories true: not experience, . . . not the world, can make a sentence true" (Prado, 1995, p. 49).

The importance of appropriating such a discourse-relative approach for evaluating the truth claims of each theory is that it opens up space for reasonable dialogue between theoretical perspectives. By not having to consider each theory in terms of traditional philosophical correctness-criteria and absolute claims to truth, the reader is less likely to reflexively dismiss alternative viewpoints. Rather, he is more inclined to make the intellectual effort to empathize with, and critically reflect on, different viewpoints. Thus, this book aims to help psychoanalysts and psychotherapists understand the "metaphysical commitment" and "fundamentally different a priori premises" about the human condition that underlie their clinical theory and practice. "Only by an analysis of an analyst's vision of human experience can his theoretical position be accurately assessed" (Greenberg and Mitchell, 1983 p. 348). Although Freud (1964, p. 158) wrote that "Psychoanalysis, in my opinion, is incapable of creating a weltanschauung of its own"—an "intellectual construction that solves all the problems of existence uniformly on the basis of one overriding hypothesis"—we believe that each theoretical position to be represented in this book has attempted to do just that, and its clinical concepts reflect this goal. For example, as Jones (1991, p. 135) has pointed out, theories of transference are implicitly theories of the nature of the self: the self fashioned by its defenses against instincts (Freud), the self formed by its inner objects (Klein), the self structured by its internalized relationships (Kohut), "the self as a narcissistic misrecognition, represented through the symbolic order of language" (Lacan) (Elliott, 1994, p. 113). Another example: Winnicott had a markedly different view of culture and individual development, which was the basis for a perspective on religion, illusion, creativity, reality, and treatment that radically differed from Freud's. As Dale M. Moyer (1995, p. 460) points out, "Freud described the process of individual development in our culture as a tragedy of disillusionment through instinctual renunciation, separation, loss, and mourning. Winnicott saw the growth of the individual as 'a creative process of collaboration' (Phillips, 1988, p. 101) and our culture as 'a medium for self-realization' (ibid., p. 119)." Moreover, Moyer indicates, Freud formulated "his theory around the core catastrophe of castration; 'for Winnicott it was the annihilation of the core self by intrusion, a failure of the holding environment' (ibid., p. 149)." Psychotherapists need to be more aware of the fact that what they are providing for their patients is a conception of life, a particular story about the nature of the world and what it means to be human in that world. What constitutes "cure" in psychoanalysis can thus be viewed as the ideal of what it means to be human in that particular version of the world.

The acrimony in psychoanalytic circles among colleagues with different theoretical orientations is a complex phenomenon that warrants at least brief comment. Such behavior is a time-honored tradition, beginning with Freud's harsh treatment of those who disagreed with him. Ernest Jones's personal attacks on Sandor Ferenczi and Otto Rank are another appalling example in the history of psychoanalysis. One reason for this acrimony may be that psychoanalysts, like religious or political fundamentalists, are profoundly built into the same world that they theorize about. For example, analysts who are trained in a particular theoretical tradition have spent considerable effort, time, and money in their psychoanalytic education. As students, they are deeply emotionally invested in their demanding training, including the theoretical tradition that guides it. After graduation, analysts frequently practice their profession and publish within the theoretical tradition in which they were trained. They also tend to affiliate with institutes and socialize with colleagues who are compatible with their theoretical outlook. What we are intimating is the extent to which an analyst's professional (and personal) identity and theoretical commitments are fused. In a sense, to be a "Freudian" or "Kleinian" analyst is to participate in a particular mode of "being-in-the-world," one that gives form, direction, and meaning to one's life. Could it be that the acrimony found in psychoanalytic circles, as well as the tendency to insularity and theoretical xenophobia, is related to the fact that analysts are trying to protect the continuity and coherence of their hard-earned identity? Are analysts so mean-spirited when it comes to dealing with their theoretical differences with colleagues because they experience challenge, criticism, and alternative viewpoints as an assault on their way of "being-in-the-world"?

In light of the declared aim of this edited collection, each contributor representing a particular theorist and/or theoretical perspective was asked to answer the following questions:

1. What is your version of the world, your conception of the human condition? What are the central problematics that the individual struggles with within his larger social context?
2. In light of your conception of the human condition, how is individual psychopathology understood?
3. How does this conception of the human condition inform your type of clinical psychoanalysis as it attempts to alleviate individual psychopathology?

The authors were encouraged to state clearly how their position is dissimilar from other theoretical perspectives. Thus, one of the important aims of this book is to help psychoanalysts and psychodynamically oriented psychotherapists acquire a deeper and more comprehensive knowledge of how their theory, both explicitly and implicitly, guides their clinical practice.

This book attempts to provide a fairly comprehensive review of the major theoretical traditions in contemporary psychoanalysis. Since each chapter is separately introduced, we will make only a few general comments here about the structure of the volume.[2] The opening chapter by Edith Kurzweil provides a historical overview of the field that helps contextualize the subsequent essays. Then follow chapters on Carl Jung (Stein), Alfred Adler (Stein and Edwards), and Karen Horney (Price), followed by selections from the "British School" of object relations, Melanie Klein (Alford), Donald Winnicott (Gargiulo), Ronald Fairbairn (Grotstein), and Wilfred Bion (Eigen). Next we move to Heinz Kohut's important contributions (Ornstein) and the influential interpersonal perspective (Wilner). The chapter by Louis Sass explicates a broadly conceived hermeneutic approach, while Paul Roth examines the innovative contributions of Roy Schafer. The work of R. D. Laing (Thompson), an exemplar of existential psychoanalysis, and the highly original contributions of Jacques Lacan (Oliner) are explored in the next two chapters. Finally, we move to the "feminist" critique (Burack).

It should be mentioned that some of the contributors invited to participate in this volume were chosen because they were not lodged in the "mainstream" psychoanalytic world. For example, Edith Kurzweil, C. Fred Alford, Cynthia Burack, and Paul Roth are not practicing analysts. Rather, they come to this book primarily as psychoanalytically inspired academics. This editorial decision was in keeping with our belief that some of the most interesting work in psychoanalysis, especially as it relates to the issue of situating psychoanalysis in the wider culture, frequently comes from those outside the discipline. Such scholars are often less impeded by the need for psychoanalytic orthodoxy. As Adam Phillips has written,

> If a lot of the most interesting psychoanalytic theory and history is now written by people outside the profession, it is partly because the people inside the profession are prone to the kinds of fundamentalism that stifle imagination in the name of something often called professional integrity

(by "fundamentalism" I mean here the assumption that something can only be legitimately criticized from within). (1994, p. 149)

Perhaps at this point the reader is asking, "Where is the Freud chapter?" The answer is that the Freud chapter (Bass) is at the end of the book rather than at the beginning as is usually the case. A few words to explain this seemingly peculiar editorial decision seem necessary.

Freud belongs to the group of authors Michel Foucault calls the "founders of discursivity" (1984, p. 114). Like Homer, Aristotle, the Church fathers, Galileo, and Marx, for example, Freud is unique in that he is not just an author of his own work. He has "produced the possibilities and the rules for the formation of other texts. . . . an endless possibility of discourse" (p. 114). That is, Freud is the point of departure for all psychoanalytic theorizing. He is the author of a theory, tradition, and discipline in which all subsequent psychoanalysts must situate themselves one way or another. Some may agree in whole or in part with Freud while others disagree with his theory. All, however, are beholden to him for making their agreements or divergences possible. In this way, as Foucault points out, Freud has "created a possibility for something other than his discourse, yet something belonging to what he founded" (p. 114). Alan Bass makes a similar point in his Freud chapter when he argues for a psychoanalysis that strives to be more like an endless movement that perpetually undoes itself. This, then, is why the Freud chapter is at the end of the book. It speaks to the need for an open-ended reading of Freud, one that is historically contingent, dynamic, and contestable (Flax, 1993). In this sense, as Bass points out, "the future of psychoanalysis belongs in its Freudian past."

Every anthology, to some extent, reflects the convictions, biases and prejudices of its editors. In other words, what is true for the theories and theorists discussed in this volume is also true for the editors. While this introduction is not the place to situate our book in its personal, historical, and ideological context, we do think it necessary to say something about our perspective as it relates to the aims of this book.

To begin with, early on we were faced with a challenge to the very assumptions of the volume, which forced us to reflect critically on what we thought we were trying to accomplish. Alan Bass (Freud) and Michelle Price (Horney) raised similar objections to our formulation of the three questions that each author was supposed to address. They argued that to ask about Freud or Horney's "conception of the human condition" assumed a systematicity that could be, and should be, objectively observed, studied, and inscribed. Both Bass and Price, in other words, raised a post-modern criticism about our request to present a theory in terms of a highly formalized, codified series of propositions, one that tends to smooth over complexities, ambiguities, and contradictions. Bass and Price want to articulate psychoanalytic theory in a way that is less susceptible to closure, that is more open-ended and contested. Such an approach would be less limiting and promote greater cross-fertilization among the many different points of view. Bass and Price thus raised very important and "disruptive" questions that forced us to consider another way of problematizing the issues that this book tries to raise. We leave it to the reader to judge the usefulness of each approach for helping us see aspects of the discipline that we have not seen before.

We will conclude by commenting on the one characteristic of this collection that is impossible to miss, namely, the large number and diversity of theories that make up the contemporary psychoanalytic landscape. As Benjamin Wolstein has noted, "the pluralism of working perspectives on psychoanalytic metapsychology may not sit well with those who seek the coherence, orderliness, and authority of a single tradition. Pluralism is, nonetheless, an irrepressible and undeniable fact of contemporary psychoanalytic life" (1993, p. 661).

We believe that the diversity of psychoanalytic theories and clinical approaches does not necessarily reflect conceptual disarray and crisis; rather, it reflects the fact that no one theory has the entire "truth" about the human condition (if we can still speak of such a truth). In today's postmodern world, it is misguided to think otherwise. As Anthony Elliott has pointed out, "no single theory will be able to confront the contemporary, multidimensional identities of the postmodern world. . . . the variety of theories in contemporary psychoanalysis . . . are therefore better understood as images of what it feels like to live in the multidimensional world of modernity" (1994, p. 168). We should recognize that the theoretical differences among contemporary psychoanalysts, at least at this time in psychoanalytic history, are too vast to be meaningfully and effectively bridged. There is little, if any, common ground. Rather, our efforts, he says, might more fruitfully be spent on "the articulation of differences" such that we shall "be able to set psychoanalysis within the wider social context, and to theorize the kinds of political [and social] effects which theories produce" (p. 167). In other words, we hope that through a method of "comparative psychoanalysis," as Schafer has called it, our book will encourage the practitioner to see the profoundly moral component to psychoanalytic discourse and practice. Psychoanalytic theorizing and clinical technique should be engaged as a politically inspired and informed social practice lodged in a particular social and historical context with both positive and negative effects. As a discursive formation it can best be judged in terms of yet to be adequately developed "discourse-specific means and tests for the production of knowledge" (Flax, 1993, p. 54). Most important, we hope that our book induces in the reader a more consciously self-critical attitude toward theory and clinical practice, for only then will the discipline better comprehend its potentially "dangerous" side, as Foucault calls it: Psychoanalysis has, says Stephen Frosh (1987, p. 268),

> partaken of reactionary political assumptions, has joined in the chorus of voices raised against dissent, has supported the oppression of women, and neglected the extent to which social behaviors and institutions are constructed rather than biologically determined. Psychoanalytic theory has also frequently been conformist, either because of its underlying assumptions or despite them.

Only by a more self-reflexive attitude toward psychoanalysis—about the politics of psychoanalytic knowledge (especially its differing claims about what constitutes the human condition), and about how the profession is situated and operates in our contemporary culture—will the discipline be better able to decide for itself what kind of psychoanalysis it wants and how its future is to be charted.

NOTES

1. The question of what constitutes a discipline is a very complex one. For an extremely interesting treatment of this problem see Foucault (1972, pp. 31–70) and Dreyfus and Rabinow's commentary on Foucault (1983, pp. 58–71).

2. The editors want to acknowledge the following books, which were especially helpful in writing the chapter introductions: Monte (1980), Greenberg and Mitchell (1983); Frosh (1987), and Elliott (1994).

REFERENCES

Cooper, Arnold M. 1984. "Psychoanalysis at one hundred: Beginnings of maturity." *Journal of the American Psychoanalytic Association* 32, no. 4: 245–67.

Dreyfus, Hubert L., and Rabinow, Paul. 1983. *Beyond Structuralism and Hermeneutics.* 2d. ed. Chicago: University of Chicago Press.

Edelson, Marshall. 1988. *Psychoanalysis: A theory in crisis.* Chicago: University of Chicago Press.

Elliott, Anthony. 1994. *Psychoanalytic theory.* Oxford: Blackwell.

Fairbairn, W. R. D. 1943. *Object relations theory of the personality.* New York: Basic Books.

Flax, Jane. 1993. *Disputed subjects.* New York: Routledge.

Foucault, Michel. 1972. *The archaeology of knowledge and the discourse on language.* Trans. by A. M. Sheridan Smith. New York: Pantheon.

————. 1984. "What is an author?" In Paul Rabinow (ed.), *Foucault reader.* New York: Pantheon, pp. 101–20.

Freud, Sigmund. 1964. "The question of a *Weltanschauung*" In *Standard edition,* vol. 22, pp. 158–86. London: Hogarth Press

Frosh, Stephen. 1987. *The politics of psychoanalysis.* New Haven: Yale University Press.

Greenberg, Jay R., and Mitchell, Stephen A. 1983. *Object relations in psychoanalytic theory.* Cambridge: Harvard University Press.

Hale, Nathan G. 1995. *The rise and crisis of psychoanalysis in the United States.* New York: Oxford University Press.

Jones, James W. 1991. *Contemporary psychoanalysis and religion.* New Haven: Yale University Press.

Kurzweil, Edith. 1989. *The Freudians: A comparative perspective.* New Haven: Yale University Press.

Monte, Christopher F. 1980. *Beneath the mask.* New York: Holt, Rinehart and Winston.

Moyer, Dale M. 1995. Book review in *Psychoanalytic Books,* 6, no. 3: 456–63.

Phillips, Adam. 1988. *Winnicott.* Cambridge: Harvard University Press.

————. 1994. *On flirtation.* Cambridge: Harvard University Press.

Prado, C. G. 1995. *Starting with Foucault.* Boulder: Westview Press.

Schafer, Roy. 1992. *Retelling a life.* New York: Basic Books.

Weinstein, Fred. 1990. *History and theory after the fall.* Chicago: University of Chicago Press.

Wolstein, Benjamin. 1993. Book review in *Psychoanalytic Review* 80, no. 4: 66.

Chapter One

Historical Overview
A Mosaic of Psychoanalytic Therapies

Edith Kurzweil

Psychoanalysis speaks in many voices. It has spawned myriads of cultural and clinical theories as well as therapies—some of them more or less classical, others hewing closely to the thought of one or another of Freud's disciples, and yet others resulting from amalgams of concepts and postmodern discourses. It is sometimes hard to find one's way among these many versions of psychoanalysis, if only because the proponents of each of them are certain that their own is superior to all others. Nevertheless, psychoanalysis has saturated our culture in less than a hundred years. When Freud wrote to one of his disciples that he had brought them the plague, he might have added, in his prescient way, that he had brought them a worldview, or, better yet, that he had brought them a multiplicity of worldviews they needed to have explained. Such explanations now are necessary precisely because psychoanalysis has become ubiquitous: most of its practitioners, involved as they are in helping their patients uncover unconscious materials, have become detached from the roots and history of the concepts they take for granted. As a rule, they share the theoretical assumptions of the colleagues within their institutes. Moreover, literary critics, feminist and postmodern theorists, and deconstructionists have superimposed their own views of psychoanalysis and have extended these discussions. But they apply psychoanalytic ideas in order to prove all sorts of cultural phenomena. Their speculations and conclusions, in turn, feed back into clinical practices. Ultimately, I believe, psychoanalysis will end up as a research tool to be used or discarded by individual therapists in line with their preference, and defended against by ever more defensive patients.

Yes, Freud was a product of his Zeitgeist, of fin-de-siècle Vienna, where philosophers, natural scientists, and other intellectuals were searching for far-reaching scientific explanations, where artistic and literary life was at a new height, where citizens danced to Strauss waltzes, gave vent to exalted eroticism, and acted on their chauvinistic double standards and new liberalism. Freud's theories subsumed all these cultural givens (and their changes over his lifetime) in his attempts to uncover and "systematize" the unconscious. And he kept reformulating and deepening his insights. These extended over almost fifty years, and are available to us in his extensive writings and correspondence. However, Freud's descendants have elaborated on the ideas that best suited their own predilections and thus have adhered to a multiplicity of "competing" Freudian Weltanschauungen, and have created clinical practices that directly or indirectly evolved from them. Indeed, many of today's therapists who may or may not consider themselves Freudian often do not know where their own concepts converge with, or diverge from, those who have had a different training. By carefully reading Alan Bass's chapter on Freud's emerging theories and practices, they will be able to better contextualize their own location within these views.

The early disciples addressed and free-associated not only to microdynamic but also to macrosocial and cultural issues. Thus it was inevitable that the rapid accumulation of multiple data on psychoanalysis, as well as the international growth of the movement, would lead to disagreements. The splitting off by some of the early followers, such as Carl Jung and Alfred Adler in 1911 and 1913, centered on conflicting principles. The differing conceptions of femininity by, for instance, Karen Horney and Melanie Klein in the 1920s, ultimately did not manage to remain under the same roof. And the so-called American ego psychology, which evolved primarily from Freud's work "The Ego and the Id" (1923), finally proved theoretically incompatible with conceptions based on Freud's "Project" of 1895 and/or on his "topographic" theory of the drives.

Before outlining the filiations and clinical consequences of specific theoretical paths to the unconscious, which in essence is what psychoanalysis (and the chapters in this book) is all about, we should recall that even in his wildest dreams Freud did not foresee that his *Interpretation of Dreams* (1900) would end up as a guidepost, as the explicit or implicit basis for what, already in 1966, Phillip Reiff called our therapeutic society. This book, of course, proves that Reiff was correct: the contributors to this volume do not question any more that therapy is central to our as-

sumptions about the human condition. Instead, they have assembled fifteen of the most consequential conceptualizations that fuel clinical psychoanalytic practices. Thereby, they are informing the readers of this volume that there are other ways to "skin the cat" than those taught in their
own institutes, and that clinical theory is based on prevalent assumptions
and on an underlying worldview.

Because psychoanalysis was international from the start, ideas grown
on "foreign" soil have tended to take root when they were thought to be
useful. These ideas include, for instance, concepts by the "British School"
of Melanie Klein, Wilfred R. Bion, Ronald Fairbairn, and Donald W.
Winnicott, and by the "French Freud," Jacques Lacan. Most recently,
Sandor Ferenczi's focus on "active" technique, "empathic" understanding, and "mutual analysis" is striking a chord, because these have recently been deemed to offer insights into some of our general preoccupations, such as child abuse and egalitarian interactions and ideals. As always is the case, these are responses to problems posed by the larger
social context within which every therapist must function. To better understand how all of this came about, we must recall the Zeitgeist and social conditions out of which Freud's thought arose. Many of the psychological riddles he tried to solve were built into his successive systems; others might be attributed to his own or some of his disciples' personalities;
and yet others were due to temporal or local preoccupations. Again, his
theoretical and clinical descendants have been at liberty to focus and
elaborate on one or more of these concerns.

Most of the handful of early followers who, in 1902, began to meet in
Freud's study on Wednesday evenings were perceiving the road to the unconscious as the best, or only, means for implementing their leftist ideals.
They were doctors and medical students, artists and writers, and they
tended to favor Marxist and socialist models of society. Thus they shared
their excitement, their biting humor and independence, along with their
dreams and disagreements. Essentially, they expected to cure neuroses
and, in the process, to learn about healing their society. That, rather than
clinical techniques and organizational questions that now divide the various psychoanalytic groups, was what they fought over, at least at first,
as becomes clear when we read the minutes of the Vienna Psychoanalytic
Society. They were rebels with a cause, and were either attacked or ignored by most of their contemporaries and by the medical establishment.

The psychoanalysts' global aims were evident, already in 1908, at the
First International Psycho-Analytical Congress in Salzburg, where San-

dor Ferenczi denounced the prevalent teaching methods as leading to faulty character development and serious illness. Schools, he said, were hothouses fostering neurosis. He promised that psychoanalysis, by doing away with excessive repression, would transform pedagogy and society. Freud as well urged teachers and nursery school workers to monitor children's emotional behavior, although he soon decided that they ought first to be analyzed in order to do so properly. Adler, on the other hand, was willing to risk losing "the gold of psychoanalysis"—that is, unveiling the unconscious—in order to implement psychoanalytic pedagogy and institute socialism sooner rather than later. The break with Jung was over his more cultural and "archaic" conceptualization of the unconscious, although there also were disagreements having to do with the direction of the movement and dissension among the disciples.

Actually, they all expected to heal their society along with their patients, but in their own way. As Freud explained in his "History of the Psychoanalytic Movement" (1914), he expected to supply a macrotheory and/or philosophy of society and a clinical theory of healing patients, and, simultaneously, to build an international movement that would further these aims. But whereas each of these three major endeavors (there are others) has depended on the success of the other two, each of them had to be advanced in its own right without, however, becoming disengaged from the others. Only by developing and improving clinical techniques, Freud's disciples agreed, would they be able to penetrate to the unconscious origins of their patients' neuroses. Fairly soon, Freud realized that these origins would remain elusive, that successive abreactions did not necessarily cure, and that patients were putting up ever more clever psychic defenses. These perceptions, in turn, generated ever greater efforts to improve clinical techniques.

Within this plethora of interests, Freud's disciples would pick those closest to their hearts or, as some have said, to their neuroses. And in addition to their priorities and personal idiosyncracies, they were inspired by the social and political preoccupations in their immediate environments. Thus they could not possibly have been as attuned to each other as Freud would have wanted them to be. On the other hand, psychoanalysis could not have taken off the way it did if the disciples had not been such a bunch of individualists who were using their own neuroses to learn about the (individual and/or collective) unconscious. In fact, the minutes of the Vienna Psychoanalytic Society demonstrate that advances were made with the help of materials and dreams they brought to the meetings and the free associations and disagreements these encouraged, which, in turn, provided the grist for Freud's theoretical formulations.

The therapies discussed in this book represent some of the dissident and divergent paths that followed from the concepts proffered by the disciples, and from those of later offshoots. To a greater or lesser extent the contributors focus on their own techniques and ways of penetrating to the unconscious of their patients (some call them clients), although a few, such as Burack, Alford, and Price, also are concerned with "theorizing" about psychoanalysis and its current role within American culture rather than with therapy. Still, all the contributors hold (explicit or implicit) views that relate to the social context within which therapy functions. I will address some of these issues as I go on to position the specific contributions in relation to the authors' views of the individual struggles their patients face, their identifications, and their understandings of the human condition, which, in turn, inform their clinical work. The very vitality of psychoanalysis, in its insistence on individual intellectual and clinical involvement, is a process rather than a fixed set of ideas; and "schools" of psychoanalysis, in order to remain viable, cannot afford to become static. Freud and his followers were keenly aware of these issues and addressed them all along. And they were conscious of the fact that they were influencing history as well as the individuals on their couches. But for my present purpose, I am leaving aside psychoanalysis's general influence, and am highlighting only issues that, I believe, impinge on the American therapeutic milieu.

The Impact of the Movement, the International Psychoanalytic Association, and the Question of Lay Analysis

I am convinced that the early disputes, which in addition to conceptions of psychoanalysis were, at least to some extent, rooted in conflicting and local politics, in specific ways of integrating psychoanalysis, and in the role it played or didn't play in national contexts, still are haunting today's therapists. This was bound to happen, for Freud's movement was set up as a loose association of individuals from around the world who were expected to disseminate psychoanalysis in very different social, religious, and cultural contexts. But Freud's Viennese disciples, for the most part, were Jewish, and he did not want psychoanalysis to be perceived as a

Jewish science. Such a designation was bound to automatically denigrate its validity and content, and thus the movement itself. That is why Freud bent over backwards to welcome and favor non-Jews, first Carl Jung and then Ernest Jones.

Volumes have been written on whether Freud fully embraced Judaism or was a god-less Jew. Indeed, he was a Viennese Jew, which meant that he neither embraced nor denied being Jewish; that he was more or less familiar with Jewish religion but did not practice it even if he (periodically and/or partially) observed the major holidays; that he was assimilated without becoming inauthentic; and that he was aware of—and tried to ignore—the pervasive but "benign" anti-Semitism in an Austria whose population was 99 percent Catholic. Whether or not Jung was anti-Semitic is yet another moot point, although one may argue that his innate religious leanings did impinge on the way he pursued and conceptualized psychoanalysis. A similar argument could be made for such American pioneers as, for instance, James Jackson Putnam and William Alanson White, for the Swiss pastor Oscar Pfister, and later on for Jacques Lacan. However, I believe that the universalistic aims of psychoanalysis and the postulate of an unconscious not tied to religion or nationality overrode the religious differences among enlightened individuals who were intent on advancing humanistic aims.

As the movement took hold, and the International Psychoanalytic Association (IPA) assumed a life of its own, its leading members were negotiating psychoanalysis's role in their own countries—adapting their practices to their society's existing and potential membership, to its laws, and to its general milieu. By 1927 Adlerians and Jungians had their own associations. Freudian analysts in most European countries originally had been doctors, psychiatrists, lawyers, artists, educators, and social workers, and most of them had been trained in Vienna's or Berlin's psychoanalytic institutes. In America, however, the American Psychoanalytic Association (APA) had been formed by physicians, and most of the founders of the New York Psychoanalytic Society (NYPS) as well had had medical rather than psychoanalytic training. Nevertheless, given the American milieu, with its lack of control over professional access, both priests and charlatans soon started to claim they were psychoanalysts. Furthermore, the existing psychoanalytic associations, unlike their European counterparts, did not have training institutes. Therefore, their medical degree alone could distinguish American psychoanalysts from the charlatans, so that they felt compelled to adamantly oppose Freud's pleas to admit laypersons even after he spelled out his argument in "On the Question of Lay Analysis" (1926). This is not to excuse the perpetuation of this practice or to explain subsequent quarrels (including the 1985 lawsuit in which American psychologists sued the American, New York, and Columbia Institutes and the International Psychoanalytic Association for loss of income because they had been training only medical doctors), but only to point out that matters extrinsic to psychoanalytic practice have weighed heavily on psychoanalytic organizations.

Later on, with the profusion of training facilities (both those created due to subsequent splits among institutes attached to the IPA and the APA, and those created in opposition to them or outside them) and with the mushrooming of "hybrid" therapies, it has become impossible to keep track of them all. This is even more true of therapists, some of whom set themselves up in private practice or run group sessions in clinics, schools, hospitals, or under other auspices. The large majority among them, however, have earned the necessary credentials in one or more of the therapies represented in this book. To distinguish among these therapies, we must recall Freud's and his disciples' early concepts, to which some contemporary therapists often return. These also contain implicit worldviews and are part of the history of the psychoanalytic movement.

As we know, Freud set out to separate psychoanalysis from philosophy and to demonstrate that by systematically pursuing the road to the unconscious he would penetrate to the roots of the human psyche. Throughout his life he insisted that this pursuit—which was inspired by his early observations based on neurophysiology—was a scientific one. The scientific aspect, of course, related most of all to the techniques he and his followers would develop, whereas the application of these techniques would become an "art." For therapists had (and have) to intuit when to use or refrain from revealing their insights, at what point to interpret or not to do so, and how to adapt, instinctively, their clinical knowledge to the analytic session. In fact, when Freud spoke of psychoanalysis as a science, he did not refer to his worldview, but to the means it offered for curing mental illness, for helping the patient come to terms with his world. However, in order to demonstrate that psychoanalysis had nothing to do with mind healers, he had to underline its scientific basis.

Neither Freud nor his early and later followers have sufficiently taken account of the fact that during the past century the human condition itself has been altering more than ever before as a result of migrations, technological changes, and the demands on modern men and women (including internal ones). In turn, these were bound to heighten whatever neurosis had been brewing since childhood. This is not to say that the capacity of the human psyche has significantly altered (another moot issue), but only that society's demands on it have grown by leaps and bounds. (These changes are discussed in the psychoanalytic literature on shifts in patients' symptoms.) Moreover, in our century, philosophy, science, and psychology have splintered into myriads of specialties, so that almost none of today's psychoanalysts are as familiar with the ins and outs of other disciplines as Freud's contemporaries were. As we will note below, some hermeneuticists, such as Paul Ricoeur and Roy Schafer, have concentrated on rectifying this situation. They attempt to "fuse" philosophical assumptions with Freud's scientific observations. Still, Freud primarily was referring to observations of the emerging unconscious by psychoanalysts, and to his own systematization of these observations into theoretical syntheses.

Inevitably, American psychoanalysts until recently have been defining themselves in relation to so-called drive theory, which in Europe often is referred to as "American ego psychology." After World War II the elaborations on Freud's structural model—as synthesized by Hartmann, Kris, and Loewenstein (1946)—hugged the limelight and became the central Freudian paradigm; therefore it was perceived as the psychoanalysts' worldview until the end of the 1960s. German Freudians, for instance, who focus on this theory's emphasis on the ego and observe the implications this has for adaptation, go on to suggest that a greater concern with the id (it alone is the drive) is called for. Such a focus would allow for a more salient analysis of unconscious aspects of individuals' socialization—that is, for ferreting out the inescapable remnants of their Nazi past. Still, German psychoanalysts, just like their American brethren, tend to analyze defenses as "the cornerstone(s) on which the whole structure of psychoanalysis rests" (Freud, 1914, p. 16) since defenses, inescapably, point to the unbearable reality the patient seeks to avoid, and which provide the psychoanalyst with clues that may assist in making it bearable.

Freud, Adler, and Jung

Freud and his disciples did not share a consistent worldview. If they had, psychoanalysis would have lost the dynamic qualities on which it thrives, or survives. According to Freud, a consistent worldview would create a "system of religion and philosophy [and thus] lay open the paths which lead to psychosis." As Alan Bass observes, such a practice would turn the psychoanalytic dyad into a folie à deux. Also, the increasing separation of psychoanalytic treatment from general medicine, and the secondary position accorded somatic symptoms, which belong to the scientific specialization of our times, have entailed putting a certain distance between what Freud always considered inseparable components of the individual—the psychic, biological, and social causes of neurosis and psychosis. In this context, we cannot emphasize enough the extent to which psychoanalysis itself has changed modern culture. Freud's Emma, Anna O., and Elizabeth von R. lived in a society that eschewed female sexuality and accepted male infidelity and adultery. To the horror of some of his contemporaries, Freud demonstrated that these factors were the bedrock of these patients' hysteria. Eventually, the recognition that he was correct led to the gradual (and public) acknowledgment that good women too are sexual beings. In the process, views about women, childhood sexuality and child-rearing practices were drastically changed, and brought forth a variety of theories and practices—not all of them Freudian. These too were incorporated into some of the offshoots of psychoanalysis and the currently popular "psychoanalytic narratives."

I tend to go along with the German psychoanalyst Alfred Lorenzer's conclusion that both Alfred Adler and Carl G. Jung theoretically rejected the sexual moment, but did so in opposite directions—Adler by stressing the rational psychic components and Jung the irrational ones. Nevertheless, as Stein and Edwards and Murray Stein, in this volume, also point out, they both held on to the notion of the unconscious. Stein and Edwards emphasize that Adler focused on the ego early on, and on the social influences that create the "realm of meanings" for individuals. They maintain that many anthropologists, sociologists, biologists, mathematicians, physicists, and psychotherapists have been motivated by Adler's thought, which, in my opinion, testifies to his global formulations about the human condition rather than his direct impact on these disciplines. Still, Stein and Edwards show that Adler's original optimism, his psychology based on feelings of community, and the continuing emphasis on the fact that every individual depends on others remain the linchpins of today's Adlerian therapists. But they do not refer to his active, socialist bent or his relations to Freud. Actually, Adler, an active member of Vienna's radical and leftist Social Democratic Party, was more influential than Freud. He succeeded not only in instituting progressive education in the city's public school system, but also in influencing social policy about mental health, rehabilitation for delinquents, and early childhood education. His concepts of personality development and of inferiority feelings still remain central to the worldview of Adlerian therapists, and to their efforts in helping their clients find better means of coping in their environment. These efforts were inspired by Adler's Marxist ideals. So, whereas Adler was most likely to sensitize his patients to social injustices, at least as part of the roots of their exaggerated feelings of inferiority, today's Adlerians focus on physical handicaps, family dynamics, and societal presuppositions and biases. By "understanding their clients' use of symptoms in order to diminish inferiority feelings and to encourage and stimulate cooperation," they no longer expect to change society.

Stein and Edwards systematically outline the twelve stages of Adlerian psychotherapy. But actual therapy, they state, is "spontaneous and creative" rather than rigidly programmatic—by "seeing and feeling what the client is experiencing," by eliciting background information, by clarifying beliefs, by encouraging new experiences, and so forth. Thereby, it seems to me, they are pursuing the same goals as the classical Freudians. Nor should we be surprised: Adler did not reject Freud's basic premises or his assumption that ultimately unconscious structures must be altered. But Freudians are reluctant to use such conscious, direct means. Maybe in a culture where more individuals are attuned to, and in need of, direct and easy ways of receiving psychotherapy to boost their self-esteem, cognitive approaches are more efficacious. In any event, Stein and Edwards correctly summarize Adler's stance by stating that "psychotherapy was to help people contribute to the social evolution of mankind." But were he alive, he would reject vehemently his follower Alexander Müller's notion of "working in partnership with God." Adler's atheism was at least as strong as Freud's.

Jung, on the other hand, was too close to religion for Freud's taste: he postulated that "the nature of the human psyche embraces . . .instinctual-somatic elements (i.e., impulses) at one end of a spectrum and spiritual-archetypal elements (i.e., images and ideas) at the other." They broke over the fact that such a formulation does not allow for the centrality of sexuality—that is, for the Oedipus complex.

We are familiar with Freud's displeasure over Jung's "divergence" and "reinterpretations" of his own concepts which, among other things, he first proclaimed in America. Freud created his Committee of the Seven Rings to counteract the damage the breaks with Adler and Jung were causing his movement. Thus Stein does well to remind us that Jung's association with Freud extended over only six years, that he was renowned before he met Freud and continued to evolve his concepts long afterwards. Actually, Jung, a psychiatrist, started a psychoanalytic group at the Burghölzli clinic in Zurich in 1907. Freud had been overjoyed to have a non-Jewish Swiss take such an active interest, soon had perceived him as his intellectual son and successor, and had entrusted him to edit the *Jahrbuch für Psychoanalyse*. Thus he did not take well to Jung's focus on spiritual psychic elements. Jung proposed his basic human instincts—hunger, sexuality, activity, reflection, and creativity—long after his break with Freud, in 1936, and stayed away from Freud's postulated instinct of aggression (thanatos) as well as from Adler's "wish for power." The archetypes that are said to shape human drives, to make up the Jungian collective unconscious, and to generate images that allow instincts to become object-related—in a realm beyond the range of the human psyche—are Jung's means of differentiating himself from Freud as well as answers to him.

Jungians too recognize repression as an indicator of psychic splintering and fragmentation. And Freud and Jung agreed that blocks to consciousness had to be removed in order to release the healing powers of the psyche into consciousness. When Jungian analysts expect to "extend the range of . . . meanings that a patient might otherwise refrain from considering" and "heal the patient's ego and arrive at a mind-body totality"—the Jungian self—their aims are those of all psychoanalysts. But the Jungian self, unlike that of self psychologists like Heinz Kohut, is a sort of God principle and exists on an axis with the ego—the human reality principle. In sum, even after their break, Jungians, Adlerians, and Freudians struggled with how to do away with psychopathology and encourage patients to better master their environment. And they all kept relying on the experience of the transference. Jungian analysts, however, expect to reach to the soul (anima and animus). Finally, this is where their worldview diverges: Freudians eschew the supernatural overtones of these terms, which some of Jung's detractors have interpreted as lacking scientific grounding and ending in mysticism.

The "British School": Melanie Klein, Winnicott, Bion, and Fairbairn

It is ironic to realize that a Hungarian born Jewish woman who was analyzed by Abraham in Berlin founded British psychoanalysis. James Strachey had been in treatment with Freud, who had referred his wife, Alix, to Abraham. As we know from her letters to her husband (Meisel and Kendrick, 1985), she had become friends with Melanie Klein, and had been impressed by her theoretical formulations and imaginative wit. Ernest Jones had started the British Psychoanalytic Society, which by 1925 had fifty-four members and associate members, among them intellectuals of the elite, such as the Stracheys, Ella Sharpe, Joan Riviere, James and Edward Glover. James Strachey was translating Freud's works, which Leonard Woolf started to publish in 1924. Jones was producing the *International Journal of Psychoanalysis* after the break with Jung, and Freud relied on him to guide his entire movement. Soon they found adherents in the important British nonconformist middle-class sector—among them Donald Winnicott, Ronald Fairbairn, Harry Guntrip, and John Sutherland.

In 1925 Alix Strachey had arranged for Melanie Klein to give a series of lectures; in the following year she emigrated to London. There, she developed her extensive theories about child development and analysis that attracted both medical and nonmedical followers. Soon it was evident that she challenged a number of Freudian assumptions, among them the theory that the child passes through the oedipal phase around the age of five: she located the roots of psychic formation at the end of the first year of life. And she conceptualized the emergence of the superego as resulting primarily from the relationship between mother and child, especially as a result of how the child experiences nurturing at the breast—rather than as the internalization of authority, as Freud did. However, Klein accepted Freud's late metapsychology, particularly the death drive (thanatos), which few American psychoanalysts have taken seriously. All in all, Kleinian "object relations," which her theories soon were called, accorded less and less with ego psychology and its principal therapeutic focus on undoing, or undercutting, psychic defenses.

These disagreements among them came to a head after Freud and his daughter Anna had emigrated to London, in what would be called the "Controversial Discussions" of 1943–44. These have been central to the development of British psychoanalysis and recently have been published in all their details (King and Steiner, 1991). Both Melanie Klein and Anna Freud knew that how psychoanalysis was conceptualized would determine its intellectual future, what candidates would be chosen, how long they would need to be analyzed, and by whom, and that the victor would be in a position to control Freud's heritage. Jones was attracted to Klein's views but did not want to cross Freud's daughter. Because he attempted to hold the movement together, he did manage an uneasy truce but could not prevent personal animosity from growing and followers from taking sides. Ultimately they agreed to have their society accommodate three distinct schools: the followers of Melanie Klein (Group A), the followers of Anna Freud (Group B), and the Middle or Independent Group, which accepted some of the ideas of each. This "gentlemen's agreement" provided a wide range of options.

Anna Freud had written "The Ego and the Mechanisms of Defense" (1966) before she left Vienna, and these were the concepts American ego psychologists were championing. Thus it was inevitable that after World War II, when the International Psychoanalytic Association again took up its activities (65 percent of its members now were in America and England), the Kleinians presented papers but were vastly outnumbered. Subsequently, as "American ego psychology" was becoming ever more institutionalized, "object relations theory" was being dismissed or submitted to *stillschweigen*. Therefore, Kleinian object relations theory and techniques were beginning to be introduced into American psychoanalysis only after the structural theory stopped promising further advances, and the more synthesizing ideas of people like Otto Kernberg, Winnicott, John Bowlby, and Bion were being heard.

Whereas Melanie Klein did not appear to have a broad worldview, Winnicott assumed that "human beings make contact and interact with the objective communal world." He had been a pediatrician and was analyzed by Melanie Klein. While working with his young patients he had noted, as Freud had, that children could deal better with the anxieties related to mother's absence after having learned to relinquish and retrieve a favorite toy with the help of a string. Some of the essays in *Playing and Reality* (1971), which introduced him to American psychoanalysts, already had appeared in England twenty years before. But then they had not found any appeal. Winnicott had observed, for instance, that "transitional objects" (emotional props) often are retained into childhood as "absolutely necessary at bed time [and] when loneliness or depressed moods threaten," and that the paradoxical uses of a baby's teddy bear or security blanket should not be analyzed because these "belong" to the infant to be cuddled, loved, or mutilated.

Klein's unremitting absorption in mother-child relations had inspired such research, and that of others in Group B and the Independent Group. Among them, John Bowlby ([1969] 1980) differentiated between behavior that initiates interactions (touching, embracing, reaching, calling) and behavior that results from mother's initiatives, such as attempts to avoid separation (clinging, crying, following), and exploration due to fear or withdrawal. He found that the child's most traumatic experience of attachment and loss was rooted in separation anxiety and subsequent mourning (for the mother rather than her breast, as Klein had postulated). Anna Freud criticized this approach as dealing with the activities of drives rather than with their mental representation, and for having understood infantile narcissism descriptively rather than metapsychologically. In any event, both Bowlby and Winnicott were adhering to Klein's focus on the good enough childhood, which was outside the classical Freudians' theoretical realm. Still, such intellectual controversies lent an openness to the ambience of the British psychoanalytic group, which ultimately allowed for more innovation than its American counterpart. As Gargiulo shows, Winnicott also dealt with adult activities and with creativity and its origins in childhood. (I ought to add that all psychoanalysts, beginning with Freud, were drawn to creative people, who, they believed, were more likely than ordinary patients to provide them with clues to the unconscious.)

Among the contributors to this book, Michael Eigen on Bion and James S. Grotstein on Fairbairn provide particularly detailed information on the personal history that influenced their theories and worldviews. This habit, of course, is as customary among psychoanalysts as it is frowned on by social scientists. However, precisely because psychoanalysts strive to invest their entire being in their work, and because this has been the habit since the earliest meetings around Freud, we must accept that Bion's "self-hate" and Fairbairn's background in Edwardian and post-Edwardian Scotland were intrinsic to their theories and practices. Bion accused American ego psychologists of being false messiahs, of being greedy and envious, and of simplifying and schematizing: their theories did not jibe with his focus on the transformations of affect or his many religious, philosophical, historical, and mathematical images to evoke psychoanalytic experiences and processes. For Bion psychoanalysis always remained an open question that may suspend both pleasure and reality principles.

Fairbairn, on the other hand, contradicted classical Freudian views about infantile sexuality, the pleasure principle and the independence of the drives. These had been fairly dominant propositions among American Freudians for a long time. Thus Fairbairn's conception of the schizoid personality and his generalizations from it to all human beings and their different types of "object relationships," along with those of the rest of the "outsiders," did not find enough appeal in America even to be seriously addressed. Grotstein carefully places Fairbairn's theoretical concerns in relation to those of Melanie Klein, to Winnicott's transitional position, and to Kohut's self psychology. He states that Fairbairn's "personology" became one of the foundations for the relations school and for self psychology. Primarily due to his practical concerns, his ideas took hold outside the milieu of the Freudians, whose history in America is too volatile to have been adequately recorded. In England, Fairbairn had opted for the Independent Group, where he started out by focusing on the infant's existential dimension and the importance of introjective over projective identification. Most psychoanalysts now agree that Fairbairn's openness to both Melanie Klein and Anna Freud, which he shared with the other members of the Independent Group, allowed for much innovation.

Existential Analysis and Jacques Lacan

"Existential psychoanalysis", as M. Guy Thompson so correctly states, is a term that tends to be associated with Sartre and his dictum that freedom is self-created through individuals' actions. It was the dominant philosophy after World War II, as well as the means of dealing with everyday modern life, and of encouraging spontaneity of action. Sartre's thought itself was based on Hegel, Binswanger, and Husserl, and especially on Heidegger's understanding of the unconscious, as conceptualized in his *Daseinsanalyse*. However, none of these philosophers were focusing on actual therapy with patients.

But Leslie Farber, Rollo May, and Erich Fromm—and even more so R. D. Laing—were psychoanalysts who incorporated existentialism into their work with patients. They emphasized the importance of identity, meaning, and responsibility as the central goals of individuals' actions. Like Sartre, they expected "complete freedom and self-creation"—due to choices that help create the individual's mode of being-in-the-world and direct his "consciousness" toward viewing the world with unlimited freedom. In the psychoanalytic dyad—consisting of two "authentic" persons—this translates into "transcendence through love and reciprocal connectedness." Past events in the patient's life are said to be recalled selectively with a sense of his/her future, and thereby establish a feeling of self unity; guilt is real and reasonable rather than judgmental; recognition of death is said to relate to the acknowledgment of freedom; the terror of freedom is perceived as the primary source of human anxiety; and patients must be in touch with their feelings and their potentialities. Ultimately, existential analysis is said to facilitate the emergence of the patient's independent will and direct him/her toward being-in-the-world.

R. D. Laing was especially bent on helping his patients uncover their self-deceptions. Unlike the majority of Freudians, he treated psychotic patients rather than neurotic ones. And he found that psychotic withdrawal was caused in early childhood, most frequently in families that systematically hid secrets and lied to the child, so that the child could not know what to believe, and was suppressing its experiences. Thompson describes the way Laing combined convictions inherent in existential philosophy with a close reading of Freud's psychoanalytic method in his radical approach to his patients' conflictual internalization of self-deception and pathology. Moreover, in the late 1960s Laing's ideas were picked up by the counterculture, mostly because these were against all authority—of parents, institutions, and government. I recall the early praise he received for assuming that patients were not sicker than psychoanalysts, and the later discredit when this did not quite hold true. However, Laing did much to underline that it is as important for a therapist to be honest as it is for him/her to be on top of the latest techniques: that it is crucial to let the patient determine the path of the treatment and to maintain true "neutrality" by means of the countertransference.

Laing's psychoanalytic thought rose to popularity around the same time as Jacques Lacan's. But whereas Laing elaborated on Freudian psychoanalysis by adding existential philosophy, Lacan chose to "reread" Freud in an entirely new manner. He caused much brouhaha among the French psychoanalysts, which later on had all sorts of repercussions in America. Marion Oliner has supplied an excellent overview of Lacan's intellectual antecedents and the excitement as well as the chaos his theories generated among French psychoanalysts and in the country's intellectual life. Along with the anthropologist Claude Lévi-Strauss, the writer Roland Barthes, the "scientific Marxist" Louis Althusser, and the philosopher-historian Michel Foucault, he was central to the "structuralist" movement. These so-called structuralists (at first) shared a new way of apprehending social reality: by reading it via (primarily) Saussurean structural linguistics. This method postulates the interplay of as

yet unconscious common mental structures with the help of semiology—
the science that studies the life of signs within society, emphasizes the ar-
bitrariness of these signs, and postulates a relationship between their signified and signifying properties. Ultimately, this technique was to uncover the general laws of language and their relations to all other areas
of human activity, including the roots of human universality. And because Lacan promised to improve psychoanalytic conceptions and insights via this method—thereby providing yet another road to the unconscious—he was at the heart of the Parisians' intellectual enterprise. In
turn, psychoanalysis was catapulted from nearly total neglect to the talk
of the town.

When the student rebellions of 1968 demonstrated that structures, in
general, can be destroyed, structuralism lost its appeal. Lacanian psychoanalysis, however, began to take its place. Its emphasis on texts, written, oral, and social, which were said to move effortlessly from conscious
to unconscious content and structure, and which were conceptualized to
thrive on multiple and crossover associations (as presented in his public
seminars), engendered free associations to whatever crossed Lacan's fertile mind. His epigrams and maxims soon were quoted around Paris. But
when they reached across the Atlantic Ocean they were taken more literally, and more seriously. There are very few Lacanian psychoanalysts in
the U.S., and these have been trained in France or in short seminars by
visitors. For the most part, American Lacanians are literary critics or
philosophers in universities who have applied some of his teachings and
free associations to feminism and other political ends. However, the fact
that structuralist thought also is said to be able to transcend time, to
move from the past to the present and back again, and that it thus is said
to be able to accommodate existential and surrealist ideas as well, does
allow for its adaptation to literary works, which, after all, rely on imagination and invention.

Feminist Psychoanalysis and Karen Horney

Cynthia Burack states correctly that "the debate [between feminism and
psychoanalysis] originates in the feminist search for a language with
which to theorize identity. . . . in the hope that more theoretically subtle
and empirically sensitive accounts of women's lives than those found in
politics can emerge." Such a conceptualization, however, tends to push

psychoanalytic feminism onto the level of language and politics and thereby to neglect its clinical focus and psychoanalytic practice. But women psychoanalysts, such as Anna Freud, Karen Horney, and Melanie Klein, among others, did contribute to the liberation of women, albeit not in the political sphere.

Periodically, feminists have charged psychoanalysis with having kept women down (emotionally and socially) by hanging on to concepts of penis envy and biological determinism; by casting mothers as causing psychopathology in their children and thus insinuating these notions into child-rearing practices; by catering to (and assuming) middle-class values for all women; and by conflating "woman" and "mother." Even though this is largely true, some feminists did put psychoanalysis to the service of feminism. Among them, Jessica Benjamin has argued that object relations is founded on the assumption that fundamentally we all are social beings. Nancy Chodorow, who found that mothers nurture their children in the way they themselves have been mothered, also argues that object relations theory best conceptualizes intersubjectivity. But many feminist theorists reject them as "conservative" and criticize them for leaving homosexuality out of their theories. Ultimately, these psychoanalytic feminists share the idea of an unconscious, but they search for it in texts—either written or social ones—rather than in the clinical encounter. Unlike Lacan, whom many of them quote, their preoccupation is with his words. But when he stated that "the unconscious is structured like a language," he was generalizing from his approach to the patients he had on his couch, a setting that is anathema to the political arena within which much of American feminism functions.

Michelle Price's essay on Karen Horney in part belongs to the American feminists' criticism whose theories, in the 1980s, began being addressed by some feminists in American universities. Essentially, Price interprets Horney's contributions to psychoanalysis in line with current discussions about gender and sex, about phallocentrism and metanarratives.

Karen Horney was born outside Hamburg, received her training in Berlin, and was analyzed by Karl Abraham. She joined Franz Alexander's psychosomatic institute in Chicago in 1932, and in 1934 became a member and training analyst at the New York Psychoanalytic Institute. But she soon criticized her colleagues for not paying enough attention to the culture within which their patients had to function. Already in the 1920s she had challenged Freud's formulations on femininity and maintained that the girl's so-called masculine (oedipal) phase is a defense against anxiety about her prospective violation by her father, and of anxiety resulting from the "biological principle" of her own sexual attraction to him. Soon she postulated that the boys' womb envy parallels the girls' penis envy—a theory that was being revived in the America of the 1970s. Price, I believe, overemphasizes the current discussions among a coterie of feminists when depicting Horney's life and work. Like other emigrés she was, at least in part, responding to her own sea change when writing *The Neurotic Personality of Our Time* (1937) and *New Ways in Psychoanalysis* (1939). She focused on the impact of life circumstances, and on the role of affection in childhood; she denounced the increasingly theoretical and intrapsychic focus the Freudians were institutionalizing in the New York Psychoanalytic Society; and she suggested that psychoanalysts first zero in on the life circumstances of their patients before getting into their childhood experiences. Horney's opponents accused her of teaching students her own methods alone; some, such as Fritz Wittels, argued for expelling her from the association. In 1941, after they barred her from teaching, Horney resigned and created her own organization, the Association for the Advancement of Psychoanalysis. She was joined by Clara Thompson, Erich Fromm, and Harry Stack Sullivan, among others. And she made yet more waves when she insisted on teaching medically trained people alone and thereby caused another organizational split. Whether or not these and other events were provoked by her prickly personality, her feminism, or the Freudians' increasing orthodoxy is one of the moot issues that pervade historical discussions. Actually, Horney was a forceful woman and a practicing feminist whose contributions, I believe, only can be diminished if they are inserted into fashionable (and waning) postmodernist discourse.

Kohut's Self and Experiential Psychoanalysis

Heinz Kohut was born in Vienna and educated in the U.S. after World War II. He studied neurology in Chicago, where he was exposed, among much else, to the psychosomatic research of Franz Alexander's group and to Bruno Bettelheim's work with autistic children. As a psychoanalyst he was increasingly dissatisfied with prevalent clinical practices, such as the "neutral" analytic setting and the analysts' preference for silence as a response to his patients' questions. Kohut first fully articulated his disagreements with "ego psychology" in *The Analysis of the Self: A Systematic Approach to the Psychoanalytic Treatment of Narcissistic Personality Disorders* (1971). He relied more on Freud's concepts of narcissism and on some of his metapsychological formulations. By then, Erik Erikson had focused on the impact of social milieu on the formation of identity; Margaret Mahler had formulated how the infant separates from its mother; and so had D. W. Winnicott. Kohut also was dissatisfied with postulating the Oedipus myth—which assumes man's dream of autochthonous origins–as central to psychic development. Instead, he favored a "countermyth" based on Odysseus's joy in the ascendance of the next generation. This is just one example of what Paul Ornstein so eloquently refers to as one of the "deeply ingrained [unexamined] personal views readily amalgamated [in every] theory-based assumption." In fact Kohut, unlike Freud, postulates "no built-in primary conflict in the psyche. Traumatic disruptions, on the other hand, lead to defects or deficits in structure building, which, in turn, lead to secondary conflicts." These, then, will also determine the ensuing oedipal conflicts, which result from both the avoidable and unavoidable shortcomings of maternal care, which, in turn, militate against constructing a cohesive self. Therefore, Kohut assumes that psychoanalytic treatment cannot focus on the "real events" the patient recalls, but only on their subjective experience.

Inevitably, Kohut's ideas were anathema to most members of the American Psychoanalytic Association. However, they did not expel him, as they had done with all previous "deviants," but debated with him at many meetings. Actually, the clinical innovations that followed from his conceptions seemed to address better the malaise that increasingly was plaguing psychoanalytic patients. Now some psychoanalysts and many psychologists based their own practices on Kohut's "changing nature of the relationship between the self and its selfobject."

Among them were those who followed an experiential approach to interpersonal psychoanalysis, which is described in this volume by Warren Wilner. Since this type of clinical practice is of recent origin, it has not much place in this chapter on the history of psychoanalytic therapies. Essentially, the experiential approach is a sort of hybrid based (in addition to Kohut) mostly on interpersonal relations as descended from Harry Stack Sullivan, on Robert Stolorow's intersubjective approach, and on Benjamin Wolstein's method that is said to bring together a focus on phenomenology with the psychoanalytic view of the unconscious. Wolstein and Wilner focus on the unique self as it undergoes a process of individuation by learning to articulate its self within the context of the psycho-analytic experiences. This experience, itself, is based on individuals' ap-prehension of their position in nature, and on the construction and inte-gration of their private selves in the actual world—that is, on the way an individual feels he or she influences, or impinges on, his/her concrete ex-perience. Within this context, the analyst must keep in mind to structure the inquiry by distinguishing between empirical, inferential, explanatory, and interpretive functions in order to help the patient attain a sense of in-tegration, of wholeness.

Hermeneutic Psychoanalysis and Schafer's Theories

Louis Sass's chapter brilliantly explains the ins and outs of the concep-tions and the history of hermeneutics, which began with Aristotle. Their more recent antecedents, primarily, are based, among others, on Dilthey's distinctions between *erklären* and *verstehen*, and on Heidegger's and Gadamer's phenomenology of lived experiences. (He also refers fre-quently to the French philosopher Merleau-Ponty, but not to Paul Ri-coeur [1970] who was more inclined to fuse modern rationality and hermeneutics with morals and the belief in God and a higher order when addressing Freud's thought.) Sass implies, however indirectly, that all psychoanalysts' practices incorporate some sort of hermeneutic stance. And he emphasizes that hermeneutics does not represent a specific school of psychoanalysis, but that its metapsychological or metaphilosophical cast may offer ramifications for a variety of psychoanalytic theories and techniques; that it points to the role of culture in molding both psyche and lived body; that we all live in "webs of significance" we ourselves have spun and in interpretations of interpretations. For the psychoana-lyst's Dasein, his culturally constituted and constituting being, is that of the double hermeneutic, insofar as "what one aims to Interpret is inter-preting itself."

Sass clarifies the implications of hermeneutics for psychoanalysts when, for instance, he states, "that a given memory or other mental en-tity is or remains unconscious is . . . a fact that must be explained on mo-tivational rather than on formal or structural grounds"; that "Dasein of-fers a different way of conceptualizing repression;" and that "the past could be said to survive . . . through disappearing, by dissolving into a background that . . . [events] mold and harden according to their own implicit form." But Freudian psychoanalysis focuses on the uncovering of past and buried trauma rather than on "the structures and rhythms of present-day experience." Hermeneutics supposes that this past "permeates the present," and in a sense "survives as a horizontal present." This implies that practicing psychoanalysts of the hermeneutic bent, it seems to me, must direct attention mostly to their patients' life situation rather than to their early experiences—a fact that led to Horney's defection over fifty years ago. Rather than locating sexuality at the pivot of experience, Sass points out, hermeneuticists conceptualize it as yet another phenomenon that needs to be understood and interpreted but that does not necessarily overdetermine the individual's life. Inevitably, hermeneuticists also view psychopathology as less mono-causal than do other schools of psychoanalysis. Finally, Sass states that such psychoanalysts as Roy Schafer have followed in the hermeneutic tradition by "rejecting the mechanistic psychoanalytic metapsychology."

Paul Roth persuasively demonstrates that Schafer's "narrational" depiction of the self offers a cogent account of how self-deception is possible. To that end, Schafer suggests an "analytic attitude" to treat the patient in order to "improve" his/her "self-identity." Because individuals come to the psychoanalyst with narratives that explain what they do and do not do, he focuses on the structure of these narratives to find the "danger situations" they face or avoid. Thus the conceptual underpinnings of his inquiries are humanistically oriented: they are derived from Kant's views of the self which ultimately rest on experience. According to Schafer, each narrative is selectively constructed—that is, how a person talks about some of his life experiences, omits others, and slants them provides myriads of clues to his personality. And his phenomenological stance strongly leans on the Kantian conception that demands formal but not thematic unity of the self, as well as on Sartre's notion of *mauvaise foi*. In fact, from philosophically questioning how self-deception is possible, Schafer moves to examining why people disclaim their own actions, or dissociate from them. He assumes that his job as psychoanalyst is to help them take responsibility, to rid them of the crippling consequences of their neuroses. By means of his hermeneutically informed analytic attitude he too expects to bring to consciousness what is unconscious.

Again, Schafer's theories, and the techniques derived from the methods of this analytic attitude, are contemporary. Their history is embedded in all of Western thought, but they remain faithful to the psychoanalytic theories that Freud and his followers developed. But his ideas are rooted as well in the discussions with informed and practicing contemporaries. Roth describes and contextualizes Schafer's problematic most intelligently.

In sum, the readers of this anthology are bound to be familiar with Schafer's ideas, as well as with those of the other contemporary theories and practices of psychoanalysis. Unlike Freud and his early followers, they take for granted that psychoanalysis most likely will never penetrate to the depths of the human psyche. And they live in a period when psychoanalytic ideas permeate the culture and much of intellectual life, so that philosophers and social scientists worth their salt must address psychoanalytic thought in a multitude of ways. This book, however, deals with the way contemporary therapists are managing to treat patients who, in turn, have been influenced by what they know about, and expect from, the therapists they confide in, from whom they expect to learn to live more or less happily ever after. Thus it is no wonder that therapists, as products of the same culture, try to find ever more novel ways to meet these demands.

Inevitably, the histories of the newer and mostly hybrid theories are short. The older ones, those that go back to the beginnings of the discipline, tend to be forgotten in the therapists' struggles to get to the bottom of each patient's psychic weakness—analyst and analysand, together try for larger generalizations from them. Such a search leads psychoanalysts to look to ever newer scientific and sociological theories, and to existentialist and hermeneutic philosophies. This quest, I believe, will stretch into the future. And because therapists primarily are concerned with adapting accepted theories to their own practices, we will periodically have to remind them of connections to earlier ideas, by updating the "History of Psychoanalytic Therapies."

Finally, this anthology counters some of the critics who have claimed that psychoanalysis has not made any progress. The wealth of new ideas in this collection is a testament to the vitality of new directions in psychoanalysis today. Perhaps a new synthesis is desirable. However, the problem, I believe, has not been with psychoanalysis but with the human condition. Its very flexibility and psychic mutability continue to evolve new defenses against treatment, which in turn demands ever new theoretical advances. At the same time, the search for shorter and simpler means to reach happiness, or some approximation to it, or at least successful functioning under more and more difficult circumstances remains yet another handicap. Perhaps only a new Freud will be able to put all of this together.

REFERENCES

Benjamin, J. 1988. *Bonds of Love: Psychoanalysis, Feminism, and the Problem of Domination*. New York: Pantheon.
Bowlby, J. [1969] 1980. *Attachment and Loss*. New York: Basic Books.
Butler, J. 1990. *Gender Trouble: Feminism and the Subversion of Identity*. New York: Routledge.
Chodorow, N. 1978. *The Reproduction of Mothering: Psychoanalysis and the psychology of Gender*. Berkeley and Los Angeles: U. of California Press.
———. 1989. *Feminism and Psychoanalytic Theory*. New Haven: Yale University Press.
Freud, A. [1936] 1966. "The Ego and the Mechanisms of Defense." In *The Writings of Anna Freud*. Vol. 2. New York: International Universities Press.
Freud, S. 1895. "Project for a Scientific Psychology." In *Standard Edition of the Complete Works of Sigmund Freud* (hereafter referred to as S.E.). London: Hogarth Press, 1:283–437.
———. 1900. *The Interpretation of Dreams*. In S.E., vols. 4–5.
———. 1914. "History of the Psychoanalytic Movement." In S.E. 14:3–66.
———. 1917. "Mourning and Melancholia." In S.E., 14:237–58.
———. 1923. "The Ego and the Id," In S.E., 19:1–66.
———. 1925. "Some Psychological Consequences of the Anatomical Distinctions between the Sexes." In S.E., 19:243–58.
———. 1926. "On the Question of Lay Analysis." In S.E., 20:251–58.
———. 1927. Postscript, "On the Question of Lay Analysis." In S.E., 20:177–258.
Hartmann, H., Kris, E., and Loewenstein, R.M. 1946. "Comments on the Formation of Psychic Structure." *Psychoanalytic Study of the Child* 3–4:9–46.
Horney, K. 1924. "On the Genesis of the Castration Complex in Women." *International Journal of Psycho-Analysis* 5:50–65.
———. 1926. "The Flight from Womanhood: The Masculinity-Complex in Women as Viewed by Men and Women." *International Journal of Psychoanalysis* 7:324–39; in Strouse, 1974, pp. 171–186.
———. 1935. "The Problem of Feminine Masochism." *Psychoanalytic Review*. 12, no. 3: 241–57.
———. 1937. *The Neurotic Personality of Our Time*. New York: Norton.
———. 1939. *New Ways in Psychoanalysis*. New York: Norton.
King, P. and R. Steiner. 1991. *The Freud-Klein Controversy. New Library of Psychoanalysis*. no. 11, 1941–1945.
Klein, M. 1926. "The Psychological Principles of Early Analysis." In *Love, Guilt*

and Reparation and Other Works, 1921–1945. London: Hogarth Press, 1975, pp. 128–38.

———. 1928. "Early Stages of the Oedipus Complex." In *Love, Guilt and Reparation and Other Works, 1921–1945.* London: Hogarth Press, 1975, pp. 186–98.

———. 1932. *The Psychoanalysis of Children.* London: Hogarth Press, 1975.

———. 1937. "Love, Guilt and Reparation." In *Love, Guilt and Reparation and Other Works, 1921–1945.* London: Hogarth Press, 1975, pp. 303–43.

Kohut, H. 1971. *The Analysis of the Self: A Systematic Approach to the Psychoanalytic Treatment of Narcissistic Personality Disorders.* New York: International Universities Press.

Kurzweil, E. 1980. *The Age of Structuralism: Lévi-Strauss to Foucault.* New York: Columbia University Press. [reissued, 1997, by Transaction Publishers].

———. 1989. *The Freudians: A Comparative Perspective.* New Haven: Yale University Press.

Lacan, J. [1966] 1977. *Ecrits: A Selection.* New York: Norton.

Lorenzer, A. 1984. *Intimität und soziales Leid.* Frankfurt: S. Fischer.

Marks, E., and Courtivron, I., eds. 1980. *New French Feminisms.* Amherst: University of Massachusetts Press.

Meisel P., and Kendrick, W. 1985. *Bloomsbury/Freud: The Letters of James and Alix Strachey, 1924–1925.* New York: Basic Books.

Nunberg, H. and Federn, E. 1962, 1967, 1974. *Minutes of the Vienna Psychoanalytic Society.* Vols. 1–3. New York: International Universities Press.

Reiff, P. 1966. *The Triumph of the Therapeutic.* New York: Harper and Row.

Ricoeur, P. 1970. *Freud and Philosophy: An Essay in Interpretation.* New Haven: Yale University Press.

Strouse, J., ed. 1974. *Women and Analysis: Dialogues on Psychoanalytic Views of Femininity.* New York: Viking.

Winnicott, D. W. 1971. *Playing and Reality.* London: Tavistock.

Chapter Two

Jung's Vision of the Human Psyche and Analytic Practice

Murray Stein

EDITORS' INTRODUCTION

Perhaps Carl Jung's most lasting influence on "mainstream" psychoanalysis has been his meticulous and wide-ranging study of symbols. For example, his investigation of the mandala, the symbol of wholeness, in part led him to the claim that intrinsic to the individual was the search for wholeness or integration of personality, what he called the process of individuation. This is regarded by many as the first discussion in the analytic literature of the concept of self and identity, which was later to play such a crucial role in psychoanalytic theory. Jung was also the first to broaden Freud's developmental theory, which focused on the first five years, to include the whole life cycle; his elaborations of the process of individuation and the psychological problems of the second half of life are important contributions to psychoanalytic theory.

As Murray Stein indicates, Jung was not able to accept the exclusively sexual nature of Freud's "libido." In working with his patients, he discovered residues of human history in their fantasies. His own childhood experiences with visions and alternative personalities had prepared him to consider the possibility that some psychic content might emanate from sources external to the individual. His self-analysis reinforced this view. Jung therefore hypothesized a personal unconscious similar to Freud's concept, and a collective unconscious that transcends the personal experiences of the individual. It is this latter aspect of Jung's theory that is most controversial and intriguing.

Within the collective unconscious, says Jung, there are stored inherited predispositions to respond with strong emotion to particular events. These predispositions, the famous archetypes, including the animus and anima, the Hero, the shadow, and the persona, were for Jung solid evidence of the innate symbol-making tendency humans had inherited from their ancestors. As Stein indicates, culture also plays an important role in shaping and forming the deployment of both archetypal and instinctual factors in the psyche.

For Jung, life does not proceed randomly. It is purposive or teleological, and shaped by beckoning goals. The purpose of an individual's life is attained when that person is fully integrated, completely in harmony with the self. Jung further believed that every human has an innate tendency to pursue this inner harmony; he called it the transcendent function. The transcendent function is the motive force behind the individual's desire to come to terms with all aspects of the self; it guides the need to accept the content of the unconscious as "one's own." Individuation and the transcendent function are thus opposite sides of the same coin. Individuation refers to the full development of all sides of oneself into a unique configuration. The transcendent function is the guiding force in the achievement of this idiosyncratic "wholeness."

As Stein points out, psychopathology for Jung is the result of personal experiences that have generated a fragmentary ego, significant blockages between ego-consciousness and the unconscious through the amassing of complexes, and pathological one-sidedness in the ego's orientation. He notes that as the virtual center of consciousness, the ego functions as the container of these polarities and splinters of consciousness within the larger psyche, as well as having the adaptational responsibility for responding to the vicissitudes of the environments. Neurosis for Jung can thus be viewed as the person's inability to create a psychological organization that can reconcile all the opposing and contradictory trends in the psyche.

"In large measure," says Stein, "the work of analysis has to do with bringing together the psychic pieces (the so called opposites) that have been split and pushed apart, so that the normal psychic equilibrating force can take over and offer its creative and healing potential. This knitting together of bits of consciousness is the work of integration in a Jungian analysis." (P. M. and A. R.)

The Nature of Healing

A wit once proclaimed that the art of the physician is to entertain the patient while nature heals. This may be as true for analysis as it is for medicine. "The best the analyst can do is not to disturb the natural evolution of this [healing] process," Jung wrote in a letter in 1960. "The process consists in becoming whole or integrated, and that is never produced by words or interpretations but wholly by the nature of Psyche itself" (1975, p. 583).

Today most experienced analysts of all theoretical persuasions would agree that they are not healers of psyche but at best only allies of the healing processes that are to be found within it. All but the most inflated clinicians recognize their limitations of skill and technique in the therapeutic process. What actually heals in psychotherapy remains a mystery. Perhaps it is a certain kind of love.[1]

What some commentators have seen as a holdover of German nature romanticism in Jung's works actually turns out to be a realistic assessment of what can happen in analysis.[2] Jung's reliance on "nature" to supply the healing forces is not some sort of woolly mysticism but a physician's recognition that human art and science have their limitations. The analyst is not omnipotent and certainly requires the cooperation of nature if healing is to occur.

Yet the practiced skill and masterful technique of the trained analyst are also important in analysis, and in some cases they are even crucial. Otherwise training would be unnecessary and training institutes an egregious waste of energy. While there may be "natural therapists" and healing personalities, the difficult analytic cases require a great deal of expertise and skill. This seems to have been true since time immemorial, as evidenced by shamanic healers, who were and are also highly trained technicians.

It is often the case that the pathways by which nature does its healing are blocked and need to be opened and cleared of obstacles. Often, weak bridges need to be built up into solid, workable psychic structures, and in some cases a whole new psychic infrastructure must be constructed if nature is to have a chance to work its healing effects. Faulty and malignant conscious attitudes and developments, acquired usually through traumatic and hurtful experiences in early life, prevent nature's healing processes from having much effect.

Actually many things can get in the way of the psyche's natural healing processes. To quote Jung from a very late work entitled "Symbols and the Interpretation of Dreams,"

> through dreams, intuitions, impulses, and other spontaneous happenings, instinctive forces influence the activity of consciousness. Whether that influence is for better or worse depends on the actual contents of the unconscious. If it contains too many things that normally ought to be conscious, then its function becomes twisted and prejudiced; motives appear that are not based on true instincts, but owe their activity to the fact that they have been consigned to the unconscious by repression or neglect. They overlay, as it were, the normal unconscious psyche and distort its natural symbol-producing function.   (1976, par. 512)

This overlay of repressed psychic material is maintained and held in place by all the psychic splits, vertical and horizontal, that are revealed through the careful scrutiny of analysis. In large measure, the work of analysis has to do with bringing together the psychic pieces (the so-called opposites) that have been split and pushed apart, so that the normal psychic equilibrating force can take over and offer its creative and healing potential. This knitting together of bits of consciousness is the work of integration in a Jungian analysis.

The Nature of the Psyche

Jung's vision of the psyche and his approach to the theory and practice of analysis unfolded over a period of some sixty years. Beginning with psychiatric studies in 1900 at the Burghölzli Clinic in Zurich and continuing through his close collaboration with Freud between 1907 and 1913, Jung went on to extend the scope of what he believed to be the true range of the unconscious from a one- (or two-) drive theory to a theory that encompasses a wide array of instinctual and archetypal foci. He also reconceptualized the relations between conscious and unconscious in a more dynamic and less mechanical way than had Freud. His early argument with Freud about the nature of libido (is it purely sexual or more general psychic energy?) turned into a thoroughgoing revision of the psychoanalytic theory that he had received in Vienna.[3]

The nature of the human psyche embraces, in Jung's view, instinctual-somatic elements (i.e., impulses) at the one end of a spectrum and spiritual-archetypal elements (i.e., images and ideas) at the other. At both extremes, psyche fades through a psychoid barrier into nonpsychic areas:

into physical matter at the somatic end and into pure spirit at the arche-typal end (Jung 1954, par. 420). The psyche itself is defined by the range of the will: whatever the will can effect or influence in principle belongs to the psychic realm, and whatever it cannot reach even in principle (e.g., autonomic system functions) lies outside the psyche. The psyche is bounded by instincts on the one side and by spirit on the other: "[T]he will cannot transgress the bounds of the psychic sphere: it cannot coerce the instinct, nor has it power over the spirit, in so far as we understand by this something more than the intellect. Spirit and instinct are by nature autonomous and both limit in equal measure the applied field of the will." (1954, par. 379).

The view much bandied about that Jung was a "mystic" is a distortion of the truth that he did take spirit into account in his theory of the psyche. And in analytic therapy it is as important to release spiritual elements as it is somatic instinctual impulses. But contrary to the popular opinion that Jung denied or downplayed the biological and instinctual side of psychic life, he actually gives it equal weight to the spiritual and archetypal. Jung's is not a purely spiritual psychology, although it takes spiritual matters more seriously perhaps than any other of the modern depth psychologies.

For Jung the unconscious contains much more than the sexual drive (the famous *Lustprincip* of Freud) and its associated materials, and more even than the total mass of repressed psychic contents of all kinds. The unconscious contains thoughts and images, impulses and desires that have not yet been experienced in an individual's life, as well as those that have been experienced and rejected for one reason or another. Certainly Jung did not deny the existence and importance of sexuality, but he found that other somatic instinctual factors also play on the psyche, not to mention the panoply of contents and factors that have more a spiritual or purely psychological identity than a biologically based one.

Jung theorized that there are a number of instinct groups, in fact, five of them. In a significant but much neglected essay entitled "Psychological Factors Determining Human Behavior," which was written in 1936 for presentation at the Harvard Tercentenary Conference of Arts and Sciences (where he received an honorary doctorate), Jung postulated that the five "instinctive factors" are hunger, sexuality, activity, reflection, and creativity. These deep human impulses, which lie beyond the levels of accultura-tion and cannot be controlled by the will, belong to human biological nature itself. They influence human behavior and supply energy and motive force ("libido") to the psyche. They are in turn shaped by several other physical, psychological, and cultural factors, which Jung calls "modalities" in the Harvard paper. These include the physical factors of gender, age, and hereditary disposition and the more psychological ones of typology, spiritual vs. physical orientation to the world, and the degree to which a person behaves consciously or unconsciously. Culture and history play a role in forming these latter three modalities and thereby influence the ways the instinct groups may be deployed in an individual's life. For Jung, history and culture play a large role in shaping and forming the deployment of both instinctual and archetypal factors in the psyche.

Jung's Harvard paper therefore also underscores his appreciation for the multitude of ways the individual psyche is embedded in and influenced by the surrounding social world. The individual is subject to social forces from both internal and external sources. As history and culture shape family life and attitudes, so family shapes the individual and, through the process of introjection, affects the ego from within the psychic matrix itself. Social disruption, war, and economic hardship are factors that contribute to the construction of an inner world that the individual carries throughout life. Jung's theory is nonsolipsistic in another sense as well: through the psychological functions, such as sensation, thinking, and feeling, the ego is able to make adjustments to the environment and to fashion a conscious response that is not fatalistically determined by the instincts or complexes. Jung's vision is profoundly appreciative of the importance of the psyche in making judgments and formulating responses and ideas about the world, but it does not see the human being as locked into a dark box from which only projections can emanate and grope at a totally unknown and unknowable "outer world." For Jung, the human being is an adaptive animal who takes cues both from intrapsychic factors such as instinctually based impulses and archetypally derived ideational processes and from the surrounding environment.

It should be noted here as highly significant that Jung does not list aggression (Freud's second drive, thanatos) or the wish for power (Adler's core drive) as basic human instincts. In this, his conception of the human condition differs from Freud's more pessimistic view, not to mention Melanie Klein's further extensions of thanatos theory into earliest childhood and infancy, as for instance in her theory of envy. He also sets himself apart from Adler, for whom the power drive was the key force in psychological life and who saw the human experience of inferiority and powerlessness as central.

This is not to say that Jung's conception of the human condition is one-sidedly and naively optimistic or depicts a psyche that is free of internal conflict or power needs. It is not. He recognizes in many places that the instincts often compete (e.g., "the system of instincts is not truly harmonious in composition and is exposed to numerous internal collisions," 1954, par. 378) and that constellations of the opposites and internal conflict within the psyche are inevitable. He also is cognizant of the power issue and its importance, especially for introverts. In fact, the existence of inner conflict is bedrock in Jungian doctrine. Conflict, inner and outer, is a normal part of human life and even provides the necessary condition for ego growth and development; politics is inevitable and universal because of the insecurity of the ego, but not instinctual.[4] Politics are driven more by the ego's need for power and grandiosity than by instinct.

If Jung does not root aggression and the need for power in instinct, he does nevertheless have a strong conception of evil.[5] The shadow (for Jung a technical psychological term) belongs to the human personality at all levels, personal and impersonal, individual and collective. But the shadow is not invariably defined by "sex and aggression," the Freudian id. It is mercurial; it depends on the particular aspects of personality that individuals and their culture choose to denigrate and attempt to eliminate. The shadow is that which does not belong in polite company, is shaming and embarrassing, and is rejected by the individual and by society as unacceptable and even intolerable. It is made up of the traits, feelings, and harbored fantasies analysands confess to their analysts with great shame and reluctance.[6] The shadow is complementary to the persona (another technical term), a person's official psychosocial identity: one side is the face we want to have seen, the other the face we want to conceal. Both exist inevitably as shadow twins. But the shadow is not drive-based and is not associated or shaped by a specific instinct.

There is in Jung's theory, then, no specific drive toward destruction or aggression for its own sake, and the shadow does not inevitably tend in that direction. Destructiveness and aggressiveness are universal among humans, or so it seems, but they are the by-products of other factors: frustration, traumatic childhood, the need to create, the urge to mate, and so on. There is no inherent human need to destroy. For Jung, this Freudian notion (the Thanatos myth) simply did not make sense from a biological or psychological standpoint, even though the idea seems to have originated with his early student, Sabina Spielrein, who passed it on to Freud (Kerr, 1993).

Belonging to the same deep level of the psyche as the instinctive factors are the archetypes. Instincts are the drives, archetypes the shapers of the drives. Together they make up the famous Jungian collective unconscious. In an essay entitled "On the Nature of the Psyche," which is perhaps his greatest single theoretical paper, Jung speculates about the relation between instincts and archetypes. He concludes that they are best conceived as lying along a spectrum, like the color spectrum, with the instincts at the infrared end and the archetypes at the ultraviolet end (1954, par. 414). But archetypes and instincts are also intimately related to one another, the first shaping and giving form to the second. By themselves the instincts would be without form and void, like the biblical *te'hom* (Genesis 1:1); the spirit (archetype) broods above this amorphous chaos and gives it shape. The archetypes structure the deep unconscious, where matter and spirit come together and meet as instinctual urge and archetypal image. In fact, one never meets an instinct without an archetypally formed structure in the psyche.

Jung would sometimes hold that the archetype is the image of the instinct. So intimately are they related that Jung often refers to archetypes and archetypal patterns without explicit or even implicit reference to instinct, simply assuming the link between instinct and archetype that drives the "pattern of behavior" that is the archetype (see 1954, par. 352). Without such a source of somatic energy, archetypal images would be lifeless and without embodiment, pure mental specters that float around in the psyche without emotional connection or impact. Taken this way, archetypes become mental abstractions and schemata for thinking rather than the numinous powers that Jung had in mind whenever he used the term "archetype."[7]

Without an image, on the other hand, an instinct would lack direction, it would be diffuse, it would not know how to find a suitable object. While instincts give energy and drive to archetypal images, archetypes generate the images that allow instincts to become object-related, to come into contact with fitting objects, which is what they inherently seek.

In Jungian theory, this linkage between instinct and archetype is the presupposition for all satisfactory object relations, beginning with the infant-breast unit (nurturance), extending through the formation of a love bond with a mate (sexuality), and including the discovery and recognition of a vocation (activity, creativity), and the persons involved and tools used for deriving meaning from experience (reflection). For Jungians, these key experiences of a "fit" in life are "archetypal," meaning that there is a good match between internal and external worlds (between need and fulfillment) and between nature and culture (between self and other, individual and society). There is also the factor of innateness: these fittings are not learned, they are discovered.

Jung would not reject the point of the object relations theorists who wish to insist that humans are innately and inherently object-oriented and object-related from the beginning of life, but he would add that the ground for this relatedness lies in the still more fundamental link between instinct and archetype. When this linkage is disrupted or broken, object relations are inevitably disturbed, perhaps even from the first moments of intrauterine life but certainly from the moment of birth onward. Without the guidance of the archetypal image, the psychic energy pouring in from the somatic base is disorganized and unfocused.

Neither instincts nor archetypes are contained within the psyche itself, according to Jung's theory, and therefore they cannot be experienced directly. The instinct groups are rooted in the somatic base, and the archetypes are formative factors that exist in a realm beyond the range of the human psyche, which Jung calls "spirit" (1954, par. 420).[8] From both extremes of the spectrum, the psyche receives signals: from the instinct groups these come as feelings of desire and as impulses, and from the archetypes they appear in consciousness as images, fantasies, ideas, visions, and intuitions. By the time they reach the psyche and even more so when they reach ego-consciousness, both types of signal have been "psychized" and related to the other type.

The empirical consciousness of individuals tends to slide back and forth between the somatic and archetypal poles of the spectrum, now experiencing desires, impulses, and the libidinal fires of passion more strongly, now images, ideas, and intuitions more intensely. Emotion can equally attach itself to either end of this polarity, and either one can at times overwhelm or swallow the other. But in the healthy psyche, which is the balanced psyche for Jung, consciousness holds instinct and archetype in tension, where they are coordinated and can work together, the one providing impulse and drive and the other contributing direction and meaning. Precisely how this coordination comes into being and operates or fails to operate successfully was a topic pursued by Jung late in life, particularly in his last great opus, *Mysterium Coniunctionis* (1955–56). The great "union of opposites" that the psyche is asked to host is that between matter and spirit. The human condition as we experience it at this point in evolutionary history is fundamentally shaped by this tension of opposites between the soma-based instincts and the spirit-based arche-types. The meeting place (or the battleground) where they converge is the psyche. As Jung saw it, the meaning of human existence in the temporal universe lies in this precise function of the psyche: to unite spirit and mat-ter within the space-time continuum of an individual human life.

When these two poles of the psyche, the material body and the tran-scendent spirit, are adequately coordinated, it makes for healthful psy-chic compensation from the unconscious. Jung's view of compensation is vastly different from Adler's. The term "compensation" for Jung does not refer to the outcome of a sense of inferiority or the attempt to over-come the feeling of smallness by imagining the opposite: It is not a "protest." Rather, compensation is conceptualized by Jung as a psychic mechanism that aims at directing a balanced dynamic movement toward individuation and wholeness. Ego-consciousness needs this compensa-tion, which is a coordinated blend of impulse and idea, from the uncon-scious because on its own and without benefit of such a relationship with "nature," it becomes rigid, sterile, and one-sided. "True instincts" or "nature" can adjust, balance, and heal the conscious personality if the way is clear for compensation to have its proper effect.

Complexes, Pathology, and Analysis

Since its beginnings in Freud's late nineteenth-century clinical workshop, psychoanalysis has been concerned with the dynamics and contents of re-pression and the problems created by this defense mechanism. Repression was, however, only the first indication of psychic splintering and frag-mentation. Early in his psychiatric career, Jung noticed the wonders of dis-sociation in his psychotic and neurotic patients. Repression is but one of several means by which consciousness is prevented from integrating parts of the psyche and extracting meaning and benefit from experience.

What the early pioneers of psychoanalysis recognized clearly from the outset was that individuals who seek treatment block much of their psy-chic wholeness from their conscious self-perceptions, usually in order to avoid psychic pain. The price for this strategy of pain avoidance and de-fensiveness is other kinds of suffering, namely, symptoms, fragmentary one-sidedness, and lack of emotional fulfillment. The way to health, as both Freud and Jung recognized, lies in removing these blocks to con-sciousness, facing the necessary pain, and constructing a container of consciousness that can hold the pieces of psyche together and keep the defenses from splitting them apart. Simultaneously, Jung believed, this would also release the healing powers of the natural psyche into consciousness.

Thus, that which has been excluded from ego-consciousness and remains unintegrated is a key issue for psychotherapeutic theory and also, or especially, for analytic practice. For Freud, the chief content of repression was sexuality in its most basic, original, and instinctual forms as he understood them. Oedipal sexuality and its attached contents of fantasy, memory, and thought were the prime targets of the repression dynamic. This accounted, in Freud's view, for childhood amnesia. Moreover, the repression of oedipal sexuality lay at the heart of culture, and for Freud this was the root of civilized humanity's psychic discontents and miseries.

Jung rather quickly recognized the inadequacies of Freud's view about repressed contents. He found that there are many other elements in the unconscious besides those that have to do with sexuality (i.e., other instincts and archetypes). Umberto Galimberti, a contemporary Italian Jungian analyst, suggests that the more damaging and far-reaching repressions in our time have to do with the spiritual end of the psychic spectrum rather than the instinctual:

> Actually, repression is carried out not so much on the level of instincts as, much more, on the level of meanings. Opinion is decided in such a one-sided and rigid fashion that the individual does not retain the possibility of expressing himself in a different way, one that could even perhaps be definitive. . . .
>
> More than being a playground for impersonal instincts, the human being is defined by the openness to meaning, and freedom is demonstrated much more by the extent of this openness than it would be by the full deployment of the instincts.   (1989, p. 91)

According to Galimberti, the task of psychoanalysis is to extend the range of possibilities for interpretation of psychological material and experience and of the meanings that a patient might otherwise refrain from considering, meanings that would consequently remain locked away in the unconscious.

These contents of the unconscious, its unthought thoughts and images, would have, if released into consciousness, the potential to transform the subject's self-concept and self-perception and provide a new map for meaning. We must understand that potential "meanings" and "ideas" can be as much the targets of repression and other splitting mechanisms as are instincts such as sexuality.

This notion vastly extends the scope of an adequate psychological hermeneutic. Not only does interpretation have the obligation of unearthing hidden sexual motives and other instinctual material, it also has the duty to expose obscured ideas and possible meanings, occluded images and experiences of the soul that are buried in the debris of personal and cultural prejudices toward what is to be allowed as true and valid for the individual. The rejection of a reductionistic hermeneutic was an essential move in Jung's break with Freud. In its place, he erected an interpretive method that could embrace a much broader range of meanings and significance.

This is not to say, however, that Jung abandoned reductionistic interpretation altogether. Rather, it was put to a different use. It was clear to him that the main hindrance to the smooth functioning of nature's psychological ecosystem lies in the personal complexes. These are psychic bodies that are developed throughout a person's life history, and most importantly in childhood. They are instigated by interpersonal traumata like emotional abandonment, sexual abuse, and lack of adequate mirroring, and then they grow by gathering associations of a similar nature around themselves and by binding them to the core of the complex with emotion. The complexes are highly charged with affect, behave autonomously (i.e., are not under the ego's control), and possess a kind of consciousness of their own. They are highly reactive to external stimuli, and when stimulated they cause both physiological and psychological distress and confusion. They are our emotional "buttons"; when pushed they can drive us to the brink of irrationality and beyond. In analysis they are interpreted reductionistically, although not necessarily bio-reductionistically. That is, the emotional reactions generated by complexes are placed in the context of their point of origination, usually childhood.

As important as their interference with the ego's so-called reality testing may be, however, a perhaps more severe problem comes about as the result of their eventual buildup into a sort of psychic barrier, often impenetrable, between the ego and the deeper, instinctive/archetypal levels of the psyche. It is this barrier of complexes that can severely block the healing compensations of the natural psyche from reaching ego-consciousness.

The complexes also form fracture points in the structure of the developing ego. They allow for ego fragmentation and dissociation along certain predictable lines of cleavage. When strongly stimulated, they splinter the psyche and cause splits within consciousness and between consciousness and the unconscious. When this happens, a person experiences a state of dissociation, high affectivity, and physiological stress. Consciousness is disturbed and the integration of experience is blocked. Memory, too, is disrupted, and distortions of every variety intrude in the ego's account of reality.

These points of vulnerability in the psyche engender ego defenses that are meant to distance the subject from suffering and pain. Unfortunately, at the same time they distance the person from valuable psychic experience and from parts of the self that are called into play at the moment of the complex stimulus. They interfere with useful instinctual responses to stressful and even dangerous situations, and they cut down on the ego's capacity to take advantage of opportunities in the environment with adaptive responses. The resultant defenses against psychic pain prevent integration and foster the chronicity of psychic patterns and partiality. The self is not unified but rather becomes compartmentalized and dissociative. This is the problematic situation found, for example, in borderline personality disorder.

As much as the fragmentariness of a poorly formed and vulnerable ego interferes with healthy functioning and utilization of healing compensation from the deep unconscious, the existence of a thick, unbreachable layer of complexes between ego-consciousness and the deeper layers of the unconscious, along with the defenses employed by the ego to keep psychic pain at bay, creates a psyche that cannot utilize the healing powers of the unconscious even when they happen to break through in dreams, impulses, or fantasies. In analytic practice, it is not uncommon for a person to report a numinous archetypal dream that should have the effect of moving the subject toward greater wholeness and meaning, but which the analyst sees as having no discernible effect. While such a dream should have a profound healing influence on consciousness, not even the added weight of the analyst's most empathic and inspired interpretation will move consciousness very far in the direction of health. Here, both dream and interpretation carry too little force within this undeveloped psychic matrix to make much difference. Psychic reality has little weight when thrown in the balance against the habits of consciousness and the power of the complexes.

The instincts, too, like the archetypes, may be ignored, overridden, or distorted by ego-consciousness and its governing complexes, or they can be turned to perverse and corrupt ends. The instinct for nurturance can be twisted into binging or anorexia (which actually denies instinct for an obsessive involvement with spirit); sexuality can be twisted into perversions by the complexes formed in childhood; activity can wither or become exaggerated, and so can reflection; and creativity can run amok in Dionysian dismemberments or cancerous inflations. Or the instincts can become so occluded and blocked off that almost nothing passes through from this level of the unconscious to ego-consciousness, at least in some of the instinct areas. Thus we find a person with no creativity, or no sexuality, or very low levels of activity or reflection or nurturance. And it is not that one of these areas is capturing all of the libido; rather, the complexes are absorbing and thwarting the impulses, and the ego is more or less bereft of energy or motivation in any direction whatsoever. This is the problematic situation the therapist often faces in neurotic chronic depression.

These various clinical pictures are the result of personal developments that have created a fragmentary ego, considerable blockages between ego-consciousness and the unconscious through the accumulation of complexes, and pathological one-sidedness in the ego's attitude. Such developments also foster and promote defenses like splitting, projection, and repression. They interfere with the way the unconscious would otherwise normally influence the ego and provide it with life-giving, healing energies from the natural instinctive/archetypal psyche. The normal and optimal function of the unconscious is to compensate the ego and to orient it thereby in the direction of psychic equilibrium and balance, but this is thwarted by faulty ego development and the formation of complexes. This is what needs to be rectified by analytic treatment. At the heart of treatment lies the analysis (ana-lysis = dismemberment) of the complexes and the synthesis of an ego attitude that can support what Jung called the transcendent function, the bridge between ego-consciousness and the deeper layers of the unconscious.

Ego and Self in Analysis

The ego is, of course, the primary object of all practical therapeutic and analytic endeavors. It is to the ego that we must answer, for it is the ego that defines a person's consciousness and is the felt center of a life. It would be foolish to attempt the healing of the psyche without healing the ego: the procedure might succeed but the patient would not know the difference!

And yet we also know that the ego is but a partial aspect of the whole psyche. The whole, of which the ego is a part, consists of the self in its totality of polarities, the most essential of which is the spectrum that stretches between the instinctual-somatic and the archetypal-spiritual extremes. This mind-body totality is what Jung conceived of as the self. The self is the God principle, as it were, and the ego is the human reality principle.

The ego is defined as a complex that constitutes a focal center for consciousness. Like all other complexes, the ego has an archetypal core, and in the case of the ego this archetypal core is very special. It is the self. This sets the ego apart from the other complexes. The ego's consciousness is privileged within the psychic universe because of its unique link to the self.

Being a complex, however, means that the ego is also deeply constituted by trauma. In fact, Jung theorizes that the ego comes into being through the "collisions" that inevitably take place between an individual and the world. He was familiar with Otto Rank's notion of the centrality of the birth trauma for ego development, and while he did not give this early experience quite the weight that Rank did, he would concede that traumata suffered at birth have a fundamental constituting force in ego formation. The ego is born in and through pain, and at its heart lies anxiety. The "reality principle" by which the ego is supposed to operate (according to Freud) in fact amounts to little more than an anxiety principle, but this is (for Jung, too) constitutive of the ego.

Like all complexes, the ego is made up of a variety of associated contents clustered around a bipolar core, and as such it is subject to fragmentation and to splitting processes that can easily break it apart into states of dissociation. In a sense, modern depth psychology begins with the study of ego dissociation. Mesmer and his followers employed "artificial somnambulism," or hypnosis (Braid's term), to create special altered states of consciousness and to induce intense rapport between "magnetizer" and subject (see Ellenberger, 1970, pp. 112ff.). What these early practitioners of depth therapy had stumbled upon was the phenomenon of ego dissociation through hypnosis. Hypnotism became what Ellenberger has termed a "royal road to the unknown mind" (p. 112) because it opened a way through the normally defended rational ego into uncharted territory. From Mesmer the trail leads to Janet, who explored the phenomena of dissociation in great detail at the Salpetriere and is often credited as the founder of modern dynamic psychiatry (Ellenberger, 1970, p. 331). Jung, like Freud and Adler, studied Janet's methods and employed some of his techniques and theories in his early work.

The existence of variety in ego states fascinated Jung from early on. His doctoral dissertation was the study of a medium (who was, in fact, his cousin Helene Preiswerk) who had an amazing ability to acquire personalities, during séances, that had vivid historical characteristics, about which she consciously knew nothing. These states of possession by foreign psychic bodies (complexes and archetypal images), as Jung found in his later investigations with psychotic patients at the Burghölzli Clinic in Zurich, can be transitory or relatively long-lasting. One goal of therapeutic analysis is to become aware of these various states of dissociation and part-personalities and to knit them together into a state of relative cohesiveness, so that an umbrella of consciousness can surround the parts and hold them together. This is different from merging them into a hybrid. Jungians speak of containing the opposites within consciousness, of maintaining the tensions inherent in the interplay and dynamics between the various pieces of the psyche and not allowing them to fall into dissociation.

As the virtual center of consciousness, the ego is responsible for playing the role of container of these polarities and splinters of consciousness within the larger psyche, as well as having the adaptational role of responding to changing environments. At its archetypal core (i.e., the self), the ego complex first comes into being even before the physical birth of the infant. This virtual center of incipient consciousness is in place and functioning already in utero, as the fetus orients itself to its environment and begins to sense the world. The self, which is the central organizing archetype of the psyche as a whole, imparts to the ego this same quality of centrality as the organism emerges into the world and gains more consciousness.

The deep connection to the self at the ego's core makes it a paradoxical psychic object. On the one hand, it is the seat of anxiety and pain, receiving its personal birth and awakening through trauma. On the other hand, it is divine and godlike because of its identity as the self. The ego is the place where time and eternity meet most intimately and crucially. The ego is at once the incarnation of the self in the time-space continuum and the fragile register of existential anxiety.

Clustered around this central bipolar core at the heart of the ego are associations that make up a person's remembered history and personal identity. Experiences of self with mother, with father, and with other significant figures in the surrounding world are introjected and woven into the fabric of consciousness and ego identity. These can be supportive and life-enhancing associations, or they can be debilitating and toxic ones. Analysis attempts to separate the ego from the pathological associations wrapped into the structure of the ego complex and to recover and support the beneficent ones.

Being a complex, however, also signifies that the ego is of only relative size and importance in the psyche's universe, not its center and not even its major body. As the putative center of consciousness, it easily succumbs to the illusion that it is the center of the whole psychological universe and in control of the other splinter psyches. This state of inflation, which is based on too close an identification between the individual ego and the archetypal self (assimilation of the ego by the self: see Jung 1966, par. 260ff.), can lead to psychic symptoms, dangerous overestimation of self-mastery and control, and illusions of grandiosity vis-à-vis the world at large. While inflation of this sort is normal in early childhood, such a state of fusion of ego and self, if it continues too long, lays the groundwork for narcissistic personality disorders. This development is seen today as being caused by inadequate relations with a primary caretaker (the "mother"); the child is abandoned (emotionally if not physically) and so compensates for the absence of the suitably mirroring "other" by clinging to an archetypal structure that replaces the person. A lack of sufficient differentiation between ego and self on the internal level is then projected into the world, where the narcissistic individual assumes an unreal and usually very fragile position of centrality and entitlement. The ego must learn through hard experience and much analysis that it is not the master of the psychic household and that it is subject to fluctuations in the psychic economy. This hard-won knowledge is the sought-for outcome of analysis.

The ego that has not disentangled itself sufficiently from the self can behave like the executive of an organization who fails to realize that he needs the cooperation of even the humblest workers in order to function well. This ego takes too much credit for the success of the organization and usually tries to avoid blame if the organization fails. The workers, on the other hand, also need the executive; if sane executive decisions and judgments are made, all may survive and prosper. This perception of interrelatedness among the parts of the intrapsychic world is where the ego needs to arrive in its awareness in order for sanity and optimal functioning to become possible. It is a position of humility and large responsibility rather than the glorification expected by an inflated ego.

If, because of its deep internal association with the self, the ego has a tendency to assume centrality in the world and to fall into grandiose illusions of specialness and importance, it can also suffer the opposite problem if the connection between ego and self is too tenuous and distant. Then the ego feels abandoned and unmoored in a frightening world of impersonal forces. It feels inadequate and suffers from low self-confidence and high self-doubt.

The proper balance in this relation between ego and self is discussed in Jungian literature under the heading of the ego-self axis. If the ego-self axis is sufficiently and properly developed, a person has the feeling of possessing a solid core of inner strength, identity, and value and has access to resources for self-esteem and confidence, but the ego is not puffed up and unrealistically inflated.

The ego develops, according to Jung, through suffering collisions with the environment. These collisions, if they are not too severe and injurious, bring challenges rather than debilitating traumas. If the ego responds positively to the challenges posed by the environment, it develops strength and mastery and begins to show increasing autonomy. It gains self-confidence and adapts more and more effectively and forcefully to the world around. For this reason, some analysts will, after having established a sound working relationship with an analysand whose ego is relatively sound and healthy, deliberately create tension in the relationship in order to facilitate ego strengthening. Some will "rotate typology," that is, assume the opposite typology from the analysand, in order to challenge the ego. Or they will play devil's advocate or make demands for adaptation that they assume the analysand can reach. This technique is, of course, not suitable for every case; with more fragile and disturbed egos, which may fall easily into mistrust or paranoia, this technique would be contraindicated. Empathy is needed there in large and steady quantities.

If the ego is severely damaged or overcome by the collisions with the environment, the traumata result in the development of split-off complexes. The traumatic event may become largely repressed because of the psychic pain involved, but the wound will leave a point of fragility in the ego where it can easily fragment and become defensive. These points of vulnerability are carefully noted in analysis, appearing typically in transference reactions and often in dreams. Interpretation and supportive insight into their origins and functioning are the usual means of treatment in Jungian analysis.

The complexes of the personal unconscious are organized around a discrete number of archetypal cores—for example, images of archetypal Great Mother and Father—and these can be identified over time as they make their appearance in the transference and through reflection on life situations as they arise in the course of analysis. The simple rule of projection is that what is unconscious can be projected, and the parental projections typically land on the analyst. When this happens, the analyst accepts it as an opportunity to allow the analysand to rework a relationship with parental complexes that has long since been in place and has controlled many of the ego's choices and decisions. Since complexes are distinguished by a high degree of affectivity and volatility, this work with transference is usually fraught with great emotional intensity. The analyst also can become "infected" (Jung's term) with the transferential material and can actually assume the feelings and roles projected into him or her by the complex (see Stein, 1992a). In analysis this is much more easily observed than controlled. What it does is give the analyst a firsthand experience of the intrapsychic conflicts suffered by the analysand, and this can be extremely useful for empathic interpretation of the analysand's struggles.

No experienced analyst labors under the illusion that complexes can be eliminated or mastered. They can be worked on and to some degree "worked through," but they are like the old bulls of the bullring: tough, experienced, and unlikely to give in to the matador under any circumstances. They function independently of the ego and will continue to do so even after many years of intense focused analysis. But knowledge about the complexes—how they work and what stimulates them—can extend the ego's range of options, so that a person knows how to stay away from likely sources of complex stimulation and learns or masters certain techniques for calming down after the inevitable complex discharge. Through analysis some of the energy is drained from the complexes, too, and can be used for ego purposes. Learning about how one's personal complexes function is a part of the educational process (Jung, 1931) that analysis engenders and is considered an important aspect of analysis by most Jungians.

In its history of interacting with the environment, the ego employs and develops certain characteristic features and manners of coping and self-protection. Some tools are at its disposal innately and are provided by nature. The ego inherits a specific "typology," that is, a characteristic tendency to assume one of two attitudes (introversion or extroversion) and one of two main functions (thinking or feeling, sensation or intuition). As this innate combination of attitude and function(s) matures in the course of development, it produces a typical cognitive style. There are introverted intuitive thinking types (the philosophers among us) and there are extroverted sensate thinking types (the managers); extroverted or introverted intuitive feeling types (the therapists and artists) and extroverted sensate feeling types (the designers and decorators). Typology forms an aspect of the personality's character structure that helps the ego cope with the environment and with the collisions that take place between itself and the surrounding world. Of course, this typology can also distort a person's reading of the environment and can, like projection, get in the way of adequate ego functioning and adaptation to the demands of life. Ordinarily a person's typology will unfold quite naturally if supported and encouraged by parents and schools. If not, a "cross-type" development can take place, which occurs when the natural typology is not accepted and the individual tries to adapt to social pressures and expectations by assuming another typology more in keeping with collective norms and expectations. This may lay the groundwork for psychological problems later in life.

Some Jungian analysts make extensive use of typology theory in their analytic work. One initial goal of therapy is typically to restore a person to natural, innate typological functioning if this has become distorted during development. In an extroverted society, for example, introverts need permission to be themselves as introverts. The depathologizing of certain typologies has a powerful therapeutic effect and goes a long way toward allowing an ego to find its own natural way of containing psyche, handling reality, and dealing with the environment. This job of ego restoration usually requires the dismantling of the parental complexes that maintain the twists in typology.

In addition to attitude and functions, the ego possesses defenses to help it cope with the world and with relationships. Typology is not seen by Jung as defensive in and of itself, even though it may be used in self-protective ways. The ego's defenses, properly speaking, include such operations as splitting, projection, introjection, and repression. Jung himself did not focus strongly on defenses in his writings, and Jungians after him have followed suit. Nor is there, in analytical psychology, great emphasis on techniques for analyzing defenses, although paradoxically the overcoming of repression and the healing of psychic splits are given great importance in discussions of the goal of maturation, which is the relative achievement of psychic wholeness. The movement toward wholeness would seem to demand as a first condition the overcoming of defenses that prevent integration from taking place. Some recent work by Jungian analysts has focused somewhat more extensively on the question of analyzing defenses (Dieckmann, 1991; Fordham, 1957; Schwartz-Salant, 1989; Van Eenwyk, 1991).

This is especially crucial in the therapeutic analysis of neurotic conditions. In neurosis, the one-sidedness of the conscious attitude is so entrenched and the repressions so tightly wired into the structures that have developed historically that the deeper unconscious activities of symbol formation and instinctual percept creation are severely blocked. The evolutionary movement toward wholeness is stunted to the point of psychic invalidism. The symptoms, which are symbolic cries for help and indicators of what is needed, are compromise formations that cannot effect actual change or have significant influence on ego-consciousness even while they speak. Here the skill and technique of the analyst in interpreting defenses is necessary and can be beneficial.

By hearing the soul's cry for help and taking a stand on the side of the wounded and distorted individuation drive, the therapist can also aid and abet the deeper unconscious processes that are striving for health and wholeness. What Jung refers to as "soul" (the anima and animus in his writings) is a level of psyche that forms a link between ego-consciousness and the instinctual-archetypal, natural psyche, which ultimately is also the link between the ego and the self (Stein, 1992b). The anima/animus structure is a "function" that corresponds to what Jung elsewhere calls the transcendent function (Jung, 1916), and its purpose is to provide a channel of communication between the ego and the deepest levels of the collective unconscious. It is also roughly equivalent to the ego-self axis if one imagines the axis as a function. To advance this cause of establishing a vital contact with the soul, almost any technique that does the job is good technique. In analytic practice, the usual Jungian move in trying to facilitate this recovery of the soul connection is to work intensively on dreams and to engage in active imagination.

Dream Analysis and Active Imagination

Dreams and fantasies are classic subverters of collective orthodoxy. They are also subverters of hardened and entrenched neurotic structure. Many dreams bypass the blockages created by the complexes and reach to the layer of soul, of anima and animus in Jung's terminology, which is the connecting link to the depths of the instinctual/archetypal psyche. It is not surprising that collective orthodoxies of all kinds seek to discount the value that might be placed on these products of unconscious process, nor is it surprising that neurotic analysands will resist bringing dreams into analysis or giving them much credence when they do. This is the resistance to soul.

The Jungian approach to analysis of the unconscious and to therapy of ego-consciousness is oriented largely by working with dreams and inner images and taking cues from them as to what kinds of intervention would be useful on the analyst's part. Dream analysis was and remains the cornerstone of classical and also of much neoclassical or post-Jungian analysis (see Samuels, 1985).

Dreams require interpretation and a method for rendering their often puzzling themes and images psychologically useful in analysis. Jung's hermeneutic for dream interpretation is basically twofold: reductive and synthetic. If the clinical picture and the dream themes point to the need to interpret dreams reductively, that is, in terms of the past and especially of childhood and pathological developmental issues, then the analyst takes this approach. This is particularly recommended for character disorders and conditions implying ego inflation. Where the clinical picture and the dreams point toward the need for a prospective, synthetic approach, the analyst will interpret in terms of future possibilities, untapped potentialities, and larger symbolic meanings. This is usually recommended for cases of depression and chronic low self-esteem and feelings of victimization. Striking the balance between these two approaches, which are typically both used at one point or another in most lengthy analyses, is a clinical art. Timing and appropriateness depend greatly on the analyst's trained intuition and the accuracy of empathic knowledge of the analysand's inner states.

In a departure from Freud's theory of interpretation, Jung did not place much value on free association as a means for discovering the meaning of dreams. Free association, he felt, does not break free of the controlling complexes and the dominant ego attitude. It goes in a circle of the already more or less known. For Jung, the dream is not meaningful until it is brought to the point of telling the dreamer something new. If you can think the thought, he felt, you do not need to dream it. So the interpretive strategy is to stay with the dream images as presented until they begin to reveal ideas, insights, patterns, or feeling states that are not already familiar to the ego. At that point, the ego can begin to benefit from the compensatory function of dreaming and can open a pathway to the deeper healing influences of the natural psyche, the instinctual and archetypal layers. The dream then begins to function as a pathway to the soul of the analysand.

A second method besides dream interpretation for reaching past the personal complexes and ego defenses into the deeper layers of the psyche was discovered by Jung in his use of active imagination. In active imagination, the analysand (in private, not in the analytic session) opens a dialogue with figures of the unconscious as they have appeared either in earlier dreams or in the active imagination itself. These imaginal figures do not represent the personal complexes—for example, mother and father—but rather figures of the archetypal, collective unconscious. Active imagination figures function much like icons on a computer screen, opening the way to programs locked deeply away in the hidden layers of the unconscious. By stimulating these iconic images, the ego is exposed to a stream of messages and information from sources of energy and insight in the unconscious that lie beyond the individual's neurotic patterns, acquired complexes, and conventional ego attitudes.

Active imagination was classically a technique invoked in analysis to help resolve intransigent transferences. It does this by replacing an outer icon (i.e., the analyst) with an inner one. As an analytic technique, active imagination may be used throughout treatment or become more emphasized toward the end of analysis as a way of preparing for termination.

Practice follows vision and theory in Jung's psychology, but practice also feeds theory and keeps it growing and evolving. The Jungian vision is a continuously expanding one. What Jung himself lays down is a powerful and compelling view of the wondrous complexity and nuanced subtlety of the human psyche. Based in two polarities—the body and the spirit—it receives material and energy from both ends of this spectrum. The human being is both an animal and a spiritual agent. Jung's theory of the psyche therefore spans the heights and depths of human experience and accounts for the similarities and differences we find among human beings throughout recorded history. The rich territory where instincts and archetypes meet is the psyche, a vast and nearly inexhaustible wonderland of figures and energies.

Jung's is also a theory that allows for human evolution and emergence. Neither the individual nor the race is a static, "given" entity but rather an evolving process in motion. The final goal is unknown and can only be surmised on the basis of what is known about the basic structures of the psyche as we can come to understand them. What Jung concluded is that there is in the individual an implacable drive toward wholeness.

Pathology is caused by a departure from this basic ground plan. In its milder forms, it amounts to simple one-sidedness that needs correction. In its more virulent forms, it presents obstacles to living a full existence that need serious, sustained analytic treatment. Even in such cases, however, assistance is usually from nature itself, for healing has its deepest source in nature rather than in the healing ministrations of therapists.

For Jung, the fundamental human struggle is to become oneself as fully and completely as possible. What this means is living the basic plan of the psyche, which is written into the fabric of nature itself. This is not without many inherent conflicts that produce necessary suffering (as opposed to neurotic suffering) and severe limitation. The narrative that unfolds from this struggle is the story of individuation, a story of limitation but also of the realization of potentials that lie hidden in the depths of the unconscious from the beginning, awaiting the quickening summons of auspiciously timed constellating life events.

NOTES

A disclaimer is in order at the outset. An essay this brief on a subject this large must of necessity represent a personal confession of the author's tastes and biases as much as it does the subject matter itself. The reader should remember, too, that forty years have passed since Jung's death, and the field of analytical psychology has continued to evolve and change dynamically during this period. In this essay, I attempt to capture something of Jung's spirit and general attitude about analysis and life as well as the particular details of what he said about theory and practice in his *Collected Works* and elsewhere. I hope to communicate what I have absorbed from reading Jung (and Jungians) over the past twenty-five years and practicing as a Jungian analyst for the past twenty. This essay is a personal but hopefully not idiosyncratic account.

1. The debate over what heals in psychotherapy continues to rage in clinical circles and beyond. For an impassioned statement about the necessity of love for healing to take place in analysis, see Aldo Carotenuto's *The Difficult Art* (Wilmette: Chiron Publications, 1992). A less heated statement of a similar view is made by Kenneth Lambert in *Analysis, Repair and Individuation* (New York: Academic Press, 1981) in his discussion of agape in analysis. Jung himself does not use the word "love" often, but he does favor the view that "kinship libido" is important in the process of psychological transformation in analysis. Most

Jungian discussions of the transference/countertransference process in analysis allude strongly to the relation between healing and love.

2. Henri Ellenberger (1970) makes a strong point of Jung's connections to the romantic movement, at least in style and tone. What this view overlooks, at least if taken to an extreme, is the equally strong, perhaps even more dominant, classical flavor in Jung's conception of the psyche as a self-regulating system of balanced forces and his preference for the rather staid number 4 over the more dynamic and lively number 3. It must also never be forgotten that Jung was committed to a medical and scientific orientation that required both practical results in treatment and responsible discussion and verification in research and publishing.

3. Liliane Frey-Rohn's detailed work *From Freud to Jung* (1974) remains the best single reference for the connections between Freud's theories (early and late) and Jung's revisions and transformations. It must be said, however, that in the long perspective of Jung's oeuvre as a whole the Freudian influence is not the crucial element. Jung's style of thinking and his cultural references were vastly different from Freud's. What Freud did was to inspire him to pursue certain lines of thought along which he might otherwise not have found his way quite so readily. Once on the track, however, Jung took his own direction, although not without a great deal of struggle and difficulty in freeing himself from the influence of Freud's genius (see Hogenson, 1994).

4. Andrew Samuels, a London Jungian analyst, in his book *The Political Psyche* (1993), takes the view that politics and political awareness are "instinctual," but he uses the word "instinct" to mean simply that most human beings find themselves thinking about politics a lot, worrying about politics, and even dreaming about politicians and political issues. He wants to make the point that analysts should concern themselves with the political consciousness (and unconsciousness) of their analysands and take politics more seriously in their daily work, not only interpreting political themes in terms of internal process and/or transference dynamics. He is not proposing a "political drive" per se, as I read him.

5. For more on Jung's views on the subject of evil, the reader can consult *Jung on Evil* (Jung, 1994).

6. Confession was seen by Jung (1931) as the first of four stages of psychotherapeutic treatment. Following confession, he listed elucidation (the "Freudian" interpretive stage), education, and transformation. Not all analytic treatments go through all four stages, but one would suppose that in all successful cases, each of the four stages would have been included to some extent.

7. The Jungian offshoot movement called archetypal psychology (founded by James Hillman) has severed the connection between image and instinct, and the consequence has been a highly cerebral theory without embodiment and having little clinical application. Archetypal psychology emphasizes conscious reflection on psychological life from an impersonal viewpoint and uses archetypal images

from classical myth, particularly Greek myth, to interpret behavior and psychic material such as dreams.

8. This view that the archetypes are at home in "spirit" has led some commentators to compare Jung's theory to Plato's, whose doctrine of eternal forms matches, in some respects, Jung's archetypal hypothesis. In temperament, however, the two thinkers are vastly different, Plato being a speculative philosopher and Jung claiming the stance of an empirical scientist.

REFERENCES

Dieckmann, H. 1991. *Methods in Analytical Psychology*. Wilmette, IL: Chiron.
Ellenberger, H. 1970. *The Discovery of the Unconscious*. New York: Basic Books.
Fordham, M. 1957. *New Developments in Analytical Psychology*. London: Routledge.
Frey-Rohn, L. 1974. *From Freud to Jung*. New York: Putnam.
Galimberti, U. 1989. Analytical psychology in an age of technology. In *Zeitschrift fur Analytische Psychologie und ihre Grenzgebiete* 20:87–120. (Author's translation).
Hogenson, G. 1994. *Jung's Struggle with Freud*. Wilmette, IL: Chiron.
Jung, C. G. 1916. The transcendent function. In *Collected Works*, vol. 8, pp. 67–90. Princeton: Princeton University Press, 1969.
———. 1931. Problems of modern psychotherapy. In *Collected Works*, vol. 16, pp. 53–75. Princeton: Princeton University Press, 1969.
———. 1936. Psychological factors determining human behavior. In *Collected Works*, vol. 8, pp. 114–25. Princeton: Princeton University Press, 1969.
———. 1954. On the nature of the psyche. In *Collected Works*, vol. 8, pp. 159–234. Princeton: Princeton University Press, 1969.
———. 1955–1956. *Mysterium Coniunctionis*. In *Collected Works*, vol. 14. Princeton: Princeton University Press, 1969.
———. 1966. *Two Essays on Analytical Psychology*. In *Collected Works*, vol. 7. Princeton: Princeton University Press.
———. 1975. *Letters*, Vol. 2. Princeton: Princeton University Press.
———. 1976. *The Symbolic Life*. In *Collected Works*, vol. 18. Princeton: Princeton University Press.
———. 1994. *Jung on Evil*. Ed. Murray Stein, London: Routledge.
Kerr, J. 1993. *A Most Dangerous Method*. New York: Knopf.
Samuels, A. 1985. *Jung and the Post-Jungians*. London: Routledge.
———. 1993. *The Political Psyche*. London: Routledge.
Schwartz-Salant, N. 1989. *The Borderline Personality*. Wilmette, IL: Chiron.
Stein, M. 1992a. Power, shamanism, and maieutics in the countertransference. In

Transference/Countertransference, ed. N. Schwartz-Salant and M. Stein. Wilmette, IL: Chiron.

———. 1992b. The role of anima/animus structures and archetypes in the psychology of narcissism and some borderline states. In *Gender and Soul in Psychotherapy*, ed. N. Schwartz-Salant and M. Stein. Wilmette, IL: Chiron.

Van Eenwyk, J. 1991. The analysis of defenses. *Journal of Analytical Psychology* 36(2):141–63.

Chapter Three

Alfred Adler
Classical Theory and Practice

Henry T. Stein and Martha E. Edwards

EDITORS' INTRODUCTION

Mainstream psychoanalysis has essentially ignored Classical Adlerian psychology, which is based on Alfred Adler's original theory of personality and style of psychotherapy. The Adlerians' alternative explanations of conscious and unconscious processes, personality development, and transference-resistance have differentiated them from mainstream psychoanalysis. Furthermore, their commitment to a unified, holistic view of personality has connected them to humanistic psychologists like George Kelly, Carl Rogers, and Abraham Maslow. We will let the readers decide for themselves whether Classical Adlerian psychology represents a depth psychology worthy of a second look by psychoanalysts.

According to Henry T. Stein and Martha E. Edwards, the Classical Adlerian approach illuminates the depth and nuances of Adler's original theory and practice; in our view, they have an interesting story to tell. This is especially true in light of Adler's historical significance to psychoanalysis and the fact that theorists have integrated many of Adler's concepts into contemporary psychoanalytic discourse without giving him adequate credit. For example, the Classical Adlerian approach is centrally concerned with a key concept that best depicts Adler's view of the human condition: "The concept of the Social Human, inextricably interconnected with others and all of nature." Adler, in other words, was one of the first to assert the importance of viewing the individual as fundamentally a social being, one that could be adequately understood only when situated in a sociocultural context. Adler's views also represented an embryonic ego psychology such that the ego was viewed not primarily as the handmaiden of the id, but as an independent, creative entity mediating intercourse with social reality.

Adler's conception of the human condition rejects libido and instinct as the fundamental human motive. Rather, he developed one of the first interpersonal models that stressed man's search for significance, security, escape from inferiority, and personal and social completeness as the fundamental coordinates on which to plot human lives in progress. Adler believed that the great human desire, more fundamental than sexual and pleasure-seeking strivings, was the striving to overcome personal, social, and environmental difficulties. As Stein and Edwards point out, the core of Adler's conception of human nature was a strongly optimistic, humanistic view of life that conceived human beings as capable of sustained cooperation in living together and aspiring for self-improvement, self-fulfillment, and contribution to the common good. Indeed, Adler referred to this essential quality of the healthy personality as *Gemeinschaftsgefühl* (feeling of community).

Psychopathology for Adler is rooted in the person's choice of his "fictional final goal," a subjective (fictional), unconscious, and creative striving to master the obstacles of his life, that is, self ideals. In the neurotic it is directed by egoistic, self-centered strivings for personal superiority and security emanating from the neurotic's inflated perception of self and overcompensation for feelings of deep inferiority; in the "normal" person, the personality's goal is largely guided by a greater feeling of community, and any compensation for felt inferiority has a more socially useful impact.

As Stein and Edwards describe it, psychotherapy for the Classical Adlerian aims at increasing the patient's feeling of community. The diagnostic indicators employed include, for example, the analysis of early recollections and the interpretation of the child's ordinal position in the family. Early recollections are important indicators because they reveal the central concerns and unconscious goals (fictions) of personality through its conscious choice of key memories. As the authors conclude, for the Classical Adlerian it is not merely a matter of gaining insight, but of using that insight to take concrete steps to improve relationships with family, friends, community, and work. This means using cognitive, affective, and even behavioral strategies to stimulate the patient's courage, help her overcome inferiority feelings, and help her develop a stronger feeling of connectedness to the community. (P. M. and A. R.)

Overview

Over the half century since Alfred Adler articulated his theory of personality and system of psychotherapy, his ideas have gradually and persistently permeated the whole of contemporary psychology (Ellenberger, 1970, pp. 645–48). The shift of psychoanalysis to ego psychology reflected Adler's original thinking, and Adler was "hailed by certain psychoanalysts as a precursor of the later developments of psychoanalysis" (Ellenberger, 1970, p. 638). Adler's observation that "human beings live in the realm of meanings" reflects the constructivist view of human behavior. An early feminist, he held that both men and women suffered from our society's overvaluing of men and undervaluing of women, and he believed that the only positive relationship between men and women was one of equality. His earliest work in which he argued for the unity of mind and body was a precursor of psychosomatic medicine.

Even the findings of anthropologists, biologists, and physicists parallel Adlerian concepts. Adler's view of the interconnectedness of all living beings and their natural proclivities toward cooperation has been echoed by anthropologists (Ho, 1993; Kim and Berry, 1993; Maybury-Lewis, 1992), and biologists (Augros and Stancui, 1988; Hamilton, 1964; Simon, 1990; Trivers, 1971; Wilson, 1975). His concept of the style of life, where one central theme is reflected in every psychological expression, suggests the concept in physics of the hologram, wherein each part of a whole is an enfolded image of that whole (Briggs and Peat, 1989). His concept of the final goal, a fictional future reference point that pulls all movements in the same direction, is similar to that of a strange attractor in chaos theory, a magnetic end point that pulls on and sets limits for a process (Nelson, 1991). He believed in the fundamental creative power of individuals and their freedom to choose and change their direction in life; this is very similar to the biological process called autopoiesis, which is the autonomous, self-renewing, and self-directing nature of all life forms (Nelson, 1991).

When sociologists, anthropologists, biologists, mathematicians, physicists, and psychotherapists begin describing remarkably similar dynamics, one wonders if we are on the brink of a new unified field theory. Forty years ago, Alexander Müller frequently referred to Adler's body of work as "philosophical anthropology," and held that it had the potential for providing the magnetic center that would draw other disciplines together (Müller, 1992).

The scientific paradigm shift and intellectual climate of the 1990s might well be ripe for a rediscovery of Adler's original and full contribution to an understanding of human beings and their relationship to the world. He created an exquisitely integrated, holistic theory of human nature and psychopathology, a set of principles and techniques of psychotherapy, a worldview, and a philosophy of living.

In this chapter we will first describe Adler's view of the human condition and his ideas of personality development, including optimal development. Second, we will outline his explanation of how this process goes astray and results in psychopathology. Third, we will sketch the Adlerian levels of intervention, which include not only psychotherapy but also preventive programs in the areas of parenting and education.

The Human Condition and Personality Development

The core of Adler's integrated complex of philosophy, theory, and practice was a vigorously optimistic, humanistic view of life. He offered a value-oriented psychology that envisioned human beings as capable of profound cooperation in living together and striving for self-improvement, self-fulfillment, and contribution to the common welfare. Indeed, Adler predicted that if we did not learn to cooperate, we would run the risk of eventually annihilating each other. Thus, if we were to distill his view of the human condition into one main idea, it would be the concept of the Social Human, inextricably interconnected with others and all of nature. The central problem that humans face is how to live on this planet together, appreciating what others have contributed in the past, and making life better for present and future generations.

The Central Concept: Feeling of Community

Following from his view of the human condition, Adler based his psychology on the central concept of *Gemeinschaftsgefühl*. It is a difficult concept to translate adequately and has been translated as social interest, social feeling, community feeling, and social sense (Ansbacher and Ansbacher, 1956, p. 134). Adler and many of his followers came to prefer the term "feeling of community" (Bruck, 1978). It is a multifaceted concept. Individuals may understand and put into practice some aspects and neglect the development of others.

If people have developed social interest at the affective level, they are likely to feel a deep belonging to the human race and, as a result, are able to empathize with their fellow humans. They can then feel very much at home on the earth, accepting both the comforts and the discomforts of life. At the cognitive level, they can acknowledge the necessary interdependence with others, recognizing that the welfare of any one individual ultimately depends on the welfare of everyone. At the behavioral level, these thoughts and feelings can then be translated into actions aimed at self development as well as cooperative and helpful movements directed toward others. Thus, at its heart, the concept of feeling of community encompasses individuals' full development of their capacities, a personally fulfilling process that creates people who have something worthwhile to contribute to one another. At the same time, the concept denotes a recognition and acceptance of the interconnectedness of all people.

These ideas also speak to the current discussion of the relationship between self and society. Unlike others, Adler saw no fundamental conflict between self and society, individuality and relatedness, self-interest and social interest. These are false dichotomies. The development of self and the development of connectedness are recursive processes that influence one another in positive ways. The greater one's personal development, the more one can connect positively with others; the greater one's ability to connect with others, the more one is able to learn from them and develop oneself. This idea has been rediscovered by recent authors (Guisinger and Blatt, 1994).

Adler saw the connections among living beings in many different spheres and on many different levels. An individual can feel connected with another, with family, friends, community, and so on, in ever widening circles. This connectedness can encompass animals, plants, even inanimate objects until, in the largest sense, the person feels connected with the entire cosmos (Müller, 1992, p. 138). If people truly understood and felt this connectedness, then many of the self-created problems of life—war, prejudice, persecution, discrimination—might cease to exist.

The feeling of interconnectedness among people is essential not only for the development of society, but also for the development of each individual person. It has long been well known that if human infants do not have emotional connections with their caregivers they will fail to thrive and are likely to die.

Furthermore, individuals need to acknowledge their connectedness to the past as well as to the future. What we are able to do in our lives depends very much on the contributions made in the past by others. A critical question that Adler saw facing each person was, What will be your contribution to life? Will it be on the useful or useless side of life?

The title that Adler gave to his system, "Individual Psychology," does not immediately suggest its social foundation. It does not mean a psychology of individuals. On the contrary, Adler's psychology is very much a social psychology in which the individual is seen and understood in his or her social context. Accordingly, Adler devised interventions not only for individual clients but also for families and schools.

In German, the term *Individualpsychologie* means the psychology of the unique, indivisible, and undivided person (Davidson, 1991, p. 6). What Adler meant by this is that, first, "Individual Psychology" is an idiographic science. How an individual develops is unique, creative, and dependent on the subjective interpretations the person gives to life. Second, Adler meant to convey that an individual behaves as a unit in which the thoughts, feelings, actions, dreams, memories, and even physiology all lead in the same direction. The person is a system in which the whole is greater than and different from the sum of its parts. In this whole, Adler saw the unity of the person. In the symphony of a person's behavior, he discerned the consistent melodic theme running throughout. This theme may have many variations in tempo, pitch, or intricacy, but it is nevertheless recognizable. Thus, to understand a person, we must look at the whole person, not at the parts isolated from one another. After we grasp the guiding theme, however, it is easy to see how each individual part is consistent with the theme.

Development of Personality

How do we come to develop this guiding theme? It is an active and creative process in which individuals attribute meaning to the life experiences they have faced. They construct out of this raw material the subjective reality to which they respond. Thus, they are not passive victims of heredity or environment (not objects) but active constructors and interpreters of their situations (subjects).

This process begins in infancy as children become conscious of felt insufficiencies in the face of normal, everyday tasks, especially when they compare themselves to older children and adults. As a result, they experience what Adler called inferiority feelings, which are the very normal reactions to the awareness of not being able to function in a way that we wish. Adler also described this as experiencing a "minus situation." These feelings become motivation for striving toward what he called a "plus situation."

Individuals strive in this direction because of the "creative power of life, which expresses itself in the desire to develop, to strive, to achieve, and even to compensate for defeats in one direction by striving for success in another. This power is teleological, it expresses itself in the striving after a goal, and, in this striving, every bodily and psychological movement is made to cooperate" (Ansbacher and Ansbacher, 1956, p. 92).

Influenced by the German philosopher Hans Vaihinger, Adler held that individuals were not always guided in their actions by reality. They were also guided by fictions, or what they believe to be true, though these beliefs are largely unconscious (Vaihinger, 1925). These ideas formed the basis of Adler's concept of the final goal. The final goal is a fictional creation of the individual—an imagined ideal situation of perfection, completion, or overcoming. Movement toward the final goal is motivated by a striving to overcome the feelings of inferiority. Although the final goal represents a subjective, fictional view of the future, it is what guides the person in the present.

In an active, courageous individual possessing a strong feeling of community, the striving toward the final goal to overcome inferiority feelings may be expressed as a lifelong movement toward optimal development—with full realization that there is no end point to this striving. This is quite similar to Abraham Maslow's view of individuals striving toward self- actualization, toward the full realization of their potential (Maslow, 1970).

The influences of the family (both parents and siblings) as well as external social influences may be critical for a person's ability to deal with inferiority feelings and develop the final goal. Children learn to cope with and/or overcome difficulties in life through the support and encouragement of significant others who promote their development, cooperation, and interdependence. Adler considered the connection with and influence of the mother the primary factor in the early development of the feeling of community. In our current social structure, fathers and caregivers are also recognized as important influences. With this positive foundation, children are likely to grow up to handle what Adler called the three tasks of life—work, community, and love—in a satisfactory way (Adler, 1992a, pp. 16–18). As a result, they are likely to develop the courage and ability to continue their growth and make a contribution to life. If, however, children do not receive the proper encouragement and support and, as a result, their feelings of inferiority become exaggerated, they are likely to be discouraged. They may adopt a final goal that is equally exaggerated to compensate for their deeply felt inferiority. Instead of developing themselves and overcoming difficulties, they pursue a goal of imagined superiority and consequently must avoid real tests of themselves. Their final goal would then be an egocentric one, on the useless side of life, rather than a goal of cooperation with others and a feeling of community. The final goal is the result of a process that is unique to each individual. Two persons with similar feelings of inferiority—for example, a deeply felt lack of intelligence—may develop very different goals. One person's goal might be to enlist others in his or her service, thus avoiding any tests of intelligence that might be failed. The other's goal might be to outdo all others, thereby demonstrating her superior intelligence in all situations.

Adler called an individual's characteristic approach to life the style of life. In various writings throughout Adler's career, he expressed this concept as self or ego, personality, individuality, the unity of the personality, an individual form of creative activity, the method of facing problems, one's opinion about oneself and the problems of life, or the whole attitude toward life (Ansbacher and Ansbacher, 1956, p. 174).

The style of life, then, becomes the way individuals approach or avoid the three main tasks of life and try to realize their fictional final goal. In healthy persons, this dealing with the tasks of life is relatively flexible. They can find many ways of solving problems and, when one way is blocked, they can choose another. This is not so for the disturbed individuals who usually insist on one way or no way.

Like others, Adler viewed the first five years of life as central in the development of personality. By that time, children have experienced enough to have adopted a prototype of their goal and style of life, although there can be some modification throughout the rest of childhood and adolescence. After that, these ways of conceiving of both self and the world seem to fashion for us a set of lenses through which we see the world. Adler called this the scheme of apperception. Individual perception, then, is limited, and there will always be a discrepancy between reality and the perception of it. For normal people this discrepancy is relatively small; for psychologically disturbed people the discrepancy is much greater.

In an optimal situation of development, adults will win children's cooperation, helping them develop a sense of significance through their contributions to others, minimizing their inferiority feelings, stimulating their courage, guiding them to be active, and helping them feel a part of the whole. These experiences will help children identify and develop their capacities and become cooperative, productive, and satisfied adults. They will be able to see and feel their interdependence with others and be challenged to develop sufficient courage to deal with difficulties, to connect intimately with others, and to improve themselves for the benefit of all. They may eventually be guided by universal values or principles—perhaps of justice, beauty, truth, and so on. They will be able to use their inferiority feelings as spurs for continued development. They will strive for superiority over difficulties rather than superiority over others. They will have solved the problems posed by the tasks of life in a mutually beneficial way.

This optimal development is different from what is commonly referred to as "normal" or "average." Although many people are reasonably cooperative, they may do just enough in relationships and in work to get by, living without deep commitment and passion and not functioning at their maximum potential. They may be somewhat bored and may endure chronic tension or "stress" without significant emotional or physical symptoms. When they face particularly difficult challenges, they may not have developed their courage and cooperation to the extent that they are able to cope adequately. At that point, they may experience a shock that might trigger psychological symptoms. Examples of challenges that might trigger such symptoms include layoffs, illnesses, marriage, the birth of children, divorce, middle age, children's departure from home, or retirement.

One potential challenge for mental health professionals is to help these "normal" individuals develop themselves to the maximum—to set an ideal of mental health that is seen as possible and inspiring, and to identify the steps needed to get there. This is described later in this chapter.

Adler's View of Psychopathology

Adler's view of psychopathology is deceptively simple. He conceived of psychological disturbances generally occurring in the presence of two conditions: an exaggerated inferiority feeling and an insufficiently developed feeling of community. Under these conditions, a person may experience or anticipate failure before a task that appears impossible and may become "discouraged." Adler tended to use this term as opposed to terms like "pathological" or "sick." When individuals are discouraged, they often resort to fictional means to relieve or mask—rather than overcome—their inferiority feelings. What they are attempting to do is bolster their feelings of self by "tricks," while they avoid actually confronting their seemingly impossible difficulties. These tricks may give them a comforting but fragile feeling of superiority.

A man who was pampered as a child may give up looking for work, become depressed, and then depend on parents or public assistance for support. Forcing others to provide for him may yield a secret feeling of power and superiority that compensates for his feelings of inferiority. Unprepared for the normal challenges that might lead to failure, he pays the price for his painful depression, but uses it to maintain his passive self-indulgence and protect himself from a real test of his capacities.

A woman who was abused by her father as a child may choose to reject and depreciate all men as vile creatures and never engage in a satisfactory love relationship. She may feel lonely, but she can always feel morally superior to all abusive males who are punished by her rejection. She would rather punish all men for the sins of her father than conquer her fears and develop the ability to love one man.

At a more extreme level, a profound and devastating feeling of inferiority might lead to a grandiose psychotic delusion of being God.

What all these situations have in common are adults whose inferiority feelings seem so overwhelming and in whom the feeling of community is so underdeveloped that they retreat to protect their fragile yet inflated sense of self. They employ what Adler called safeguarding devices to do this (Ansbacher and Ansbacher, 1956, pp. 263–80).

Individuals can use safeguarding devices in attempts to both excuse themselves from failure and depreciate others. Safeguarding devices include symptoms, depreciation, accusations, self-accusations, guilt, and various forms of distancing. Symptoms such as anxiety, phobias, and depression can all be used as excuses for avoiding the tasks of life and transferring responsibility to others. In this way, individuals can use their symptoms to shield themselves from potential or actual failure in these tasks. Of course, individuals may be able to do well in one or two of the tasks of life and have difficulties in only one, for example, in work, community, or love.

Depreciation can be used to deflate the value of others, result in a sense of relative superiority through aggressive criticism or subtle solicitude. Accusations attribute the responsibility for a difficulty or failure to others. Self-accusations can stave off criticisms from others or even elicit comforting protestations of value from them. Guilt may create a feeling of pious superiority over others and clear the way for continuing harmful actions rather than correcting them. Distancing from tasks and people can be done in many ways, including procrastination, avoiding commitments, abuse of alcohol and/or drugs, or suicide.

These safeguarding devices are largely unconscious and entail very real suffering on the part of individuals who employ them. For them, however, the protection and elevation of the sense of self is paramount, and they prefer to distress themselves or others rather than reveal their hidden exaggerated feeling of inferiority.

There are three categories of influences that might stimulate the development of these exaggerated inferiority feelings in children: (1) physical handicaps, (2) family dynamics, and (3) societal influences (Adler, 1992a).

Children can either be born with or develop physical handicaps (e.g., deformity, illness) with which they may feel overburdened. The care and attention given to them because of their difficulties may result in their expectation that others should always make their lives easy and keep them the center of care and attention. They may never test their own strengths. The pity or scorn they might also receive may negatively influence their self-evaluations. In any case, their inferiority feelings are likely to become exaggerated.

Family dynamics, including parenting styles and position in the family constellation, is the second category of influences on the development of the inferiority complex. Parenting styles that cause trouble for children are divided into two main categories: pampering, and neglect and abuse. Children who have been pampered have come to expect being the focus of attention and having others serve their whims. They have been trained to take rather than to give and have not learned how to face and overcome problems by themselves. As a result, they have become very dependent on others and feel unsure of themselves or unable to face the tasks of life. Thus they demand undue help and attention from others. These demands may be expressed through aggression (e.g., commands) or through weakness (e.g., shyness), by positive means (e.g., charm) or by negative means (e.g., anger). Furthermore, when pampered children grow up and others no longer do their bidding, they may interpret this refusal as aggression against them, which may lead to their taking revenge on these others.

Children who have been neglected, rejected, or abused have not experienced love and cooperation. They do not know what it means to feel a positive connection to others and, as a result, often feel isolated and suspicious. When faced with difficulties, they tend to overrate these difficulties and underrate their own abilities. To make up for what they did not receive as children, they may feel entitled to special consideration or compensation. They may want others to treat them well but do not feel an obligation to respond in turn. Remarkably, both pampered and neglected or abused children may have similar expectations as adults. The first group expects the familiar pampering to continue; the other demands pampering as compensation. Both may feel entitled to everything and obligated to nothing.

Adler was one of the first to recognize that children's positions in the family constellation of siblings also could affect their development in critical ways (Adler, 1992b, pp. 126–32). Being a significant member of the family is important, and children may become discouraged if they think they have a disadvantageous position.

For example, oldest children's experience of being "dethroned" by their younger siblings may stimulate them to decide that regaining their power is the most important thing they could do. Later in life, the pattern of striving for preeminence may continue at work, where they control subordinates excessively, and at home, where they may become domestic tyrants.

Second children, experiencing their older siblings as pacemakers, may respond by continually striving to surpass and conquer them. If this appears to be too difficult, these children may give up and withdraw from the competition. Youngest children have many pacemakers and can become quite ambitious and accomplished, or they may not develop the courage necessary to realize their ambitions and remain helpless babies. Only children tend to spend their lives in the company of adults, frequently as the center of attention. As a result, these children may fail to learn how to cooperate with peers.

Of course, Adler realized that the examples listed above are only a few of many possible outcomes. The objective position of the child is not the influencing factor; what are crucial are the psychological position and the meaning that the child gives to that position. Thus, two children born several years apart may grow up in ways that are quite similar to those of only children. On the other hand, if parents help their children cope with the unique demands of their positions in the family constellation, and if there is a cooperative rather than a competitive home atmosphere, the children are likely not to develop the characteristics associated with each of the positions.

The third category of influence is the societal factors outside the family that also shape how individuals develop their views of themselves and the world. Adler recognized the school as a dominant influence and spent much of his time training teachers and establishing child guidance clinics attached to the schools throughout Vienna.

Social discrimination on the basis of poverty, ethnicity, gender, religion, or educational level can also exacerbate inferiority feelings. Adler emphasized that it was not just the objective facts or influences that had an impact on the child, but the interpretation the child gives to them. Children who are discriminated against because of physical deformities or socioeconomic status, for example, may find maintaining a positive sense of self difficult. But doing so is possible if someone provides sufficient contact, understanding, and encouragement.

Finally, in a way that was far ahead of many others of his day, Adler recognized the destructive influence of our culture's archaic view of men and women. He observed that women were typically devalued and that this was a major influence in their exaggerated feelings of inferiority. But he also realized that men, too, were adversely affected. The overvaluing of men often leads to extremely high expectations, and when men begin to see that they cannot meet these expectations, their inferiority feelings also increase. Adler felt that the healthiest arrangement is a recognized equality of value between men and women, which would then result in a higher level of cooperation between them (Adler, 1980).

Early experiences, both inside and outside the family, in combination with hereditary attributes and physiological processes, are used creatively by children to form an impression of themselves and life. A final goal of success, significance, and security is imagined and a style of life is adopted to prepare for that goal. Individuals who are not self-pampering or discouraged hold opinions of themselves and the tasks of life that are reasonably close to what Adler called "common sense." These individuals feel connected to one another and have developed their ability to cooperate.

People who do not feel connected to others and have not developed the ability to cooperate will develop a private logic that becomes increasingly more skewed and divergent from common sense. This private logic involves an antithetical scheme of apperception that the person uses rigidly to classify self, others, and experience. In child development, an antithetical scheme is related to children's need for security. They quickly slot their perceptions into very simple categories, often based on whether the stimulus is considered "good" or "bad." Under normal conditions of development, however, children gradually develop the ability to perceive the subtle gradations of qualities in themselves and others. Disturbed individuals, however, because of their heightened feelings of insecurity, remain at the more primitive level of an antithetical scheme of apperception. They may, for example, see only the antithetical extremes of absolute stupidity or total brilliance. Thus, if others do not recognize their brilliance, they assume that others think they are stupid. If they are not adored by all, they may feel neglected or humiliated. If they are not totally powerful, then they must be totally powerless.

While the scheme limits the person's ability to make realistic judgments, it does serve the purpose of protecting the person's choice of a final goal and life style. If an individual feels totally powerless, then it is perfectly logical (from the point of view of his private logic) and is seemingly in his best interests to compensate by grabbing all the power he can, even if this harms others. The person ignores or justifies this harm because of his feeling of being totally powerless. In reality, however, he is not totally powerless. But if he recognized this, he would lose the justification or motivation to strive in the direction of the final goal.

Discouraged individuals may function relatively well for some time. Their functioning, however, is based on a pretense of value or significance that emerges from their private ideas, which do not hold up in reality. Eventually their private views clash with reality and lead to a shock—for example, difficulties in work, friendships, love relationships, or family—which may lead to the development of symptoms.

These symptoms, however, are not the main focus of an Adlerian understanding of psychological difficulties. What is important is how individuals use their symptoms. Symptoms are actually the smoke covering the fire of inferiority feelings. The symptoms create a detour around and distance from the threatening tasks of life, protecting the pretense. Three factors distinguish mild psychological disorders from severe disorders: the depth of the inferiority feelings, the lack of the feeling of community, and the height of the final goal.

In focusing too much on the symptoms per se, we run the risk of neglecting what underlies the symptoms—the inferiority feelings. Unless the severity of these inferiority feelings is diminished, the client will continue to use the symptoms like a crutch for an injured, unhealed limb. And until this process is uncovered and resolved, the person may just substitute one symptom for another.

Adlerian Interventions

Adler's contributions to mental health included several levels of intervention. While the art of psychotherapy was his primary work, he also had a major impact on the field of education in efforts to prevent psychological disorders (Adler, 1957). Adler started by training parents, but realized that in order to reach the majority of children he needed to switch his focus to teachers. In Vienna he spent a great deal of time lecturing to teachers and demonstrating how to understand and influence children. In addition, he was asked to establish child guidance clinics attached to the schools throughout Vienna. He saw prevention through education as the first level of intervention and as a great investment in the future. Continuing in these efforts, many of Adler's followers simplified some of the ideas for use by teachers and parents (Dreikurs and Soltz, 1964; Dreikurs and Grey, 1968), thus furthering Adler's influence.

The next level of intervention is counseling. Adlerian counseling is generally time-limited, supportive therapy that is usually focused on specific problems. It leads to moderate insight, attitude change, and behavioral change. Anthony Bruck, an associate of Adler, developed brief counseling to a fine art, including the use of explanatory graphics and charts (Bruck, 1978). Examples of the focus of counseling include parenting, marital relationships, and career choice and development. These interventions can help individuals cope with developmental milestones, life crises, and change points in their lives. The potential for personality change at a deep level, however, lies in psychotherapy.

The overall goal of Adlerian psychotherapy is helping an individual develop from a partially functioning person into a more fully functioning one. "Fully functioning" means able to solve each of the areas of life more cooperatively, more courageously, with a greater sense of contribution and a greater sense of satisfaction. To do this, an individual must identify and work toward becoming her best self. In other words, the overall goal of therapy is to increase the individual's feeling of community. This is very practical. It is not merely a matter of gaining insight, but of using that insight to take concrete steps to improve relationships with family, friends, community, and work. In its largest sense, the goal of therapy is not to improve just the client's life; the therapist is working to improve the quality of life for everyone in the client's circle of contact, as well as improving society through the client.

Thus, the first specific goal of therapy is not necessarily fulfilling the client's expectation. The client may want instant, and somewhat magical, relief of symptoms, or he may want to continue what he is doing without feeling so uncomfortable. The therapist has to be sympathetic to this desire, but must clarify and establish, as quickly as possible, the cooperative working relationship that is required for genuine improvement of a difficult situation.

Adler suggested that we must provide a belated parental influence of caring, support, encouragement, and stimulation to cooperate. When courage and creativity are reawakened in the client, a new, unfamiliar feeling of community may develop as he discovers that he has something valuable to offer. Some people have been cared for in a mistakenly indulgent way and have absorbed it, but they have not learned to feel or express a genuine caring for others. These people, although they need to be cared for in a new encouraging way, also need to be challenged to start caring for others in this new way.

Stages of Classical Adlerian Psychotherapy

For teaching purposes, Adlerian psychotherapy can be divided into twelve stages; in each stage cognitive, affective, and behavioral changes are gradually promoted (Stein, 1990). At the last three stages, the spiritual domain can also be addressed. The stages reflect progressive strategies for awakening a client's underdeveloped feeling of community. What we must remember, however, is that the actual therapy is very spontaneous and creative and cannot be systematized into steps to which we rigidly adhere. Empathy and encouragement, although emphasized at certain points, are present in every stage of effective psychotherapy. A highly abbreviated overview of the twelve stages follows.[1]

Stage 1: Empathy-Relationship Stage

The initial therapeutic goal is to help the client become a more cooperative person, and this starts with learning to cooperate in therapy.

When the client's cooperation is lacking, the therapist can diplomatically point to this. If the client attempts to assign full responsibility for change to the therapist, the therapist can suggest that the rate of progress will depend on the degree of cooperation between them. Therapists may help in the discovery of some new helpful ideas, but the ideas must be applied to improve a situation. Initially, the client may need to express a great deal of distress with little interruption. In response, the therapist offers genuine warmth, empathy, acceptance, and understanding. To understand the uniqueness of each client, the therapist must be able to "stand in the shoes" of the client and "see and feel" what the client is experiencing. If the client is feeling hopeless, the therapist must be able to feel the client's hopelessness without feeling sorry for her, but then step back and provide hope for change. Thus, the therapist must be able to come close enough psychologically to the client in order to empathize, but withdraw neutrally at some point in order to generate hope and discuss possible improvements. An atmosphere of hope, reassurance, and encouragement enables the client to develop the feeling that things can be different.

Stage 2: Information Stage

The therapist gathers relevant information: the presenting problem and its history, the client's level of functioning in the three life tasks, information about the family of origin, early memories, and dreams. Religious and cultural influences may also have significance. When appropriate, intelligence, interest, and psychological testing are included.

The information given always contains a degree of distortion, as well as significant omissions. After studying the parallel patterns of childhood and the present and analyzing the rich projective material in early recollections and dreams, the therapist develops preliminary hypotheses about the inferiority feelings, goal, life style, private logic, and antithetical scheme of apperception.

Stage 3: Clarification Stage

Socratic questioning clarifies the client's core beliefs about self, others, and life. Then the consequences of these beliefs are evaluated and compared with new possibilities. Mistaken ideas and private logic are corrected to align with common sense. The client's ideas must be unraveled to trace how she first adopted them in childhood. A client may have the idea that if his wife doesn't give him what he wants, then she doesn't love him. The therapist might ask a series of questions to illuminate the private logic behind this statement: "Is it your idea that love is only giving you what you want? What if what you want is no good for you? Should your wife give you what is unhealthy for you? Is that really being loving?" These questions will help the client explore the meaning he gives to love and marriage and may come to change his private views of these matters.

Symptoms may serve as excuses for avoiding something that the client is not doing. One way the therapist can ferret this out is to ask the question, "If you did not have these symptoms, what would you do?" The client's answer is often quite revealing about what she is avoiding.

Stage 4: Encouragement Stage

The therapist cannot give clients courage; they must find it in themselves. The therapist can begin this process by acknowledging the courage in what the client has already done: for example, coming to therapy. Then therapist and client together can explore small steps that, with a little more courage, the client might take. It is through actually trying new behaviors and realizing that disaster is not an inevitable consequence that the client's courage grows.

Clients may have exaggerated inferiority feelings that they want to eliminate totally, believing that if they realize their goal these painful feelings will disappear. The therapist must first reduce these feelings to a manageable level and then convince the clients that normal inferiority feelings are a blessing that they may "use" as a spur for improvement.

Genuine self-esteem does not come from the approval or praise of others. It comes from the person's own experience of conquering difficulties. Therefore, small progressive action steps, aimed at overcoming previously avoided difficulties, must be taken, one at a time. For many clients, this is equivalent to doing the "felt impossible." During and after these steps, new feelings about efforts and results are acknowledged and discussed.

In attempting to avoid failure, discouraged people often decrease their level and radius of activity. They can become quite passive, wait for others to act, and limit their radius of activity to what is safe or emotionally profitable. Gradually, the level, radius, and quality of a client's activity must increase. A move in the wrong direction is often a necessary first step, which the therapist can correct after commending the attempt. Without new activity and experimentation there will be little real progress. Some new success must be achieved so that the client prepare for the next stage.

Stage 5: Interpretation and Recognition Stage

Psychological movements are the thinking, feeling, and behavioral motions that clients make in response to the external tasks facing them. Thus, in addition to listening to what the client says, the therapist must be attuned to what the client actually has done and currently does in relation to life tasks. Movements in therapy are the most visible. Does the client come on time or late; get off the track; talk all the time and leave little opportunity for the therapist to say anything; agree with everything but "forget" to put it into practice between sessions? The therapist's job is to describe these movements precisely and help the client identify the immediate goals or final goal to which they lead.

Depreciation and aggression are tactics clients use to elevate artificially their self-esteem and punish others for not living up to their mistaken expectations. Clients are often quite clever in adopting the weapon that will hurt others the most. The therapist must show the client how ineffective or childish the weapons are or that they eventually hurt the client more than they hurt the intended victim.

To dissolve the client's antithetical scheme of apperception, the therapist must dialectically question it. However, the client will probably resist this dialogue because the scheme provides certainty and supports the pursuit of the childlike, egocentric final goal. Clients' final goals represent visions of what they imagine will help them feel absolutely superior, safe, significant, and secure. When they are faced with changing these final goals, the alternative often looks like being nobody, worthless, and vulnerable. The client's scheme uses cognitive rigidity to generate very strong feelings. It locks the client into a dichotomized, superior/inferior way of seeing the world, evaluating experiences, and relating to others. Thus, to dissolve the antithetical scheme of apperception, the therapist must help the client see the real and subtly distinguishing qualities of people and experiences rather than dividing impressions into "either-or," rigidly absolute categories.

All behavior is purposive and is aimed at moving toward the final goal. If clients have goals that are on the useless side of life, then their emotions will also serve these goals. Frequently, emotion is used to avoid responsibility for actions. This is reflected in the often-heard claims of the client: "He made me angry; I couldn't help it." Each individual's use of emotions is unique, and the therapist must be sensitive and precise in identifying the underlying purposes of these emotions.

The final goal includes expectations of the roles that others should play. If the final goal is to be adored, then others must play the role of adorers; if the final goal is to dominate, then others must be submissive. The therapist must help the client identify these expectations and their actual impact on relationships. Rather than having such demands of others, clients need to learn how to generate self-demand, determining what they will do to contribute to their own development and to other people and situations.

After unfolding the meaning of the client's movements and their immediate goals, the therapist eventually leads to interpreting the core dynamics of the client's inferiority feeling, final goal, and style of life. Family constellation and experiences, current behavioral patterns, early recollections, and dreams are integrated into a unique, vivid, and consistent portrait.

In revealing the client's goal, diplomacy, good timing, and sensitivity are essential. The client must feel the encouragement of new successes before she will feel open and ready to face a clear picture of the mistaken direction she had previously followed. The therapist helps the client evaluate the goal and discover what is really gained or lost in this pursuit—using logic, humor, metaphors, reduction to absurdity, and what Adler called "spitting in the soup." In this last strategy, the therapist makes the final goal—for example, being powerful, intimidating, and demanding respect—"taste bad," perhaps by comparing it to being a Mafia don. The discussion around the client's final goal reflects a very vigorous form of thinking about the meaning of life and what the client is doing with it and what else he could or should be doing.

Stage 6: Knowing Stage

Previously, the client relied on the therapist to interpret her movements and their connection to the life style and goal. Now the client interprets situations, sharing his or her insights with the therapist. Many clients are tempted to terminate at this point, feeling that they know enough, even though they have not actually applied their insight and changed their main direction in life.

Stage 7: Missing Experience Stage

Some clients cling to strong negative feelings through powerful images and memories from childhood. These feelings may inhibit or poison their contact with people. Others may lack a depth of positive feeling in their work and relationships. They try to do "the right thing" but do not have a feeling of enjoyment or affection in the process. They may have sufficient insight but not have enough positive emotional anticipation to take new action. While it is possible with some clients to promote change through cognitive interpretation, with others an emotional breakthrough is more effective. The therapist can use role-play, guided imagery, or eidetic imagery exercises to dissolve negative imprints from parents and siblings and replace them with new nurturing, encouraging experiences and images. Ongoing groups or one-day group marathons are preferable for role-playing techniques, utilizing group members for the parental or sibling figures. Longer individual sessions can also be effective.

Stage 8: Doing Differently Stage

Insight and newly found courage are mobilized to approach old difficulties and neglected responsibilities. Small, experimental steps are ventured in the main arenas of life. Initially this is going to be hard for clients because they will not expect a positive feeling as a result of taking steps in a new direction. However, it is possible to start with what the person is willing to attempt and gradually make it more socially useful. A very aggressive person who verbally attacks others might be encouraged to attack his problems vigorously and productively instead.

Generally, all the behavioral steps that clients are encouraged to take in therapy are directed toward increasing their level of confidence and changing their life style. However, profound change occurs after the client and therapist have together identified and discussed the client's final goal and life style. On the basis of this insight, then, the client can work to change the main direction of movement and approach to the three main tasks of life (community, work, and love).

Stage 9: Reinforcement Stage

Most of the client's actions have been egocentric, providing imagined protection or self-enhancement, and neglecting the needs of others. The therapist helps clients learn to let go of themselves and focus on others, on tasks, and on the needs of situations.

All these new positive actions are encouraged and supported. As the client begins overcoming major difficulties that had been previously avoided, courageous efforts, good results, and feelings of pride and satisfaction are affirmed. As a result, the egocentricity gradually dissolves. The client may need emotional coaching to experience and express the new positive feelings.

Stage 10: Community Feeling Stage

The therapist has demonstrated his feeling of community to the client continuously, since the very first meeting, by accepting him unconditionally as a fellow human being, expressing a deep interest through listening and concern for his distress, and indicating a willingness to help. Perhaps skeptical of the therapist's good will at first, the client has felt and appreciated the genuine caring and encouragement.

The conquering of obstacles has generated courage, pride, and a better feeling of self, which now leads to a greater cooperation and feeling of community with the therapist. The client should now extend this feeling to connect more with other people, cooperate with them, and contribute significantly to their welfare. As the client's new feeling of community develops, she will become motivated to give her very best to her relationships and her work.

Stage 11: Goal-Redirection Stage

When the client begins to let go of an old goal and life style of self-protection, self-enhancement, and personal superiority over other people, he experiences a temporary feeling of disorientation as a new horizon opens up. Now, after exploring and experimenting, he may adopt a new, conscious life goal that is inspiring and socially useful. He abandons his former direction and pursues the new one because it yields a more positive feeling of self and greater appreciation from others.

Clients constantly observe their therapists and may use them as positive or negative models. How therapists behave is critical, as it may interfere with the therapy process if clients see that their therapists do not embody what they are trying to teach the clients.

Maslow explored the characteristics of many fully functioning people and concluded that what we usually refer to as "normal" or "average" functioning is actually a commonly accepted form of very limited psychological development. He set the standard of psychological health many notches higher than the benchmarks of most of his contemporaries. Adler and Maslow were in agreement on this issue, which was not to set our therapeutic sights merely on the "normal" or "average," but to aspire to the ideal of what people could become. Not many clients may be willing to reach this far, but some will be interested, and the therapist should be prepared to facilitate this journey.

As clients improve, the therapist can help them see that they can use new, more liberating and inspiring guides for their lives. These alternative guides are what Maslow called metamotivation or higher values—for example, truth, beauty, justice (Maslow, 1971). The values that individual clients choose will depend on their unique sensitivities and interests.

Stage 12: Support and Launching Stage

The client has learned to love the struggle of overcoming difficulties, now prefers the unfamiliar, and looks forward to the unexpected in life. Feeling equal to others and eager to develop fully, she expresses a spirit of generosity and wants to share what she has accomplished. Now the client can become a generator of encouragement to other people.

Feeling stronger and functioning better, the client may need a self-selected challenge to stimulate the development of his best self. The very best in a person does not simply flow out, but is a response to a healthy self-demand. It may be stimulated by an unexpected situation or a chosen challenge. The therapist may prompt the search for such a challenge and can help the client evaluate what would be a worthy, meaningful, stimulating, and socially useful challenge—one that is neither too big nor too small for the client's capabilities. For some clients, it may be the recognition of a "mission" or "calling" in their lives.

Therapeutic Techniques

The creative freedom inherent in Adlerian practice demands a variety of strategies that suit the uniqueness of each client and capture the spontaneous therapeutic opportunities the client hands to us in each session. Although the twelve stages represent a conceptual center line of treatment, essentially, a unique therapy is created for each client. The specific techniques used at any one time depend on the direction that seems currently accessible. Four main strategies characterize current classical Adlerian therapeutic technique: assessment, Socratic questioning, guided and eidetic imagery, and role-playing.[2]

Assessment

A thorough life style analysis serves as the guide to the therapeutic process; generally this occurs during the first three stages of treatment. A central technique that Adler pioneered to assess life style is the projective use of early memories (Adler, 1933). These memories, whether they are "true" or fictional, embody a person's core beliefs and feelings about self and the world. They contain reflections of the person's inferiority feelings, goal, scheme of apperception, level and radius of activity, courage, feeling of community, and style of life.

In addition to these early memories the therapist uses the following to do the assessment: (1) description of symptoms, the circumstances under which they began, and the client's description of what he would do if not plagued with these symptoms; (2) current and past functioning in the domains of love relationships, family, friendships, and school and work; (3) family of origin constellation and dynamics, and extended family patterns; (4) health problems, medication, alcohol, and drug use; and (5) previous therapy and attitude toward the therapist. While much of this information can be collected in the early therapy sessions, the therapist can also obtain it by asking the client to fill out an Adlerian Client Questionnaire (Stein, 1993). This permits the client to answer in detail many important questions and increases the client's level of activity in the therapy process. In addition, it saves some therapeutic time and enables the therapist to obtain a binocular view from both the client's written and verbal descriptions.

Socratic Questioning

The Socratic method of leading an individual to insight through a series of questions lies at the heart of Adlerian practice (Stein, 1990, 1991). It epitomizes the relationship of equals searching for knowledge and insight in a gentle, diplomatic, and respectful style, consistent with Adler's philosophy. In the early stages of psychotherapy, the therapist uses questions to gather relevant information, clarify meaning, and verify feelings. Then, in the middle stages of therapy, more penetrating, leading questions uncover the deeper structures of private logic, hidden feelings, and unconscious goals. The therapist also explores the personal and social implications of the client's thinking, feeling, and acting, in both their short- and long-term consequences. Throughout, new options are generated dialectically, examined, and evaluated to help the client take steps in a different direction of her own choosing. The results of these new steps are constantly reviewed. In the latter stages of therapy, the Socratic method is used to evaluate the impact of the client's new direction and to contemplate a new philosophy of life. The Socratic style places the responsibility for conclusions and decisions in the lap of the client. The role of the therapist is that of a "cothinker," not a superior expert. Just as Socrates was the "midwife" attending the birth of new ideas, the Adlerian therapist can serve as "midwife" to the birth of a new way of living for a client.

Guided and Eidetic Imagery

For many clients, cognitive insight and new behavior lead to different feelings. Some clients need additional specific interventions to access, stimulate, or change feelings. Guided and eidetic imagery, used in an Adlerian way, can lead to emotional breakthroughs especially when the client reaches an impasse. Eidetic imagery can be used diagnostically to access vivid symbolic mental pictures of significant people and situations that are often charged with emotion. Guided imagery can be used therapeutically to change the negative imprints of childhood family members that weigh heavily on a client and often ignite chronic feelings of guilt, fear, and resentment. These techniques are typically used in the middle stages of therapy. Alexander Müller recommended the use of imagery when a client knew that a change in behavior was sensible, but still did not take action (Müller, 1937). Some clients need a vivid image of themselves as happier in the future than they presently are, before they journey in a new direction that they know is healthier.

Role-Playing

In the middle stages of therapy, role-playing offers clients opportunities to add missing experiences to their repertoire, and to explore and practice new behavior in the safety of the therapist's office. To provide missing experiences—for example, support and encouragement of a parent—a group setting is recommended. Group members, rather than the therapist, can play the roles of substitute parents or siblings. In this way, a client can engage in healing experiences and those who participate with him can increase their own feeling of community by contributing to the growth of their peers. When learning and practicing new behaviors, the therapist can offer coaching, encouragement, and realistic feedback about probable social consequences. This is somewhat equivalent to the function of children's play as they experiment with roles and situations in preparation for growing up. Clients need to be treated with gentleness and diplomacy, yet offered challenges that strengthen their confidence and courage.

Creativity in Psychotherapy

Adlerian psychotherapy is an art, not a science, and must be practiced with the same integrity of any artistic endeavor. Though it is based on theory, philosophy, and principles, its practice must come honestly from the heart. It is not a mere technology that can be practiced "by the numbers," nor is it a bag of tricks that can be added successfully to an eclectic pile of value-free tools.

The uniqueness of each client requires constant invention. Similarly, the personality of each therapist makes his or her approach inimitable. However, as Adler himself (Hoffman, 1994) and his followers demonstrated, the personality of the therapist must be congruent with the philosophy of the therapy.[3] Through a vigorous study analysis, an Adlerian therapist assesses and reduces to a manageable level his own inferiority feelings, identifies and redirects the final goal and style of life, and develops on all levels a strong feeling of community. In addition, the person struggles with the philosophical issues of life and engages with the study analyst in a search for higher values that would be most uniquely suited to that individual.

Metatherapy

Maslow labeled this latter aspect of therapy "metatherapy" (Maslow, 1971). He suggested that the fullest development of human potential might require a more philosophical process, one that went beyond the relief of suffering and the correction of mistaken ideas and ways of living. Müller (1968) described the last phase of therapy as a "philosophical discourse." For those clients who need and desire this experience, classical

Adlerian psychotherapy offers the psychological tools and philosophical depth to realize their quest.

We summarize Adler's psychology in six central principles.[4]

1. Unity of the individual: The individual is not internally divided or a battleground of conflicting forces. Thoughts, feelings, and behaviors are consistent with the person's style of life.

2. Goal orientation: A central personality dynamic originates from the growth and forward movement of life itself. It is a future-oriented striving toward a goal of significance, superiority, or success, which is frequently out of a person's awareness. In mental health, the goal is superiority over general difficulties; in mental disorder, it is superiority over others. The early childhood feelings of inferiority, for which an individual aims to compensate, lead to the creation of a fictional goal. The depth of inferiority feeling determines the height of the goal, which then becomes the "final cause" for the person's behavior.

3. Self-determination and uniqueness: The goal may be influenced by hereditary and cultural factors, but it ultimately springs from the creative power and opinion of the individual.

4. Social context: As an indivisible whole, a system, the human being is also part of larger wholes or systems—family, community, culture, nation, humanity, the planet, the cosmos. In these contexts, we meet the three important tasks of life: community, work, and love. All are social problems. The way individuals respond to the first social system, the family, may become the prototype of their worldview.

5. Feeling of community: Each human being has the capacity for developing the feeling of interconnectedness with other living beings and learning to live in harmony with society. The personal feeling of security is rooted in a sense of belonging and embeddedness in the stream of social evolution.

6. Mental health: Social usefulness and contribution are the criteria of mental health. Maladjustment is characterized by an underdeveloped feeling of community, a deeply felt inferiority feeling, and an exaggerated, uncooperative goal of personal superiority. The goal of therapy is to increase the feeling of community, promote a feeling of equality, and replace egocentric self-protection, self-en-

hancement, and self-indulgence with self-transcending, courageous social contribution.

Does psychotherapy directly benefit a society or only the individual? Adler believed that the ultimate purpose of psychotherapy was to help people contribute to the social evolution of mankind. Müller added a spiritual element to this idea. He suggested that a human being's mission in life was to work in partnership with God to complete an unfinished world (Müller, 1992). However Adler's philosophy is expressed, in essence, it offers a socially responsible answer to the question of what it means to be a human being.

NOTES

1. The stages were suggested by Sophia deVries who studied with Adler. They were then developed by Henry Stein.

2. These strategies are rooted in the original Adlerian treatment style and are enriched by the contributions of Sophia deVries, Alexander Müller, and Henry Stein.

3. This comes both from personal knowledge of Sophia deVries, Anthony Bruck, Alexander Müller, and Kurt Adler and the description of Lydia Sicher's work (Davidson 1991).

4. Based on propositions listed in Ansbacher and Ansbacher 1956, 1–2.

REFERENCES

Adler, Alfred. 1933. First Childhood Recollection. *International Journal of Individual Psychology*. 11:81–90.

———. 1957. *The Education of Children*. London: George Allen and Unwin.

———. 1980. *Cooperation between the Sexes: Writings on Women, Love and Marriage, Sexuality and Its Disorders*. Ed. and trans. Heinz L. Ansbacher and Rowena R. Ansbacher. New York: Jason Aronson.

———. 1992b. *Understanding Human Nature*. Trans. from the 1927 edition by Colin Brett. Oxford: Oneworld Publications.

———. 1992a. *What Life Could Mean to You*. Trans. from the 1931 edition by Colin Brett. London: Oneworld Publications.

Ansbacher, Heinz L., and Ansbacher, Rowena, eds. 1956. *The Individual Psychology of Alfred Adler*. New York: Basic Books.

Augros, Robert, and Stancui, George. 1988. *The New Biology*. Boston: New Science Library.

Briggs, John, and Peat, David. 1989. *The Turbulent Mirror.* New York: Harper and Row.

Bruck, Anthony. 1978. Twenty Lives. Unpublished manuscript.

Davidson, Adele K., ed. 1991. *The Collected Works of Lydia Sicher: An Adlerian Perspective.* Fort Bragg, CA: QED Press.

Dreikurs, Rudolf, and Grey, Loren. 1968. *A New Approach to Discipline: Logical Consequences.* New York: Hawthorn Books.

Dreikurs, Rudolf, and Soltz, Vicki. 1964. *Children: The Challenge.* New York: Hawthorne/Dutton.

Ellenberger, Henri. 1970. *The Discovery of the Unconscious: The History and Evolution of Dynamic Psychiatry.* New York: Basic Books.

Guisinger, Shan, and Blatt, Sidney J. 1994. Individuality and Relatedness: Evolution of a Fundamental Dialectic. *American Psychologist,* 49:104–11.

Hamilton, W. D. 1964. The Genetical Evolution of Social Behavior. *Journal of Theoretical Biology.* 7:1–52.

Ho, D. F. 1993. Relational Orientation in Asia Social Psychology. In U. Kim and J. W. Berry, eds., *Indigenous Psychologies: Research and Experience in Cultural Context.* Newbury Park, CA: Sage, pp. 240–59.

Hoffman, Edward. 1994. *The Drive for Self.* New York: Addison-Wesley.

Kim, U. and Berry, J. W., eds. 1993. *Indigenous Psychologies: Research and Experience in Cultural Context.* Newbury Park, CA: Sage.

Maslow, Abraham H. 1970. *Motivation and Personality.* 3d ed. Revised by Robert Frager, James Fadiman, Cynthia McReynolds, and Ruth Cox. New York: Harper and Row.

———. 1971. *The Farther Reaches of Human Nature.* New York: Penguin.

Maybury-Lewis, D. 1992. *Millennium: Tribal Wisdom and the Modern World.* New York: Viking.

Müller, Alexander. 1937. The Positive Emotional Attitude. *International Journal of Individual Psychology.* 3:30–37.

———. 1968. Alfred Adler's Individual Psychology. Unpublished translation of *Die Indivdualpsychologie Alfred Adler's.*

———. 1992. *You Shall Be a Blessing.* San Francisco: Alfred Adler Institute of San Francisco.

Nelson, Andrea. 1991. The Application of Chaos Theory to the Understanding of Psychological Transformation. Ph.D. diss., Pepperdine University.

Simon, H. A. 1990. A Mechanism for Social Selection and Successful Altruism. *Science,* 250:1665–68.

Stein, Henry. 1988. Twelve Stages of Creative Adlerian Psychotherapy. *Individual Psychology.* 44:138–43.

———. 1990. Classical Adlerian Psychotherapy: A Socratic Approach. Audiotape study program. San Francisco: Alfred Adler Institute of San Francisco.

———. 1991. Adler and Socrates: Similarities and Differences. *Individual Psychology*, 47:241–46.

———. 1993. Adlerian Client Questionnaire. San Francisco: Alfred Adler Institute of San Francisco.

Trivers, R. 1971. The Evolution of Reciprocal Altruism. *Quarterly Review of Biology*, 46:35–57.

Vaihinger, Hans. 1925. *The Philosophy of "As If": A System of the Theoretical, Practical and Religious Fictions of Mankind.* New York: Harcourt, Brace.

Wilson, E. O. 1975. *Sociobiology: The New Synthesis.* Cambridge, MA: Belknap Press.

Chapter Four

Karen Horney's Counterdiscourses
Contemporary Implications

Michelle Price

EDITORS' INTRODUCTION

Michelle Price begins her discussion of Karen Horney somewhat "disruptively." She suggests that it is impossible to write an essay on "the Horneyan view of the human condition" since her work went through different phases of theoretical construction and development. The quest for unified answers can eclipse and misrepresent her work and its complexities, contradictions and intricacies. "A postmodernist era," Price says, emphasizes "multiple and continuously shifting registers of identities encased in semiotic and linguistic orders," and this means we "can view Horney only through the lens of our own historical and cultural stories, which inform . . . her ideas with our own." Horney's views must thus be situated within her own historical and cultural context; this implies acknowledging that in many ways her work was shaped by the dominant discourses and communities that she was embedded in. Horney developed what Price calls "counterdiscourses" to the Freudian "metanarrative," one that to some extent intimated various postmodern, feminist, and cultural themes.

Karen Horney has been regarded as one of the great spokeswomen for what has frequently been called the "cultural school" of psychoanalysis. These theorists claimed that what Freud formulated as biologically ordained was actually culturally fashioned and that psychoanalysis should be reinterpreted as a theory of the way the person is socially constructed. Price's "read" of Horney's writings indicates that Horney accepted certain Freudian assumptions about the human condition but drastically differed from his views on a number of points. For example, Horney accepted Freud's view of psychological determinism; she believed that the cause of each mental event may be found in unconscious processes and motives; she too focused on the rational capacities of selfhood; and she appropriated from Freud the basic concept of unconsciously motivated defenses against self-threatening perceptions, as evidenced by her detailed discussion of defensive strategies for coping with others.

However, Horney dramatically disagreed with Freud in the area of motivational content. She reinterpreted the Oedipus complex, for example, as a culturally driven, episodic process of jealousy and aggression within some families. For Horney, the origins of the oedipal situation were not so much sexual urges as interpersonal needs. Similarly, Horney found Freud's libido theory to be a grossly inaccurate representation of feminine psychology. The concept of "penis envy" by which Freud tried to explain women's feelings of inferiority and later development into the role of motherhood Horney found to be based on inadequate and prejudiced interpretations of "evidence" from neurotic women. Moreover, these interpretations reflected male ignorance, degradation, and possible envy of the female capacity for having children. By desexualizing the Oedipus complex and situating it in the realm of disturbed interpersonal relationships, she challenged Freud's biological essentialism and reductionism. Similarly, by rejecting the universality of penis envy in women, she gave social and cultural realities greater motivational importance than Freud's unconscious instinctual necessity.

For Horney, neurosis occurs when the "basic anxiety" experienced in childhood and coupled with "basic hostility" that could not be expressed causes alienation of the individual from her "real" self (approximately the "true core" of one's being and the urge for "self-realization"). The central neurotic conflict is further elaborated by an adoption of an idealized self at the expense of one's spontaneity, self-confidence, and autonomy. In other words, the neurotic attempts to fashion herself into something she is not in order to acquire security. Since other people are the main protagonists in what has become a menacing world, the neurotic fashions rigid defensive strategies for managing them. According to Price, anxiety and the striving for safety are the basis of neurotic problems, but only in their contrast to the normal cultural patterns and hence related to an individual's personal form of expression and family culture. Such views differ from Freud's, she says, in that cultural and interpersonal factors antecede intrapsychic ones as opposed to the reverse, which is the foundation of classical theory. Also Horney rejects sexual impulses as the cause of psychopathology and suggests that "the center of psychic disturbance are unconscious strivings developed in order to cope with life despite fears, helplessness, and isolations"—the so-called neurotic trends. The contemporary sensibility in Horney's thinking is here expressed in the idea that we can never step out of our own culture and time, which define particular knowledges and the chains of signification. The analyst "can only sort our structures of signification that are inherently culturally produced and saturated with multiple meanings."

The main aim of treatment for Horney was to provide the analysand with the means to liberate the "real self," to accept its character, and to foster its maximum and spontaneous expression without neurotic defensiveness. Neurotic individuals tend to have an idealized self that they strive to realize and actualize in therapy. Lack of success in attaining this "idealized image" generates rage, terror, and fragmentation. This image has furnished an inauthentic sense of wholeness and integration, subsituting for spontaneity and aliveness. In a word, the highly pragmatic Horneyan analyst tries to assist the analysand in self-realization. Recasting this program in a more contemporary, postmodern idiom, with its emphasis on multiple narratives of self-identity, we could say, following Price, that the aim of a Horneyan analysis is to "focus more on the elucidation and recognition of various internal/external pulls and their affective and historical elaborations" in the service of learning how to creatively live with a multiplicity of selves. (P. M. and A. R.)

What is Karen Horney's view of the human condition? This question assumes a coherence and evolution that can be objectively observed, studied, and inscribed. It asks that a logic and order be imposed on Horney's work that renders it comprehensible and useful to others. Although such an endeavor is quite seductive and appealing, to quote Sampson (1993), it raises serious questions. The initial question is, to whom does that order and coherence belong, Horney, the inscriber, or both? Additionally, the question assumes one Horney, with one identity, whose theory is unitary and accessible to such an interpretation. The theory is highly suspect in a postmodernist era that emphasizes multiple and continuously shifting registers of identities encased in semiotic and linguistic orders. By attempting to locate Horney's theory and views, I inevitably lose her with all her complexities, contradictions, and intricacies. I must acknowledge a distortion and alienation from Horney's ideas, developed in a different time and context. To give her an identity and location is to provide her with a scripted part in a contemporary discourse. We can view Horney only through the lens of our own historical and cultural stories, which infiltrate, define, and permeate her ideas with our own. This is in concordance with the view that the dominant discourses of Horney's time defined her, as they did her colleagues.

Additionally, the idea of a clear view of human existence presents itself as problematic; it conflicts with certain psychoanalytic ideologies that embrace multiplicity, difference, conflict, unconscious processes, and endless mystery. Psychoanalysis originated as a discourse in which particular rational and positivist notions of humanity could be destabilized and unpacked. The question therefore appears to be a product of Enlightenment thinking that assumes positions of objective truth, knowledge, and structure. My version of psychoanalysis attempts to decenter such integrated, linear "truths." Nonetheless, the task of categorizing Horney has been tackled by many. Horney has been postulated as an interpersonalist (Greenberg and Mitchell, 1983), compatible with object relations theory (Ingram and Lerner, 1992), self psychology (Paul, 1989; van den Daele, 1981), Guntrip (Lerner, 1985), and Mahler (Lerner, 1983). Rendon (1991) has written extensively on the influence of Hegel in Horney's work, while feminists have claimed Horney as their own, citing her early papers on feminine psychology (Westkott, 1986; Symonds, 1991; Fliegel, 1986). Her work has also influenced the treatment of trauma victims (Symonds, 1975), the treatment of incest victims (Price, 1992, 1993), psychoanalysis (Ingram, 1987), and literary criticism (Paris, 1991). These attempts point either to the flexibility, accessibility, and profundity of Horney's ideas or to the ability of individuals to write her work and thinking into their own. Either conclusion indicates that any essay on her views reflects that of the author, which inevitably transforms the subject of the text.

In consideration of this, I propose and prefer to write and contemplate on the early Horney. This is not to ascribe to her a distinct philosophy of life, but rather to elucidate certain trends and presumptions in her work. In this preference I join Eckardt (1991, 1994) and Ingram (1994), who point to Horney's early work on feminine psychology and culture as being not only substantial and significant, but also in line with contemporary concerns. I am further influenced by Ingram's attempts to situate Nietzsche's influence in her work and demonstrate her affinity to current deconstructionist and postmodernist trends. This is not to imply that Horney can be classified by the signifier "postmodernist." She wrote and lived in a time when positivist ideas permeated and dominated intellectual discourse. Her ideas and texts contain many essentialist, positivist, and universal claims. Yet despite this, her early work can be read as a beginning consideration of ideas that are compatible with or, at best, considerate of postmodern thinking. In doing this type of reading of Horney, I inevitably reveal my own political and academic agenda. Whether such an agenda delegitimizes the content of my essay is a valid question. It is my proposition that in writing such a semihistorical text or in being involved in an analytic interaction, we are constantly interpreting and representing each other's discourses. Our voices are situated in the text, as they are in the construction of history. This essay is as much an interpretation as the words of any analyst to his/her analysand. Interpretations can be constructed as fictions (Geertz, 1973) and cannot be accepted as "Truth," based only on their coherence, tightness, or the assurance with which they are argued (Geertz, 1973, p. 18).[1] I therefore present in the following pages my constructed narratives of Karen Horney, situated in my own personal, cultural, and historical context and linguistic order.

Horney and the Feminists

Horney's essays on feminine psychology were written from 1922 to 1933 and published as an edited volume in 1967. They appear to reflect Horney's beginning dissatisfaction with Freudian metanarratives, particularly constructs regarding penis envy, feminine development, and sexuality. They are the subjugated discourses that would stand as contrast to the smoothness of Freudian metapsychology. These papers were alternately dismissed by Freud as resulting from some feminists' inability to work through their penis envy or co-opted by some members of the Freudian inner circle as their own. Eckardt (1991, 1994), Westkott (1986), and Fliegel (1986) have discussed these papers and their insights in depth.

What is of particular relevance for this essay is that Horney presented a counterdiscourse to Freud, a trend that was also followed by Ferenczi, Adler, Jung, and others. The existence of such discourses was extremely relevant to the newly created psychoanalytic community and essential to its expansion and later developments.[2] Despite her attempts to present ideas that were different from Freud's, the language and theoretical presumptions of these essays by Horney read like Freud. Horney maintains biological and essentialist constructs and metaphors in discussing masculine and feminine development, while simultaneously attacking them. This can be indicative of her struggle to sever ties with Freudian doctrine and her own analytic experiences. She may have been reluctant to openly challenge Freud at that particular time and stage of her professional career. It can additionally be representative of the influence of Freudian thinking in her own constructions and her compliance with it. This would be in line with power/knowledge factors and Freud's domination of available and acceptable psychoanalytic discourses. Horney, like Freud, cannot be viewed outside her own historical and cultural context. His views as well were reflective of a larger view of individual life. It is not until the publication of *The Neurotic Personality of Our Time* (1937) that Horney begins to abandon Freudian metaphors and utilize a different type of language. Understanding the language she utilized is essential for deconstructing her text and its rhetorical strategies and intents. The voice of the text indicates the other to whom Horney or any author may be speaking (M. Kaminsky, personal communication). Her papers on feminine psychology are presented in dialogue with her colleagues, while later works speak directly to the public. Initially Horney attempts to accommodate to Freudian discourse and accepts a scripted part within it. She speaks like them. In her later works she attempts to transform the discourse and the form of her talk.[3] Inherent to this is the assumption that without Freud, there could have been no Horney.

In the papers on feminine psychology Horney begins to use cultural contexts in her construction of theoretical propositions and women's symptoms. According to Horney, the assumption that women are dissatisfied with their sex is a product of the phallocentric biases of the psychoanalytic community.

> In this formulation we have assumed as an axiomatic fact that females feel at a disadvantage because of their genital organs, without this being regarded as constituting a problem in itself—possibly because to masculine narcissism this has seemed too self-evident to need explanation. Neverthe-

less, the conclusion drawn so far from the investigations—amounting as it does to an assertion that one half of the human race is discontented with the sex assigned to it and can overcome this discontent only in favorable circumstances—is decidedly unsatisfying not only to feminine narcissism, but also to biological science.   (Horney, 1924/1967, p. 38)

Although still maintaining the popular essentialist ideology regarding the categories of gender and sexuality, she exposes some of the discursive factors and phallocentrism that are part of Freud's constructions and the community in which he lived. Freud is transformed into a signifier and metaphor for a certain philosophy. By asserting that it is unsatisfying to biological science, Horney utilizes and attacks Freud's own rhetoric and home base. She additionally challenges Freud's concept of penis envy and the idea that a baby is a substitute for the castrated penis. "At this point, I as a woman, ask in amazement and what about motherhood? And the blissful consciousness of bearing a new life within oneself? . . . And the deep, pleasurable feeling of satisfaction of suckling it and the happiness of the whole period when the infant needs her care?" (1926/1967, p. 60).

Although the idealization of motherhood that is inherent in this statement is indicative of Horney's historical/social context and certain essentialist views of women, she articulates the silenced voices and outrage of women to disclaim Freud's proclamations. In this counterdiscourse, she challenges what is constituted as real, natural, and scientific fact. She then proceeds to write of womb envy in men and their fear of the maternal figure, which has strongly influenced the work of Chassguet-Smirgel (1970) and Fast (1994). She critiques the patriarchal view of women evident in the Freudian metanarrative. She proposes that Freud and his followers' ideas have been influenced by the fact that they were men and consequently had a vested interest in suppressing women and maintaining an illusion of male superiority and authority. This stance clearly and strikingly challenges Freud's claims to developing a grand universal theory that is scientific and objective. Horney contemplates how analysts' own values, interests, and gender influence their thinking and discourse. In this broad stroke, she attempts to reveal what Sampson (1993), decades later, in line with social constructionism, would refer to as the "absent standard." This is the hidden agendas, the backgrounds, the constructed "normal" that are present in the text and the culture and organize one's theoretical propositions and normative practices.

Horney further attributes some of the findings regarding women to the cultural biases against women. She writes in "The Flight from Womanhood" (1926/1967) that women have been continuously studied by men and have yielded to their observations and claimed them as their true nature. Given the general landscape of a "masculine society" (Simmel, 1984), Horney wonders how accurate a psychology of women analysis has yielded. In this type of thinking and speaking one hears preludes to a Foucaudian analysis of culture, psychiatry, and domination. By this I refer to Foucault's focus on the discursive and regulatory practices that are embedded in discourse and the construction of identity and pathology. The theories of female psychology and subjectivity are constructed within particular political contexts and their agendas.

In "The Overvaluation of Love" (1934/1967), Horney inserts cultural and social considerations into the cases of women who become overly dependent on men and their love. She focuses on the importance of the role of women and characterological factors as opposed to biological and instinctual destiny. Women's psychological struggles are viewed through the lens of the culture's conflicting definitions of femininity (Westkott, 1986). For example, she writes of women's overdependence on men and need for their approval due to internal feelings of worthlessness. Social factors are linked to feelings of worthlessness. This particular narrative is further developed in Benjamin's (1988) contemporary work on femininity and domination. Inherent to Benjamin's conceptualization is the young girl's need for recognition from and identification with the father as signifier of power and representative of the outside world. Since she rarely receives this recognition, severe feelings of inadequacy and worthlessness can be produced. There follows a reactive idealization of men in their socially sanctioned roles. If I can't be like you or recognized by you, then I will try to have you. This sets the stage for relations that are characterized by idealization, domination, and submission. Both Benjamin and Horney reveal how women are complicit in their own domination by accepting and colluding with the voices of those who dominate. This is also an essential aspect of Lacanian theory (1977), which requires that men and women accept the Law of the Father in order to acquire personhood and avoid psychosis. Horney and Benjamin challenge what Lacan and Freud accept as culturally normative. Horney's discussion may present as local knowledge in our time, but was highly radical and innovative for the period of psychoanalysis in which she was developing her ideas.

Horney acknowledges the influence of Georg Simmel (1984), a sociologist who critiques society as being masculine. This masculinity then becomes the standard by which we examine civilization. This places man in an advantageous position of being the constructor and creator of reality. Man controlled the discourse and was the implicit standard for normal development and identity in psychoanalytic theory. This type of thinking reveals the discursive factors utilized to create particular knowledges and truths, whose deconstruction is one of the crucial agendas of postmodern philosophy. The use of sociological findings reveals Horney's holistic treatment approach and a consideration of social/cultural influences on individuals' lives and character structures. The integration of narratives from the social sciences, humanities, and cultural studies in psychoanalytic theory is an essential aspect of Horney's thinking. It places men and women in a social context that is invariably connected to formulations regarding development, symptom formation, and pathology. This is particularly evident in the essay "The Problem of Feminine Masochism" (1935/1967), where she critiques the work of Deutsch, Rado, and Freud, most notably in their ignorance of the influence of cultural factors and differences. "The onesideness or positive errors in the results obtained by a partial examination of the picture are due to a neglect of cultural or social factors—an exclusion from the picture of women living under civilizations with different customs" (pp. 223–24). These threads of social critique that are intertwined in this work are more fully drawn out and elaborated in her later texts.

Cultural Discourses and Psychoanalysis

In Horney's subsequent works, two significant changes are noted in her language and writing style. She ceases to write about women's experience and adopts a gender-neutral theoretical approach. This move from female psychology to human psychology foreshadows the current work of Butler (1990), who radically critiques the very categories of gender and sexual identity as being socially constructed. Horney relinquishes use of the binary opposition of masculine and feminine, with its inherent hierarchy and positioning of male dominance. Although not necessarily her intent, Horney does not accept the position that women can possess knowledge only regarding women, while men can discuss male and female experience.[4] This further distinguished and segregated her from mainstream psychoanalytic discourse. Many feminist thinkers express dismay over this erasure of gender from her work or believe that her character descriptions were still predominantly about women (Westkott, 1986). I would argue that this change in focus from feminine psychology to men and women presented an opportunity to enlarge the scope of her work and the discourses that women were permitted to engage in. Additionally, by talking only about women, Horney would continue to maintain a binary hierarchy, with women being posited as different, the "other." This would collude in male dominance and maintain men as the regulatory standard.

Secondarily, Horney ceases to utilize Freudian metaphors and speaks in a simple, direct voice regarding "everyday" problems and "neurotic" development. In her change of language style, she begins to speak to the public. She no longer is merely addressing her colleagues and involved in a dialogue with them, in which Freud defines the rules and acceptable conversations. In the traditional analytic discourse, her voice is marginalized and subjugated and she is relegated to the position of Freud's spokesperson. If she does not speak in the dominant Freudian voice, then she is not acknowledged and basically silenced, as was Sandor Ferenczi. In those circles, dialogue was merely a masqueraded monologue (Bakhtin, 1984). If she had continued to speak in their voice and ignored her own, she would also be silenced. Her way out of this conundrum was to go to the people and consequently establish herself as a speaking subject. This additionally reveals Horney's belief that psychoanalysis is not some mysterious knowledge that is the privilege of the few. This "knowledge" can be shared with the public and pragmatically assist them in understanding themselves. Although her language style has been criticized as simplistic, it does provide individuals with information that can be used to promote self-reflectiveness and introspection.

The change in the form of her language further served an economic and political purpose. Horney could not promote herself or her narratives without followers. She appealed to the public in a language and style that were comprehensible and experience-near. This is not to imply that Horney did not maintain particular ideas regarding the human condition or psychopathology, but that she attempted to speak directly to her constituents in their local language. Traces of a continued discourse with Freudian theory may be noted in her later texts, where there is a tendency to (over)state the constructive forces in humankind and an overly optimistic view of human potential. This could be constructed as her continued commentary on Freud's philosophy of mankind and biological destiny. It is evidence of her struggles with Freud's exclusive focus on sex and aggression as constituting subjectivity.

In *The Neurotic Personality of Our Time* (1937), Horney continued the thread of thought that she began in her earlier essays and intertwines psychology and cultural studies. She anticipates expected criticism and responds in writing to her critics that her theoretical philosophy is still psychoanalysis as it is concerned with unconscious processes and the way these processes find expression in daily life (pp. 8–9). Implicit to this is a definition of psychoanalysis that privileges unconscious processes over a developmental hierarchy. In Horney's alternative view of humankind, she proposed a new way of thinking about ourselves, our world, and what defined symptoms and pathology. Horney also believed that psychoanalysis contained ethical positions. She was deeply concerned with morality and the belief systems of analyst and analysand, which replaced developmental schematas (Horney, 1946, 1950). Self-realization and actualization of one's potentiality are moral responsibilities. The manifestations and details of this are embedded and constituted in the cultural discourses and practices. "For Horney, we are all children of our culture. . . . Contemporary philosophy has increasingly vindicated Horney's view that these values ramify even pure science" (Ingram, 1987, p. 123). Belief systems, values, and identities emanate from the cultural context that one is situated in, which contests particular universal proclamations. What is considered normal varies not only within the culture but also over time (Horney, 1937, p. 15). The culture approves of certain standards of behavior and feelings in a certain group, which then imposes those standards on its members; the standards are defined as normalcy and truth. Our very feelings, attitudes, and self-narratives are molded by the conditions in which we live.

Horney viewed neurosis as a reification and hardening of cultural values regarding freedom, love, and mastery (Rendon, 1991). Neurosis is generated by specific cultural configurations that determine the particular forms of health and pathology, and what is signified as such. Horney constructs neurosis as related to rigidity in a person's options of choice and reaction, as well as the discrepancy between an individual's potential and his or her accomplishments. Anxiety and the quest for safety are the foundations of neurotic development, but only in its contrast to the "normal" cultural patterns and hence related to an individual's personal idiom and family culture, to borrow Bollas's (1987) term. A person or his actions cannot be signified as neurotic if they are commensurate with the cultural belief system and knowledges. They must differ from the particulars of a given culture, in regard to quantity or quality, in order to be termed pathological (Horney, 1937, p. 26).

Horney additionally writes that the majority of individuals within a culture have to face the same problems (1937, p. 30), thereby suggesting that these problems have been created by specific life conditions and not predominantly intrapsychic and instinctual factors. Cultural and interpersonal considerations precede intrapsychic ones, as opposed to the reverse, which is the foundation of classical theory. This form of cultural consideration illustrates her synchronicity with the work of interpersonal, object relations, and relational theorists. This trend is further elaborated on in her discussion of the origins of basic anxiety, which she constructs as the basis of neurotic development. Basic anxiety is related to the child feeling alone and helpless in a potentially hostile world, whereby the parents are insensitive and do not recognize the child's individuality and needs (Horney, 1950). The child does not receive an adequate amount of warmth and affection, leading to immense insecurity, terror, and related adaptive strategies. This replaces sexual impulses as the cause of anxiety and pathology (Horney, 1937, p. 54). Fear and anxiety are caused by external dangers, forms of relationships, and cultural conditions.

Horney illustrates how particular conflicts are embedded within the culture and can promote confusion, symptom formation, and neurotic development for an individual. For example, the American focus on the need to be popular and the simultaneous need to be successful can be diametrically opposed and create internal conflict and neurotic symptomatology.[5] This type of thinking is commensurate with her earlier work on feminine psychology, where the cultural coding of women's identity can create various phenomena, such as penis envy. These types of conditions are culturally produced, not instinctual. Additionally they are labeled pathological only in certain cultural contexts.[6] She is skeptical of the universal in regard to construction of pathology and normalcy, which is in line with Nietzsche and Derrida (Ingram, 1994) and favors Geertz's (1983) local knowledges and focus on locating the particulars of a culture.

Structures of Meaning

In Horney's shift from a developmental hierarchal paradigm, she additionally repositions analytic theory from a linear to a temporal and circular model. This is in line with current trends in contemporary analytic discourses, which have been eloquently introduced and discussed by Mitchell (1993). In Horney's theoretical narratives, individuals acquire identities through early interpersonal transactions and positions in the culture. These acquired selves do not remain static, nor does she envision a dialectic between different stages of development. She does not discuss stages but rather the continuous evolving individual who negotiates, adapts, and struggles with self, other, and life. Neurosis and psychopathology are constructed as the individual's inability to be flexible and develop a repertoire of responses. Rigidity consists of a repetition of reflexes to individual life experiences, foreclosing on spontaneity, aliveness, and uniqueness. "The presentation of homogeneity, of integration can be constructed as a mask, a masquerade that falsely unifies diverse aspects of experience and forecloses on others" (Price, 1995a). Horney's concept of the vicious circle has individuals interpreting and responding to events in a rigid, constricted manner that colludes with particular neurotic patterns and fixed interpretive themes. This can be read as individuals organizing their lives and events in the same narrative manner, reauthoring events to fit a particular script. By reframing it in current postmodernist lingo I may be somewhat guilty of distortion, but clearly it is similar to current trends that depict therapy as a "therapy of literary merit" (White and Epston, 1990) and text analogies (Schafer, 1992; Spence, 1982).

By shifting the focus from the past and developmental schemata to the present, Horney is interested in who the person is in the present, rather than who he was. She is concerned with internal structures of meaning and the construction of the person's interactions with others, as opposed to their genesis. However, Horney does not totally erase the past or the question of how one's present identity has been constructed. She relies on the concept of adaptation to explain current levels of meaning and functioning. We adapt to our individual cultures by imaginatively creating ways of being that achieve some form of safety for us. The particulars of our individual backgrounds in their cultural contexts determine the forms of our creations. These adaptations can become rigidly situated, rendering us unable to abandon them, even when they cease to be adaptive. Adaptation replaces defenses, which signifies an abandonment of linguistic metaphors of a combative, militaristic nature, inherent in Freudian metanarratives.[7] She is concerned with how these adaptations interfere with a person's ability to live life in a full and wholehearted manner.

Horney postulates that most individuals enter analysis not necessarily to change their adaptive ways of being, but to effectively improve them. They have an idealized self that they seek to realize and actualize in therapy. Lack of success in achieving this "idealized image" evokes rage, terror, and fragmentation. This image has provided a fictive sense of wholeness and integration, replacing spontaneity and aliveness. Part of the analysis lies in deconstructing this image and its historical origins in familial and cultural narratives, and reducing the individual's alienation or dissociation from aspects of the "real self."

Horney's concept of the idealized self is concordant with her emphasis on and belief in authenticity, aliveness, and a true self. As the child and adult try to maintain a sense of safety, there is a renouncement of the real self and an identification with various adaptations. These adaptations become the central focus and are often infused with idealizing qualities. As this process continues, the person becomes increasingly alienated from the real self. The real self delineates one's authenticity, spontaneity, and potential. It is "the fundamental core of aliveness that, though universally present in each of us, finds its unique expression in each individual's development of his/her potential for self realization" (foreword to Horney, 1950). Implicit to this is Horney's quest for authentic moments in life and a decrease in alienating qualities. It poses the quest for a richer and deeper appreciation of the aliveness of self and other. In this sense, her work strongly borrows from the philosopher Soren Kierkegaard in its emphasis on man's potential alienation from self and the quest for self realization and authenticity.

Alienation from self is comparable in Horneyan theory to a loss of identity and connection to the spiritual and material self (Horney, 1950, p. 156). It involves a dissociation from one's aliveness, feelings, beliefs, and wishes. It situates one in a position of continuous not knowing. She quotes Kierkegaard: "The loss of self, says Kierkegaard (1941/1844), is 'sickness unto death'; it is despair—despair at not being conscious of having a self, or despair at not being willing to be ourselves. But it is a despair (still following Kierkegaard) which does not clamor or scream" (Horney, 1950, p. 158).

The implications of this reposition psychoanalysis as a psychology of self-representation. In Horney's philosophy we become interested in how people construct themselves and idealize and devalue various aspects of self. We listen in their words for what is privileged (idealized) and what is marginalized (despised). In transforming monologues to dialogues through the analytic discourse, we reconsider previously disenfranchised self-narratives and related values. This allows for the generation of alternative narratives, of questions and responses to fixed positions and representations. We search out the seams, the gaps in apparently seamless constructions and utilize them to create new possibilities and ideas (Price, 1995b).

Postmodern Critique and Implications

All analytic and theoretical texts can be viewed as historical documents that trace the genealogy of our discipline. Horney's texts can be examined as moments in time and a voice located in particular cultural/social contexts and linguistic orders. She is not transhistorical. By situating Horney's work, we can evaluate her within our current discourses for her continued relevance and insightfulness. Horney's work is basically positivistic and permeated with essentialism. This is no surprise, considering the time in which she lived and practiced. She maintained beliefs in such ideas as innate heterosexuality, and there is a strong idealization of motherhood and its physicality. Although she challenges the construct of penis envy, which is one of her more important contributions, she did maintain a belief in other "essentialist" and "biologically bedrock" constructs. This is evident in Horney's concept of the "real self."

The construct of a real self reflects a belief in a true essence that is located within the person. The goal of psychoanalysis is to liberate and reveal this essence. Although Horney places a strong emphasis on culture, the real self appears to exist outside cultural contexts. It is pure and reified, reflecting an innocence and romanticism to her thinking. The existence of other selves, such as the idealized and despised, are presented in a hierarchal order to the real self. Although there is a consideration of multiple selves, only the unitary self is posited as healthy. Integration is the goal and multiplicity is a pathological construction. This presents as problematic when we contrast it with current ideas regarding culture, context, and multiple identitie(s) and reveals the gaps in her conceptualizations. These current ideas contest the notion of a unified singular self. We are different selves in different contexts—cultural and relational. Attempts at unification would be considered attempts to erase difference and dissociate from multiple experiences.

Horney's view of culture is additionally problematic. Although she was successful in her attempts to situate neurotic development and interpersonal difficulties in a cultural context, she reifies the concept of culture. She often evokes culture as a separate category, as if there were times when one can step outside of it. She additionally evokes it in a negative context, to use it as an explanation for what is wrong and what we don't like. One can insinuate from her text that it is possible to be free of culture and view it somewhat objectively. Current anthropological texts, heralded by Geertz (1973), contest such an idea. According to Geertz (1973, p. 14), "culture is not a power, something to which social events, behaviors, institutions, or processes can be causally attributed; it is a context, something within which they can be intelligibly—that is, thickly—described." In this narrative of Geertz, cultural analysis guesses at meanings and is aware of cultural contexts without ever discovering essential Meaning and Truth. Culture is the air, that which we live and breathe, it is in our pores and we are never without it. Horney's separation of culture and the real self appears as an artificial binary, constructed as a way of maintaining some sense of an essence to human subjectivity.

Horney's insertion of culture as forming the signification of pathology and health, however, does coincide with Gergen's (1991) contemporary idea that we can never step out of our own culture and time, which defines particular knowledges and the chain of signification. She does not take her ideas of culture as far as Gergen does, but they are complementary. It follows from both of their texts that as analysts we can only sort out structures of signification that are inherently culturally produced (Geertz, 1973) and saturated with multiple meanings.

Despite the areas of Horney's theory that present as problematic within certain narratives, Horney struggled with issues that are currently at the forefront of postmodernism, social constructionism, feminist psychoanalysis, and cultural studies. Although she lacked the discourses to discuss those concerns and ideas, they can be read in her texts. The elucidation of these themes in her work is relevant to contemporary concerns in psychoanalysis. Individuals like Horney, Ferenczi, Sullivan, Winnicott, and others struggled with issues that are receiving attention in contemporary psychoanalysis.

Pragmatic Applications

Despite the above noted concerns, Horney's approach is a pragmatic one, continuously concerned with how to assist individuals in what she deemed the moral task of self-realization. Her language is one of education, not of necessarily impressing others or of melting into the dominant psychoanalytic and scientific discourses of her time. Her clarity of language makes her work accessible to even those not fully trained in analytic theory (Ingram, 1987). This is particularly evident in Horney's *Final Lectures* (1987), which are permeated by her viewpoints and ideas regarding the clinical principles of psychoanalysis (Ingram, 1987). It is additionally evident in the frequent claims by individuals to have found themselves situated within her texts. "It felt as if she was talking directly to me."

In a world where truth and ultimate knowledge have been destabilized in favor of particulars (Lyotard, 1984) and multiple truths (Derrida, 1981), the pragmaticism and experience-near style of Horney's ideas are relevant. According to Flax (1990), the current standard for truth is a pragmatic one, whereby some ways of talking and acting fit in better in the context of the needs of a particular culture at a particular time. As she quotes Derrida (1981), knowledge and truths assist us in coping, not in revealing. Noncontextual truths and metanarratives are viewed with skepticism and cynicism (Flax, 1990). Pragmaticism itself must additionally be viewed skeptically in regard to the alignment of power factors and silenced voices within cultural inequalities and biases. This is inclusive of political factors of domination organized around race, class, sexualities, and gender hierarchies and distinctions. Taking this into account, I nevertheless have found Horney's privileging of cultural, interpersonal, and gender factors relevant to my clinical work. This does not attempt to posit it as truth or metatheory, but elaborates its usefulness in interpreting various phenomena. Let me illustrate with a clinical example that I have written about in another essay (Price, 1995a).

A female patient who clearly defines herself as a feminist is experiencing serious fertility problems, and it seems more than likely that she will be unable to conceive a child. In discussion of this in session, she cried out, What kind of woman am I, if I can't have a child? She then added, I can't believe I said that, but I really believe it, it's natural for real women to have babies. For this woman, despite other narratives and convictions, to be a woman means to conceive and be a mother. Not to do so puts her own sense of femininity and womanhood in jeopardy. The signifier of feminist causes additional problems for her. To be a feminist, for her, means to not define herself as a woman by her fertility. Yet she does. To admit so means to feel guilty and unable to be a "real" feminist (like a "real" woman). To not admit so means to dissociate and suppress an aspect of her experience, causing alienation and underlying despair. One possible way of analyzing and representing my patient's conflict is that the conflict itself is a signifier of various cultural narratives fighting for dominance, manifesting themselves in an identity struggle.

This type of analysis incorporates Horney's ideas regarding cultural dictates and context, as well as the pressures on women in this particular culture. This includes the defining and potentially conflicting terms of femininity that can be organized as totalizing demands. Where Horney (that I find in her texts) and I may differ is in the direction of the analysis. Horney, in accordance with the cultural privileging of a unitary, integrated real self, could attempt to assist this woman in locating her "real" wishes and desires. She would assist her in decreasing her alienation and freeing herself from various cultural restraints and her own self-effacing trends. These trends, as well as the patient's possible grandiosity, may force her to be a "perfect" feminist, woman, and mother. This type of approach can lead to pathologizing these aspects of my patient's dilemma and consequent adaptations.[8]

I would tend to view my patient's struggle as a product of various cultural narratives that are intertwined with her own personal idiom and familial background. It additionally is not static and continues to evolve and serve different purposes in different contexts. Regardless, the analysis would not be aimed at assisting her in arriving at a unified, integrated solution. It would focus more on the elucidation and recognition of various internal/external pulls and their affective and historical elaborations. The focus is not necessarily on adaptation but in decreasing alienation and dissociation and a greater appreciation of multiplicity. This utilizes the Horneyan concepts of alienation and realization in a particularly contemporary style.[9]

I have attempted in this essay to discuss some of Horney's contributions to psychoanalytic and philosophical discourses and their relevance to contemporary clinical thinking and practice. I have further attempted to provide a postmodern critique of some of her ideas. In the construction of this essay, I have taken the liberty of highlighting particular aspects of her texts and omitting others. By evoking the concepts of pragmaticism and the mutual construction of texts I provide a rationalization for my essay. This is directed toward the anticipated response that this is not Horney. It implies that there are many Horneys that are dialogic and personal creations. This stands as my representation and memory of her, infused with my own individual particularities. I chose not to reveal in this essay my own idiosyncratic and highly personal path that led me to this analysis of Horney, but I evoke its presence. Additionally my interest in Horney's cultural theory has led me to the work of Geertz. It seems fitting and appropriate to conclude this essay with a quote from him. Although he refers to interpretive anthropology, the term can easily be replaced with interpretive psychoanalysis.

> To look at the symbolic dimensions of social action—art, religion, ideology, science, law, morality, common sense—is not to turn away from the existential dilemmas of life for some empyrean realm of de-emotionalized forms; it is to plunge into the midst of them. The essential vocation of interpretive anthropology is not to answer our deepest questions, but to make available to us answers that others, guarding other sheep in other valleys, have given, and thus to include them in the consultable record of what man has said. (Geertz, 1973, p. 30)

NOTES

1. This literary deconstructive strategy is the same one that Horney utilized to critique Freud's theories regarding feminine psychology and sexuality. In doing so, she exposed the biases and phallocentric views that influenced his and his world's ideas. She inserted gaps in his seemingly coherent and smooth narrative. Her exposé also postulated an explanation as to the willingness of his audience to accept his views, which strengthened its coherence. It was in the male society's vested interest to accept and support his phallocentric view of women and their development. Women, as well, accepted this view and colluded in their own suppression. Horney's counterdiscourse created new ways to think and talk about men and women and exposed Freudian facts as constituted by sociopolitical and gendered agendas.

2. This is in concordance with the idea that Freudian psychoanalysis was created as a counterdiscourse to Enlightenment thinking and rationality. It presented alternative ways of thinking about people and the world. In addition, it presented a new way of talking about people that gave new meaning to what we do (Bruner, 1990). Horney's critique of Freud maintained this circular discourse regarding the philosophy of personhood. This discourse continues to be essential to the expansion and enrichment of the psychoanalytic community.

3. This type of discourse analysis is heavily influenced by the works of Eagleton (1983), Foucault (1973a, 1973b), Derrida (1974), Bakhtin (1984), and Flax (1990). Additionally, Sampson (1993) provides an excellent discussion of accommodative and transformative forms of discourse in his article "Identity Politics."

4. This same idea can be traced in common practices regarding referrals. Female analysts are usually referred female patients, while it has been more accepted that male analysts can treat men and women. It is only recently that this is being destabilized and the analytic literature is attending to the transference/countertransference configurations of female analysts/male analysands.

5. This type of duality is constructed as a problem in a world that defines health as belonging to a unitary, integrated self. The idea of the self as multiple opens up spaces in which different moods, states, and wishes can coexist. The demand for unity and smoothness pathologizes these contrasting states, as does the signifier, conflict. Multiplicity allows for a dialectic to exist, as well as the shifting from different states, needs, and desires. Horney lived in a time when an integrated, nonconflicted self was still seen as the norm. In our current time and culture, the focus would be less on multiplicity than the degree of disassociation and alienation (Bromberg, 1993; Rivera, 1989).

6. Horney does not perform the same thorough critique on culture as she does on feminine psychology. In this work, she is more willing to accept cultural dictates regarding normalizing truths without revealing their underlying discursive factors and absent standards.

7. This trend is continued in the remainder of Horney's work. She replaces defenses with adaptations, transference with the analytic relationship, resistances with blockages, splitting with compartmentalization, and so on. This seems to indicate her separateness from Freudian discourse and the creation of a new way of speaking.

8. In Horney's texts one can read of her beginning dissatisfaction and discomfort with the concreteness of the concept of the real self. She fluctuates in the delineation of it as a reified entity or as a signifier for the goals of potentiality and authenticity in life. As I have already illustrated, due to her situation in the history of psychoanalytic discourses, Horney was limited in her ability to speak of or consider this concept in other ways.

9. I would also consider the implications of context on the discourse. By this I refer to the fact that it is two women—analyst and analysand—who are discussing issues regarding femininity, sexuality and success. The potential relational transactions and transference/countertransference configurations would be part of the analytic dialogue.

REFERENCES

Bakhtin, M. 1984. *Problems of Dostoevsky's poetics*, Trans. E. Emerson, Minneapolis: University of Minnesota Press.
Benjamin, J. 1988. *The bonds of love: Psychoanalysis, feminism and the problem of domination*. New York: Pantheon.

Bollas, C. 1987. *The shadow of the object: Psychoanalysis of the unthought known*. New York: Columbia University Press.

Bromberg, P. M. (1993). Shadow and substance: A relational perspective on clinical process. *Psychoanalytic Psychology*. 14(2): 147–68.

Bruner, J. 1990. *Acts of meaning*. Cambridge: Harvard University Press.

Butler, J. 1990. *Gender trouble: Feminism and the subversion of identity*. New York: Routledge.

Chasseguet-Smirgel, J. 1970. Feminine guilt and the Oedipus conflict. In *Female Sexuality*, ed. J. Chasseguet-Smirgel. London: Maresfield Library, pp. 94–135.

Derrida, J. 1974. *Of grammatology*. Baltimore: The Johns Hopkins University Press.

———. (1981). *Positions*. Trans. A. Bass. Chicago: University of Chicago Press.

Eagleton, T. 1983. *Literary theory: An introduction*. Minneapolis: University of Minnesota Press.

Eckardt, M. H. 1991. Feminine psychology revisited: A historical perspective. *American Journal of Psychoanalysis*. 51 (3): 235–43.

———. (1994). Karen Horney's themes of self-realization and mental health: An historical perspective past and present. Paper presented at the American Academy of Psychoanalysis, Philadelphia, May 20.

Fast, I. 1994. Women's capacity to give birth: A sex-difference issue for men? *Psychoanalytic Dialogues*, 4 (1): 51–68.

Flax, J. 1990. *Thinking fragments: Psychoanalysis, feminism and postmodernism in the contemporary West*. Berkeley and Los Angeles: University of California Press.

Fliegel, Z. O. 1986. Women's development in analytic theory: Six decades of controversy. In *Psychoanalysis and women*, ed. J. L. Alpert. Hillsdale, NJ: Analytic Press.

Foucault M. 1973a. *The order of things*. New York: Random House.

———. 1973b. *Madness and civilization*. New York: Random House.

Geertz, C. 1973. *The interpretation of cultures*. New York: Basic Books.

———. 1983. *Local knowledge: Further essays in interpretive anthropology*. New York: Basic Books.

Gergen, K. J. 1991. *The saturated self: Dilemmas of identity in contemporary life*. New York: Basic Books.

Greenberg, J. and Mitchell, S. A. 1983. *Object relations in psychoanalytic theory*. Cambridge: Harvard University Press.

Horney, K. 1924. On the genesis of the castration complex in women. In *Feminine psychology*, ed. H. R. Kelman (1967). New York: Norton, pp. 37–53.

———. 1926. The flight from womanhood: The masculinity complex in women as viewed by men and by women. In *Feminine psychology*, ed. H. R. Kelman (1967), New York: Norton, pp. 54–70.

————. 1934. The overvaluation of love. In *Feminine psychology*, ed. H. R. Kelman (1967). New York: Norton, pp. 182–213.

————. 1935. The problem of feminine masochism. In *Feminine psychology*, ed. H. R. Kelman (1967). New York: Norton, pp. 214–33.

————. 1937. *The neurotic personality of our time*. New York: Norton.

————. 1946. *Our inner conflicts*. New York: Norton.

————. 1950. *Neurosis and human growth*. New York: Norton.

————. 1967. *Feminine psychology*, ed. H. R. Kelman. New York: Norton.

————. 1987. *Final lectures*, ed. D. H. Ingram, New York: Norton.

Ingram, D. H. 1987. Horney's psychoanalytic technique. In *Psychotherapists' casebook: Theory and technique in the practice of modern therapies*, ed. I. L. Kutash, and A. Wolf, Northvale, NJ: Jason Aronson.

————. 1994. Discussion of the papers by Susan Quinn and Marianne Horney Eckardt. In *Women beyond Freud: New concepts of feminine psychology*, ed. M. M. Berger, New York: Brunner Mazel.

Ingram D. H., and Lerner, J. A. 1992. Horney theory: An object relations theory. *American Journal of Psychoanalysis*, 52 (1): 37–44.

Kierkegaard, S. 1941/1844. *Sickness unto death*. Princeton: Princeton University Press.

Lacan, J. 1977. *Ecrits*. Trans. A. Sheridan. New York: Norton.

Lerner, J. A. 1983. Horney theory and mother/child impact on early childhood. *American Journal of Psychoanalysis*, 43 (2): 149–57.

————. 1985. Wholeness, alienation from self and the schizoid problem. *American Journal of Psychoanalysis*, 45 (3): 251–58.

Lyotard, J. 1984. *The postmodern condition: A report on knowledge*. Minneapolis: University of Minnesota Press.

Mitchell, S. A. 1993. *Hope and dread in psychoanalysis*. New York: Basic Books.

Paris, B. 1991. A Horneyan approach to literature. *American Journal of Psychoanalysis*, 51 (3): 319–37.

Paul, H. A. 1989. Karen Horney's theory of self. *In Self Psychology*, ed. D. W. Detrick and S. P. Detrick, Hillsdale, NJ: The Analytic Press.

Price, M. 1992. The psychoanalysis of an adult survivor of incest: A case study. *American Journal of Psychoanalysis*. 52 (2): 119–36.

————. 1993. The impact of incest on identity formation in women. *Journal of the American Academy of Psychoanalysis*, 21 (2): 213–28.

————. 1995a. Gender Talk: Psychoanalysis, postmodernism and feminism, Discussion of The third step, by M. Dimen. *American Journal of Psychoanalysis*, 55(4), pp. 321–331.

————. 1995b. The illusion of theory: Discussion of R. Chessik's "Postmodern psychoanalysis or wild analysis." *Journal of the American Academy of Psychoanalysis*. 23 (1): 63–71.

Rendon, M. 1991. Hegel and Horney. *American Journal of Psychoanalysis*, 51 (3): 285–99.

Rivera, M. 1989. Linking the psychological and the social: Feminism, poststructuralism and multiple personality. *Dissociation*. 21 (1): 24–31.

Sampson, E. E. 1993. Identity politics: challenges to psychology's understanding. *American Psychologist*, 48 (12): 1219–30.

Schafer, R. 1992. *Retelling a life: Narration and dialogue in psychoanalysis*. New York: Basic Books.

Simmel, G. 1984. On women, sexuality and love. New Haven: Yale University Press.

Spence, D. P. 1982. *Narrative truth and historical truth: Meaning and interpretation in psychoanalysis*. New York: Norton.

Symonds, A. 1991. Gender issues and Horney theory. *American Journal of Psychoanalysis*, 51 (3): 301–12.

Symonds, M. 1975. Victims of violence: Psychological effects and aftereffects. *American Journal of Psychoanalysis*, 35: 19–26.

van den Daele, L. 1981. The self-psychologies of Heinz Kohut and Karen Horney: A comparative examination. *American Journal of Psychoanalysis* 41 (4): 327–37.

Westkott M. 1986. *The feminist legacy of Karen Horney*. New Haven: Yale University Press.

White, M., and Epston, D. 1990. *Narrative means to therapeutic ends*. New York: Norton.

Chapter Five

Melanie Klein and the Nature of Good and Evil

C. Fred Alford

EDITORS' INTRODUCTION

In terms of the history of psychoanalytic thought, the work of Melanie Klein represents the situating of object relations at the hub of theoretical and clinical discourse. While she accepted Freud's view that it was the sexual and aggressive drives that motivate human behavior, she radically differed from him in her claim that these drives are inherently related to others rather than being directionless, tension-producing stimuli that become secondarily connected to objects acting as the medium for their satisfaction. As we shall see, Klein's mental universe of "internal objects," of phantoms, images that occur in phantasies that are reacted to as "real," is very different from Freud's with its fundamentally objectless energies.

As C. Fred Alford suggests, two aspects of the Kleinian worldview are especially distinctive. First is her metaphysics, "an absolute idealism in which the ideas of our inner-world constitute external reality." This, he says, leads to a certain lack of existential seriousness in her account. Her idealism does not adequately take into account the external world, real relationships, and the real self. In addition, Klein's privileging of the internal realm of fantasy leads to a profound neglect of the role of social and cultural factors in the structuring of human relationships and the construction of the self. This lack however, is compensated for in the therapeutic technique, which, Alford claims, accentuates individual responsibility, and so speaks to the real self in the world, not solely the self as container of its objects. Kleinian technique focuses almost exclusively on transference, but not, as some have claimed by minimizing reality; rather, says Alford, "everything is in the transference, and the transference is now. . . . The transference isn't about the analysand's relationship to parents and others transferred to the analyst. It's about the analysand's relationship to the analyst right now, in this room, at this moment."

The second distinctive aspect of Klein's worldview, says Alford, is the moral quality of her outlook. Rather than claiming that Kleinian morality is insinuated in her worldview, it would be more correct to say that her morality is her worldview. For Klein, the central human struggle is "between love and hate, between care and concern for others and their malicious destruction." Psychopathology for Klein thus emanates largely from internal, constitutional sources, primarily from one's aggression. The role of external reality as a determinant for most psychopathology is circumscribed and limited in the Kleinian system. However, says Alford, for all its emphasis on greed, hatred, envy and rage, Kleinian theory and practice are constructed on and rooted in hope: that the power of love and gratitude is as inherent, and strong as hatred, though much more fragile. The "real" goal of Kleinian analysis, Alford says, is not the diminution of depressive guilt and paranoid-schizoid anxiety, not (as some have argued) the integration of oneself and one's experience of others, but the activation of compensatory reparative activities. The "healthy" person for Klein is the one who has worked through the splits in the psyche that are sustained by unresolved primitive conflicts and that inhibit the creative and life-affirming desires. This accomplishment, along with the internal acceptance of pain and conflict as being intrinsic to existence, tends to foster a balanced assessment of the world. (P. M. and A. R.)

More than any psychoanalyst since Freud, Melanie Klein has created a worldview, a picture of human nature and the world it inhabits. Klein's theory contains, or rather is, an epistemology (a theory of knowledge), a metaphysics (a theory of ultimate reality), and an ontology (a theory of what exists). Unlike Freud, Klein never developed these implications of her work, so that at first glance hers seems the very opposite of a worldview, merely an account of the passionate and destructive inner-world of children. The most distinctive aspect of Klein's worldview is her metaphysics, an absolute idealism in which the ideas of our inner-world constitute external reality. One sympathetic critic calls her theory Platonic. I will question this designation, but the insight behind it is not misleading.

Klein's theory is complex, widely known in some aspects, hardly at all in others. To many it is extremely implausible. Though it is not my intent to explain or explore her theory for its own sake, it makes no sense to explore her worldview independently of her theory. They are one, even if it takes some work to spell out the philosophical implications, the view of man, woman, and reality implicit in it. I begin by exploring her relationship to Freud, particularly the way she used Freudian terms to designate un-Freudian concepts and some quite un-Freudian terms to develop Freud's thought further, particularly his late metapsychology. It is in her complex relationship to Freud that Klein's theory as worldview is best explored.

In 1925 Klein was invited by Ernest Jones to give a series of lectures on child analysis in England. Two years later she emigrated there, where she remained for the rest of her life. Klein was the first psychoanalyst to practice genuine analysis, as opposed to educative techniques, with young children. At first Klein's work was in harmony with that of the British Psycho-Analytical Society. On the publication of Klein's work *The Psycho-Analysis of Children* in 1932 (*Writings*, vol. 2), the president of the society, Edward Glover, wrote a glowing review, treating the book as a breakthrough in the development of psychoanalysis (Segal, 1981, p. 73). This harmony began to dissolve in 1935 with the publication of "A Contribution to the Psychogenesis of Manic-Depressive States," Klein's first major theoretical paper. In this and subsequent papers Klein began to challenge key Freudian assumptions, all the while arguing that she was only elaborating them. Whereas Freud saw the superego as arising during the resolution of the oedipal phase at the end of early childhood, Klein pushed back the beginning of the oedipal stage, and with it the emergence of the superego, to the first year of life.

Framing the issue as a question about the age at which the Oedipus complex emerges, as both Klein and her critics did, only disguised more fundamental disagreements. By the term "oedipal" Klein meant not a sexual interest in mother but a pregenital desire to possess and control the riches and goodness of mother's body. By superego Klein meant not the internalization of father's authority, but the young child's innate sense of guilt at its own greed and aggression toward mother, and later father. While trying to establish her theoretical continuity with Freud, Klein was evolving along different lines, in which the key developmental events are pre-oedipal, centering not so much on eros as aggression. Yet there are genuine continuities with Freud. In *Beyond the Pleasure Principle* (1920), Freud revised his instinct theory, combining self-preservation and libido into eros, the instinct to preserve and extend life, setting this instinct against what would later be called thanatos, the death instinct. Klein is one of the few psychoanalysts to take the *Todestrieb* seriously. It is the basis of her worldview, a view rooted in Freudian metaphysics, and misleadingly expressed in Freudian concepts.

For Freud, the drives originate as tensions within the body. This physical tension affects the mind, whose function is to meet the needs of the body by eliminating drive tensions and preserving a state of equilibrium. Libido and aggression produce experience by means of the bodily sensations to which they give rise. For Klein, on the other hand, libido and aggression are always contained within, and always refer to, relationships with others, either real or imaginary. For Klein the body is not so much the source of the drives as the means of their expression. In a word, the drives are passions. Rather than referring to directionless, objectless psychic energy that only later becomes attached to objects of love or hate, Klein sees the drives as patterns of feelings toward real and imaginary others. For this reason Klein is regarded as the founder of object relations theory, our passionate relations to others the foundation of her worldview. "Passion is the essential force of man energetically bent on its object." Karl Marx (1978a, p. 116), not Melanie Klein said this. But she would have understood.

Klein never confronts the difference between her view and Freud's. The closest she comes is in her discussion of the nature of a psychological object. For Freud the object is always "the object of an instinctual aim," whereas Klein (*Writings* vol. 3, p. 51) holds that it represents "in addition to this, an object-relation involving the infant's emotions, phantasies, anxieties and defenses." Greenberg and Mitchell (1983, p. 146) put it simply and powerfully. "Drives for Klein are relationships." An important consequence is that Freud's distinction between id and ego (that is, between energy and structure) becomes redundant. For Klein the central conflict in human experience is between love and hate, between care and concern for others and their malicious destruction. In Klein's theory, it is not so much the ego or superego that constrains aggression, but love. Here is the core of Klein's worldview, a world divided into love and hate because all who inhabit it are. The continuity with Freud's late metapsychology should be noted, but also the difference. Love and hate are born in relationships. Throughout life we struggle to prevent our loving relationships from being overcome by our destructive hate.

In 1941, W. R. D. Fairbairn had used the term "schizoid position" to describe the way the infant's ego splits almost at birth into loving (idealizing) and hating (persecutory) aspects. Earlier Klein herself had written of the way aggression is split off from love and experienced as paranoia. In 1942 she linked Fairbairn's phrase with hers, calling the earliest developmental stage the paranoid-schizoid position to stress the coexistence of splitting and persecutory anxiety.[1] Freud had argued that while the infant may experience anxiety, he does not, and cannot, fear death because he does not yet have an ego. Klein, on the other hand, argued that there is enough ego present at birth for the child to fear death, which it experiences as a fear of disintegration in the face of its own hatred. "The terror of disintegration and total annihilation is the deepest fear stirred by the operation of the death instinct within" (Segal, 1981, p. 116). The deepest terrors stem from within, products of our own hatred. Nothing is more characteristic of Klein's worldview than this inner-focus, the worldview of the infant active throughout our lives, constituting an external world in its own image.

The infant projects not only his aggression, but also his primitive love, which through interaction with unconscious phantasy creates a good object, what Klein calls the good breast.[2] In this simple statement one sees two fascinating but troubling aspects of Klein's thought. First, the focus on particular fantastic objects, like the good breast, as though they exist. One of my students suggested that we read Klein by focusing on the verbs and ignoring the nouns. It is the passionate, directed relatedness that is important in her account, not the part objects it is directed toward. Tempting advice, but I would offer a single caveat. Part-objects, like the good and bad breast, stem from the fragmented and fragmenting intensity of primitive desire, and may help remind us of this experience, a world torn into pieces that never coalesce to make a whole: a whole self or a whole other.

The second troubling aspect of Klein's thought suggested by the statement that begins the previous paragraph is that real parents, and their reactions to the infant, whether loving or frustrating, have relatively little to do with the infant's response. The bad breast and good breast are generated internally, seeming to live a life of their own independently of actual parental response. Klein is an object relations theorist for whom the most fundamental relationships are internal, between and among mental objects. This is the strength of her theory, and its weakness.

The aim of the infantile ego in the paranoid-schizoid position is to introject and identify with its ideal object, while keeping the bad objects away via a continuous process of projection and internalization. The infant's foremost anxiety at this stage is that his persecutors will destroy him and his good object. The primary defense is not projection (already employed to create good and bad objects and externalize them) but splitting and idealization, in which the infant holds good and bad objects rigidly apart, as though they exist in separate, watertight psychic worlds that never touch. Though fixation at the paranoid-schizoid stage is characteristic of schizophrenia and other severe emotional disorders, this stage should not be seen as pathological, but as a crucial step in emotional development, by which the infant learns to overcome his fear of disintegration by introjecting and identifying with the good breast.

Consider, in this regard, Donald Meltzer's study (1978, pt. 2, p. 64) of Klein's *Narrative of a Child Analysis* (*Writings*, vol. 4), her record of treating a ten-year-old boy named Richard. Richard's core problem was not excessive but inadequate splitting-and-idealization. He "could not keep the destructive and Hitleresque part of himself from crowding in on and taking over the good part." Because of his inadequate splitting-and-idealization (Meltzer runs the terms together with hyphens as though they were a single process), Richard tended to confuse good and bad, leading to greatly heightened paranoia (for example, he was uncertain whether the helpful maid was a good object or a bad one), hypocrisy, and confusion. From the perspective of a Kleinian morality this is the fundamental problem humans face. Socrates said that no one ever does wrong knowingly, but only because the wrongdoer fails to understand that doing right will benefit him more in the long run. In a similar fashion, Klein's account implies that people want to do good, by which she means love and care for others. Reparation she calls it. Too often, however, people are too scared, too overwhelmed by their confusion, their inability to keep their good and bad parts separate. Kleinian analysis is a moral enterprise, oriented toward overcoming confusion over good and bad, and the terror this generates (the terror of mistaking good for bad and destroying it), so that the natural desire to care and repair others may be liberated. In the end, Klein's is a moral and optimistic teaching. Hers is not, however, an optimism that is purchased cheaply.

As early as three months of age, says Klein, the infant begins to recognize that the bad mother who frustrates him, and whom he has destroyed in phantasy a thousand times, is also the good mother who tenderly meets his needs. It is this recognition that good and bad object are one that is the foundation of the depressive position. It is, I would argue, the foundation of morality as well. The world is not divided into black and white; only our primitive mental processes are. It is the task of morality to come to terms with gray, which means with our own ambivalence. About everything. Though this is not the place to spell out the formal, philosophical implications of Kleinian morality, its outlines are apparent, a way of thinking that has little room for the categorical imperative and universal strictures, and all the room in the world for the complexities of actual relationships. Not Immanuel Kant but Carol Gilligan (1982), to put it as simply as possible.

By helping to mitigate the intensity of paranoid anxiety, decent, loving parents may help this integrative process along. Nevertheless, Klein seems to understand the internal integration of the good and bad parent as driven more by the increasing sophistication of the child's cognitive apparatus (making it more difficult—but not impossible under the stress of severe anxiety—to deny that good parent and bad parent are one) than by the responsiveness of his environment. Klein calls it the depressive position because attempts to restore the destroyed object to wholeness are coupled with depression and despair, the young child doubting that he is powerful enough to make whole all that he has destroyed. The child attempts to resolve his depressive anxiety through reparation: the mother and others are repaired through restorative phantasies and actions that symbolize love and reparation. If depressive anxiety is strong enough, however, it may lead the child to employ defenses more characteristic of the paranoid-schizoid position, such as splitting the mother once again into good and bad. By making mother bad, the child need not confront his guilt and depressive anxiety over destroying what he loves and depends on.

Whereas paranoid anxiety involves fear of destruction by external forces, depressive anxiety concerns fear regarding the fate of others, both real and imagined, in the face of the child's own hatred and aggression. As a result of his rage and hatred the child fears that he has damaged and destroyed all that is good in the world, as well as within himself. Attempting to lessen his anxiety and guilt through phantasies and actions, the child seeks to re-create the other it has destroyed, first by phantasies of omnipotent restoration, later by affectionate and healing gestures toward real others. This suggests an important point. At the earliest stages of the depressive position, the love and concern for others seem primarily motivated from anxiety and guilt, as in "I have destroyed those who care for and love me; how will I survive?" Klein is insistent, however, that this concern for the fate of the other soon comes to reflect a genuine concern for the object qua object, which Klein sees as stemming from the child's gratitude for the goodness it has received from mother.

Though Klein's emphasis on interpreting aggression is generally stressed (she has been called an id psychologist), the central role of love and reparation in her thinking can hardly be overemphasized. Joan Riviere (1952, p. 60), one of Klein's earliest associates, argues that her studies on reparation are "perhaps the most essential aspect of Melanie Klein's work." Just as much as aggression, care and concern for others are inherent features of the child's earliest relationships. "Feelings of love and gratitude arise directly and spontaneously in the baby in response to the love and care of his mother," says Klein (1964, p. 65). In a word, love is neither an aim-inhibited expression of libido nor merely an attempt to identify with a powerful other. Rather, it expresses concern—caritas—regarding the welfare of the other qua other (Alford, 1989, pp. 9–10). Furthermore, caring is not simply a reflection of the child's great dependence on others. The child does not care for others solely to have his desires better satisfied. Care and concern express "a profound urge to make sacrifices," to make others happy out of genuine sympathy for them (Klein, 1964, p. 65).

As Klein elaborated the depressive position, it came to include more and more aspects of psychic life traditionally viewed from a Freudian perspective, such as the Oedipus complex. Whereas Klein had earlier suggested that greedy hatred at the mother's self-contained goodness motivates the pregenital oedipal conflict, she came to see the conflict as part of the depressive position, in which jealousy toward the father endangers the child's relationship to the good breast, as well as the goodness of the father himself, leading to heightened feelings of anxiety and loss. Whatever one may think of Klein's argument, nothing is gained by continuing to call this phenomenon the oedipal conflict. Klein is writing about a different psychic world, whose relationship to Freud's is virtually incommensurable, at least as far as the Oedipus conflict is concerned.

Rather than saying that Kleinian morality is an implication of her worldview, it would be more accurate to say that her morality is her worldview. In this worldview, men and women are capable of genuine love and concern for others. While Klein recognizes that morality originates in aggression (the paranoid-schizoid position reflects—or rather, is—a primitive talion morality, in which every phantasied act of aggression against mother is returned in kind), this is only its starting point, not its mature basis. Klein also recognizes that love and concern for others may be fundamentally selfish ("I love you because you make me feel so good"). Yet this is not the foundation of Kleinian morality either, but only its origin. Klein reveals the potential of individuals to love and care for others out of a genuine, unselfish concern for the other's welfare. She does suggest that this concern stems from the individual's ability to identify himself with the sufferings of others. We are not dealing here with disinterested altruism or a categorical imperative. But neither are we dealing with an emotional transaction modeled on hydraulics or economics.

Donald Meltzer (1981, p. 179) calls Klein's a "theological model of the mind." By this he means that a person's internal objects are his gods, giving meaning and purpose to his life. We might, however, extend this observation to include the recognition that Klein's basic categories are fundamentally ethical or moral in character. As Michael Rustin (1982, pp. 82–83) observes, "Kleinian theory is impregnated with moral categories, and its developmental concepts . . . incorporate moral capabilities (notably concern for the well-being of other persons) into their theoretical definition." It could be argued that such a claim commits the naturalistic fallacy: the derivation of "ought" from "is." This would not be correct. For Klein, human nature has more to do with hypothetical features of universal relationships than it does with biology (a point noted previously in the discussion of Klein's difference from Freud regarding the status of the *Todestrieb*). Rather than deriving morality from human nature, Klein discovers morality in the earliest human relationships. Humans are about "ought" from the day they are born.

The German philosopher Jürgen Habermas (1980, pp. 11–12) has stated that in his last philosophical conversation with his colleague Herbert Marcuse shortly before Marcuse's death, Marcuse said, "I know wherein our most basic value judgements are rooted, in compassion, in our sense for the suffering of others." It is precisely this sense of morality whose roots Klein uncovers. It is a morality based not merely on the desire to make sacrifices, to make reparation for real and phantasied acts of aggression. It is also based upon an ability to identify deeply with others, to feel connected with their fates. Their pain becomes our own. Klein states that in the act of reparation, "the ego is identified with the sufferings of the good objects" (*Writings*, vol. 4, p. 273).

That morality might stem from compassion is an insight expressed by Jean-Jacques Rousseau (1979, p. 222) when he posits pity (*pitié*) as the prerational basis of morality.[3]

> Thus is born pity, the first relative sentiment that touches the human heart according to the order of nature. To become sensitive and pitying, the child must know that there are beings like him who suffer what he has suffered, who feel the pains he has felt, and that there are others whom he ought to conceive of as able to feel them too.

From pity Rousseau (1964, p. 131) derives all the virtues. For what are generosity, clemency, and humanity but pity applied to the weak, the guilty, and the species in general? Though he does not call it that, Rousseau is writing of the morality of the depressive position, reparative morality it might be called. It depends, it is apparent, on the interaction of pity and identification. Or rather, pity is identification with the suffering of others in the depressive position.

Like Freud in *Civilization and Its Discontents*, Klein bases morality on guilt. Unlike Freud, she systematically distinguishes between two kinds of guilt. The guilt associated with the paranoid-schizoid position is experienced in terms of the talion principle, an eye for an eye. It is not a pretty picture: "The child lives in dread of his objects' destroying, burning, mutilating, and poisoning him, because these activities dominate his own phantasies toward them. . . . Thus, in the child's psychic economy, as on the Lord High Executioner's list, the punishment always fits the crime" (Greenberg and Mitchell, 1983, pp. 132–33).

I would add only that whereas these unconscious phantasies of persecution are mitigated by the reparations of the depressive position, they never disappear. They are not merely the child's unconscious fears but also those of adults when they are operating in the paranoid-schizoid position.

Though I shall discuss the therapeutic implications of Klein's worldview shortly, an important point can best be made here. Analysis can serve to reduce paranoid-schizoid anxiety by showing its origins in unconscious and unrealistic fears of persecution. Analysis cannot, however, do much by itself to reduce depressive guilt, because the analysand really did want to ravage and destroy those he loves. From this perspective, one should feel guilty for one's phantasies, whether one has acted on them or not. Or rather, one will feel guilty about them no matter how many times the therapist says one need not. Depressive guilt can be denied, but not eliminated, because it is a product of the unconscious, in which there is no distinction between phantasy and reality. It is more productive to focus on reducing paranoid-schizoid anxiety, which is mitigated by the analyst's interpretation of aggression, so the analysand's natural reparative impulses can be liberated. The real goal of analysis is not the reduction of depressive guilt but the mobilization of compensatory reparative activities. In this respect, Freud's classic characterization of emotional maturity takes on new meaning. Creative work and love are signposts of maturity because they are primary ways adults may make reparation, symbolic and real, in our culture.

If Klein's is a theological model of the mind, then it must have a place for evil. "The imagination of man's heart is evil from his youth, says the Lord" (Genesis 8:21). Klein doesn't write of evil, but she does write of envy. Like evil, envy isn't just something bad. Like evil, envy seeks to destroy the good because it is good. Carefully distinguishing among envy, jealousy, and greed, Klein sees jealousy as an attempt to exclude another from the source of good. The Oedipus conflict is exemplary. Greed wants all the good for itself. The damage done to the object, or a third party, is incidental. Envy seeks to destroy the good itself. Frequently it does so out of sheer spite: if the envious person cannot have all the good himself, if he cannot be the good itself, then no one else shall have it either. In a word, envy empties the world of goodness because it hates the good, raging at the thought that there might be goodness beyond the self, a goodness that can only make the self feel bad and empty by comparison. Sometimes, says Klein (*Writings* vol. 3, pp. 217–21), patients are unable to accept the analyst's help precisely because they see the analyst as having something useful and good to offer. It is as though the patient must remain ill to deny the worth of the analyst and his technique. As usual, Klein does not restrict herself to strictly analytic insights, but implies (without working out the implication) their more general relevance. There are, she states (*Writings* vol. 3, p. 189), pertinent psychological reasons envy ranks among the seven "deadly sins."

> I would even suggest that it is unconsciously felt to be the greatest sin of all, because it spoils and harms the good object that is the source of life. This view is consistent with the view described by Chaucer in "The Parson's Tale": "It is certain that envy is the worst sin that is; for all other sins are sins only against one virtue, whereas envy is against all virtue and against all goodness."

Toward the conclusion of *Civilization and Its Discontents*, Freud (1961, p. 77) writes that

> the aggressive instinct is the derivative and the main representative of the death instinct, which we have found alongside eros and which shares world dominion with it. And now, I think, the meaning of the evolution of civilization is no longer obscure to us. It must present the struggle between Eros and Death, between the instinct of life and the instinct of destruction as it works itself out in the human species. This struggle is what all life essentially consists of, and the evolution of civilization may therefore be simply described as the struggle for life of the human species. And it is this battle of the giants that our nursemaids try to appease with their lullaby about Heaven.

We can now appreciate the claim of Klein and some of her followers that she actually came closer to Freud's worldview, as expressed in his late metapsychology, than Klein's critics, especially Freud's daughter, Anna. For Klein too the world is a titanic battleground between two forces, love and hate, between the impulse to destroy and the impulse to repair and create.

Still, it would be a mistake to equate Klein's worldview with Freud, changing eros and thanatos to love and hate. Kleinian love is different. Meltzer (1978, pt. 1, p. 84) compares the Freudian view of love with a capital investment aimed at making a profit, Klein's with endowing a charity. For Freud, you do not invest your libido unless you hope to get back more than you give. "You cannot exactly think of yourself as a benefactor of mankind when, by loving, you set up a factory, as it were, rather than endowing a charity." Kleinian love, on the other hand, gets from the very act of giving. It gets the chance to repair the self by repairing and restoring the world, or at least a little part of it.

Seen from this perspective, the Kleinian account locates the source of psychopathology in thanatos, the sheer intensity of human aggressiveness, the innate desire to rend, spoil, and destroy. To be sure, the thanatos that Klein writes of is not Freud's, not an innate desire to return to the stasis of death, but an innate propensity to destructive rage in the face of frustration; not just the extreme frustration of deprivation, but the everyday frustration of imperfect satisfaction of need. To write of human nature is not a popular exercise these days, and Klein no more proves its existence than those who deny it prove its nonexistence. We are really talking about terms; thanatos is a way of characterizing passions that challenge our ability to love and care for others from virtually the day we are born. Were there no desire to love and care for others, to make reparation for our hatred, there would be no psychopathology either—and no civilization. Psychopathology resides in the dynamic conflict between our hatred and our love, a conflict rooted in the nature of human passion, but expressed in as many different forms as there are cultures, and as many ways as there are individuals.

To see this more clearly, we need to examine the epistemic status of Klein's theory, which is a fancy way of saying we need to look at what it says is real, and whether this claim makes sense. A worldview isn't just about what's good and bad; it is about what is (ontology). Freud's worldview is starkly materialistic and naturalistic, at least in its stated intent. Klein's is not. Meltzer (1981, p. 179) calls Klein's view of the mind "Platonic," referring to the way meaning is generated from within and projected onto a formless world. However, to put it this way seems to stand Plato on his head. For Plato, only the forms (Eidos, or Ideas) are real, and the forms exist independently of our knowledge of them. Instead of being Platonic, the Kleinian view is actually sophistic. Our mind is a cave, our unconscious phantasies a parade of shadows across the back of that cave, shadows that we subsequently impose on the external world. While the world may prove incompatible with some phantasies, such as its idealization as an ever-giving mother, all we may know for sure is the content of our own phantasies. The result is an emphasis on internal reality at the expense of external. To be sure, Klein changed her view in this regard throughout the course of her work, granting ever more importance to real relationships in her later writings, particularly "Envy and Gratitude" (1957). Certainly later Kleinians, such as Hanna Segal, have developed this focus further. Nevertheless, the somewhat misnamed "Platonic" character of Klein's thought matters.

Meltzer (1978, pt. 2, p. 86) suggests that we must change our way of thinking to come to terms with Klein's idealism (in the literal sense of idealism: the world is my idea), coming to recognize that psychic reality is the paramount reality, the locus of all truth and meaning.

> It requires an immense shift in one's view of the world to think that the outside world is essentially meaningless and unknowable, that one perceives the forms but must attribute the meaning. Philosophically, this is the great problem in coming to grips with Kleinian thought and its implications.

In fact, the world is meaningless, in the sense that many (but hardly all) moderns hold that its meaning is not given by God or the movement of the absolute spirit but by the collective actions of humans in society over time. Nevertheless, most men and women experience the world as replete with meaning, filled to overflowing with it. Rather than being born into an empty cave, as Meltzer implies, we are born into a cave in which every shadow has a thousand meanings associated with it, the work of millennia of cultural history.

Necessary is the development of cultural values (meanings) that encourage the transformation of reparative impulses into constructive reparative activities directed toward those most in need of reparation. Needed is the channeling of reparation from its earliest emergence as an inchoate impulse to its constructive cultural practice in good works. It is no accident that Kleinians have not developed this intimation of her work, limiting their extensive art criticism to the work of individual artists, or the nature of art in general (Stokes, 1961). The "idealistic" quality of the Kleinian worldview leads some Kleinians to downplay what I would call the absolute seriousness of reality and the absolute reality of other persons. There is, in other words, nothing in her way of thinking that connects us to the world with the proper gravitas human life deserves.

Thomas Ogden (1986, p. 82) writes that Klein's term "depressive position" is misleading. It could better be called the "historical position," in order to stress the continuity of experience, and the experiencing self, which emerges with the capacity to know whole objects existing in time. The paranoid-schizoid position is Orwellian, history rewritten a thousand times a day, as the other is magically destroyed, repaired, disappeared (think of the *desaparecidos* of Argentina), and replaced with another just as good. The depressive position understands that one cannot rewrite history, but only live in it, experiencing a connectedness with the flow of events that brings so much joy and sorrow. Such a conception is not "idealistic"; nor is it materialistic in the reductive manner in which Freud sometimes, but by no means always, wrote. It is realistic, taking human relatedness in the world seriously. I believe Ogden is correct. Where he is mistaken is in suggesting that one can simply rename the "depressive position" and be done with it. One cannot; there is a lack of historical understanding inherent in the Kleinian concept that is not changed by a name.

Two examples will help show the difference between the depressive position and the historical position.

In *Narrative of a Child Analysis*, her account of her analysis with ten year old Richard, Klein (*Writings* vol. 4, pp. 43–44) writes,

> In the present stage of analysis, Richard's capacity to integrate the ego and to synthesize the contrasting aspects of his objects had clearly increased and he had become more able, in phantasy [!] to improve the bad object and to revive and recreate the dead ones. . . . In the dream, Richard could also bring the two parents together in a harmonious way.

Sure, Richard is just ten years old, but this way of thinking permeates Klein's thinking, confirming one's worst fears about psychoanalysis in general—that phantasies of reparation, dreams of harmony, and symbolic representations of reconciliation might substitute for the real thing. It is a view not without consequence.

Consider Klein's discussion (1964, pp. 104–5) of how colonizers, having ruthlessly exterminated native populations, might make reparation: by "repopulating the country with people of their own nationality." Klein's comments were made in 1936, and one could argue that they reflect no more than the spirit of the times. Yet this would let her off the hook too easily. From a Kleinian perspective the psychological effect of an act of reparation is considerably more important than its external consequences. It's this that leads to a certain thoughtlessness, a lack of complete seriousness about the effects of one's acts on others, their impact on the world. Without such seriousness, morality is not fully formed. Klein's theory itself exhibits characteristics of paranoid-schizoid thinking (actually, the manic phase of the depressive position, in which paranoid-schizoid defenses are employed against loss), in which natives and colonialists are interchangeable, because both are not quite real. Ogden (1986, p. 89) states that "The 'depression' of the depressive position is more accurately thought of as a feeling of sadness involved in the acknowledgment that history cannot be rewritten." To know this one must know, and feel, the weight of history. The Kleinian account doesn't always make this easy.

The reasons Klein writes like this are various, but one deserves more attention than it usually receives. Klein lacks a concept of the self in the world, often writing as though the self were the stage on which internal objects destroy each other, repair each other, and generally play out their internal roles. That is, Klein sometimes writes as if internal objects lived a life of their own, more interesting and important than the lives of the selves whom they just happen to inhabit. "But what are our selves?" asks

Klein (1964, p. 104–5). "Everything, good or bad, that we have gone through from our earliest days onwards." The self, it seems, is little more than the container of its objects and the flow of its experiences. This absence of subjectivity, contributing to the implicit characterization of self as object rather than subject of experience, an entity to which things happen, is a prime attribute of the paranoid-schizoid position. This position, I am suggesting, is itself characteristic of Kleinian theory, and hence the Kleinian worldview, *überhaupt*. Meltzer (1978, pt. 2, p. 115) alludes to this aspect of Klein's thought in his comment (immediately following his discussion of Klein's characterization of Richard's improvement quoted above) that "all this sounds like an active process by the ego and not something that happens to it through the mysterious agency of the 'core of goodness'" (that is, through the influence of good internal objects). It is no less a characteristic of paranoid-schizoid thinking (in its manic phase) to see goodness and reparation as something that happens than to see destruction and chaos as products of the mere desire to harm.

Generally this issue is dealt with in terms of the absence of psychic structure in Klein's account. Since the focus here is on her worldview, I shall approach the same issue slightly differently, in terms of the relationship between self and external world. Instead of thinking of the self as a stage on which internal objects act out their roles, we should think of the world as a stage on which selves torn by love and hate struggle to find some accommodation between these passions. It is this accommodation that constitutes psychic structure. It is the task of every individual and every society to find ways to tolerate ambivalence, and so forgive oneself for the harm done to others in phantasy and reality by acts of reparation that take the reality of other individuals and their needs into account. It is the way we make ourselves whole. "All the world's a stage, And all the men and women merely players"—a cliché even before Shakespeare has Jaques utter it. It is well to recall its context: the seven ages of man, from sobbing and puking infancy to senility. The world's a stage because it is man's lot to act: to be and do in the world, from birth to death, and be done to in turn. What I am calling for here is similar to Roy Schafer's (1976) action language; only whereas Schafer stresses the language, I stress the action. If doing does not come first, if acting is not given the attention it deserves, then the result is likely to be a worldview that is in some way effete, not fully serious. I would not claim this for Klein's work as a whole, certainly not for its implications for a worldview that sees man as a creature torn between his love and his hate, his capacity to create and his urge to destroy. Her worldview is as real and profound as classical tragedy, to which she has rightly compared it (*Writings* vol. 3, pp. 275–99). But it remains a risk in Klein's account. One might argue that to make external reality paramount is incompatible with a thoroughgoing psychoanalytic worldview, which must put inner reality first. It's a false dichotomy, a tendentious choice. To take external reality seriously is not so much an ontological choice, a claim about what exists, as it is an existential one, a claim about what is important and valuable, our relatedness to others in love and hate. Klein knows this, but sometimes it gets lost in the drama of internal objects, perhaps because for all its terrors the internal world is still easier to bear. Or at least easier to repair and make whole.

Implications for Therapeutic Technique

Reluctant to tamper with her theory, Klein's epigones have transformed Kleinian technique, so thoroughly in many cases that objections to Kleinian theory no longer apply in practice. Admirable in some respects (better to change the practice to address lacunae in the theory than not to change it at all), this strategy makes Kleinian theory and technique all the more confusing, as a continuity is assumed that does not actually exist. This is not unlike the original situation, in which Klein claimed to be working out the implications of Freudian concepts while actually developing her own. Thomas Ogden (1986) is one of the few to have actually transformed the theory without abandoning it, and he is no Kleinian.

R. D. Hinshelwood's *Dictionary of Kleinian Thought* (1989) tracks recent developments in Kleinian therapeutic technique well, as does Elizabeth Spillius (1988). I focus only on a couple of aspects of Kleinian practice that illuminate, and are illuminated by, her worldview. Though Kleinians remain especially interested in analysis with children, I address only their work with adults.

Kleinians hold that most of what goes on in an analytic setting is an expression of unconscious phantasy. Early and deep interpretation of this phantasy can reduce the anxiety behind it, Kleinians directing their interpretations toward the anxiety, not the defense. Precocious and aggressive interpretation of unconscious phantasy is the hallmark of Kleinian technique, especially in the early years, Klein justified her approach in terms of its success in reducing anxiety. Most criticism of Kleinian technique has been directed toward this aspect of her practice—that Kleinian interpretation is too aggressive too early, imposing its strange part-object language on the patient. No wonder the patient feels persecutory anxiety. The intrusive analyst causes it! More recent Kleinian therapeutic practice has taken this criticism to heart, though the principle remains the same: interpret the persecutory and depressive anxiety, so that the integrative reparative impulses might have room to emerge (Spillius, 1983, p. 325).

Everything is in the transference, and the transference is now; this is the other hallmark of Kleinian technique. The transference isn't about the analysand's relationship to parents and others transferred to the analyst. It's about the analysand's relationship to the analyst right now, in this room, at this moment. Apparently talking about figures in his external world, the analysand is actually talking about split-off parts of the analyst, fragmenting his experience of the analyst in order to manage his ambivalence, perhaps protecting the analyst from his own hatred. Kleinians are noted for aggressively interpreting the negative transference, feelings of hatred, rage and envy toward the analyst. Naming names, putting these unpleasant realities out in the open, is believed to almost immediately reduce anxiety, allowing the analysand's affection and gratitude to come to the fore. Critics hold that such an approach does not fully appreciate the contribution of defenses to psychic structure. Take them apart too early, and the analysand may fall apart. More recent developments in Kleinian thought have stressed the need to move slowly in this area as well.

Beginning as early as 1934 with James Strachey's account of how the analyst (and the analysand's relationship with him or her) can act to moderate unconscious phantasy, and so help the patient integrate good and bad, Kleinian technique has appreciated real relationships and their structure-building properties. Strachey (1934) argued that the analyst is not merely a good object, but a real object, both good and bad, who makes himself or herself available for use as a framework around which the analysand can build a more integrated emotional life. Later accounts, such as Wilfred Bion's (1962), have explained this process in terms of the analyst as container, the analyst's mind helping to contain the fragmented and fragmenting experiences of the analysand, eventually allowing the analysand to reappropriate these lost parts of himself in a more integrated manner (Hinshelwood, 1989, pp. 21–23). Klein, like Freud, was deeply suspicious of the countertransference, believing the patient used projective identification to act out the transference by putting parts of himself into the analyst. Klein's followers do not reject this analysis, but they deny its conclusion: avoid being drawn into the transference. On the contrary, many post Kleinians see the counter transferential experience of the analyst as grist for the mill, the mill that recognizes the alien and intrusive quality of its experience, neither accepting nor rejecting it out of hand, but processing it in the analyst's own way and time, allowing the analysand to reappropriate it in his or her own way and time.

Much that is problematic in Kleinian theory is corrected in this practice. Rather than being the stage on which objects act out their dramas, the self becomes their container, first the self of the analyst, then the analysand. This is how analysis cures. The reality of the analytic relationship is recognized, as is the impact of the personality of the analysand; his or her capacity to contain and process primitive anxiety becomes a key variable.

From the idealism of Kleinian theory, in which the most real and important relationships are intrapsychic, among internal objects, Kleinian therapeutic practice arrives at a materialistic account in which it is actual relationships that feed back to transform psychic structure. No more than in philosophy can Kleinian theoretical idealism and practical materialism be reconciled. Idealism and materialism are axiomatic, about worlds so different that from the perspective of a thoroughgoing idealism it makes no sense to talk about the material feeding back to modify a world of ideas, as the ideas make the world in the first place. Not merely a philosophical problem, this issue must be confronted in any thoroughgoing reformulation of the Kleinian project. Until that time, a modus vivendi seems to have been reached, in which Kleinian practice continues to develop and prosper not in spite of its incompatibility with the theory, but because of it. Sometimes inconsistency fosters progress.

Much more remains to be said about Kleinian therapeutic technique, particularly its elaboration of projective identification, a concept developed by Klein. This is not the place. Here is the place to compare and contrast technique with worldview. About the Kleinian worldview, I suggested that its idealism risks not taking seriously the external world, real relationships, and the real self. The same cannot be said about Kleinian technique. On the contrary, Kleinian technique emphasizes individual responsibility, and so speaks to the real self in the world, not merely the self as container of its objects. It is not the fault of mommy or daddy that the patient is so hurt and angry; it is the responsibility of the patient to come to terms with his or her own rage and envy at the analyst in the transference right now. To be sure, such a perspective risks downplaying the contribution of real relationships to the patient's distress. On the other hand, what we know about these real relationships is that they get encoded in psychic structure, so that they become the patient's own—including his own responsibility.

Reality impinges in the consulting room in a way it never does in theory: real patients, real relationships, and the pressing need to alleviate suffering and sorrow. So too the real gratitude of patients whose lives have been helped. In this environment only an ideologue or a fool could ignore reality. Klein certainly didn't, nor have most Kleinians. But this reality has not made its way back fully to theory, to worldview.

If Kleinian theory and technique have not kept pace, neither are they out of sync. Both express a powerful optimism in the face of darkest reality, a rose set against black velvet, the natural desire to love and care for others blocked by paranoid-schizoid as well as depressive anxiety: fear that one's own love is not strong enough or good enough, which is unfortunately too often the case. For all its concern with greed, hatred, envy, and rage, Kleinian theory and practice are built on hope: that the power of love and gratitude is as natural and powerful as hatred, though infinitely more fragile. Remove the barriers and it will flow freely.

I have argued that this flow must be channeled properly, for while the urge to make reparation is natural, it is not for this reason naturally moral. It must be directed properly; this is the most important thing society and culture can do. It must be directed outside, not just inside (in reality, not just phantasy), toward those most in need, toward those truly damaged by our (including "our" nation's or ethnic group's) hatred, greed, and carelessness. In a word, reparation must become historical; we must recognize that precisely because we cannot undo our acts of aggression and carelessness, we must do what we can as best we can to make amends to real people, if not to those we have harmed, then their legatees. Klein's idealism does not encourage this, and in this regard the Platonic quality of her worldview is troublesome, leading to a failure to confront history with the gravity it deserves. "Men make their own history, but they do not make it just as they please; they do not make it under circumstances chosen by themselves, but under circumstances directly found, given and transmitted from the past. The tradition of all the dead generations weighs like a nightmare on the brain of the living" (Marx, 1978b, p. 595).

The Kleinian account has the potential to wake us from the nightmare of history, revealing how the battle of love and hate in the unconscious of each member of the species creates a world in its image, a world no less real because we make it. Not just Freud's materialism, but that of Marx, is an important corrective to Kleinian idealism, reminding us that while men and women make history what it is, they are not for this reason free to ignore it.

If Klein's Platonism is troublesome, as it is, it is also liberating. Plato's Socrates wonders whether goodness can be taught. While he's not sure if it can be taught, he's more sure that it can be learned. We must only remove obstacles to its pursuit, so that the student might open his eyes and find it on his own. In this sense too Klein's account is Platonic, and properly so. Goodness is innate; mitigate the paranoid-schizoid and depressive anxiety that stands in its way, and it will naturally emerge, always vulnerable but remarkably persistent, like a green plant. On this point the worldview and the therapeutic technique are one. Nurture goodness by confronting and interpreting badness.

NOTES

1. In her attempt to maintain a continuity with Freud, Klein sometimes wrote of what she calls "positions" as though they were tantamount to developmental stages. This is misleading. Position is not a chronological or developmental concept, but Klein's key structural term, referring primarily to the way the ego is organized, its internal object relationships, its characteristic anxieties and defenses. Although the paranoid-schizoid position precedes the depressive position, these positions actually coexist, or rather alternate, throughout life. Earlier in her work Klein wrote of overcoming the depressive position. Her late works, however, stress the goal of attaining or preserving it. The depressive position is a developmental achievement that must be constantly defended and regained throughout life.

2. Kleinians always spell "phantasy" with a *ph*, in order to stress its unconscious reality. I follow that practice when writing about the Kleinian concept.

3. Pity stems from the Latin *pietas*, "piety," as does Rousseau's *pitié*. The English and French meanings are not identical, but similar.

REFERENCES

Note: with one exception, all references to the work of Melanie Klein are to her collected writings, *The Writings of Melanie Klein*, 4 vols. (New York: Free Press, 1984). The exception is "Love, Guilt and Reparation," which appears in a widely available paperback, *Love, Hate and Reparation*, by Klein and Joan Riviere.

Alford, C. Fred. 1989. *Melanie Klein and Critical Social Theory*. New Haven: Yale University Press.

Bion, Wilfred. 1962. *Learning from Experience*. New York: Basic Books.

Freud, Sigmund. 1961. *Civilization and Its Discontents*. Trans. J. Strachey. New York: Norton.

Gilligan, Carol. 1982. *In a Different Voice*. Cambridge: Harvard University Press.

Greenberg, Jay, and Stephen Mitchell. 1983. *Object Relations in Psychoanalytic Theory*. Cambridge: Harvard University Press.

Habermas, Jürgen. 1980. "Psychic Thermidor and the Rebirth of Rebellious Subjectivity." *Berkeley Journal of Sociology* 24–25: 1–12.

Hinshelwood, R. D. 1989. *A Dictionary of Kleinian Thought*. London: Free Association Books.

Klein, Melanie. 1964. "Love, Guilt and Reparation." In *Love, Hate and Reparation*, by Melanie Klein and Joan Riviere. New York: Norton.

Marx, Karl. 1978a. "Economic and Philosophical Manuscripts of 1884." In *The Marx-Engels Reader*, ed. Robert Tucker. New York: Norton.

———. 1978b. "The Eighteenth Brumaire of Louis Bonaparte." In *The Marx-Engels Reader*, ed. Robert Tucker. New York: Norton.

Meltzer, Donald. 1978. *The Kleinian Development*. 3 pts. in 1 vol. Perthshire, Scotland: Clunie Press.

———. 1981. "The Kleinian Expansion of Freud's Metapsychology." *International Journal of Psycho-Analysis* 62:177–84.

Ogden, Thomas. 1986. *The Matrix of the Mind*. Northvale, NJ: Jason Aronson.

Riviere, Joan. 1952. "On the Genesis of Psychical Conflict in Early Infancy." In *Developments in Psycho-Analysis*, ed. Melanie Klein, Paula Heimann, Susan Isaacs, and J. Riviere. London: Hogarth Press.

Rousseau, Jean-Jacques. 1964. "Discourse on the Origin and Foundations of Inequality Among Men." In *The First and Second Discourses*, trans. R. Masters and J. Masters. New York: St. Martin's.

———. 1979. *Emile*. Trans. A. Bloom. New York: Basic Books.

Rustin, Michael. 1982. "A Socialist Consideration of Kleinian Psychoanalysis." *New Left Review* 131:71–96.

Schafer, Roy. 1976. *A New Language for Psychoanalysis*. New Haven: Yale University Press.

Segal, Hanna. 1981. *Melanie Klein*. Harmondsworth: Penguin Books.

Spillius, Elizabeth Bott. 1983. "Some Developments from the Work of Melanie Klein." *International Journal of Psycho-Analysis* 64:321–32.

———. 1988. *Melanie Klein Today*. Vol. 2. London: Routledge.

Stokes, Adrian. 1961. *Three Essays on the Painting of Our Time*. London: Tavistock.

Strachey, James. 1934. "The Nature of the Therapeutic Action of Psycho-Analysis." *International Journal of Psycho-Analysis* 15:127–59.

Chapter Six

D. W. Winnicott's
Psychoanalytic Playground

Gerald J. Gargiulo

EDITORS' INTRODUCTION

Thanks to Winnicott's skillful amalgamation of Freudian and Kleinian ideas into his own highly original and personalized form of object relations theory, the struggle of the self for an individuated existence became a crucial concern for psychoanalytic theory. Perhaps Winnicott's entire corpus can in part be viewed as an answer to the question of how a newly born infant develops a sense of self—an authentic, whole, "true" self, from its original state of "unintegration"—that simultaneously is capable of intimate connection to others. Gerald J. Gargiulo's essay focuses on Winnicott's concepts of "play" and "transitional space" as paradigms for the experience of cultured man and of the therapeutic encounter.

As Gargiulo points out, for Winnicott play was creative, progressive, and developmental. In its most basic form, play expands the evolving relationship between the feeding infant and the mother through the infant's use of toys and other play articles within a metaphorical, potential, transitional space. As the "true" self (the "inherited potential" that constitutes the "kernel" of the infant) evolves through spontaneous gestures, playing becomes the medium for the expression and elaboration of this true self. Most important perhaps, says Winnicott, the true self develops in an atmosphere of acceptance and care by the "good enough mother" who values and empathizes with the child's spontaneous play. Extrapolating from this last point, Gargiulo comments that object relations . . . [for Winnicott] is not a special brand of intrapsychic discourse (not a descriptive term for internal imagoes), but rather an obvious statement about man's essential communal makeup. Our "selves" are formed by everything that comes to pass between us, everything that constitutes our personal and/or social history. Human beings, consequently, do not have relationships; they are relationships.

Gargiulo further indicates that for Winnicott, human cultural experience, such as religious phenomena and aesthetic creation, largely occurs "within" this "overlapping circle of personal illusion and objective reality"; the "place" where the pressure of differentiating inner and outer reality need not be sustained.

Winnicott believed in the importance of the environment in generating personal problems and psychopathology. Without a "facilitating environment" the child was likely to develop a "false self"— a schizoid-like form of self-experience in part characterized by compulsively anticipating the reactions of others. The false self is both a defense against the failure of the maternal object and an effort by the person to establish some kind of object relationship. As Gargiulo indicates, for Winnicott the important issue was to understand the early failure in adaptation (on the part of the parent to the child), which had become frozen in the child. Says Winnicott, it was normal "to defend the self against specific environmental failure by a freezing of the failure situation." Psychopathology thus involves the distortion and restriction of the self that results from the lack of "good enough" parenting. Psychosis, for example, was viewed as an "environmental deficiency disease."

Psychoanalytic treatment, for Winnicott, meant creating a "holding" environment—like the constancy of care and love of the "good enough" parent—that would allow the analysand to unfreeze and reexperience that original failure situation. Winnicott says that the analyst, like the mother, "would be reliably there, on time, alive and breathing"; he "would keep awake and become preoccupied with the patient;" he would be "free from temper tantrums, free from compulsive falling in love." As Gargiulo notes, however, Winnicott believed that the facilitating environment alone was not sufficient to bring about change: interpretation and working through of intrapsychic conflict and of early primitive anxieties were essential components of any analysis. However, this work was conceptualized by Winnicott as the play of two subjectivities, the analysand and the analyst, with the aim of fostering the expression of the analysand's "true" self, the whole and unified self that is genetically predetermined. A "successful" analysis for Winnicott, Gargiulo intimates, is correlated with a more robust, alive, and spontaneous self. Post-analytically, such a person is characterized by a greater capacity for play, illusion, and solitude, and greater relatedness and responsiveness to others. (P. M. and A. R.)

Man and Culture

It might seem odd that in *Playing and Reality* (1971), D. W. Winnicott quotes the Hindu poet Rabindranath Tagore as a backdrop for his psychoanalytic reflections. But as one gets to know the man, one realizes that the choice is not odd at all. Tagore muses on the countless cycles of life,[1] while Winnicott invites us down to the seas, to the timeless sand, and reminds us that if we are to experience the world as interesting, worthwhile, and fertile, play must go from a theoretical possibility to a personal experience.[2] What this means for the practice of psychoanalysis, however, is still being explored. Freud's concern that his reflections and observations be classified as "science" still casts its shadow over our theoretical formulations and everyday practice.[3] Winnicott's growing appeal is due, I believe, to the promise he holds out that an analyst can do credible work without sacrificing individual creativity and spontaneity.

Although clearly acknowledging the import of subjective phantasy, Winnicott stands in the philosophical tradition that presumes that human beings make contact and interact with the objective communal world: that is, what we are capable of knowing is reality itself, that which stands in the shadow of internal phantasy, so to speak, but which is knowable as objective. Such reality is usually encountered, developmentally, in the mothering person, the mother as existing in the outside world. The "ego," consequently, is not simply libidinal. Rather, the child's "libido" comes to be through all his/her experiences with a minimally good enough mother. Object relations, as applicable to Winnicott, is not a special brand of intrapsychic discourse (not a descriptive term for internal imagoes), but rather an obvious statement about man's essential communal makeup. Our "selves" are formed by everything that comes to pass between us, everything that constitutes our personal and/or social history. Human beings, consequently, do not have relationships; they are relationships. No meaningful analytic work can be done without that awareness.

In contradistinction to other analytic thinkers, Winnicott was not concerned with structuring a formalized psychoanalytic theory of man. To read Winnicott is not to enter the arena of logical argumentation, but rather to experience an invitation to muse and to create along with him. Ever desirous of encouraging personal spontaneity and creativity, he was reluctant to codify his approach lest the very qualities he deemed essential for human life be rigidified through submission to a "knowing other."[4] Instead he spoke, almost casually, about the route we humans must travel in our task of achieving personal maturation, the necessary processes we need to traverse in order to step outside the circle of mother-self-world to find the wider circle of the world of self and other. Such a world is one in which we are destined to spend our lives either with a sense of personal aliveness or with conforming deadness.

Play, as we know, belongs to personal aliveness and therefore presumes that an individual has come together into a useable self. This process of coming together as a person was, for Winnicott, intrinsic to his understanding of people. He studied the ingredients, as it were, that enabled humans to be capable of love and hate, and to recognize their selves and other selves, those whom we can meet on shared ground—the endless sand—and build a place to be. Winnicott (1971, pp. 65–85) would eventually call such building creative, and the fruits of such labor the gifts of culture. But to step into the circle of culture is, in Winnicott's thought, to refind the "transitional space" of early childhood, that overlapping area, that gentle mixture of self and other; the world, as it were, waiting to be found with all of a person's history active in the searching. All such finding is, of necessity, a creating.

To be alive means that the overlapping circle of personal illusion and objective reality,[5] (the seedbed of culture) is experienced as likable and entertaining, inviting as well as challenging. As teddy bears negotiate a child's many selves, for example, the world is put to new and personal uses, and culture is fertilized.

Winnicott (1971, p. 14) considered psychoanalysis one of the primary inheritors of the transitional space of childhood play, that is, one of the cultural outcomes of a good enough childhood; he thought of it along side such other achievements as art, philosophy and religion. Bridges, all of them. They are, in Winnicott's thought, links between our insides (forgotten as well as remembered), and the world around us, between the "me" and the "not me."[6] In the creation of culture man weaves the not me with his subjective phantasies and produces a world in which he feels safe enough to play. When we experience ourself as giving and receiving, the very world that defines us as human comes to be. And so Winnicott (1971, p. 100) can write that "cultural experiences are in direct continuity with play, the play of those who have not yet heard of games."

Another way to explore Winnicott's notion of transitional space is to reflect on his concept of "mind" (1958). Winnicott denies the existence of mind as some type of Leibnitzian monad, as an "entity" inside one's head.[7] (He was clearly reacting to one psychoanalytic model, influenced by both Descartes and Kant, that locates "mind" and "meaning" as locked within the individual psyche.[8]) One fruitful way to read Winnicott's thoughts on psyche/soma is to speak of "mind" as a personal referent term for a communal accomplishment, that is, communication in all its possibilities. Language, for example, is one such experience of communication enabling us to experience and create mind.[9] We are persons by the very force of being social, being relational. Human "meaning" comes about, consequently, only as a result of a shared environment, within a particular cultural context. Although "mind as community" was not a specific turn of phrase for Winnicott, it does reflect what I believe is an essential implication of his approach, the appreciation of man as creative, as cultural. Lewis Thomas (1984), the scientist and essayist, has written persuasively of persons as constituted by their human communities, not as separate entities definable in terms of self-regulating mechanisms.[10] To isolate the psyche in terms of drives and phantasies, forces and counterforces is to reduce spontaneity to reflex, creativity to formula, and culture to control.

To be alive, for Winnicott, means more than being a compliant response to a particular environment—the triumph, all too frequently, of a false self-organization. Being alive is more than mere sanity and clearly some steps beyond instinctual satisfaction.[11] Instincts are understood, in Winnicott's thoughts, as fortifiers for an existent ego, that is, for the individual who has achieved personal integration.[12] Otherwise the experience of "drives" is as "persecutory-like intrusions," and their satisfaction a guarantee of nothing more than physical stimulation.[13] Only when we feel personally alive can relationships be humanly satisfying. Grounded in our capacity to both hear and respond to others, instinctual gratifications have a chance to be personally fulfilling, enabling us to experience thereby that we are not lost stars in an endless night but are, in fact, tied to each other by the need to feel real, desired, imaginative, and responsive. Winnicott's therapeutic hope is that as we aid in the process of personal integration, we are contributing not merely to an individual acceptance of "Ananke,"[14] but to a careful building of the human enterprise.

Only when we feel effective in our personal interactions, rather than perpetually accommodating, can aggression be experienced as a stabilizing force for our personal identity and sexuality a pleasurable securing of the me and the not me. In the moments of self-forgetful orgasm of self and other, just as in man's great cultural achievements, we are allowed to give up the "experience" of separateness (one might say the "delusion" of separateness). Adult autonomy has more to do with a capacity to depend on and interact with others than the ability to function "independently." Not only does creativity enter psychoanalytic diagnostic categories, but also a capacity for civility. For civility has to do with the careful treatment of others; it is a maturational achievement that reflects something of what Winnicott means by "using" the object, that is, recognizing the other's separateness and interacting accordingly.[15] To be civilized means to live cooperatively in a world of others. An analysis that results in anything less has not reached its goal.

The Therapeutic Place

Winnicott believed that most parents, particularly mothers, not only had their child's best interest at heart but were also equipped to foster their child's maturational processes.[16] When all did not go well, however, the resolution of such developmental tasks, for either child or adult, became the focus of therapy. As analyst, Winnicott grew convinced that only an individual who could give to and receive the rewards of play had fulfilled the potential of creativity that is the mark of a true self organization. Progressively, throughout his writings, he saw the goal of treatment as enabling a patient to be in a place where such play was possible; where the ebb and flow of life would be both accepted and lived. Not insignificantly does he quote Tagore, a poet who spoke of the utter and complete unity of all things, especially the interdependence of life and death. In the drama of man, "play" and "illusion" (Lila and Maya) formed the backdrop to both Tagore's and Winnicott's reflections.

Winnicott (1958) made of his psychoanalytic office a transitional space: something contributed to by both analyst and patient; a common playground where they might both meet and create a world, as it were, precisely because there would be a world there to be found.[17] Sometimes that "world" would have small beginnings: drawing squiggles, by turns, on a piece of paper. Squiggly games were one way Winnicott (1971, p. 16) found of coming together with a patient and finding a new way of speaking, a unique creation. And finding a new tongue by which to speak of the paradoxes of human existence is to make of the psychoanalytic encounter a place where creativity enters technique, the experience of which is as important for an analyst as it is for a patient. One does not, consequently, just "undergo" an analysis, nor does one simply "conduct" an analysis. One has to be developing, all the time, a place where memory can be trusted, aloneness can be safe, and love and hate can be traveled repeatedly without any loss of direction. Analysis, then, depends on "who" is doing it, just as each work of prose or poetry depends on "who" is doing it, and this does no violence to literary rules or tradition.

Although there is a body of knowledge about human experience and maturation that is essential to a practitioner, each analyst is, as we know, as distinctive a guide as a Virgil to a Dante. Who, therefore, is doing an analysis determines whether it is a stale repetition of formulae or a personalized embodiment of psychoanalytic principles. Winnicott, as the analyst and as the poet that he was, had no interest in establishing a "school" of thought, no interest, as I have mentioned, in codifying his reflections into a "teaching." He was opposed, for example, to Melanie Klein's insistence that her followers use "her" terms. Such insistence, he felt, would rob the individual practitioner of the chance to find his or her own words for what was going on.[18]

Clinical Perspectives

An individual's achievement of "personal aliveness" was, for Winnicott, the linchpin for his reflections on human pathology as well as his therapeutic focus. The resolution of intrapsychic conflict was subordinate to this goal. We live through all kinds of experiences growing up, most of which we cannot hold in our hands but which, nevertheless, we carry with us all our lives. Winnicott knew, particularly because of his work with children, that when the therapeutic playground was "safe," an analyst could help a patient bring to light what had been condemned to darkness, or bring into focus what had been looked at from aside. As patient and analyst experienced continuity they could begin to experience contiguity; standing on level ground, they could gradually allow for the play of metaphor, the work of knowing and not knowing, the paradox of love and hate, life and death: the repetitive road marks of an analytic encounter. And in the amiability that could follow from such activity, what had been eclipsed could emerge, what was sidetracked in personal development could begin healing, and even what was missing in the analyst's understanding and approach could be supplied.

It becomes obvious, I believe, why Winnicott would not, could not, organize a "school." He merely reminds us what each person, in the analytic meeting, brings to the "place" of therapy. And on this "ground" there is no automatic indication that a psychoanalysis has begun, certainly not the use of the couch. Since a patient's contribution to the analytic space is crucial, Winnicott highlighted the need for an analyst not to intrude, or to interpret too early, or, for that matter, too correctly. One safeguard against this last possibility is, I believe, for an analyst to allow himself the experience of "forgetting." There are "rules" to the play, but one must frequently forget prior experiences and expectations if the present is not to be overshadowed by too much thinking, or too much need for an analyst to be in the "know" as to what is happening.[19]

The Patient

For all of Winnicott's understanding of the observable developmental stages, he never lost sight of the complexity of the human situation. As easily as he can speak of the good enough mother's adaptation to her child's needs, he can speak of the necessary, although hidden, role of illusion in a child's coming to be. Illusion, that is, as the subjective phantasy whereby a child creates the world, the satisfier of his/her needs, as a first and necessary step in dialoguing with the other.[20] When the other, usually the mother, meets such phantasies with her own responsiveness, the world is experienced as giving and welcoming and so a child can engage it with minimal anxiety. That engagement means that a person finds that s/he is not alone, not a solitary island, not lost. Winnicott's thoughts are clear: dialogue with the world, personally and culturally, is what should define human experience. Erik Erikson speaks in the same vein when he notes that, from a more observational stance, both mother and child truly do create each other in their different roles. When the mother is able to experience the child as her own, responsive to his/her individual timings, as well as be created by the child as its own, we have the first dance of reciprocity, from which civility and culture follow. When this does not occur, personal integration gets sidetracked and rage and desolation roam the psyches of both caretaker and cared for. The experience of personal aliveness is either aborted or eclipsed.

In such circumstances Winnicott would interview both mother and child; he would employ the whole family, if necessary, to find the "thread" of personal "ongoing-in-being" that had gotten sidetracked into reactive compliance or defiant isolation. He would proceed so since, when things had gone badly, a child's personal history was all too often a chronology of objective environmental misalignments. What had occurred in childhood was Winnicott's lens through which he understood adult patients as well. Such developmental misalignments would issue, all too easily, in hatred coming to the fore, not the unconscious hatred that psychically kills the other, just as it delights in its resurrection (which we will speak of later when discussing his thoughts on reparation and concern), but an angry disjunction between the self and the world. He would come to speak of this as the antisocial tendency.[21] Hatred eventually acknowledged, however, is one of the important steps toward personal integration; hatred understood is not just lethal, it is already receding to make way for some usable personal contact. The raged-at-world can become the usable world, just as the raged-at-analyst can become usable also. Angry disjunctures are not easy to work with, and so Winnicott (1958) could talk of his own response of hatred to a patient, which he might hold in isolation till a patient could hear of it and the hearing could be helpful.[22]

When things have gone badly in Eden, when the world has been found short of being "good enough," other symptoms, as we have spoken about, come to the fore. The transitional space between the child and his/her personal world becomes garbled and the precursor of mind, as communication, is aborted. The child, or adult, is forced to retreat, as it were, into his own ruminations, back into observation rather than response, back into fearful, skewed perceptions, reacting to an environment more with compliance than spontaneity. This compliance is the forerunner of what Winnicott calls the "false self," as against spontaneity, the hallmark of a "true self" organization.

When the stage is cluttered with deadening experiences, impulses that have lost a personal grounding, memories that eclipse the self, then a person has no alternative but to reenact such a history, repeatedly, with all those with whom she/he comes in contact. Transference, then, is an inability to find new lines for the play of our lives. The old lines are repeated and defended as a person tries to author himself with a script that is not his/her own. It is as if the dead of the past outnumber the living present, as if one is having a dialogue with masks.[23] In the new speech, the new language between analyst and patient, and the new hearing, the voices of the past can find a resting place.

Winnicott was content to limit himself to a few comments during a session; he understood—and was comfortable communicating—that he was, at times, the patient's father or mother. No need for psychotic labels, just history unfolding. The play of transference, however, is more than allowing and clarifying its occurrence; its resolution is fostered only within a context of an analyst's personal presence, one that is neither confessional nor intimate, but available, sensible, and concerned. A presence, I believe, that knows how important it is to convey to patients that we are as committed to holding their dreams as we are to interpreting them.

The Therapist

Winnicott (1965) spoke of countertransference as the lack of professionalism in a therapist's conduct vis-à-vis a patient (1965, pp. 159–61). One example of professionalism, in Winnicott's context of the psychoanalytic encounter, is the therapist's appreciation of the patient's developmental needs and the willingness to foster their integration. Developmental needs, in the task of personal integration (personalization and realization), are by definition different from instinctual gratifications. Because he knew the significance of this distinction, Winnicott (1971, pp. 56–64) did not hesitate to provide milk and cookies, for example, for those patients for whom he thought it would be helpful. He wrote, also, of rocking a particularly regressed patient in his arms until there was a quiet, personal experience of breathing, enabling the patient thereby to touch the ground of his/her life, so to speak.[24] He had extended sessions for those people who were not able to get to his office with the usual frequency. And he was quite content to let a patient come upon an inexact interpretation, which might be close enough to the mark, rather than offer—even presuming he knew it—the "correct" interpretation himself.

Thus it becomes clearer that "who" is doing the work is no call to wild analysis but an awareness that the psychoanalytic encounter is as distinctive as good prose, or as personally affirming and consoling as the best of poetry. And just as a land without a bard is desolate, just so is the psychoanalytic place empty if it is filled, as I have mentioned, with correct formulae rather than personal experiences. In this sense Winnicott stands in the tradition of the experimental work of Sandor Ferenczi (1988) while likewise fulfilling the analytic task so ably described by Andre Green (1975). Green reminds us that to simply repeat what has been handed down to us would be to effectively kill analysis; keeping this knowledge alive and vital means innovation.[25] And innovation is possible only when one can trust one's good will toward a patient and toward oneself, and indulge in enough forgetfulness to be surprised, in Theodor Reik's (1948) sense, by what may transpire.[26] A "forgetfulness" that is close to what Freud (1913) meant by free hovering attention. Self-awareness can be, all too easily, a by-product of the anxious ego (Fingarette, 1963, pp. 71–112), a hindrance to inventiveness.

And Winnicott was inventive. Some of his interventions are open to conflicting interpretations. Yet for him, I am certain, rocking a patient in the hope that some primal memory would be touched, and the patient's personal experience of "ongoing-in-being" resumed, was not seen as either seductive or harmful. With good will toward oneself, an analyst need not be totally right in his interpretations in order to avoid being totally wrong. Occasionally an analyst might even have as a goal that his/her patients would thereby experience their analyst's limitations in understanding. Winnicott did (1965, pp. 50,54).

Countertransference, for Winnicott, as we have mentioned, is anything that interferes with an analyst's professional stance. How frequently, we might ponder, might psychoanalytic theory itself be a countertransference? How often, Masud Khan (1975, p. xxviii) writes, do analysts see their patients as more integrated than they, in fact, are, in order that they might experience themselves functioning as analysts (conducting an analysis, frequently for years, on the false assumption, in Winnicott's [1965, p. 152] terms, "that the patient exists")? Meaning, I believe, that when pathology has had the upper hand we have the experience of "mind" as a solipsistic entity, a "locked-in-ness," so to speak, which comes about when an individual has had to take over the protective functions that should have been provided by his/her caretaking environment. The individual becomes consequently, both caretaker and cared for, overly self-conscious and apprehensively cautious; the caretaker-self is caught in a hall of mirrors. When such a turn of events comes to be, obsessive ruminations predominate, and the capacity for playful metaphorical interchange is eclipsed. When a patient is locked into his/her mind, and not at home in his/her soma, we have the breeding ground of an analysis lasting for years but getting nowhere. In such cases Winnicott would search beyond the rubble of intellectual awareness for what was life-giving, be it a patient's need to find forgotten rage[27] and/or protective (managerial) care in order to begin a personal self.[28]

Winnicott, as we have mentioned, reminds analysts that a patient must learn to play first before any productive investigative or clarificatory process can be undertaken. Squiggling games can be done with more than lines on a paper; they can be done with words that need not issue in anything more than moments of basic trust. A human life is made of such moments. It is against such a backdrop that we can understand Winnicott's poetic hope that death would find him "alive."[29]

A Case in Point

Let us conjure up a case he wrote about. A man, somewhere in his midforties, comes to his office, a man who has tried analysis for the past twenty-five years with different analysts. He is a successful man, by many worldly standards, but a man unable to resolve a persistent feeling that all was not well within. With such a case Winnicott allowed himself to forget even himself, because he trusted himself, and to say to the patient one day that although he knew the patient was male, he heard a female in the room, he saw a female in the room. And to complete the circle he told the patient that of course he (Winnicott) knew that he was mad for saying this. Winnicott's "madness," he would later assure the patient, was not to be taken metaphorically, but rather as a moment of suspension of perception of external reality in order to contact a hidden experience that the patient was unknowingly carrying around. What conjectured experience? That his mother, now dead, during the earliest periods of his life, saw a girl, out of her own madness, before she was able to handle and see her son as male.

One foot in the past, eyes toward the future, hopes grounded in timeless, mostly hidden images, our nameable selves reflecting how we were called, how we were spoken to. Winnicott's patient had been spoken to as if he were a girl every time his mother interacted with him during his earliest months; and the confusion as to who he was, who he was supposed to be, came down as an echo into his present life. Content to think that in many cases poetic listening was more helpful than diagnostic categories, Winnicott could let his mind wander to a place where we all may be confused as to who we are, or are supposed to be. Reaching such a place in himself, without repudiation, he could hear the echo of that little girl in the consultation room and name it for his patient.[30]

Self, Other, and the World

Man is, I believe, not so much alone as lonely until another hears him, with his/her whole self, as it were. Only then can the potential transitional space between ourselves and what is not ourselves become actual. By "actual" Winnicott means something analogous to a bridge being built, a cocreation between a child and the mothering environment, between analyst and patient, cocreation where what is created is also simply found; creation meaning finding it for oneself. And finding the world for oneself, making it a real place where spontaneity is possible, is an essential prologue to what we call the works of man's hands, the world of culture (in traditional psychoanalytic language the world of sublimation; not the sublimation of certain people at special moments, however, but the everyday creation of the alive enough person).[31]

How important, then, Winnicott's therapeutic focus on enabling a patient to feel personally alive, since without such experience the world is a dead place. It is with such a goal of aliveness in mind that Winnicott (1965) explored the roots of childhood phantasy, finding there, as a necessary stage, a destruction of the world, which is, paradoxically, a backdrop for experiencing the world as separate, outside our omnipotent control. Experiencing the world as separate enables a child (or adult) to "use" it, as such, and not simply "relate to" the other as provider.

Experiencing the world as separate means achieving a capacity for reparation, a Kleinian concept that Winnicott made his own. Such a capacity is able to come about, Winnicott wrote, when guilt over a "psychic" killing is "held but not felt as such," so that the experience of concern predominates.[32] Reparation and concern are, then, the building blocks of communal civility. Achieving such a developmental capacity establishes, on firm ground, the child as separate, as aggressive, and as essentially related. As a child goes from relating to the mother-world to developing a capacity to use—that is, to appreciate as separate—the mother-world, he experiences a gradual change over from unintegration to integration, all of which fosters the experience of being a unique person.[33] Such uniqueness entails, Winnicott (1965) notes, not only a "capacity to be alone" (1958, p. 36), but an aloneness that comes about through our objective relatedness. Alone, that is, in the presence of someone else. Alone, also, even to oneself.[34] An aloneness that must be recognized, and not violated, by an analyst. Consequently Winnicott's (1965, p. 39) remark that "there is no such thing as an infant" (without a mother) is more than a clever phrase; and that there is no such thing as a patient (without an analyst) is more than an obvious implication.[35] They are, in fact, fundamental statements about man/woman as symbolic, that is, as relational; most obviously experienced in our creation and use of language in the service of understanding ourselves, others and our human world.

Erik Erikson (1966) also spoke of the early dialogue of mother and child as the "ontology of ritualization," a "place" where the capacity for the symbolic is born[36] (the divided coin, as it were, half mother, half child, the unification of which is both a creation and a refinding of mother and child, of self and of other).[37] The baby creates the mother as mother, that is, the baby's response, when things go well, evokes motherliness, just as mother's response, in experiencing the child as her own, creates him/her to her own image. When an individual is not locked in deadly combat for the fulfillment of basic needs, a healthy relationship can predominate. And the capacity for symbolization can begin since mother, as herself, and as the found world, is not experienced with terror but rather with possibility.

What possibility? The possibility to come upon, through symbolization, forgotten aspects of the self and/or of the other, of love or hate, sexuality and/or loss, hidden in the world, tucked inside the most common of things or images, transforming the place where we live into a playground for the Muses. Symbolization and, by implication, sublimation are not isolated achievements; they are the consequence of being personally alive and contributing to the communal, dialogic world in which we live.[38] The triumph of play, if you will.

Play, however, is always free, not imposed.

Winnicott was convinced that the more we are able to raise children respecting their "personness," the more morality—a necessary prerequisite for living in an adult communal world—would follow. In his thought, quite rightly I believe, the fact that morality is taught, frequently by some external religious authority, is a statement of our still as yet inadequate child-rearing practices. In his respect for a person's individuality and internality, Winnicott was essentially a profoundly spiritual man; he was not interested, however, in polemics about religion. Anyone familiar with Zen thought or Vedantic Hinduism will hear echoes while reading him; particularly, for example, in his understanding of the role of breathing in establishing a personal soma. (To live in the body is the start of life.) In this vein we can understand Winnicott's reflections on the "madness" of attempting to impose one's personal world upon another as their necessary world. Such missionizing is a violation of sanity and civility. He was not an advocate for missionaries of any sort—religious, political, or psychoanalytic. There is, we can conclude, a "madness" in possessing the truth. A "capacity for compromise is not a characteristic of the insane," Winnicott notes(1988, p.138).[39] Compromise entails not eclipsing, by denial, our solitariness in all its roles, nor our own death in all its epiphanies, avoiding thereby what Winnicott calls the manic defense.[40]Compromise is essential if we are to live in ourselves and with others.

End-Thoughts

Winnicott understood, as I read him, that holding our patients' dreams was a necessary task, so that they could eventually hold themselves, confident that the world would not let them go until, of course, it was time for them to say good-bye—alive. He preferred, I believe, to traverse the landscape of man rather than simply observe it. Concerned with what it means to be alive, to be in health, he replaced empirical detachment with personal experience. It is a lingering prejudice not to hear this as scientific, a commitment to understanding "without preconceived notions,"[41] in lieu of an appeal to the gods.

It is not without reason that the ancient Greeks spoke of happiness as residing in the full exercise of personal competence; this was the civilization that read nature and told us that love begets love forever. Winnicott, from all appearances, achieved both competence and love, and shared these with us.[42]

We are indebted to his generosity.

NOTES

1. Tagore (1941). "On the seashore of endless worlds children meet" (p. 41). Note Winnicott's parapraxis of meet = play, quite in keeping with the intent of the poet.

2. Winnicott (1971): "psychotherapy is done in the overlap of the two play areas, that of the patient and that of the therapist. If the therapist cannot play, then he is not suitable for the work. If the patient cannot play, then something needs to be done to enable the patient to become able to play, after which psychotherapy may begin" (p. 54). ["p]sychoanalysis has been developed as a highly specialized form of playing in the service of communication with oneself and others" (p. 41).

3. Winnicott, Shepherd, and Davis (1989). In his review of "Memories, Dreams, Reflections" (C. G. Jung), Winnicott writes, "If I want to say that Jung was mad, and that he recovered, I am doing nothing worse than I would do in saying of myself that I was sane and that through analysis and self-analysis I achieved some measure of insanity. Freud's flight to sanity could be something we psycho-analysts are trying to recover from" (p. 483).

4. Roustang (1982): "If the analyst relies entirely on himself in practice, he cannot rely on someone else in theory. To dissociate the two makes no sense, because theorization can take place only during practice" (p. 72).

5. Winnicott (1971): Note: "We experience life in the area of transitional phenomena, in the exciting interweave of subjectivity and objective observations, and in an area that is intermediate between the inner reality of the individual and the shared reality of the world that is external to individuals" (p. 64).

6. Winnicott (1958): "The intermediate area to which I am referring is the area that is allowed to the infant between primary creativity and objective perception based on reality-testing. . . . The mother's adaptation to the infant's needs, when good enough, gives the infant the illusion that there is an external reality that corresponds to the infant's own capacity to create" (p. 239).

7. Winnicott (1958): "In the study of a developing individual the mind will often be found to be developing a false entity, and a false localization" (p. 244).

8. Cavell (1993): "Like the Cartesian, Freud draws here a radical distinction between the 'internal' and subjective world, which we can know, and the real, external world, which he claims we cannot. . . . So Freud is led to the traditionalist's skeptical view that all knowledge begins and ends with first-person experience" (p. 19).

9. Cavell (1988): "For an interpersonal or third-person view, on the contrary, meanings are not in the head . . . but adhere to thoughts, ideas, and propositions, in virtue of their relationship to this community, to the history of their use, to events and things in the world, and to other ideas" (p. 597).

10. Thomas (1984):"we get along together in human society because we are genetically designed to be social animals, and we are obliged, by instructions from our genes, to be useful to each other" (p. 104).

11. Winnicott (1958):"Through artistic expression we can hope to keep in touch with our primitive selves whence the most intense feelings and even fearfully acute sensations derive, and we are poor indeed if we are only sane" (p. 150n).

12. Winnicott (1971): "It is the self that must precede the self's use of instinct" (p. 141).

13. Winnicott (1965): "but id-excitements can be traumatic when the ego is not yet able to include them" (p. 141).

14. On "Necessity," see Ricoeur (1970, section 3)

15. Gargiulo (1989). "Accordingly" is of course the point. "To do this is to be freed from the search for the all-powerful knowing Other. When one is no longer subject to the transference desire, one is able to live freely and creatively, in the world. Freud was not Reichian when he said the goal of analysis was to be able to love and to work; nor do I think he was, in using the word love, arguing for a delusional state" (p. 159).

16. Winnicott, (1957): "what we need is mothers [and fathers] . . . who have found out how to believe in themselves. These [parents] build the best homes" (p. 42).

17. Winnicott (1965). See "The Aims of Psychoanalytic Treatment" (pp. 106–70) for reflections on his work.

18. See: Rodman (1990): "This artificially integrated phenomenon must be attacked destructively"(p. 33).

19. Winnicott (1965): "I have always felt that an important function of interpretation is the establishment of the limits of the analyst's understanding" (p. 189). Also Winnicott (1971): "It does not really matter, of course, how much the therapist knows provided he can hide his knowledge" (p. 57). Winnicott is indicating the need for an analyst never to violate a patient's inner core, that center from which the true self organization springs.

20. Winnicott (1958): "It will be seen that fantasy is not something the individual creates to deal with external reality's frustrations. This is only true of fantasying. Fantasy is more primary than reality, and the enrichment of fantasy with the world's riches depends on the experience of illusions"(p. 153). But also note Winnicott (1971): "fantasying interferes with action and with life in the real or external world, but much more so it interferes with dream and with the personal or inner psychic reality, the living core of the individual personality" (p. 31). Therefore my use of phantasy.

21. Winnicott (1958): "The antisocial tendency is characterized by an element in it which compels the environment to be important. The patient through unconscious drives compels someone to attend to management. It is the task of the therapist to become involved in this the patient's unconscious drive, . . . The antisocial tendency implies hope" (p. 309).

22. Winnicott (1958): "In analysis of psychotics the analyst is under greater strain to keep his hate latent, and he can only do this by being thoroughly aware

of it. . . . If the patient seeks objective or justified hate he must be able to reach it, else he cannot feel he can reach objective love" (p. 199).

23. Calvino (1974): "You reach a moment in life when . . . the dead outnumber the living. And the mind refuses to accept more faces. . . . on every new face . . . it prints the old forms, for each one it finds the most suitable mask" (p. 75).

24. Little (1990): "Treatment is needed, rather than 'technique'; and intuitive behavior and management, not verbal interpretation" (p. 88). "Through his reliable 'holding' . . . and acceptance of a direct relationship, I began to trust D. W. and to find continuity and something of a 'mutual feeding situation'" (p. 98).

25. Green (1975): "an analyst cannot practice psychoanalysis and keep it alive by applying knowledge. He must attempt to be creative to the limits of his ability" (p. 18a). Also: "In the end the real analytic object is neither on the patient's side nor on the analyst's but in the meeting of these two communications in the potential space which lies between them. . . . the analyst . . . constructs a meaning which has never been created before the analytic relationship began" (p. 12a).

26. Reik (1948): "On the threshold of psychological research we find, not familiarity with ourselves, but astonishment at the phenomena of our own minds" (p. 239).

27. Winnicott (1971): "If, in the fantasy of early growth, there is contained death, then at adolescence there is contained murder. . . . In the unconscious fantasy, growing up is inherently an aggressive act" (p. 144).

28. Winnicott (1958): "In the third grouping I place all those patients whose analyses must deal with the early stages of emotional development [when] . . . the personal structure is not yet securely founded. . . . the accent is more surely on management" (p. 279).

29. Rodman (1990): "Oh God! May I be alive when I die"(p. 5).

30. Winnicott (1971): "Creativity and Its Origins" (1971, pp. 72–75).

31. Gargiulo (1992): "We can understand sublimation, consequently, as closely related, if not identical, to the symbolic use of objects in this place of play, manifested by the capacity to play. . . . Ideally, therefore, sublimation starts in the first year and progressively continues throughout an individual's life. It is the capacity to adaptively use symbols at different developmental levels; that is, in a way that makes play, as Winnicott understands it, possible" (p. 32).

32. Winnicott (1965): "Failure of reparation leads to a losing of the capacity for concern, and to its replacement by primitive forms of guilt and anxiety" (p. 82).

33. Phillips (1988): "So for Winnicott the healthy integration made possible by a holding environment is always reversible; states of unintegration can be tolerated and enjoyed. But if integration is 'incomplete or partial' the unintegrated parts of the infant become, in Winnicott's view, dissociated" (p. 81).

34. Winnicott (1965): "each individual is an isolate, permanently non-communicating, permanently unknown, in fact unfound" (p. 187).

35. For a clinical discussion of this approach see Gargiulo (1991, pp. 155–66).

36. Erikson (1966): "In all epigenetic development, however, a ritual element, once evolved, must be progressively reintegrated on each higher level, so that it will become an essential part of all subsequent stages" (p. 613).

37. Winnicott (1965): "In between the infant and the object is some thing, or some activity or sensation. In so far as this joins the infant to the object (viz. maternal part-object) so far is this the basis of symbol-formation. On the other hand, in so far as this something separates instead of joins, so is its function of leading on to symbol-formation blocked" (p. 146).

38. Gargiulo (1992): "Winnicott's experience of man as 'playful' (*homo ludens*) enabled him to create a playground where culture and personal consciousness mirror each other" (p. 332).

39. Note the preceding sentence as well: "If development proceeds well the individual becomes able to deceive, to lie, to compromise, to accept conflict as a fact and to abandon the extreme ideas of perfection and an opposite to perfection that make existence intolerable" (Winnicott, 1988a, pp. 137–38), also Winnicott, Shepherd, and Davis: "When Jung deliberately lied to Freud he became a unit with a capacity to hide secrets instead of a split personality with no place for hiding anything" (p. 487).

40. Note Winnicott's (1958) thoughts on the manic defense, which is "intended to cover a person's capacity to deny the depressive anxiety that is inherent in emotional development, anxiety that belongs to the capacity of the individual to feel guilt, and also to acknowledge responsibility for instinctual experiences, and for the aggression in the fantasy that goes with instinctual experiences" (pp. 143–44). "[It] is characteristic of the manic defense that the individual is unable fully to believe in the liveliness that denies deadness, since he does not believe in his own capacity for object love; for making good is only real when the destruction is acknowledged" (pp. 131–32).

41. Winnicott (1988b): "Freud gave us this method which we can use, and it doesn't matter what it leads us to. The point is, it does lead us to things; it's an objective way of looking at things . . . for people who can go to something without preconceived notions, which, in a sense, is science" (p. 574).

42. Lear (1990): "The creation of the individual and the caring for the individual are of a piece. For it is only with the internalization of these caring relationships that there emerges a creature sufficiently reflective and self-aware to deserve the title of 'individual' (p. 187).

REFERENCES

Calvino, Italo. 1974. *Invisible Cities*. London: Pan Books.
Cavell, Marcia. 1988. "Solipsism and Community." *Psychoanalysis and Contemporary Thought*. 11, no 4.

———. 1993. *The Psychoanalytic Mind*. Cambridge: Harvard University Press.

Erikson, Erik.1966. "Ontogeny of Ritualization." In *Psychoanalysis: A General Psychology*, ed. Rudolph Loewenstein, Lottie Newman, Max Schur, and Albert Solint. New York: International Universities Press.

Ferenczi, S. 1988. *The Clinical Diary of Sandor Ferenczi*. Ed. Judith Dupont. Cambridge: Harvard University Press.

Fingarette, Herbert. 1963. *The Self in Transformation*. New York: Harper and Row.

Freud, Sigmund. 1913. "On Beginning Treatment (Further Recommendations on the Technique of Psychoanalysis)." In *Standard Edition*. London: Hogarth Press, vol. 12, 121–45.

Gargiulo, Gerald J. 1989. "Authority, the Self, and Psychoanalytic Experience." In *Psychoanalytic Review* 76, no. 2.

———. 1991. "Reflections, Musings and Interventions: A Personal Communication on Psychoanalytic Work." In *Psychoanalysis Today*, ed. Elizabeth Thorne and Shirley Herscovitch Schaye. Springfield: MA: Charles C. Thomas.

———. 1992. "Sublimation, Winnicottean Reflections." *Psychoanalytic Review*, 79, no.3.

Green, Andre. 1975. "The Analyst, Symbolization and Absence in the Analytic Setting." *International Journal of Psychoanalysis*, 56, Part 1.

Khan, M. 1975. Introduction to D. W. Winnicott's *Through Pediatrics to Psychoanalysis*. New York: Basic Books.

Lear, Jonathan. 1990. *Love and its Place in Nature*. New York: Farrar, Straus and Giroux.

Little, Margaret. 1990. *Psychotic Anxieties and Containment*. Northvale, NJ: Jason Aronson.

Phillips, Adam. 1988. *Winnicott*. Cambridge: Harvard University Press.

Reik, Theodor. 1948. *Listening with the Third Ear*. New York: Grove.

Ricoeur, Paul. 1970. *Freud And Philosophy*. New Haven. Yale University Press.

Rodman, Robert. 1990. "Insistence on Being Himself." In Tactics and Techniques in Psychoanalytic Therapy, vol. 3, *The Implications of Winnicott's Contributions*, ed. Peter Giovacchini, Northvale, NJ: Jason Aronson.

Roustang, Francois. 1982. *Dire Mastery*. Baltimore: Johns Hopkins University Press.

Tagore, R. 1941. *Collected Poems and Plays*. New York: Macmillan.

Thomas, Lewis. 1984. *Late Night Thoughts on Listening to Mahler's Ninth Symphony*. Toronto: Bantam Books.

Winnicott, C., Shepherd, R., and Davis, M. (eds.) 1989. *D.W. Winnicott: Psychoanalytic Explorations*. Cambridge: Harvard University Press.

Winnicott, D.W. 1957. *The Child and the Family*. London: Tavistock.

———. 1958. *Collected Papers: Through Paediatrics to Psycho-Analysis*. London: Tavistock.

————. 1965. *The Maturational Processes and the Facilitating Environment.* New York: International Universities Press.

————. 1971. *Playing and Reality.* New York: Basic Books.

————. 1988a. *Human Nature.* New York: Schocken Books.

————. 1988b. *Psychoanalytic Explorations.* (Compilation.) Cambridge: Harvard University Press.

Chapter Seven

W. R. D. Fairbairn and His Growing Significance for Current Psychoanalysis and Psychotherapy

James S. Grotstein

EDITORS' INTRODUCTION

As James S. Grotstein points out, it is only in recent years that Fairbairn's contributions of a half century ago are undergoing a fundamental reevaluation. The emergence of relational and self psychology, occupying as they do a postmodern, relativistic perspective that highlights intersubjectivity, has, says Grotstein, evoked a reemergence of interest in Fairbairn's original conceptions that now, in retrospect, seem so prescient.

Fairbairn developed what he called an object relations theory of personality: "Psychology," says Fairbairn, is the "study of the relationships of the individual to his objects." This reconceptualization of psychoanalysis deviated from Freudian theory in at least two important ways. First, Fairbairn viewed the ego as a structure that existed from birth rather than emanating from the id as a consequence of its interactions with reality. The ego was self-energizing; it did not derive its energy from the id; it was also a dynamic structure. Fairbairn's rejection of the notion of a separate id was in part rooted in his belief that libido was a function of the ego and aggression was a response to real-life neglect and frustration of the individual's attempt to establish satisfying connections with others. As Grotstein indicates, Fairbairn also deviated from Freud in his assertion that libido was object-seeking, not pleasure-seeking; its goal was not discharge of tension but the creation of gratifying relationships. In other words, for Fairbairn there is a fundamental human striving to relate to others, and the infant therefore is "hardwired" toward reality from birth. This relations-seeking and relations-maintenance has adaptive value in terms of biological survival. For Fairbairn, says Grotstein, "the human being was born and lived his lifetime with such an inescapable need for the object that this object dependence informed all stages of development, from immature to mature dependency." Moreover, indicates Grotstein, for Fairbairn the inevitable frustrations in the mother-infant relationship lead to the internalization of an object that is gratifying and ungratifying. Ambivalence, anxiety, and insecurity are stimulated in the infant, leading to the activation of defenses, especially splitting, which Fairbairn viewed as a universal mental phenomenon necessary to manage frustration and overstimulation in early relationships. Says Grotstein, "the human condition predicates man as having a schizoid nature by virtue of the splitting dissociations that inevitably characterize the formation of his endopsychic structure" (the unitary, all-embracing psychic structure Fairbairn called the ego).

Psychopathology for Fairbairn, unlike Freud (who saw it as a consequence of conflict over pleasure-seeking impulses), was rooted in disturbances and interferences in relationships to others. Understanding the infant's real-life experiences with his early significant others was thus crucial for understanding healthy and unhealthy development. For Fairbairn, intimates Grotstein, maternal deprivation in particular was the basis for psychopathology. Fairbairn believed that psychopathology was best conceptualized as the ego's effort to maintain old connections and yearnings represented by internal objects. As Grotstein has indicated, the main problematic that undergirds all psychopathology for Fairbairn is between the developmental inclination toward mature dependence and more differentiated and satisfying relations, and the childish refusal to relinquish infantile dependence and connections to undifferentiated objects, emanating from the terror of losing connection of any kind. Says Grotstein, "in his emphasis on the importance of introjective over projective identification," Fairbairn "formulated object relations theory as being fundamentally traumatic; that is, objects are internalized only when they are felt to be endangering. Thus, strictly speaking, the term 'object relations' constitutes a default category of failed interpersonal relations where the responsibility lies with the external parental objects." Thus for Fairbairn, "only bad objects are internalized; good objects do not have to be because they are satisfying." Psychopathology for Fairbairn, in other words, emanates from the ego's self-fragmentation as it tries to maintain the connection to the object and control its unsatisfying elements.

Psychoanalytic therapy for Fairbairn, says Grotstein, is best understood in terms of how it differs from Freud. Unlike Freud, who believed that the analytic experience is constituted by the working through of unconscious conflict about one's id impulses, Fairbairn thought it should aim at reconstituting the individual's capacity to form and maintain authentic, real relationships with others. "Mature dependence"—Fairbairn's term for the theoretically possible but practically unreachable ideal state of emotional health—is manifested in terms of the individual's ability to sustain intimate, mutual connections to other people. Moreover, says Grotstein, the individual no longer has the need to introject and identify with the realistic badness of one's early and later objects so as to preserve their needed goodness. In the healthy person, there is no need to self-fragment in order to sustain connection and loyalty to the contradictory and irreconcilable aspects of significant objects. (P. M. and A. R.)

Fairbairn's Worldview

In considering Fairbairn's worldview, one must first consider its background. Fairbairn was a physician and psychiatrist in Edwardian and post-Edwardian Scotland who, like Winnicott below the border, was grounded in the immediacy of the clinical situation with patients. His educational background, however, was deeply influenced by ancient Greek philosophy (particularly that of Aristotle) and, as was the custom at Scottish universities at the time, by Continental philosophy, especially including Kant, Hegel, Leibnitz, and Nietzsche. He had also closely followed the ideas of the English philosophers Hobbes and Berkeley, of his fellow Scotsman Hume, and of the American James. Hegel's influence on Fairbairn can be seen in the latter's emphasis on the dichotomy of love and hate in object relations and in the nature of the slave-master relationship as one of the principal relationships that occur between endopsychic structures.

Many of his nonmetapsychological papers deal with common sociopsychological problems, such as child molestation, for example. Dicks (1963) readily applied his ideas to marital therapy, and Guntrip (1961, 1963, 1969, 1971) employed it as a starting point for his own pragmatic theory of "personology," which became one of the foundations for the relations school and for self psychology. Fairbairn's religious background instilled in him a deep respect for the spiritual as well as the demonic capacities of humans. His formal education was classical. The Anglo-Scottish Zeitgeist in which he developed was characterized by Harry Guntrip (personal communication) as the preeminence of pragmatism and humanism. These last two qualities seem to be the Ariadne's thread that courses through virtually all his contributions. They were the qualities that allowed him to challenge the experience-distant aspects of contemporaneous Cartesian (dualistic) Freudian orthodoxy and transform it into a unitary psychology involving a self (ego) that was unitary though unformed from the beginning, was object-seeking, and whose "drives" were inseparable from its unitary nature.

Utmostly, he believed that the infant was a "person in his own right," not a psychoanalytic construct from autoerotic libido theory. Though he stated it simply, the metapsychological ramifications for psychoanalytic theory and practice were profound. It conveyed the existential dimension for the first time and also espoused a rationale for the inextricability of deficit theory from conflict theory, that is, the infant was in conflict *because* of the impact on him of environmental deficits. In minimizing the importance of primary process and, instead, privileging the infant's capacity to perceive reality as it was, as Stern (1985) was to proclaim later, he became a veritable ombudsman for the infant, whose ontological insecurity he believed was the parents' prime responsibility to support and encourage. In detailing the schizoid withdrawal that inescapably results when the infant and child are critically unattuned or abused, he not only anticipated the "true/false-self" dichotomy that Winnicott (1960b) later proffered, he also fundamentally addressed the alienated existential nature of human existence. To my mind he was and remains the only analyst within the orthodox/classical framework to have done so, with the possible exception of his fellow Scotsman R. D. Laing.

In his emphasis on the importance of introjective over projective identification, he formulated object relations theory as being fundamentally traumatic; that is, objects are internalized only when they are felt to be endangering. Thus, strictly speaking, the term "object relations" constitutes a default category of failed interpersonal relations where the responsibility lies with the external parental objects.

An Introduction to His Work

William Ronald Dodds Fairbairn was a quiet, diffident lowland Scotsman in his private life, but his other self betrayed a respectful yet almost messianic zeal to reform—but not to overthrow—some of the canons of the then so-called Freudian orthodox psychoanalysis. That this term is no longer in current usage and has been replaced by its now-embattled successor, "classical psychoanalysis" is due in no small measure to Fairbairn's impact. The enormity of the effect of his works on current psychoanalytic thinking would have astonished his contemporaries, yet his publications are few compared to those of others. For many personal reasons, he seldom traveled, lectured, or spoke outside Edinburgh. He visited London only a handful of times in his lifetime. Were it not for a few people who had personal contact with him, John Sutherland (1963, 1980, 1989) and Harry Guntrip (1961, 1963, 1969, 1971, 1975), he might not have been known at all except for a few analysts or therapists around the world who occasionally wrote about him and valued his work, for example, Sullivan (1963) and Modell (1965, 1968).

I cannot help likening Fairbairn to another Scotsman, Robert Burns, whose line, "A man's a man for a' that" succinctly describes perhaps the main thrust of Fairbairn's work. Fairbairn, the lowland Scottish aristocrat and scion of an ancient family, was really the great psychoanalytic "commoner"; he was perhaps the first psychoanalyst to address the existential perspective of the human being ("the infant is a person in his own right"), as well as one of the first to discuss the necessity for an empathic relationship between parents and children, as well as analyst and patients.

Following in the groundbreaking object relations tradition of the Hungarian school (Ferenczi, 1909, 1913, 1925; Hermann, 1936; Balint, 1937, 1956, 1958, 1965, 1968), and following on the heels of another even more eclipsed personality of his time, Ian Suttie (1935), the real founder of the object relations school in Britain, Fairbairn (1940, 1941) was quick to take issue with what has become the bête noire of orthodox *and* classical psychoanalysis, the instinctual drive theory.

In retrospect, it seems that Freud (1911) may have taken the wrong road and found himself in a cul de sac when he chose to privilege the concept of the pleasure principle and infantile sexuality and to conjoin them with his drive theory rather than emphasizing infantile dependence. Fairbairn, steeped as he was in the philosophy of science, was intent on updating the scientific status of psychoanalysis by removing it from the nineteenth-century hydraulic mechanics of von Helmholtz (pleasure-unpleasure principle, discharge of tension, etc.) and reformulating it instead with the new scientific principles of the twentieth century, such as relativity, where valent selves and objects interact. Fairbairn became the first metapsychologist for the object relations point of view, which differed from the pleasure principle perspective of the drive theory. Fairbairn's basic thinking was the obvious: "The infant is oral not because he is autoerotic but because he seeks a breast."

An extension of that simple but profound conception was Fairbairn's notion that the existence of the object is implicit to the infant's libido and that autoerotism develops, not as a primary organization, but as a secondary *default* because of frustration in primary object-seeking. These two points were to find their way quietly but profoundly into the mainstream of psychoanalytic thinking on both sides of the Atlantic, particularly in the United States. Under other names, they were to alter the way we think about infants and children and their interrelationships with their parents. They anticipated the later works of Winnicott (1945, 1947, 1949, 1954, 1958, 1960c, 1969, 1971d) and Bowlby (1958, 1960, 1969, 1973, 1980).

Another of his concepts that deserve far more explication is his general theory of object relations itself. Although Fairbairn believed in the conflict theory, he was perhaps the first analyst to exposit the deficit position. The infant suffers for "not being treated by his mother as a person in his own right." Further, he postulated, in contradistinction to Freud and orthodox theory, that secondary process was primary and that primary process was secondary; that is, the infant is born with a sense of reality (perception of the realness of neglect, deprivation, and abuse by his real objects) from the very beginning. He does not operate primarily from the pleasure principle but defaults into using the pleasure principle when object relations are realized—realistically—to be untenable.

Fairbairn discovered and laid bare the existentialism of the schizoid patient and explored schizoid phenomena for the first time in the history of psychoanalysis. To this day, the deeper implications of his work in that regard have not been sufficiently understood or appreciated. It is only lately that dissociation in multiple personalities, for instance, is becoming highlighted in the wake of studies on adult survivors of child abuse.

As Kohut (1971, 1977) was later to do with narcissism, Fairbairn had already done with the schizoid phenomenon. He distinguished between the schizoid personality, the schizoid state, and the fundamental schizoid pattern that occurs in all human beings. As Kohut (1971, 1977) was later to do with self disorders, Fairbairn conceived that the quality of being schizoid applied not only to the distinct entity, the schizoid personality, but also more generically to all human beings, since everyone—normals included—is characterized by a multiplicity of different ego states within themselves. For instance, the very existence of a separation between the id, ego, and superego constitutes a schizoid phenomenon insofar as it is a splitting of the ego. An intrinsic part of the schizoid personality is a withdrawal from untrustworthy interpersonal relationships, which are then taken into the patient's internal world where they constitute internalized "object relationships."

In other words, the infant needs a "satisfying person" on the outside. Failing that, he introjects the image of that person into his internal world as an unsatisfying object. This unsatisfying object, in turn, is identified with an unconscious aspect of the ego. Thus, the internalized object is treated as if it is indistinguishable from the ego itself. This unsatisfying object is then split and divided into a rejecting object and an exciting object. Along with this, the unconscious ego that is identified with the unsatisfying object splits and becomes an antilibidinal ego, which is identified with the rejecting object, and the libidinal ego, which is identified with the exciting object.

I shall go into Fairbairn's endopsychic structure shortly, but for now I should like to discuss his view of internalizations and identifications. One of the most evocative of Fairbairn's conclusions, and one that has paradoxically remained largely unnoticed, is his concept of internalization and identification. Unlike virtually any other theoretician, Fairbairn states that only bad objects are internalized; good objects do not have to be because they are satisfying. Thus, from Fairbairn's point of view, all identifications can be thought of as actually or potentially pathological. I think Fairbairn would have exempted trial identifications, that is, identifications that were transitory and not permanent. Freud (1914) himself hinted at this when he said that the shadow of the object falls on the ego. If we follow that metaphor to its conclusion, we see that the ego must conform to the shadow of its object, thereby restricting its own agenda in favor of the object's. The infant introjects the badness of the object because the object is needed, and its badness in the external object is all the more threatening. On the inside of the self it can be controlled, albeit in phantasy.

What does the infant or, for that matter, the normal person of any age do with good objects or the goodness of the object? Fairbairn states that the goodness of the object does not have to be internalized. He does not explain this fully, but one inference is that the goodness of the object produces good experiences that allow the infant to grow properly. An analogy would be that the infant must take in the milk from the breast, but not the breast itself unless the breast is felt to be bad and therefore must be taken in.

The Moral Defense

An offshoot of Fairbairn's ideas of introjection and identification is his concept of the moral defense, or the defense of the superego. The infant takes in the badness of the parent, as mentioned above, in order to control it within and also to restore the external object to a suitable state. In other words, the infant takes over (that is, takes over the responsibility for—by identifying with) the parent's badness in order to "cure" the parent, that is, to "launder" the parent's image so as to have a fictively reconstructed parent that is serviceable for the infant's needs.

Fairbairn believed that the objects that were taken into the internal world, along with the dissociated egos that joined each of the objects, constituted "endopsychic structures" that, in turn, related to each other as unconscious dynamic structures. Since Fairbairn's, as well as Klein's, theory of psychoanalysis derives so heavily from Freud's prestructural theory, particularly his pivotal object relations paper "Mourning and Melancholia" (Freud, 1917), I believe that it would be useful to outline Freud's only substantial contribution on internal object relationships.

In that paper, Freud differentiated between the clinical and metapsychological aspects of mourning as distinguished from melancholia. He pointed out that melancholia is a pathological phenomenon that typifies the pattern of object loss by patients who are rooted in narcissism, that is, who are so narcissistic that they cannot bear—or even conceive of—the loss of the object. Whereas healthy individuals can accept the loss of the object, then contemplate its value and pine for it during the mourning period, they do not lose self-esteem in the process. In fact, they gain self-esteem because of their identification with the value they attribute to the departed object.

In melancholia, on the other hand, the loss of the object is not able to be borne or conceived of, as I mentioned; it is therefore denied by virtue of internalization (i.e., introjective identification). By virtue of becoming the object in phantasy, the narcissist obviates the experience of loss. When the lost object is now internalized and introjectively identified with, it is split into two objects and subordinated egos, which identify with these internalized objects. One object joins up with the ego ideal (a "gradient in the ego," as Freud was wont to call it), and the other aspect of the object is identified in the ego itself—at the lower end of the gradient.

The anger that the narcissist feels about the loss undergoes an involution. It does not become conscious because the object is not experienced as being lost. Instead, the hostility toward the putatively departing object is directed internally toward that internalized object in the ego and toward the ego that is identified with it. The authorizing subject of the hostility is the ego ideal and the other aspect of the object with which it is identified. Thus, as Freud pointed out, a maximum of sadism by the ego ideal and its associated internalized object is directed toward the ego in identification with *its* respective internalized object.

Using Freud's format for the splitting, internalization, and introjective identification with the lost or disappointing objects whose loss or disappointment has to be narcissistically denied, Fairbairn constructed a veritable dynamic anatomy of the unconscious, perhaps the only one, in my opinion, that exists in psychoanalysis in meaningfully personal (object relations) terms. It differs considerably from the so-called internal world of orthodox analysis, which did not contemplate the dynamic relationships between internal objects to any great extent. It also differs from the object representational world of American ego psychology, which characterizes relationships as "shifts of cathexis" of object representations, "neutralizations," "de-neutralizations," "changes of function," and so forth.

Further, since Fairbairn (1944, 1946, 1949, 1951, 1952, 1954), unlike any other analyst at the time, did away altogether with the primacy and independence of the pleasure principle and with the separation between drives and objects, he substituted for the above the notion that the infant's needs (drives) were always object-related and never independent of the object. Thus, one cannot speak of a drive without an infant or without an object, a hypothesis that was to be copied sometime later by Winnicott (1945, 1951, 1952, 1960a, 1960b, 1960c, 1969, 1971a, 1971b, 1971c, 1971d): "There is no such thing as an infant; there is only an infant and its mother!"

Fairbairn (1943a, 1943b) was quick to see that Freud's internalized bad object, which was identified in the ego, represents a split-off aspect of the internalized bad object represented to the ego. Fairbairn quickly hypothesized that the ego attached to this bad object was none other than Freud's (1923) id itself. Since Fairbairn did not believe in the id separated from an ego or an object, he renamed the id the libidinal ego.

Next he realized that the object with which the libidinal ego was identified and to which it was attached was a tantalizing and exciting version of the original unitary bad object that was internalized at the beginning of the melancholic process. He renamed the more sadistically aggressive internalized bad object that was attached to the ego ideal the "rejecting object," and its associated ego was the antilibidinal ego. In so doing, Fairbairn provided the provenance for four substructures (occupying two endopsychic units in the internal world). These four substructures, in turn, had been originally split off from the original ego and the original object. The latter remain in consciousness as well as in unconsciousness as the central ego and its associated ideal object.

In this manner, Fairbairn (1944) had constructed a unique system and anatomy of the internal world, one that accounted for psychic functioning in ways that eluded other conceptions. It is interesting to note, for instance, that Fairbairn not only does away with the id, but recasts it as an instinctual ego (libidinal ego) directed toward a forbidden object that is conditionally good and conditionally frustrating and rejecting, but he also has constructed the equivalent of two separate superegos. The one is the more sophisticated and moral superego, which consists of a central ego and its relationship to the ideal object. The other is the more primitive and more sadistic one, which consists of the rejecting object and its antilibidinal ego. It is very important to recognize that the antilibidinal ego and the rejecting object constitute a primitive, unconscious, premoral system, one with pseudomoral authority that has power to threaten or even crush the libidinal ego and its relationship to the exciting object.

The concept of endopsychic structure is unique in many other ways as well. First, Fairbairn has accounted for the internalization of a psychic family, where the parts are "cannibalized" from living, external needed objects and become internalized as virtually demonic beings who interact with each other much as a troubled family does. Thus, Fairbairn's scheme is eminently applicable to system theory, family therapy, child abuse, and other areas.

Second, Fairbairn's endopsychic concept accounts for the dynamic psychopathology of the two-person relationship (mother and child and/or father and child) as well as the Oedipus complex (triangular situation).

Yet another eminently useful aspect of Fairbairn's conception of dynamic endopsychic structures has to do with what in analysis has been called the negative therapeutic reaction and what in daily life is called the fear of progress or success. It also helps to account for the enormous sense of guilt and, even more profoundly, the sense of shame that patients experience in primitive conditions.

Why, for instance, do people who are raped or severely traumatized feel guilty and/or ashamed, especially when they are innocent in the first place? Fairbairn's answer to this paradox is unique. One who is overcome by trauma feels "broken" by the abuser and retroactively (as well as retrospectively) reconstructs a belief about oneself that one is inhabited by bad objects with *whom one is identified*! Shame emerges from the retroactive and retrospective emergence of the sense of being unprotected by good objects and laden with bad ones with whom one is in identification.

The problem of success is similar. The more one is inclined to achieve success, the more one seems to be reminded by the shameful objects of the internal world that one does not deserve success, which is associated with good objects, because those had been forfeited in the identification with the bad ones. As a further corollary of this principle, there seems to be a sadistic injunction by the rejecting object against the self as if it is exclusively identified with the libidinal ego whose entreaties toward the exciting object are intercepted by the primitive internal saboteur (antilibidinal ego and rejecting object), which then boycotts it under threats of annihilation.

Put another way, Fairbairn's conception of the progress of psychotherapy or progress through life outside therapy is one of the return of bad objects, his term for Freud's return of the repressed, associated with the lifting of repression. Thus, what we repress are not instinctual drives but rather the relationships between internal objects and their subsidiary egos. As I pointed out in another contribution, I believe that Fairbairn had somewhat diminished the profundity of his explorations by employing the conventional term "object relations" instead of "demonology" (Grotstein, 1994a, 1994b, 1994c).

I should now like to spell out some more valuable inferences to be drawn from Fairbairn's conception of endopsychic structure. First, we see that there is a two-tier system of repression, as mentioned before. One tier is topographically horizontal and represents the repression of the internalized bad objects by the ideal object and the central ego. The second tier of repression is vertical, that of the secondary repression of the libidinal ego and its exciting object by the rejecting object and its antilibidinal ego. Thirty years later, Kohut (1971) was to expound on the vertical and horizontal divisions of the self, apparently totally unaware that Fairbairn had uncovered this topographical phenomenon much earlier.

Second, we see, as also mentioned earlier, that the endopsychic structures account for the two-person (mother-infant and/or father-infant) situation plus the oedipal triangular situation. Third—and this concept was truly innovative—Fairbairn placed love at the very bottom of the structure as the victim/scapegoat, as it were, of a double attack, one by the central ego and its idealized object and the other by the antilibidinal ego and its rejecting object.

A clinical translation of this phenomenon would be that one's love for the object is the most perilous and endangered aspect of the self. One would much rather risk being rejected by virtue of being bad than rejected for being loving. Love makes one vulnerable to a two-pronged attack, in other words, whereas if one hates, one at least is identified, supposedly safely, with the aggressor. Thus, safety is exchanged in a Faustian bargain for ultimate humiliation because of one's love.

It must be remembered that, even though the concept of endopsychic structure schematizes the patient's experience of his internal world, the defense mechanisms of repression and splitting are really fictions about the existence of separate selves and objects. In other contributions (Grotstein, 1994a, 1994b, 1994c, 1998) I postulated that the original unitary ego and object persist on a dual track, side by side with the experience of splitting so that there is, consequently, always an unconscious awareness of the frightening unity of the badness and the goodness of the object and the terror that inheres in the dissociations of the self. In other words, there is always a fear of reintegration because of the return of the terror that caused the schizoid dissociation(s) in the first place.

Even though Fairbairn has emphasized that the human condition predicates man as having a schizoid nature by virtue of the splitting dissociations that inevitably characterize the formation of his endopsychic structure, nevertheless he is describing the melancholic picture of the internal world originally portrayed by Freud (1917) and considerably extended by Klein (1940, 1946, 1950, 1957, Klein et al., 1952). From the orthodox Freudian and Kleinian points of view, endopsychic structure is, in other words, the picture of the melancholic, one in which there is an introversion of hatred, which is then directed inward toward a weakened, diffident self. Fairbairn has turned the melancholic picture around and shows that though it is melancholia from one point of view, the structure of this melancholia is essentially schizoid.

Endopsychic structure is a very useful way of understanding the plight of most individuals in their development, but it is particularly apposite, for instance, in children who are raised in dysfunctional homes and especially in homes where there is child abuse and/or molestation. Freud (1923) emphasized that the infant first tries to maintain a purified pleasure ego by splitting off and projecting outward all unpleasant experiences; similarly, Klein's (1952a, 1952b, 1952c, 1955, 1958) concept of projective identification largely describes how the infant wishes to rid itself of bad aspects of itself and of its internal objects so as to remain omnipotently invulnerable. By contrast, one of Fairbairn's foremost assumptions is that the infant and child are primarily realistic rather than primarily phantasmal and consequently seek to maintain the security of their attachments with their parents by introjecting and identifying with their perception of the parents' badness.

Fairbairn calls this the moral defense, or the defense of the superego, thus noting that this occurs not only in terms of external objects but also with internal ones, thereby accounting for how a cruel superego progressively becomes more omnipotent and even more cruel at the expense of the vulnerable ego who is the donor of its own power in order to spare the superego.

The relationship between these endopsychic structures helps us understand why, for instance, children who are abused or molested have such a difficult time discussing it with others, including therapists. The sense of shame is enormous. They believe they are identified with bad objects, retrospectively—*res ipse loquitur*, as I mentioned earlier. Yet another aspect of this situation is that many of these children may take on the so-called martyr defense. That is, they may introjectively identify with what is felt to be the bad or cruel external object, experience self-abuse, act the loser, avoid success, and carry out other forms of self-punitive behavior, but in such a passive-aggressive way that one quickly realizes, as Freud (1917) did, that their guilt has a projectively provocative effect on their caretaking objects. Often behind this unconscious action narrative is the hope to "bust" their parents, that is, to bring them to the public at large by virtue of the suffering victim's agony.

Fairbairn's developmental scheme is also of considerable importance. He followed a dual-track system insofar as he followed the stages of the maturation of the ego's relationship to its object corresponding to the autoerotic stages founded by Abraham (1924), but at the same time integrated the successional stages, in part, with Klein's (1940) positions, the paranoid-schizoid and depressive, being ongoing dialectical positions of the ego in its relationship to the object (see Grotstein, 1998).[1]

Fairbairn probably would have been better off to have made a cleaner separation between Klein's positions and their stages. He formulated that in the oral stage of development, which he termed the period of infantile dependence, "psychotic anxiety" occurred because of a primary split due to intolerable frustration. The fear that its love is bad causes the infant to dissociate and to take on, at its own expense, the badness of the object, as mentioned above, in order to preserve the goodness of the external object.

Whereas Klein (1940, 1955), in her own scheme of development, first came up with the so-called paranoid position, out of deference to Fairbairn, she renamed it the "paranoid-schizoid position." However, it should be noted that her use of the term "schizoid" in "paranoid-schizoid" is significantly at odds with Fairbairn's concept of "schizoid position." For Fairbairn, schizoid was a primary ontological statement of the experience of object betrayal, whereas for Klein schizoid simply meant the splitting off of bad feelings and of bad internal objects prior to their projective relocation (projective identification) into objects and object images. Put another way, Fairbairn's schizoid position conveys the infant's realistic withdrawal from its disappointing objects, whereas Klein's paranoid-schizoid position is characterized by persecutory anxiety that originates from the infant's *phantasies* about the object. Fairbairn clearly had a more profound ontological concept in mind by the use of the term "schizoid." To him it conveyed the idea of an alienated self, one that was to be renamed later by Winnicott (1960b) the "true self," in contrast with the compliant "false self."

In terms of the depressive position, Fairbairn tended to follow Abraham very closely and, in my opinion, failed to understand the fuller ontological implications of Klein's depressive position (the need to institute reparational and restorative procedures for the object, etc.). Fairbairn analogized the depressive position to the schizoid position insofar as the danger of love was the critical challenge of the infant in the schizoid position, and the crisis of hate (because of teething) was the principal endangering experience in the depressive position.

Fairbairn (1941) next envisioned a transitional phase, a term that was to be made more famous by Winnicott (1951) a decade or so later without any reference to Fairbairn. In Fairbairn's view of psychopathology, the transitional phase is the stage where neurotic techniques for relating to internal objects developed. Thus, Fairbairn believed that neurosis was constitutive of at least four discrete techniques of splitting between objects and selves.

Originally emphasizing the objects and their splits, Fairbairn described the four neurotic techniques as (1) the obsessional, (2) the paranoid, (3) the phobic, and (4) the hysterical. He envisioned that the paranoid technique sought to rid the ego of its bad objects and seek to hold onto the good, whereas in hysteria the reverse was true, that is, the latter seeks to identify with the badness of the object (like the true schizoid patient) and projects outward the good internal object into the good external object for safekeeping.

Whereas the obsessional is undecided about whether or not to get rid of an object that he also at the same time does not wish to hold onto, he is stuck in a "Mexican standoff." The phobic is intolerant of both the good object and the bad and seeks to project both of them outward and thus is denuded of objects altogether, feeling all the more hopeless and terrified without them.

The next stage of development is mature dependency, which Fairbairn contrasted with the then Freudian goal of genital maturity. Kohut (1977) once again picked up on this notion of mature dependency and incorporated it into his own conception of self psychology. Fairbairn's conception of the Oedipus complex is also worthy of note. He assigned the Oedipus complex to a position of lesser importance than it held and still holds in orthodox and classical theory. For orthodox and classical analysis, the Oedipus complex is a constellating stage of development. In their respective theories, infantile fixations in the oral and anal zones (pregenital) are of importance *only as regressive elaborations from the Oedipus complex, not primarily in their own right.* This privileging of the Oedipus complex over the pregenital positions had to do with the overall importance they gave to the concept of primary narcissism, a concept that disallowed significant infantile mental life prior to the Oedipus complex.

Fairbairn (1944, 1946, 1949, 1951, 1952, 1954), following in the footsteps of Suttie (1935) and Ferenczi (1909, 1913, 1925), and parallel with Klein (1928, 1940, 1945, 1952a, 1952b, 1952c, 1955, 1958; Klein et al. 1952), helped to eclipse the then patristic nature of psychoanalytic emphasis on the father complex, the Oedipus complex, and castration anxiety—for that matter, on infantile sexuality altogether—and replaced them with an emphasis on the primal importance of *infantile dependency*, both for normal development and for psychopathology. Thus, the most important aspects of human development constitute the destiny of infantile dependency as it normally evolves into mature dependency, and abnormally fails to evolve but devolves into neurotic and/or psychotic detours—as defined by pathological relationships to internal objects.

For Fairbairn (1940), the Oedipus complex was simply a continuation of earlier infantile mental life and the factors of its dependency relationships to objects. Thus, in the oedipal phase, the child now faces two sets of split parents: a good and a bad mother, and a good and a bad father. The male child will reconcile the four internal objects by condensing them into two objects. Thus, the son will assign the good mother and the good father object images to his mother and idealize her, whereas he will extract the bad object aspects of his mother, conjoin this bad image with the counterpart bad image of the father, and project both of those into the external father object. The daughter will do exactly the opposite.

Developed mainly in the 1940s and early 1950s, Fairbairn's ideas were largely eclipsed because of the battle of the titans (Melanie Klein and Anna Freud). He suffered an eclipse similar to that of Winnicott, but both men's works are now becoming much more highly regarded thanks to the new atmosphere of object relations and intersubjectivity.

In summary, one can say that Fairbairn belonged to the very loyal opposition to Freud, and his work was complementary to the work of Klein. He helped to emphasize the primary importance of the infant's relationship to its mother from a realistic standpoint, believing that the infant's phantasmal mental life was not primary but was, rather, secondary to his/her distress with real objects. He formulated the concept that the greatest danger the individual faces is the fear that his love is bad—and only secondarily and defensively that his/her hate is bad.

Fairbairn's concept of endopsychic structures is perhaps the best way of accounting for how the infant and child internally experience abusiveness, frustration, impingement, and disappointment. He conceived that the unconscious consists of bad internal objects, and that the fear of the return of the repressed is always the fear of the return of bad objects—or, more nearly exactly, the fear of the return of bad internal object relationships with dissociated egos. He conceived of the moral defense, which is the child's compliantly adaptive way of trying to defend the intactness of its attachment to its object at its own expense by selectively identifying with the bad aspects of the needed parent. This is how the pathological components of endopsychic structure are formed.

Fairbairn's humanistic, relativistic, postmodern worldview informs his metapsychology and his ideas about treatment. He abandoned the couch for chairs placed facing each other so that he could actualize his conception of the intersubjective couple. Most important, he believed that the human being was born and lived his lifetime with such an inescapable need for the object that this object dependence informed all stages of development from immature to mature dependency, which he would today certainly have called interdependency. His postmodern worldview propounds relativism, not absolutism or hierarchy. Thus, he is one of the legitimate forebears of the relational, self psychology, and intersubjective schools.

NOTE

1. By "ongoing dialectical positions of the ego," I am referring to Klein's (1940) assumption that the ego's relationship to the object, rather than proceeding through *stages*, is constrained by two dialectical ontological *positions*, the paranoid-schizoid and the depressive positions.

REFERENCES

Abraham, K. 1924. A short study of the development of the libido. In *Selected Papers on Psycho-Analysis*. London: Hogarth Press and Institute of Psycho-Analysis, 1948, pp. 418–501.

Balint, M. 1937. Early developmental states of the ego. Primary object-love.

Imago 23:270–88. Shortened trans. In *International Journal of Psycho-Analysis* (1949) 30:265–73.

———. 1956. Pleasure, object, and libido: Some reflexions on Fairbairn's modification of psychoanalytic theory. *British Journal of Medical Psychology* 29:162–67.

———. 1958. The concepts of subject and object in psychoanalysis. *British Journal of Medical Psychology* 31:161–72.

———. 1965. *Primary Love and Psycho-Analytic Technique.* London: Tavistock.

———. 1968. *The Basic Fault.* London: Tavistock.

Bowlby, J. 1958. The nature of the child's tie to his mother. *International Journal of Psycho-Analysis* 39:350–73.

———. 1960. Separation anxiety. *International Journal of Psycho-Analysis* 41:80–113.

———. 1969. *Attachment and Loss.* Vol. 1, *Attachment.* New York: Basic Books.

———. 1973. *Attachment and Loss.* Vol. 2, *Separation: Anxiety and Anger.* New York: Basic Books.

———. 1980. *Attachment and Loss.* Vol. 3, *Loss: Sadness and Depression.* New York: Jason Aronson.

Dicks, H. V. 1963. Object relations theory and marital studies. *British Journal of Medical Psychology* 36:125–29.

Fairbairn, W. R. D. 1940. Schizoid factors in the personality. In *Psychoanalytic Studies of the Personality.* London: Tavistock, 1952, pp. 3–27.

———. 1941. A revised psychopathology of the psychoses and psychoneuroses. In *Psychoanalytic Studies of the Personality.* London: Tavistock, 1952, pp. 28–58.

———. 1943a. The war neuroses: Their nature and significance. In *Psychoanalytic Studies of the Personality.* London: Tavistock, 1952, pp. 256–87.

———. 1943b. The repression and the return of bad objects (with special reference to the "war neuroses"). *British Journal of Medical Psychology* 19:327–41.

———. 1944. Endopsychic structure considered in terms of object-relationships. In *Psychoanalytic Studies of the Personality.* London: Tavistock, 1952, pp. 223–29.

———. 1946. Object-relationships in dynamic structure. In *Psychoanalytic Studies of the Personality.* London: Tavistock, 1952, pp. 137–51.

———. 1949. Steps in the development of an object-relations theory of the personality. In *Psychoanalytic Studies of the Personality.* London: Tavistock, 1952, pp. 152–61.

———. 1951. A synopsis of the development of the author's views regarding the structure of the personality. In *Psychoanalytic Studies of the Personality.* London: Tavistock, 1952, pp. 162–82.

————. 1952. *Psychoanalytic Studies of the Personality.* London: Tavistock.

————. 1954. *An Object Relations Theory of the Personality.* New York: Basic Books.

Ferenczi, S. 1909. Introjection and transference. In *Sex in Psychoanalysis.* Vol. 1. Trans. Ernest Jones. New York: Basic Books, 1950, pp. 35–37.

————. 1913. Stages in the development of the sense of reality. In *Sex and Psychoanalysis.* New York: Robert Brunner, pp. 213–39.

————. 1921. The further development of an 'active therapy' In psychoanalysis. In *Further Contributions to the Theory and Practice of Psycho-Analysis,* comp. John Rickman, trans. J. Suttie. New York: Bruner Mazel, 1980, pp. 198–217.

————. 1925. Contra-Indications to the 'active' psycho-analytic technique. In *Further Contributions to the Theory and Practice of Psycho-Analysis,* comp. John Rickman. trans. J. Suttie. New York: Bruner Mazel, 1980, pp. 217–29.

Freud, S. 1911. Formulations of the two principles of mental functioning. In *Standard Edition,* 12:213–26. London: Hogarth Press and Institute of Psycho-Analysis, 1958.

————. 1914. On narcissism: An introduction. In *Standard Edition,* 14:67–104. London: Hogarth Press and the Institute of Psycho-Analysis, 1957.

————. 1917. Mourning and melancholia. In *Standard Edition,* 14:237–60. London: Hogarth Press and the Institute of Psycho-Analysis, 1957.

————. 1923. The ego and the id. In *Standard Edition,* 19:3–59. London: Hogarth Press and the Institute of Psycho-Analysis, 1961.

Grotstein, J. 1994a. Notes on Fairbairn's metapsychology. In *Fairbairn and the Origins of Object Relations,* eds. D. Rinsley and J. Grotstein. New York: Guilford, pp. 112–48.

————. 1994b. II. Endopsychic structures and the cartography of the internal world: Six endopsychic characters in search of an author. In *Fairbairn And The Origins of Object Relations,* eds. D. Rinsley and J. Grotstein. New York: Guilford, pp. 174–94.

————. 1994c. A reappraisal of W. R. D. Fairbairn. *Bulletin of the Menninger Clinic* 57 (4): 421–49.

————. 1998. The dual-track theorem and the "Siamese-twinship" paradigm for psychoanalytic concepts. Manuscript in preparation.

Guntrip, H. 1961. *Personality Structure and Human Interaction: The Developing Synthesis of Psychodynamic Theory.* London: Hogarth Press.

————. 1963. Psychodynamic theory and the problem of psychotherapy. *British Journal of Medical Psychology* 36:161–72.

————. 1969. *Schizoid Phenomena, Object Relations, and the Self.* New York: International Universities Press.

————. 1971. *Psychoanalytic Theory, Therapy, and the Self.* New York: Basic Books.

———. 1975. My experience of analysis with Fairbairn and Winnicott (How complete a result does psycho-analytic therapy achieve?). In *Essential Papers on Object Relations*, ed. P. Buckley. New York: New York University Press, 1986, pp. 447–68.

Hermann, I. 1936. Sich-Anklammern-Auf-Suche-Gehen ["Clinging-going-in-search"]. *International Zeitschrift für Psychoanalyse* 22:349–70. Reprinted In *Psychoanalytic Quarterly* (1976), 45:5–36.

Klein, M. 1928. Early stages of the Oedipus conflict. In *Contributions to Psycho-Analysis, 1921–1945*. London: Hogarth Press and the Institute of Psycho-Analysis, 1950, pp. 202–14.

———. 1940. Mourning and its relation to manic-depressive states. In *Contributions to Psycho-Analysis, 1921–1945*. London: Hogarth Press and the Institute of Psycho-Analysis, 1950, pp. 311–38.

———. 1945. The Oedipus complex in the light of early anxieties. In *Contributions to Psycho-Analysis, 1921–1945*. London: Hogarth Press and the Institute of Psycho-Analysis, 1950, pp. 339–90.

———. 1946. Notes on some schizoid mechanisms. In *Developments in Psycho-Analysis*, ed. M. Klein, P. Heimann, S. Isaacs, and J. Riviere. London: Hogarth Press and the Institute of Psycho-Analysis, 1952, pp. 292–320.

———. 1950. *Contributions to Psycho-Analysis, 1921–1945*. London: Hogarth Press and the Institute of Psycho-Analysis.

———. 1952a. Some theoretical conclusions regarding the emotional life of the infant. In *Envy and Gratitude and Other Works, 1946–1963*. New York: Delacorte, 1975, pp. 61–93.

———. 1952b. The origins of transference. In *Envy and Gratitude and Other Works, 1946–1963*. New York: Delacorte, 1975, pp. 48–56.

———. 1952c. Mutual influences in the development of ego and id. In *Envy and Gratitude and Other Works, 1946–1963*. New York: Delacorte, 1975, pp. 57–60.

———. 1955. On identification. In *New Directions in Psycho-Analysis*, ed. M. Klein, P. Heimann and R. Money-Kyrle. London: Tavistock, pp. 309–45.

———. 1957. *Envy and Gratitude*. New York: Basic Books.

———. 1958. On the development of mental functioning. In *Envy and Gratitude and Other Works, 1946–1963*. New York: Delacorte, 1975, pp. 236–46.

Klein, M., Heimann, P., Isaacs, S., and Riviere, J., eds.. 1952. *Developments in Psycho-Analysis*. London: Hogarth Press.

Kohut, H. 1971. *The Analysis of the Self: A Systematic Approach to the Psychoanalytic Treatment of Narcissistic Personality Disorders*. New York: International Universities Press.

———. 1977. *The Restoration of the Self*. New York: International Universities Press.

Modell, A. H. 1965. On having the right to life: An aspect of the superego's development. *International Journal of Psychoanalysis* 46:323–31.

————. 1968. *Object, Love, and Reality.* New York: International Universities Press.

Stern, D. 1985. *The Interpersonal World of the Infant: A View from Psychoanalysis and Developmental Psychology.* New York: Basic Books.

Sullivan, C. 1963. *Freud and Fairbairn: Two Theories of Ego-Psychology.* Doylestown: Doylestown Foundation.

Sutherland, J. 1963. Object-relations theory and the conceptual model of psychoanalysis. *British Journal of Medical Psychology* 36:109–24.

————. 1980. The British object relations theorists: Balint, Winnicott, Fairbairn, Guntrip. *Journal of the American Psychoanalytic Association* 28:829–60.

————. 1989. *Fairbairn's Journey into the Interior.* London: Free Association.

Suttie, I. 1935. *The Origins of Love and Hate.* New York: Matrix House, 1952.

Winnicott, D. W. 1945. Primitive emotional development. In *Collected Papers.* New York: Basic Books, 1958, pp. 148–56.

————. 1947. Hate in the countertransference. In *Collected Papers.* New York: Basic Books, 1958, pp. 194–203.

————. 1949. Birth memories, birth trauma, and anxiety. In *Collected Papers.* New York: Basic Books, 1958, pp. 174–93.

————. 1950. Aggression in relation to emotional development. In *Collected Papers.* New York: Basic Books, 1958, pp. 204–18.

————. 1951. Transitional objects and transitional phenomena. In *Collected Papers.* New York: Basic Books, 1958, pp. 229–42.

————. 1952. Psychoses and child care. In *Collected Papers.* New York: Basic Books, 1958, pp. 219–28.

————. 1954. The depressive position in normal development. In *Collected Papers.* New York: Basic Books, 1958, pp. 262–77.

————. 1958. *Collected Papers: Through Paediatrics to Psycho-Analysis.* New York: Basic Books.

————. 1960a. The theory of the parent-infant relationship. In *The Maturational Processes and the Facilitating Environment.* New York: International Universities Press, 1965, pp. 140–52.

————. 1960b. Ego distortion in terms of true and false self. In *The Maturational Processes and the Facilitating Environment.* New York: International Universities Press, 1965, pp. 37–55.

————. 1960c. Counter-Transference. In *The Maturational Processes and the Facilitating Environment.* New York: International Universities Press, 1965, pp. 158–65.

————. 1969. The use of an object and relating through identification. In *Playing and Reality.* London: Tavistock, 1971, pp. 86–94.

———. 1971a. Playing: A theoretical statement. In *Playing and Reality*. London: Tavistock, pp. 38–52.

———. 1971b. Playing: Creative activity and the search for the self. In *Playing and Reality*. London: Tavistock, pp. 53–64.

———. 1971c. Mirror-role of mother and family in child development. In *Playing and Reality*. London: Tavistock, pp. 11–118.

———. 1971d. Interrelating apart from instinctual drive and In terms of cross-identification. In *Playing and Reality*. London: Tavistock, pp. 119–37.

———. 1971e. *Playing and Reality*. London and New York: Tavistock.

Chapter Eight

Wilfred R. Bion
Infinite Surfaces, Explosiveness, Faith

Michael Eigen

EDITORS' INTRODUCTION

Bion was one of the most original thinkers in psychoanalysis and perhaps the most difficult theorist to understand for those who have not been immersed in his thought. There are at least two reasons for this. First, Bion drew from a variety of disciplines, such as philosophy, mathematics, science, and the psychology of perception, in his effort to create a theory of thinking that used the psychotic mind as its starting point. Psychotic processes and experiences are exceedingly difficult to make intelligible, to communicate and to codify (codifying clearly went against Bion's intentions). Second, Bion's often deliberately ambiguous, idiosyncratic, and mystical presentation of his views makes it exceedingly difficult for the uninitiated reader to grasp his most profound insights about being and relating, especially within the psychoanalytic encounter. Bion wanted to use words that were devoid of saturation or "understandability"; he did not want to represent reality as most psychoanalytic authors tend to do. Rather, Bion wrote in an extremely emotionally evocative manner that was meant to be "disruptive" to the reader. He encouraged his readers, as he did analysts in their clinical work, to suspend "memory, desire, and understanding." While it is tempting to try to summarize and codify Bion's work in a didactic style similar to the other introductions in this volume, we feel in this case to do so is an act of editorial violence that is better resisted. Thus, in the spirit of Bionic disruption, rather than give the reader a customary rendering of Bion's work, we have asked

Michael Eigen, whose chapter is crafted in a similarly novel and emotionally evocative manner, to introduce his own essay. While we think this editorial decision is most "true" to the spirit of Bion's oeuvre (and Eigen's essay), we are also well aware that it makes engaging their work much more difficult and effortful for the reader. Perhaps a bit of advice from James S. Grotstein, one of the most thoughtful explicators of Bion, would be helpful: "One more truly learns from experience by listening to oneself responding to the input; that is, one learns by listening to oneself listening! If you do not get it the first time, read it again but without trying!" (personal communication). Says Michael Eigen,

A sense of catastrophe pervades Bion's work. It links personality and life together, much as Freud's libido does. It is as if there is an empty category, a preconception, a felt sense of catastrophe that is virtually omnipresent and built into our hardware, a "nameless dread." It is more than annihilation anxiety or death drive, although these are in the ballpark. In its most lethal mode, Bion calls it "a force that continues after . . . it destroys existence, time and space." But catastrophic dread pervades generative experiences as well.

There are creative and destructive big bangs, creative explosions as well as wipeouts. For example, we do not yet know what to do with emotional truth, truths about our lives. There are individuals who cannot take truth, or misuse it. People who cannot tolerate the experience of truth may explode when a truth hits. There is anxiety about truth, as well as about death, sex, money, and status. Our equipment is very much in infancy when it comes to reconciling tensions between survival and integrity.

Catastrophic dread pervades the evolution of our equipment, a kind of growth anxiety. How do we help ourselves grow a psyche capable of tolerating the buildup of experience? How do we grow the ability to be true to ourselves in ways that are not lethal? Imagine being an embryo or fetus undergoing momentous developmental waves. What an astronomical growth rate, what changes of form! Imagine being psychically embryonic today in some important way. How terrified one might be if one began growing emotionally at the rate an embryo grows physically! Yet something like that *can* happen, and we are afraid of current possibilities for psychic movement. In response to dread of catastrophe, Bion writes of faith. Faith can be dread-full too. But psychic movement is even more dreadful without it. Bion describes the psychoanalytic attitude as an act of faith, an incessant opening to evolution of experiencing. There is faith one can open in spite of all the ways one closes and shuts life out. There is faith that one can be true to the impact of life and let living grow. Nameless dread blows all structure away. There is nothing to hold on to. Faith, too, goes beyond everything nameable, and there are no forms to hold on to. There seem to be positive and negative infinities in tension with each other. Bion enjoins us to become infinite. We *are* infinite infinities, alternating currents, capable of maximum-minimum emotions, good and evil. How do we become partners with the capacities that constitute us and evolve well together?

(P. M. and A. R.)

No psychoanalyst I know has confessed more self-hate in print than Bion. Reading his autobiography (1982, 1985) is an exercise in tolerance of self-laceration. Yet vivid pictures of his life emerge: his devastating yet rich early childhood in India, the horrors of an 8-year-old's school life in England, the gradual emerging of a tough, supersensitive man with insect endurance, an athlete, a war hero, a doctor, a psychiatrist, a psychoanalyst.

One of the most painful passages in Bion's autobiography depicts his walled-off immobility when his young daughter tried to reach him across a yard. He sat in autistic-schizoid silence, unable to reach out to her. I think Bion was permanently horrified by himself (his inability to respond), horrified by what people did to each other, what *he* did. He felt he lost his daughter and was grateful when his second wife made family come alive, and saved him from himself. He felt he died in the First World War. His first wife's death as a result of childbirth during the Second World War heightened his embittered sense that there was no end to dying. His writings are concerned with interweavings of destruction of personality and affective intensity, with deadness and aliveness of self.

One of Bion's most terse and telling depictions of destructiveness was of "a force that continues after . . . it destroys existence, time and space" (1965, p. 101). How can a force continue after it destroys existence, time, and space? Isn't that a contradiction in terms? Yet it is just such impossibility that gives his formulations their special punch. The idea of destruction going on in subzero dimensions, feeding on deadness, endless worlds of deadness: it brings us up short and deepens our realization of what we are up against. Destructiveness challenges us and we dare not ignore it.

More Preliminary Remarks

Most psychoanalysts would be surprised to find no use of the term "drive" in Bion's major works. One would think he has Freud's life and death drives in mind, especially the latter as developed by Melanie Klein. Yet he calls himself an object relations theorist, a field theorist, and the term "drive" is glaring in its omission.

Bion focuses on transformations of affect. Instead of drive language, he uses affect language. For example, he traces the play of love (L), hate (H), knowledge (K), and faith (F). The value of any of these elements depends on its function in a given context. Any can be more creative or destructive, contribute to or impede personality growth at a particular moment. The analyst needs to stay open to fresh perception of relations, close to the impact of the moment.

Bion uses many images drawn from diverse fields as intuitive models for impacts he experiences in psychoanalytic sessions, as tools for making observations, and as tracers to illuminate the interplay of variables, functions, and attitudes. Many analysts would be bewildered, even alarmed, at the array of religious, philosophical, historical, and mathematical images Bion uses to describe or evoke psychoanalytic experiences.

He uses the garden of Eden, the flood, the tower of Babel, the Sphinx, and Tiresias in *Oedipus Rex* to depict psychoanalytic dramas involving curiosity, the passion to know, punishment, anxiety and guilt, and the omniscience that prevents learning from experience. Bion is also drawn to mystics, like Jesus and Rabbi Luria, who show that not only do curiosity and the desire to know get one in trouble, but birth processes of new experiencing involve cataclysmic processes. Faith, as well as knowledge, opens doors of perception that unleash disturbances. Faith that is merely comforting is probably as deleterious to growth as knowledge that is cut off and schizoid (although comfort and cuts have uses too).

Ideas and images from Plato, Kant, Poincaré, Frege, Milton, Freud, Klein, Scholem, physics, astronomy, medicine: Bion battled to feel free to select what he needed from the writers and influences that mattered to him. He drew deeply from the well of his experience. If psychoanalysis does not grow from the depths of being and reflect who one is, what good can it do? How can psychoanalysis be a catalyst for growth if the analyst evades his personal destiny? Bion always seems to be wondering what psychoanalysis is and what it can do. He takes running leaps, opens, comes back with another bit of the elephant. He encourages us to do the same with our version of whatever it is we are doing. For Bion psychoanalysis is no fixed thing to be subsumed by formulas, but an unknown to be created and discovered.

His famous formula for the radical openness of the psychoanalytic attitude (an act of faith) expresses his passion for fresh starting points. He describes the psychoanalytic attitude as being without memory, desire, understanding, or expectations (1970). Over and over the analyst stays open to the impact of the patient. Of course, understanding, memory, and expectations grow from this impact. But it is to the impact that the analyst returns, an affective core of experience, which gives birth to images, which give birth to symbols, which give birth to ideas.

Bion's brand of openness leads him to depict, in varying ways, states involving maximum-minimum emotion. We might place double arrows between heightened emotionality and emotional vacuum or void (e.g., maximum emotion $\rightleftharpoons$ minimum emotion) to suggest interchangeability, reversibility, oscillation, opposition. An extreme would be catatonic excitement-stupor. But silence and explosiveness play a role in many phenomena. Bion was fascinated with various ways emotion-emotionlessness could be structured, and he leaves us a rich treasure of observations.

My suspicion is that Bion did not, finally, alienate those closest to him (he remained endearing) because he could be *felt* experiencing the desolation that haunted him. Even when he was in black-hole states, *someone* was there, clinging to life. The vacuum or void was a measure of intensity in reverse. At times the formless infinite void became thoroughly alive and enlivening. Nevertheless, I believe Bion knew the zero states whereof he spoke, and weathered them. Life never lost its relish in a final way.

How can maximum emptiness-fullness exist together? The law of contradiction does not hold in any simple way for emotional space, where one *can* be in two places at once, perhaps must be. How can a dead man be alive, and an alive man be dead? Bion bears witness that such simultaneity is possible, necessary. After immersion in the Bionic universe, one wonders whether it wouldn't be less than human not to taste something of the everythingness-nothingness that forms the background of experiencing.

Another example of the well-nigh indistinguishability of seemingly opposite currents is Bion's discussion of the commingling of health and sickness in certain psychotic individuals. A person may feel that his "well being and vitality spring from the same characteristics that give trouble. The sense that loss of the bad parts of his personality is inseparable from loss of that part in which all his mental health resides, contributes to the acuity of the patient's fears" (1965, p. 144). One suspects that Bion partly has his own eccentricities in mind when he speaks of aliveness and disturbance flowing from the same source. Such sentences in Bion's work are barriers against analytic smugness.

As is typical, Bion maximizes the tenacity, provocativeness, and acuity of his formulation by listing a group of traits that might be taken as indices of illness or health, depending on how they function, or one's view of them: ambition, intolerance of frustration, envy, aggression, and uncompromising belief in a fulfilling ideal object (1965, p. 144). Most of these belong to what Melanie Klein describes as the paranoid-schizoid position (more infantile, primitive, pathological). Bion emphasizes that they are or can be part of the patient's endowment of health and virility, with origins "in a *normal* physical state" (1965, p. 144; italics Bion's).

Kleinian writers note the contributions paranoid-schizoid capacities make to normal functioning (e.g., the importance of splitting, projection, denial, idealization), but the overall thrust is on "making" the depressive position, where one is capable of perceiving/introjecting a whole object, feeling remorse over one's destructiveness, and undertaking reparative activities. Bion's emphasis is on the back-and-forth, the incessant contributions of both poles, the life- (as well as death-) giving aspects of the most elemental resources. He is a spokesman for what is valuable in what seems most ill (and the ill in what seems healthy by conventional standards).

In my sessions with Bion in New York (in 1977), he startled me by talking about the Kabbalah (Eigen, 1993, pp. 272–74). He seemed to feel that the Kabbalah was relevant for my problems, but also for his, and for the sort of psychic processes that interested him. As I struggle now to convey something of the essential quality of his work, I think of a teaching of Lurianic mysticism. God contracted to make room for the world. This resulted in divine sparks being buried in dead and evil places. It is up to us to recover these sparks and unite God with himself. Bion has done his job. He has gone into realms of evil and deadness, and redeemed what he could. He joins Freud and Luria, too, in helping us live with what is unredeemable, although we do not know exactly what that might be. Wherever we turn (including subzero worlds of infinite horror and deadness), there is much we *can* do, together with the ever present can't.

Multiplicity and Explosiveness

The next sections of this chapter spring from two images Bion uses, one from geometry and one from physics: (1) a geometric solid with an infinite number of surfaces; and (2) explosiveness (*à la* the big bang vision of the universe's origin). The former pertains to the many ways any moment of a session can be viewed (by analyst or patient), and to the sort of space an individual is able to constitute. The latter points to turbulence that is part of change, beginnings, and destruction. It is tempting to say that the former has to do more with cognition and the latter with emotion, but there is so much overlap and reversibility that a clear-cut distinction would be misleading. For example, there is explosive thought and deadening interpretation. Nevertheless, we will follow, as space permits, some of Bion's uses of these images. In so doing, we get a sense of the flavor and thrust of his vision through selected details.

Infinite Surfaces

Suppose two people agree that what they say to each other is selected from other things they do not say, and that what they notice about what they say is selected from other things they do not notice. Neither insists his view is the only view, yet both try to communicate some bit of experience. It is possible that these individuals will make room for the impact of each other's communications, partly because neither claims that his contribution is exhaustive or excludes the other's. Neither negates communicative efforts on the basis of what is unable to be communicated. These lucky individuals are able to work with the restrictive nature of communication. They go on speaking, while tolerating recognition that what they say (or paint, or write, or compose, or build, or legislate) is possible only on the basis of what is left out or not sayable.

However, there are individuals who remain silent in the face of the unsayable. They are unable to communicate what they might, because they are held captive by what evades the limits of communication. They cannot take their eyes off what they are not saying, in order to say what they can. At other moments, such individuals may say too much too quickly and jump around in dizzying fashion, trying to say everything at once (again, nothing can be left out). To such a person, nothing the analyst says seems usable, as there is always something that is not said, and what is not said may seem more important than what is said.

In the fable I am developing, the *everything-at-once* or *all now* individual is unable to take for granted the infinite in every moment. He cannot abide representational restrictions, not even restrictions meant to represent the infinite in every moment. Bion offers images to convey infinite possibilities of timing and meaning in a session. This situation "could be represented by a visual image of a figure in which many planes meet or lines pass through a common point," or "a visual image of a geometric solid with an infinite number of surfaces" (1970, p. 8). The *everything-at-once/all now* individual cannot suffer spatial representation of infinite possibilities, even in pretend (analogical) fashion. To represent the infinite in terms of a visual image is idolatry, and psychoanalysis, like ordinary daily life, is blasphemy.

The medical model of psychoanalysis commits the opposite error, since it treats the psyche like a physical body. The physician uses his senses to study instruments and see and touch bodies. But thoughts and feelings are not localizable: "anxiety has no shape or colour, smell or sound" (1970, p. 7). The analyst works with the felt impact of the patient and affective-ideological transformations of this impact. The felt subject-to-subject link (or lack of it) is crucial.

The analyst who goes beyond the medical model neither treats the psyche like a physical thing nor evades use of spatial models. With the psychotic, he intuits the infinite unsayable. But he allows ineffable intimations to contribute to personality growth. A vision of infinite surfaces of a moment or session can be awesome, but the fact that this can be represented and talked about can make for shared appreciation. Part of therapeutic work involves finding expressive language (images, narratives, metaphors, statements, outbursts, drawings, songs, movements, etc.) for aspects of the impact we have on each other, and aspects of the impact life has on us.

Bion is especially interested in individuals who cannot endure growth of experience. They cannot take the impact of events, nor can they communicate disability in a way that might help. If the presence of the analyst is a challenge to grow, the very being of the analyst must be obliterated. Obliteration may be out of envious hate, but also results from being too damaged to support the impact of the other. Part of the task of therapy is to help build a capacity to work with the interchanges therapy generates. This places considerable pressure on analyst and patient alike.

Individuals who cannot tolerate evolution of the capacity to support growth of experience may evade this painful challenge by discounting anything the analyst says on the grounds that the analyst is saying it. For example, an individual with eyes glued on the formless infinite (and who unconsciously demands everything at once now) may be hyperaware that whatever we do reflects selection processes. If the analyst says something about the patient, he must also be saying something about himself. Whatever the analyst says may be used against him. The patient may not be wrong in arguing that the analysis is more about the analyst than the patient.

Similarly, an analyst cannot cover all possible meanings of any moment. A patient may move the analyst to try more inclusive interpretations, until the analyst is driven to impotent silence in the face of incapacity or impossibility. The analyst may react against this pressure by adopting a subtle moralistic stance or by some other urge to action (implosion leads to explosion of the analysis). Thus the analyst is brought to the point where he, too, is unable to tolerate experiencing, particularly when experiencing is of destruction or collapse or undoing of experiencing.

The analyst must become an expert or artist or adept at living through collapse of analysis. He studies processes that undo themselves. Little by little he learns something of what working with destructive processes entails. His growth in capacity to live through and work with destruction signals the patient that such a capacity is possible. If the analyst can survive therapy, perhaps the patient can as well.

Instead of negating growth because it is too hard or uncertain (why bother—one's going to die and know nothing anyway!), the analyst models the realization that only uncertain growth is possible. When he tries to communicate with colleagues, he must struggle to find models for his experience that are not too general or concrete, not too inclusive or exclusive. A parallel struggle goes on to find intuitive models or images to communicate with patients. Myths of destruction and creation encode processes that go on in sessions. Which image is valuable when? What lens, at what distance, provides most mileage at a given time?

Bion never tired of painting problems inherent in the communication of mental states. How do we communicate what goes on inside? What is inside? What does it take to discover a feeling? How do we know what we feel, or feel what we feel, or let another know? Can we know without an other? We discover our feelings as we speak them, but aren't they changing as we discover them? We cannot keep up with affective transformations, but we also *are* them. How do we communicate with ourselves and others? Often we discover that the other has heard something quite different from what we said, or thought we meant to say. Dare the analyst ever take for granted his and the patient's understanding of one another? Bion knew from experience how difficult it is to feel understood, to understand oneself, to understand another. One wonders, from reading Bion, if it is more unusual for people to understand each other than is ordinarily imagined. The violence issuing from misunderstanding testifies to the importance of the difficulties he highlights.

The infinite surfaces of time and meaning of every session always give analyst and patient a way out. They may never have to pass through the eye of the same needle. They can always find ways of being somewhere else, of pointing elsewhere, of failing to meet. Even when they want to meet, it is always possible to miss each other. Nevertheless, multiplicity and uncertainty do not completely obliterate impact.

Meeting flows from impact. Authentic therapeutic struggle gravitates around points of impact analyst and patient have on each other. The sense of impact is the raw datum analyst and patient have to work with. Part of the adventure of therapy is learning to discover and communicate bits of impact that make a difference—not only impacts of events and people, but impacts of thoughts, feelings, sensations, our own impacts on ourselves. Can we take a little more, let a little more intensity build and work its way through affective expressions, so that we begin to notice what calls us into life or prevents us from living?

Explosiveness

Bion (1970, pp. 12–15) uses a reverse big bang image to describe individuals who cannot let experience build. He imagines an explosion so violent that constitution and use of viable mental space is obliterated. Psychic life is blown up. The individual or the analogical space that involves symbolic life is blown away. Coordinate or mapping systems are useless. The individual cannot find a workable orienting frame of reference. What might pass for thoughts or feelings turn out to be bits of flotsam and jetsam floating away from each other with accelerating velocity, scraps of an explosion eons away.

This is a reverse big bang because it destroys rather than creates potential for living. A well-meaning analyst may think the patient is making meaningful communications, only to seethe in frustrated bewilderment when the work keeps collapsing. It may take some time for the analyst to realize that the patient is no longer there, that the latter's emissions are light years away from what is left of the patient by the time they reach the analyst. An analyst who enters such a patient's force field is in danger of having his own mental processes blown away as well. Meaning is jammed because the kind of emotional/symbolic space meaning depends on has been obliterated. What reaches the analyst might more profitably be taken as signals of a self-obliterating process that began long ago, is ongoing, and sweeps up whatever comes near.

Thus Bion allows for the possibility that a good deal of what the patient says or does is incoherent and meaningless, indices of catastrophe in progress. The individual who sees the analyst may be very far from the point of the original explosion. A second, or third, or fourth personality may have grown in place of the original. These, too, are parts of catastrophic processes. An analyst who has some inkling of the catastrophic processes he faces tries to avoid inflicting the surplus torment of talking to the wrong patient. Finding which patient to talk to when is a major part of the therapist's struggle.

A psychoanalysis, like a person's life, "can be seen as a transformation in which an intense catastrophic emotional explosion O has occurred (elements of personality, link, and second personality having been instantaneously expelled to vast distances from their point of origin and from each other)" (Bion, 1970, p. 14). The analysis is like "one moment in time stretched out so that it becomes a line or surface spread out over a period of years— an extremely thin membrane of a moment" (1970, p. 14). The analyst uses temporal-spatial images to portray his sense of the patient's loss of space-time. He uses images like explosive obliteration in hopes of bringing the patient's non-existence into focus, a lens to allow the one who isn't there to achieve a measure of visibility.

Bion (1970, pp. 13–14) traces the fate of a scream as an example of transformations explosive processes can undergo. He puts together a psychotic patient's references to not being able to get ice cream over two years. The patient begins by saying he could buy no ice cream, and after two years says there was no ice cream. Such remarks triggered in Bion a vision of the patient's linking capacity. In the beginning there was the link with a good object (ice cream), which underwent destruction or spoiling. When destructiveness showed up, the individual's scream became a link between two personalities. Screaming over loss or destruction of goodness replaces the good feeling link.

Screaming provides a link (or calls for linking) as goodness vanishes. Screaming may demand restoration of goodness, but can also blindly feed further destruction. The good object turns into an "I scream" link, which builds its own momentum. As the scream builds, the individual may become less accessible, more caught in panicky fury. The other may not be able to respond suitably, and even if there is response, the latter may not be able to fan the good link into life, or sustain the bad link for long. Insofar as "I-scream" fails as link, it transforms into "no-I-scream." The scream dies out or implodes, or is lost in stupor.

Destruction snowballs. The good link transforms to the scream link, which transforms to no scream or nothing at all: mute stupor, deathly silence, or meaningless, chaotic noise. One could imagine a happy infant becoming a screaming infant becoming a stuporous infant. Yet Bion goes farther. The explosion of linking processes he depicts involves also a succession of explosions. The dying out of the scream (fatigue, hopelessness, negativistic refusal, stupor, numbness) ignites explosion of mental space as such.

The congealed scream may at first be a refusal to scream. Why scream if it does no good, if it fails as link? At first, the individual may be alive enough to ragefully stifle reactivity. But negativism spirals, eats itself up. The no scream (silent refusal) starts as desperate linking attempt, silence meant to draw the other in (silent people hope to be unseen, but may also hope others will come to them). But stifled reactivity can lead to dying out (loss) of reactivity. The numbing process swallows the individual. The linking capacity explodes into nothingness, an agony of anesthesia forever reaching a vanishing point.

The link moved from nourishing connection, to screaming connection, to no screaming connection (a mutated mute connection, void connection). The no link is a connection of sorts for a time. But the no link (no scream) itself explodes, and loses much of its capacity to attract or repulse. The individual may finally be lost in spacelessness, no individual at all. Explosion and black hole become the same.

A scream can be an explosion that grows from pain and then obliterates pain. One might take screaming as a sign of the explosiveness inherent in our nature. But, it is important to note, the destructive explosive process Bion points to sweeps the scream along with it. A scream is usually on the side of life. It expresses pain or distress or terror or fury. It is failure of the scream to meet with corrective measures that furthers the subject's spin out of existence. Even the no scream (angry or frightened silence) may harbor the hope or demand or wish for a saving presence or a righting of affairs.

Bion does not develop a causal account of the explosive destructiveness he envisions. He sights it and traces its moves. It appears to aim at linking processes. Wherever one finds it, it is destroying links or mushrooming through nothingness after links have been destroyed. It destroys the good, sweet link (ice cream), it destroys the scream link, it destroys the no scream link. It drives the subject further and further out of existence. The destructive force seeks and destroys any place the individual tries to make contact with himself and others. The linking capacity undergoes successive detonations, its generative ability ever nulled.

The analyst may imagine fragments of a link as "dispersed instantaneously over infinite space" (1970, p. 14). But psychotic destruction in the patient may be so immense that the idea of infinite space is not viable, since any space may be too restrictive. The challenge for the analyst is how to link up with a patient in whom the space where links are possible has been destroyed. How does one grow or regrow a world and psyche in which linking processes can evolve and in which life is possible?

One can imagine that Bion knew well the destruction of existence he depicts. As mentioned earlier, he felt he died in the First World War. Years later he could be imprisoned in immobility (compressed into a sepulchral self) in the face of his child's spontaneous needs. He knew in his own being what it is like to lose goodness, to become a scream stretched over years, to become a scream that dies out (a useless scream), an impacted silence collapsing into nothingness.

His writings are like SOS messages sealed in a bottle thrown into the sea. We open them and at first it is like reading in the dark. When our eyes adjust, we glimpse worlds of deadening processes in ourselves we dared not imagine. Bion used to remark that by reading him, at least, one gets to know what having a patient like Bion is like. I suspect there are many psychoanalytic writers who write from the depths of their beings, hoping to create a therapist who can cure them, or communicate through deaths with another living flame.

Generative Explosiveness

Bion uses the image of explosiveness to describe generative as well as destructive processes. There are positive as well as negative aspects to explosive processes. The birth of a new idea or feeling or intuition may have explosive properties. Growth can be explosive. Beginnings have explosive aspects.

Bion's emphasis on explosiveness in development can partly be understood in terms of the resistance of any established status quo state to change. The saying "The good is enemy of the better" touches on a certain inertia in human nature. Bion is especially sensitive to barriers, walls, blockages on both individual and social levels. He uses terms like Establishment vs. Genius or Messiah to depict conflict between conservative and radical elements in life (1970, pp. 62–82). The new idea or intuitive vision is experienced as life-giving yet also destructive from the vantage point of the established order. Ideally, the old and new achieve a useful symbiotic relationship, each contributing to the other, facilitating growth of knowledge and being (of individuals, of society). However, one must not expect things to go too smoothly, since boundary tensions can be incendiary.

In addition to the explosiveness of the new in relation to the old (and, conversely, the violence of the old vis à vis the new), Bion points to something inherently explosive about psychic birth processes in themselves. The big bang that begins the biography of the universe is not simply an explosion of the old. The beginning is itself explosive, an explosiveness intrinsic to beginning. As a model for psychic processes, new beginnings would be expected to be explosive, not merely because they disturb the old, but because they *are* explosions: explosions into life, life explosions.

In Dante's *Paradiso*, the soul keeps opening. More and more heaven is possible, no end to opening. It is no longer a matter of resistance of the old. There is only more and more opening, more and more divinity. It is only a matter of what the soul can tolerate. Apparently for Bion there is something intrinsically explosive about the journey toward infinite opening. Opening is explosive.

In our conversations, Bion brought up the importance of the Kabbalah in thinking about psychic reality. He used it not only to locate psychic life, but also to experience more intensely. Kabbalah (Steinsaltz, 1988) has its own versions of big bang processes, explosive beginnings. The *Ein Soph* or Infinite Infinite is beyond conceptualization. As it descends toward knowledge and understanding, a kind of explosion takes place. At times divine movement is depicted as a lightning flash, or white light (all colors contained). It explodes downward (into knowledge, understanding, feeling, action) and upward (through and beyond intuition) simultaneously. The birth of consciousness is likened to a blast of light. For Bion consciousness is an explosion.

Bion uses the experience of truth as one example of explosive consciousness. If lies poison, truth explodes. Facing truths about one's life explodes the lie one lives. Psychoanalysis can be dangerous because it can overturn lives. The analyst is necessarily (partly) a subversive support, insofar as he midwives the resetting and reshaping of lives.

Many people fear going into analysis because they sense that the truth of their lives will upset what they've built up. They fear they will have to act on truths they keep closeted. Their adaptations include comforts, pleasures, and habits that are reassuring. They would like analysis to diminish pain or dysfunction without too much cost. Perhaps, in some ways, analysis is "easier" for those who feel that their lives and persons are disasters, who do not have too much to lose. They are already so badly injured that analysis cannot cause them too much harm. They have reached such a level of desperation that truth seems saving, cleansing, nourishing, rather than disastrous.

Bion is keenly aware of the destructive and generative impact of emotional truth. On the one hand, he feels that truth is necessary for psychic growth, as food is for the body (1970, chap. 1). On the other hand, he is aware that people may be ill equipped to take the impact of truth. He suggests there may be evolutionary as well as individual factors involved. A mental apparatus that evolved to handle problems of survival may need further evolution to work with problems of integrity, emotional truth, and *how* we survive (*quality* of *being*, and not simply material being).

The human psyche's concern with issues of emotional integrity is an evolutionary explosion, a new dimension. Humans discover it is possible to live a lie, to be poisoned by the lies they live. Bion is one of those who suggest that this "sense" of emotional lying-truthing has an aesthetic element that needs nursing. How do we "know" we are on a track that is right or good for us? What is this intimation of being "off" or "on" as we go along, this *feeling* of linking with ourselves, or being far from the mark? Under what conditions do these intimations work generatively, destructively? And aren't terms like "generative-destructive" awesomely crude?

Bion is attracted to difficulties inherent in psychoanalysis. He has a way of exploding hypocrisy with laconic black humor. One example is the question, Can a liar be psychoanalyzed? Bion suggests that if a liar can't be psychoanalyzed, no one can, since a liar (the psychoanalyst) also does the analyzing. Is anyone exempt from lying? Bion trenchantly remarks that only a liar could disregard lying's pervasive nature (1970, p. 2). Analyst and patient struggle with the same basic problems. Our common task is how to become better partners with the capacities that constitute us, a never ending journey. Our job is not to stop lying (an impossibility), but to evolve further in our relationship with this tantalizing capacity.

Part of wisdom involves dosage, a sense of context. Truth kills as well as frees. In an earlier work (Eigen, 1992, Chap. 4 & 5), I described an analyst, Ben, who used truth to ax others (and himself). He was a truth addict, gorging on truth orgasms. He had a scent for what was false in life and went for the jugular. In doing so, he was in danger of destroying his closest relationships and losing everything dear to him. His sense of truth-falsehood needed deepening, broadening, contextualizing. He did not see the destructive way he used truth, the megalomanic bludgeoning, the lie.

Among other things, Ben needed to metabolize or process his destructive use of truth. He needed to develop a more resonant context for himself and others, a larger psychic field. He needed to grow a psyche capable of tolerating more of himself and others, one that could let the impact of the other grow, one that could let his own being grow. His precocious (intolerant) use of truth short-circuited growth of experiencing and its Möbius strip "truth-lie" mix. My writings on Ben document his (our) struggle to grow more of a psyche capable of tolerating more growth.

Bion's discussions of consciousness as an explosion, the ubiquity of lying, the need for truth as psychic nutrient, and truth's destructive and generative shift the center of therapeutic gravity toward what it takes to let experiencing evolve. It is not a matter of the Oedipus complex, maternal envy, sibling rivalry: all these (and more) are useful at particular moments. They represent particular organizations of relational tensions, pressures of diverse affective intensities. What is at stake is whether an individual (or group) can take its own capacity for experiencing. To what extent is emotional life, and mental life in general, too much for us? How much of ourselves can we take and allow to develop? Can we do so in life-giving ways? How do we relate to our destructive tendencies? How best can we make room for ourselves? Are we creatures destined always to have relatively low tolerance for ourselves, or can tolerance for ourselves and each other truly grow? Psychoanalysis is always an open question as to how far or in what ways analyst and patient can constitute themselves with reference to the conditions and capacities that make their lives possible.

Faith in O

The radical openness of the psychoanalysis Bion envisions is given dramatic expression in his description of the analyst's attitude as an *act of faith* (F) (Bion, 1970, pp. 41–54). One feels that Bion's description of faith is itself an act of faith, and that there has been a growth of the O in faith as Bion's writings evolved. In earlier works there was more of an emphasis on evolution of K (knowledge, insight, understanding) and attacks on K links. He traced psychotic hatred of emotional reality and destruction of knowledge of emotional life. By his last major, formal work (1970), Bion was explicit in grounding psychoanalysis on something deeper than the drive to know. It is not simply knowledge that psychotic intolerance destroys. The faith that supports living is at stake. In his writings on faith, Bion comes close to envisioning what must be a contradiction in terms: a psychoanalysis without words.

Of course, psychoanalysts and their patients go on speaking. Bion wrote and spoke to the end of his days. But he affirmed something more important than words. For Bion, nonverbal emotional reality has a certain privilege or primacy that gives words value. If words do not grow out of and mediate or signal movement of the emotional substrate, they are useless, even dangerous (since high-altitude verbalization can lose contact with or falsify the affective core). The greater part of psychoanalytic movement is wordless.

Psychotic processes not only attack the analyst's capacity to know and put things together and make sense out of a life (or segments of a life). Psychotic processes undermine the faith that makes meaning meaningful. In psychosis the faith that makes emotional aliveness possible (and desirable) is undermined. The faith that makes an alive analysis possible is threatened. What comes under attack is the analyst's faith in the analytic process. The analyst is in danger of losing not only his mind, but also his faith that mind and life are worthwhile. What suffers damage or destruction is his conviction that being in the analysis is worthwhile, that *being* is worthwhile.

As mentioned earlier, Bion envisions (a real experience, I believe) a destructive stripping of everything worthwhile, a denudation of personality and life past the null point into subzero dimensions: "a force that continues after . . . it destroys existence, time and space" (1965, p. 101). What can possibly meet or face or address such a force or state or deadening process? To the death without end, Bion proposes its counterpart: a faith in infinite O'ing. Can this faith outflank, outlast, undercut, absorb and partly metabolize, or somehow go beyond ever increasing deadness? Can faith survive analysis? Can faith survive (and contribute to) life?

Bion describes faith as a stripping away of mind. He advocates a disciplined eschewing of such mental capacities as expectation, understanding, desire, memory, and sense impressions. He relates this generative zero state or radical openness to Freud's free-floating attention, an artificial blinding (suspension of usual use of mind) so that intuition of psychic reality builds. He writes, "If the mind is preoccupied with elements perceptible to sense it will be that much less able to perceive elements that cannot be sensed. . . . It is important that the analyst should avoid mental activity, memory and desire, which is harmful to his mental fitness as some forms of physical activity are to physical fitness" (1970, pp. 41–42).

It is as if Bion tries to find an Archimedean point of being that destruction can't destroy. He achieves a state (or a vision of a state) in which there is nothing for the destructive force to feed on. One must ask, if one contracts until nothing is left but naked intuition, can't the destructive force feed on that? Bion seems to feel that (at the point of ultimate contraction) it may always be possible to open a little more, to keep on opening, so that faith provides more room (because it is "spaceless," infinite) than destruction can exhaust. Faith keeps opening as destruction keeps destroying: one infinity opening vis à vis the other. Such a statement, of course, is an act of faith.

The attitude of faith provides a "resistanceless" medium in which it is possible to observe destructiveness at work. Bion is concerned with how it is possible to make a correct clinical observation, especially observations of destructive processes: "I am concerned with developing a mode of thought which is such that a correct clinical observation can be made, for if *that* is achieved there is always hope of evolution of the appropriate theory" (1970, p. 44).

The starting point is always the impact of being on being, psyche to psyche, and the transformations that experiences of impact undergo. What state of being best registers these impacts and their transformations? To what extent can we let experience of the other's impact "ob-trude" and build? For Bion theory is secondary and follows observation of waves of impact. Theoretical work, indeed, can be part of the ripple effect of one being impacting on another, ceaseless attempts to provide orienting frames of reference for mutual sensitivity.

Of course the term "resistanceless" is a fiction, since nothing is resistanceless. The pain, disorientation, and insecurity the analyst feels in trying to achieve the openness Bion calls faith show how difficult the analytic attitude is to find and sustain. It is not simply a matter of blowing dust off a mirror. It is human for patient and analyst to share difficulties in their work, since they are both defensive creatures struggling with disabilities. Analytic time is a mixture of hardship and joy for both parties, as they fight for and against each other and work with processes that support, defeat, and challenge them.

Bion blasts the idea of the analyst as *knower*, since it is openness to *unknowing* (perhaps the unknowable) that grounds the analytic attitude. One tries to keep opening to shifting impacts and transformations of impacts. Can one ever know what is impacting on what? The analyst's experience of the patient is not the same as the patient's of the analyst. Furthermore, the analyst (or patient) may have difficulty achieving consensus with himself as to what he is feeling, or what his feelings mean. Nevertheless, one speaks from the point of impact, or from experience of evolution of impact. To connect with and voice intimations, hunches, and convictions from the pressing plethora of alternatives is itself a kind of faith. No two voices can be identical.

The voice that comes through Bion's climactic writings expresses and conveys the faith he speaks of. It is a strong and passionate affirmation of the human spirit via the analytic attitude, almost a musical evocation of the faith he fights to live from. His writing is an act of faith: it tries to convey the faith domain it grows from, alive in twists and turns of the living moment. Let me quote a passage that is a clarion call: "Investigation of the problems involved depends on F. This means that the understanding of the patient and the identification with him that have been regarded as sufficient hitherto must be replaced by something quite different. The transformation in K must be replaced by transformation in O, and K must be replaced by F" (1970, pp. 45–46).

One cannot know O. One *is* O. The center of gravity shifts from knowing to being. We can talk about O and work with this or that bit of knowledge (always open to revision) about O. But we also *are* O and evolve in O as O evolves. "The problem in discussing O is that the discussion can only be about evolved characteristics of O (K) whereas F is related to O itself" (1970, p. 45).

The analyst's true home, when being an analyst, is living transformations in O, evolving in O, being in O through F. Since Bion associates O with infinity, "The analyst has to become *infinite* by the suspension of memory, desire, understanding" (1970, p. 46).

Tall order! Not the usual description of the analyst and the analytic function! The analytic attitude is F in O, and can never be rationalized. Insofar as it is rationalized, it is not the analytic attitude, not F in O, not radical openness to impact, not living transformations in O. We are explosive nutrients for one another. Only by living O through F do we stand a chance of connecting with and hearing each other, as we speak through and from our O's, our shared O.

O

I have postponed to the last discussion of what Bion might mean by O. My inclination is to use the notation as the moment suggests, and let usage acquire tonality with time. In Milner's (1987, pp. 258–74) chapter on mysticism, Bion's O is zero, a null state, emptiness, void, nothingness, a quasi-oriental O. She associates analytic openness with pregnant emptiness, creative darkness, the power of nonexistence, the goodness of absolute vacuity, the matrix of the sense of self, the divine ground of one's being, the experience of breathing. It is as if we surface momentarily at different points of an infinite pool. If we live only at the surface, we cut each other (we are very pointy). But it is also possible to dip into background interlacings, where our roots interlock.

For Milner O is inherently orgasmic, albeit a muted (and extended) orgasm in analytic work. Bion tends to emphasize negative aspects of experiencing O in his explicit "descriptions" (analogical evocations). For him the impact of O tends to be dreadful: "The emotional state of transformations in O is akin to dread"(1970, p. 46). This is not so much a matter of psychodynamic resistance as of equipment insufficiency and unfamiliarity. Not even an analyst is used to *being* an analyst. Few of us are used to exercising the capacity Bion calls F in O. Bion is actually calling for an evolution of our O, our capacity to be an analyst, our capacity to live F in O. To let go usual modes of being and knowing is frightening.

One wonders if too much analytic training goes into making believe the beast isn't there. What happens if one discovers that the psyche is alive? An analyst discovering the living psyche is akin to a praying person overturned by prayer, shocked by more than he bargained for. If one of the faces of O is emotional truth, one is always in danger. One can, perhaps, control falsehood more easily than truth (it is possible to own or claim a lie as one's own, but truth belongs to everyone—although any ideology of control is insufficient).

Bion (1970, p. 47) presses the point home by suggesting a kinship between increase in the power of F (as the analyst practices it) and experiences of severely regressed patients. At a certain phase of opening one may feel the pull of sleep akin to stupor. As contact with O sharpens, experience heightens and intensifies, so that emergent perceptual and sensory configurations may be painful. Not only must the analyst evolve with these shifts. Intimations of the latter are possible only by letting go one's ordinary grip on reality. Artificial blindness is also a kind of artificial madness.

Bion touches on a sort of necessary analytic madness when he points out that the analytic attitude suspends both pleasure and reality principles. The deprivation of desire, memory, understanding, and sensation that opens F in O

> corresponds to displacement of the pleasure-pain principle from its dominant position. This would not matter were it not for a simultaneous apparent deposition of the reality principle. . . . The disciplined increase of F by suppression of K, or subordination of transformations in K to transformations in O, is therefore felt to be a serious attack on the ego until F has become established. (1970, p. 48)

O can be the ultimate reality of a session, emotional truth of a session, growth of experience of an analysis, the ultimate reality of the personality. It can be creatively explosive, traumatically wounding, crushing, uplifting. To a certain extent, one can select what O to focus on when. One spends a lifetime discovering one's O, tuning in, connecting with, becoming at-one with whatever one imagines it to be, whatever it makes itself known as. If one is lucky, one learns more about working with one's O as one goes along.

But I still have not said what O is. Kant's thing-in-itself, Plato's Form, Eckhart's godhead, Milton's formless infinite, Kaballah's *Ein Soph*, the Christian Incarnation, the weekend break in analysis, the weekly session in psychotherapy, the point of meeting or of not meeting, the impact two people have on each other and how they process their impact, the awesome shock of being alive, revelation of who one is or isn't, gifts and horrors of history, the shell that entombs one and the fire that burns the shell: O keeps changing meaning, finding new forms of expression, evolving, transforming. O as a notation explodes itself.

Our ideas of what science is must be transformed by what science is asked to deal with. A science (psychoanalysis) of the ultimate reality of the personality, O, has nothing to hold on to. It is a search for ways of making correct observations of what is unknown and ultimately unknowable, "a science of at-one-ment," since one *is* the O one studies (1970, pp. 88–89). It is more important to *actually* evolve than to talk about evolution. But it is also possible that what we say provides analogies for processes beyond words. The evolution of the relationship between the wordy and wordless is ongoing, and we are very much engaged in mediating quality connections, gaps, leaps.

What Has Bion Done?

Let us stand on both sides of the looking glass: on the one side, faith, and on the other, a force that goes on working after it destroys existence, time, and space. Two immense denudations, strip downs. One eats up everything, infinite Pac Man, feeding on true self, false self, no self. The other keeps Opening. O'ing and O'ing. I suspect, finally, that there is a primacy of Opening over Oblivion. But Bion retains a certain democracy, equality of voices, a perennial binocularity (or multiocularity).

William Blake somewhere writes of heaven as a war in which all voices have their maximum say to the benefit of all: no compromises, total fullness of expression of all realities of Reality. O seems to have endless plasticity, transforming into what the avenue of approach of the moment can use. Yet Bion's O is not prior to the moment of creation, the living now. O is evolving now and we with it, as it is us and we are it. Our oneness with it is part of the psychoanalytic method, one with the evolving O of moment.

One has to admire the achievement of one who felt denuded of life, and uses denudation as a means of finding life. I think of Zen masters who speak of becoming like a dead man as a way of opening. It is also possible for life to open life, a more orgasmic path than Bion explicitly describes. The senses, of course, are nutrients, not only nuisances or barriers to enlightenment. Bion does not deny this. However, one of his special achievements is to pull away the skin of sensory goodness, insofar as the latter masks destructive processes that are crucial for us to learn about.

His analysis has wide application in a time when materialistic pleasures are substituted for emotional realities, when addiction to sensory goods (often manipulated by media images and market research) obscures destructive forces. Can we even tell what is destructive and what isn't? Bion suggests that F in O is a way of cleansing our equipment to the point where what is happening to us can begin to register. We discover our naked sensitivity to life's impact at the point where everything has been thrown overboard.

REFERENCES

Bion, W. R. 1965. *Transformations.* London: Heinemann.

———. 1970. *Attention and Interpretation.* London: Tavistock.

———. 1982. *The Long Week-End: 1987–1919.* Abingdon, Oxon: Fleetwood Press.

———. 1985. *All My Sins Remembered* and *The Other Side of Genius.* Abingdon, Oxon: Fleetwood Press.

Eigen, M. 1992. *Coming through the Whirlwind.* Wilmette, IL: Chiron.

———. 1993. *The Electrified Tightrope.* Northvale, NJ: Jason Aronson.

Milner, M. 1987. *The Suppressed Madness of Sane Men.* London: Tavistock.

Steinsaltz, A. 1988. *The Long Shorter Way.* Northvale, NJ: Jason Aronson.

Chapter 9

Heinz Kohut's Vision of the Essence of Humanness

Paul H. Ornstein

EDITORS' INTRODUCTION

Perhaps it is Heinz Kohut's "psychology of the self" more than any other "master narrative" that has challenged the Freudian hegemony in the United States. Indeed, as Paul Ornstein claims, Kohut ultimately viewed his theory not as a complement to Freud's but rather as a different paradigm. This assertion was rooted in part in Kohut's conviction that his theory provided a markedly different view of the human condition, one that illuminated aspects of human experience that were largely ignored by Freudian theory. In particular, it is self-experience (its coherence, continuity, integrity), especially as it is transformed by real and imagined relationships, that Kohut put at the center of his psychoanalytic theorizing.

As Ornstein points out, Kohut's narrative on "the nature of man" is dramatically different from Freud's: Freud's infant is born into an antagonistic environment with which it is immediately in conflict and which it has to oppose; Kohut's infant is born into a potentially harmonious, empathic milieu in which there is a "fit" between the infant and its environment; for Freud the basic motivational source is lodged in the sexual and aggressive drives, whereas for Kohut it is the creation and sustaining of selfobject ties that are fundamentally motivating. For Freud, the Oedipus complex is the universal, central developmental-instinctual conflict that largely determines personality development, including its disfigurement. Kohut, on the other hand, viewed the oedipal phase in terms of its potential strengths. Healthy oedipal experiences involve the joyful assertion of newly attained capacities that are empathically and supportively responded to by one's selfobjects, usually one's parents. Oedipal conflicts are universal, says Ornstein, but not the Oedipus complex, since Kohut considered the latter, which is characterized by intense conflict and murderous wishes, to be already a manifestation of a failed self-selfobject relation. Classical theory, in other words, posits the individual as "Guilty Man," struggling under the domination of the pleasure principle to reduce the tension of the instincts. Kohut's "Tragic Man," in contrast, struggles to fulfill the aims of the ambitions and ideals contained in the bipolar nuclear-self. For Guilty Man the central anxiety is castration anxiety, while for Tragic Man it is the dread of complete disintegration.

Adult psychopathology for Kohut is largely determined by endowment, coupled with the changes of the infant's and child's experiences in the selfobject context. In particular, it is the frequent failure in empathy by the parents that weakens the child's self. However, traumatic impact is not restricted to early life; it can occur in later life when selfobject experiences are unavailable, unreliable, or inconsistent. As Ornstein says, "defects and deficits in the functioning of the self and the inevitable massive defensive structures erected to protect a thus enfeebled and fragmentation-prone self constitute the bases of the patient's psychopathology."

Treatment, in Kohut's version of self psychology basically involves the patient establishing a selfobject transference (e.g., mirroring, idealizing, or twinship), which temporarily supports the enfeebled or fragmentation-prone self. The working through of the transference facilitates "transmuting internalization" of the analysand's selfobject functions. Thus the analytic experience becomes the foundation of a compensatory self-structure. In other words, it is the internalization of the analyst's selfobject functions, brought about through empathic understanding and explaining, that leads to change. Insight may accompany or follow the belated acquisition of missing psychic structures. Says Ornstein, "acceptance of the remobilized archaic needs in the transference. . . and the two steps in the interpretive process, understanding and explaining, are the vehicles of cure." The aim of such a treatment, he says, is "belated structure building"; "the capacity to find an em-

pathically responsive selfobject milieu post-analytically . . . characterizes the essence of a psychoanalytic cure." (P. M. and A.R.)

[P]sychoanalysis has hardly yet scratched the surface of
the fascinating mystery of man.
　　—Heinz Kohut, "Introspection, Empathy and the
　　　　　　　　Semicircle of Mental Health"

Every psychoanalytic theory has been suffused with its originator's particular image of man and woman—his or her conception of the human
condition. This image has two separate components from two separate
sources, which later coalesce into one firmly held Weltanschauung. One
component appears to have preexisted in the theoretician's mind, having
been built up throughout life, prior to psychoanalytic experience and
knowledge, decisively determining the direction of later theorizing. The
influence of preexisting assumptions is clearly discernible in each theoretician's basic hypotheses, regardless of the usual insistence on the
purely empirical origin of the clinical-theoretical enterprise of psychoanalysis. The initial formulation of each theory already bears the imprint
of the originator's preexisting and frequently hidden assumptions about
the human condition. The other component emerges in the unfolding and
continued refinement of the theory itself, on the basis of expanding clinical experience, which usually enlarges and buttresses these preexisting
assumptions and vice versa. It follows that each psychoanalytic system
embodies its originator's preexisting, direction-giving, personal views as
well as those that later emerge from the evolving theory itself.

We who adopt any of these theories also gravitate in part toward the
one that embodies *our* preferred vision of the human condition.

Because these deeply ingrained personal views readily become amalgamated with our theory-based assumptions about human nature, both remain unexamined. We tend to accept our personal views, once they become amalgamated with our theories, as "scientific facts." Thus, our outlook on man (and woman), our Weltanschauung or worldview, our
assumptions about what our abiding human characteristics are across cultures and across the ages, become solidified. And this solidified worldview
inevitably affects all we think and do as [psychoanalysts].

(Ornstein, 1993a, p. 194)

So fundamental and direction-giving has each theoretician's preconception been, so far-reaching the impact of their respective amalgamated images of the human condition on both theory and clinical practice that it is a veritable puzzle why there has been such scant attention paid to the exploration of the implicit or explicit assumptions about human nature in the various psychoanalytic theories.[1]

My task, then, in this chapter is to present Heinz Kohut's image of the essential nature of man, as this has emerged in his writings and in my prior considerations of this issue (Kohut, 1971, 1977, 1979, 1980, 1981, 1984, 1985; Ornstein, 1978, 1983, 1990, 1993a), amplified by other relevant works (especially those of Tolpin, 1980; Kriegman, 1988, 1990; Kriegman and Slavin, 1989, 1990; Slavin and Kriegman, 1992). I shall then connect this image—as Kohut himself had done—with the nature of individual psychopathology as well as the psychoanalytic curative process that is correlated with it.

Weltanschauung in Psychoanalytic Theories

It might be best to begin with the statement that Kohut considered psychoanalysis an empirical science, just as Freud did.[2] While Kohut fully embraced the scientific worldview just as Freud had done, he did not follow Freud's insistence that psychoanalysis did not have—and did not need to have—its own Weltanschauung. Kohut considered that Freud's attitude expressed unacknowledged value judgments, that had been masquerading as value-neutral theory, (supposedly) based entirely on the empirical data of the analytic treatment experience, fused with the (supposedly) value-neutral "scientific worldview."

Whether psychoanalysis did or did not need its own Weltanschauung is irrelevant, since willy-nilly each of its multiple variants inevitably appears to have a compelling—albeit often unrecognized or disavowed—built-in worldview. The issue is only that we need to become aware of what this built-in worldview is, make it explicit, and study its impact on theory building and clinical practice. Kohut explicitly recognized that his version of psychoanalysis contained a view of the human condition that drastically differed from Freud's implicit, unacknowledged, value-laden view. Kohut went so far as to claim that his conception of the nature of man and woman was one of the most significant distinguishing features of his self psychology—a distinguishing feature that in itself (aside from other characteristics of his theory) set it apart from other psychoanalytic theories. It was this view, he maintained, that precluded self psychology's integration with other psychoanalytic theories (Kohut, 1980, pp. 474–82).

Because of the importance of the issue of integration of theories (and the controversy that surrounds such endeavors—see, for example, Shane and Shane, 1980; Tolpin, 1980; Pine, 1990), a general comment about integration and Kohut's own statement in this regard should be offered, as a prelude to the discussion of his conception of the image of man and woman and its clinical and theoretical consequences.

Some Obstacles to an Integration of Psychoanalytic Theories

A decisive obstacle to an integration of the various psychoanalytic theories lies in the very nature of theoretical systems. Each theory claims to offer a comprehensive account of its empirical data, and its specific concepts make sense only in the context of the whole system. The data themselves and the concepts they give rise to are method- and context-bound. It is therefore impossible to export such concepts (based on different observational methods) into the foreign territory of another theoretical system and place them into this new context without drastically altering their meaning and significance. Another way of saying this is that "translation is impossible between different theories" (Goldberg, 1988, p. 32).[3] Furthermore, theories are inherently antagonistic to each other, as depicted by Kuhn (1962), and their proponents fight for their supremacy in the quest to make their own theory the leading paradigm of their respective fields.[4]

Already on these accounts, then, theories are ultimately unintegratable—even if to many the integration of theories appears desirable (for example, Shane and Shane, 1980), possible, and necessary (for example, Pine, 1990). Attempts to force such integration have thus far been without discernible success or demonstrable benefit. Since no theory accounts for all observed facts in any one area—theories are notoriously "underdetermined" (Gedo and Goldberg, 1973; Goldberg, 1988; Hesse, 1978)—instead of trying to integrate them, we should expect each theory to account independently for most of the hitherto observed facts in the field. The question will then remain, which of the theories demonstrate a more encompassing explanatory power and a higher heuristic potential? By no means is this an easy decision. Meanwhile, registering what the theory does not seem to explain, that is, registering the "anomalies" as they multiply (Kuhn, 1962), is what will spark further progress within each theoretical system, ultimately leading to a new paradigm.

Kohut, however, focused on a different set of obstacles in the way of integrating the "findings, concepts and theories [of self psychology] with those of other modern schools [of psychoanalysis, which he was challenged to consider]. . . . in particular with those of Mahler and Winnicott" (Kohut, 1980, p. 474). It was his impression—right or wrong from our current perspective—that

> however valid and important their findings and insights [referring to Mahler and Winnicott], they focus on circumscribed periods of individual development and, with the exception of certain applications in pathography (see for example, Lynch, 1979) their work does not furnish us, as does classical analysis and self psychology, with *a broad concept of man that would illuminate human pursuits and human fate "beyond the bounds of the basic rule"* [meaning outside the confines of the psychoanalytic situation].   (1980, p. 475, italics added)

Although this objection alone would not yet be insurmountable, instead of accepting the idea of integration, Kohut strongly favored the cross-fertilization of "genetic data obtained by reconstruction from the analyses of adults and the findings obtained by psychoanalytically sophisticated child observers and child analysts." He insisted on the fact that for this cross-fertilization "to be carried out successfully, i.e., in order that it eventuate in significant results, the basic stance of the child observer and those who reconstruct childhood experience via the analysis of transferences must be compatible" (1980, p. 475, italics added). Kohut was referring here to the use of the observational method of empathy, which, if systematically used by psychoanalysts and child observers alike, would make their data more compatible and cross-fertilization more successful.

Focusing on what he considered the "overriding" or "real" obstacle to the integration of the findings of self psychology with those obtained by other methods, Kohut began with two telling anecdotes. In the late 1960s Otto Kernberg asked Kohut what he thought was the difference between his work and Kohut's. Kohut answered that Kernberg "looked on narcissism as *in essence pathological* and he, Kohut, looked on it as *in essence healthy*" (1980, p. 477, italics added). Around the same time, Mahler asked Kohut a similar question in a letter. Kohut responded to her by saying that "we were digging tunnels from different directions into the same area of the mountain" (p. 477). These replies were still correct, Kohut maintained a decade or so later, but he could no longer give such short and simple answers to the same kinds of questions, since he now considered the differences between his own and Kernberg's as well as Mahler's ideas much more basic.

On later reflection, he did not consider his earlier responses to Kernberg and Mahler as representing "unbridgeable obstacles blocking . . . integration." The bottom line regarding the impossibility of integration, *"the unbridgeable obstacle . . . is the basically different outlook regarding the scientific evaluation of the nature of man and the significance of his unrolling life"* (1980, p. 478, italics added). This concise statement underscores the central importance Kohut attributed to his view of "the nature of man" and the significance of the unrolling of each human being's life-plan, basic design, or program laid down in the nuclear self—that is, the fate of this inner design throughout "the curve of life" (p. 480).

Kohut expressed this unbridgeable obstacle once more in relation to the suggestion that self psychology integrate the findings of the mother-child observers: "[T]he differences between these two outlooks are basic and . . . they are of such magnitude that we would have to demand from either the other schools of thought or from self psychology the relinquishment of the central value system that determines the content of scientific observation and the significance assigned to the data" (1980, p. 481).

In this context, as well as dispersed throughout his writings, Kohut spells out his different outlook—to which we should now turn.

Kohut's Conception of the Human Condition

A description of Kohut's image of man and woman shall be based here on three sources in his writings: (1) his explicit statements of his views; (2) what various aspects of his theory reveal; and finally, (3) what his clinical reports convey.[5]

To begin, let us briefly juxtapose Freud's basic premise to that of Kohut's for a quick comparison and contrast, in order to show that each of these premises already embodies the foundation of a more comprehensive view of the human condition.[6] This more comprehensive view will emerge here later along with the fuller articulation of the theory beyond its basic premises. The choice of one or the other of these premises has to be made (and there are obviously more than these two to choose from); the choice cannot be evaded and it cannot be made on scientific grounds alone; it is guided by an implicit, a priori worldview, as mentioned earlier, which then becomes imperceptibly amalgamated to the evolving theory and viewed as intrinsically a part of it.

The Basic Premises

Schematically put, Freud's basic (axiomatic) premise is as follows: The infant is born with the innate propensity for

> incestuous lustfulness, pleasure seeking and murderous wishes as primary and basic, [and these are from the beginning] on a collision course with the culture and society [represented by the caregivers] into which the human infant has to be civilized. . . . This taming, controlling and proper channeling of the drives occurs against the infant's and child's will and selfish interests. The results are at best an acquisition of a thin veneer of civilization that can, and frequently does, easily peel off, laying bare the original lustfulness and bestiality beneath. . . . to restate . . . [it] in theoretical terms . . . the human infant born as a "bundle of drives" evokes the caregiver's efforts at curbing, controlling and channeling these drives. This leads inevitably to conflicts between the drives and the representatives of culture. Conflict is thus built into the mental apparatus from the very outset and culminates in the prototypically conflict-ridden Oedipus complex. From then on this conflict pervades every human activity in health and disease (Ornstein, 1993a, p. 198)

Schematically put, Kohut's basic (axiomatic) premise, his fundamental hypothesis, is as follows:

> [T]he human infant arrives into this world preadapted— we might now say "hard-wired"—for the capacity to elicit the needed responses from its surroundings. Hence [the infant's] primary need is for connection and for response. . . . To express this in theoretical terms, the infant is born, with all of its biological givens, into a "self-selfobject matrix" in which an empathically responsive milieu will provide physically, nutritionally, and emotionally what it needs for its prolonged development. The infant is thus a social being to begin with, reaching out actively to a harmonious and receptive rather than to an antagonistic and coercively civilizing environ-

ment. So there is no built-in primary pathogenic conflict in the human psyche. However, conflict is inevitable because the milieu can never respond
perfectly to the needs of a budding self. Hence, there will always be conflict. Such conflict becomes pathogenic or pathological, however, only if, in
response to empathic failures of the selfobject milieu, the development and
consolidation of the self is thwarted. (Ornstein, 1993a, p. 200)

The difference is immediately obvious: Freud's human infant is born
into an antagonistic environment, with which it is immediately in conflict
and which it has to oppose.

Freud's hypothesis derives psychic development from the clash of forces of
the primary drives with the socializing demands of the parental imagoes as
the earliest representatives of the social environment. A psyche that is conceived as developing out of such a matrix is *by definition*, full of *primary*
conflicts. Thus, the notion of psychoanalysis as a conflict psychology *par
excellence* is thereby built into our view of human development. (Ornstein,
1983, p. 357)

In stark contrast, Kohut's human infant is born into a potentially
harmonious, empathic milieu; there is an assumed "fit" between the infant and its environment, rather than a built-in antagonism to begin
with:

Kohut's hypothesis derives psychic development from within the self-selfobject matrix, where the relation between the rudimentary self and its empathic selfobject constitutes the primal unit of psychological experience
[rather than the drives and their vicissitudes]. . . . Thus, there is here, *by definition*, no built-in primary conflict in the psyche. Traumatic disruptions,
on the other hand, lead to defects or deficits in structure building, which,
in turn, lead to *secondary* conflicts. (Ornstein, 1983, pp. 357–58)

We should now follow the evolution of Kohut's theory beyond his
basic premise in order to gain a fuller picture of his version of the human
condition, and to identify the central problems that each individual
struggles with in the larger social context.

Further Development

In keeping with his core developmental hypothesis, Kohut's human infant actively strives for connection to its selfobject-surround in order to
attain a cohesive, vital, and harmonious nuclear self by means of the responsiveness to the needs of its budding self. Based on endowment (in-

nate skills and talents) and the prideful, enthusiastic, affirming responses of the caregivers (mirroring selfobjects) as well as the availability of others to look up to and partake of their strengths (idealized selfobjects), a unique inner program or life-plan will develop and become an essential part of this cohesive and vital nuclear self. A central task of early development will thus be the acquisition of this cohesiveness, vitality, and inner program or blueprint-for-life. Once these are attained and reasonably consolidated, the individual's struggle will involve the maintenance of the cohesiveness and vitality of the self as well as the living out or the fulfillment of the inner program of the nuclear self. In fact, Kohut defines mental health as the capacity to employ (at least in one sector of the personality) one's innate skills and talents self-assertively, in keeping with one's ideals and values. A central task of later development (persisting throughout life) will thus be the maintenance of the cohesiveness of the self and the implementation of this life-plan—to become what we are in the deepest layers of our being.

Since all of personality development and later life occurs in a self-selfobject milieu and is fundamentally influenced by it, self psychology focuses on the state of the self (its cohesiveness and vitality or its fragmentation and depletion, and so forth) in its relatedness to others and sees *this* as the core issue in human existence.[7] Kohut expressed this in a powerful language of metaphors:

> In the view of self psychology, man lives in a matrix of selfobjects from birth to death. He needs selfobjects for his psychological survival, just as he needs oxygen in his environment throughout life for physiological survival. Certainly the individual is exposed to the anxiety and guilt of unsolvable conflict and to the miseries of lowered self-esteem following the realization that he has failed to reach his aims or live up to his ideals. But so long as he feels that he is surrounded by selfobjects and feels reassured by their presence—either by their direct responses to him or, on the basis of past experiences, via his confidence in their lasting concern—even conflict, failure and defeat will not destroy his self, however great his suffering may be. Self psychology does not see the essence of man's development as a move from dependence to independence, from merger to autonomy, or even as a move from no-self to self. We do not disregard man's anxieties and depressions, in infancy, in adulthood, and when face to face with death. And while we certainly do not ignore man's greed and lust and his destructive rage, *we see them not as primary givens but as secondary phenomena due to disturbances in the self-selfobject unit.*
>
> (Kohut, 1980, pp. 478–79, italics added)

There are, of course, innumerable variations and details of this struggle depicted by Kohut, which make up the picture of man and woman in their social context. We can only hint at the richness and variety of this struggle by a schematic reference to the development of the self as Kohut envisaged this on the basis of his reconstructions from the working through of the various selfobject transferences.

In one line of development the "grandiose self" (an archaic configuration) becomes progressively transformed through the affirming, validating, and admiring responses of the "mirroring selfobject" into unencumbered, healthy self-assertiveness—representing one pole of the bipolar self. In this sector of the personality self-esteem and its regulation, as well as the enjoyment of one's physical and mental capacities and the unhindered pursuit of one's goals and purposes, will signal a felicitous structuralization of the self.

In another line of development the "idealized parental imago" (an archaic configuration) becomes progressively transformed, in response to the availability of idealizable others ("idealized selfobjects") and the slow, step-wise, phase-appropriate disillusionment in them, into internalized values and ideals—representing the other pole of the bipolar self. In this sector of the personality the capacity for self-calming and self-soothing, the channeling of one's drive-needs; the containment of affects, and the capacity to attach oneself to higher causes and ideals with sustained enthusiasm will signal a felicitous structuralization of the self.

In still another line of development the "twinship-" or "alterego-selfobjects" (i.e., those others we experience as similar to ourselves, kindred souls—and by whom we feel supported in becoming a part of the human community) create the preconditions for the unfolding of talents and skills. Their unhindered functional availability to the self will signal a felicitous structuralization in this sector of the personality.

Kohut spelled out further some of the broader implications of his developmental theory, first by paraphrasing M. Tolpin and then adding his own comment:

> "Kohut's baby" as Marian Tolpin put it humorously . . . is not dependent, clinging or weak, but independent, assertive, strong—it is psychologically complete so long as it breathes the psychological oxygen provided by contact with empathically responsive selfobjects, and in this respect, it is no different from the adult who is complete, independent, and strong only as long as he feels responded to.

If we accept the presence of a milieu of responsive selfobjects as a necessary precondition of psychological life, if, moreover, we acknowledge the fact that the healthy, normal human being is psychologically constituted in such a way that he survives only in such a milieu and is equipped with the ability to search for and find such a milieu, *then our outlook on man—on his psychopathology and on his behavior in the social and historical arena—will be determined by this basic assumption.*

(Kohut, 1980, pp. 481–82, italics added)

It is important to note here that Kohut no longer uses the hypothesis of a "psychosexual development" (based on the vicissitudes of the sexual and later also of the aggressive drive) to conceive of the attainment of health or disease. He replaced this classic core assumption of development with the idea that it is the availability of mirroring, idealized, and alter-ego or twinship selfobjects—the requisite phase-appropriate *experiences* with them—that are the *sine qua non* of normal development, the basic nutrients for the development of the self.[8]

This drastically altered developmental hypothesis puts its distinctive stamp on what emerges as Kohut's view of the human condition. This view will come into sharper relief as we consider development beyond the phase of the attainment of the cohesiveness and consolidation of the nuclear self (i.e., the nuclear self-assertive ambitions, nuclear internalized values and ideals, and nuclear skills and talents). Cohesiveness and consolidation are prerequisites for entering the oedipal phase of development with a reasonable structural intactness, which provides the capacity to master the ubiquitous oedipal conflicts.

The Oedipus Complex

"[T]he presence of a firm self is a precondition for the experience of the Oedipus complex. Unless the child sees himself as a delimited, abiding, independent center of initiative, he is unable to experience the object-instinctual desires that lead to the conflicts and secondary adaptations of the oedipal period." (Kohut, 1977, p. 227). Kohut's view of the oedipal phase and the Oedipus complex (1977, pp. 220–48; 1981, pp. 553–56) is most revealing of his vision of the human condition and is in sharp contrast to that of Freud's.

[An oedipal] conflict either can or cannot be resolved, depending on the consolidation of the self. A cohesive, vital, vigorous self can deal with its conflicts successfully. An enfeebled, fragmentation-prone, or fragmented self cannot. This determines the nature of the oedipal experience. The child with a cohesive self will enter the oedipal period exhilarated with the new challenges in spite of guilt, anxiety, and conflict. The normal oedipal experience is not a violent, conflict-ridden phase as long as the oedipal selfobjects respond to the child's oedipal longings and hostilities with acceptance and empathic understanding rather than seductively or punitively. Such an oedipal experience further consolidates the male and female self. Thus it is the harmony between the self and its selfobject milieu that determines the outcome. Both the dark side and the bright side of the personality develop from innate givens within an essentially empathic or unempathic self-self-object matrix.

There is one additional striking difference [in Kohut's conceptualization as compared to Freud's]. It is the child's innate potentialities, emerging talents, and skills that are responded to. The responses of the selfobject-milieu to the child's own potentialities (as opposed to the caregiver's ideas of what the child ought to be like) will safeguard the successful unfolding of the child's own talents and skills. What develops, develops, therefore, from within. The environment facilitates this development [by providing the necessary emotional nutrients] or thwarts it [by not being able to provide them]. Personality features are therefore not mainly the result of a civilizing force; not an imposition from without—as Freud thought—that the child has to fight off tooth and nail; not developments born out of a natural antagonism but out of a natural fit. There will, of course, be antagonisms, but those will be secondary, even if extremely important.

(Ornstein, 1993a, p. 200)

While the oedipal period with its experiential content remains important in Kohut's view, it is no longer as pivotal as it was in Freud's conceptualization. For Kohut, the oedipal *conflicts* are universal, not the Oedipus *complex*, since he considers the latter already a manifestation of a failed self-selfobject relation. In other words, the Oedipus complex is the expression of an underlying self-pathology. What we see as the drama of the Oedipus complex, the various forms of incestuous lustfulness and hostility in symptom- and character-formation, are often desperate efforts at self-healing rather than efforts at holding on to infantile pleasures and destructiveness instead of renouncing them.

Kohut, in connection with comparing and contrasting his view of the Oedipus complex with the classical view, introduced the concepts of pleasure-seeking "Guilty Man" to characterize the classical view and fulfillment-seeking "Tragic Man" to characterize the view of self psychology. He thus postulates "two major aspects of the psychological nature of man." This is how he put it:

> [V]iewed from a broad perspective, man's functioning should be seen as aiming in two directions. I identify these by speaking of *Guilty Man* if the aim is directed toward the activity of his drives and of *Tragic Man* if the aims are toward the fulfillment of the self. . . . Guilty Man lives within the pleasure principle; he attempts to satisfy his pleasure-seeking drives, to lessen the tensions that arise in his erogenous zones. The fact that man, not only because of environmental pressure, but especially as the result of inner conflict, is often unable to achieve his goals in this area, prompted me to designate him Guilty Man when he is seen in this context. . . . Tragic Man, on the other hand, seeks to express the pattern of his nuclear self; his endeavors lie beyond the pleasure principle. Here, too, the undeniable fact that man's failures overshadow his successes prompted me to designate this aspect of man negatively as Tragic Man rather than "self-expressive" or "creative man".   (Kohut, 1977, pp. 132–33)

In another context he says,

> [Freud's is] a conception of man as endowed with either a well functioning or malfunctioning psychic apparatus—of man spurred on by his drives and shackled by castration anxiety and guilt. It is . . . a concept that . . . does adequate justice to the problems of the structural neuroses, and, *in the broad arena of societal and historical development, encompasses the conflicts of Guilty Man.*   (Kohut, 1977, p. 233, italics added)

Kohut valued classic metapsychology as having "illuminated and explained a vast area of human psychic life that had heretofore been covered by darkness. . . . [but it] left a significant and important layer of human experience essentially untouched" (1977, p. 238). Applying the understanding of Guilty Man to the understanding of this other layer of experience, that of Tragic Man, remained unsuccessful.

> Classical theory cannot illuminate the essence of fractured, enfeebled, discontinuous human existence: it cannot explain the essence of the schizophrenic fragmentation, the struggle of the patient who suffers from a narcissistic personality disorder to reassemble himself, the despair—the guiltless despair, I stress—of those who in late middle age discover that the basic pattern of their self as laid down in their nuclear ambitions and ideals has not been realized. Dynamic-structural metapsychology does not do justice to these problems of man, cannot encompass the problems of Tragic Man.
>   (1977, p. 238)

In a further comparison and contrast Kohut focuses on the fact that in classical analysis the Oedipus complex is par excellence the nucleus of the neurosis, whereas in self psychology the oedipal phase—"whether or not it leaves the individual beset by guilt and prone to neurosis—is the matrix in which important contribution to the firming up of the independent self takes place, enabling it to follow its own pattern with greater security than before" (1977, p. 238-39).

Kohut clearly states that contrasting the classical view with that of self psychology does not imply a pessimistic versus an optimistic philosophy; either position could stress the positive or the negative aspects. However, "the emphasis in self psychology is . . . more on the growth-promoting aspects of this [oedipal] period and in classical conflict psychology more on the pathogenic ones" (1977, p. 239).

Kohut then elaborates on the fact that self psychology's focus is drawn to the positive aspects of the oedipal period, which adds a significant dimension to Kohut's view of the human condition.

> True enough, the classical theory is fully compatible with an appreciation of the positive features of the oedipal experience. But it sees the positive qualities that the psychic apparatus acquires at that period as the results of the oedipal experience [its possible felicitous outcome, namely, the resolution of the Oedipus complex], not as a primary intrinsic aspect of the experience itself. (1977, p. 229, italics added)

Kohut describes the "primary intrinsic aspect" of the normal oedipal experience itself in moving words:

> [T]he normal child's oedipal experiences—however intense the desire for the heterogenital parent, however serious the narcissistic injuries at recognizing the impossibility of their fulfillment; however intense the competition with the homogenital parent, and however paralyzing the correlated castration anxiety—contain, from the beginning and persisting throughout, an admixture of deep joy that, while unrelated to the content of the Oedipus complex in the traditional sense, is of the utmost developmental significance within the framework of the psychology of the self. (1977, p. 236)

Kohut sees the fate of oedipal conflicts as closely tied to parental responses. The joy he discovered in the oedipal child (by reconstructing from the working through of his adult patients' selfobject transferences)

> is fed from two sources . . . [although in the child this is] essentially a unitary experience . . . [from](1) the child's inner awareness of a significant forward move into a psychological realm of new and exciting experiences,

and—of even greater importance—(2) his participation in the glow of pride and joy that emanates from the parental selfobjects despite—indeed, also because of—their recognition of the content of their child's oedipal desires.   (1977, p. 236)

Kohut was aware of the complexities and extreme variability of parental responses; his remark on "optimal parents" or rather "optimally failing parents" is of interest: "[Such parents] are people who, despite their stimulation by and competition with the rising generation are also sufficiently in touch with the pulse of life, accept themselves sufficiently as transient participants in the ongoing stream of life, to be able to experience the growth of the next generation with unforced nondefensive joy" (1977, p. 237).

Intergenerational Relations: Odysseus versus Oedipus

Kohut recognized the ubiquitous occurrence of intergenerational strife (as an expression of the Oedipus complex), but he interpreted its *significance* very differently, in keeping with his new view of the nature of the oedipal experience and of the Oedipus complex.

> Traditional analysis believes that man's essential nature is comprehensively defined when he is seen as *"Guilty Man,"* as man in hopeless conflict between the drives . . . that spring from the biological bedrock of homo natura [Freud's view of man in nature] and the civilizing influences emanating from the social environment as embodied in the superego. Self psychology believes that man's essence is defined when seen as a self and that homo psychologicus [as contrasted with homo natura] is, on the deepest level, *"Tragic Man,"* attempting, and never quite succeeding, to realize the program laid down in his depth during the span of life.   (1977, p. 558)

Kohut ascribes the quasi-"magical," persistent hold on us of the oedipal narrative to Freud's "great ability to mythologize the key concepts of his scientific system" (1977, p. 559) and thereby implant them firmly into our Western minds. There are two ways to counter the entrenched view, Kohut suggests. One is a logical but weak argument; the other is a bit of a "countermagic," another myth; supposedly the stronger argument. Logic would dictate that a reinterpretation of the Oedipus myth would undermine Freud's view, in that the story begins not with Oedipus's lusting for his mother and wanting to murder his father, but with his parents' rejection and abandonment of him. This recognition of the full story has been around for a long time, barely making a dent in the firmness with which the Freudian narrative dominates psychoanalysis and the wider Western culture. Kohut's "countermagic" is derived from the story told by Homer, according to which Odysseus is a "striving resourceful man, attempting to unfold his innermost self, battling against external and internal obstacles to its unfolding; and warmly committed to the next generation, the son in whose unfolding and growth he joyfully participates—thus experiencing man's deepest and most central joy, that of being a link in the chain of generations" (1977, p. 561).

The essence of the story, as Kohut retells it, is this: The Greeks were preparing for the Trojan War and drafted all the chieftains with their men, ships, and supplies. Odysseus, in the prime of his life, with a young wife and an infant son, refused to join. A delegation sent by the Greek states came to see him. He faked insanity by plowing his land with an ox and an ass yoked together and flinging salt over his shoulder into the furrows with a silly, conically shaped hat on his head. He clearly behaved as if he had taken leave of his senses. But one of the visitors suspected foul play and picked up Odysseus's infant son, Telemachus and threw him in front of the plow. Odysseus, without the slightest hesitation, made a semicircle around the child with his plow to avoid hurting him. The delegation immediately concluded that Odysseus was sane.

Kohut insists that the story of Odysseus and Telemachus portrays a healthy father's primary wish to protect the son, while Laius's and Oedipus's story portrays an already disturbed, pathological relationship.[9] What, then, is psychopathology from a self psychological perspective?

Kohut's Conception of the Nature of Psychopathology

For Kohut, assumptions regarding normal development (as reconstructed from the working through process of analysis and correlated with the findings of modern mother-child observations) lead directly to his conception of the nature of psychopathology. Endowment, coupled with the vicissitudes of the infant's and child's experiences in the selfobject milieu, determines the nature and extent of the adult's later psychopathology. Traumatic impact is not restricted to early life; it can and does occur with later traumata as well. It is the unavailability or unreliable and inconsistent availability of selfobject experiences (at times coupled with actively inflicted traumata to the infant or child) that will be responsible for the specific defects or deficits in the self. Defects and deficits in the functioning of the self and the inevitable massive defensive structures erected to protect a thus enfeebled and fragmentation-prone self constitute the bases of the patient's psychopathology.

In the realm of self-assertive ambitions the inadequately or inconsistently mirrored self will suffer from low self-esteem, a lack of capacity for its regulation, and an inability to enjoy mental or physical activities. Such a self will be blocked in pursuing its goals and purposes; it will feel "empty." Pervasive defensiveness will lead to massive inhibition, emotional withdrawal, social isolation due to an extreme sensitivity to slights, lack of initiative for fear of failure and criticism, and many other problems. Free pursuit of any activity is impossible if one constantly expects to be foiled.

In the realm of values and ideals, the unavailability of idealizable selfobjects or their massive and traumatic de-idealization leaves the person without the capacity to withstand being buffeted by ever-present daily injuries to self-esteem. The person is left with little ability to rebound from such experiences, and hence suffers from chronic anxiety and depression. Affect regulation, its free expression or its appropriate containment, are both impaired; there is a marked incapacity for self-soothing and self-calming; the ability to turn outward, toward higher ideals, becomes impossible when the self is preoccupied with its own survival. Disintegration anxiety is the deepest central threat to the self.

When skills and talents did not have an opportunity to unfold during development or were traumatically stunted, the individual will be deprived of self-esteem restoring capacities through performance of any of its physical or mental functions that may engender self-approval as well as expressions of creativity. Such individuals will take this state of affairs as proof of their unworthiness and inferiority.

The essential point here is that these different clusters of disturbances will inevitably lead to secondary conflicts, further disabling and often paralyzing the self. Manifest passivity, severe inhibition, and lack of initiative are frequently based on the underlying deficits just described. Only the development of one of the selfobject transferences will disclose the specific nature of the deficit, its pathogenesis and treatability.

Here, "real events" (as they were perceived by the child), that is, lived experiences and not drive-related fantasies, are at the root of psychopathology. Of course, these experiences do lead to fantasies, which exert their impact on the manifestations of psychopathology. The psychoanalytic treatment principles and the processes that develop in the course of analysis can never remain focused on the "real events." They have to proceed to the patient's subjective experience of those events. Whatever actual events occurred in the patient's infancy and childhood cannot be erased from the patient's past, but analyst and patient together can rework and more accurately rewrite the experiencing of that past in the present.

What kind of psychoanalytic curative process did Kohut envision for these deficit-based, rather than primarily conflict-based, disorders of the self?

Kohut's Conception of the Curative Process in Psychoanalysis

Kohut's portrayals of healthy development and psychopathology reveal a tight, logical connection between them and an equally tight and logical connection of both to the curative process. The derailment or arrest of healthy development can occur at two junctures. The first one is at the point of the attainment of the cohesiveness and vitality of the nuclear self and the simultaneous acquisition of its basic-program or life-plan (as described earlier). The lack of early mirroring, the unavailability of idealizable caretakers, and the lack of wholesome twinship experiences lead to basic structural defects in the bipolar self or in the development of skills and talents, including the inadequate laying down of its nuclear program. The second is at the point where basic structuralization is attained, and the self may no longer be as enfeeblement- and fragmentation-prone as it had been before. However, it may now become encumbered in its ability to fulfill its basic design or nuclear program, which requires a continued empathic milieu for its unfolding. It is at this second point that the parent's seductive and/or punitive responses to the child's budding oedipal wishes may turn into an unresolved Oedipus complex. This then interferes with the free and unencumbered unfolding of the personality. But even these unresolved oedipal struggles unmistakably contain the ubiquitous self-healing efforts self psychology sees in every human being.

Kohut described the nature of psychoanalytic cure very much in keeping with what he considered to be the essence of psychological health and psychopathology. This is how he put it:

Self psychology holds that self-selfobject relationships form the essence of psychological life from birth to death, that a move from dependence (symbiosis) to independence (autonomy) in the psychological sphere is no more possible than a corresponding move from a life dependent on oxygen to a life independent of it in the biological sphere. The developments that characterize normal psychological life must, in our view, be seen in the changing nature of the relationship between the self and its selfobjects, but not in the self's relinquishment of selfobjects. In particular, developmental advances cannot be understood in terms of the replacement of the selfobjects by love objects or as steps in the move from narcissism to object love.

(Kohut, 1984, p. 47)

In keeping with these ideas, the analytic process is predicated on the remobilization of thwarted needs in the various selfobject transferences. This remobilization regularly occurs against inner resistance: the fear of retraumatization. The patient's psychopathology, however, always expresses, even through the most maladaptive symptoms and behaviors, the urge for belated acquisition of those capacities whose development and unfolding were traumatically thwarted. The patient always reaches out, but this reaching out is often covered over with often difficult to penetrate defensive layers. This may therefore lead to the mistaken view that the patient resists and refuses to relate. Acceptance of the remobilized archaic needs in the transference (however disguised for self-protection) and the two steps in the interpretive process, understanding and explaining, are the vehicles of cure. Optimum frustration[10]—inevitable in the treatment process—leads to belated structure building through "transmuting internalization." Transmuting internalization refers to the belated maturation of archaic inner needs and potentialities and their transformation into abiding psychological funtions (psychic structures).[11] Insight may accompany such a process, precede it, or follow it—but insight is no longer viewed as the main vehicle of cure. Belated structure building accomplishes the "cure." Kohut then went beyond structure building as the ultimate expression of cure by claiming that it is the capacity to find an empathically responsive selfobject milieu post-analytically that characterizes the essence of a psychoanalytic cure.[12]

Having thus far described how Kohut views development, health, illness, and the treatment process, and how this view reveals his conception of the human condition, we should now look at what he considers to be the factors distorting our view.

What May Distort the Psychoanalyst's View of the Human Condition

Kohut (1959 and especially 1981) singled out the biologically understood concept of the "drive" and the sociopsychologically understood
concepts of "dependence" and "adaptation" as having led to an undesirable shift in the essence of analysis, both as theory and as treatment.
In his view these concepts have become "the unacknowledged and un-
questioned total view of the essence of man and the essence of life"
(Kohut, 1981, p. 549). As a result, psychoanalysis has

> become less of a science and more of a moral system, and psychoanalysis
> as therapy has become simultaneously . . . less of a scientific procedure
> based on the elucidation of dynamic and genetic relationships and more an
> educational procedure, aiming at predetermined and thus extraneous
> goals—which, again are unacknowledged and unquestioned—toward
> which the patient is led and which, on the basis of an unacknowledged and
> unquestioned dimension of his transference, the patient tries to reach.
>
> (1981, p. 549)

Kohut added that when "knowledge-values" and "independence-val-
ues" remain unacknowledged, these too distort the analyst's scientific
perception and interfere with his or her ability to allow analysands to develop in accordance with their own nuclear program and destiny.

> I hold the view that these two values have prevented us from recognizing
> the central position of the self and its vicissitudes in man's psychological
> make-up par excellence as concerns the man of our time and his era-spe-
> cific psychopathology. They have prevented us, in other words, from ac-
> knowledging the significance of the innermost program of the self, and the
> importance which the realization or nonrealization of its potential has for
> the individual in deciding whether he feels psychologically ill or whether he
> feels that he is healthy. (1981, p. 551)

In Kohut's view, what emerged from Freudian psychoanalysis was
not—as Freud envisioned—"homo natura" (man as he was in nature)
that is, "a biological unit interacting with its surroundings," but "Guilty
Man," reflecting "a psychological and moral view of man." Kohut also
felt that within "certain strict limits" this explanatory framework was
useful. "But unless it was supplemented by and subordinated to the self
psychological point of view which can put the self into the center of a
psychological view of man, the traditional outlook will be misleading."

Kohut asserts that self psychology has

> freed itself from the distorting view of psychological man espoused by tra-
> ditional analysis because, having accepted the fact that the field-defining
> observational stance of introspection and empathy is *absolute* and indeed
> *axiomatic* it does not pose as biology or psychobiology but accepts itself as
> psychology through and through.
>
> The "biologized" version of psychoanalysis offers us a distorted psycho-
> logical view which will be misleading because it considers a frequently en-
> countered set of pathological phenomena [the Oedipus complex] as consti-
> tuting "normality" and leads thus to a serious misunderstanding of man in
> the therapeutic setting and of man in the arena of history.   (1981, p. 556)

A serious debate about Kohut's view of the human condition and its contrast with the Freudian view has not yet taken place in the psychoanalytic
literature. Evolutionary biologists, on the other hand, have made several
noteworthy, in-depth studies of Kohut's view of human nature in comparison with Freud's, in their various writings (Kriegman, 1988, 1990;
Kriegman and Slavin, 1989, 1990; Slavin and Kriegman, 1992). They
argue that evolutionary biology is a proper external platform from which
to examine psychoanalytic propositions, since in a broader sense biology
is "the study of life" and so is psychoanalysis. They were able to confirm
the validity of some of Kohut's views of human nature from their own independent perspective. Kriegman recognizes the validity of "conflict-free
motivational sources of the human tendency toward empathic union
with others" (Kriegman, 1988, p. 271). Thus, he asserts that self psychology recognizes "a deep emotional wellspring . . . for compassion,
that can give rise to altruistic behavior and that need not—and, Kohut
(1984) argued, cannot—be understood within the context of a drive
based conflict psychology."

Importantly, evolutionary biology also confirms Kohut's notion of a
prideful and joyful parenthood, and Kriegman suggests that "human capacities for compassion and joyful empathic union were shaped by the
selective pressures that created altruism (kin altruism and reciprocal altruism)" (1988, p. 271). "It is the inborn yearning for empathic union
with others, the natural parental tendency to succor the child, and spontaneous compassionate caring that account for the powerfully rewarding
experience that can result from the intimate participation in the maturation and healing of another through a lengthy empathic immersion in the
other's psyche."

Modern evolutionary theory suggests that Kohut's interpretation of the clinical data may have the same degree of biological foundation in the human motivational system as we assume instinctual drives have. Guilty Man, riddled with conflict, may in fact be, as Kohut viewed him, a result of the failure of the human tendency to seek out and maintain empathy-based self-selfobject relationships. The theory of evolution suggests that there is a direct biological basis for this human tendency; that this tendency was selected for because of the adaptive advantage conferred on those who possessed it.

This is just a sample of the far-reaching and intriguing conclusions the evolutionary biologists cited here have been able to formulate in their profound discourse with traditional psychoanalysis and self psychology, greatly enriching any ensuing further dialogue. Self psychology will still have to continue its search with its own method of introspection and empathy and compare and correlate its findings with the boader study of life.

NOTES

1. To my knowledge Kohut was the only psychoanalytic clinician and theoretician who has systematically articulated his own vision of human nature and considered it intrinsic to his self psychology. In addition, he repeatedly compared and contrasted his views with those of Freud. For some notable additional exceptions, see, for instance, Becker, 1969; Dilman, 1983; Kriegman, 1988, 1990; Slavin and Kriegman, 1992; Kriegman and Knight, 1988; Kriegman and Slavin, 1989, 1990; Greenberg and Mitchell, 1983.

2. Kohut was not a "radical empiricist," and his approach fits in well with the modern, constructivist view of reality. For further comments on the nature of self psychology as an empirical science, see Ornstein, 1993b, pp. 9–10.

3. Goldberg has recently shown this by examining the concepts of "part-objects," "transitional objects," and "selfobjects" as to their meaning and respective theoretical position. He concluded that they each belong to such different theoretical contexts and refer to such different observational data that they cannot even remotely be equated with each other, or "translated" into each other (Goldberg, 1988, pp. 33–36)—as this is so often cavalierly attempted.

4. There are many sociocultural, sociopolitical, and individual- and group-narcissistic reasons for the unwillingness or inability to give up one's favored theories even when they are under prolonged siege. The relentless demand for the integration of the new *findings, concepts, and theories* with the older ones (seen as reflecting commendable broad-mindedness) may in no small measure be due also

to the particular, unexamined, and perhaps therefore unyielding worldview embedded in each theory, as this essay proposes.

5. It should be noted here in passing that Kohut mainly spoke of "the image of Man" and of the "human condition" or the "essence of humanness" in his later writings and only occasionally "lapsed" into speaking of "human nature," most likely in order to avoid any semblance of biologizing his psychology or embracing the frequently assumed implication of human nature as universal, fixed, and unchangeable.

6. Proceeding from the basic premises to the more fully articulated theories and to what these reveal about each theory's vision of the human condition is not meant to indicate that these have been deductively arrived at. In whatever fashion and sequence they have ultimately emerged, it is now, in retrospect, appropriate to look at their structure and inner logic with the basic premises as their starting point.

7. Because connection and relatedness are preconditions for evoking needed responses for self-development, self psychology is generally grouped with other "relational theories." While this is on the whole correct from a certain perspective, it is also a misleading and inadequate characterization of self psychology. Self psychology, in its essence, is a "structural psychology." Developmentally, connection and relation to archaic selfobjects are in the service of "structure building," that is, the acquisition of the various capacities of the bipolar self. Later on, connection and relation to "mature selfobjects" are in the service of maintaining self-cohesion and living out the self's nuclear program, its blueprint for life. Self psychology's central concern is with the structural intactness or structural deficiencies of the self—not adequately covered by the term "relational psychology."

8. Kohut spoke of "selfobjects"—a neologism for an intrapsychic concept. The term refers to the "self's objects", to how the self experiences its objects. Thus it clearly points to the variety of phase-appropriate experiences of being admired and validated, of being allowed to merge with, or being attached to, an all-knowing, powerful other and being associated with like-minded others, kindred spirits. We clearly need both terms, "selfobjects" and "selfobject experiences," in order to be able to speak of "connecting to" or "evoking from" others what we need. Speaking of selfobjects is often a convenient shorthand for the relevant experiences. Thus the term "selfobject experiences," more prevalent in the literature these days, does not reflect conceptual innovation. It merely reflects at times greater linguistic precision and consistency.

9. Kohut, however, was also aware of the fact that Freud's mythology-based rhetoric could not so easily be corrected by the less dramatic Odysseus myth, which (to my knowledge) was never fashioned into the kind of popular dramatic form that the Oedipus myth was by Sophocles and others later. Thus the Oedipus myth appeared to have further shaped and anchored the Weltanschauung of

the receptive mind of Western men and women after Freud made of the myth what he did.

10. Contemporary self psychologists prefer the term "optimum responsiveness." But as long as we retain the word "optimum" in either phrase we are likely to have difficulty in defining what optimum is; the word invites an external observer's judgment and frequently induces us to rationalize all sorts of interventions as necessary. I have always preferred the term "empathic responsiveness," which expresses the analyst's recognition that it is from the patient's perspective alone that we can determine what is needed for an analytic process to develop.

11. The acquisition of psychic structures through transmuting internalization is in sharp contrast to their acquisition through identification. In the latter the characteristics of the parental imagos and others have to be made one's own (introjected); whereas in the former, the child's own intrinsic potentialities will have to be responded to in order for their maturation and internalization to take place. Identification is by now a murky and confusing concept, but in this context it is a sign of inadequate mirroring of the child's own innate capacities; more akin to "identification with the aggressor" than to the normal process of structure building.

12. To avoid the frequent misconception, I should emphatically underline that this analytic endeavor inevitably includes the search for understanding and explanations, hence insight. There is no other analytic approach to convey those necessary key elements of the curative process that are "carried" by the specific relationship between patient and analyst, than through the interpretive process.

REFERENCES

Becker, Ernest. 1969. *Angel in Armor: A Post-Freudian Perspective on the Nature of Man.* New York: George Braziller.

Dilman, Ihlam. 1983. *Freud and Human Nature.* Oxford: Blackwell.

Gedo, John, and Goldberg, Arnold. 1973. *Models of the Mind.* Chicago: University of Chicago Press.

———, ed. 1980. *Advances in Self Psychology.* New York: International Universities Press.

Goldberg, Arnold, 1988. *A Fresh Look at Psychoanalysis: The View from Self Psychology.* Hillsdale, NJ: Analytic Press.

Greenberg, J., and Mitchell, S. 1983. *Object Relations in Psychoanalytic Theory.* Cambridge: Harvard University Press.

Hesse, Mary. 1978. Theory and Value in the Social Sciences. In *Action and Interpretation*, ed. C. Hookeway and P. Petit. Cambridge: Cambridge University Press.

Kohut, Heinz. 1959. Introspection, Empathy, and Psychoanalysis. *Journal of the American Psychoanalytic Association* 8: 567–83.

―――. 1971. *The Analysis of the Self.* New York: International Universities Press.

―――. 1977. *The Restoration of the Self.* New York: International Universities Press.

―――. 1979. The Two Analyses of Mr. Z. In *The Search for the Self*, ed. P. H. Ornstein. Madison, CT: International Universities Press, 1991, vol. 4, pp. 395–446.

―――. 1980. Reflections on Advances in Self Psychology. In *Advances in Self Psychology*, ed. A. Goldberg. New York: International Universities Press, pp. 473–554.

―――. 1981. Introspection, Empathy and the Semicircle of Mental Health. In *The Search for the Self*, ed. P. H. Ornstein. Madison, CT: International Universities Press, 1991, vol. 4, pp. 537–67.

―――. 1984. *How Does Analysis Cure?* Ed. A. Goldberg with P. E. Stepansky. Chicago: University of Chicago Press.

―――. 1985. *Self Psychology and the Humanities: Reflections on a New Psychoanalytic Approach.* Edited with an Introduction by Charles B. Strozier. New York: Norton & Company.

Kriegman, Daniel. 1988. Self Psychology from the Perspective of Evolutionary Biology: Toward a Biological Foundation for Self Psychology. In *Progress in Self Psychology*, ed. A. Goldberg. Hillsdale, NJ: Analytic Press, vol. 3, pp. 253–74.

―――. 1990. Compassion and Altruism in Psychoanalytic Theory: An Evolutionary Analysis of Self Psychology. *Journal of the American Academy of Psychoanalysis* 18:342–67.

Kriegman, Daniel, and Knight, C. 1988. Social Evolution, Psychoanalysis, and Human Nature. *Social Policy* 19:49–55.

Kriegman, Daniel, and Slavin, Malcolm Owen. 1989. The Myth of the Repetition Compulsion: An Evolutionary Biological Analysis. In *Progress in Self Psychology*, ed. A. Goldberg. Hillsdale, NJ: Analytic Press, vol. 5, pp. 209–52.

―――. 1990. On the Resistance to Self Psycholgy: Clues from Evolutionary Biology. In *Progress in Self Psychology*. Hillsdale, NJ: Analytic Press, vol. 6, pp. 217–50.

Kuhn, T. 1962. *The Structure of Scientific Revolutions.* Chicago: University of Chicago Press.

Lynch, David. 1979. *Yeats: The Poetics of the Self.* Chicago: University of Chicago Press.

Ornstein, Paul H. 1978. The Evolution of Heinz Kohut's Psychoanalytic Psychology of the Self. In *The Search for the Self: Selected Writings of Heinz*

Kohut, 1950–1978, ed. Paul H. Ornstein. New York: International Universities Press, vol. 1, pp. 1–106.

———. 1983. Discussion of Papers by Drs. Goldberg, Stolorow and Wallerstein. In *Reflections on Self Psychology,* ed. Joseph D. Lichtenberg and Samual Kaplan. Hillsdale, NJ: Analytic Press, pp. 339–84.

———. 1989. The Fate of the Nuclear Self in the Middle Years. In *New Psychoanalytic Perspectives—The Middle Years,* ed. John M. Oldham and Robert S. Liebert. New Haven: Yale University Press, pp. 27–39.

———. 1990. The Unfolding and Completion of Heinz Kohut's Paradigm of Psychoanalysis. In *The Search for the Self. Selected Writings of Heinz Kohut: 1978–1981,* ed. Paul H. Ornstein. Madison, CT: International Universities Press, vol. 4, pp. 1–82.

———. 1993a. The Clinical Impact of the Psychotherapist's View of Human Nature. *Journal of Psychotherapy Practice and Research* 2:193–204.

———. 1993b. Introduction: Is Self Psychology on a Promising Trajectory? In *The Widening Scope of Self Psychology: Progress in Self Psychology,* ed., Arnold Goldberg. Hillsdale, NJ: Analytic Press, vol. 9, pp. 1–11.

Pine, Fred. 1990. *Drive, Ego, Object, and Self: A Synthesis for Clinical Work.* New York: Basic Books.

Shane, M., and Shane, E. 1980. Psychoanalytic Developmental Theories of the Self: An Integration. In *Advances in Self Psychology,* ed. Arnold Goldberg. New York: International Universities Press, pp. 23–46.

Slavin, Malcolm Owen, and Kriegman, Daniel. 1992. *The Adaptive Design of the Human Psyche: Psychoanalysis, Evolutionary Biology, and the Therapeutic Process.* New York: Guilford.

Tolpin, Marian. 1980. Discussion of "Psychoanalytic Developmental Theories of the Self: An Integration," by Morton Shane and Estelle Shane. In *Advances in Self Psychology,* ed. Arnold Goldberg. New York: International Universities Press, pp. 47–68.

Chapter 10

An Experiential Approach to Interpersonal Psychoanalysis

Warren Wilner

EDITORS' INTRODUCTION

In Warren Wilner's essay we have an interpersonal perspective that is in one way similar to many of the object relations theorists discussed in this book, namely, it puts real and imagined relationships with others at the center of its theorizing. In all the theories that tend to fall under the rubric of a "relational/structural" viewpoint, it is the need to create and sustain relationships that motivates behavior. However, Wilner and others (like Benjamin Wolstein), who are lodged in an experiential interpersonal perspective, give a most interesting "spin" to the broadly conceived relational/structural position by focusing on the phenomenology of immediate experience between two people. In this view, gaining clarity of one's experience and deepening relatedness to others are the goals toward which analysands, and individuals in general, need to strive.

As Wilner points out, the worldview that undergirds such an interpersonal position is that human "nature, which is intimately connected with the fabric of life as well as having a private self of its own, is constituted by the struggle to bring these dual aspects into synchronicity with one another through the quest for whole and integral experience." Whole experience, Wilner's key concept, is experience that is a seamless composite of subjective and objective experience. It is, he says, its own dimension of awareness that is the apprehension of personal self with life as a whole at once. It should be emphasized that, in contrast to Freud, who tended to characterize the individual and culture as in opposition, the experi-

ential interpersonal point of view as articulated by Wilner conceptualizes culture, along with biology, as constitutive of the "unique
self" but not reducible to or separate from them. That is, the self is
not a standardized epiphenomenon of social discourse or biology;
rather, it subsumes both of them in its psychic uniqueness.

Psychopathology, from this point of view, tends to develop when
an individual excludes immediate experience from consciousness.
Such individuals are unable "to bring subjective and objective experience into synchronicity" and cannot therefore undergo whole
experience. These individuals are alienated from the felt immediacy
of their own experience; subjective and objective experience become indirectly and covertly related to each other, fostering a sense
of inner chaos, anxiety, and fear. In other words, one's unique self,
one's psychic center, is undermined and obscured. Such blocking of
one's felt experience frequently occurs in relation to others, especially in the context of increased demands for direct, open, free-
flowing encounter and relatedness.

In terms of psychoanalytic treatment, says Wilner, an experiential interpersonal approach is a system of clinical operations that
promotes understanding and change by bringing about increasing
clarity about one's engagements in life as they are experienced and
conarrated within the interactive, therapeutic context. What makes
interpersonal analysis unique, he claims, is that this procedure is
carried out with minimal introduction of external metaphor such as
a statement about sexual or aggressive drives, the need for proper
structure, the importance of internal or external relationships, or
developmental considerations. Clear and accurate descriptions accomplish for the experiential interpersonalist what interpretation
and metapsychologically based metaphor do for an analyst from
one of the other psychoanalytic approaches.

Interpersonal analysis, suggests Wilner, also differs from other
analytic orientations in its privileging of the reality of events in
treatment. Interpersonal analysts attend to the sequential unfolding
of experience and behavior as they actually occur in sessions for
both patient and analyst; they are interested in the evocation and
explication of behavior and psychic events; and they believe that reacting to, carrying out, and viewing all experience and behavior are
expressive of what is "really" transpiring in the analytic setting.
The goal of treatment, if one can speak of such a thing, is an en-

during sense of psychic center and self-awareness, a fundamental sense of unmediated personal being. Wilner concludes that "whole experience is . . . essential in enabling one to act from within in a way that allows the integrity of world, physically and socially, to be preserved and enhanced, and in making it possible for one to react to world in such a manner that the character of one's self is similarly sustained and enriched." (P. M. and A. R.)

The worldview that informs my interpersonal psychoanalytic position is that man's/woman's nature, which is intimately connected with the fabric of life as well as having a private self of its own, is constituted by the struggle to bring these dual aspects into synchronicity with one another through the quest for whole and integral experience (Wilner, 1982, 1987). Experience, the key concept of this essay, refers to a personal undergoing of a life's events (*Webster's New World Dictionary*, 1964); a happening in the context of the individual's "personness" that is brought to awareness through experience at the same time as he/she becomes cognizant of his/her connection to world as something that extends beyond the boundary of personal self.

In an effort to bring together a phenomenological approach and the psychoanalytic theory of the unconscious, Wolstein (1974) frequently refers to unconscious experience. To make the concept of unconscious experience consistent with the above definition of experience implies that one may undergo a psychic event that impacts on the self and helps connect one with certain aspects of the larger nature of life, but that remains outside awareness. The apprehension of this event as actual experience may have to await an opportunity for conscious realization, which renders this formulation consistent with Wolstein's own that a person's unique self, which is individuated through experience, may have to lie dormant until conditions are safe enough for it to emerge more openly in awareness. My focus in this essay, however, will be on the psychoanalytic undergoing of conscious experience.

The sense of whole or simple experience as pure makes such experience difficult to describe. One is aware of this experience as simply occurring, without volitional action or without an attitude of receptivity appearing to be called for. Nothing stands out. There is only experience. Neither one's own sense of personal being nor the larger nature of life is highlighted in awareness. Nor is subjectively felt experience contrasted from a sense of things as being external to the self. All aspects of experience that may otherwise appear phenomenologically differentiated and contrasted from one another present themselves seamlessly as one within whole experience. Whole experience, as I define it, is, therefore, not unified experience. No separate aspects exist to be unified. Whole experience is instead its own dimension of awareness that is the apprehension of personal self with life as a whole at once. Experience assumes the character of simplicity and wholeness in ordinary life. One observes water falling from the sky at the same time that one feels wet, which is the experience of being in the rain. Objective and subjective experience are present concurrently, in that one knows that it is raining and undergoes the experience of wetness. Were we simply to look at water falling from the sky without also being outside, we would objectively know that it was raining, but we would not be experiencing the wetness of rain. Similarly, if while out-of-doors one suddenly felt wet while having one's head buried in a book, one would subjectively be experiencing wetness. We might then infer that it had begun to rain, but we wouldn't know unless we looked. We might, after all, have gotten wet from the spray of a neighbor's garden hose, or from someone spilling water out of a window above our heads.

The ability to psychoanalytically undergo whole experience is tempered by the great complexity of the analytic experimental field. An analyst's own ability to undergo such experience and his/her further ability to help patients realize whole experience are difficult ends to achieve. However, the significance of whole experience within psychoanalysis, if it can be attained, is, I believe, manifold. Such experience provides a base line against which to discern fragmented experience. In addition, due to the clarity and strength that personal presence infused with whole experience brings, a person is in a better position to be sensitive to how he/she is being affected by events and others in life, as well as more clearly able to discern how he/she is influential in life as well. To experience such reciprocity of effect between self and world is to better learn about and realize both.

In psychoanalysis the interpersonal position provides, I think, a suitable conceptual model for how whole experience in an analytic treatment may be generated. The word "interpersonal" calls attention, first, to the personalizing of experience as it occurs in analysis, and, second, to how the analyst uses his/her own personal experience in engaging a patient.

If "personalized" is taken to mean that aspect of being and becoming the unique person that one is and may continue to become, then this sense of the word is consistent with Wolstein's discussion of how a unique self must undergo a process of individuation—that is, to articulate itself within the context of experiences in life—before an individual can be said truly to become a person. And "personal" here would refer to the significance that experience may be found to have for a person in expressing his/her own unique vision of life, way of putting things together, and individual strivings. In psychological life, personal experience is not automatic. An individual must be willing to be a person in order to undergo potentially transformative personal experience, which may further help him/her become a yet more individuated person. In the absence of such willingness, experience may be little more than fragmentary bits and pieces of objectivistic and subjectivistic awareness connected by inference. The clarity of knowledge that may well derive from joining together personal experience and the awareness of the immanent presence of world would not likely be present.

The second important aspect of the term "interpersonal" concerns the relationship to world. In analysis one is reminded of one's ever-present connectedness to the other, as one who affects oneself, who is engaged as an object of one's psychological attention, and with whom one is joined with in generating potentially fresh psychological experience that may never have been undergone by either before.

The term "interpersonal" may be understood as pointing to the space or psychological field between the persons who are engaging one another as well. The interpersonal analyst is reminded that it is this larger field of potential whole experience of which patient and analyst are part that sometimes enables what could become an intimate psychic engagement between patient and analyst to take place. The presence of this field, as a concept, alerts the analyst to how he or she is being called on "personally" to carry the analysis in the sense of having to rely only on his/her own psychic resources, which may include his/her estimate of patient/psychic resources in order for the analysis to work. The field, as constituted by the patient and analyst together, has a life of its own, much as in the gestalt principle of the whole being greater than the sum of its parts. Consequently, the interpersonal analyst, attuned as he/she would be to the presence of this field as a psychic resource, would be able to treat all experience of whatever nature, seemingly relevant or irrelevant, coherent or incoherent, as arising from this field and as being of potential psychoanalytic significance. One therefore does not have to rely only on that experience that is felt to have been processed. In an extreme reading of the term "interpersonal," as it pertains to this psychic field, one may eventually see how all experience that is undergone may indeed reflect one's person, but then it may be equally true that all such experience may similarly reflect what is nonpersonal as well. This would be consistent with the dual dimensionality of experience as involving both the person and what extends beyond the person as world.

One of the direct implications of this view for doing analytic treatment is that all experience, both fragmentary and whole, that is undergone in the analysis, experience that is therefore understood to arise from the interpersonal field, is considered a function of the analysis. With regard to experience that is of a nonlinear and noncoherent nature, with the concept of an ever-generative interpersonal field, the analyst is sensitized to how additional experience may be generated, which may place such awareness, as well as much of one's previous experience, in a different light. This is an important consideration as it pertains to the development of an experiential interpersonal approach to the treatment. With a conception of such a source of ongoing experience, the analyst becomes aware of a tension between his/her efforts to direct the focus of his/her inquiry in a more linear and goal-directed way, in relation to the natural movement of analytic experience itself, as that which is going on independently of one's efforts. It becomes important, therefore, that an analyst permit experience to play itself out even as he/she searches out particular pathways for psychoanalytic exploration.

These two different analytic functions, which are analogous in ego psychology to the analyst's experiencing and observing egos (Sterba, 1934), may also be seen as paralleling the Eastern and Western ways of engaging experience. Allowing oneself to undergo whatever experience that one might in a nonjudgmental and nondirected way is what is done in meditation (Engler, 1984). However, there is in meditation no examination of content for meaning, and one's reactions to whatever experience one undergoes are not a call to begin directing experience; rather, they are considered to be just other experiences. Experiencing in this fashion is relevant to the position being developed here of psychoanalytic experience being its own dimension of significance without having to be anchored immediately to meaning or causative factors, whether they be considered to inhere inside or outside the person. In the Zen Buddhist philosophical tradition, one is said to ultimately arrive at the realization that both the experiencing self and the world that is being experienced are illusory, constructions of one's mind and without substance of their own, including the mind that is thought to be doing the constructing. The dimension of human experience need not be concerned with the truth or falseness of such experience in relation to an assumed independent external or internal reality. The Western philosophical side of the analyst's functioning would, of course, be reflected by the more directed and focused inquiry and the determinations that the analyst would be undertaking. Interestingly, just as Zen goes to one extreme in using the natural movement of human experience as a call for proclaiming the self and world as illusion, so do psychoanalysts move to the other extreme in using what in analysis is referred to as free association, instead of the natural movement of experience, to affirm how such experience is reflective of essentialistic psychological factors and constellations that are thought to have substantive and enduring psychological presence. The position being taken here is that in addition to the ways one might use experience either to support or to counter the assertion concerning the substantive nature of self and world, the existence of experiencing as a distinct analytic modality is in itself significant and may be undergone as such on its own. Determinations may be made regarding the substantive or nonsubstantive nature of self and world, but from the present perspective these are viewed as ideally arrived at through the effects and process of the analysis, rather than imposed through one's previously held views. The quality of the analytic experience is, therefore, considered to be inseparable from the act of making such determinations. Whole experience in the context of a particular psychoanalysis may yield a very different sense regarding these ontological considerations than experience that is fragmentary, or mostly objective or subjective. It is possible, for example, to experience oneself and the world substantively for compensatory reasons, for example, in order to try to fill in what is experienced to be a deficiency in the actual strength of one's experiences. At the same time, one might also experience such substance as the natural end product of the analytic process. Ultimately, experiencing self and world to be illusory may come about for similar reasons—as a possible compensation for one's being too concretely anchored in reality, or as the result of an organic experience of seeing, for example, how experienced aspects of self and world may be unnecessary psychic constructions that dissolve in the natural flow of self-moving experience, experience that William James has referred to as "sciousness" (Miller, 1987). As with Rothenberg's (1983) discussion of Neils Bohr's work on complementarity in physics, actual life, which experience may to some degree and nature reflect, may be both substantive and nonsubstantive, depending on one's contextual relatedness to it, just as Bohr determined that a phenomenon that appeared capable of being either a particle or a wave could be conceived of as being both at once. The issue of the way different actual modalities of experience may be deeply constitutive of the quality and nature of the psychoanalytic experience that one may undergo has been explored in different ways by various analytic writers (Ogden, 1989; Weedon, 1987; Wilner, 1989).

Subjective and Objective Experience

Common to most ways of studying the nature of experience is its division into subjective and objective aspects, which is related to the interpersonal concept of the analyst being a participant observer within the process of analysis. In a concretistic reading of these two abstractions, I place subjective experience, which commonly means experience that is inwardly felt and not bearing directly on the nature of outside reality, in an interpersonal or field context. Subjective experience then becomes that modality of awareness that arises as a result of one's being *subjected* to some influence. The concept of subjective experience therefore is related to participation and reflects the larger nature of life, since it is being assumed for the sake of conceptual clarity that the subjecting influence or influences that may be evoking this type of experience is or are originating from outside what one would determine to be the boundaries of self. The phenomenology of subjective experience is such that whereas such experience is assumed to be evoked from without, the venue of the experience undergone takes place within the boundaries of self.

In contrast, the concept of objective experience is literally understood to reflect a person's objectives or intended purpose. Contrary to subjective experience, which appears to be beyond one's control, an individual feels that he or she is the author of objective experience. Such objective experience is assumed to originate from within the self, but the locus of the actual experience is outside the boundary of psychological personhood, on the objects of focus. Where subjective experience reflects one's participation in life, objective experience is an outgrowth in psychoanalysis of the analyst's observing function and sense of separate self. Dialectically, self is presupposed in being able to observe other, and may even be said to be constituted by such an act. Subjective experience has the character of movement in that one is vulnerable to further subjecting influence. Objective experience, on the other hand, seeks to establish islands of permanence and stability, which themselves may not immediately have to be subject to outside influence and pressure for change. Objective experience, in essence, declares that something is reality. Subjective experience, on the other hand, reflects the impermanent and contingent nature of life.

It is unusual for people to undergo subjective experience without trying to know why. The proverbial jaded New Yorker, for example, might be said to be capable of hearing an explosion without looking around to see what may have caused it, or a person may be too apathetic or depressed even to think about food, let alone try to eat some, when starting to suffer from hunger pangs. Furthermore, a student or practitioner of an Eastern religion might wish to experience a pure physical sensation in his or her fingers without attending to what it is that he/she might be touching. In contrast, one commonly observes things that one does not wish to subject oneself to. One may not be interested in an event that one finds aversive. On the other hand, one naturally wishes to place oneself in the midst of what looks as though it will be satisfying and enjoyable. As an offshoot of this, although one may not presently experience the actual desired situation, one might be said to be undergoing the "experience of desiring" what may be this objectively apprehended situation or person.

One of the major ways of viewing the field of psychoanalysis concerns itself with how experience may be organized in the mind of an analyst. In the most traditional mode, the analyst objectivistically sees what is assumed to be actually or metaphorically present in the patient's, and perhaps also the analyst's, unconscious in an experience-near sense—their thoughts, feelings and fantasies—and as experience-distant—the state of their psychic apparatuses, selves, internal object worlds, various hermeneutic positions concerning what certain things may mean, and so on. This latter mode of organization is represented primarily by the classical and object relational positions, though it may apply to more metapsychologically based views arising out of interpersonal, broadly relational, and self psychological positions as well (i.e., the dynamisms of the self system, developmental considerations, and the structure of the self).

A second major way of organizing analytic experience involves the analyst's attempts to view as an objective reality the patient's and the analyst's own experience directly. Donnel Stern (1983) looks at the way we formulate unformulated experience; Hoffman (1991) and the social constructivistic school understand experience to be a socially influenced personal construction of an ambiguous and incomplete external reality; and the self psychologically oriented Stolorow and his associates (1987) view experience within psychoanalysis as having no bearing on possible determinations regarding the actual nature of reality. They claim that the significance of experience for psychoanalysis lies solely in what its personal meaning is for the patient. Stern's and Hoffman's positions concern the construction of experience itself, whereas Stolorow et al. attend to the subjective meaning of experience that has already been formed.

A third way of seeing how analytic experience is organized in the analyst's mind is Levenson's (1993) interpersonal position concerning how the data of analysis refer most significantly not to things that are in our minds, such as the relativistic ways we experience things, nor to objectivistic metapsychological "truths" that require mediation and interpretation in order to be brought to light, but to actual and real interpersonal events that are said to be occurring in the treatment room between the patient and the analyst, and to the patient and the analyst in their respective lives.

Hoffman appears to take a position midway between Stolorow's focus on trying to objectivistically view subjective experience and Levenson's attempt to get directly at objective reality. Hoffman asserts that there is a reality, but it is ambiguous as well as unknowable in its totality. One therefore can know only a part of what is out there. All we are said to be able to ascertain are the ways we construct relativistic images of this reality, and the influences, interpersonal and endogenous, upon these constructions. Many of the differences between Hoffman and Levenson are well explicated in two articles in which they challenge one another's positions directly (Hoffman, 1990; Levenson, 1990). Protter (1988) offers a similar classification of analysts' schemas to that outlined above. He refers to existential, textual, and contextual modalities. In contrast, I am referring more to the ways organized experience first appears in the analyst's mind. Protter's focus, as I see it, is to define modalities of knowing as they are primarily determined by the way the analyst defines the analytic situation, whereas I am looking more at what is being experienced with special regard to the relationship between subjectivity and objectivity.

Beyond the ways analytic experience is organized are the metapsychological explanations that concern themselves with how the experience that is being undergone is then accounted for. This is a difficult distinction in actuality to make, since the two areas interpenetrate. Nevertheless, Wolstein (1971) has developed a clear and comprehensive formulation regarding the structure of psychoanalytic inquiry in which he delineates clear distinctions between the empirical, inferential, explanatory, and interpretive functions of the analyst.

Psychopathology

From the present perspective, psychopathology is the individual's inability to bring subjective and objective experience into synchronicity. Subjective and objective experience become instead indirectly and covertly related to each other. This inability to achieve synchronicity is, in turn, related to a person's fundamental inability to undergo whole experience. To loosely paraphrase Baratt (1988), there is a subverting of objective experience by subjective experience, and an attempt to bind subjective experience that may be associative and nonvolitional to organized stable and ostensibly rational objective experience.

The consequent fragmentation of experience often manifests itself in the mistaking of private self for the workings and nature of one's actual participation in life, and to confuse the nature of participation with the life of the self. As Noy (1969) put it, there is an attempt to treat the self as though it were an external object, and to deal with external objects as being capable of fulfilling self experience. I see, for example, Stolorow and his associates as being to focused on self, and relational and classically oriented analysts as overemphasizing the importance, respectively, of the social and biological spheres of one's being.

Psychoanalysts are attentive primarily to objective awareness. They are inclined to use inwardly felt experience in the service of arriving at objective appraisals or "truths," rather than allowing such experience to follow its own course. An analyst's lack of attention to subjectively felt experience interferes with his/her ability to undergo whole experience, which is constituted of what is freely moving as well as stable and phenomenologically real. From the perspective of this essay, such inattentiveness further preempts the possibility of apprehending how one's subjective experience may be a function of the psychological forces present in the immediate clinical context.

An example of an analyst allowing his inwardly felt experience to develop in awareness before placing it in a more cognitive frame is Kernberg's (1975) account of his vivid experience of white bands of light produced by the slats of a Venetian blind in his office, which coincided with his sense that the patient he was with was not a real human being at all. This experience was sufficiently disorienting to impel Kernberg to have a fresh experience about the patient: that she was depersonalizing herself in order to block sexual feelings toward him. This formulation was only one of many that the therapist may have to come up with, but allowing his subjective experience to play itself out did serve to help open up Kernberg's awareness.

An inner experience that proved to be directly linked to an area of interest for a supervisee was reflected in a dream that I had had about Eisenhower the night before I was to see the supervisee. The dream suddenly came to mind while I was with the supervisee, and I decided to tell him about it, despite the fact that he is too young to have been able to be very aware of Eisenhower when the latter was president, nor did I think that he would be very interested in him. It was with surprise that I then heard the supervisee say that he had "an Eisenhower fetish." We went on to discuss my dream and the supervisee's interest in Eisenhower in many ways, including how the Eisenhower theme might be relevant to the patient this therapist was discussing with me.

In actual psychoanalytic experience it is often difficult to distinguish the subjective from the objective. We commonly think of subjective experience as being reflective solely of one's self—thoughts, sensations, feelings, and fantasies that bear on the nature and condition of the self, experiences that are themselves not thought to actually reflect what may be considered outside reality. What is deceptive is that some subjective experiences assume an objectivistic form. For example, an entire reverie may appear in one's mind in which one may be thinking about another person in such-and-such a way, or one may find oneself musing about what one may have to do later. One can argue that such experience, being subjective as it is, does address the needs and strivings of the self. But in what is for the present study an important conceptual distinction, the fact that experience is subjective in nature no more necessarily reflects the state of the self than does objective experience necessarily provide an accurate picture of a reality that is assumed to exist independently of this experience. Contrariwise, the content of one's subjective experience may indeed be reflective of outside reality, though a clinical inference would usually be required to bring this relationship into focus, just as undergoing objective experience at a particular time may bear upon the state of the self. Whatever form experience may take, the criterion of being subjective can from the present perspective be fulfilled only if such experience, through either being allowed to play itself out or by being actively and analytically traced, could be found to have arisen as a result of the person being subjected to some influence.

Objective experience may contain subjective elements as well. In the act of directing one's attention in a particular way in order to ascertain something, one may during the course of this process be subjected to a feeling of love or anger, for example, but the essential experience remains an objective one. Objective experience is the cognitive counterpart to behavioral acts of mastery. One tries to know the way things are, to see a certain order, to bring about an effect. One may even attempt to bring within one's conscious control certain ordinary subjective experiences, such as feelings or sensations, through trying to induce them on one's own. A focus on objective experience is compatible with what we have traditionally been trained as psychoanalysts to do. Unless we believe with Lacan (1977) that analysis entails an endless association of signifiers that never arrive at what is being signified, most analysts believe that they are trying to get at something, no matter how this may be formulated. Thus, we may be willing to undergo a series of subjective experiences because we believe that they will lead to some finite point. As will continue to be explicated in the ensuing discussion, allowing experiences simply to emerge "for experience's sake" without actively looking to make some determination at the end is a challenging proposal.

An objectivistic focus in psychoanalysis is essentially involved in trying *to account for* whatever experience one is undergoing. This is ordinarily not simply carried out as a metaphysical exercise, since our valuation, as analysts, of the power of cognition is such that we believe that if we can objectively understand, for example, a subjective experience of pain, know its source, cause, mechanism, and function, we will be able to tolerate it better if need be, or be able to eradicate it completely, as with neurotic plan. Likewise, to be able to see and understand the objective correlates of an experience of pleasure, we believe, can help enable us sustain or repeat this experience.

Objective experience, when used in this way, is the servant of mastery. It may, however, become an instrument of servitude as well. When we have a hunch about an issue in treatment, for example, it becomes after a time difficult not to follow this line of objective inquiry and to be able to see anything else. As a result we organize, bind, hold, contain, and neutralize—all terms familiar to psychoanalytic theory—overly charged or unpredictably moving aspects of our experience in order to remain on a particular track, which tends then to perpetuate this focus. Carveth (1984) quotes Wittgenstein in conveying a similar idea, but with regard to the influence of language on experience. Wittgenstein writes, "a picture held us captive and we could not get outside it, for it lay in our language and language seemed to repeat it to us inexorably" (p. 515).

While we may try to use subjective experience to arrive at objective ends, as psychoanalysts we have come to appreciate how our objective efforts are often undertaken at the unconscious behest of subjective beginnings; that is, we may try to maintain or bring about certain objective experiences in order to either help perpetuate, avoid, or attenuate other subjective experiences.

Another aspect of being "subjected" by an external influence concerns how an analyst's metapsychology shapes his/her experience with a patient. The extent to which the analyst may become so influenced by his/her metapsychology, to the point of selectively inattending to other significant experiences, can indeed contribute to rendering how an analyst undergoes his/her immediate experience a more salient clinical issue than the manifest issues that the patient is presenting. The analyst's relationship to his/her own experience, an aspect of countertransference, becomes then a subject of the analysis along with the focus on the patient. The presence of such metapsychology-tinged influence may be illustrated by the following case, which I have discussed at greater length elsewhere (Wilner, 1981), and which concerns a patient of a supervisee of Kohut (1977), Mr. W., whom Kohut is at this point supervising. At some point, the patient was recounting the contents of his front pants pocket in a way that bored the therapist and that neither therapist nor supervisor could make much sense of. They had dismissed the idea of the behavior being a manifestation of negative transference, or of it having a sexual reference, despite the proximity, as the therapist pointed out, of the pants pocket to the patient's genitalia. In Kohut's actual theory of the self, much that the patient experiences is thought to be an expression of the self's fragmented state. However, in a metapsychological shift that foreshadowed a significant revision by Stolorow, Brandchaft, and Atwood (1987) of some of Kohut's ideas, Kohut himself suggested that not only was this patient not in such a state of fragmentation, but that he was giving a proud account of his possessions for the therapist to mirror, attesting thereby to his growing self-confidence and solidity of self. Kohut went on to say that the present behavior was related to the patient's having been separated from his parents when he was a little boy, when he had been sent to live with relatives on a farm. The patient as a young boy was left alone in the house, and used to check the contents of his dresser drawers while the family was out working in the fields. Following the supervisor's formulation, the therapist was able to listen to the patient with renewed interest.

I have already stated that one cannot observe another's subjective experience directly, just as one cannot observe one's own observing eye while in the act of observing (Organ, 1968). One can "observe" only one's own objectivistic reading of one's own or another's subjectivity. There are strong grounds to consider in this case that Kohut's "objective" view of the patient's subjectivity may have, in turn, been influenced by the therapist's and Kohut's own subjectivity. This is to say that their view, which was dependent on a belief in their ability to step outside the influence of the analytic process, was itself a function of this same process. An alternative way of proceeding, for example, would have been for the therapist to stay with his/her subjective experience of being bored and to see where it may have led, without having to try to get an objective handle on things. Thus, had the therapist allowed this experience to continue, including as part of this experience his own efforts to combat it, it might then have occurred to the therapist that the patient may have been doing what he was doing because he himself may have been bored. We might speculate that such boredom was caused by what was experienced by him as the therapist's pulling things out of his/her own metaphoric pocket in a theoretically predictable way. What was mentioned about the patient going through the objects of his drawer when the family was out doing work in the fields might have, at least, been considered as being a metaphoric reference to the "family" of therapist and supervisor not paying attention to the patient sufficiently because of their preoccupation with their theoretical position, that is, their own work in the analytic field.

It is also possible to read the patient's actions as being directly related to the therapist and supervisor in a positive way, as Kohut, again anticipating Stolorow, had suggested. The patient may unconsciously have been attempting to point to how Kohut and the therapist should look at his actions, not solely as fragmentary products of the self, or as defenses or compensations for a fragmented self, but as affirmations of a strong self. In this view, the patient, in that he responded well to the new formulation, might originally have been pushing therapist and supervisor into generating new actions and perceptions, which he might later mirror.

The problem as I see it in the above case is the therapist's and supervisor's attempt to account for the experience that the therapist was undergoing without allowing the subjective nature of the experience to further unfold first. The bias that is again usually present in analysis is for the analyst not to let the subjective nature of the experience play itself out. There is, in contrast, rarely failure on the analyst's part in coming up quickly with new objectivistic observations and formulations. Whole experience, as I see it, cannot occur in the presence of such a unimodal focus, as it requires both subjective and objective experience in order to occur.

Treatment

I conceive of whole experience as bringing self and man-in-world together at once. In treatment, a therapist working from this perspective would not allow his/her organized and formulated experience to inform the bulk of his/her therapeutic action, regardless of how involved such experience may become in the undergoing of the process. Instead the therapist, in quest of whole experience, would allow whatever experience he/she would undergo to be given a chance to take on a life of its own. As an agent for the explorations of the natural movement and mysteries of unconscious psychic process, a therapist working from this perspective would become increasingly sensitive to how the desire to shape and control experience leads to the phenomenon of experiential repetition, with the consequent loss of what might otherwise be the opportunity to become unique and whole.

Different analytic orientations accentuate different aspects of the analyst's clinical experience with the patient. The consequences of these emphases, in terms of both what is heightened in the analyst's awareness and what is de-emphasized or inattended to, are important as experiential signposts. These signposts may be viewed as, perhaps at first, impediments, then ultimately as conductors or conduits of whole experience, if the analyst is later able to bring these emphases into awareness.

Levenson (1993), for example, believes that when the patient is himself/herself anxious, confused, enacting something in treatment, he/she is often reacting to what Levenson sees as the analyst's own anxiety. It is the dimension of analysis in which one participant subjects the other to a possible immediate experiential effect, which Kohut and the therapist in the previous case appear to neglect, but that Levenson and Hoffman, coming as they do from a more interpersonal position, attempt to address. Levenson calls for a freer interaction between patient and analyst in which the analyst, if he/she can, tells the patient about his/her experience with the latter in order to enlarge upon whatever is being presently experienced and behaved between them.

However, believing that one's anxiety is evoking a reaction from the patient, such as avoidance, anxiety, or a move to comfort the analyst, may lead the analyst to undergo feelings of guilt, fear, sadism, or despair. Similarly, with regard to Hoffman's (1991, 1993) social constructivistic position, patients' and analysts' reactions to one another are considered to be largely socially influenced constructions of experience, and not reactions to things that are thought to be essentially real in the other. From this perspective, then, it would be important for a social constructivistically oriented analyst to go into his/her likely to be experienced feelings of uncertainty about the reality of what he/she might be experiencing, feelings of personal insecurity, urges to dogmatically assert, and a desire, for example, to rush into enacting feelings and hunches with less concern for consequences and with less caution about what one believes to be the contingent nature of one's experience. This is a position that Hoffman (1993) has actually moved toward in recent writing. It is, on the other hand, also possible, of course, for an analyst with the above orientation to become extremely cautious and obsessional regarding the reasons he/she may be experiencing what he/she is.

A more objectivistically oriented classical analyst, for example, might feel a sense of pride and power about being able to make sense out of analytic muddles, or harbor a fear of being subjectivistically controlled by the patient, and, as a result, experience concern about being blind to what the patient may actually be like. However, the experience that may ensue could not likely be predicted beforehand. It must await a particular psychoanalysis.

It would seem to follow that if objective experience, as I have suggested, tends to organize and restrict the free movement of subjective experience in the analyst's mind, the analyst might be more able to reach whole experience, in which one might truly be able to say that one knows what is now happening, as well as allows to happen what one knows, if one allowed oneself to undergo subjective experience first. This is a formidable conceptual dilemma to resolve in terms of organized and rational experience alone. For if the objective is to allow for the free movement or liberation of experience in one's awareness, how can this come about through directed effort that is by nature objectivistic? Such efforts, it would seen, would only serve to reinforce the attempt to make something happen by capturing an experience, paradoxically not the experience of movement within experience itself—a maneuver that is likely to keep experience from actually being able to move on its own, or within the present perspective, to keep it from being able to expand.

As stated with regard to the above case, the therapist might have stayed with his/her feeling of boredom to see what it might have led him/her to further experience. Another possibility is to allow whatever fragmentary experience one might undergo, such as fleeting thoughts, partial impressions, awareness of sensations, whatever may appear on the margin of one's awareness, to come more into focus. Since the interpersonal field is constituted by all experiences that are undergone in the analytic process, these same phenomenologically fragmented experiences is seen as a function of the analysis as well, the meaning and significance of which may not be able to be determined until a full unfolding of such experience may be permitted to take place.

Part of the difficulty in undergoing whole experience is, I think, that one is accustomed to objectifying things and may not realize that one is doing so. For example, in the following clinical vignette I was able to become aware of how I ordinarily make an effort to construct objective experience, as Hoffman has suggested we do, because the nature of this particular clinical situation enabled me to realize suddenly that there was nothing that needed to be done in order for the experience at hand to seem complete. The actuality of the event in this instance appeared to be exactly what I separately within my own psyche was undergoing. Hence, I did not have to build objective experience, or undergo an experiential process of finally coming to realize that I was being psychologically influenced. My objective and subjective experience appeared immediately to be one, which is to say that individually they did not appear to functionally exist as separate modalities of awareness at this time. My assertion dialectically evokes the counterargument that we can never get outside our own experience in order to know what exists "in reality." I believe that this counterassertion can be challenged in instances where one is able to "catch oneself in the act" of constructing experience in order, I will assume, to match an existing reality. This presupposes that one has some apprehension of this reality in order to know what experience would match it. But again, when one possibly is experiencing "what is," there is then nothing that need be constructed. The issue experientially might then be as much being able to apprehend one's reflexive proclivity to experientially construct as it is to apprehend reality as it might be. Space does not permit an exploration of the relativistic and perspectivistic issues that the above assertion naturally elicits.

A patient is recounting a complex dream that I find hard to follow, which involves his offering help to a man who is sick. He interrupts his telling of the dream to ask me if I would rather not hear it. I'm surprised by his question and ask him why he's asking, though I realize—in an instant of what I think of now as whole experience—that he's right. This was for me whole experience because what I was observing at the instant coincided exactly with what I was subjectively experiencing as a participant who was being influenced by the process, much as in the simple experiences of everyday life that I have come to realize is rare in psychoanalysis, at least experience that is of psychological significance. In asking the patient why he had asked me what he did, I was already beginning to construct objective experience and build complexity in order, I think, to avoid a possible unfolding of what I believe now could have been experience of direct contact between us. A fuller discussion of this case may help to elucidate something of the relationship between whole experience and objective and subjective awareness.

The patient replies that I was grimacing and looked in pain as he was talking. For the sake of avoiding this direct encounter with the patient, and also in order to pursue my own objectivistic analytic ends, I tell him that I am fine and want to hear the rest of the dream. I reflect later that I may have been grimacing because of straining to integrate the various elements of the dream. I, again, was aware of feeling the discomfort that the patient was pointing out to me, but I chose to try to ignore this subjective experience. I could have inquired further of the patient about his experience of seeing me in this way, but this felt to me at the moment like a ploy, since he was, in fact, right, and seemed comfortable in his experience. But, in addition, since I was avoiding my own subjective experience at that moment, I probably did not feel free to pursue this.

The possibility of my having told the patient that I was feeling uncomfortable, and, furthermore, that I may even have wanted him to suspend the narration of his dream, had probably been too threatening to me as a possible giving up of control to the patient, whose scope of awareness at that moment appeared to extend beyond the horizon of my own. But what is also of interest is how my own need to preserve the objectivistic analytic continuity of my experience through understanding the patient's material served to reinforce my refusal to accept this possibility for direct contact with him. In addition, the patient's dream, as I will indicate, suggested that he may have known what would happen in the session before it actually took place.

Later in the session, I went back to explore with the patient the possibility that the person that he was trying to help in the dream may have stood for me—a thought that at this point suggested itself because I had by then gotten over the shock of undergoing my own whole experience, evoked as it was by his actions. At this point I was finally able to make the connection between the content of the dream and the patient's observation that I looked in pain. He found the comparison interesting, but the idea fell flat, as it aroused no strong apparent interest in either of us at this point. In thinking about the dream after the session, I became aware of yet another parallel. The sick man in the dream, whom the patient knew, was sitting in a movie theater when the patient approached him; he wanted only to continue watching the movie. This struck me as being in a sense what I was trying to do in the session when the patient asked me his question. As if I were objectivistically watching a movie, I wanted to hear the end of the dream, regardless of my apparent discomfort. Furthermore, despite my interest in Levenson's (1972) discussion of how what is said in a session may be interpersoanlly enacted in the process, I was interested only in trying to locate the patient's issues through seeing what he may have been projecting about himself in the dream, just as a movie screen is a projection screen.

These parallels may be analytically explained by metapsychologically and experience-near informed references to the patient's and my own psychologies as follows: the patient may have perceived me (perhaps correctly, since I did act this way) as feeling sick, looking at life, or at least analysis, despite my many protestations to the contrary over the years, as though it is a movie and not real, while refusing to acknowledge my situation and accept help. A more Kleinian view would place the patient as sadistically torturing me by telling me this complex dream, and then trying to make restitution by offering to help me. From a classical perspective, the patient may have been trying to get me to submit to him physically; thus the dream that I found hard to follow, I may also have found hard to swallow. Furthermore, the patient may either treat others in such a way that they end up needing help, or he may choose people who need help to begin with, but he feels thwarted in his efforts to render assistance because they are also unable to accept what he tried to provide. A further consideration is that the patient is highly competitive and has overpowered me with his dream. He then pointed out to me that he had indeed conquered me in the guise of telling me that he thought that I could not tolerate listening to the dream, thereby attesting to his power. In addition, the dream may suggest a reversal of the above possibilities as well: here, the sick man may stand for the patient, with him standing for myself, as I am trying to help him. The dream figures may also, of course, refer to various configurations of a parent-child relationship. My efforts to fit the contents of the dream, along with its transferential and countertransferential implications, into a steady stream of self-continuous analytic experience, or, in other words, to try to make analytic sense out of the material, thus interfered with my ability to, and reinforced my resistance to, experience direct contact with the patient during the session itself.

The vignette illustrates the possibility that acceptance of genuine contact and the possibility of whole experience when these are available may be alternatives to enacting repetitive psychological patterns in the process. Thus, had I attended initially to my discomfort in listening to the dream, I would have been helping myself. Not only would this have shifted my experiential focus, but I would no longer have been in the same position of needing the patient's help. He would not have to offer to stop telling me the dream and therefore, I would no longer be in the position of the man in the movie theater who was interested more in watching the movie than in being cognizant of how he was feeling. What might have transpired between the patient and myself through such a turn of events is unknown, as each of us might have become real others to one another, with our actions and experiences at this point no longer being able to be understood either through our separate individual psychologies or through a dovetailing of these psychologies. Then again, had I been capable of reacting directly, maybe the patient might not have dreamed this dream to begin with.

The fulfillment of man and woman's quest to realize their natures as constitutive of world and as separate selves has been represented in this essay by the concept of whole experience. The attainment and elucidation of such experience, in turn, have been traced through an analysis of objective and subjective experience.

Objective experience emanates from a differentiated personal self that is separated from world, but is about world. Subjective experience has been described here as resulting from impingements of what is outside self, which is experienced within the self as inner experience. Whole experience is viewed as being essential in enabling one to act from within in a way that allows the integrity of world, physically and socially, to be preserved and enhanced, and in making it possible for one person to react to world in such a manner that the character of one's self is similarly sustained and enriched.

The problematics or pathologies surrounding the relationship between objective and subjective experience, and the therapeutic actions undertaken to resolve them are complex matters to study. What appears clear is that one's sense of self and ability to act and understand are limited and organized by the structure of the context of which one is part, just as the potential of context to duplicate itself in a person is tempered by each individual man's/woman's unduplicatable uniqueness.

It is finally the ability of each of these reference points to maintain its own integrity and not succumb to transformation into the other that enables humankind to unearth more of the contextual systematics that both affect it as human and are constitutive of its nature, and to continue to refine its individuality as human, thereby enabling it to be capable of nondeterministic acts and experiences. Whole experience, as I see it, is reflective of a person's ability to attain this sense of integral wholeness, and his/her own personal uniqueness, while it is simultaneously reflective of the whole context within which one is engaged. In a social sense, whole experience, in that it affirms what is whole in others, as well as providing an impetus for what is fragmentary to become whole, engenders its own perpetuation.

REFERENCES

Barratt, B. B. 1988. Why is psychoanalysis so controversial? Notes from left field. *Psychoanal. Psychol.* 5:223–40.

Carveth, D. L. 1984. The analyst's metaphors: A deconstructionist perspective. *Psychoanal. and Contemp. Thought* 7:491–560.

Engler, J. 1984. Therapeutic aims in psychology and meditation: Developmental stages in the representation of the self. *J. Transpers. Psychol.* 16:25–62.

Hoffman, I. Z. 1990. In the eye of the beholder. *Contemp. Psychoanal.* 26:291–99.

———. 1991. Toward a social-constructivist view of the psychoanalytic situation. *Psychoanal. Dialogues.* 1:74–105.

———. 1993. The intimate authority of the psychoanalyst's presence. *Psychologist Psychoanalyst* 13:15–23.

Kernberg, O. 1975. *Borderline Conditions and Pathological Narcissism.* New York: Jason Aronson.

Kohut, H. 1977. *The Restoration of the Self.* New York: International Universities Press.

Lacan, J. 1977. *Ecrits.* New York: Norton.

Levenson, E. A. 1972. *The Fallacy of Understanding.* New York: Basic Books.

———. 1990. Reply to Hoffman. *Contemp. Psychoanal.* 26:299–304.

———. 1993. Shoot the messenger: Interpersonal aspects of the analyst's interpretations. *Contemp. Psychoanal.* 29:383–96.

Miller, I. S. 1987. William James and the psychology of consciousness. *Contemp. Psychoanal.* 23:299–313.

Noy, P. 1969. A revision of the psychoanalytic theory of the primary process. *Int. J. Psychoanal.* 50:155–78.

Ogden, T. H. 1989. *The Primitive Edge of Experience.* Northvale, NJ: Jason Aronson.

Organ, T. 1968. The self as discovery and creation in Western and Indian philosophy. In *East-West Studies on the Problem of the Self,* ed. P. T. Raju and A. Castell. The Hague: Martinus Nyhoff, pp. 163–76.

Protter, B. 1988. Ways of knowing in psychoanalysis. *Contemp. Psychoanal.* 24:498–526.

Rothenberg, A. 1983. Janusian process and scientific creativity. *Contemp. Psychoanal.* 19:100–19.

Sterba, R. F. 1934. The fate of the ego in analytic therapy. *Int. J. Psychoanal.* 15:117–26.

Stern, D. 1983. Unformulated experience. *Contemp. Psychoanal.* 19:71–99.

Stolorow, R. D., Brandchaft, B, and Atwood, G. B. 1987. *Psychoanalytic Treatment: An Intersubjective Approach.* Hillside, NJ: Analytic Press.

Webster's New World Dictionary of the American Language. 1964. Cleveland: World Publishing.

Weedon, Chris. 1987. *Feminist Practice and Poststructuralist Theory.* New York: Basil Blackwell.

Wilner, W. 1981. The psychopolitics of Heinz Kohut's theory of narcissism. *Compreh. Psychother.* 3:33–53.

———. 1982. Philosophical approaches to interpersonal intimacy. In *Intimacy*, ed. Martin Fisher and George Stricker. New York: Plenum, pp. 21–38.

———. 1987. Participatory experience: The participant-observer paradox. *Amer. J. Psycholanal.* 47:342–57.

———. 1989. Experiential confinement as a condition of psychological change. *Amer. J. Psychoanal.* 49:51–66.

Wolstein, B. 1971. *Human Psyche in Psychoanalysis*. Springfield, IL: Charles C. Thomas.

———. 1974. Individuality and identity. *Contemp. Psychoanal.* 10:1–14.

Chapter Eleven

Ambiguity Is of the Essence
The Relevance of Hermeneutics for Psychoanalysis

Louis A. Sass

EDITORS' INTRODUCTION

"Hermeneutics," as Woolfolk, Sass, and Messer have pointed out in *Hermeneutics and Psychological Theory*, is an umbrella term for a group of related approaches that have evolved as an antidote to scientism—the modern tendency to view the natural sciences as modes for all forms of inquiry. Hermeneutics, they write, strives to "provide cultural, philosophical, or methodological alternatives to the quantification, naturalism, objectivism, ahistoricism, and technicism that have increasingly come to dominate the modern 'weltanschauung.'" It follows that hermeneutics in the psychoanalytic context "does not represent a distinct school of psychoanalysis, on the same level with, say, classical psychoanalysis, ego psychology, self psychology, or British object relations theory." Rather, as Sass argues in the following chapter, it is perhaps best viewed as a "metapsychological or even metaphilosophical position with implications for the understanding and application of a wide variety of psychoanalytic theories and techniques." Drawing from what he designates the central tradition of contemporary hermeneutics, the work of Martin Heidegger and Hans-Georg Gadamer ("ontological hermeneuticists"), Sass focuses on "philosophical anthropology—the image of man or fundamental conception of human existence that guides theory and practice."

For Heidegger, according to Sass, the most basic mode of human existence, on the basis of which all other modes must be comprehended, is not detached knowing but engaged activity. In his view, other modes of experience, like the detached contemplation of the scientist, philosopher, or psychoanalyst, are preceded, both temporally and logically, by everyday situations of engagement with the world. Thus for Heidegger "everydayness is not just a possible mode of existence; everyday engagement, as it is lived prereflectively, is both the primordial foundation from which derive all other modes and the key for understanding all other modes." One of the main ramifications of Heidegger's insight, says Sass, is that the sphere of subjectivity no longer appears as an epistemologically privileged realm, a refuge of certainty in a world of unfounded assumptions and assertions. Dasein ("Being-there," Heidegger's term for human existence) can thus know its own being only in an inexact, provisional, and circuitous way, not through some quasi-scientific method of direct intuition, with access to certain and foundational data. Human subjectivity, indicates Sass both here and in *Hermeneutics and Psychological Theory*, cannot be comprehended as an analyzable combination of isolatable and fully specifiable mental entities or elements that either do or do not exist in a determinate form. It is rather "an interweaving texture of only partially specifiable themes and backgrounds that exist at various levels of implicit and explicit awareness, often merging imperceptibly with one another." To recognize the "horizonal" aspect of experience (the role of the context, totality, or horizons within which experience occurs) is to realize that understanding can never be at the foundational beginning of some flawless methodology; as Sass points out, in the hermeneutic view, "experience is not transparent to itself; it is a kind of text analogue, an intrinsically obscure object that needs to be interpreted to bring light to its hidden meaning, and that can be evoked only by an approximate and metaphoric, perhaps even quasi-poetic mode of description." Sass is here intimating the primacy of Being and the unity of the subject and world. For the ontological hermeneuticists, then, "human beings are constituted by their self-interpretations, but for the most part, these interpretations are not unique, freely chosen, or consciously recognized, since they are deeply embedded in the public and determining facts of language, culture, and history, and are so pervasive as to be nearly invisible." Hence the title of Sass's essay, "Ambiguity Is of the Essence" ("of human existence" concludes the quote from Merleau-Ponty).

As Sass points out, a hermeneutic approach to psychopathology would concentrate less on crucial childhood experiences or particular conscious or unconscious contents, "emphasizing instead the overall . . . lived context, the prereflective stylistic-horizonal features of experience that are so readily ignored." Such a view, he says, does not necessarily contradict more traditional psychoanalytic formulations such as those "involving a punitive-superego figure, a grandiose selfobject, or . . . an oedipal fixation." However, "the particular representation or preoccupation would have to be understood . . . as emblematizing or as having generalized outward into the horizon." The emphasis, he says, is thus on "pervasive, formal features rather than specific childhood conflicts and traumas or particular mental contents." Pathological horizons tend to express themselves in inauthentic modes of experience, such as "calculative thinking, a loss of authentic temporality or spontaneity, a failure fully to inhabit or take responsibility for one's own actions," a tendency to go along with convention in a passive way, a too rigid, narrow, and structure-bound lifestyle, or "forms of subjectivism or objectivism that distort or disguise the primordial relationship of Dasein to its world and other human beings." The case studies of Ludwig Binswanger and Medard Boss and the analyses of Maurice Merleau-Ponty are classics in depicting such pathological modes of being-in-the-world.

Hermeneutically inspired psychotherapy, Sass claims, would foster greater awareness of the impact of social, cultural, and historical factors in the fashioning of the patient's life and behavior, as well as greater concern with action in the "real" world as opposed to the inner life. There would be less emphasis on the supposedly unique and private aspects of the patient's internal world, including the personal origins of individual qualities and quirks. While Sass indicates that these foci are not viewed as "off-limits," he suggests that the hermeneuticist would tend "to focus on exploring one's relationship to shared ethical norms, on the truth or adequacy of one's understanding of external social reality, and of the meaning, interpersonal impact and appropriateness of one's concrete actions in the world." As he conceives it, where the psychoanalyst sees the truth of experience as something preexisting and determinate, residing in the inner space of the patient's unconscious and passively waiting to be discovered, a hermeneutic appreciation of the horizonal nontransparency of human experience would see insight as an inquiring, dialogic, interpretive enterprise in which patient and analyst assume more or less comparable roles. Ideally, each uses habitual preconceptions in a nonrigid, nondoctrinaire fashion for the purpose of investigating meanings that reside, in a way, "not in the patient's mind but in the text-analogue they have before them," that is, the patient's behavior and narrated experiences. In this context, the aim of treatment is centrally concerned with "a global or horizonal transformation affecting the unseen but foundational basis of one's entire capacity for experiencing, acting, and communicating with others." (P. M. and A. R.)

"All concepts in which an entire process is semiotically concentrated elude definitions; only that which has no history is definable," wrote Friedrich Nietzsche in his *Genealogy of Morals* (1967, p. 80). This statement, eminently hermeneutic in spirit, applies to nothing so much as to hermeneutics itself, a concept whose antiquity is matched by a striking—at times maddening—ambiguity.

Hermeneutics has been and, in some quarters, continues to be understood in a fairly restrictive sense, as denoting a specific methodology or set of rules and techniques for the interpretation of written texts. Others assign it a wider significance, as referring to the specific modes and methods appropriate to the social or human sciences, in contradistinction to those forms of experiment and explanation relevant to study of the natural world. Yet a third group understands hermeneutics more generally still, as a reflective inquiry into the nature of human understanding and interpretation in the broadest sense, not excluding scientific knowledge, and thus as concerned with "our entire understanding of the world and . . . all the various forms in which this understanding manifests itself" (Gadamer, 1976, p. 18).

Concern with textual interpretation as well as the term "hermeneutics" itself can be traced back to the ancient world (the term is used by Aristotle). It was not, however, until the Renaissance and Reformation that hermeneutics was born as a distinct discipline, largely as a result of Protestant efforts to establish the basic intelligibility and coherence of the holy scriptures as an alternative to papal authority and church tradition, but also due to renewed interest in classical texts and in Roman law and jurisprudence (Mueller-Vollmer, 1985, pp. 1–2). Many later writers broadened and deepened hermeneutics by suggesting principles and techniques for the proper understanding of all utterances, spoken or written, sacred or secular, classical or modern, and by contributing in various ways to a comprehensive theory of interpretation and understanding. The Enlightenment scholar Johann Chladenius, for instance, called attention to the important role of point of view or relativity of perspective in historical accounts. The romantic theorist Friedrich Schleiermacher argued for the necessary role of active interpretation not just with difficult or seemingly contradictory texts but in all acts of human understanding: "Nothing is understood that is not construed," he argued (Mueller-Vollner, 1985, pp. 7, 8).

In the course of the nineteenth and early twentieth centuries, a number of thinkers concerned themselves with the specific methodological and epistemological status of the human sciences, especially history. Borrowing from Johann Gustav Droysen the *erklären-verstehen* distinction (explanation versus understanding), Wilhelm Dilthey attempted to formulate a *Critique of Historical Reason* that would furnish knowledge of the human world with the kind of analysis, justification, and potential certitude that Kant's *Critique of Pure Reason* had provided for the sciences of nature. Whereas explanation is causal and knows its object from without, understanding, being directed at persons and human productions, knows its object from within and by way of grasping the interconnections of a coherent tissue of meanings.[1] What is understood, for Dilthey, is always some kind of outer expression—gestures, language, works of art, and so forth—that externalizes lived experiences (*Erlebnisse*) such as states of mind or emotional attitudes (Mueller-Vollmer, 1985, pp. 24–25); these latter being understood, in accordance with Dilthey's "life-philosophy" orientation, as dynamic, ever-changing, and deeply historical in nature. Dilthey (1985) considered the capacity for understanding to be rooted in the humanist's or human scientist's capacity for modes of experience akin to those of his (human) object; and he tended to conceive such understanding as a kind of pure empathic identification whereby the interpreter sheds all his or her own biases or parochial concerns and achieves "perfect co-living" with or "re-experiencing" of the *Erlebnisse* of the other.

The two most important figures of twentieth century hermeneutics are Martin Heidegger and Hans-Georg Gadamer. Both were steeped in the older tradition of hermeneutic thought, and Gadamer was Heidegger's student; their thoughts are similar and closely intertwined. Heidegger developed what might be termed hermeneutic phenomenology. This involves a more precise delineation of the historicity of human existence as well as a decisive universalizing or ontologizing of hermeneutic methodology—that is, a recognition that processes of understanding and interpretation not merely are tools of the human sciences, but constitute the very essence of human existence itself. (Hence we can speak of the tradition of "ontological hermeneutics," as distinct from the "methodological hermeneutics" of Dilthey and others.) As Heidegger puts it in *Being and Time* (1962, p. 62), "The phenomenology of Dasein [Being-there, human existence] is hermeneutic in the original sense of the word, because it signifies the business of interpretation."

Gadamer's contributions are best described as pertaining not so much to hermeneutic phenomenology as to what could be called phenomenological hermeneutics. His primary concern is not with phenomenology per se, not with the modes of experience or existential dilemmas of the human being taken as an individual. Gadamer focuses instead on the classic problems of the hermeneutic tradition, problems concerning interpersonal communication and the possibility of knowledge of the other, in life as well as in the human sciences. His innovation, however, is to ground this in a (Heideggerian) phenomenology of Dasein as inescapably embedded in a particular existential-historical context and as itself inherently hermeneutic in nature, that is, as always already endowed with interpretations and preconceptions that can be changed but never entirely shed (Linge, 1976). Gadamer argues that the kind of pure empathic knowing or epistemological certainty that Dilthey sought is an impossibility for such a being; and from this he derives pluralist and antifoundationalist conclusions regarding the nature of knowledge in the human sciences. (Hermeneutic phenomenology and phenomenological hermeneutics differ only in focus or emphasis; I shall use "hermeneutics" as a generic term covering both these variants of the ontological-hermeneutic tradition.)

Given this long and variegated history, it is hardly surprising that the relevance of hermeneutics for psychoanalysis has been understood variously by psychoanalysts themselves as well as by those philosophers who have written on the topic. For some, the essential message to be derived is that psychoanalytic explanations or interpretations should be couched in a language of meanings, purposes, and intentions, not of energy, efficient causation, or reified entities of any kind. Others emphasize the primacy of empathy as the route to psychological knowledge; the need for accounts of a specifically narrational form; the appropriateness of coherence rather than correspondence theories of truth; a general rejection of objectivist assumptions in favor of relativism regarding explanation and understanding; or aestheticist or pragmatist views of therapeutic impact that question the possibility or deny the relevance of veridical insight—and of course there are various combinations of the above. To survey these approaches would be a major task and is not my purpose here. I should like, rather, to return to sources, considering what implications can be derived from what many would consider the central tradition of contemporary hermeneutics, the work of Heidegger and Gadamer—which I will, somewhat with tongue in cheek, refer to as the "hermeneutically correct" position.[2] At this point their ideas must certainly seem abstruse in the extreme. It will be the task of this chapter to clarify and flesh out their views, and to sketch their relevance for theory and practice in psychoanalysis.

Before I proceed, it should be stressed that hermeneutics does not represent a distinct school of psychoanalysis, on the same level with, say, classical psychoanalysis, ego psychology, self psychology, or British object relations theory. It is better seen as a metapsychological or even metaphilosophical position with implications for the understanding and application of a wide variety of psychoanalytic theories and techniques.[3] It is true that ideas akin to those of hermeneutics have most often been introduced by analysts of particular persuasions, especially adherents of interpersonal and intersubjectivist schools (e.g., Gill, 1994; Hoffman, 1991; Stern, 1991; Mitchell, 1993; Cushman, 1995; Orange, 1995; Stolorow et al., 1988).[4] This is partly because these schools have developed quite recently, in a perspectivist, post-Kuhnian climate, but also because their particular concerns with interpersonal factors and intersubjective realities have led them to question traditional methodological and epistemological assumptions about the analyst's privileged role in psychoanalytic knowing and interpretation. Still, for the most part, the dimensions of concern to hermeneutic theory are, if not orthogonal, at least oblique to those that have traditionally divided the various schools of psychoanalytic theory and practice. Hermeneutics operates at an abstract level, which places it in some sense above the fray; indeed, it should be possible to recuperate the insights of most of the traditional psychoanalytic schools, from classical psychoanalysis to self psychology, by reconstructing them in a more hermeneutic spirit.[5]

Husserl's Cartesian Phenomenology

Given our present purposes, we can best approach Heidegger's hermeneutic phenomenology by considering his disagreements with Husserl, the founder of the phenomenological movement and a thinker who shared certain crucial assumptions with Freud. It is worth dwelling on these philosophical differences at some length, for, as we shall see, the hermeneutic conception both of human existence (hence of personality and psychopathology) and of human communication (hence of psychotherapy and the possibility of psychological knowledge) derives from them.

Like Freud, Husserl had been a student of Franz Brentano in Vienna, and he accepted Brentano's key concept of "intentionality" (the term is used in a technical sense), namely, the notion that the mark of the mental, the essence of consciousness, is its quality of aboutness, its directedness toward a meant (or "intentional") object that can be characterized as the content of that act (Frede, 1993, p. 52; Hall, 1993, p. 122). Husserl assumed that there was a strict phenomenological correspondence between intentional acts and the mental objects—or representations—they intend; all phenomena were the objects of mental acts of various kinds, such as thinking, imagining, seeing, or desiring. He also made an assumption that is familiar since Descartes's postulation of the clarity and certainty of the *cogito* (the "I think"), namely, that the existence as well as the contents of one's own consciousness can have a kind of transparency and certitude that facts about the external world must necessarily lack. One may not be able to be utterly certain that the table one perceives is really out there in external space. However, the fact that the object or representation *of* or *within* one's experience is indeed experienced *as* a table, and further, as a table that one has the experience of perceiving rather than of imagining or remembering—*these* facts, at least, seem beyond all possibility of doubt (see Lauer, 1965).

It would appear to follow, then, that one possesses forms of implicit knowledge concerning essences of two types: the first pertaining to (experiential) objects, the second to acts of conscious awareness. One must have an implicit awareness, for example, of what it is for something to be a table, rather than, say, a chair or a stool, and also of what it is to perceive an object rather than to remember or imagine it. Husserl refers to these two aspects of conscious experience as the noema and the noesis, respectively. Presumably, given Husserl's Cartesian assumptions, it should be possible to describe the noematic and noetic aspects of consciousness, and thereby to obtain complete and certain knowledge concerning the essential defining characteristics of all objects of experience as well as of their possible modes of existence. To render explicit these implicit awarenesses is the goal of Husserlian phenomenology. Getting at these essences is not easy, however, for it is necessary to guard against certain natural tendencies that are inherent in normal or everyday forms of consciousness.

Generally we exist in what Husserl called the "natural attitude," in which we assume, for example, that visual objects are *actually* out there in space. And our immediate and naive characterization of both experiential objects and modes of experience (of what it is to be a table, say, or of what remembering involves) is likely to be contaminated by nonessential features inherent in the example or two of these phenomena that most immediately come to mind. Phenomenological rigor requires using the method of eidetic variation whereby we consider numerous possible instances in order to discover the constant or essential features running through all instances of "chairs" or all instances of "remembering." It also requires us to set aside our assumptions of *actual* reality (existence "out there"), to bracket the natural attitude in order to focus on a purely phenomenal realm and to become fully aware of the mode or form of our *experiences* of reality. (The latter might mean noticing, e.g., the way one always assumes the existence of a multiplicity of hidden facets existing beyond, yet coordinated with, what is before our eyes.) In addition we must set aside any theoretical or metaphysical assumptions we may have adopted, unwittingly or not, from philosophy, from any particular science, or from what passes for common sense in a given culture or milieu. If, however, we learn these purifying techniques, if we properly carry out what Husserl called the various "reductions," we can then discover the "absolute intelligibility of Being" (Gadamer, 1976, p. 169); then we shall be able to carry out a complete and precise inventory—an inventory not of the empirical or actual world, but of all types of objects and modes of being that can possibly exist *for us.* Husserl's famous catchphrase, "To the things themselves," is a call to return to the objects and the world as they really are, not as theory may imagine them to be but as they actually manifest themselves in human experience itself.

Hermeneutic Phenomenology and Phenomenological Hermeneutics

Like Husserl, Heidegger thought philosophy should be the attempt to grasp things as they really are, free of all distorting assumptions, and he too considered phenomenology, the process of attending carefully to our actual experiences of self and world, to be its appropriate method. He also shared (at least in the period of *Being and Time*) Husserl's transcendental subjectivism and anthropocentrism, the assumption that the being of entities, of the world, and of the self is rooted in the sense we have of them in our understanding (Frede, 1993, p. 53). But how was the phenomenological project to be carried out? What *kind* of being does one thereby discover? Here lie the differences between Husserl and Heidegger.

From very early on Heidegger had strong reservations about Husserl's conception of intentionality, of the nature of the fundamental correlation between subject and world. In Heidegger's view, Husserl's method of rigorous phenomenological intuition (direct viewing), the centerpiece of his project of "philosophy as rigorous science" (Husserl, 1965), was not faithful to the phenomena after all. What Husserl (1970, p. 153) termed his project of "self-reflective clarity carried to its limits" did not, in fact, give us "the things themselves" as they are manifest in primordial, prereflective experience, but rather things as they have been conceived within the deeply rooted but profoundly misleading tradition of Western thought, a tradition in which, to mention but one feature, things have been conceived as bare material substances having qualities and value-characteristics as secondary, add-on features. Heidegger argues that such assumptions, which have close analogues in Husserl's ontology, derive from a privileging of the cognitive, theoretical, or passive-contemplative stance over what is in fact the more primordial relationship with the world that is inherent in practical activity. "The Being of those entities which we encounter as closest to us can be exhibited phenomenologically," writes Heidegger (1962, p. 95), "if we take as our clue our everyday Being-in-the-World"—the latter being not the detached contemplation or "bare perceptual cognition" brought about through the various Husserlian reductions, "but rather that kind of concern which manipulates things and puts them to use; and this has its own kind of 'knowledge.'"[6]

The paradigmatic entity for Heidegger is a tool in use, such as a hammer, a door handle, or the turn signal on a car. When they are employed in the normal fashion, we do not have direct focal awareness of such entities. They are not intentional objects in the Brentano/Husserl sense of the term. The entity as such, with its physical or sensory characteristics—its weight, color, or shape, the qualities it would have if experienced as what Heidegger calls a "present-at-hand" object of contemplation—recedes from awareness. We see through it, as it were, focusing instead on the goals or purposes to which it is subsidiary. Heidegger (1962, p. 97) speaks of tools or equipment as having an "in-order-to" structure. This is the essence of their "equipmentality." It is what imbues a given piece of equipment with a practical significance; and, simultaneously, it links the tool together with other parts or aspects of the world that have some related role in a given practical context or set of concerns: "To the Being of any equipment there always belongs a totality of equipment . . . : inkstand, pen, ink, blotting pad, table, lamp, furniture, windows, doors, room" (p. 97). But these qualities of purposive significance and holistic interconnectedness are genuinely manifest only when the equipment is being used. Then, however, these qualities are not manifest as objects of knowledge, not even as implicit objects of knowledge akin to Husserlian noemata or the schemas of contemporary cognitivist psychology (pp. 121–22).

It would, in fact, be just as wrong to think there is knowledge, even of an implicit kind, of equipmentality (as, say, an abstract representation of hammerness, contained somewhere in the unconscious mind) as it is to think present-at-hand experiences of objects are necessarily prior to, and presupposed in, experiences of meaningful entities such as tools: "[I]n such dealings [e.g., hammering with a hammer] an entity of this kind is not *grasped* thematically as an occurring Thing, nor is the equipment-structure known as such even in the using" (Heidegger, 1962, p. 98). Neither hammering nor the hammerer have knowledge *about* the hammer's character as equipment—not, at least, knowledge existing in the form of representations or rules. There is no implicit or unconsciously held abstract structure, no objectively real (though of course nonmaterial) entity that, like a Husserlian noema or Fregean "sense," underlies, organizes, and directs our actual experience and behavior, and which it might be possible to discover once and for all if only one looks carefully enough and employs the proper techniques. "The less we just stare at the hammer-Thing [and, one might add, the less we contemplate it theoretically], and the more we seize hold of it and use it, the more primordial does our relationship to it become, and the more unveiledly is it encountered as that which it is—as equipment," writes Heidegger (1962, p. 98). "Readiness-to-hand" is Heidegger's favored term for this quality of equipmentality, the kind of being characteristic of equipment-in-use.

We might say, then, that a hammer, in its authentic equipmental hammerness, its readiness-to-hand, is "understood" only when it is used; only then is it appropriated understandingly. But understanding always involves "interpretation" of some kind. There is always a *way* in which Dasein takes or construes its world, in this instance, for example, by taking the world as a context for a certain kind of practical action, thereby coming to understand entities in certain ways (nicely illustrated by the story about the child with a hammer—to whom everything looks like a nail).[7] It would be wrong to think of this "activity" of interpretation as necessarily implying either volition or reflective self-awareness or a dominant role for the individual human actor—as seems to be assumed by some advocates of humanistic psychology and of a more humanistically oriented psychoanalysis (e.g., the Sartre-like "action language" of Schafer [1976; for a critique, see Sass, 1988], which stresses "acknowledging personal agency"). Actually we interpret all the time—indeed we are never *not* interpreting—and generally we do so in quasi-automatic ways and in conformity with cultural habits and practices that are deeply sedimented in our bodily and prereflective being; hence the need for psychologists and psychoanalysts to appreciate the role of culture and society in molding the psyche and the lived body (see Bruner, 1990; Shweder, 1991; Csordas, 1994). "In fact history does not belong to us, but we belong to it," writes Gadamer (1984, p. 245). "Long before we understand ourselves through the process of self-examination, we understand ourselves in a self-evident way in the family, society and state in which we live. . . . The self-awareness of the individual is only a flickering in the closed circuits of historical life." It may be true, then, that we live in "webs of significance" we ourselves have spun (Geertz, 1973, p. 5), but this does not mean that we spin them at will, by choice, or on our own.

I have said that these habitual modes of action and experience, these practices and webs of significance, need not be encoded in the form of rules or abstract representations of any kind. Postulating the existence of such rules—as is characteristic of cognitivism and structuralism of various forms, including Chomsky, Lévi-Strauss, and much of contemporary cognitive psychology—is usually taken to imply that interpretation is not ubiquitous; that at some level, perhaps of unconscious processing, the need for construal falls away and rules just operate automatically, like mechanisms or algorithms, simply telling us how to proceed. Ludwig Wittgenstein's (1958) famous discussions concerning the nature of rule-following, which are profoundly congruent with the spirit of hermeneutic thought, show, however, that this is an illusion—given that, outside logic and mathematics, it is always necessary to construe or interpret a rule in order to apply it (unless one wants to postulate rules for the interpretation of rules, but this would lead to an infinite regress). The hermeneutic slogan, "interpretation all the way down" (Geertz, 1973, pp. 28–29), acknowledges this truth. The domain of human practices is highly articulated and differentiated, of course; it contains inertias and constancies of all kinds; but it is a mistake to view these enduring patterns as but the reflections or instantiations of some purer world of Platonic essences, Fregean "senses," Chomskyan structures, or Husserlian noemas. There are just the practices themselves, being constituted ever anew by the interpretive habits of the beings who live them (see Bourdieu, 1990).

Such a view does deflate a certain kind of cognitive ambition, the aspiration to burrow deep and emerge with a single, shimmering truth that puts everything in its place once and for all. But it does not imply that there is nothing to be discovered or nothing to be said, nor need it have the relativistic implication that there is no way to choose between one interpretation and the next. The domain of human existence is not a rebus, hiding beneath its surface complexities a single hidden message from which everything else is generated; but neither is it a Heraclitean flux, defeating any conceivable generalization.[8] We should recall, after all, that Heidegger himself speaks of essences—the essence of equipmentality or the essence of Dasein, for instance. The very meaning of "essence" has changed, however, once the hermeneutic turn has been made: for now essences can no longer be conceived as phenomena that are discrete, clear-cut, waiting out there to be discovered; rather, they are themselves interpretations, or, more accurately, Interpretations of interpretations. (Henceforth I follow the convention of using "interpretation" uncapitalized to refer to spontaneous acts of understanding/interpretation that occur in everyday experience, while capitalizing the word when referring to those explicit Interpretations that psychologists or philosophers may offer of particular individuals or of Dasein more generally.)

Neither the toolness of the tool nor the larger equipmental context in which it participates is, then, the kind of phenomenon that is readily conceived as an intentional object in Brentano's sense, or readily made the object of Husserlian description. Neither is in fact objectlike at all, if by this we mean to refer to the sort of thing that is the end point or target of a perceptual or cognitive act. (Hence Heidegger [1962, p. 69; Dreyfus, 1991, pp. 66–68] speaks of such phenomena as appearing not to perception but to "circumspection" [*Umsicht*].) The way the tool, as tool-in-use, makes itself manifest is precisely by withdrawing, since only when it is *not* focused on, when it is known only tacitly, does it fully play out its role *as* tool. This is also true for the larger equipmental context: the context *as such* recedes precisely in order to let particular elements or features of the context show up as obstacles, tools, or goals. Heidegger (1962, pp. 37, 59) makes much of this seeming paradox—the withdrawal of what is in some sense nearest, the invisibility of what is most important or most encompassing.[9] The same point holds, in fact, not just for particular equipmental contexts such as carpentry or penmanship, but for every encompassing context within which entities can have significance for human beings, and indeed for the most encompassing context of all, what Heidegger refers to as our general sense of worldhood, which includes our most pervasive understanding of objects of any kind and our basic abilities to move closer or further away, to pick them up or set them down, and so forth (see Hall, 1993, p. 132).

Heidegger (1962, p. 172) puts considerable stress on the importance of what he calls "mood" or "state-of-mind" (*Stimmung* or *Befindlichkeit*), the feeling-tone or sense of attunement that pervades one's world at a given moment, or, for that matter, that may characterize a given person, culture, or epoch of history. (Heidegger speaks, e.g., of the "wonder" so characteristic of the early Greeks, by contrast with the "anxiety" more distinctive of the modern age [Held, 1993].) Mood, like understanding, is a constant and constitutive feature of experience—even neutrality, "pallid, evenly balanced lack of mood," is itself a kind of mood, notes Heidegger (1962, p. 173). Ontologically, it is more primordial than volition, objectifying cognition, or reflective self-awareness. "[S]o far from being reflected upon," writes Heidegger, moods "assail Dasein in its unreflecting devotion to the 'world' with which it is concerned" (p. 175), thereby determining in the most pervasive way how things can show up within the "horizons" or "clearing" of human experience, whether, for example, as poignant, fearsome, colorless, or amazing. Mood, like various equipmental contexts, like worldhood in general, is crucial, all-determining; yet precisely *because* it is everywhere, it is also nowhere, hence inaccessible to the kind of pure object-oriented beholding or direct inspection of Husserlian phenomenology.[10]

The crucial dimension of human existence, for Heidegger, always concerns these pervasive contexts, clearings, or horizons where subject and world interpenetrate.[11] They are the source or locus of Being, of the way things are or show up in general. In Heidegger's view the most persistent error of Western thought is the failure to appreciate this Being-dimension, the existence, nature, or role of these clearings or horizons—whether by ignoring them entirely or by attempting somehow to understand them on the model of the sorts of objectlike (often present-at-hand) entities that, in fact, could appear only within such contexts.[12] The latter is what Heidegger refers to as the forgetting of the ontological difference—the effacing of the distinction between the ontological or Being aspect of existence and that which pertains to particular entities or things.[13]

Only if one grasps the horizonal nature of Dasein, and all the complex interplay of disclosure and concealment that is bound up with the ontological difference, can one appreciate the particular challenges and advantages characteristic of such disciplines as psychoanalysis.[14] We human scientists—psychologists, anthropologists, psychoanalysts, whatever we may be—are of course human beings ourselves, thus condemned to interpretation whatever we examine; but in such cases our object is also an interpreting creature, an embodied, culturally constituted and constituting being—Dasein. The situation of the human scientist or psychoanalyst is then that of the double hermeneutic, since what one aims to Interpret is interpreting itself—the mode of understanding of a creature such as oneself.

If we reject the rather mystical notion of an empathic co-living with the other (a notion championed by certain nonhermeneutic advocates of phenomenological and humanistic psychology, as well as by the self psychologist Heinz Kohut, who understands empathy as "vicarious introspection"), we must then recognize that our knowing of the other's being—our Interpretation—necessarily operates on a different level, a more reflective, abstract, or objectifying plane, than does the object we seek to know (the interpreting and the interpretations that are the patient's Dasein). The psychologist or psychoanalyst is not in the position of the patient; it is not his own being or his own horizons that he seeks to know. This means that, at least with regard to the patient's horizons, he is not confronted with the standard situation of Dasein—which is necessarily to neglect the enabling horizon (the horizon that one is, that constitutes one's very being) in favor of the entities showing up within it. In this sense it may be easier to know another than it is to know oneself.[15] At the same time, however, it must be recognized that our Interpretation is never simply a description but always itself a construal—which is grounded in our own (only partially recognized) concerns and presuppositions, and which is likely to conceal some part of the truth even as it illuminates others. There is also the further problem that Interpretations of Being are liable to "degenerate" when communicated in the form of explicit verbal assertions. Language, notes Heidegger, is more naturally suited to the characterization of entities; repetition of verbal descriptions renders them empty, as they become progressively detached from their originating source in some insight into phenomenology.

Implications for Psychoanalysis

The importance of Being and the horizonal nature of consciousness are two ways of characterizing Heidegger's central message. To see the relevance for psychoanalysis we shall consider notions about the unconscious, early childhood, and sexuality—the central themes of psychoanalytic theory.

Freud seems to have imagined the unconscious in largely spatial and atomistic terms, as a sort of place, vessel, or reservoir containing mental entities—"ideas" he sometimes called them—that could be charged with various kinds and amounts of affective or instinctual energy. Freud's affinity with Brentano is evident in his way of conceptualizing these entities, for he clearly imagines them in representational terms, that is, as having a distinct, almost objectlike quality (Dreyfus and Wakefield, 1988, p. 273). In this sense Freud's conception of the unconscious, at least in its formal characteristics, is remarkably similar to his conception of the conscious mind. What is experienced at both levels are the sorts of entities that could be the objects of Brentanean intentionality, the focal targets of discrete mental acts that are themselves conceived in largely cognitive terms. The fact that a given memory or other mental entity is or remains unconscious is therefore a wholly contingent fact that must be explained on motivational rather than on formal or structural grounds. It is not due to any intrinsic obscurity, to any formal characteristic that makes it incompatible with focal conscious awareness, but only to the fact that its content, for instance, memories of oedipal desire, happens to be such as to occasion repression (a defense operation that, not incidentally, is itself conceived as a kind of targeted Brentanean act).

This way of conceiving things is largely responsible for what has struck many as the paradoxical quality of the Freudian conception of the unconscious, a view that appears to postulate a realm that is in some crucial respects identical to consciousness yet nevertheless *not* conscious at all. It can seem as if Freud is describing what could only be some kind of lighting process, yet all the while insisting that this process must somehow be occurring in the dark.

Heidegger's conception of Dasein offers a different way of conceptualizing repression, one that better understands its frequent and constitutive role in human experience. At least in many instances, the blindnesses Freud accounts for with his concept of acts of repression can be understood as consequences of the revealing/concealing dynamic inherent in Dasein's horizonal nature. The repressed need not be thought of as composed of intentional mental contents—representations—that happen to be kept out of awareness by targeted acts of repression, but rather as involving aspects or features of experience that have a fundamentally horizonal mode of existence, whether because they were never the objects of explicit awareness (as, e.g., in a family where an exaggerated, sadistic pattern of power relationships was so pervasive as never to have been explicitly conceived as such by the child) or because they have, as it were, deliquesced outward into a clearing, spreading out to constitute a general but now unnoticed set of expectations or way of seeing the world. One implication of such a view is to bring out the "positive" side of repression, the way it does not merely extrude phenomena from awareness but also constitutes alternative possibilities of experience.[16]

Maurice Merleau-Ponty (1962, p. 83), a hermeneutic phenomenologist influenced by Heidegger, rejects the view that the traumatic experience survives "as a representation in the mode of objective consciousness and as a 'dated' moment." Rather, "it is of its essence to survive only as a manner of being and with a certain degree of generality." On Merleau-Ponty's account, what is distinctive about the sort of clearing repression creates or perpetuates is its rigidity and persistence. It is as if one momentary world persisted, forcing all subsequent worlds into its mold: "One present among all presents . . . displaces the others and deprives them of their values as authentic presents. We continue to be the person who once entered on this adolescent affair, or the one who once lived in this parental universe" (p. 83). New experiences do register, of course; new emotions do occur—but they affect only the content, not the general form or structure of one's way of existing.

According to this hermeneutic phenomenological account, the (traumatic and repressed) events of the past could be said to survive, in the specific sense of having their constant effect on the present, precisely through disappearing, by dissolving into a background that they mold and harden according to their own implicit form. This is the opposite of Freud's view that the psychologically most important memories, memories of repressed traumatic events and thoughts from childhood, are also the ones that remain most unchanged (because, on Freud's account, such mental contents are not "worked over" and connected with new associations in the process of occasional recall to conscious awareness). The effect of repression, as Freud views it, can be likened to the freezing of a prehistoric mammoth beneath layers of ice: it is a concealing that simultaneously preserves by isolating what would otherwise deteriorate or dissolve over the course of time. On such a view, excavation of the past may well seem a possible and appropriate goal for psychoanalytic investigation. By contrast, if one adopts the hermeneutic phenomenological point of view, one sees the past as having its most significant existence not in the repositories of memory but in the structures and rhythms of present-day experience.

Given the hermeneutic conception of human existence, the connections between aspects or features of a person's experience—within focal consciousness, within the prereflective or unconscious penumbra, as well as *between* these two realms—primarily involve what philosophers term "internal" (or logical) rather than "external" (or causal) relationships. It is a matter not of contingent, merely associative relationships between distinct elements that have their significance in advance—relationships that could be fully understood, for example, by a causal analysis—but of a mutually implicative holistic structure in which the very meaning of the elements is constituted by their relationships with each other; indeed, where it is even misleading to speak of elements at all. The past, as we have seen, does not exactly distort the present, or impose on it a kind of secondary charge. It permeates the present. In a sense, one might say, it *is* our present; it *is* our world, surviving as a horizonal presence (Merleau-Ponty [1962, p. 442] speaks of the "atmosphere of my present") that reveals and constitutes as much as it conceals. This conception may, in fact, be perfectly compatible with the Freudian notion of transference (some might even say it is inherent in Freud's notion); but if so, we must avoid thinking of the past (or the unconscious) as something that lies behind or beneath the present like some shadow-world or Pompeian parallel universe, as Freud was wont to think.[17] What is most crucial about the past will not at all take the form of present-at-hand facts waiting there to be discovered (for this sort of uncovering Heidegger used the term *entdecken*). Instead it will have the revealing/concealing being of Dasein, and this can only be *disclosed* (*erschlossen* is Heidegger's term)—that is, it can be grasped only through the nonobjectifying, never-final modes of understanding and interpretation.[18]

On the hermeneutic account, then, memory is not a storehouse, museum, or photo album in which prior experiences are preserved in more or less their original form. It is precisely through losing their salience as particular *contents* of experience (whether conscious or unconscious), by dissolving outward into the horizons of awareness, that past events can retain such a grip on us, structuring our present orientations and projects toward the future. This, however, is but half the story. One must also recognize that the past, at least the living or relevant past, is actually molded by one's present attitudes and projects. These latter may themselves derive from and express the past, yet they also have a reciprocal, in a sense retroactive effect *on* the past, for example, by bringing out certain themes and events as important while letting others fade out into obscurity and near irrelevance.[19]

Heidegger (1962, p. 41) writes that "any Dasein is as it already was. . . . It *is* its past, whether explicitly or not," but he also points out that "Dasein 'is' its past in the way of *its* own Being, which, to put it roughly, 'historizes' out of its future on each occasion." Heidegger gives, in fact, a certain priority to the future in the constitution of "primordial and authentic temporality" (p. 378). The past could be said to "happen" out of the future (Guignon, 1992, p. 133), in the sense that each projected possibility sets up a kind of retrospective force field in which past events are made to line up—rather like iron filings in a magnetic field—whether as detours, obstacles, or stations along the way. In this sense the past, whether of an individual or of a culture as a whole, cannot possibly have any single or constant meaning. Its significance will depend, as indeed it should depend, on the standpoint from which it is seen, on the questions that have come to seem relevant in present circumstances, which, in turn, must derive from a sense of where one is currently heading.[20]

And all this occurs not only at the level of thematization, as in the explicit narratives offered as Interpretations in a psychotherapeutic session, but, more primordially, in the spontaneous, ongoing historizing interpreting that is life itself. From a Heideggerian or hermeneutic point of view, Sartre's famous line from his novel *Nausea*—"You must choose: live or tell"—is therefore quite misleading; and so is any analysis that would treat narrative form as an after-the-fact add-on whose very structure necessarily distorts the authenticity of experience as originally lived (this, it seems to me, is the flaw in Donald Spence's [1982] important but, in this particular respect, hermeneutically "incorrect" book, *Narrative Truth and Historical Truth*). Dasein is "an entity for which, in its Being, that Being is itself an *issue*" (Heidegger, 1962, p. 458)—that is to say, an entity that is constantly projecting itself into future possibilities, constantly revealing its own "potentiality-for-Being" by placing itself in a temporal sequence that has all the narrational qualities of development and suspense. "[A]ll prospection is anticipatory retrospection," writes Merleau-Ponty (1962, p. 414) in his chapter on temporality, but "it can equally well be said that all retrospection is prospection in reverse: I know that I was in Corsica before the war, because I know that the war was on the horizon of my trip there. . . . Time is thought of by us before its parts, and temporal relations make possible the events in time."

This essential historicity of spontaneous human existence implies a certain ambiguity, given the multiplicity of projects and retrospections that are always weaving their way in and out of our awareness, sometimes fairly explicitly but often in ways more inchoate or obscure. At the same time it implies that there is no utter ontological rift between knowledge and life—between the Interpretations developed during a psychoanalytic session and the more spontaneous, inchoate interpretations that are the stuff of our everyday existences.

Traditional psychoanalysis has often been criticized for having too linear a notion of time, for adopting too static a notion of the past and viewing later events as simple products of earlier ones. The criticism seems valid, at least for psychoanalysis in North America. Freud's writings do, however, contain some neglected resources that encourage a more dynamic and less linear-deterministic conception, in particular the notion of *Nachträglichkeit*. *Nachträglichkeit*, a concept central to Jacques Lacan's (Heidegger-influenced) rereading of the Freudian canon (Bowie, 1991, p. 182), might be translated as "deferred action" or "retroaction." It refers to the way "experiences, impressions and memory-traces may be revised at a later date to fit in with fresh experiences or with the attainment of a new stage of development" (Laplanche and Pontalis, 1973, p. 111). The classic example comes from Freud's account of the Wolfman, whose memory-impressions of his parents' coitus, observed at age one and a half, became traumatic only at the time of a dream at age four, owing, in Freud's words, "to [the Wolfman's subsequent] development, his sexual excitations and his sexual researches" (quoted in Laplanche and Pontalis, 1973, p. 113).

The conception of temporality implied by the *Nachträglichkeit* notion is certainly consistent with a hermeneutic phenomenological perspective. Freud, however, appears to have conceived retroaction rather narrowly, as applying not to lived experience in general but only to those (largely sexual) traumatic events that had undergone repression. Also, his descriptions of retroaction frequently suggest either some kind of mechanistic process, such as a delayed discharge, abreaction, or recathexis, or else some fairly deliberate activity of recollection, as opposed to the more spontaneous, prereflective, virtually automatic, and unceasing activity of reconstruing implied in Heidegger's notion of temporality. Freud does not, in fact, extrapolate his concept into a more general, perspectivist appreciation of *all* attempts to understand or transform the influence of the past, including his own case histories and those developed in the course of any psychoanalytic treatment. The latter has, of course, become a central theme in the writings of narrativist analysts who recognize that human beings are constantly telling stories about themselves, and that no one of these stories could ever be final or correct since each story, like the remembering that supports it, will be largely determined by the context or question to which it responds (e.g., Schafer, 1983, pp. 204, 219; 1980).

We have considered conceptions of the unconscious and the role of the past; it remains to make some related points concerning the role of sexuality in human existence. Psychoanalysis has often succumbed to the temptation of thinking of sexuality as some kind of separate and primary realm that contains the key for understanding all the ambiguities of present existence. But as Merleau-Ponty points out in some particularly rich pages in his *Phenomenology of Perception* (1962), sexuality would not have the immense significance it has were it not for the fact that it already contains within itself all the general dilemmas and riddles of human existence. Sexual experience is an opportunity, he writes, "of acquainting oneself with the human lot in its most general aspects of autonomy and dependence. The embarrassments and fears involved in human behavior are not explicable in terms of the sexual concern, since it contains them already" (p. 167).

This by no means implies that sexuality can be ignored in favor of a more general analysis of abstract philosophical or psychological concerns, as if the body's issues were but epiphenomena of the movements of Spirit, Consciousness, or the Self (as sometimes seems to be implied by self psychological analyses of sexual symptoms as but "disintegration products" of disturbances really pertaining to the Self). Like Heidegger, Merleau-Ponty is opposed to idealist no less than to materialist forms of reductionism, and thus to any attempt to reduce human existence to the playing out of some abstract principle. The body, and sexuality in particular, do have a particularly central place in our lives; but to grasp this role one must take account of all the particulars of physical desire and appreciate the body's inherent ambiguities—how it is traversed by all the major dimensions of human existence.

Thus Merleau-Ponty (1962, p. 168) writes that there are two mistakes to be avoided if one is to understand a phenomenon like sexuality: "one [mistake] is to fail to recognize in existence any content other than its obvious one, which is arrayed in the form of distinct representations, as do philosophies of consciousness; the other is to duplicate this obvious content with a latent content, also consisting of representations, as do psychologies of the unconscious." Merleau-Ponty agrees with Heidegger's (1962, p. 60) statement that, in some sense, "'Behind' the phenomena . . . there is essentially nothing else"; but, also like Heidegger, he recognizes that uncovering the meaning of the phenomena requires interpretation since it lies everywhere and nowhere, hiding in the visibility of the clearing.

Merleau-Ponty is particularly good on the essential ambiguousness of this domain, the realm of Heideggerian Being, which he compares to an atmosphere or an individual haze through which the world is perceived. In what he calls "that ever slumbering part of ourselves which we feel to be anterior to our representations," there are "blurred outlines, distinctive relationships which are in no way 'unconscious' and which, we are well aware, are ambiguous, having reference to sexuality without specifically calling it to mind" (1962, p. 168). That interpretation or understanding of the world that we call eroticism or sexuality is itself ambiguous. Hence any Interpretation of it will have to echo this quality, acknowledging the ineffability it implies.[21] But this applies not only to sexuality but to all of human life—which is everywhere imbued with the subtleties and concealments inherent in its horizontal nature. For "ambiguity," Merleau-Ponty writes, "is of the essence of human existence. . . . Thus there is in human existence a principle of indeterminacy, and this indeterminacy is not only for us, it does not stem from some imperfection of our knowledge. . . . Existence is indeterminate in itself, by reason of its fundamental structure" (1962, p. 169).[22]

The hermeneutic assumption of fundamental ambiguity should not be confused with the Freudian notion of overdetermination, which also acknowledges a multiplicity of meanings. Overdetermination presupposes not ambiguity but what I would prefer to call complicatedness. It views a given psychological event as the end point of a number of different trains of association or other causal chains, perhaps more than one is ever likely to uncover, yet each of which links a discrete and determinate set of events. Hence, on principle at least, the causal chains could all be discovered, thereby providing a complete explanation of the phenomenon in question. This assumption, influential if seldom articulated, of the possibility of a complete illumination is one reason Freud remains a child of the Enlightenment. Despite links to romanticism and considerable awareness of many possibilities of self-deception, Freud seems not, in fact, fully to have registered the problematization of human self-knowledge that occurred in the wake of the Kantian and romantic recognition of the human mind's active but largely unconscious role in constituting its own being and world.

Relativism, Truth, and the Hermeneutic Virtues

By contrast with the confident Enlightenment aspiration toward total illumination, rigorous description, and causal explanation, the hermeneutic position may well seem weak and unsatisfying. Its extreme holism and antireductionism (whether to principles or to prior causes) rule out many familiar forms of explanation. Its perspectivism suggests that any account that *is* given will be partial at best, certainly subject to revision, inevitably misleading in some respects. In a bitter passage written after he read *Being and Time*, Edmund Husserl characterized the disillusionment that would seem to follow from accepting—as he himself most emphatically did not—the viewpoint of Heideggerian hermeneutics. "Philosophy as science, as serious, rigorous, indeed apodictically rigorous, science— *the dream is over*," Husserl (1970, pp. 389–90) wrote. "Philosophy once thought of itself as the science of the totality of what is [but] these times are over—such is the generally reigning opinion of such people. A powerful and constantly growing current of philosophy which renounces scientific discipline, like the current of religious disbelief, is inundating European humanity."

Of course, from the hermeneuticist's standpoint, giving up the dream of rigor and certitude is no real loss, for the dream is in fact only that, not a realistic goal but a phantasm conjured up by a certain kind of self-deluding will-to-truth. The hermeneuticist believes, after all, in the ubiquity of interpretation. According to this view, scientific knowing is rooted in a more primordial kind of understanding: the present-at-hand objects of scientific description are not waiting there to be discovered by the unbiased eye; they are artificial abstractions from a more fundamental readiness-to-hand.[23] On such an account, the positivist or empiricist is a victim of what has been termed the "myth of immaculate perception" (Nietzsche): Failing to recognize the necessity and ubiquity of interpretation, the fact that seeing, for instance, is always a seeing-*as*, he or she falls victim to what Gadamer calls the "prejudice against prejudices," the aspiration, rooted in Enlightenment scientism, toward a perception that would slough off all preconceptions and traditions and somehow make direct contact with The Real.

By contrast, both Heidegger and Gadamer, like their predecessors in the hermeneutic tradition, note that the meaning of any part, fact, or individual percept can be obtained only from the larger context or whole in which it participates. In understanding linguistic expressions, one projects before oneself a meaning for the text as a whole as soon as some initial inkling of meaning emerges in the text. The same holds with human action, when, for example, a cultural anthropologist endeavours to understand (to Interpret) an unknown ritual or, for that matter, when someone in everyday life "reads" (interprets) the nonverbal cues of her conversation partner. Thomas Kuhn's *Structure of Scientific Revolutions* (1970) makes a similar point concerning scientific knowledge of the natural world, pointing out that prevailing "paradigms" always prestructure and give meaning to the facts that are observed.[24] This is one moment of the famous hermeneutic circle: that "to-and-fro movement between partial understandings and the 'sense of the whole'" (Baynes, Bohman, and McCarthy, 1987, p. 320; Heidegger, 1962, pp. 194–95).

Neither Heidegger nor Gadamer is, however, a relativist. Neither believes that reality is merely a projection of prejudices or foreconceptions, or that all interpretations are equally valid because they simply manufacture their own confirmation, molding perceptual input to their own design. Obviously, neither Heidegger nor Gadamer believes we ever encounter the bare fact or thing-in-itself; both also recognize the inexhaustibility of potentially valid interpretations. Yet both are in some sense "realists" or, at least, are imbued with the "realistic spirit"—if we understand by this not belief in the bare fact but acknowledgment of the world's capacity to resist us, to disconfirm expectations we project before us (see Gadamer, 1984, p. 236; Warnke, 1987, p. 146; also Diamond, 1991). "Only through negative instances do we acquire new experiences. . . . Every experience worthy of the name runs counter to our expectation," writes Gadamer (1984, p. 319), acknowledging on this point the wisdom of the Enlightenment empiricist Francis Bacon. If, as Gadamer (1976, p. 8) has written, "prejudices are biases of our openness to the world," this is, in part, because they open us, or should open us, to the ways the details or facts as we have been understanding them may fail to harmonize with each other in the contexts we have been projecting, thereby demanding that we revise this whole or cast about for an entirely different one.[25] And this, by the way, is the other moment of the famous hermeneutic circle—what Geertz (1983, p. 69) describes as that "characteristic intellectual movement [or] conceptual rhythm . . . namely, a continuous dialectical tacking between the most local of local detail and the most global of global structure in such a way as to bring them into simultaneous view."[26]

To believe in the potential inexhaustibility of possible interpretations need not, then, lead to the assumption of undecidability *between* interpretations, as some postmodernists tend to think. Though it may be impossible to discover some final, unassailable Truth, this does not preclude selecting, in a provisional way, between better and worse interpretations of a given phenomenon. It does not imply relativism or subjectivism (see Sherwood, 1969, pp. 244–57). Hermeneutics cannot then be categorized in accordance with the usual dichotomies. It is situated at a sort of midway point, equidistant from empiricism or positivism, from naive objectivism, as well as from certain forms of absolute skepticism and fictionalism sometimes propounded under the banner of postmodernism.[27] The real enemy of hermeneutics, we might say, is any form of dogmatism, and this includes dogmatic skepticism.

In *Truth and Method*, Gadamer explicitly eschews any prescriptive intent. The aim of his (ontological) hermeneutics, he explains, is not to develop "an art or technique of understanding," not to "make prescriptions for the sciences or the conduct of life, but to try to correct false thinking about what they are" (Gadamer, 1984, pp. xiii, also xvi) by clarifying the understanding and interpretation that are ubiquitous in human existence.[28] In fact we are all already—and inevitably—hermeneuticists. The "truth" and the "method" referred to in his title can be read as opposed to each other, for Gadamer doubts that rigorous techniques or rules of understanding are the best route to achieving understanding.[29] It would be wrong to conclude from all this, however, that Gadamer's work (or Heidegger's) has no implications for how the goal of adequate understanding might most appropriately be pursued. Gadamer does in some sense derive "ought" from "is": he clearly believes that a careful examination of successful acts of understanding/interpretation uncovers certain constitutive processes or moments, and that the most successful acts of understanding/interpretation will generally be those that most fully realize each of these aspects or moments.

The first requirement is, of course, to recognize (and exploit) the necessity of prejudice, indeed, at times, of bold conjecture, without which revelation would be impossible. The second, however, is to pay close attention to the phenomena one is trying to understand, in particular to potential inconsistencies and resistances to our prejudices or conjectures. The third is to maintain a self-conscious, potentially self-critical awareness of the nature, sources, and impact of one's own prejudices, of their necessity but also of their capacity to blind and of the dangers inherent in overcommitment to any single or too narrow perspective.[30] "All correct interpretation must be on guard against arbitrary fancies and the limitations imposed by imperceptible habits of thought and direct its gaze 'on the things themselves,'" explains Gadamer (1984, pp. 236–37).

> A person who is trying to understand is exposed to distraction from foremeanings that are not borne out by the things themselves. . . . Thus it is quite right for the interpreter not to approach the text directly, relying solely on the foremeaning at once available to him, but rather to examine explicitly the legitimacy, i.e., the origin and validity, of the foremeanings present within him.

Acceptance of bias and bold conjecture; openness to resistance from the world; constant awareness of prejudice—and to these we should add flexibility, the wit and imagination to see things under a variety of different aspects: these we might call the four virtues of hermeneutic understanding. The first hermeneutic virtue (use of bias and bold conjecture) is one that psychoanalysis appears to display in the strongest of terms. With its propensity for shocking reversals of overt meanings, its predilection for what has been called a hermeneutics of suspicion, psychoanalysis has been the most fecund source of nonobvious, nontrivial hypotheses—of revelatory prejudices—about human motivation in modern psychology. For most of its now nearly century-long history, psychoanalysis has not, however, been particularly conspicuous for its adherence to the virtues of openness to disconfirmation or a critical self-consciousness, nor were its major figures particularly flexible. It should be noted, however, that many rather recent psychoanalytic writers have been far more open, versatile, and self-critical; and also that, when taken as an eclectic whole (as several more recent writers are inclined to do, e.g., Gedo and Goldberg, 1973; Pine, 1990), the entire psychoanalytic tradition, with its ceaselessly warring schools, does look far more promising from a hermeneutic standpoint. Still, a certain procrusteanism seems to have been endemic in the psychoanalytic tradition and, in my view, remains remarkably persistent in many quarters.

From a Gadamerian standpoint, this psychoanalytic procrusteanism largely derives from a failure to recognize the inevitable contribution of the knower to the known.[31] The point to be grasped, however, is not merely that such a contribution is unavoidable, but that it is, in fact, by no means lamentable. For, even if the analyst were, *per impossibile*, able to fulfill the Diltheyan ideal—to shed his own skin, or rise up out of his own context or horizons before descending, wraithlike, into that of the patient—it is not at all evident that a truly satisfying form of understanding would be thereby achieved, for then one's grasp of the other would have to mirror or invoke all the ramifying complexity and elusive ambiguity of experience as lived from moment to moment. Instead of Interpretation, which classifies and organizes, one would have full evocation of the teeming, intertwining flux of conscious and unconscious life—perhaps in the manner of a novel by Virginia Woolf or a surrealist experiment in automatic writing. Truth, on Gadamer's account, is best conceived as an *event*. It is an event that occurs when there is a fusion of horizons, for instance, when a patient's rather inchoate recollections and feelings come together with the analyst's more abstract, conceptual, and consistent mode of awareness. What is wanted, then, is a map, not the entire territory itself; and while the map must in some way correspond to its object, it must also abstract from the realm it describes, bringing out certain potential saliencies while neglecting others. A problem arises when the active, constructive, or transformative nature of one's inter-preting is not acknowledged, for then the abstraction is, in a sense, placed out there in the world and treated entirely as a discovery. A most inter-esting example of this occurs with Freud's theory of dreams, which as we know he viewed as the royal road to the unconscious.

Freud considered the manifest level of the dream to display all the ir-rationality of primary process forms of experience. Given that the latent content of the dream exists at a more deeply unconscious level, the level that contains wish-fulfillment fantasies of a primordial and motivating sort, one might expect him to treat the latent level as still more primitive, illogical, and unrealistic, and thus as still more alien to conscious under-standing and refractory to direct verbal expression. Oddly enough, how-ever, Freud says just the opposite. Underlying the manifest content, lying prior to it in the chain of mental events that produces the actual dream-experience, contained within (and expressing) the infantile wish that mo-tivates the dream, is what Freud calls a latent "dream-*thought*"—some-thing that Freud (1900, pp. 506, 312, 277) himself describes as "entirely rational," indeed, as having "all the attributes of the trains of thought fa-miliar to us in waking life" and as being, in contrast to the manifest con-tent, "immediately comprehensible, as soon as we have learnt them." Freud's conception of motivated disguise is based on this notion, for he takes it for granted that the obscurity of the dream that the patient ex-periences and reports is not intrinsic to the matter itself but results in-stead from transformative processes—the "dream work"—that serve the purpose of preventing conscious recognition of something inherently clear. (Recall Freud's use of the analogy of the political cartoonist, who must render in oblique and visual form what could more directly be ex-pressed by means of explicit verbal statement.) Thus, on Freud's (1900, p. 597) account, "perfectly rational dream-thoughts, of no less validity than normal thinking," are "submitted to abnormal treatment" (the dream-work) which "is in the highest degree bewildering and irrational."

Why should Freud have adopted such an implausible view, a view that seems inconsistent with his own assumptions about the nature of uncon-scious mentation and human motivation? I think this can be understood as resulting from a certain objectivism in his conception of human sci-ence. Freud's own Interpretations of a given dream are, of course, the product of conscious, verbal thought, and they are meant to clarify and explain; it is therefore not surprising that they should be given in explicit, linguistic terms. But if a person assumes that a valid truth must be, in effect, a mere uncovering or a simple mirroring of a prior reality, he will then be motivated to treat his own Interpretations as discoveries rather than construals, as excavations of a hidden or prior truth that (by a happy coincidence) was lying there all along, in precisely the form in which it is now described.

There are problems with such a view. It downplays the multifarious, inexhaustible nature of the unconscious mind, indeed of the human psyche in general. It encourages the quixotic search for single truths. And finally, it implies that obscurity is really only superficial, a reflection not of an ambiguity or mystery inherent in human existence but of dynamic forces that, on principle at least, could always be uncovered and overcome.[32]

Hermeneutics and Psychopathology

What is the relevance of hermeneutics, of hermeneutic phenomenology and of phenomenological hermeneutics, for the understanding of psychopathology? First, of course, there is the general tendency to encourage a certain tentativeness in one's formulations, a perspectivist recognition of the role of bias or point of view and a concomitant appreciation of the incompleteness of any single diagnostic concept or interpretive formulation. Beyond this, we can see hermeneutics as relevant on two different planes.

On the first, most general level, hermeneutic phenomenology has implications for how any particular form of psychopathology will be conceived, without, however, providing, from itself, a definition of either the essence of the psychopathological-as-such or any particular type of psychopathology. These general implications include eschewing too linear-deterministic a conception of etiology or an overfocus on developmental or causal questions that would neglect present structures of action and experience. Another error to be avoided is that of conceiving psychopathology in terms of discrete, present-at-hand objectlike phenomena in causal or quasi-causal interaction. A good example of the latter, non-hermeneutic approach is Freud's (1911, p. 63) famous interpretation of paranoia as a double transformation of male homosexual desire, in which each of a sequence of distinct attitudes (I, a male, love him; I hate him; he hates [persecutes] me) is treated as a discrete mental representation akin to a Husserlian noema.

A hermeneutic approach would focus less on purported childhood antecedents or particular mental contents (conscious or unconscious), emphasizing instead the overall clearing or lived context, the prereflective stylistic-horizonal features of experience that are so readily ignored (in accordance with what Heidegger calls the "forgetting" of the ontological difference). Such a view does not necessarily contradict more traditional or standard psychoanalytic ways of formulating the pathological element—as, for instance, involving a punitive-superego figure, a grandiose selfobject, or a specific pathogenic conflict such as an oedipal fixation. The particular representation or preoccupation would have to be understood, however, as emblematizing or as having generalized outward into the horizon.[33] This is exemplified in Binswanger's focus not on the content of dreams, but on the particular ways of structuring time and space that are revealed in them (Foucault and Binswanger, 1993). Though developed in a different intellectual tradition, the structural/characterological approach to psychopathology espoused by David Shapiro (1965), which stresses pervasive, formal features rather than specific childhood conflicts and traumas or particular mental contents, is in many respects consistent with hermeneutic phenomenology. Shapiro (1981) demonstrates, for example, that paranoia and unconscious homosexuality might, in some cases, better be understood not as distinct phenomena existing in some kind of external relationship with each other (as in the Freudian sequence mentioned above), but as two different features—or better, aspects—that can be implicit in a rigid personality structure with characteristic anxieties and ambivalences.[34]

So far we have considered the importance of understanding psychological illness or dysfunction in formal or structural terms. Beyond this we must consider the specific criteria of pathology that hermeneutic thought generates from itself through specifying either salient themes or other general qualities that characterize the lived horizon of pathological forms of existence.

Pathological horizons can be understood to be those that are dominated by what, from a Heideggerian standpoint, would be considered relatively inauthentic modes of experience—for example, the "present-at-hand," calculative thinking, a loss of authentic temporality or spontaneity, a failure fully to inhabit or take responsibility for one's own actions, or forms of subjectivism or objectivism that distort or disguise the primordial relationship of Dasein to its world and other human beings (e.g., Heidegger, 1988; Foucault, 1987, pp. 44–57; Dreyfus, 1987; Sass, 1990,

1992a). Both Ludwig Binswanger and Medard Boss, the (existential) psychiatrists who first applied Heideggerian thought to issues in psychopathology and mental health, often associate pathology with a tendency to go along with convention in a passive way, that is, by "falling" into the mode of being of "the They," to adopt Heidegger's jargon. This, however, may be too existentialist a reading of Heidegger (a reading that Heidegger explicitly rejects in the period after *Being and Time*). Heidegger, it seems, has a more subtle appreciation of the social nature of the human being, and conceives authenticity as involving not simple rejection of or distancing from convention so much as a kind of resoluteness and "clear-sightedness" about the *way* one takes up existing cultural possibilities (Guignon, 1993).

Another way of conceiving psychopathology is to focus on more general or formal characteristics of the horizons in question, such as their rigidity or narrowness. This is what Binswanger (1975, pp. 111–19, 284) does in defining psychological disorder as domination of the personality or lived-world by one "world-design," a condition in which what he calls a single "existential a priori" has come to dominate virtually all forms of experience. Binswanger understands this as involving a paradoxical loss of freedom, a "self-chosen unfreedom" whereby a world-design that does, in some sense, derive from the patient himself nevertheless gets reified and eventually dominates the patient's entire being, rendering him passive and thus depriving him of his basic human freedom. Similarly Medard Boss (1988, p. 72) views pathology as being, in essence, "privation, blocking, impairment or restriction of the original openness and freedom"; and Merleau-Ponty (1962, pp. 83, 442) describes how particular preoccupations can generalize and come to dominate the entirety of one's world. Recent psychoanalytic writers of a constructivist persuasion have also equated pathology with rigidity, while associating health with openness to various perspectives and the development of a certain self-consciousness and distance from one's own biases. Patients, they say, need to adopt a more "constructivist" attitude, or else to become "more versatile, sophisticated and relativistic historians of their lives" (Schafer, 1980, p. 43; also Hoffman, 1991, p. 96; Gill, 1994; Protter, 1985; Mitchell, 1988; for criticisms, see Sass, 1994, 1995).

A more specifically Gadamerian approach might focus more directly on the interpersonal encounter as the key index of both pathology and health.[35] Phenomenological hermeneutics would tend to emphasize how the rigidity and narrowness can preclude a true fusing of horizons in the encounter with others. (For Gadamer the truly experienced person is the one who is open to new experiences, who is able to accommodate to the horizons of the other; this Gadamer sees as the consequence of true *Bildung*.) But Gadamer's criticisms of the prejudice against prejudices and of interpretive aestheticism suggest the possibility of rather different forms or sources of pathology as well. Openness, flexibility, and self-critical distance are not, after all, the only hermeneutic virtues. One must also be able to take seriously, hold on to, and apply an enabling set of prejudgments or forestructures.

In emphasizing only rigidity or limitedness as the key to pathology, Binswanger and Boss, like the constructivists and interpersonalists of contemporary psychoanalysis, seem rather one-sided—perhaps because they are too influenced by Western individualism, hence too inclined to adopt a humanistic rather than a truly hermeneutic position (Sass, 1989). After all, it is also possible for the opposite to be the case, for a given individual's horizons to be overly weak or fluid, insufficiently persistent, or to feel too arbitrary or provisional to be fully inhabited, as perhaps in borderline and as-if personalities and in some schizoid and schizophrenic cases (see Sass, 1992b, pp.119–74). More than a century ago, Friedrich Nietzsche (1980, pp. 7, 11, 41, 50) described a "madly thoughtless fragmentation and fraying of all foundations, their dissolution into an ever flowing and dispersing becoming," as among the characteristic illnesses of our age. Modern man, he wrote, is exposed to "much too bright, much too sudden, much too changeable light"; and as a result, "the lines of his horizon restlessly shift again and again," rendering him incapable of both action and desire.[36] In sum, any definition of psychological health or illness needs to bear all the hermeneutic virtues in mind; neither openness nor freedom nor self-consciousness can serve as the sole criterion of health.

Hermeneutics and Psychotherapy

Let us consider implications for psychotherapy. How should therapy be conceived and conducted? What are its pitfalls and what can it hope to accomplish?

One must not expect to discover some radically new set of techniques or rules of procedure. Hermeneutics, after all, questions the very appropriateness of technical or methodological approaches in matters of human knowing and interaction. Also many key thinkers—not only Binswanger and Boss but also more recent writers influenced by the hermeneutic tradition (e.g., Roy Schafer)—have considerable respect for Freud's contributions and are inclined to adopt many of his suggestions, especially on the practical level of therapeutic practice.[37] Hermeneutics' relevance must be sought on a more general or foundational plane: it offers not a new technology but a different vocabulary and way of orienting one's thinking about the nature, purpose, and limitations of psychotherapy. The aspects of hermeneutics that have had the greatest influence include Heidegger's refusal of mechanistic and deterministic visions of human nature and Gadamer's rejection of methodology and of objectivist conceptions of truth.

In Boss's view (1988, pp. 71–72) the central aim of psychotherapy is "to give back to neurotically crippled men and women their own original openness and freedom," to provide people with "the freedom to dispose of the possibilities of their own existence in a way that accords with their own-most perceptions, judgements and talents." Most proponents of Daseinanalysis, existential psychotherapy, and humanistic psychology would agree. If psychological suffering can be understood as "loss of freedom," as the (self-deluded) sense of being fundamentally determined and constrained, then therapy, as one humanistic psychologist puts it, must attempt "to free individuals of their own restrictions, to restore the sense of existential command" (Craig, 1988b, p. 3). Freedom also emerges as the central value of the self-described hermeneutic approach of Roy Schafer (1976), who rejects the mechanistic psychoanalytic metapsychology and advocates an "action language" that would restore the patient's sense of being a unitary agent who initiates and is responsible for the meaningful aims he or she pursues.

As I have already suggested, this emphasis on freedom does seem, from a hermeneutic-phenomenological standpoint, to be exaggerated, putting too existentialist a slant on things. Freedom, at least in the sense of exercising conscious choice or having awareness of a variety of explicit alternatives, is not the only or even the cardinal virtue for Heidegger, who was hostile to many aspects of subjectivism and modern individualism. Acceptance of "thrownness," of the ways one is determined by circumstances entirely beyond one's control, is also part of an authentic existence. In addition Heidegger emphasizes resoluteness and, particularly in his later writings, a respectful and patiently waiting openness to Being. Accordingly, Boss (Craig, 1988c, p. 27) speaks of needing to help other human beings "to come into their being," and describes psychotherapy as helping "to allow that which appears to us to come to its own best fullness." Some patients may in fact have too great a sense of their own control and responsibility (Hicklin, 1988, p. 137), and may need to achieve a more profound sense of their groundedness, mortality, and limitations.

Also, from a Gadamerian point of view, too much emphasis on loosening up restrictions is disturbingly reminiscent of the prejudice against prejudices. In this perspective the goal of psychotherapy would be restoration of the possibility of authentic dialogue. Openness is certainly a part of what is required, but there is also a need for commitment and a degree of constancy, without which one would lack or fail to apply those biases that are, in fact, a *sine qua non* of true openness to the world. Gadamer is acutely aware of the value of tradition and of the need to root oneself in a perspective in order to encounter existence in a meaningful fashion.

But however one imagines the process of therapy—whether as a matter of broadening or loosening or, alternatively, as some kind of grounding, deepening, or centering—it must clearly involve not an alteration of discrete and isolatable features, such as specific memory traces, but something more difficult to bring about: a global or horizonal transformation affecting the unseen but foundational basis of one's entire capacity for experiencing, acting, and communicating with others. But how can one get a patient to experience the nature and consequences of his or her implicit construal of the world, or to conceive and live out alternatives to this construal? Change of this sort will not be easy to facilitate; it is not something one can do for another person by, for example, providing advice or explicit insights.

Freud was obviously well aware of the difficulty of bringing about therapeutic changes and, in particular, of how unavailing mere insight can be; but for the hermeneuticist, his way of accounting for the difficulty fails to get to the heart of the matter. The psychoanalytic notion of "resistance" postulates the existence of specific and targeted mental acts or processes when, in fact, the relevant insights are difficult to achieve for more basic, structural reasons—namely, because they pertain to aspects of one's existence so encompassing and foundational as to be, of necessity, virtually invisible to the person who lives them. Recall that, in the hermeneutic perspective, every illumination is also a concealment. Among the things that get concealed are, of course, the (enabling) presuppositions of the knower in the very moment of his knowing. A full awareness of this fact, of the inevitable falling-short of full self-knowledge (the "eternal penultimacy of consciousness," Gilbert Ryle termed it [Weinsheimer, 1985, p. 39]), must inevitably undermine or at least problematize belief in the ideal of insight, since it indicates that new insights will always be accompanied by new forms of obscurity.

The hermeneutic rejection of objectivist epistemology has implications for the understanding of transference and countertransference and, more generally, for grasping the epistemological situation of the therapeutic encounter. Certainly one must reject the traditional tendency to polarize the analyst as valid knower versus the patient as (self-deluding) object of knowledge. Indeed, if prejudices are biases of our openness to the world, if knowledge is an interpersonal event (Gadamer's "fusion of horizons"), then it is difficult to sustain the traditional view of either transference or countertransference as necessarily being distortions that can or should be overcome. Rather, as Irwin Hoffman (1983, p. 394) notes, "the perspective that the patient brings to bear in interpreting the therapist's inner attitudes [must be regarded as] one among many perspectives that are relevant, each of which highlights different facets of the analyst's involvement." A similar point applies to the analyst and his or her countertransference; here too the ideal of neutral, dispassionate observation comes to seem not merely unattainable but even undesirable. Only from within a perspective, only from a position of embeddedness within attitudes both theoretical and emotional, is it possible to understand another human being in any depth. Escaping such biases is impossible (there *is* no neutral observation point), but one may seek a certain flexibility in shifting among sets of biases, and at least a degree of self-awareness regarding their engulfing and constituting presence (see Hoffman, 1991).[38]

Clearly, then, hermeneutics would dispute the objectivism or naive realism inherent in traditional psychoanalytic views about the role of insight in the psychoanalytic cure (Gadamer [1976, 122] himself speaks of the "naivete of reflection")—a view implied in what has been termed Freud's "tally theory" (Grunbaum), whereby therapeutic effectiveness is taken as an index of historical accuracy. At the same time, a Gadamerian or Heideggerian hermeneutic position need not be assimilated to the more extreme narrativist and relativistic positions espoused in recent years by certain psychoanalytic writers. It is not that a hermeneutically correct position would deny the psychotherapeutic importance of narrative coherence, self-aware perspectivism, or a certain fluidity of horizons (the preoccupations of works by Spence [1982], Schafer [1983], and

Barnaby Barratt [1993] respectively; for critiques of these writers, see Sass and Woolfolk, 1988; Sass, 1988, 1994, 1995). A full grasp of what I have called the hermeneutic virtues will show, however, that it would be a mistake to overemphasize any one of these goals at the expense of the others, or to the point of denying all concern with approximating reality. To understand the latter point, we may find it helpful to review Gadamer's views on the mimetic aspect of art.

As Gadamer notes, the object "out there" that is depicted in, say, a painted portrait is not entirely separate from the representation "in here" but, rather, is transformed by how it is viewed. A compelling portrait of a friend does not merely imitate but actually makes us see her differently; hence the living face cannot provide a constant, unchanging standard of comparison against which to compare the painted image (as correspondence theories of truth might seem to imply).[39] Yet, as Gadamer also notes, it is true as well that a good portrait will pick out and render salient features that were already there and of which we were, in some sense, always aware (Gadamer, 1984, p. 102; Warnke, 1987, pp. 56–60). It also *fits* the face portrayed, even if it caricatures and exaggerates; and in this sense we must acknowledge that the correspondence theory of truth does itself contain at least some measure of truth. Similarly, an optimally effective Interpretation in a psychoanalytic session is creative as well as accurate: it would not have the power to transform unless it also captured its object in some fashion; in this sense narrative truth and historical truth are not opposed but rather potentially complementary (see Wachterhauser, 1994).

The ethics of conversation espoused by hermeneutic theory has implications for the conduct of psychotherapy. A hermeneutics of suspicion—whereby the interpreter looks for deep-lying and motivating meanings of which the speaker or writer is unaware—certainly needs to be part of any therapist's orientation. Gadamer (1989; also Warnke, 1987, pp. 127) suggests, however, that such a stance should be adopted only after the failure of more straightforward attempts to see the coherence and validity of what the other is saying. Such advice runs counter to the more Procrustean tendencies of psychoanalytic interpretation, and would encourage adoption by psychoanalysts of a somewhat more (though by no means entirely) phenomenological orientation, one that pays greater attention to the patient's own sense of his or her meanings. Gadamer (1984, pp. 164–65; Warnke, 1987, p. 14; Linge, 1976, p. xx) has, however, also criticized the aestheticism inherent in treating the other's speech as an object of contemplation, rather than respecting his or her claims about the world enough to disagree with them; and this suggests, at least in some instances, the value of something closer to a Kernbergian confrontation than to a Kohutian empathizing, a Rogerian unconditional positive regard, or the mere fashioning of coherent narratives.

In a confrontational approach, one (tactfully, of course) draws the patient's attention to internal inconsistencies in his attitudes or to features of the world that seem to contradict her claims or assumptions. This would seem to be one way to foster awareness of the nature and, ultimately, the nonnecessity of the particular framework (for example, a polarizing and vacillating one) with which the patient lives. Another possible way of breaking through the totalizing tendencies of a patient's horizons would involve a demonstration, by the psychotherapist's very being, of a world constituted by different values and assumptions. Michel Foucault, a philosopher-historian much influenced by Heidegger, was particularly interested in the totalizing stances that can develop on a general cultural scale.[40] As ways of breaking the lock of these visions, he suggests focusing on attitudes, interpretations, and social practices that have been neglected or marginalized yet that still exist in some corners of society, as well as pursuing a "genealogical" perspective that traces contingent historical pathways that brought the dominant horizons into being, thus illustrating their lack of inevitability. These recommendations could also be applied on the scale of individual psychotherapy—for example, by encouraging recall of forms of existence from periods of childhood that preceded rigidification of the patient's horizons or by exploring the circumstances under which these rigidifications came about (Dreyfus and Wakefield, 1988, p. 281).

The irreducible complexity of the therapeutic situation should be obvious enough. The analyst/therapist will need to shift appropriately between empathy and confrontation, between surface comprehension (hermeneutics of intention) and a hermeneutics of suspicion, between reticence and self-expression. He or she will also need to move gracefully through a variety of differing epistemological attitudes or orientations— at times looking for anomalous facts or potentially recalcitrant details, at other times pressing a narrative frame, and at still other moments reflecting on his own biases or seeking new ones. No formula could possibly indicate when each of these attitudes should be adopted, for how long or how exclusively it should be maintained, or, for that matter, just how it should be applied. This will hardly be news to the experienced clinician, who knows very well that therapy is a kind of art; that in the absence of clear-cut rules one necessarily relies on a half-conscious sense of tact, good judgment, and human intuition. *Phronesis* is the term Gadamer borrows from Aristotle to describe this kind of moral judgment and practical wisdom, the sort that is required, he says, in all true conversation or in any meaningful encounter with a text.

Phronesis is to be distinguished from *episteme*, the kind of general, abstract knowledge epitomized by mathematics, but also from *techne*, which is the technical know-how of the craftsman (Gadamer, 1984, pp. 278–89). One distinctive feature of this sort of knowing, the kind demanded by psychotherapy or legal decision making, is that one's general knowledge may be fundamentally altered or improved by the circumstances of application. In some sense, in fact, one does not even understand key concepts in such domains—what counts, for instance as just or unjust, as self-destructive or insane—except insofar as one applies the concept in question to particular cases (though it is also the case that the particulars are determined by the concepts, in accordance with the hermeneutic circle). Understanding does not precede application because, as Gadamer (1984, p. 23) puts it, "everything decisively depends on the circumstances." To recognize the crucial yet always unpredictable role of context and circumstance is to see that uncertainty (like bias) is quite unavoidable in the therapeutic situation. "The real event of understanding," Gadamer notes (1976, p. 58), "goes beyond what we can bring . . . through methodical effort and critical self-control. Indeed, it goes far beyond what we ourselves can become aware of." Hence it is absurd for the analyst or therapist to be too controlled or too rigidly on guard. It follows that detailed therapeutic manuals and specific protocols of procedure, like general abstract knowledge, can be of but limited value; it may be more useful, in fact, to cultivate a certain spontaneity and to court the unexpected (Stern, 1990).[41]

In closing let us recall a second feature of *phronesis*, the characteristic self-awareness it demands, what Gadamer (1984, p. 288) terms "the virtue of thoughtful reflection."[42] As we know, the proper exercise of moral judgment and practical wisdom requires epistemological self-awareness on our part, a recognition (always incomplete) of how our prejudices can limit or distort what it is that we see. To recognize that human existence is intrinsically ambiguous, that all knowledge brings, as its inevitable complement, a vaster penumbra of ignorance, makes it impossible to think of ourselves as simply seeking *the* correct explanation or the entirety of correct accounts. We can no longer see ourselves in the image of the white-coated scientists or technicians of the popular imagination—led on by a simple quest for the truth, merely following wherever the facts may lead. Instead we must recognize the inevitable partiality of all that we know, and with this, the element of commitment in all knowing along with the sense of responsibility this entails.

The sense of responsibility becomes greater still once we grasp the ontological implications of our embeddedness, once we recognize how abiding biases and orientations affect not only our knowledge but also the world in which we live and have our being. For psychotherapists this is especially crucial: it should be obvious that the theories we wield and techniques we apply do not merely analyze, explain, or treat, but actually help to constitute the modern psyche. As both Philip Rieff and Michel Foucault have argued, psychoanalysis, and modern psychology more generally, not only reflect but also create the individualized and divided, the entitled and self-obsessed kind of self that is characteristic of our culture and our time—contributing to each person's sense of inhabiting a private interior domain that may feel richly furnished or empty but that, in either case, often seems to be at the root of a common modern malaise. The hermeneutic appreciation of human embeddedness, of the role of culture and historical tradition in molding both our knowing and our being, should disabuse us of any tendency to universalize our own predicament, to view Western individualism or inwardness as a higher, purer, or more authentic expression of the essential human condition. It should make us recognize that, whatever else it may be, psychoanalysis is also an ethnopsychology—and as such both a reflection and a constituent of our own peculiar horizons. Finally it should help us see that along with the help we provide, we psychologists, psychoanalysts, and other psychotherapists may be simultaneously contributing to some of the more problematic aspects of modern Western civilization, fostering "that form of alienation that turns [the human being] into *Homo psychologicus*" (Foucault, 1987, p. 74).

NOTES

1. Dilthey describes *verstehen* as "understanding of meaningful connections within the mental realm" (quoted in Boss, 1963, p. 85).

2. I recognize, of course, that other usages of the term "hermeneutics" are perfectly defensible. For a brief introduction to three kinds of hermeneutics—termed

methodological, ontological, and critical—see Woolfolk, Sass, and Messer, 1988. The hermeneutics discussed in the present chapter corresponds to "ontological hermeneutics."

3. Reflecting on the relationship of ethnology and philosophy, Heidegger (1962, p. 76) states that "the positive sciences [these, presumably, would include psychoanalysis] neither 'can' nor should wait for the ontological labours of philosophy to be done"; more philosophically informed work in such a field would not constitute a straightforward advance in knowledge, he says, but a "recapitulation," a reconstruction of what has already been discovered in a more sophisticated, "ontologically more transparent" way.

4. These are the theorists whose views most closely approximate the vision of hermeneutics outlined in the present chapter. The writings of Schafer and Spence, though extremely valuable, are by my lights less hermeneutically "correct." For an overview on hermeneutics and psychoanalysis, see Phillips (1991). For hermeneutic phenomenology in a Jungian vein, see Brooke (1991).

5. Schafer, for example, an analyst much influenced by hermeneutics, nevertheless prefers the narratives provided by classical psychoanalysis. One might also pose the question of whether psychoanalysis has any greater affinity with hermeneutics than do other schools of psychology or psychotherapy. Psychoanalysis has an especially acute appreciation of the role of the past, forms of awareness that are not fully conscious, and, in general, the elusive complexity of human existence; also, it lacks the prejudice against prejudices. All these features are congruent with the hermeneutic perspective.

6. In this way, says Heidegger (1962, p. 187), pure intuition (*Anschauen*), the essential method of Husserlian phenomenology, is deprived "of its priority, which corresponds . . . to the priority of the present-at-hand in traditional ontology."

7. The concepts of understanding and interpretation are closely related in the hermeneutic tradition, indeed often virtually indistinguishable. We might think, however, of "interpretation" as stressing the more active contribution of subjectivity (Dasein, in Heidegger's terminology) to the constitution of the world, whereas "understanding" connotes a more passive or recipient role, emphasizing not the intelligibility given to the world so much as the significances received from it. But for Heidegger and Gadamer, these are not distinct processes that could ever be separated ("All understanding is interpretation," writes Gadamer [1984, p. 350]), but rather ways of calling attention to aspects of a unified process or event.

8. For Freud's use of the rebus metaphor, see Freud (1900, vol. 4, p. 277).

9. Dasein's "own specific state of Being . . . remains concealed from it. Dasein is ontically 'closest' to itself and ontologically farthest; but pre-ontologically it is surely not a stranger" (Heidegger, 1962, p. 37). "What is it that phenomenology is to 'let us see'? . . . Manifestly, it is something that proximally and for the most

part does *not* show itself at all: it is something that lies *hidden* . . . but at the same time it is something that belongs to what thus shows itself, and it belongs to it so essentially as to constitute its meaning and its ground" (p. 59).

10. Being, writes Heidegger, "is both nowhere and everywhere. It *has* no place as something other than itself. It is itself the placeless dwelling place of all presencing" (1977c, p. 43). There is controversy about the extent to which Husserl himself came to recognize some of the limits of a "phenomenological positivism" that would seek exact knowledge via a pure beholding. Merleau-Ponty (1982–83, p. 70) sees Husserl's phenomenological program as having "brought to light fragments of being which disconcerted his frame of reference." In Merleau-Ponty's view (1962, p. xiv), "The most important lesson which the reduction teaches us is the impossibility of a complete reduction." Merleau-Ponty's "optimistic" reading of Husserl's *Crisis of European Sciences and Transcendental Phenomenology* makes the later Husserl sound virtually indistinguishable from Heidegger; but this is not the usual interpretation. See Husserl (1970, pp. 148–51) on the possibility of objectifying the entire background or "vital horizon" by means of a universal epoche (transcendental reduction).

11. Dasein "*is* itself the clearing," writes Heidegger (1962, p. 171).

12. "The Interpretation of the world begins, in the first instance, with some entity within-the-world, so that the phenomenon of the world in general no longer comes into view" (Heidegger, 1962, p. 122).

13. Husserl would be included among those whom Heidegger sees as being concerned only with beings, "that which is" (*das Seiende*), and not with Being (*das Sein*), the more primordial ground of existence (Lauer, 1965, p. 49 n).

14. "Being" may be the most universal of concepts; this does not mean, however, "that it is the one which is clearest or that it needs no further discussion. It is rather the darkest of all" (Heidegger, 1962, p. 23).

15. "Ontically, of course, Dasein is not only close to us—even that which is closest: we *are* it. In spite of this, or rather for just this reason, it is ontologically that which is farthest" (Heidegger, 1962, p. 36). See also Gadamer's statement, "We are dark to ourselves, and that means that we are. It co-constitutes the being of our Dasein" (Weinsheimer, 1985, p. 169 n).

16. One might think of hermeneutic phenomenology as furthering the telos inherent in psychoanalysis itself: as "bring[ing] to psychoanalysis certain categories, certain means of expression that it needs in order to be completely itself" (Merleau-Ponty, 1982–83, p. 67), something it can do only by separating itself from a certain scientism or objectivism. The Heideggerian analyst Medard Boss appears to have taken this view: "In fact, I think I'm a more Freudian, a more truly Freudian, a more faithfully Freudian therapist, than Freud himself," he said. "Freud spoiled his insight and his genius by his belief that only natural scientific thinking leads to truth" (Craig 1988c, p. 43).

17. See Stern (1991, pp. 54–55) re several recent psychoanalytic formulations

of the unconscious as "unformulated experience" or "absence of explicit reflection." See also Orange (1995) on "emotional memory."

18. Both classical psychoanalysis and some of its critics have focused almost exclusively on issues of discovery. In *Narrative Truth and Historical Truth*, a powerful critique of psychoanalytic procrusteanism often cited as a central text of psychoanalytic hermeneutics, Donald Spence (1982) demonstrates very convincingly the great difficulty of avoiding inaccuracies of an atomistic, factual sort in psychoanalytic reconstructions of a patient's past; and based on this argument he gives up entirely on historical truth, suggesting that only pragmatic or aesthetic criteria can be used for selecting among psychoanalytic accounts. Nowhere, however, does Spence consider the possibility that a given narrative may perfectly well capture broader themes or modes of past experience even though it may be wrong on certain factual details. Spence focuses too much on *entdecken* and too little on *erschlossen*.

19. A great deal of empirical research in cognitive psychology illustrates these tendencies; see, for example, Rubin (1986).

20. "[T]he essential nature of the historical spirit does not consist in the restoration of the past, but in thoughtful mediation with contemporary life" (Gadamer, 1984, p. 150). At times Freud (1899, p. 322) acknowledges something akin to this truth, as in his screen memories paper, where he notes that we do not have memories *from* childhood so much as memories *relating to* our childhood—memories that show "our earliest years not as they were but as they appeared at the later period when the memory was aroused."

21. In Merleau-Ponty's view (1962, p. xviii), our relationship to the world cannot be further clarified by analysis; philosophy can only place it before our eyes for ratification.

22. Merleau-Ponty (1962, p. 23) speaks of phenomenology as "a new way of looking at things," which, far from privileging the clear and the distinct, "reverses the relative positions of the clear and the obscure."

23. "By looking at the world theoretically," writes Heidegger (1962, p. 177), "we have already dimmed it down to the uniformity of what is purely present-at-hand."

24. Kuhn calls himself a hermeneuticist, by the way. See Hesse (1980) for criticism of the assumption that there is something less hermeneutical about the natural as opposed to the human sciences.

25. "A consciousness formed by the authentic hermeneutical attitude will be receptive to the origins and entirely foreign features of that which comes to it from outside its own horizons. Yet this receptivity is not acquired with an objectivist 'neutrality'" (Gadamer, 1979, pp. 151–52).

26. The latter process may involve selection of a different theory of a similar type or, more rarely, a more fundamental shift in mode of understanding, as with

Kuhn's distinction between the puzzle solving of "normal science" versus the paradigm shifts of scientific revolutions.

27. Gadamer questions the adequacy of both inductivist and deductivist models of concept formation as being too hierarchical and unidirectional. The more intuitive, oscillating process of metaphoric comparison may provide a better model of human knowing (Gadamer 1984, pp. 387–97; Weinsheimer 1985, pp. 237–38).

This characteristic refusal of the various "isms," with their clear-cut metaphysical and epistemological assumptions, can make statements of the hermeneutic stance sound rather paradoxical at times, but this is because hermeneutics rejects any kind of oversimplifying "rigor." An interesting passage in *Being and Time* (Heidegger, 1962, p. 454), quoted from Count Yorck, approvingly describes paradoxicality as "a mark of truth" and as being opposed to common opinion, which is characterized as "an elemental precipitate of a halfway understanding which makes generalizations."

28. "My real concern was and is philosophic [as opposed to methodological]: not what we do or what we ought to do, but what happens to us over and above our wanting and doing" (Gadamer, 1984, p. xxviii). Gadamer does not, in fact, deny the worth of methodological approaches in the human sciences; he only denies that method is all we need, that it has a monopoly on truth (Weinsheimer, 1991, p. 28).

29. Gadamer agrees with the 19th-century philologist Philip August Boeckh, who wrote, "Correct understanding is an art, and therefore rests on a half-conscious competence" (Mueller-Vollmer, 1985, p. 22).

30. Gadamer (1984, pp. 305–41) refers to this as "effective-historical consciousness" (*wirkungsgeschichtliches Bewusstsein*). It is part of what Risser (1989, p. 176) describes as a characteristic "vigilance against the pretension of knowing."

31. This is the source of what Gadamer (1984, p. 239) calls "the tyranny of unrecognized prejudices."

32. It would be absurd to argue that Freud lacks all appreciation of the elusiveness of human existence. He mentions, for example, the "dream's navel," "the spot where it reaches down into the unknown." A passage often exists, he notes, "in even the most thoroughly interpreted dream which has to be left obscure" (Laplanche and Pontalis, 1973, pp. 236, 294; Freud, 1900, vol. 5, p. 525); there the "tangle of dream-thoughts" is so richly intertwined as to make one realize that the "intricate network" of our inner world of associations could never be fully unraveled. As with the notion of overdetermination mentioned earlier, however, Freud seems to account for this in de facto rather than on-principle terms (i.e., as due to immense complicatedness), thus stopping short of a full (and hermeneutically "correct") acknowledgment of human ambiguity.

33. On the need to supplement this "breadth psychological" approach with an account of more focal forms of repression, see Dreyfus and Wakefield (1988).

34. To the extent that psychoanalytic writers adopt a more structural, stylistic, or horizonal way of understanding psychopathology, their work tends to be more congruent with a hermeneutic approach than is much of classical psychoanalysis.

35. According to Karl-Otto Apel, the goal of psychoanalytic treatment is to restore the possibility of true dialogue with the patient (Warnke, 1987, p. 122).

36. "[O]nly by forgetting that he himself is an *artistically creating* subject does man live with any repose, security, and consistency," writes Nietzsche (1979, p. 86), in a line one can read as a rebuke to the exaggerations of some narrativist, constructivist, and postmodernist psychoanalysts.

37. Boss (1963, pp. 285, 59) spoke of "Freud's unsurpassed practical recommendations" for the conduct of therapy, describing his own project as an attempt to "restore the original meaning of Freud's actual, immediate, concrete and most brilliant observations."

38. Such ideas have been proposed in psychoanalysis for several decades now, generally without explicit reliance on hermeneutic thought; but as Donnel Stern (1991, pp. 59, 69 n) has suggested, it is Gadamerian hermeneutics that provides the most cogent justification for accepting this relatively new standpoint.

39. Mimetic art, on Gadamer's account, is a form of knowledge; "one learns to see the object represented in terms of the truth that the representation reveals about it," explains Warnke (1987, p. 59). "[W]e do not understand what recognition is in its profoundest nature," writes Gadamer (1984, p. 102), "if we only see that something that we know already is known again, i.e., that what is familiar is recognized again. The joy of recognition is rather that more becomes known than is already known."

40. "For me Heidegger has always been the essential philosopher" (Foucault, 1985, p. 8).

41. Gadamer (1984, p. 279) states that "knowledge which cannot be applied to the concrete situation remains meaningless and even risks obscuring the demands that the situation makes."

42. Heidegger (1977b, p. 116) defines reflection as "the courage to make the truth of our own presuppositions and the realm of our own goals into the things that most deserve to be called in question."

REFERENCES

Barratt, Barnaby. 1993. *Psychoanalysis and the postmodern impulse.* Baltimore: Johns Hopkins University Press.

Baynes, Kenneth, Bohman, James, and McCarthy, Thomas, eds. 1987. *Philosophy: End or transformation?*. Cambridge: M. I. T. Press.

Binswanger, Ludwig. 1975. *Being in the world*. Trans. and intro. Jacob Needleman. London: Souvenir Press.

Boss, M. 1963. *Psychoanalysis and daseinanalysis*. Trans. L. B. Lefebre. New York: Basic Books.

———. 1988. Recent considerations in Daseinanalysis. In Craig, ed. *Psychotherapy for freedom*, pp. 58–74.

Bourdieu, Pierre. 1990. *The logic of practice*. Stanford: Stanford University Press.

Bowie, M. 1991. *Lacan*. Cambridge: Harvard University Press.

Brooke, Roger. 1991. Phenomenological analytical psychology: A clinical study. *Harvest* 37:88–100.

Bruner, Jerome. 1990. *Acts of meaning*. Cambridge: Harvard University Press.

Craig, Erik, ed. 1988a. *Psychotherapy for freedom: The daseinanalytic way in psychology and psychoanalysis*. Special issue of *Humanistic Psychologist* 16.

Craig, Erik. 1988b. Introduction: Daseinanalysis: A quest for essentials. In Craig, ed., *Psychotherapy for freedom*, pp. 1–21.

Craig, Erik. 1988c. An encounter with Medard Boss. In Craig, ed., *Psychotherapy for freedom*, pp. 24–57.

Csordas, Thomas, ed. 1994. *Embodiment and experience: The existential ground of culture and self*. Cambridge: Cambridge University Press.

Cushman, Philip. 1995. *Constructing the self, constructing America: A cultural history of psychotherapy*. Reading, MA: Addison-Wesley.

Diamond, Cora. 1991. *The realistic spirit: Wittgenstein, philosophy, and the mind*. Cambridge: M. I. T. Press.

Dilthey, Wilhelm. 1985. The understanding of other persons and their life expressions. In Mueller-Vollmer, ed., *The hermeneutics reader*, pp. 152–65.

Dreyfus, Hubert. 1987. Foucault's therapy. *PsychCritique* 2:65–83.

———. 1991. *Being in the world*. Cambridge: M. I. T. Press.

Dreyfus, Hubert and Wakefield, Jerome. 1988. From depth psychology to breadth psychology: A phenomenological approach to psychopathology. In Messer, Sass, and Woolfolk, eds., *Hermeneutics and psychological theory*, pp. 272–88.

Foucault, Michel. 1985. Final interview. *Raritan* 1 (summer).

———. 1987. *Mental illness and psychology*. Trans. Alan Sheridan. Berkeley: University of California Press.

Foucault, Michel, and Binswanger, Ludwig. 1993. *Dream and existence*. Trans. Forrest Williams. Atlantic Highlands, NJ: Humanities Press.

Frede, Dorothea. 1993. The question of being: Heidegger's project. In Charles Guignon, ed., *The Cambridge companion to Heidegger*. Cambridge: Cambridge University Press, pp. 42–69.

Freud, Sigmund. 1899. Screen memories. In *Standard edition of the complete psychological works of Sigmund Freud* (hereafter *SE*), trans. and ed. James Strachey. London: Hogarth Press, 1958, vol. 3, pp. 301–22.

———. 1900. *The interpretation of dreams*. In *SE*, vols. 4 (all) and 5, pp. 339–625.

———. 1911. Psycho-analytic notes on an autobiographical account of a case of paranoia. In *SE* vol. 12, pp. 9–82.

Gadamer, Hans-Georg. 1976. *Philosophical hermeneutics*. Trans. David Linge. Berkeley: University of California Press.

———. 1979. The problem of historical consciousness. In Paul Rabinow and William Sullivan, eds., *Interpretive social science: A reader*. Berkeley: University of California Press.

———. 1984. *Truth and method*. New York: Crossroad.

———. 1989. Reply to Jacques Derrida. In Diane P. Michelfelder and Richard E. Palmer, eds., *Dialogue and deconstruction*. Albany: State University of New York Press, pp. 55–57.

Gedo, John and Goldberg, Arnold, eds. 1973. *Models of the mind*. Chicago: University of Chicago Press.

Geertz, Clifford. 1973. *The interpretation of cultures*. New York: Basic Books.

———. 1983. *Local knowledge*. New York: Basic Books.

Gill, Merton. 1994. *Psychoanalysis in transition: A personal view*. Hillsdale, NJ: Analytic Press.

Guignon, Charles. 1992. History and commitment in the early Heidegger. In Hubert Dreyfus and Harrison Hall, eds., *Heidegger: A critical reader*. Cambridge, MA: Blackwell, pp. 130–42.

———. 1993. Authenticity, moral values, and psychotherapy. In Charles Guignon, ed., *The Cambridge companion to Heidegger*. Cambridge: Cambridge University Press, pp. 215–39.

Hall, Harrison. 1993. Intentionality and world: Division I of *Being and time*. In *The Cambridge companion to Heidegger*, ed. Charles B. Guignon. Cambridge: Cambridge University Press, pp. 122–40.

Heidegger, M. 1962. *Being and time*. Trans. John Macquarrie and Edward Robinson. New York: Harper and Row.

———. 1977a. The question concerning technology. In *The question concerning technology and other essays*, trans. William Lovitt. New York: Harper and Row, pp. 3–35.

———. 1977b. The age of the world picture. In *The question concerning technology*, pp. 115–64.

———. 1977c. The turning. In *The question concerning technology*, pp. 36–49.

———. 1988. On adequate understanding of Daseinanalysis. In Craig, ed., *Psychotherapy for freedom*, pp. 75–98.

Held, Klaus. 1993. Fundamental moods and Heidegger's critique of contemporary culture. In John Sallis, ed., *Reading Heidegger: Commemorations*. Bloomington: Indiana University Press, pp. 286–303.

Hesse, M. 1980. *Revolutions and reconstructions in the philosophy of science*. Brighton, UK: Harvester Press.

Hicklin, Alois. 1988. The significance of life history in Daseinanalytic psychotherapy. In Craig, ed., *Psychotherapy for freedom*, pp. 130–39.

Hoffman, Irwin Z. 1983. The patient as interpreter of the analyst's experience. *Contemporary Psychoanalysis* 19:389–422.

———. 1991. Discussion: Toward a social-constructivist view of the psychoanalytic situation. *Psychoanalytic Dialogues* 1:74–105.

Husserl, Edmund. 1965. *Philosophie als strenge Wissenschaft*. Frankfurt: Klostermann.

———. 1970. *The crisis of European sciences and transcendental phenomenology*. Trans. David Carr. Evanston, IL: Northwestern University Press.

Kuhn, Thomas. 1970. *The structure of scientific revolutions*. 2d ed. Chicago: University of Chicago Press.

Laplanche, J. and Pontalis, J.-B. 1973. *The language of psychoanalysis*. Trans. Donald Nicholson-Smith. New York: Norton.

Lauer, Quentin. 1965. *Phenomenology: Its genesis and prospect*. New York: Harper and Row.

Linge, David E. 1976. Editor's introduction, In Gadamer, *Philosophical hermeneutics*, pp. xi-lviii.

Merleau-Ponty, Maurice. 1962. *The phenomenology of perception*. Trans. Colin Smith. London: Routledge and Kegan Paul.

———. 1982–83. Phenomenology and psychoanalysis: Preface to Hesnard's *L'oeuvre de Freud*." Trans. Alden L. Fisher. *Review of Existential Psychology and Psychiatry* 18: 67–72.

Messer, Stanley, Sass, Louis, and Woolfolk, Robert, eds. 1988. *Hermeneutics and psychological theory*. New Brunswick: Rutgers University Press.

Mitchell, S. 1988. *Relational concepts in psychoanalysis*. Cambridge: Harvard University Press.

Mitchell, S. 1993. *Hope and dread in psychoanalysis*. New York: Basic Books.

Mueller-Vollmer, K. 1985. Introduction: Language, mind, and artifact: An outline of hermeneutic theory since the Enlightenment. In Mueller-Vollmer, ed., *The hermeneutics reader*. New York: Continuum, pp. 1–53.

Nietzsche, Friedrich. 1967. *The genealogy of morals*. Trans. Walter Kaufman and R. J. Hollingdale. New York: Vintage.

———. 1979. On truth and lies in a nonmoral sense. In *Philosophy and truth: Selections from Nietzsche's notebooks of the early 1870s*, trans. Daniel Brazeale. Atlantic Highlands, NJ: Humanities Press, pp. 79–97.

———. 1980. *On the advantage and disadvantage of history for life*. Trans. P. Preuss. Indianapolis, Hackett.

Orange, Donna. 1995. *Psychoanalytic epistemology: The process of emotional understanding.* New York: Guilford.

Phillips, J. 1991. Hermeneutics in psychoanalysis: Review and reconsideration. *Psychoanalysis and Contemporary Thought.* 14:371–424.

Pine, Fred. 1990. *Drive, ego, object, and self: A synthesis for clinical work.* New York: Basic Books.

Protter, B. 1985. Toward an emergent psychoanalytic epistemology. *Contemporary Psychoanalysis* 21:208–27.

Risser, James. 1989. The two faces of Socrates: Gadamer-Derrida. In Diane P. Michelfelder and Richard E. Palmer, eds., *Dialogue and deconstruction: The Gadamer-Derrida encounter.* Albany: State University of New York Press, pp. 176–85.

Rubin, David C., ed., 1986. *Autobiographical memory.* New York: Cambridge University Press.

Sass, Louis. 1988. The self and its vicissitudes: An "archaeological" study of the psychoanalytic avant-garde. *Social Research* 55:551–608.

———. 1989. Humanism, hermeneutics, and humanistic psychoanalysis. *Psychoanalysis and Contemporary Thought* 12:443–505.

———. 1990. The truth-taking stare: A Heideggerian interpretation of a schizophrenic world. *J. of Phenomenological Psychology* 21:121–49.

———. 1992a. Heidegger, schizophrenia, and the ontological difference. *Philosophical Psychology* 5:109–32.

———. 1992b. *Madness and modernism: Insanity in the light of modern art, literature, and thought.* New York: Basic Books.

———. 1994. The epic of disbelief: The postmodernist turn in contemporary psychoanalysis. *Partisan Review* 61:96–110.

———. 1995. Review essay re: Barnaby Barratt, *Psychoanalysis and the postmodern impulse. Psychoanalytic Dialogues* 5:123–36.

Sass, Louis, and Woolfolk, Robert. 1988. Psychoanalysis and the hermeneutic turn: A critique of narrative truth and historical truth. *Journal of the American Psychoanalytic Association* 36:429–54.

Schafer, Roy. 1976. *A new language for psychoanalysis.* New Haven: Yale University Press.

Schafer, Roy. 1980. Narration in the psychoanalytic dialogue. In W. J. T. Mitchell, ed., *On narrative.* Chicago: University of Chicago Press.

Schafer, R. 1983. *The analytic attitude.* New York: Basic Books.

Schafer, R. 1992. *Retelling a life: Narration and dialogue in psychoanalysis.* New York: Basic Books.

Shapiro, David. 1965. *Neurotic styles.* New York: Basic Books.

Shapiro, David. 1981. *Autonomy and rigid character.* New York: Basic Books.

Sherwood, M. 1969. *The logic of explanation in psychoanalysis.* New York: Academic Press.

Shweder, Richard A. 1991. *Thinking through cultures: Expeditions in cultural psychology*. Cambridge: Harvard University Press.

Spence, Donald. 1982. *Narrative truth and historical truth*. New York: Norton.

Stern, Donnel B. 1990. Courting surprise: Unbidden perceptions in clinical practice. *Contemporary Psychoanalysis* 26:452–78.

———. 1991. A philosophy for the embedded analyst: Gadamer's hermeneutics and the social paradigm of psychoanalysis. *Contemporary Psychoanalysis* 27:51–80.

Stolorow, Robert, Brandchaft, B., and Atwood, G. 1988. *Psychoanalytic treatment: An intersubjective approach*. Hillsdale, NJ: Analytic Press.

Wachterhauser, Brice R. 1994. Gadamer's realism. In Brice R. Wachterhauser, ed., *Hermeneutics and truth*. Evanston, IL: Northwestern University Press.

Warnke, G. 1987. *Gadamer: Hermeneutics, tradition and reason*. Stanford: Stanford University Press.

Weinsheimer, Joel. 1985. *Gadamer's hermeneutics*. New Haven: Yale University Press.

———. 1991. *Philosophical hermeneutics and literary theory*. New Haven: Yale University Press.

Wittgenstein, Ludwig. 1958. *Philosophical investigations*. 2d ed. Oxford: Blackwell.

Woolfolk, Robert, Sass, Louis, and Messer, Stanley. 1988. Introduction to hermeneutics. In Messer, Sass, and Woolfolk, eds., *Hermeneutics and psychological theory*.

Chapter Twelve

The Cure of Stories

Self-Deception, Danger Situations, and the
Clinical Role of Narratives in Roy Schafer's
Psychoanalytic Theory

Paul A. Roth

EDITORS' INTRODUCTION

As Paul Roth suggests, Roy Schafer has been one of the most provocative and philosophically sophisticated theorists in recent years. Although deeply lodged in the orthodox tradition in terms of his acceptance of what he calls Freudian "storylines"—the infantile psychosexual and aggressive conflicts that he thinks are the basis for an analysand's problems in living—Schafer has nonetheless rejected classical metapsychology, the theoretical superstructure of Freudian psychoanalysis. The main problem with metapsychology, according to Schafer, is the tendency for metapsychological explanation, in both its mechanistic and anthropomorphic variants, to deny or underplay the role of the analysand's intention, volition, and responsibility in favor of deterministic interpretations. For Schafer, says Roth, experience is always an active construal, never just a passive reflection of a determining external reality, hence Schafer's "reformulation of Freudian metapsychology into 'action language.'" In contrast with Freud's "premodern language of mind," says Schafer, the main principle of action language is that all human experience should be designated by verbs in the active mode and understood as "actions," as "intentional or goal directed performances" "for which the analysand accepts some significant measure of responsibility." Only in this way will we "unquestionably require there to be a specific author of the action in question."

Schafer, while remaining in the Freudian tradition in terms of his acceptance and clinical use of Freudian "retellings," has developed a "narrational" account of the self, a "psychoanalysis without psychodynamics," as he has described it. It is this theory of the self, says Roth, that helps illuminate a crucial philosophical problem that challenges psychoanalytic theory. The challenge was best formulated by Sartre: how to conceptualize a unified self without postulating a metaphysical splitting of the self, and a splitting of the nature in which a self can be conscious of itself. Says Roth, "insofar as psychoanalytic theory speaks of an unconscious, and, in particular, a self that is deceived as to its own (unconscious) motives, then psychoanalytic theory doubles the epistemological dualism deriving from Hume and Kant. For now the self cannot only not be an object to itself, it both is and is not aware of itself." Schafer's thoughtful reflections on the problem of self-identity and self-deception, says Roth, resolve these problems and lead him to conceptualize psychopathology and psychoanalytic treatment in a novel manner.

As Roth indicates, Schafer's notion of the self can be described as "the self-as-storyteller about who one is" or, in the words of Schafer, "the self is a kind of telling about one's individuality." This view, argues Roth, has the advantage of relinquishing Freud's effort to formulate a physics of the mental and puts in place instead a unified person who is acting and doing. This is Schafer's move away from Freud's motivational mechanisms driven by instinct, in which the person is more or less passive, to what Roth calls an existential/humanistic view that stresses the individual's agency. People are "authors of their existence," Schafer says. Psychoanalysis, according to Schafer, must reject Freud's "Newtonian idea of psychodynamics" and adopt "a thoroughly non-mechanistic, non-organismic language," a language of reasons, not causes.

For Schafer, psychopathology is in part conceptualized in terms of "disclaimed actions." That is, there is no confusing splitting of the self as in conventional psychoanalytic explanations of self-deception; rather, he acknowledges that "people can be unaware of the reasons for their actions." Disclaimed actions, says Roth, are a fundamental form of self-deception inasmuch as individuals speak of themselves as not in control of their desires and behavior. Schafer, influenced by existentialism, is here talking about the evasion of responsibility for one's feelings, thoughts, and behavior. The goal of Schaferian psychoanalysis, says Roth, is to help the analysand "reclaim" these happenings as his actions.

Roth then raises a most important question regarding Schafer's view of self-deception, namely, why does a person's narrative cause him pain? If individuals create their own meanings, why do people feel discomfort with the meaning they have placed on their actions? These questions are crucial to understanding Schafer's view of psychopathology, formulated in part in terms of what he calls "danger situations." Danger situations are the noncognitive personal constructions, rooted in one's preverbal or traumatic past, that are inaccessible or overwhelming such that they cannot be articulated. It is through these inchoate experiences, these unarticulated storylines, that a person defines and constructs experiences. Thus, says Schafer, "a neurosis is created and arranged and protected. It is, correlatively, the construction of danger situations and the construction of emotional action to take in these situations."

Schaferian psychoanalytic treatment, says Roth, is "the cure of stories." It consists of clarifying, in terms of a psychoanalytic narrative, what the analysand is doing, and to make sense of it in terms of unconsciously defined and disclaimed danger situations. The therapeutic task is to identify and "deconstruct" the interpretation given experiences that are thematized in terms of one's particular unconscious danger situations. Psychoanalytic interpretation expands the conceptual resources available to the person to make his behavior intelligible and to take responsibility for it. Says Roth, "Words free not by magic, but by providing new shape and form through which to construct, analyze, and articulate experience." Schafer's narrative thus offers us a somewhat different version of the human condition than Freud, Kohut, and Klein, three "masternarratives," as Schafer calls them. As Roth says, paraphrasing Schafer, "if Freud offers us the narrative of 'the taming of the beast within,' Kohut narrates according to 'the discovery of the self within,' and Klein postulates the 'mad person within raging about,' Schafer's narrative concentrates on the enhancement of responsibility, from 'self-as-victim of unknown psychic forces' to 'master in one's own house.'" (P. M. and A. R.)

Talk about the self or self-identity invokes a number of interrelated philosophical puzzles. A key puzzle concerns the fact that, *contra* Descartes, there is no pure or simple *cogito* that one apprehends. Hume famously put this as follows: "For my part, when I enter most intimately into what I call *myself*, I always stumble on some particular perception or other, ... I never can catch *myself* at any time without a perception, and never can observe any thing but the perception" (Hume, 1988, p. 252) No *particular* perception turns out to be the perception of *oneself*. There are available only congeries of perceptions that one speaks of as related to a single self. Call this the "no-self puzzle": what is the nature of the self who is conscious but not also an object for that consciousness?

Kant extended Hume's insight by arguing that the existence of a unified consciousness is necessary for there being a self. If one could not identify experiences as one's own, one would lack a basic prerequisite for self-identity. But the unity that makes self-identity possible must be constituted *prior to* experience, for, as just noted, no particular experience provides the experience of a self. Rather, Kant observed, the thought that an experience is mine accompanies our experiences. "Through this I or he or it (the thing) which thinks, nothing further is represented than a transcendental subject of thoughts = X. It is known only through the thoughts which are its predicates, and of it, apart from them, we cannot have any concept whosoever" (Kant, 1933, A346/B404). The senses in which the self is constitutive of but not an object in experience creates what one commentator terms "epistemological schizophrenia" (Todes, 1967, p. 166) with respect to the nature of self-knowledge. A radical dissociation seemingly exists between the self as knower and the self as known. Even more, one has no "privileged access" to the knowing self; we know who we are only through experience.

To appreciate the relevance of such questions about the self to psychoanalytic theory and practice, one need only consider, for example, how these issues bear on the critical notion of self-deception. Self-deception, in one form or another, constitutes a *raison d'être* of psychoanalysis. Analytic work aims to identify and bring to consciousness motives, intentions, and meanings involved in one's own actions of which one is, in some sense or other, unaware. Without a coherent account of self-deception, psychoanalysis is a cure for which there is no identified disease.[1]

Self-deception implies that one does not have available to oneself the meanings and intentions of one's actions and experiences. Thus, the dissociation noted by Hume and Kant between the self as unified consciousness and the self as object of knowledge is reproduced in psychoanalysis as a split between the knowing subject and that subject's understanding of his or her own actions. Moreover, the epistemological split arises with particular force and significance within the theoretical framework of classical psychoanalysis inasmuch as what is "hidden" from view is not just the self as unity, but one's own motives and intentions as agent. In order to generate an account of self-deception, psychoanalytic theory must double the split that philosophers acknowledge.[2]

But further splitting (that is, beyond that of the pure and empirical self) leads only to theoretical incoherence regarding the notion of the self. Positing an unconscious does not avoid the epistemological and metaphysical necessity for having a single self of whom all the various conflicting parts are true. Without a unified consciousness, self-deception would be impossible. For if there is no such unified self, then who is it that is deceived?[3] In order to have even prima facie plausibility, psychoanalytic theory must provide an account of self-deception that respects the unity of the knowing subject.[4] In this respect, the cogency of a theory's notion of self-deception represents a key test of its plausibility.

In what follows, I explore aspects of the "narrational" account of the self advocated and developed by Roy Schafer. Schafer's narrative theory of the self commands attention, I suggest, because of the particularly cogent solution it offers to the problem of self-deception and the general question of self-identity. In this connection, I indicate how Schafer, through his formulation of a philosophically sophisticated account of how self-deception is possible, creates in turn a distinctive vision of the "analytic attitude." That is, I indicate how Schafer's account of the self and self-identity determines his approach to treatment.

Somewhat ironically, my reconstruction of Schafer gives less pride of place to what Schafer himself considers his main theoretical innovation—the reformulation of Freudian metapsychology into "action language." My account underscores, rather, how the narrativist perspective provides a well-articulated theoretical framework for identifying and dealing with "danger situations." Danger situations are experiences that are perceived as threatening and that, by virtue of how the experience is subjectively interpreted, trigger patterns of defensive behavior. That is, the key achievement of Schafer's theory, at least on my telling of it, lies in his development of the notion of a danger situation and how he uses this to link to a theoretically cogent concept of the self that is clinically useful for the task of the analysis.

More specifically, the narrational view, as I present it, shows how the narrative construction of the self provides, for the analytic situation, a way of literally giving voice to the analysand's concerns. In an analysis of danger situations, one is reaching back to a time when adequate words were not available to express or give shape to what one, at that age and time, experienced. Schafer's clinical theory emphasizes the role of analysis in giving words to and a narrative structure for the character of danger situations. It highlights as well how and why the process of articulating the partially or wholly inchoate past is best analogized to story construction and is not to be thought of as the recovery of a past with some intrinsic or determinate meaning. The therapeutic function of narratives I term the "cure of stories."[5]

Moreover, an understanding of the constructed nature of the psychoanalytic narrative helps explain how tales told to and from the couch have therapeutic effect. The narrational notion of the self provides a particularly plausible and theoretically elegant explanation for the therapeutic efficacy of psychoanalysis.

In outline, my reconstruction of Schafer's view traces the connection between self-identity, narrative, and the nature of psychoanalytic therapy. First, I indicate that Schafer explicitly endorses what I shall term an existential vision of human existence. Whatever significance or meaning there is to human life must be created by people themselves. People do this by forming a narrative, a storyline by which they organize and explain their actions, if only to themselves. It is Schafer's underlying existential vision of how meaning is conferred to human action that gives narrative the particularly central role it has in his overall account of therapy.

This leads to the second point, which concerns why, given Schafer's initial views on the existential origins of meaning, people come to disown or disavow their actions. That is, Schafer needs an analogue to Jean-Paul Sartre's famous notion of *mauvaise foi* (bad faith) in order to explain why people disown actions without involving himself in a convoluted notion of a split consciousness, which he otherwise rejects.[6] Appreciating how Schafer reconciles the accounts of self-identity and self-deception helps reveal the critical importance of his notion of "danger situations."

In the third section I indicate how, in view of Schafer's account of danger situations and his existential view of meaning, the cure of stories is possible. Psychoanalytic stories help cure, the argument goes, by providing a thematic and narrative structure to early, often inchoate experiences and reactive patterns that otherwise unknowingly control one's life. Psychoanalytic dialogue offers to analysands the possibility of articulating, and so reinterpreting and perchance changing, their reactions to life situations. In brief, psychoanalytic stories cure by breaking the interpretive grip imposed on how one lives by early fears and associated ongoing patterns of reaction.

In an essay reviewing psychoanalytic concepts of the self, Lewis Kirshner (1991) correctly notes that Schafer rejects the type of self that is presumed by the self psychology of, for example, Kohut. As Kirshner remarks, "Following Schafer, it can readily be seen that hypostatization of a presumptive entity inside the mind, a 'self,' may lead to a mystification of analysis, in which the quest for self-realization or actualization takes on an absolute quality, and pursuit of a 'true self' evokes the mirage of psychic perfection" (p. 164). More generally, Schafer frequently and characteristically locates his own position by contrasting it with the idealizations of the self he finds in Kohut's writing, on the one hand, and, on the other hand, with the view of the self as born mad and destined to remain so he attributes to Melanie Klein.[7]

In addition to rejecting those theories, which invest individuals with an essential or core natural self, Schafer distances his view as well from the mechanistic and positivistic conception of psychoanalysis on which Freud relied. To the contrary, Schafer identifies psychoanalysis with humanistically oriented inquiry. One consequence is that human beings, no longer seen through mechanistic and reductionistic lenses, are understood as agents, that is, authors of their own acts. A second is that psychoanalysis itself is perceived as more akin to history than to, say, physics or even biology (Schafer, 1978, p. 6). It is by developing the parallels between historiography and psychoanalytic theory as narrativizing projects that Schafer proposes to break psychoanalytic theory of the positivist legacy bequeathed it by Freud.[8]

Schafer's humanist/narrativist turn leads him to focus, as well, on the philosophical problems surrounding understanding the self that were discussed above.[9] On the one hand, Schafer maintains that any cogent theory requires that the unity of the self be respected. Following Hume and Kant, he sees no theoretical alternative to this. He concurs with them, as well, in viewing the unified self as only a formal and not a substantive concept. There is no intrinsic self waiting to be born. Yet, on the other hand, he recognizes the need to provide an account of how psychic conflict is possible that avoids the pitfalls inherent in the notion of self-deception noted earlier.

Schafer reformulates the Kantian split self distinction as one between the self-as-agent and the self-as-object (e.g., Schafer, 1968, p. 80). The self-as-agent (the "I") is the narrator/synthesizer of the self-as-object ("me"). "A thought does not deal with anything, for it is not an agent. It is the thinker of the thought who is the agent. It is the thinker who deals with things. . . . The self is a kind of telling about one's individuality" (Schafer, 1978, p. 86).[10] The view of the self-as-storyteller about who one is has the virtue, as Schafer insists throughout his writings, of doing away with Freud's attempt to formulate a physics of the mental. It puts in place instead a unified person who is acting and doing (1978, p. 102).

Schafer uses the term "narrative" broadly but with sufficient consistency that there is no difficulty in identifying the family resemblances among the activities he groups under this term. The generic feature of narratives is that they offer ways of characterizing (human) action over time. Terming these tellings "narratives" emphasizes that the descriptions offered are human constructions, not reports of what occurs *sub specie aeternitatis*. In this respect, narratives "create" truth; descriptions of human actions are not true or false *simpliciter*, but relative to a narrative/context.[11]

> It is especially important to emphasize that narrative is not an alternative to truth or reality; rather, it is the mode in which, inevitably, truth and reality are presented. We have only versions of the true and the real. Narratively unmediated, definite access to truth and reality cannot be demonstrated. In this respect, therefore, there can be no absolute foundation on which any observer or thinker stands; each must choose his or her narrative or version. Further, each narrative presupposes or establishes a context, and the sentences of any one account attain full significance only within their context and through more or less systematic or consistent use of the language appropriate to the purpose. (Schafer, 1992, pp. xiv–xv, 114).[12]

One authors one's life, in the relevant sense, to the extent that one has the categories or concepts in which to do so. However, there is a twist. On the narrative account which Schafer develops, one constructs narratives about oneself working *selectively* from one's experience. "An author of existence is someone who constructs experience. Experience is made or fashioned; it is not encountered, discovered, or observed, except upon secondary reflection. . . . The introspecting subject extracts from the plenitude of potential experience what is wanted. . . . Introspection does not encounter ready-made material" (Schafer, 1992, p. 23). What is selected from experience as relevant to one's narrative is a matter of, so to speak, authorial discretion.

Although one works selectively from experience in authoring a view of oneself, one need not always draw consistently from experience, or tell only one tale about oneself. Schafer's narrativist version of the Kantian conception of the self demands formal but not thematic unity.

> I suggest that the analysand's experiential self may be seen as a set of varied narratives that seem to be told by and about a cast of varied selves. And yet, like the dream, which has one dreamer, the entire tale is told by one narrator. Nothing here supports the common illusion that there is a single self-entity that each person has and experiences, a self-entity that is, so to speak, out there in Nature where it can be objectively observed, clinically analyzed, and then summarized and bound in a technical definition . . . . [W]e analysts may be said to be constantly dealing with self narratives— that is, with all the storylines that keep cropping up in clinical work—such as storylines of the empty self, the false self, the secret self, and so on.
>
> (Schafer, 1992, p. 26)

Authors are articulators. Analysands are authors who employ a special theory and vocabulary; they differ from those never exposed to psychoanalysis only in the vocabulary with which they are provided.[13]

What marks Schafer as a latter-day existentialist is not only his view that each of us constructs the meaning of our actions, but also his particular way of crafting a theoretically satisfying account of the self. The charge that psychoanalytic theory lacks any such satisfactory account is found, for example, in Sartre's exposition of the notion of *mauvaise foi* (bad faith) (Sartre, 1966, p. 56–86).[14] The problem, Sartre contends, is that psychoanalytic theory requires not just a metaphysical splitting of the self, but a splitting of the nature in which a self can be conscious of itself. In particular, insofar as psychoanalytic theory speaks of an unconscious, and, in particular, a self that is deceived as to its own (unconscious) motives, then psychoanalytic theory doubles the epistemological dualism deriving from Hume and Kant. For now the self cannot only not be an object to itself, it both is and is not aware of itself.

But this additional splitting, Sartre goes on to complain, is inconsistent on the face of it. For, he insisted, there must be a self who is the author, and not just the subject, of self-deception. And that self just is oneself. Who else could it be? But, then, in what sense is oneself deceived?[15]

While rejecting the Freudian notion of the unconscious, Sartre also recognized the need to explain self-deception. Some of his remarks, in fact, point to a more satisfying theoretical solution to the problem. In an apt and striking phrase, Sartre refers to the unified consciousness that is deceived as an instance of a "mystery in broad daylight." We can be mysteries to ourselves, for example, in cases where our own behavior puzzles us. This mystery is possible, Sartre speculates, because "this possession is deprived of the means which would ordinarily permit *analysis* and *conceptualization*" (Sartre, 1966, p. 699). The suggestion, I take it, is that what makes for inaccessibility is not a mind divided against itself, but a lack of conceptual resources to make sense of what one is doing.

Schafer's concern is to answer the foregoing conundrums regarding the self—to answer the question of how self-deception is possible—in a way consistent with his move toward humanism and away from mechanism. This concern drives his well-known reworking of Freudian metapsychology in terms of "action language." "Action language" is a way of viewing analysands that takes them to be agents, not mechanisms subject to impersonal forces over which they have no control. Schafer characterizes the purpose as follows: "The project . . . is one by means of which psychoanalysts may hope to speak simply, systematically, and nonmechanistically of human activities in general and of the psychoanalytic relationship and its therapeutic effects in particular" (1978, p. 7). More specifically, action language accepts the apparently paradoxical view that there is no splitting of the self (as the notion of self-deception appears to require) but people can be unaware of the reasons for their actions. This failure of awareness stems, however, not from some convoluted conception of the mind whereby one part "hides" or "deceives" the other.

From his existentially influenced perspective regarding the meaning of action, Schafer puts the problem of how self deception is possible as one of learning why analysands typically disown responsibility for or control of their desires and behavior. Schafer terms such denials or disownings "disclaimed actions." The act of disclaiming is, for Schafer, the fundamental form of self-deception inasmuch as individuals, in disclaiming actions, speak of themselves as not in control of themselves. "It is the defining feature of psychoanalytic interpretation to retell certain crucial happenings as actions. . . . One may say that, through analysis, disclaimed actions are narratively transformed into acknowledged or claimed actions" (Schafer, 1981a, p. 4).[16] The problem posed by the fact that people disclaim responsibility for their own actions is the problem of how one could not know, or not control, what one is doing.

From the analysand's perspective, the problem appears as one of dissociation from his or her own actions, a failure to identify the actions taken as his or her own. "[W]hen patients present symptoms as afflictions or happenings, as by definition they must, psychoanalysts on their part understand them to be disclaiming certain intricate actions that they are performing unconsciously" (Schafer, 1981a, p. 19). The goal of psychoanalysis, on the Schaferian perspective, is to help the analysand "reclaim" these happenings as actions, that is, as doings under the person's control.

In this passive way of regarding their own agency, classical psychoanalytic theory too readily conspires. The usual mode of constructing an analytic story, Schafer complains, permits analyst and analysand to construct an account of the patient as a creature of instinctual drives or as a mere spectator with regard to his or her wishes, desires, and intentions.

> Drives appear to be incontrovertible facts of human nature. Even the most casual introspection delivers up a passive picture of the self being driven by internal forces. It might therefore seem perfectly justified to distinguish being driven from wishing, in that wishing seems clearly to be a case of personal action. The distinction is, however, untenable. It takes conscious and conventional testimony of drivenness as the last or natural word on the subject; but to do so is to ignore the proposition that introspection is itself a form of constructed experience based on a specific narration of mind.
>
> (Schafer, 1981a, p. 36)

But why, Schafer asks, countenance narratives in which "the subject tells himself that he is passive in relation to a drive rather than that he is a[n] . . . agent?" (Schafer, 1981b, p. 37). Schafer rejects, then, both the science and the morality that the narratives countenancing moral passivity presume. Instead, he seeks to show that "people are fantasizing whenever they disclaim action. That is to say, they are imagining their selves or their minds as spatial entities, existing in a split up and split off way" (1983, p. 243). The notion of the split self, then, is morally as well as theoretically undesirable.[17]

Emphasis on the primacy of the individual as agent is a classic theme in existential thought. The narrativist perspective introduced by a Schaferian analyst invites analysands to see themselves as akin to the "unreliable narrator" of contemporary literary theory, that is, someone who is "relating" the story to the reader, but whose perspective is also shown, by other plot devices, not to be totally trustworthy.

[T]he analyst listens and interprets in two interrelated ways. First, the analyst retells what is told from the standpoint of its content, that is, its thematic coherence. . . . The specific content then becomes merely illustrative
of an unrecognized and probably disavowed set of attitudes that are held
by the analysand who is shown to be an unreliable narrator in respect to
the consciously constructed account. Ultimately, the unreliability itself
must be interpreted and woven into the dialogue as an aspect of resistance.
(Schafer, 1981b, pp. 38–39)

What makes them "unreliable" in the relevant sense is that the
analysands do not see themselves as the authors/agents of their own actions.

Against, then, both the mechanistic view of the psyche inherited from
Freud and the analysands' own narratives of bondage to unknown
forces, Schafer constructs a conception of the self within psychoanalytic
theory that empowers the self by creating a narrative structure by which
to reclaim responsibility for, and therefore control of, disclaimed actions.
"An essential feature of analytic insight is the increasingly limited use of
self-narratives of the sort that amount to flagrant disclaimers" (Schafer,
1983, p. 249). Indeed, a defining element of the analytic enterprise is the
analyst's insistence on eliminating the analysands' perceived tendency to
split their thought into those within their control and those not so controlled.

Recall that, for Schafer, no action has a preordained meaning. The
meaning is supplied by some interpretive context or other.[18] In this regard, the crucial assumption of the narrational perspective, the one I
have labeled from the outset its existential assumption regarding meanings, is that people are seen "as continuously selecting, organizing, and
directing a neurotic existence" (Schafer, 1983, p. 145). The fundamental
virtue of the Freudian interpretive context, he maintains, is that it provides a transformative account, one that offers the opportunity for alternative understanding of one's own action via a different vision of one's
experiences.

[O]ne must bear in mind that these constructions both presuppose and further the process of changing the analysand's point of view of himself or
herself in relation to others; that is to say in the interpretive circle, the significant observation, memories, insights, and modes of feeling that are
made possible by the Freudian constructions also document and extend
these very constructions. Under the influence of the psychoanalytic perspective, the analysand not only begins to live in another world but learns

> how to go on constructing it. . . . It is a world of greater personal author-
> ity and acknowledged responsibility.   (Schafer, 1978, p. 25)

In part, reinterpretation enhances self-control and responsibility by being able "to identify a network of intelligible actions where none was thought to exist" (Schafer, 1976, p. 127). A reinterpretation of experience, in turn, allows one to perceive new options for behavior or breaks the grip of interpretations unwittingly applied.

However, Schafer's reworking of the concept of the self in this way creates a problem, namely, why is not the existential self infinitely plastic? If meaning is of one's own creation, why should a person not be perfectly content to assign any significance whatever to his or her actions? What creates a discordance or a need to deny one's own actions? The narrational notion of the self must be shown not to lead to the untenable consequence that one can make of one's life story whatever one wants.

The preceding account of the self poses at least two important problems. First, how is it possible, on Schafer's narrational view, for someone to disclaim or disown actions, much less to be mistaken about which actions are in his or her control? On the existential view he endorses, the meaning of actions is the interpretation given to them. Hence, there is no mistake, it would seem, that one could make about the understanding of one's own actions. A second, and deeper, question challenging the plausibility of the Schaferian narrativist strategy is why someone's narrative should cause him or her pain. Why, if meaning is created, do people come to feel discomfort with the meaning they have placed on their actions?

Schafer confronts these problems directly. With regard to the first question, concerning how one could possibly be "wrong" in interpreting one's own actions, Schafer readily admits that the "correction" analysis offers is evident only after the analytic perspective is accepted.[19] What recommends the psychoanalytic perspective is its capacity, if properly applied, to alleviate the puzzles and problems an analysand's own narrative has led him or her to encounter.[20]

Answering the second question brings us to Schafer's crucial theoretical notion of danger situations. Although building in his characteristic fashion on Freud's own work,[21] Schafer expands and develops this notion in a way that makes it central for his version of psychoanalytic theory. For Schafer, as for Freud, a fairly limited range of situations constitute the main danger situations infants and children initially face. What is critically important is understanding that "all later dangers in psychic reality are considered to be derivative of these early ones" (Schafer, 1992, p. 37). The psychic reality is that in which a person lives, or, perhaps, with which a person lives.

There are two fundamentally important aspects of danger situations so understood. The first is that they are, Schafer insists, noncognitive. They are noncognitive because they refer, by and large, to experiences that either were preverbal or outran or overwhelmed any conceptual resources available for articulating the experiences.

The meaning of danger situations is, one might say, a bodily meaning, a "gut" reaction to events. The "recognition" of a situation as a danger situation, in other words, rests primarily on its affect.[22] They have this conceptually rudimentary or inchoate status because danger situations represent responses to very early experiences.

> Once we develop our explanations in a universe of meanings rather than forces, we cannot avoid viewing the person as the interpreter of circumstances and needs, that is, as the definer and assigner of meanings. Danger situations are thus personal constructions, and whether or not a person constructs a danger situation will depend on his or her conceptions and estimates of self relative to circumstances. It also follows that, strictly speaking, the earliest traumatic situations, starting with birth, are not situations at all in that they refer to noncognitive events. A newborn cannot conceive situations, and physiological stress or disequilibrium is not yet a situation.
> (Schafer, 1983, p. 99)

> A situation, of course, is not created out of whole cloth. From the dawn of mental activity, each person takes into account necessity and accident, but he or she can only do so in phase-specific and individually characteristic ways. However much one agrees with others in certain "objective" respects, and however limited and directed one may be by bodily makeup, maturation, and the conditions and language of one's upbringing, one may still be viewed as authoring one's own life. . . .
> . . . But my thesis applies to more than the construction of a situation. It applies as well to the actions of the person in the situation thus defined. For an essential aspect of maintaining the nonbehavioristic orientation of psychoanalysis, of its concern with psychical reality or unconscious fantasizing, is to remember always that what to an outside observer might look like identical items of behavior may mean different things to different agents or to one agent at different times. Here we come directly to the way in which the concept of action is integrally related to the concept of situation.
> (Schafer, 1983, p. 100)

The patterns represent modes of coping developed during early developmental stages. Because the patterns were established before one could conceptualize what one is doing, a result is that what the pattern is, what triggers it, and what fears it connects with remain unarticulated. That which was never articulated is, for all intents and purposes, inaccessible to discursive understanding.

Through these acquired senses of certain situations as threatening, a person defines and constructs experiences. Even though these modes of understanding are initially wholly or partially inchoate, they set the themes for how experience is understood. Hence, they may be termed part of an analysand's own narrativizing practice.

> Once we develop our explanations in a universe of meanings rather than forces, we cannot avoid viewing the person as the interpreter of circumstances and needs, that is, as the definer and assigner of meanings. Danger situations are thus personal constructions, and whether or not a person constructs a danger situation will depend on his or her conceptions and estimates of self relative to circumstances.   (Schafer, 1983, p. 99)

According to Schafer, "What we call a derivative or compromise comes into being in the terms of, and by virtue of, a narrative strategy. The analysand uses the storyline to develop ever new opportunities for repeating and perpetuating unconsciously maintained infantile psychosexual dilemmas and dangers. And these prototypes are themselves narrativized" (1983, p. 271). The point about the psychic reality of a danger situation is that these are constructions that individuals put on their experience. Indeed, "[m]ore than construct these fantasies, the analysand constructs actual situations which, psychically, verify and justify imprisonment" (Schafer, 1983, p. 270). It is pointless, and besides the point in any case, to argue that, "objectively," no danger exists.

This determines the second of the crucial features of the notion of a danger situation. This is that the therapeutic task, from this perspective, is to identify and "deconstruct," so to speak, the interpretation given particular types of experiences.

> We say we diagnose psychopathology; however, by the word pathology we refer to that which one suffers, thereby implying passivity and affliction. But . . . it is wrong to think that a neurosis befalls one. A neurosis is created and arranged and protected. It is, correlatively, the construction of danger situations and the construction of emotional action to take in these situations.   (Schafer, 1983, p. 111)

If by a diagnosis we refer to what someone is doing, then we may designate a psychoanalytic therapy in comparable action terms. In the case of neurosis, the service we render is inappropriately called the cure of pathology. Rather, we should say it consists of clarifying what the "patient" is doing, and to make sense of it in terms of unconsciously defined danger situations.

(Schafer, 1983, p. 112)

For Schafer, identifying and addressing such situations define the analytic encounter. That is, what makes danger situations seemingly inaccessible to consciousness is not some intrapsychic happening that leaves individuals, Humpty-Dumpty-like, with split psyches needing to be put back together again. Rather, on the account owing to Schafer, the problem is that the experiences defining danger situations elude conscious understanding because they belonged to a time when words were not adequate to characterize the fear, or no words were available at all.

[I]t is largely on the basis of these unconsciously perpetuated infantile and fantastic dangers that analysands fear the prospect of changing and "getting well." For when they first become analysands, and for a very long time afterwards, they envision "getting well" only as a full actualization of those infantile danger situations. If, as we believe, they have developed their disturbing modes of functioning as static accommodations to such dangers, why should they risk changing and "getting well"? The analyst cannot empathize too strongly with this desperate, locked-in position.

(Schafer, 1983, p. 70)

The threat of analysis, on this perspective, is that one must confront something dreaded but unknown, at least to words.

In this context, the analyst and analysand are engaged not in reconstructing the past, in the sense of stating what happened inasmuch as, in Schafer's view, this is literally impossible. It is impossible because the analysand has, *ex hyposthesi*, no terms or concepts in which the past experience, whatever it was, could be expressed.

The point is that psychoanalytic interpretation expands the conception of actions and that this expansion is an essential constituent of insight. Insight combines both the old and the new. The new comprises all those conceptions of life-historical actions, relations, and situations that the analysand may never before have defined as such. . . .

. . . Absurdity enters at the point where one ascribes this retrospective designation of the action to the early infantile mind . . . . Put in historical perspective, there is far more to an action than could have entered into its creation at the moment of its execution. It is the same as the effect of a new and significant literary work or critical approach on all previous literature; inevitably, fresh possibilities of understanding and creation alter the literary past.   (Schafer, 1978, p. 21)

What is available is just the viscera, the reactions to some element that defines certain experiences as danger situations (Schafer, 1981a, p. 28). Because the pattern of responses to danger situations reflects only a rudimentary grasp of what is feared and why, people experience their own reactions to such situations as alien to themselves. Such actions may result from no intentions or motives that one can clearly articulate

The important point is that a pattern of responses emerges in an attempt to cope with perceived threats to oneself. These patterns manifest themselves as other, later-life events are construed in terms of the early, prototypical danger situations. Psychoanalysis, in turn, provides the words—and so allows us to bring to consciousness—by which to characterize and systematically comprehend what we are reacting to when we react in particular ways. How this is thematized in the analysis is not a discovery, but a creation of a new narrative, one with, hopefully, therapeutic efficacy.

So when, throughout his writing, Schafer emphasizes that no description has pride of place, this is because, at least in part, it is only in the present that the analysand can give a manageable shape to the past. "My special point is that, within the analytic method, accounts of the past and the present become increasingly dependent on one another; more exactly, neither account is finally conceivable without the other" (Schafer, 1981a, p. 40). This is why Schafer dismisses debates about "evidence" for interpretations as "meaningless" (1981a, p. 40). The psychoanalytic narrative—the putting into words in a particular causal sequencing—is the conferral of a special and theoretically created meaning, namely, a psychoanalytic meaning. "[T]hrough redescription, the same action has undergone a number of narrative recontextualizations and so has had multiple meanings conferred on it" (1981a, p. 42). Thus, Schafer freely acknowledges, key psychoanalytic concepts such as regression do not represent pure recall of the past. Rather, they stand as "a new mode of constructing experience and, as such, it is a mode of reconstructing the experience of the past in radically new ways" (Schafer, 1981a, p. 47).

Psychoanalytic narration confers meaning by recontextualizing experience, and not by the recovery of some past and determinate memory context with an already (but unconsciously) articulated structure and affect. This is why Schafer insists that psychoanalytic interpretation is not reductive with regard to past experience, but thematic and organizational, "no different in principle from any sophisticated thematic analysis of literary texts and historical data" (1981a, p. 49). Contrary to those who would insist that the narrativist strategy does not dignify the analysand's actual experiences with the title of "reality," Schafer insists that what primarily matters is a person's "second reality," his or her life's experience as narrativized by that person.[23] The visceral interpretation given experience is what matters. Analysands live unarticulated storylines. Their own narratives are lost to them, due not to some strange mechanism of repression, but to the fact that the available conceptual resources were (prior to analysis, anyway) inadequate to bring them to discursive awareness.

In an earlier work, I argued that accounts like Schafer's narrativist view are interestingly and importantly analogous to Thomas Kuhn's famous discussion of the role of paradigms—exemplars—in the natural sciences (Roth, 1991a). In particular, I maintained that experience, once narrativized, became a personal paradigm or template for interpreting all later experience. This is partially right. However, my earlier account did not give proper emphasis to the way danger situations possess an importantly unformed but psychologically persistent character akin to habits. By assimilating later experiences to the prototype, such habitual interpetations construe some situations as danger situations. By appreciating the role of danger situations in creating what may be termed affectual paradigms, we can appreciate how the narrativist strategy nicely connects experiences early and late to patterns of self-understanding, emotional pain, and therapeutic relief.

Past experiences do not exist somewhere in conceptual space, awaiting rediscovery. When Schafer insists, throughout his extensive *oeuvre*, that thought represents a type of action, his point, I take it, is that we must not fool ourselves about the origins of the meaning that experience has for us. The interpretation is by us, and so represents an action, a doing on our part. The rub is that the action may be largely reflexive, insofar as it is in response to a danger situation, and so not "present" at a conscious, that is to say, articulatable, level.

The cure of stories is possible, then, because the analytic process possesses the potential to rethematize those interpretations given previous experience that held one unwittingly in their thrall. Words free not by magic, but by providing new shape and form through which to construct, analyze, and articulate experience.

Among its many potential accomplishments, psychoanalytic interpretation prepares or assists the analysand to be independently and regularly self-correcting or less self-deceiving. Through interpretation, it reduces the desperateness of the prototypic danger situations of childhood in terms of which, unconsciously, the analysand has continued to construct experience. It also familiarizes the analysand with her characteristic, hitherto unconsciously employed repertoire of defensive activities. . . . It does so in order to help her recognize signs that she feels endangered and is already beginning to respond defensively in a way that now she mostly does not want.   (Schafer, 1992, pp. 43–4)

Again, there is an extremely close parallel here between Schafer's vision of how stories cure and Kuhn's account of paradigm change, an account Schafer echoes by speaking of the analysand as living in a different world (Schafer, 1978, pp. 24–25).[24]

In formulating a notion of the core self as the constructor of narratives about the empirical self, we come full circle. The problems about the self and self-deception with which this discussion began permit an appreciation of how Schafer's analytic attitude resolves the sort of problems about the self to which psychoanalytic theory is prone. Agency resides not in the power of a thought—there is no mental physics—but in the narrativizing template applied to experience. "The self is a kind of telling about one's individuality. . . . [T]he self is a regulated mental action, a telling rather than a teller" (Schafer, 1978, p. 86). How experience affects us depends on how, in part, we integrate it into our own ongoing understanding of ourselves and the world.

Psychoanalytic interpretations permit the possibility of change by making visible the generic features both underlying and triggering one's reactions, that is, why certain experiences are perceived as threats. Such interpretations alter one's narrativizng strategy about danger situations by providing an articulated pattern of understanding that better befits the person one has become.

The psychoanalyst continues to define the psychoanalytically familiar conflictual themes and to trace the same sorts of infantile origin of these themes, though perhaps he or she does so more lucidly now owing to a clearer conception of what it is possible to say coherently. The important task of the psychoanalyst is to decide on those psychoanalytic descriptions of problematic actions and situations that are the most illuminating and potentially the most conducive to beneficial personal transformation.

                                                 (Schafer, 1978, p. 97)

The unconscious ceases, on this view, to be some mysteriously split off and inaccessible realm. If we identify the unconscious with the tendency to interpret ever more nuanced and complex life experiences as a species of a previously defined danger situation, self-deception is no more mysterious than any other pattern of behavior to which we are habituated, and no less real or controlling.

Self-deception has its basis, in other words, in the fact that there is a continuity of self from our earliest infancy to our present stage. This continuity carries with it the fact that later narrativizing strategies do not so much replace earlier ones but simply overlay them with words. What Schafer calls the "adultomorphism" of experience involves just this unwitting accretion of later narrativizing strategies on infantile ones.

> Adultomorphism is involved, for example, when reference is made to infantile feelings and fantasies. . . . But the analysand's infantile modes and contents of experience can only become analytic data in formulations that necessarily recognize and enhance the analysand's "observing ego" or "mature psyche." One may, therefore, say of analytic interpretation that, far from unearthing and resurrecting old and archaic experiences as such, it constitutes and develops new, vivid, verbalizable, and verbalized versions of those experiences. Only then can these new versions be given a secure place in a continuous, coherent, convincing and up-to-date psychoanalytic life history. This is the history that facilitates personal change and further development. (Schafer, 1983, pp. 189–90; see also pp. 222–24)

> I have emphasized that the origin of many of the disclaimers we issue is to be found partly in the infantile "bodily ego" or sensorimotor antecedents of thinking in words. What distinguishes this infantile mode is its concretized and animistic rendition of psychological activity. . . . As body centered beings, we corporealize our mental actions from the first; the learning of ordinary figurative language facilitates and consolidates this apparently unavoidable way of constructing experience.
> (Schafer, 1983, pp. 242–43)[25]

Understanding ourselves is comprehending a vast and complex process by which life experiences are selectively assimilated into some general pattern for making sense of things. These patterns originate in infancy and, however obscure to the discursive beings we become, are never extinguished from our narrative repertoire. But insofar as analysis brings the noncognitive under the sway of the cognitive, it amounts to a type of conceptual/interpretive revolution.

The unconscious is not a lost realm of experience; it comprises, as

Sartre hinted, unconceptualized yet habituated patterns of action. Combined with the assumption that it is the person who gives meaning to his or her actions, this opens the possibility for providing new meaning, new ways of dealing with a world that, at least, transcends near instinctual, habitual modes of reacting. "For what has also changed is the analysand as life-historian, as maker of sense, as definer and designer of possible futures. I have described what amounts to a cognitive revolution on the part of the analysand" (Schafer, 1983, p. 191). The self is and remains a unity. The difference that psychoanalytic intervention may make concerns only the resources available to the self *qua* narrator with regard to organizing and understanding experience.[26]

An analyst, in helping analysands give voice to what were previously habitual, influential, but unrecognized patterns of action, is not making a discovery of some psychological *terra incognita*, but is giving shape to what previously had none. In this respect, an analyst is more like an astronomer charting constellations in the night sky by which one may guide oneself through what would otherwise be a journey without sign or marker. Just as a constellation is simultaneously fashioned from "real" elements but is also a fabrication on the part of the astronomer, so too is an analyst's narrative real and fabricated. We need not compromise its use, for this sort of case, by calling it a fabrication. Without it, experience has no shape or coherence, and so offers no guide. With it, one has important and stable signposts by which to navigate.[27]

"Danger situations" define the analysand's world and mark the route which the psychoanalytic narrative must chart to effect a cure—a relief from one's neurotic misery. I have sketched how Schafer remains faithful both to the existential dictum that humans create, rather than find, meaning in their lives, and to the psychoanalytic credo that it is the meanings of which we are not aware, but repetitively relive, that imprison us.

NOTES

I would like to thank Stephanie Ross, Roy Schafer, Marilyn Wechter, and the editors for helpful comments on an earlier draft of this chapter.

1. This is, at least, Schafer's view as I understand it and one with which I am in deep agreement. As Schafer observes, "The idea of unconscious mental processes is the foundation of psychoanalytic theory." He goes on to add that what is of psychoanalytic moment is the discrepancy that arises between events understood at the conscious level and how these are comprehended at the un-

conscious level. "[T]he point to emphasize is that, typically, the versions of events that are told unconsciously do not conform to those told consciously" (Schafer, 1981a, p. 6).

2. There is "doubling" at least with respect to the process of interpreting and integrating experiences as one's own. The notion of self-deception, that is, implies the integration of experience into at least two different organizing accounts; similarly, there is a doubling as well of intentions, motives, and desires. I argue below that there cannot be a doubling of the transcendental self.

Put another way, Kant and Hume still leave us with an image of a person as a unity with respect to understanding his or her experiences. A notion of self-deception shatters this unity. Freud may be read, some suggest, as changing our self-understanding by forcing the notion of a unitary empirical self to give way to competing and comflicting selves, all of whom "are" the person. For a development of this theme, see Rorty, 1986.

3. For related reflections on these problems and their relevance to psychoanalytic theory, see Krischner, 1991.

4. I leave aside here questions of the nature of multiple personality disorder, and the issue of whether or to what extent individuals suffering from it lack, in some interesting sense, true self-identity.

5. The notion of narrative invoked here is imported by Schafer from debates in the philosophy of history. There, as in the version of psychoanalytic theory championed by Schafer, narrative explanations are contrasted to explanatory structures favored by positivists. The contrast is between explanations that mimic the form of explanations in the natural sciences and those that have a story-like form. For a somewhat minimalist, but quite adequate, definition of narration, see Schafer, 1981a. I have elaborated on issues surrounding narrative as a form of explanation in a number of places. For some references, see Roth, 1988, 1991a, 1991b.

6. The *locus classicus* here is Sartre, 1966, esp. pp. 82–86.

7. Typically, Schafer locates his own view via triangulation with respect to Freud, Kohut, and Melanie Klein or Merton Gill. See Schafer, 1981b or 1985 for characteristic exercises in this way of situating himself. For purposes of understanding the notion of the self, the contrast could be put in terms of alternative narrative lines. If Freud offers us narrative of "the taming of the beast within," Kohut narrates according to "the discovery of the self within," and Klein postulates the "mad person within raging about," Schafer's narrative concentrates on the enhancement of responsibility, from "self-as-victim of unknown psychic forces" to "master in one's own house."

This characterization of Schafer's view is my own. In correspondence, Roy Schafer indicates that, regarding Kohut, he (Schafer) primarily thinks that "his [Kohut's] theory lacks the scope and depth and therapeutic efficacy of some other approaches." With regard to Kleinians, he suggests that his account is more congruent with theirs than my quick summary might suggest.

8. Schafer's account contains a number of interesting and important points of congruence with the work analyzing the parallels between historiography and literary theory expounded over the last twenty-five years by Hayden White. Although Schafer is clearly familiar with White's work and occasionally even acknowledges it (see, e.g., references listed in Schafer, 1981a), he cites White much less often than one might expect. There may be, behind this, some issue of who deserves credit for the development of the importance of literary tropes for historiography. Compare, in this regard, Schafer's 1970 essay, "The Psychoanalytic Vision of Reality" (Schafer, 1976), and White's important introduction to his magisterial work, *Metahistory* (1973).

A very readable, intelligent, and comprehensive introduction to the vagaries of narrative theory can be found in Martin, 1986. Martin is particularly good at locating both Schafer and White in the context of their respective disciplines and relative, as well, to the larger debates regarding the nature of historical explanation, which form the philosophical background for much of what Schafer and White do. Martin nicely presents the issues that make plausible the constructivist and literary approach to history championed by the two. As Martin observes, with respect to accounts of historical and psychoanalytic narrative, "at present we have no standards or even suggestions for determining how the connections between events in fictional narratvies might differ from those in history" (1986, p. 73; see, more generally, pp. 71–80).

9. These discussions occur in many of Schafer's work. For a characteristic instance, see Schafer, 1992, pp. 21–26.

10. In *Language and Insight*, (1978), Schafer employs a distinction between "person" and "self" that is similar to Kant's contrast between the pure and empirical selves. See, e.g., p. 87.

11. I have developed and defended this view elsewhere. In particular, see Roth, 1988, 1991a, 1991b.

12. A word of caution is in order here. There are schools of thought that call themselves "existential psychoanalysis," but it would be a mistake to identify Schafer with these thinkers, for reasons Schafer himself cogently provides in several works (see, e.g., Schafer, 1976). As he explains it in that work, Schafer's existentialism is, in part, a reaction to what he correctly perceives as Freud's mechanistic conception of the psyche, a conception that permeates Freud's metapsychology. Against this, Schafer maintains that "identity is phenomenological, existential, and intentionalistic at its core" (1976, p. 114).

13. Schafer offers at least two different formats involved in the thematizing (or, one might say, following Hayden White, emplotting) experience. One mode is formal, the other substantive. What I call the formal mode Schafer discusses as alternative visions of reality. See, e.g., "The Psychoanalytic Vision of Reality" in Schafer, 1976. The substantive mode is discussed in Schafer, 1967, esp. p. 153.

14. For Schafer's explicit recognition of this concept and the challenge it poses to psychoanalytic theory, see, e.g., Schafer, 1981a, p. 17 n. 7.

15. See. For example, Schafer's remarks on self-deception in Schafer, 1976, pp. 234–45.

16. Regarding the centrality of the notion of disclaimed actions to Schafer's general, nonmechanistic reformulation of Freudian theory, see, e.g., Schafer, 1978, pp. 73–77. It is crucial, as well, to the ultimately unitary theory of the self that Schafer seeks to construct. See, e.g., Schafer, 1983, pp. 142–43, 241–49.

17. This criticism of the moral orientation of classical psychoanalysis flows form Schafer's position that this orientation is less psychologically functional than Schafer's preferred alternative. Schafer does not assume that some one moral outlook is objectively correct.

18. See, in particular, Schafer's essay "The Psychoanalytic Vision of Reality" (Schafer, 1976, pp. 22–56).

19. It would be appropriate here to distinguish, following Schafer, between an analysand's primary and secondary reality. The primary reality is the world as one initially experiences and understands it. The analytic situation creates, Schafer maintains, a "second reality" within which this primary interpretation is challenged and a new mode for interpreting and understanding experience is developed. Analysis is a process of learning to reinterpret experience and making this interpretation one's own, i.e., one's primary interpretation. I discuss this at greater length in Roth, 1991a.

20. See, e.g. Schafer, 1983, p. 244. I argue (Roth 1991a) that Schafer's account of the different realities, and what prompts one to change between them, closely and importantly parallel Thomas Kuhn's famous discussion of paradigms, anomalies within paradigms, and the process of paradigm change discussed in his now classic work, *The Structure of Scientific Revolutions* (1970).

21. See, e.g., Schafer, 1992, p. 37. For the central role that Schafer assigns this notion in his own reworking of Freud, see Schafer, 1983, chap. 7, esp. p. 96.

22. This is not to claim that it is by affect alone that one identifies danger situations as being of a particular type or otherwise individuates them.

23. See "The Psychoanalytic Vision of Reality" (Schafer, 1976).

24. For detailed development and discussion of the parallels between Kuhn and Schafer, and the implications for the understanding of psychoanalysis, see Roth, 1991a, esp. pp. 190–96.

25. See also Johnson, 1987.

26. As Schafer rightly insists, this account does away with the stock distinction between explanation and understanding. See Schafer, 1976, pp. 210–11. This is a central theme I develop in Roth, 1991a.

27. The question of what is real and what is a narrative construction in one's life is, like analogous questions in the philosophy of science, a vexed issue. My astronomy analogy is meant to suggest why the distinction between "the real"

and "the constructed" is yet another dualism we can do without. I have attempted to develop a defense of this view in a number of essays. See especially Roth, 1991b.

BIBLIOGRAPHY

Hume, David. 1888. *Treatise on Human Nature*. Ed. L. A. Selby-Bigge. Oxford: Clarendon.

Johnson, Mark. 1987. *The Body in the Mind: The Bodily Basis of Meaning, Imagination, and Reason*. Chicago: University of Chicago Press.

Kant, Immanuel. 1933. *The Critique of Pure Reason*. Trans. N. Kemp Smith. London: Macmillan.

Kirshner, Lewis A. 1991. "The Concept of the Self in Psychoanalytic Theory and Its Philosophical Foundations." *Journal of the American Psychoanalytic Association* 39:157–81.

Kuhn, Thomas. 1970. *The Structure of Scientific Revolutions*, 2d. ed. Chicago: University of Chicago Press.

Martin, Wallace. 1986. *Recent Theories of Narrative*. Ithaca: Cornell University Press.

Rorty, Richard. 1986. "Freud and Moral Reflection." In *Pragmatism's Freud*, ed. J. Smith and W. Kerrigan. Baltimore: Johns Hopkins University Press.

Roth, Paul A. 1988. "Narrative Explanation: The Case of History." *History and Theory* 27:1–13.

———. 1991a. "Interpretation as Explanation." In *The Interpretive Turn: Philosophy, Science, and Culture*, ed. J. Bohman, D. Hiley, and R. Shusterman. Ithaca: Cornell University Press, pp. 179–96.

———. 1991b. "Truth in Interpretation: The Case of Psychoanalysis." *Philosophy of the Social Sciences* 21:175–195.

Sartre, Jean-Paul. 1966. *Being and Nothingness*. Trans. H. E. Barnes. New York: Washington Square Press.

Schafer, Roy. 1967. "Ideals, Ego Ideal, and Self Ideal." *Psychological Issues* 5:131–74.

———. 1968. *Aspects of Internalization*. New York: International Universities Press.

———. 1976. *A New Language for Psychoanalysis*. New Haven: Yale University Press.

———. 1978. *Language and Insight*. New Haven: Yale University Press.

———. 1981a. *Narrative Actions in Psychoanalysis*. Worcester, MA: Clark University Press.

———. 1981b. "Narration in the Psychoanalytic Dialogue." In *On Narrative*, ed. W. J. T. Mitchell. Chicago: University of Chiacgo Press, pp. 25–49.

————. 1983. *The Analytic Attitude.* New York, Basic Books.

————. 1985. "Wild Analysis." *Journal of the American Psychoanalytic Association* 33:275–99.

————. 1992. *Retelling a Life: Narration and Dialogue in Psychoanalysis.* New York: Basic Books.

Todes, Samuel J. 1967. "Knowledge and the Ego." In *Kant: A Collection of Critical Essays,* ed. R. P. Wolff. New York, Anchor Books.

White, Hayden. 1973. *Metahistory.* Baltimore: Johns Hopkins University Press.

Chapter Thirteen

Existential Psychoanalysis
A Laingian Perspective

M. Guy Thompson

EDITORS' INTRODUCTION

Existential psychoanalysis is probably best viewed as a mode of orientation emanating from a wide range of loosely associated theorists who have (mostly indirectly) influenced the mainstream of psychoanalytic theory and practice. For example, as Paul Roth points
out in this volume, Roy Schafer's rejection of Freud's motivational
mechanisms driven by instinct in which the person is more or less
passive, in favor of a view that stresses the individual's agency (people are "authors of their existence")—suggests the influence of existentialism on Schafer's work. As M. Guy Thompson indicates, existential psychoanalysis has also been an important and frequently
unacknowledged forerunner of the now modish intellectual movements of deconstructionalism, postmodernism and hermeneutics,
viewpoints that have influenced psychoanalytic theorizing.

Existential psychoanalysis was initiated by Ludwig Binswanger
and Medard Boss, both of whom were lodged in the existential
philosophical tradition of Martin Heidegger. Although Binswanger
and Boss found much in Freud that was illuminating, their work
can be historically understood as a reaction to Freudian psychoanalysis. Most important, for Binswanger and Boss man is "being-
in-the-world," that is, man and world are always merged and each
is intelligible only in terms of the other. From this fundamental difference in perspective flowed other disagreements between the existentialists and Freud: where Freud had articulated a deterministic
view of behavior as a consequence of past experiences, Binswanger

and Boss conceptualized the individual as a composite of conscious processes, continuously in flux, and continually struggling toward a future state of self-fulfillment; where Freud formulated psychoanalysis as the explication of the linkages between psychological states and their underlying physical processes, the existentialists aggressively challenged any assumption of a mind/body split. Unfortunately, the ambivalence that Binswanger and Boss shared toward Freud's conception of psychoanalysis served to inhibit rather than encourage a deeper connection between existentialists and the psychoanalytic movement. It was 1960 before existentialism—in the words of Jean-Paul Sartre—would ultimately "find its Freud" in the person of the Scottish psychiatrist and philosopher R. D. Laing, a trained psychoanalyst who moved easily between the two camps.

As Thompson points out, R. D. Laing's conception of existential psychoanalysis emanated from his lifelong identification with the existential philosophical tradition, especially as articulated by Heidegger, Sartre, Søren Kierkegaard, and Friedrich Nietzsche. Laing felt that Binswanger and Boss had failed to do justice to what he thought was the essence of Heidegger's contribution, that is, his conception of truth, which Laing characterized as "literally that which is without secrecy, what discloses itself without a veil. This concept has practical interpersonal implications in terms of telling the truth, lying, pretending, [and] equivocating." According to Thompson, Laing based his clinical theory largely on the existential concept of "authenticity" and its correlate, self-deception (i.e., "inauthenticity"). The basic thrust of existential psychoanalysis, as Laing conceptualized it, is rooted in the dialectic between truth and falsehood and how the conflict between them engenders a split in the self that results in so-called psychopathology. Laing, says Thompson, adopted the skeptic view that knowledge is intrinsically personal and that the totality of everything we believe is rooted in experience. In turn, experience engenders suffering, so it is in our nature to mitigate that suffering by deceiving ourselves about what our experience tells us. We adopt false "truths," Thompson indicates, that are more pleasing than the ones we actually experience, and split ourselves accordingly.

Hence "existentialism is a subversive and inherently skeptical philosophy that seeks to undermine established truths, whether they assume the form of edicts that are popularized by 'the crowd' or neurotic fantasies that are substitutes for an irrepressibly disturbing reality." Laing's existential brand of psychoanalysis, says Thompson, is characterized by main ideas: (1) all human knowledge is based in personal experience; and (2) the weight of experience is so burdensome and painful that we foreclose and evade it through self-deception.

As Thompson describes it, what makes Laing's clinical approach specifically psychoanalytic is the affinity between Freud and many of the existential themes that Laing cherished. For example, Freud also believed that virtually all forms of psychopathology are the consequence of secrets that human beings manage to conceal from themselves. He believed that we repress those secrets in the first place due to personal experience, the nature of which engenders intolerable suffering.

In turn, Freud's method of treatment, psychoanalysis, was the model upon which Laing based his existential approach. Like Freud, Laing believed that the only way to undo the consequences of self-deception is to take part in a therapeutic relationship wherein the two participants endeavor to be as honest with each other as they can. Whereas Freud believed that psychopathology is due to the difficulty that every human being has with an intrinsically harsh reality, Laing concluded that some realities are harsher than others. Hence Laing believed that psychotic and other forms of psychopathology are the consequence of having been deceived by the very people one is most dependent on; generally speaking, this implicates society at large, but, closer to home, it comes down to the family to which each of us belongs.

Laing's emphasis on the interpersonal dimension to one's reality and the capacity that each of us possesses to subvert each other's experience through lies and deception characterizes the specifically existential aspect of Laing's interpretation of psychoanalysis. This view of psychopathology prompted Laing to expand even further on Freud's observation that the therapeutic relationship must be rooted in a strict adherence to truthfulness. In turn, Laing adopted Freud's fundamental rule of psychoanalysis, to be completely honest with one's therapist, and its correlate, the rule of neutrality, to be unequivocally accepting of one's patients.

Laing, according to Thompson, devoted most of his clinical career to arguing that conventional psychiatric treatment, including certain trends in psychoanalysis, are inherently manipulative. This view was derived from Laing's observation that humans, when their backs are against the wall, can be surprisingly devious and even mean-spirited in order to preserve those self-deceptions that protect them from anxiety. Consequently, he argued that therapists are just as likely to engage in duplicity as the patients they treat. (P. M. and A. R.)

What is "existential" psychoanalysis?[1] This may seem like a rather arcane question at a time when few practitioners of psychoanalysis identify themselves with an existential orientation. In the 1960s, when terms like existential analysis, existential psychoanalysis, and existential therapy were on the lips of every psychology student in America, no one knew what it meant then, either. Everyone talked about it all the same. Why? There's no denying that the word sounds good. The term "existential" has a wonderful flavor to it, full of depth, resonance, meaning. It sounds at once European and personal; humanistic yet vaguely wise; intellectual but not academically so. It was the perfect word for anybody who professed to be "in the know," streetwise but learned. To be existential was synonymous with being hip, modern, on the cutting edge. Existential psychoanalysis seemed to define itself, epitomized by spontaneous, in-the-café encounters. Surely specialized training was irrelevant, if not obscene. Existentialism, a philosophical school of thought, was somehow related to the technique of existential analysis, but one was discouraged from making too much of the relationship between them. If you did, you might be accused of confusing treatment with philosophy. Yet existential analysis—whatever it is—is based on the work of a group of philosophers who are bound by *existentialism*. It's no wonder it was hard to fathom the nature of a clinical school whose roots were frequently suppressed.

Today, the question, What is existential psychoanalysis? is still being asked, but now because it's fallen out of fashion. All the people who made existential psychoanalysis a driving force in Continental psychiatry have died. Ludwig Binswanger, Medard Boss, Victor Frankl, R. D. Laing, David Cooper, Rollo May, Ludwig Lefebre, and Eugene Minkowski are only some of the psychiatrists and psychologists who promoted the cause of the existential approach to psychoanalysis. Their passing has struck a near-death blow to the intellectual movement they inspired. While terms like deconstructionalism, postmodernism, and hermeneutics have assumed a cachet that once belonged to the existentialists, many today have forgotten it was the existentialists who initiated these now fashion-able—and inherently subversive—intellectual movements.[2]This is why the question, What is existential psychoanalysis? is as relevant now as ever, and why it is important to answer it.

It is one of those supreme ironies that even while the newer intellec-tual schools are openly courted by contemporary analysts, a protracted antipathy has historically undermined the relationship between existen-tialism and psychoanalysis. This mutual animosity is perhaps the most intractable obstacle to delineating the elements of a school that was os-tensibly rooted in their reconciliation. Indeed, one has to ask if it still makes sense to speak in terms of an existential "school" of psychoanaly-sis when it has never been recognized by the psychoanalytic community; nor have the existentialists sought to become bona fide members of the analytic culture. In fact, one of the principal aims of the existentialist movement was to challenge analytic orthodoxy, epitomized by its ten-dency to objectify the human condition and its advocacy of an excessive detachment in the treatment situation. The existentialist complaint with psychoanalysis was deftly summarized by R. D. Laing's observation that "psycho-analytic theory in its weaker aspects ignores the active consti-tuting, making, moulding moment of personal unity, thereby reducing the person to a resultant of instinctual vector-abstractions which leave no place for intentionality in each life" (Laing and Cooper, 1971, p. 23).

A Brief History of Existential Psychoanalysis

The earliest existential analysts emphasized their differences with Freud even while they were indebted to his inherently subversive conception of treatment. Both Binswanger and Boss, though loyal to Freud personally, favored the existential philosophy of Martin Heidegger over Freud's more conventional model. Binswanger began his psychiatric career under the tutelage of Eugen Bleuler and Carl Jung, who in turn introduced him to Freud (Spiegelberg, 1972, pp. 194–200). Though he initially embraced Freud's ideas, Binswanger became dubious of his positivistic conception of the unconscious. After reading Heidegger's *Being and Time* ([1927] 1962), he converted to existentialism and developed his own clinical the-ory, *Daseinsanalyse*.[3] Binswanger's conversion to Heidegger's philoso-phy coincided with a myriad of Continental psychiatrists who were in-corporating Heidegger's views into their clinical practice. Other versions of "existential analysis" emerged—notably that of Medard Boss—all rooted principally in Heidegger's work, not Freud's. Boss nevertheless took Freud seriously enough to commission a study of his clinical technique (1963), though it had a negligible impact on the psychoanalytic movement and is now out of date.[4] To make matters worse, Heidegger's pronounced lack of interest in Freud's theories further discouraged an entire generation of existential psychiatrists from taking the latter's radical—if sometimes convoluted—theories more seriously. Many chose to dismiss psychoanalysis entirely and opted for an eclectic approach instead.[5] Yet, beneath the din of their purported differences, the views of Heidegger and Freud share a remarkable proximity, seldom noted in the literature.[6]

It wasn't until Sartre's *Being and Nothingness*, published in 1943, that an existential philosopher initiated a reconciliation between the two camps. Unlike Heidegger, Sartre recognized the profundity of Freud's thought and devoted a considerable amount of time to studying his ideas. Sartre even demonstrated his own version of psychoanalysis in biographical studies of Genet and Flaubert (Laing and Cooper, 1971). This established a precedent that encouraged others to pursue a relationship with psychoanalysis outside its sanctioned societies. Sartre's daring—and typically French—combination of defiance and devotion inspired his friend Jacques Lacan to found a renegade school of his own after being expelled from the International Psychoanalytical Association for unorthodox training methods (Roudinesco, 1990, pp. 373–478). Lacan even claimed to be the rightful heir to Freud's disturbing views about the human condition and devoted the rest of his life to condemning the establishment's "friendlier," more popular version. Though Lacan subsequently aligned himself with the structuralist and surrealist movements, a significant portion of his clinical technique was indebted to the phenomenology of Heidegger and Sartre.[7] Ironically, Lacan's refusal to disavow his identification with psychoanalysis—despite his "excommunication" by its principal accrediting body—inadvertently solidified the precarious ties between psychoanalysis and the existentialists.

Unlike the psychiatrists who based their clinical work exclusively on Heidegger, R. D. Laing was especially drawn to Sartre, a philosopher much closer to his age and temperament. When he devoted one of his books to a study of Sartre's philosophy (Laing and Cooper, 1971), Sartre graciously included a foreword that praised Laing's "perfect understanding" of his work. In turn, Laing lauded Sartre's brand of existential psychoanalysis as a courageous testament to Freud's foundation (pp. 22–25). Laing and Sartre shared a genuine appreciation for the latent affinity between psychoanalysis and existentialism, just as many of Laing's views about the human condition were indebted to Sartre's philosophy (Kirsner, 1976). But it would be misleading to depict Laing's existentialism as "Sartrean." Laing insisted that his clinical theories were not derived from any one philosopher, and a careful reading of his work confirms that the views of Heidegger, Merleau-Ponty, Scheler, Kierkegaard, Nietzsche, Tillich, Jaspers, Minkowski, Buber, Hegel, and even Montaigne are among the many sources of Laing's treatment philosophy—a list that doesn't even include the considerable influence of Eastern philosophy.

Laing was one of the few existentialists who were actually trained and qualified as a psychoanalyst, though his experience at the British Psychoanalytical Institute was not an altogether enjoyable one. Some of the faculty perceived Laing as a renegade and insisted he repeat his final year of training because he had missed so many classes, an argument that Laing bitterly refuted and eventually won, with the support of his training analyst and supervisors (Burston, 1996). After graduation he drifted away from the institute to pursue a more independent path. Even D. W. Winnicott, one of Laing's supervisors, kept a cautious distance from his former pupil, apparently dubious of Laing's ties to existential philosophy. Shortly thereafter, Laing and a group of colleagues founded the Philadelphia Association and established a training program that integrated psychoanalysis and phenomenology. A born maverick, Laing rejected his former ties to the mainstream, and his subsequent rift with orthodox psychoanalysis hardened even further over the years. Yet the antipathy that Laing's British colleagues expressed toward existential philosophers wasn't an isolated affair; it characterizes the sentiments shared by psychoanalysts the world over, especially in the United States.[8]

Ironically, though Heidegger was the principal inspiration for Binswanger's and Boss's respective conceptions of existential analysis, neither was able to translate his philosophy into a readily accessible clinical language. Binswanger's famous "Case of Ellen West" (in May, 1958) is a typical—and embarrassing—example of the inherent difficulty in translating the extraordinary subtlety of existentialist philosophy into a clinical technique that reflects its essential message. Though Binswanger utilized a new nomenclature that was inspired by Heidegger's terminology, he continued to "diagnose" and depict the patients he treated according to conventional psychiatric nosology. The "Case of Ellen West" reads like an encyclopedia of psychodiagnostic classifications, reducing the plight of this pathetic young lady to little more than a plethora of diagnostic categories, repeating the very kind of objectification and even "depersonalization" that Heidegger's philosophy was intended to overcome. As far as the treatment itself was concerned, Binswanger made little effort to understand her tormented history from the perspective of her *personal experience*. He even sanctioned her decision to kill herself as an existentially "authentic" act because Heidegger conceived inauthenticity as the consequence of denying the inevitability of one's death! Contemporary psychoanalysts—whom Binswanger condemned for *their* dehumanizing tendencies—would be rightfully horrified at the cavalier and insensitive manner in which Binswanger treated this desperate young girl. If this is an example of the "Daseinsanalytic" perspective, it's little wonder that it so quickly fell out of fashion.[9]

On the other hand, Medard Boss was considerably more successful in translating Heidegger's views into a form of clinical practice, no doubt due to the personal friendship they shared and Heidegger's extended efforts to educate Boss in the mysteries of his philosophy. During the 1960s Heidegger even gave seminars at Boss's home in Zollikon, Switzerland, to a group of his fellow psychiatrists. Though not available in English translation (Heidegger, 1987), these seminars present a penetrating critique of medical and psychological sciences and their failure to grasp the fundamental nature of the human condition. Unfortunately, these seminars also reveal Boss's limited understanding of Heidegger's philosophy, which is only superficially represented in Boss's writings. Even Boss's grasp of Freud's psychoanalytic technique is suspect. In his *Psychoanalysis and Daseinsanalysis* (1963), Boss chided Freud at length for his positivistic conception of the transference. But to give Freud his due, the open manner in which he showed every facet of his treatment philosophy, including his mistakes, was daring compared with Boss's often vague and elusive characterization of his own therapeutic technique. Read today, his book ultimately fails to formulate a clear treatment philosophy and methodology, hardly a testament to Heidegger's radical "deconstruction" of psychology and medicine.

More surprising still is Binswanger and Boss's failure to systematically explore the one feature of Heidegger's philosophy that is most relevant to clinical practice: the relationship between truth and authenticity.[10] This is especially disappointing since this is the feature of existential philosophy that so easily resonates with the aims of psychoanalysis. Only in Laing's work is this theme situated at the heart of his clinical theory. In fact, as we shall see, Laing's version of existential psychoanalysis was entirely devoted to this theme. Echoing Freud, he believed that virtually all versions of psychopathology can be traced to the incidence of both self-deception and deception between humans. No other existentialist has made this the central theme of his treatment philosophy. This is the principal reason I believe Laing's work epitomizes the essential contribution of existential psychoanalysis. His preoccupation with the pervasiveness of deception and dishonesty in our everyday affairs with one another owes as much to his fidelity to Freud as it does to his existentialist sources. Unlike the typical existential psychiatrist and psychologist, Laing never abandoned his principal identity as a *psychoanalyst*. In every meaning of the word, his contribution is truly an existential "psychoanalysis."

On the other hand, while Laing could hardly be characterized as a "Heideggerian," his debt to Heidegger's philosophy was explicitly noted in his *Self and Others* (1961) when he depicted his conception of truth as "literally that which is without secrecy, what discloses itself without a veil. This concept has practical interpersonal implications in terms of telling the truth, lying, pretending, [and] equivocating" (p. 111). In other words, being truthful with oneself about what one genuinely believes characterizes Laing's conception of authenticity—or, more colloquially, being honest with oneself. While this conception of authenticity no doubt owes as much to Sartre and Kierkegaard as it does to Heidegger, both views emphasize the anguish of isolation that is imposed by our relations with others.[11] In Laing's own words, "To be 'authentic' is to be true to oneself, to be what one is. . . . To be 'inauthentic' is to not be oneself, to be false to oneself: to be not as one appears to be, to be counterfeit" (pp. 108–9). Hence, the basic thrust of existential psychoanalysis, if it aspires to be at all existential, may be characterized by two principal themes: (1) all human knowledge is rooted in personal experience; and (2) the weight of experience is so painful that we avoid and corrupt it through *self-deception*.

Hence, human beings have a hard time accepting the truth about themselves and circumvent it by devising convoluted means of escape. Existentialism is a subversive and inherently skeptical philosophy that seeks to undermine established truths, whether they assume the form of edicts that are popularized by "the crowd" or neurotic phantasies that are substitutes for an irrepressibly disturbing reality. In that spirit, Kierkegaard attacked Christianity for the distortions it espoused about Christ's teachings, and Nietzsche—arguably the first postmodernist thinker—railed against those who pretended to be authorities of any kind. In turn, Heidegger and Sartre founded their philosophies on the proposition that truth is embedded in experience, but that the toll of experience is so harsh that no one can bear it. What philosophy could be more relevant to the aims of a treatment attitude whose goal is liberation from self-inflicted illusions? While existentialists have always been critical of those psychoanalysts whose behavior belies what they stand for, they have done so in order to reconcile their own views with the person whose work is still closest to their sensibilities: Sigmund Freud. What is inherent in Freud's conception of psychoanalysis that existentialists find so appealing?

Freud's Conception of Psychoanalysis

Freud's abandonment of hypnosis in favor of the free association method officially inaugurated his technical innovation of "psychoanalysis." To free associate simply means to utter the thoughts that come to mind during the therapy session. This entails the willingness to refrain from keeping those thoughts to oneself, no matter how personal or private they are. The rule of free association was only introduced when Freud arrived at the conclusion that neurotic conflicts are the consequence of extremely personal secrets we manage to conceal from ourselves. These secrets are repressed from consciousness in the first place because they concern painful disappointments we experienced in childhood. Suppressing our knowledge of these experiences by "forgetting" them magically relieves the anguish and frustration they elicited. Freud concluded that the suppression of thwarted desire produces psychical conflicts, which in turn lead to psychopathology, symptomatic expressions of the anguish that was previously repressed.

In order to render the practice of free association compelling and not a mere adjunct to treatment, Freud subsequently introduced the "fundamental rule," the patient's explicit *pledge* to be candid. If exercised with sufficient discipline, the patient's candor should serve to untangle the conflicts that had been instigated earlier. In other words, the fundamental rule of psychoanalysis is nothing more than the promise to be honest, by unreservedly "free associating" with one's analyst (Freud, 1913, pp. 134–36). Hence, Freud's conception of psychotherapy was really a form of moral therapy because its curative power lay in the patient's capacity for honesty. One of the implications of this thesis is that the principal cause of psychopathology is self-deception.

Laing recognized the inherently existential nature of Freud's views about the etiology of psychopathology, that it is rooted in the patient's experience. But he also felt that Freud's thesis needed further development. After incorporating the fruits of his research into the etiology of pathology with families of schizophrenics,[12] Laing concluded that our tendency to conceal painful experiences from ourselves is significantly compounded in families where secrets are systematically hidden from one another. I know what you are thinking, but you deny it and pretend to think the opposite. Or I know how I feel, but you insist that I really experience the opposite. This kind of "mystification" can be so extreme that the child no longer knows what he believes (Laing, 1965). In fact, his sense of reality may become so compromised that he seeks refuge through psychotic withdrawal (Thompson, 1985, pp. 88–117).

Laing believed that the treatment of psychosis should serve to reverse the pathogenic process that had been initiated in order to escape an intolerable situation. To make this transition possible—the transition from the treatment of neurotic conflict to that of psychotic loss of reality— Laing needed a more encompassing conception of experience than Freud's formulation provided. He turned to Hegel and Heidegger, both of whom had published extensive critiques on the phenomenology of personal experience (Hegel, 1949, pp. 131–45; Heidegger, 1970). Hegel, for example, showed how the foundation of experience is much deeper than the simple awareness of an act, in the sense that I have an experience of writing this sentence. When I truly experience something, I'm affected by it because it entails confronting the unexpected. In other words, my experiences violate my familiar view of reality as a consequence of perceptions or insights that unexpectedly force their way into consciousness. It is just this kind of experience that characterizes the shock that existential analysts depict as the therapeutic "encounter," when we're suddenly taken out of our depth.

Due to its intrinsically unsettling nature, Hegel concluded that experience elicits despair. Hegel, however, also noted that despair is essentially positive because the experiences that elicit it occasion transformations in consciousness, which in turn account for maturation. Consequently,

Hegel was the first to recognize that experience isn't merely subjective; it's also transcendental because it takes me "outside" myself and puts me in situations that alter my perspective. The effect that my experiences have over me also changes, to a significant degree, the person I am. Hegel's term for my relationship with the things that affect me through my experience of them was his famous "dialectic": "This dialectical process which consciousness executes on itself-on its knowledge as well as on its object-in the sense that out of it the new and true object arises, is precisely what is termed Experience" (1949, p. 142). Hegel arrived at this unusual conception of experience while exploring the nature of consciousness and its relation to change and history. It had an enormous impact on the way philosophers saw the relationship between thought and action.[13] Heidegger was so taken with Hegel's views about the nature of experience that he critiqued it in a book (1970). There, Heidegger emphasized the *revelatory* aspects of experience as well as the transformative ones. According to Heidegger, experience not only changes the world I inhabit, it also reveals things I hadn't realized by bringing them into the open. Hence, experience elicits truth. Heidegger was particularly interested in the "handy," inherently practical aspects of experience. He noted, for example, that my capacity to experience can be nudged this way or that in order to prepare myself for "undergoing" experiences of a wide variety. By anticipating my experiences purposefully I can even utilize experience to gain knowledge about myself. In other words, there are *degrees* to which I experience things; it isn't all or nothing.

On the other hand, experiences don't just happen to me whether I want them to or not. I'm also capable of resisting experiences I'm afraid of. In turn, the degree to which I'm able to experience is determined by my willingness to submit to it. According to Heidegger,

> To undergo an experience with something—be it a thing, a person, or a god—means that this something befalls us, strikes us, comes over us, overwhelms and transforms us. When we talk of "undergoing" an experience, we mean specifically that the experience is not of our own making; to undergo here means that we endure it, suffer it, receive it as it strikes us and submit to it. It is this something itself that comes about, comes to pass, happens. (1971, p. 57)

The extent to which I am able or willing to listen to what my experience tells me determines how fully I experience what I happen to be doing, whether I'm eating a meal, solving a problem, or undergoing a psychoanalysis. Heidegger recognized that because experience is transformative, I fear it and resist by holding back. I'm perfectly capable of suppressing my experiences and even repressing the significance or memory of experiences I've just had in order to "forget" them. In effect, I can resist change by suppressing my experience or elicit change by succumbing to it.

This conception of experience enabled Heidegger to develop a radical conception of subjectivity—Dasein—that virtually erased our everyday notion of "person" or "ego" and substituted in its place an ontological dimension to our existence. In Heidegger's view there is no fixed "person." We are constantly changing as our experiences shape and alter the direction our existence takes. Being human, we resist these changes and attempt to hold on to the person we no longer are. Then we try to "make" ourselves into someone—or something—that is artificial. Psychopathology—if it makes any sense to use that term—is simply a flight from the changes that experience fosters, by denying what our experience is about.

Laing and Experience

Heidegger's phenomenological critique of experience had a profound impact on the way Laing conceived the nature of psychopathology and, by extension, the therapeutic process.[14] He saw psychotic withdrawal, for example, as a desperate attempt to stay true to one's experience when the people in one's environment are violently opposed to it. This is paradoxical because psychosis, as Laing understood it, is an attempt to escape the experience of an intolerable situation while clinging to the very thing one wants to escape. The convoluted compromise that ensues constitutes "psychotic breakdown." In other words, the psychotic is actually trying to be true to his or her experience when forbidden by others to give voice to it.[15] This theory of psychosis, though somewhat radical, conforms with Freud's view that psychotic symptoms are a desperate attempt to heal the rift with reality that the psychotic, by employing denial, has just created (Freud, 1924, pp. 185–86). The problem with this strategy is that it usually—though not always—ends in failure: the psychotic gets lost and can't find a way out.[16]

Laing believed that anything we are capable of experiencing can't, in and of itself, be truly "pathogenic." Rather, it is the *suppression* of experience—by self or others—that gives rise to the distortions in consciousness we associate with psychopathology. Hence anything that we're called upon to experience—even "psychotic" experience—must have a meaningful purpose. Following Heidegger, Laing concluded that the ability to submit to wherever our experience leads us is the principal vehicle for psychic change.[17]

Laing's emphasis on the transformative nature of experience epitomizes the existential component of his clinical technique. Existential psychoanalysis strives to deepen experience by giving voice to it, irrespective of the kind of psychopathology being treated. Freud's free association method—a verbal form of meditation that relies on the patient's utterance of experience—was a clinical variation of the transformative and revelatory dimension to experience articulated by Hegel and Heidegger. Its efficacy rests on the patient's willingness to submit to the experience of the analytic hour by verbalizing what those experiences are.

Laing's relationship with Freud was developed gradually and extended over the breadth of his clinical career. When he was training as a psychoanalyst, Laing, like most existentialists, was critical of Freud and readily identified with the views of Melanie Klein, Ronald Fairbairn, and D. W. Winnicott. But subsequent to his training Laing became disenchanted with the object relations theorists (including the Middle group) and grew increasingly appreciative of the subtlety of Freud's position. Though Laing published nothing about this "conversion," by the time I began my psychoanalytic training with him at the Philadelphia Association in 1973, Laing was convening seminars in which he characterized Freud as having obtained a grasp of the human condition that rivaled even that of the existentialists, including Binswanger and Boss.

Truth and Trauma

Laing's relationship with Freud was complex, but one of the most significant points of convergence between them probably entailed their views about the nature of deception and trauma. Deception was a cornerstone of Freud's theory about the etiology of psychical conflict and the formation of psychopathology. Freud, like most conventional psychiatrists today, initially believed that hysterical symptoms were the consequence of a psychological *trauma*: sexual abuse by one of the child's parents. In his essay "On the History of the Psychoanalytic Movement," published in 1914, Freud described his initial attraction to Charcot's theory of hysteria: "Influenced by Charcot's view of the traumatic origin of hysteria, I was readily inclined to accept as true and aetiologically significant the statements made by patients in which they ascribed their symptoms to passive sexual experiences in the first years of childhood—to put it bluntly, to seduction" (1914b, p. 17). The weight of contradictory evidence, however, eventually demolished the efficacy of Charcot's theory. While sexual molestation was probably just as common in 1914 as it is now, it couldn't explain the prevalence of hysterical symptoms in patients who couldn't have been molested. This conclusion was initially disheartening, but it also provided Freud with a crucial insight. If some patients are capable of complaining about "traumas" they hadn't actually *experienced,* then mightn't their phantasies concerning those alleged traumas account for the emergence of their neurotic conflicts? Freud concluded that "If hysterical subjects trace back their symptoms to traumas that are fictitious, then the new fact which emerges is precisely that they create such scenes in phantasy and this *psychical* reality has to be taken into account alongside *practical* reality" (pp. 17–18). The implications of this discovery completely altered Freud's conception of trauma. Literally meaning wound, the concept of trauma was adopted from medicine and the procedure that was used to treat injuries. When one thinks of trauma, the words violation, shock, and violence readily come to mind. Whereas Freud initially assumed that neurosis was the consequence of a traumatic experience—an act of violence—his subsequent rejection of the "seduction theory" altered his way of conceiving the child's experience of pain and disappointment.

Freud concluded that the *anticipation* of trauma can be even more "traumatic," in a manner of speaking, than one's actual experience of it. In a stroke of genius, Freud grasped the degree to which young children are vulnerable to disappointment and how difficult it is for them to bear it. Children are capable of repressing virtually anything that becomes too painful to accept, and it is notoriously easy for them to substitute objectionable realities with more pleasing phantasies. By defending themselves from painful disappointments—that is, "traumas"—in this way, children avoid *experiencing* their disappointments in the ordinary sense, even though they occur in "reality." A child's phantasy of being seduced, for example, may harbor a wish to be special in order to counter the disappointment of occupying a subsidiary role. In effect, the child's phantasy displaces a disappointing reality and serves to keep the repression of that reality in check.

Having repressed what the child doesn't want to know, it becomes anxious that it will *discover something it can't permit itself to learn.* In other words, children intuitively ward off painful experiences they unconsciously anticipate in order to ease the anguish of disappointment. Freud's appreciation for how terribly painful the experience of disappointment is and the liberties children take to avoid them characterizes the existential dimension to his work.

Truth and Deception

This view of trauma explains the nature of "psychical conflict" in Freud's model, whether the pathology in question is neurotic conflict or psychotic withdrawal.[18] People who suffer such conflicts are of two minds: they struggle against the intrusion of a reality that is too painful to bear, while harboring a phantasy that is incapable of being realized.[19] Their lives are in abeyance. Following this conception of psychopathology, the goal of psychoanalysis is to help analytic patients face the realities they avoid by *experiencing* them in the analytic situation. To paraphrase an axiom of Nietzsche in a different idiom, we allow the dreadful, which has already happened, to happen!

Freud's analysis of Dora, though the treatment was a failure, is a prototypical example of how the relationship between truth and deception is decisive in the etiology of neurosis (Freud, 1905). Dora, who was only eighteen when she began her analysis, had been subjected to the most extraordinary deceptions and intrigues imaginable. Her father had been involved in a love affair with a married woman right under Dora's nose— and presumably her mother's—for years. He even conspired to look the other way while his mistress's husband, the infamous Mr. K, attempted to seduce Dora, a child only fourteen years of age. Though he failed in his efforts, two years later he tried again. This time Dora took the matter to her father, not realizing he was aware of Mr. K's intentions and even supported them. Dora's father went through the motions of confronting Mr. K, who (ostensibly) denied everything. Dora subsequently fell into a prolonged depression, compounded by a host of related hysterical symptoms.

By the time she was eighteen and suicidal, Dora'a father took her to see Freud. Her brief analysis uncovered the intrigues that Dora had "known" of, but repressed. Perhaps the most remarkable aspect of

Freud's inquiry into the causes of Dora's condition concerned the question: what specifically drove Dora to her pathological condition, the traumatic events that transpired at the hands of her family, or the consequent *self*-deceptions Dora employed to protect herself from disappointment? Freud suspected that Dora was secretly in love with Mr. K but that her devotion to her father and jealousy over his affair with Mrs. K made it impossible for her to confront the reality of her situation. As unsettling as her family's duplicity must have been, Freud believed it was Dora's unwillingness to face the truth about her own feelings that provoked the neurotic conflict she subsequently suffered.[20]

One of the most surprising aspects about this case concerned Freud's novel conception of trauma. Whether the reality one is confronted with is so terrible that *no one* could be expected to accommodate it, or whether that reality simply doesn't suit the individuality of the person who is embroiled in it, it still comes down to the same thing: *the rejection of reality, for whatever reason, gives rise to a "dual reality" that manifests a pathogenic conflict*. But what if the reality in question differs according to the type of pathology that is manifested? Inspired by the interpersonal theories of Harry Stack Sullivan and Frieda Fromm-Reichmann, Laing suspected that the reality schizophrenics are trying to get away from must be more harrowing than one that engenders simple frustration. In other words, psychotics must have a good reason to be even more terrified of reality than neurotics, who don't go to such lengths to escape it.

He concluded that frustration alone couldn't account for the crippling effects of psychotic withdrawal. If Freud's principal thesis—that the psychotic rejects reality because it's so painful—was correct, then what would compel someone to withdraw in such a radical fashion? Isn't it possible, Laing conjectured, that the reality psychotics reject is qualitatively different from the one we ordinarily encounter? This is the type of question (what is going on in the *real world* that might account for the pathology in question?) that an existentialist is more likely to ask. This is the same question that prompted Laing to seek an alternative to narcissism as the principal motive force in schizophrenia. Laing applied Freud's conception of psychic trauma to his research into extreme forms of delusional confusion, but in a more dialectical framework. While Freud emphasized the use of phantasy as a way of avoiding objectionable realities, Laing was interested in the means by which people systematically employ deception on one another in order to manipulate the other person's experience and hence, that person's reality. This dialectical dimension to my experience of others—what I think they think about me; and what they in fact think but conceal from my awareness—was derived from Laing's debt to Hegel's "master-slave" dialectic: *my internal critique of how others affect-and help constitute-my experience.*

Whereas Freud conceived of trauma in terms of the frustration that thwarts the experience of pleasure, Laing envisioned a different form of trauma that could convincingly account for psychotic symptoms. He saw it in terms of a state of confusion that follows when one's reality has been compromised, not through self-deception alone but as a consequence of being deceived by somebody else. The two forms of deception—Freud's intrapsychic version and Laing's more dialectical one—are not mutually exclusive. In fact, they typically interact. What's more, Laing believed that both forms of deception are discernible in virtually every form of psychopathology.

Deception and Madness

The nature of deception was a common theme in Laing's writings throughout the 1960s, his most prolific decade as an author. Ironically, *The Divided Self* (1960), Laing's first and most famous book, is the only one in which deception *between* persons doesn't play a major role. It was a classic existentialist study about the experience of going mad but said little about the social context that would subsequently play such a critical role in Laing's thinking. It did, however, presage his later work with a compelling exploration of the relationship between self-deception and psychopathology.

Laing's next book, *Self and Others* (1961), examined the relationship between interpersonal relations and the etiology of severe psychological disturbance. Many of the terms that Laing introduced in that book for the first time—for example, collusion, mystification, attribution, injunction, untenable positions—were coined for the purpose of providing a conceptual vocabulary that could explain how human beings, in their everyday interactions with each other, distort the truth so effectively that they are able to undermine the other person's sense of reality. It was just this vocabulary that Laing suggested was missing in Freud's theories. Even the object relations theorists who were critical of Freud's drive model were unable to formulate the kind of phenomenological critique of psychotic experience that Laing's interpersonal focus provided.

For example, in 1964 Laing and his research colleague Aaron Esterson published a study of eleven schizophrenic patients emphasizing their interactions with the members of their respective families. *Sanity, Madness and the Family* (Laing and Esterson, 1964) stands out as one of the most impressive phenomenological studies of this kind ever undertaken.[21] It demonstrated how massive forms of trickery, deception, and mystification were systematically employed against each of the schizophrenic family members by their parents. One of the patients, whom Laing called Maya, is typical of the families studied. Her parents, who come across as pretty crazy themselves, believed that their daughter had special powers that enabled her to read their minds. The father spoke openly—when his daughter wasn't present—of having systematically employed surreptitious tests on his daughter to "confirm" that Maya knew what her parents were thinking. Maya, in turn, suspected that something of the sort was going on, but when she was finally able to confront her parents in one of their family sessions, they coyly winked at Laing and brazenly denied it, as they had done all her life.

In case after case Laing and Esterson unearthed a casual and often chilling array of deceptive maneuvers of this kind, employed by devoted parents against their unsuspecting children. The parents also systematically distorted the truth about their efforts to manipulate their children so that, by means of this double-distortion they effectively nullified the child's efforts to determine the truth. Laing's approach to this problem prompted many parents to accuse him of blaming them for the plight of their schizophrenic children. In fact, Laing attributed the conflicts that parents so easily get embroiled in to the human condition. The blood is on all our hands. Laing adopted and in turn incorporated into his clinical theory the existentialist view that all human beings are inherently devious and, without giving it much thought, deceive one another as a matter of course. Schizophrenia is only one of the inevitable consequences of this state of affairs.

In *The Politics of Experience* (1967), his most popular book, Laing directed his efforts to a more complicated and inherently convoluted "politics" of interpersonal experience where he delineated how others are able to determine my experience through the power they possess to obfuscate what my experience is. Beneath the mask of our carefully crafted social veneer, all of us, Laing suggested, are "murderers and prostitutes" at heart (Laing, 1967, p. xiv). The theme throughout this study was as compelling as it was provocative: human beings employ acts of casual deception on one another, which Laing depicted as carefully disguised acts of "violence," often in the service of the most well-intentioned motives.

The book had an explosive impact on an entire generation of psychology students in America at a time when the counterculture had lost its faith in a government that was dragging its children into a meaningless war. Laing suggested that virtually anyone in a position of power over others—whether government officials or generals, even parents and psychiatrists—is invariably corrupted by that power when used to gain influence over others. Indeed, depending on the situation, each of *us* finds ourselves committing treasons against others just as often as we are victimized by *them*. The implications of this view for analytic technique were immense.

While this arguably stark critique of human nature owed much to Nietzsche, Heidegger, and Sartre, it was a view that Laing also attributed to Freud. In his papers devoted to the technical rules of psychoanalysis, Freud went out of his way to admonish analysts to be truthful with their patients even when it is painful to do so, and to dispense with the "lies and pretenses which a doctor normally finds unavoidable" (1915, p. 164). Similarly, Laing argued that the most important element in the therapeutic experience is the honest and straightforward manner with which patients are treated, not the cleverness or complexity of the psychoanalyst's techniques.

Laing and Dora

Ironically, Freud's analysis of Dora is a prototypical example of the kind of manipulation and deception that Laing believed are typically employed in families of schizophrenics (Freud, 1905). Laing once told me that the case had a profound impact on his thinking and that he was even startled, in subsequent readings of it, by the degree of mystification Dora's father employed against her. The most blatant example of the kind of deception employed against her was when Dora's father conspired with Mr. K (who had accosted her while walking by a lake) to convince her she had only imagined his attempt at seduction. In other words, Dora's experience of the incident was reinterpreted back to her, by the two men she loved the most, as *the inventions of a disturbed and over-*

sexed imagination. This is the kind of mystification—the reinterpretation of one's experience as phantasy—that Laing attributed to the etiology of psychotic disintegration.

If Laing's thesis is correct, why did Dora not develop a psychosis instead of the most celebrated case of hysteria ever documented? In fact, Laing never suggested that mystification is exclusive to families of schizophrenics. While mystification is a necessary determinant to schizophrenia, it doesn't necessarily engender a psychotic reaction. One needs to take into account the purpose for which deceptions are employed as well as the intentionality that prompts the victim of those deceptions to respond in the particular manner that she does. There were numerous factors that distinguished the interpersonal "politics" of Dora's family from a typical schizophrenogenic one.

For one thing, there is generally a naivete about the prepsychotic individual that belies the precocious sophistication that characterized Dora's behavior. And while the prepsychotic will typically comply with the mystifying parent by abdicating his or her perception of reality in deference to the parents, Dora knew that Mr. K was lying when he contradicted her version of what occurred by the lake; she wasn't the least confused by the disparity between their respective accounts of what happened. Another important distinction between the way Dora's family employed deceptions and the way the family of a schizophrenic might is that, in Dora's case, the purpose of the mystification was to simply *deny Dora's accusations*. Dora's father and Mr. K colluded together in their deception of Dora to avoid the potentially embarrassing revelation of the secret pact they had instigated between them. They didn't want Dora, now that she had seen through their scheme, to expose their plans. On the other hand, the mystification employed in families of schizophrenics serves a more subtle purpose: to subvert the children's *experience of reality* by bending their intentionality to the parents' will.

The point Laing wanted to emphasize is that the line between neurotic and psychotic forms of deception isn't so easy to determine. What they share in common is far more instructive than what sets them apart. Whether deceptions are employed for the purpose of safeguarding uncomfortable secrets, or whether the purpose served is to gain control over somebody's mind, virtually every form of psychopathology is the consequence of lies employed by human beings against each other and ultimately against themselves. In fact, the line between psychopathology and "normality" is even more difficult to discern than the one between neurosis and psychosis—an observation that Freud was the first to point out. Secrecy and deception are axiomatic in every culture. All of us have been subjected to deviousness of one kind or another as children. Years later, when we become analytic patients, we instinctively employ deceptions of our own against anybody who endeavors to determine what we're hiding. Deception is so ingrained in each of us that it has become our currency for relationship and the principal source of resistance to psychotherapy.

The Truth about Technique

The reason Laing went to such pains to labor this aspect of human existence was that he believed human deviousness isn't a matter that can be relegated to the "sick" members of society alone. All of us employ deception for the same reason. Whenever we're thwarted in our endeavors we feel disappointment and frustration; we're afraid that behaving honestly will expose us to even greater vulnerability. We resort to guile and manipulation, but because this entails subterfuge we experience an even greater measure of anxiety and guilt. Then, in order to protect ourselves from increased anxiety, we increase our deceptive practices even more.

It is ironic that children and mental patients are the most defenseless victims of these tactics. They lack the credibility to make their case heard, even when they know they're being manipulated, which isn't often. Laing argued that psychiatrists and even psychoanalysts, in their zeal to effect change, frequently resort to tactics of this nature. They become manipulative and, without realizing it, transform analysis into a sort of contest where the more clever protagonist "wins."

Freud was the first to recognize the dilemma every psychiatrist encounters when trying to effect change without resorting to coercive maneuvers. Indeed, the abandonment of such maneuvers epitomized the ethical foundation of psychoanalysis from its inception. Freud coined a number of terms—neutrality, abstinence, countertransference, therapeutic and educative ambition—that were intended to alert analysts to the inherent dangers of their power. Similarly, Laing's therapeutic technique embodied a simple overriding concern: how honestly are therapists treating their patients; and how honest are they committed to being?

Laing's approach to this problem owed an undeniable debt to the "basic rule" of psychoanalysis: the fundamental rule and its correlate, the rule of neutrality. The fundamental rule was rooted in the premise that it is imperative to establish a rule of thumb at the beginning of treatment whereby patients agree to be as truthful as they can by concealing nothing that comes to mind. Second, analysts by the same token should take everything they're told with a grain of salt. In other words, they should assume that their patients are telling the truth while reserving judgment about the veracity of what they say. More importantly, analysts themselves shouldn't try to determine the direction that the treatment follows, even when they're convinced that they know which direction is "best." They should permit their patients to proceed in the manner to which they are predisposed, in the manner that is true to their experience. This second rule of thumb became the "rule of neutrality."

Laing endorsed these two rules as axiomatic of existential psycho-analysis. He cautioned, however, that the fundamental rule shouldn't be reduced to a means of obtaining knowledge "about" a patient's unconscious. On a deeper level it entails each patient's willingness to plumb the depths of his or her experience and accepting the consequences of whatever comes to light, for better or worse. This can't possibly happen unless the analyst, in his or her neutrality, is capable of accepting the person we turn out to be. Though Laing was uncomfortable with the idea of exacting an "oath" from patients in the manner that Freud advocated, he believed that some form of implicit understanding has to exist that is rooted in mutual respect.

Since candor is the principal means of overcoming neurotic conflict, Freud was concerned that the *analyst's* behavior may inadvertently inhibit rather than encourage the patient's efforts to comply with this rule. Deviousness on the part of analysts would render analytic treatments negligible, or worse. Hence the rule of neutrality—keeping an "open mind" to whatever patients say—should encourage patients to express themselves more freely. Indeed, the real danger to analysis, Freud believed, doesn't lie in analysts making their views known to their patients but in pretending to entertain views that aren't really theirs. Why was Freud so concerned that analysts might deliberately distort their views to their own patients?

Freud discovered that some analysts, eager to guide the treatment into a more predictable course, resorted to techniques he considered unanalytic because they were dishonest. Some analysts were uncomfortable with their patients' seductive demands, for example, while others went to the other extreme and urged their patients to fall in love with them. Some even encouraged their patients to believe that if they "behaved" a certain way they would ultimately be rewarded with their analyst's love, even though the analysts knew that such a reward was impossible. It was in this context that Freud condemned the use of trickery as a tool of analytic treatment and introduced the rule of neutrality, to serve as a foil to these temptations. In Freud's words,

> My objection to this expedient [i.e., the use of trickery] is that psycho-analytic treatment is founded on truthfulness. In this fact lies a great part of its educative effect and its ethical value. . . . Since we demand strict truthfulness from our patients, we jeopardize our whole authority if we let ourselves be caught out by them in a departure from the truth.   (1915, p. 164)

In their neutrality, analysts should neither encourage nor discourage patients from expressing whatever feelings they happen to experience, whether love, hatred, spite, or jealousy, nor to compel patients to feel what they don't. Hence, the rule of neutrality is rooted in the same premise as the fundamental rule: truthfulness. The gist of Freud's message is quite simple. The only way anyone can hope to resolve the effects of *self-deception* is to submit to a relationship with another person wherein they endeavor to be as honest *with each other* as they can.

It isn't hard to appreciate how Freud's views about the relationship between deception and psychopathology, on the one hand, and honesty and treatment, on the other, would inspire an existentialist like Laing to recognize the existential dimension to his thought. Laing's analytic technique was epitomized by neutrality: taking care to never manipulate the behavior of one's patients (Thompson, 1997). Since Freud's death, however, analytic neutrality has become confused with the rule of abstinence—deliberately withholding one's sympathy. Contemporary analysts tend to incorporate those aspects of neutrality that involve attending to the analyst's experience of the treatment situation into a revised conception of countertransference, whereas Freud conceived of neutrality as a foil to countertransference, in the sense that he originally intended (Freud, 1915, p. 164).

From a contemporary perspective, Laing's treatment philosophy was almost exclusively rooted in attending to the analyst's "countertransference" (i.e., neutrality, properly speaking). He saw his role as one of helping patients "untie" the knots they had managed to tie themselves in. He believed this entailed exercising extraordinary care to not repeat the same types of subterfuge and coercion that had got them into their knots in the first place. He followed the same practice in his training methods. In my supervision experience with him Laing treated students with the same degree of openness and noninterference that he brought to bear with his patients. He refused to dictate the course that candidates should follow, nor did he try to "correct" the mistakes they invariably committed.

This degree of noninterference in the context of analytic treatment and training has become such a rarity that the idea of it is increasingly dismissed as unprofessional, irresponsible, even unethical. Those analysts who believe it is incumbent on them to run a "tight ship," to maintain their authority over patients (and students) at all costs, and who attribute analytic failures to "insufficient treatment" or, worse, "inadequate training," aren't likely to embrace a method of treatment that is as modest in its claims as it is cautious with its interventions. It is worth keeping in mind that this measure of uncommon restraint and skeptical caution epitomized Freud's clinical behavior as much as it did Laing's. We correct or improve such matters at our peril if, when seeking "progress," we lose sight of the need we each have to find our own way and to commit our own mistakes.

And what of Laing' relevance today? Or is he merely an interesting chapter in history to be studied for the sake of posterity? The last few years of Laing's life were difficult ones. He endured a devastating divorce and then drifted away from his colleagues in London. His books became increasingly autobiographical as he turned inward to relieve his shattered existence. Yet even in his suffering Laing epitomized the existentialist sensibility like no other figure of his generation. He "deconstructed" the dark side of the family that each of us has survived; he fostered a technique that replaced "treatment" with an uncommon humanity; and for his labors to subvert orthodoxy he took the heat and, perhaps, paid the price for challenging the hegemony of health institutions that increasingly seek profit as their principal motive. Like Freud, Laing was a visionary and ahead of his time. He invited us to look at ourselves through a lens that would drive the fainthearted to despair or, perhaps, crazy. His work remains a beacon to the existential philosophers whom few have read for themselves, but it is also a culmination of their mission to depict our profound alienation and to repair it.

There are encouraging signs that some are beginning to recognize the relevance of Laing's message—and existentialism—for the postmodernist era. Psychoanalysts who shunned existentialism or thought Laing was irrelevant are beginning to reference his work (Bollas, 1987; Burston, 1994; Frank, 1990; Levenson, 1991). With new works about Laing on the horizon, a new generation of "existential analysts" may emerge as we approach the culmination of this pivotal century. They, too, will be faced with the same question: What is existential psychoanalysis? Like those before them, they will have to answer it for themselves.

Whatever answer they come to, I would like to add a word of caution. Existential psychoanalysis isn't now nor was it ever supposed to be an alternative to psychoanalysis, nor is it a radically new vision of what psychoanalysis never was but should have been. It is what psychoanalysis was always intended to be and, in its latency, always was. It is at once Freudian and heretical, tolerant and deviant, respectful of the limitations to human knowledge but never content to rest on its laurels. It is perhaps appropriate to give Laing the last word on the matter:

> Existential thinking offers no security, no home for the homeless. . . . It addresses no one but you and me. It finds its validation when, across the gulf of our idioms and styles, our mistakes, errings and perversities, we find in the other's communication an experience of relationship established, lost, destroyed or regained. We hope to share the experience of a relationship, but the only honest beginning, or even end, may be to share the experience of its absence.   (1967, p. 34)

NOTES

Some portions of this essay were included in a lecture, "Deception, Mystification, Trauma: Laing and Freud," presented at Duquesne University, March 11, 1994, under the auspices of the Simon Silverman Phenomenology Center. Permission to include them in this publication is gratefully acknowledged.

1. For the sake of simplicity, I include under the rubric "existential psychoanalysis" any efforts to integrate the phenomenology of Edmund Husserl, Martin Heidegger, Jean-Paul Sartre, or Maurice Merleau-Ponty into the psychoanalysis of Freud.

2. Heidegger's impact on contemporary intellectual thought is enormous. Deconstructionalists such as Jacques Derrida (1978), hermeneuticists such as Hans-Georg Gadamer (1994) and Paul Ricoeur (1974), and postmodernist thinkers such as Emmanuel Levinas (1981), Jean-Luc Nancy (1993), and Philippe Lacoue-Labarthe (1990) are all indebted to aspects of Heideggers's philosophy for the formulation of their views.

3. Dasein was Heidegger's term for what is typically depicted as the "self," but

with this crucial qualification: it is a concept of subjectivity that constitutes and in turn is constituted by our experience of the world, emphasizing the ontological rather than strictly psychological ("individualistic") dimension of one's existence. It includes the spatial and temporal dimensions of each person's life as it unfolds instead of the more simplistic and inherently solipsistic notion of a "personality" that is alienated from its intrinsic nature and accordingly compartmentalized.

4. Indeed, a reading of the representative papers published by the "existential analysts" at that time (see Rollo May's [1958] collection of papers by Continental existential psychiatrists, *Existence*) shows a disappointing tendency to encapsulate their theories in an excessively arid and technical fashion, no doubt contributing to the movement's eventual demise.

5. This is mirrored by the so-called Americanization of existential psychotherapy, epitomized by "popular" West Coast practitioners such as Rollo May, James F. T. Bugental, and Irvin Yalom, all of whose treatment philosophy is more idiosyncratic than, strictly speaking, phenomenological.

6. For a closer look at the compatibility between Freud's and Heidegger's views, see Thompson, *The Truth about Freud's Technique: The Encounter with the Real* (1994a).

7. For a more detailed treatment of Lacan's relationship with phenomenology see Thompson, *The Death of Desire: A Study in Psychopathology* (1985) and Anthony Wilden, *The Language of the Self* (1968).

8. This prompted my decision to train with Laing and his colleagues at the Philadelphia Association in the 1970s. For a personal account of my experiences there, see "The Fidelity to Experience in R. D. Laing's Treatment Philosophy" (1997).

9. See Laing's scathing critique of Binswanger's application of existential analysis in *The Voice of Experience* (1982, pp. 53–62.)

10. Though many clinicians attribute its origins to Kierkegaard (May, 1958, p. 118), it was Heidegger who introduced this concept as one of the pivots of his philosophy (Heidegger, [1927] 1962, pp. 219–24). While the term "authenticity" never actually occurs in Kierkegaard, it is generally acknowledged that his preoccupation with mortality and self-deception significantly inspired Heidegger's views. Whereas Heidegger emphasized the need to resign oneself to one's death, Kierkegaard was more troubled by the universality of human hypocrisy and self-delusion.

11. While undeniably influenced by Heidegger's more ontological preoccupation with our relation to Being before death, Sartre—following Kierkegaard—was more interested in the lack of authenticity typically manifested in interpersonal relations. In terms of the aims and limitations of clinical practice, the latter emphasis would appear to be the more relevant.

12. At the Tavistock Institute for Human Relations, from 1958 to 1964.

13. Hegel's views about the dialectic of desire influenced an entire generation

of French intellectuals—including Jean-Paul Sartre, Maurice Merleau-Ponty, and Jacques Lacan—through Alexandre Kojeve's lecture course on his work (1969).

14. Even the concept of "psychopathology" bothered Laing because of the inherently medical connotation that one is suffering from some type of illness, which Laing held was antithetical to the existentialist perspective. He eventually dropped the term entirely.

15. This conception of psychosis was also indebted to D. W. Winnicott, who construed various forms of psychopathology as a desperate effort to feel real (Winnicott, 1964).

16. The bulk of Laing's contribution to the treatment of schizophrenia was based on the notion that psychotic breakdown is an attempt to "break through" the existential impasse one is in. Laing's treatment center at Kingsley Hall was devoted to permitting its inhabitants the opportunity to do just that, without being medicated by the psychotherapists they were seeing.

17. For more on the relationship between experience and psychical change see Freud 1914a and a synopsis of that paper in Thompson 1994a, pp. 192–204.

18. In Freud's model, both neurotic and psychotic individuals seek a means of escaping a frustrating reality. The neurotic endeavors to conform with reality by repressing a thwarted desire, whereas the psychotic seeks to protect his desire narcissistically by simply denying the troublesome reality and withdrawing from it.

19. See Kierkegaard's conception of double-mindedness outlined in *Purity of Heart Is to Will One Thing* (1956).

20. See Thompson 1994a, pp. 93–132 for a more thorough discussion of Freud's analysis of Dora.

21. See also *Interpersonal Perception* (Laing, Phillipson, and Lee, 1966), in which Laing and his research colleagues provide a phenomenological critique of communication patterns among married couples.

REFERENCES

Bollas, C. 1987. *The Shadow of the Object.* New York: Columbia University Press.

Boss, M. 1963. *Psychoanalysis and Daseinsanalysis.* New York: Basic Books.

Burston, D. 1994. Freud, the Serpent and the Sexual Enlightenment of Children. *Int. Forum Psychoanal.* 3:205–19.

———. 1996. *The Wing of Madness: The Life and Work of R. D. Laing.* Cambridge: Harvard University Press.

Derrida, J. 1978. *Writing and Difference.* London: Routledge and Kegan Paul.

Frank, J. A. 1990. Listening with the Big Ear: A Laingian Approach to Psychotic Families. In *Psychoanalysis and Severe Emotional Illness,* ed. A.-L. Silver and M. B. Cantor. New York: Guilford Press.

Freud, S. 1905. *Fragment of an Analysis of a Case of Hysteria*. In *Standard Edition*: vol. 7, London: Hogarth Press, 1953, pp. 3–122.

———. 1914a. Remembering, Repeating and Working-Through (Further Recommendations on the Technique of Psycho-Analysis II). In *Standard Edition*: vol. 12, 1958, pp. 145–56.

———. 1914b. On the History of the Psychoanalytic Movement. In *Standard Edition*: vol. 14, 1957, pp. 3–66.

———. 1915. Observations on Transference-Love (Further Recommendations on the Technique of Psycho-Analysis III). In *Standard Edition*: vol. 12, 1958, pp. 157–71.

———. 1924. The Loss of Reality in Neurosis and Psychosis. In *Standard Edition*: vol. 19, 1961, pp. 183–7.

Gadamer, H.-G. 1994. *Heidegger's Ways*. Albany: State University of New York Press.

Hegel, G. W. F. 1949. *Phenomenology of Mind*. New York: Macmillan.

Heidegger, M. [1927] 1962. *Being and Time*. Oxford: Basil Blackwell.

———. 1970. *Hegel's Concept of Experience*. San Francisco: Harper and Row.

———. 1971. *On the Way to Language*. New York: Harper and Row.

———. 1987. *Zollikoner Seminare*. Ed. M. Boss. Frankfurt: Vittorio Klostermann.

Kierkegaard, S. 1956. *Purity of Heart Is to Will One Thing*. New York: Harper and Row.

Kirsner, D. 1976. *The Schizoid World of Jean-Paul Sartre and R. D. Laing*. St. Lucia, Queensland: Queensland University Press.

Kojeve, A. 1969. *Introduction to the Reading of Hegel*. New York: Basic Books.

Lacoue-Labarthe, P. 1990. *Heidegger, Art and Politics*. Oxford: Basil Blackwell.

Laing, R. D. 1960. *The Divided Self*. New York: Pantheon.

———. 1961. *Self and Others*. New York: Pantheon.

———. 1965. Mystification, Confusion, and Conflict. In *Intensive Family Therapy*, ed. I Boszormenyi-Nagy and J. Framo. New York: Harper and Row, pp. 343–63.

———. 1967. *The Politics of Experience*. New York: Pantheon.

———. 1982. *The Voice of Experience*. New York: Pantheon.

Laing R. D. and A. Esterson. 1964. *Sanity, Madness and the Family*. New York: Basic Books.

Laing, R. D., Phillipson, H. and Lee, R. 1966. *Interpersonal Perception*. London: Tavistock.

Laing, R. D. and Cooper, D. G. 1971. *Reason and Violence*. 2d ed. London: Tavistock.

Levenson, E. 1991. *The Purloined Self: Interpersonal Perspectives in Psychoanalysis*. New York: Contemporary Psychoanalysis Books.

Levinas, E. 1981. *Otherwise Than Being or Beyond Essence*. Hague: Martinus Nijhoff.

May, R., ed. 1958. *Existence: A New Dimension in Psychiatry and Psychology*. New York: Basic Books.

Nancy, J.-L. 1993. *The Experience of Freedom*. Stanford: Stanford University Press.

Ricoeur, P. 1974. *The Conflict of Interpretations: Essays in Hermeneutics*. Evanston: Northwestern University Press.

Roudinesco, E. 1990. *Jacques Lacan & Co*. Chicago: University of Chicago Press.

Spiegelberg, H. 1972. *Phenomenology in Psychiatry and Psychology*. Evanston: Northwestern University Press.

Thompson, M. Guy 1985. *The Death of Desire: A Study in Psychopathology*. New York: New York University Press.

———. 1994a. *The Truth about Freud's Technique: The Encounter with the Real*. New York: New York University Press.

———. 1994b. The Fidelity to Experience in Existential Psychoanalysis. In *The Psychology of Existence: An Integrative, Clinical Perspective*, ed. K. Schneider and R. May. New York: McGraw-Hill, 1995, pp. 233–247.

———. 1996. The Rule of Neutrality. *Psychoanalysis and Contemporary Thought*. 19, no. 1.

———. 1997. The Fidelity to Experience in R. D. Laing's Treatment Philosophy. *Contemporary Psychoanalysis* 33(4): 595–614.

Wilden, A. 1968. *The Language of the Self*. Baltimore: Johns Hopkins University Press.

Winnicott, D. W. 1964. Fear of Breakdown. In *The British School of Psycho-analysis*, ed. G. Kohon. New Haven: Yale University Press, 1986, pp. 173–182.

Chapter Fourteen

Jacques Lacan
The Language of Alienation

Marion M. Oliner

EDITORS' INTRODUCTION

In our view, Lacan's novel theorizing can be regarded as one of the most important contributions to contemporary psychoanalysis. His work emphasizes the subversive potential of psychoanalysis, specifically, he offers an original way of understanding how the individual becomes constituted in the structure of language and culture.

Lacan has fashioned a compelling view of how what appears to be our primary reality, our "being," is in fact fashioned through a sequence of shifts in which we become inserted into the symbolic order of culture. Perhaps most important, these shifts are conceptualized as inherently alienating. That is, for Lacan, being is always alienated from its own history, it is formed in and through otherness, and it is thrown into a symbolic world that is external to itself. Thus, for Lacan, the so-called ego, the "I," is an alienating screen, an illusion, that conceals the divided and fractured character of unconscious desire. This is Lacan's famous critique of ego psychology and its claim that the ego should be the center of psychological life. In contrast, Lacan offers us a "decentered" subject, a subject who is formed in the context of social relationships, and who is characterized by constant fragmentation and disintegration that is inflicted by the unconscious.

As Marion M. Oliner points out, it was Lacan's conviction that psychoanalysis and, perhaps, even Freud himself were untrue to the meaning of the unconscious, and that the emphasis on the ego, with its function of synthesis, constituted a regressive move with regard to the revolutionary aspects of Freud's discovery. Lacan's "return to Freud" was as a spokesman for the unconscious. He preferred a style of writing that resembled free association, so that his formulations are evocative rather than descriptive. Nevertheless, says Oliner, he was emphatic in his belief in an unconscious that is totally divorced from its biological underpinnings and that is structured according to the rules of linguistics, metonymy and metaphor, and a concept of "desire" that aims at a return to merger with the mother, which is rendered impossible by the prohibition of the father. Foreclosure, typical of psychosis, signifies the absence of the prohibition of the father. Lacan, Oliner claims, saw man as attempting to become that which would satisfy the desire of (for) the other but never attaining this goal. In other words, man's essence is the chain of signifiers that define his desire; this is the sense that psychoanalysis can reinstate to him. Says Oliner, "the paradox of the Lacanian universe consists in the notion of a being that is liberated through submission to the inevitability of self-alienation. It is the acceptance of being lived through a structure that constitutes Lacan's notion of the human condition" For Lacan then, ontologically speaking, humans are essentially split and alienated precisely because needs must be expressed in language, and must be directed to an other who exists separately and independently of us.

As Oliner emphasizes, Lacan never wavered in his opposition to the notions of a cohesive individuality or autonomous and coherent ego, and he repeatedly admonished analysts not to respond to the demands made by the analysand. Ultimately, he considered the job of the analyst to be the restoration to the patient of the dividedness that is his essence and the meaning of the inner structure that lives in and through him. For Lacan, in other words, the purpose of analysis was to confront the analysands with the impossibility of their desire through frustration of their wishes and hence to induce them to accept self-estrangement as the necessary foundation of "being." Lacan's controversial "techniques," such as unpredictably abbreviated sessions and other "disruptive" and frustrating behavior, were thus meant to bring the analysand to an understanding of his internal discontinuities and ruptures and ultimately to accept alienation as fundamental to the human enterprise. That is, for Lacan, the fact of living in any society presupposes alienation from certain personal possibilities and desires. To not embrace that fact is part of what constitutes psychopathology. Analysis thus aims to help the analysand "to speak what heretofore been unspeakable," that is, to reclaim the voice for one's desires, by untangling the familial experiences, the signifiers that have had an interpretive grip on one's life. As Oliner indicates, for the Lacanian, the analyst remains the Other, but not the other whose pleasure rules the analysis, but the other as in Freud's "other scene," the unconscious. In this, she notes, Lacan was consistent in that he avoided the unity between analyst and analysand inherent in such concepts as "the therapeutic alliance" or "holding environment" and replaced them with the notion of an analysis that confronts the person with his unconscious from which he has been alienated because of the search for sameness and cohesion. (P. M. and A. R.)

Lacan has been mistakenly considered the representative of psychoanalysis in France. This error is based on the novelty of his approach and on his notoriety, which eclipsed those analysts in France who accepted psychoanalysis on the basis of the same view of the human condition as Freud had done, when he treated man as an extension of the animal kingdom. Although Lacan was a psychiatrist by training, he took the road of those artists and philosophers who used the discovery of the unconscious as a tool for the overthrow of reason in life and art. He came from the same milieu as the poets André Breton and Louis Aragon, who celebrated the fiftieth anniversary of the study of hysteria as the "greatest poetic discovery of the end of the nineteenth century" (Anzieu, 1975, p. 131). Like Breton, the surrealist, Lacan elevated the role of the unconscious and attempted to return to Freud in a specific way, that is, before Freud (according to Breton and Lacan) became untrue to his own discovery by introducing and in a sense enthroning the synthetic function of the ego, derived from eros. Lacan could not accept the notion of the domination of a psychic agency that aims at harmony within the personality and a gratifying relationship to external reality.

Lacan's departure from the belief in a cohesive, integrated subject, except as subjected, i.e., enslaved, is also the product of his study of Hegelian philosophy, but Lacan's return to Freud was predicated on his wish to abolish the synthesis inherent in Hegel's dialectic and in Freud's structural theory. Thinking based on similarity and identity, stems, according to Lacan, from the realm of the Imaginary. His is an attempt to continue the revolutionary aspects of the Freudian discovery by maintaining the image of a divided subject alienated from his desire, which cannot and should not be satisfied because it is not man's fate to attain unity and thereby breach the gap of his separateness. Philosophically, this is a radical departure from Freud's "biologism" and the excesses of Marie Bonaparte, who, at the time Lacan's theories were enunciated, was considered Freud's leading representative in France. Lacan abandoned completely the theory of mental life as an outgrowth and extension of the cohesive experience of the instinct of self-preservation. He brought into psychoanalysis the notion of the decenteredness of man's existence, also spelled ex-sistence, thereby introducing an approach that was equally inspired by philosophy, art, and his clinical experience. As instinct and drive give way to the term "desire" in the Lacanian terminology, its ancestry is philosophical rather than biological: "it is Sartre who speaks of man being torn between a 'desire to be' and a 'desire to have', and who defines desire itself in terms of a 'lack of being' [*manque d'être*]" (Macey, 1988, p. 116). Lacan completes Sartre's thought by introducing the other or the phallus as the metaphor for the object of desire but also the guarantor of separateness. The desire depicts the quest for a "signifier," not a body part, that maintains itself as an indispensable motivator. This approach generated for psychoanalysis in France a much wider following than elsewhere because it addressed the concerns of feminists, revolutionary politicians, contemporary philosophers, and artists, and earned the enmity of the International Psychoanalytic Association.

Lacan had a large following, but there were many disaffections even during his lifetime, so that many French analysts were influenced by him but would not call themselves Lacanians. One of his former disciples, Pontalis (1979), suggests that the issues around Lacan were not centered on substance but on transference. He said that when the "veterans" got together, "we all said: at this date no one could not be a Lacanian; at this other, one could no longer be Lacanian. But the dates were not at all the same depending on the person concerned" (p.9). After Lacan's death in 1981 his successors were not able to maintain the unity of his heritage, so that at the present time, the Lacanians are only a fraction of the numbers who adhered to him at the height of his success in the 1960s and early 1970s. In this work, I shall attempt to convey the theory and practice of Lacan's return to Freud. It is not necessary to spell out the details, which are confusing, inconsistent, and variable over time; instead it is possible to stay with the essentials that make Lacan radically different from all other post-Freudians, whom he rejected vehemently and repeatedly, lending his writings a polemic character.

Alienation and the Celebration of the Unconscious

Lacan spent his life fleshing out his basic convictions by leaning on linguistics, mathematics, philosophy, Freud's writings, and his own clinical experience; the dismantling of the ego and the celebration of the unconscious, even more than the stress on language, run like a Leitmotiv through his work. With regard to linguistics, Macey (1988, p. 122) suggests that Lacan's interest in language and dicta such as his famous phrase "the unconscious is structured like a language" have to be regarded as the fascination of an analyst with language and not the result of work by an expert linguist. And Laplanche (1981, p. 262) suggests that the rapprochement between the unconscious and language necessitates a reformulation of either the Freudian unconscious or the linguistic notions of metonymy and metaphor. Lacan introduces language epitomized by Fort-Da in Freud (1920) and the "Nom-du-Père" (the name—also sounding in French like the no—of the father) to theorize about the division occurring at the time of the dissolution of the unity between mother and child. In this theory language is the cornerstone of human existence before which and beyond which there is nothing. Lacan is not entirely successful or consistent in this, but this does not concern the centrality of his attempt for most of his creative life: the study of the individual's insertion into the symbolic order as a result of the prohibition against the return to being the desire of the mother, the mother's phallus. He considers the ensuing symbolic castration to be the necessary condition for human psychic existence and therefore postulates the existence of a gap at the heart of being. Time and again, Lacan attacks the ego, with its identifications and search for wholeness, synthesis, and mirroring, because it aims at abolishing the gap of separateness. I shall attempt to concentrate on this aspect of his work and avoid as much as possible the many digressions and inconsistencies in a man who attempted through his style to make himself the embodiment of the discourse of the other—the other meaning, in this case, the unconscious.

The opacity of Lacan's style is deliberate. He does not hesitate to associate freely in texts that might call for a rational and very deliberate argument. His writings are replete with terms borrowed from foreign languages or other fields of specialization, puns, neologisms, and word plays, thus epitomizing Lacan's distrust of reason and cohesion. He said:

> Writing is distinguished indeed by a prevalence of the text, in the sense that this factor of discourse will assume here—a factor that makes possible the kind of tightening up that I like in order to leave the reader no other way out than the way in, which I prefer to be difficult. In that sense, then, this will not be writing. (1966, p. 493)

> Every return to Freud leading to a lesson worthy of this name will only come about through the way (road) from where the most hidden truth becomes manifest in the revolutions of the culture. This way (road) is the only training that we can pretend to transmit to those who follow. It is called: a style. (1966, p. 458)

The style he has chosen aims at maintaining the irony of speaking with the conscious mind for that other part, which has different or even opposite meanings. Therefore, the clarity that I am attempting has to rely on an overall view of the Lacanian terrain. Lacan himself was contemptuous of the pedantry of discourse that calls itself rational, because it can be so easily compared to the ego in paranoia, a condition in which there is a cohesive interpretation of a world in which the ego takes a central place and in which that which does not synthesize is projected.

Lacan based his doctoral thesis on paranoia: the study of Aimée, a patient who attempted to murder an actress. She first attracted the attention of the surrealists because they were fascinated with the convulsive beauty of murderesses. Eluard, a poet, called Aimée's writings "involuntary poetry." According to Roudinesco (1986, p. 130), Lacan's thesis received recognition by writers and young psychiatrists but not in psychoanalytic circles. He sent a copy to Freud, but he received nothing but an acknowledgment. Lacan's subject and its reception illustrate the degree to which his psychiatric training dovetailed with the revolutionary movement in the arts.

The antagonism to the ego and the privileging of the unconscious was "in the air" in France. Already in the nineteenth century, French artists were fascinated by the invisible: the symbolists attempted poetry and painting that would make the invisible visible. Redon, the painter, and Malarmé, the poet, were among those. Others, the *poètes maudits*, epitomized madness. Among them was Rimbaud, who is frequently cited for having said, "Je est un autre" (I is another), which Lacan took up when he said, "'I'm a man' . . . at most can mean no more than, 'I'm like he whom I recognize to be a man, and so recognize myself being such.' In the last resort, these various formulas are to be understood only in reference to the truth of 'I is an other.'" (1966, p. 118; 1977, p. 23).

In the twentieth century André Breton actually studied Freud's writings in order to further his own attempt at living the life of the unconscious and to undermine the conventional notions of art.[1] He practiced automatic writing inspired by Janet, the psychologist. Lacan recalls a similar celebration of madness in the graffiti in a guardhouse saying: "Not everyone who wants to be mad can become mad" (Lacan, 1966, p. 176).

Underlying the interest in madness were firm philosophical convictions concerning the human condition and the wish for a revolution: Lacan denounces Darwin for justifying the exploitation of Victorian society and the social devastation it inaugurated by the law of the survival of the fittest, or as Lacan says very poetically, "by the image of a laissez-faire of the strongest predators in competition for their natural prey" (1966, p. 121; 1977, p. 26). Lacan stresses that before Darwin, Hegel's theory had changed all that forever.[2] The latter, according to Lacan, considered the subjective and objective progress of history to be based on the conflict between Master and Slave. "If, in the conflict of Master and Slave, it is the recognition of man by man that is involved, it is also promulgated on a radical negation of natural values, whether expressed in the sterile tyranny of the master or in the productive tyranny of labor" (Lacan, 1966, p. 121, 1977, p. 26). Lacan blames this on the ego: "It is clear that the promotion of the ego today culminates, in conformity with the utilitarian conception of man that reinforces it, in an ever more advanced realization of man as individual, that is to say, in an isolation of the soul ever more akin to its original dereliction" (1966, p. 122, 1977, p. 27). He links aggressivity to the narcissistic aim at conquering space:

> Nevertheless, we have a few psychological truths to contribute there too: namely the extent to which the so-called "instinct of self-preservation" deflects into the vertigo of the domination of space, and above all the extent to which the fear of death, the "absolute Master", presupposed in consciousness by a whole philosophical tradition from Hegel onwards, is psychologically subordinate to the narcissistic fear of damage to one's own body.   (1966, p. 123, 1977, p. 28)

Narcissism prevails over biological survival in this Lacanian assessment.

Lacan was well acquainted with Heidegger's work. His direct references to Heidegger in his own writings do not reflect the degree to which some of his key concepts derive from the thinking of this difficult author. Lacan credits Heidegger with having shown how man is conditioned by this temporality through death, and he applies it, rather mysteriously, to psychoanalysis when he says that "the death instinct essentially expresses the limit of the historical function of the subject" (1966, p. 318, 1977, p. 103). He also credits Heidegger with having discovered that truth lies there where it hides. It appears that this gave Lacan the foundation for his notion of speech as the key to the unconscious, which it intends to hide. According to Macey (1988), Lacan's division of speech into empty and full speech resembles Heidegger's distinction between *Gerede* and *Rede*.

> Heidegger insists that the latter category has no "disparaging signification" in that "terminologically, it signifies a positive phenomenon which constitutes the kind of Being of Dasein's understanding and interpreting", but it is a mode of speaking which does not allow any real interpretation of Being and which cuts the subject off "from its primary and primordially genuine relationships-of-being-towards the world, towards Dasein with, and towards its very Being-in. Discourse [*Rede*] alone can truly appropriate Being." (pp. 147–48)

Without capitalizing the term, Lacan frequently alludes to "being" in his writings, treating it as if its meaning were self-evident. This habit causes the reader untold difficulties because he has synthesized and borrowed from thinkers who do not necessarily harmonize. By taking elements of Heidegger's thinking and applying them to the Freudian legacy, has he furthered it or has he used concepts like the death instinct in such a way that they contradict the implications implicit in the biological underpinnings of Freud's theory? The answer to this question depends on the importance one attributes to Freud's philosophy. Lacan's work is clearly unthinkable without its close relationship to a philosophy that stresses death, division, and nothing, whereas Freud posited and never revised his conviction that there were no negatives in the unconscious.

Therefore, when Lacan studies madness, a term dear to the nineteenth-century romantics and philosophers, and stresses alienation, he appears to bring psychoanalysis closer to Marxism than it ever was. It is not surprising, therefore, that he became linked with the student rebellion of 1968, but since his thinking only "borrows" and never coincides, the bridges that others wanted to walk on soon collapsed. In the long run Lacan could not be identified with any other thought but his own which was that of a brilliant, rebellious psychoanalyst who saw his task as liberating others by giving them back "the way to their own, sense" (1966, p. 124).

Departure from Freud's "Biologism" and Ego Psychology

Clearly, the way to their own sense lies for Lacan in the realm of meaning or signification and not in biological fulfillment. Sexual gratification as such appears to be of little interest to Lacan, because it could take place within the world of the imaginary without revealing the truth. The truth or the meaning of the individual is based on the destruction of the object (also called the murder of the thing) that takes place in infancy. This idea is derived from Freud's description in his article "Beyond the Pleasure Principle" (1920, pp. 14–15), in which a toddler uses a spool to play the game of Fort-Da (gone and back again). Freud emphasizes that this is a means for the child to master his mother's absence. Lacan adds that it is the birth of desire: "the moment when desire humanizes itself is also the moment when the child is born to language" (1966, p. 319). With the introduction into psychoanalysis of the term "desire," Lacan initiates another rapprochement with philosophy. According to Macey (1988), the term is descended from Descartes and "seems designed to conjure up echoes of Kojève's definition of desire as being human only to the extent that it is oriented towards 'other Desire and an other Desire'" (p. 117). Lacan (1966) suggests that the child who is overfed refuses the food and his refusal becomes his desire in anorexia. Through this refusal to satisfy the mother, he attempts to diminish her desire for him so that he can evolve his own desire. Anyone familiar with the Freudian concepts of the "wish" that strives toward gratification either through action in reality or by means of fantasy recognizes that "desire" is designed to convey motivation that is based on the frustration necessary for the existence of the individual. To a lesser degree, this could be said of the Freudian "wish" as well. An individual who is totally satisfied, if such a one could exist, would not be an individual. Developmentally, separateness depends on optimal frustration by the environment. But in the Lacanian system, wishing is not desire. A wish can be gratified, however briefly, by making itself acceptable to the ego, which finds an object in external reality that can put an end to the frustration. Desire depends on the other for its very existence; it is the desire for recognition, the desire to be the desire of the other, which has to be frustrated, for if it were eliminated through gratification, there could be no separation from the other, that is, the mother. Lacan's formulation would not be based on the term "separation," reminiscent of Mahler's theories, but could be expressed by stressing that without the gap, there is no being.

The Freudian "wish" motivates the pleasure principle which can use the reality principle in such a way that it can be gratified, mostly through compromises with the demands of reality and conscience. In the case of a conflict that prevents the wish from being gratified, it can be repressed and remain part of unconscious fantasy, where once more it seeks gratification through derivatives. These notions are incompatible with the fundamentals of the Lacanian "desire," which has to exist in order for there to be a being. Desire must forever seek its object, but since the father forbids it, it is the search that constitutes the individual.

Lacan is vehement in his denunciation of the notion of an ego that can and does synthesize the drive with its own defenses in such a way that it can find gratification in external reality. For him such wholeness is death and constitutes a step backward from the discovery of the unconscious. It is man's fate to be divided, and the division stems from the structure of the unconscious, which contains in it the prohibition of the father. Once more, this constitutes an inversion of the Freudian notion, in which it is the function of the ego to prohibit, to oppose, and to structure. For Lacan, the conscious part of the mind, with its narcissism, search for wholeness, mirroring, totality, and identity, forms the Imaginary as against the Symbolic, the unconscious, linked to the father and structured like a language. The Lacanian unconscious is inserted into the symbolic order, which is epitomized by language and the family structure. Thus it is social as against Freud's cauldron of biologically derived urges. Nevertheless, it is not immediately apparent why this evolution, whereby psychoanalysis postulates that the individual is born into a social order that structures his unconscious, had such a liberating effect on Lacan's followers. It was a view that appealed to leftists, as other branches of structuralism did, yet Lacan was vehement in his assertion that alienation is fundamental to man's condition, and the law of the father, far from being overthrown by means of a revolution, must be obeyed because abolishing it throws man into the realm of the Imaginary, with its destructuring effects. The hope for change in society came more from Lacan's political bedfellows and his own conduct within the established psychoanalytic institutes than from his theory of man's fate.

Lacan's relationship to the women's liberation movement is equally puzzling. He was the hero of feminists for a while because he called "symbolic castration" the moment at which the infant accepts not being the mother's desire, that is, her phallus, and lives with the gap thus created. Since this constitutive moment cuts across gender lines, it could be said that it did not attribute special status to boys. There is good reason to argue that Lacan's theory—based on anatomy, as is Freud's—is not so impartial after all. Not being the mother's phallus leads to the wish to have it, so that along with the law of the father, the name of the father, and the desire to be the desire of the other (the mother), "desire" appears in a phallocentric universe. Of course, with the deliberate slipperiness of Lacanian concepts, there are also statements that contradict this view, but it is safe to say that the majority of his statements on structure, language, and the father go in the direction of phallocentrism, illustrated by the following reference to the Wolfman's "burning curiosity that tied him to the phallus of his mother, that is to say this eminent lack-of-being of which Freud has revealed the priviliged signifier" (Lacan, 1966, p. 522). Much as Lacan calls upon Freud's name, the reference to the phallus as signifier (without ties to a fixed signified such as the penis) constitutes a fundamental and deliberate departure from Freud but not necessarily from phallocentrism:

> Viewed in a perspective of this sort, the phallus does indeed begin to seem neutral, and only adventitiously connected with the male body. It becomes the indispensable theoretical device that allows sexual differences to be measured—not an organ but a structure, not a token of virility but the foundation for a new combinatorial science. All this would be unexceptional if Lacan's plea for dialectic did not also involve him in a monomaniacal refusal to grant signifying power to the female body. . . . Lacan himself tirelessly suggests that any such transfer of symbolic power to the female would be heresy, and bring the Symbolic order itself on the verge of ruin.   (Bowie, 1991, pp. 146–47)

As Macey (1988) noted in reference to the castration complex, "It is difficult to see what has been gained from the substitution of one signifier for another, unless there is some advantage to be had by replacing the notorious 'anatomy is destiny' with 'symbolization is destiny'" (p. 188). Ultimately, therefore, it appears that in Lacan's theory the alienation of women is greater than that of men because women's desire is even more elusive than that of men:

> A man is nothing else but a signifier. A man looks for a woman as—this will appear strange to you—that which cannot be situated in discourse,

since . . . that is to say that woman is not-all, there is always something in her that escapes discourse. A man seeks a woman because there is something in her which escapes discourse. (Lacan. 1975, p. 34)

Considering the importance Lacan attributes to discourse, there is no answer relating to the place of women. But Lacan deliberately left his texts ambiguous enough to be open to various interpretations. The basis for this belief in evocative as against informative language will be discussed in greater detail in relationship to his theories concerning language and meaning. Despite Lacan's recourse to a poetic, evocative style, he leaves no doubt about the importance he attributes to the fundamental division within the individual. He expressed it repeatedly in his opposition to American ego psychology, and he stressed time and again that desire is dependent on the lack, the absence, and the prohibition through the law of the father. The split is constitutive of the unconscious, whose beginnings Lacan studied in relation to the Fort-Da game, which postulates this split, a *Spaltung*, as he often called it. The child's subsequent insertion into the symbolic universe maintains this division so as to prevent the unity in the unconscious that would plunge the individual into nonbeing. From the gap, desire, tied to language and following its laws of metonymy and metaphor,[3] is activated and with it the search for the other in its manifold manifestations, but not for sameness that would undo the division.

However, the search for wholeness typifies the Imaginary whose advent is caused by the mirror stage, that privileged moment when the child identifies with a specular image that is not himself. The identification with a reversed picture of himself is the first in a series of misidentifications based on the gaze of the mother or her desire for the child. "The essential point is that in this way, the first effect of the imago in the human being is the effect of alienation of the subject. It is in the other[4] that the subject identifies himself and experiences himself at the outset" (Lacan, 1966, p. 181). These precocious identifications based on visual elements serve an anticipatory function in that they become the supports of narcissism. Lacan posits, rather idiosyncratically, that these alienating identifications constitute narcissistic suicide.

At the outset of [psychic] development, a primordial Ego as essentially alienated is linked to the primitive sacrifice as essentially suicidal:
This is the fundamental structure of madness:
This primordial discordance between the Ego and being is the fundamental note [that resonates throughout psychic life]. (Lacan, 1966, p. 187)

It is not easy to be certain about the nature of the 'primitive sacrifice' mentioned here. In the language of American psychoanalysis, it concerns the sacrifice of individuation, but Lacan calls it "being." Thus he appears to say that for the sake of attaining an imaginary wholeness that is not the human condition to achieve, man is willing to abolish the desire for the other, in its many guises. Hence the apparently contradictory statement concerning a suicidal narcissism for the sake of narcissistic wholeness, entailing the "successful" synthesis by the ego.

The use of the term "being" does not explain adequately the entity that he discusses and compares with the ego, but it does introduce the possibility of the idea of not being caused by alienation. This is an encounter with Lacan's free use of Freud's death instinct, although once more, he applies the term in his own special way when he says,

> Only at the intersection of these two [temporal and spatial] tensions should one envisage that assumption by man of his original splitting, by which it might be said that at every moment he constitutes his world by his suicide, and the psychological experience of which Freud had the audacity to formulate, however paradoxical its expression in biological terms, as the "death instinct."   (1966, p. 124; 1977 p. 28)

In another context, Lacan connects the father with death:

> How, indeed could Freud fail to recognize such an affinity, when the necessity of his reflection led him to link the appearance of the signifier of the Father, as author of the Law, with death, even to the murder of the Father—thus showing that if this murder is the fruitful moment of debt through which the subject binds himself for life to the Law, the symbolic Father is, in so far as he signifies this Law, the dead Father.
>   (1966, p. 556, 1977, p. 199)

To a Freudian, these references to suicide and death in the unconscious illustrate clearly that Lacan does not adhere to the traditional assumption of an unconscious that does not contain negatives. However, both concepts, that of being and that of death, take on central importance in Heidegger's philosophy. Lacan, like Heidegger before him, uses death as a much-needed limit in a theory where all other concepts slip along an almost infinite chain of signifiers. The Lacanian world, which never goes further than admitting to a privileged signifier (the phallus), does not allow for the signified underneath the signifier. Once more, this is a departure from Freud's biologism and leads to a theory that defines meaning by "want" in search of a chain of signifiers.

Living with Paradox

The paradox of the Lacanian universe consists in the notion of a being that is liberated through submission to the inevitability of self-alienation. It is the acceptance of being lived through a structure that constitutes Lacan's notion of the human condition, and because of his emphasis on a structured unconscious that must be allowed to live through our superficial sense of identity, he has been associated with structuralism. But as in the case of other similarities between Lacan and leaders in related fields, it is more important to assess the meaning than to stay with a label. Lacan went from the Cartesian "I think" to the Lacanian "it (id) speaks" and emphasized the paradox when he said, "I think where I am not therefore I am where I don't think" (1966, p. 517). If there is an "I" that represents the subject, it is in his speech.

The Central Role of Language

Of course, nothing in Lacan's theory is uncomplicated, and it cannot be expected that Lacan's emphasis on language means that he trusts speech. He does not, but to him it is the only means through which the individual can eventually reveal his meaning. He differentiates between full and empty speech. The latter appeals for a reply and does not address the void behind speech. It must be remembered in this context that, as Laplanche and Pontalis (1973) observe, Lacan "refuses to acknowledge that the signifier can be permanently bound to the signified" (p. 440). Empty speech attempts to do precisely that, whereas full speech would allow for the gap behind the word. This gap can be illustrated by the example of the person who says, "I am an analyst," but who recognizes that there is no one-to-one correspondence between the I and the analyst even if he or she functions as such. Any closer correspondence would mean that the individual "takes himself" for what he says he is, and this is madness in which "we must recognize the singular formation of a delusion which—fabulous, fantastic, or cosmological; interpretative, demanding, or idealist—objectifies the subject in a language without dialectic" (Lacan, 1966, p. 280; 1977, p. 69). The dialectic takes place in the gap between the spoken word and what it means; it opens the road to the unconscious and the chain of signifiers leading to truer meaning.

Lacan bases his whole theory on the possibility of finding the truth of an individual's desire through speech, the only possible instrument of analysis. The analysand "manifests this truth . . . by opening him forever to the question about knowing how that which expresses the lie of his particularity eventually formulates the universality of his truth. . . . A question upon which is inscribed the whole history of philosophy. . . . down to the radical ambiguity indicated by Heidegger for all that truth signifies revelation" (Lacan, 1966, p. 166). He has been criticized for this approach. Revelation has religious connotations that appear alien to the intent of psychoanalysis, and the emphasis on language leads to a neglect of affects and behavior. This criticism is amply deserved. It is equally true that Lacan has allowed no substitute for the Freudian "thing representation" behind the "word representation" and that this creates a "philosophy of the human subject [that] is self-consciously thin, empty and weightless. He invents a subject without subject matter" (Bowie, 1991, pp. 75–76). He no more allows for the thing behind the word than he admits to Saussurian linguistics: "The unity of Saussure's sign, a compound of signifier and signified, has been decisively broken" (Macey, 1988, p. 132). This break is intended because "The unconscious is that part of concrete discourse insofar as it is transindividual, which is not at the disposal of the subject to reestablish the continuity of his conscious discourse" (Lacan, 1966, p. 258). Much as Lacan's emphasis is on discourse, which we generally do not consider a solitary endeavor, it appears in his writing as the vehicle for the wish for recognition and mirroring. "Human language constitutes a communication where the sender receives from the receiver his own message in inverted form" (Lacan, 1966, p. 298). It is the portrait of a self-enclosed world in which language, without fixed meaning except as a link in a chain, is the only substance to which Lacan admits. According to Leavy (1977), an American analyst who has studied the work of Lacan and language

> Lacan's theoretical position demands further elaboration, which does not depart from the linguistic mode of thought but includes a derivative of that mode—namely, the idea of the "symbolic order" more or less in the sense in which the term "symbolic" is used by Lévi-Strauss. That is, the whole system of signifiers is organized in advance of any individual's appearing on the scene. We are ushered into it by our acquisition of language, to be sure, but also by our introduction to all the other social forms, which, as Lévi-Strauss . . . has tried to show, are themselves "structured like a language."   (p. 209)

Being as consistent as he is about his emphasis on the psychic, for Lacan nonpsychic reality per se does not exist. He has postulated *le réel* as the third agency along with the symbolic and the imaginary. It is nonsymbolizable and the result of foreclosure; it is the impossible, and it is, in keeping with Freud, that which, because it cannot be symbolized, comes back as the real in psychosis.

I have shown that in his view of the human condition, Lacan was of his time. With his emphasis on a structure that lives through the subject, he joined the revolt against humanism that had placed man at the center of the universe and was implicated in the disaster that befell Europe. Nevertheless, inasmuch as he was the spiritual leader for many students and analysts who were in revolt against established societies, his was an ambiguous position whose inherent insubordination was clearer than its positive assumptions because that Other, that unconscious, that desire structuring man could ultimately be a return to a notion like God's will. It has been said that Lacan's Catholic beginnings are evident in his psychoanalytic theories. Making himself the spokesman for the Other certainly enabled him to assume a powerful, if not autocratic, role in French psychoanalysis.

Because of the difficulties of his concepts and the resistance to them in the Anglo-Saxon psychoanalytic circles, his ideas were important only to Latin America and to academicians elsewhere. He remains an enigma to most analysts, especially to those who followed Hartmann's endeavor to expand psychoanalysis into a general psychology. Yet, however idiosyncratic Lacan's approach may have been, he was a powerful counterforce to the attempt to take psychoanalysis out of the exclusive realm of the psychic. He said, "If the place of the master is left empty, it is due less to his death than to the growing obliteration of the meaning of his work" (1966, p. 244). And Lacan's interpretation of this meaning was the portrait of man alienated from his transindividual unconscious, seeking only similarity and self-confirmation in his relations to the outside world.

Individual Psychopathology

Whereas Freud came to psychoanalysis through hysteria and thereby the problem of sexuality, Lacan became most interested in paranoia, that condition that typifies a faulty cohesiveness of the personality in which "the other scene," as Freud called the unconscious, is projected into the other existing in the external world. The emphasis Freud placed on the homosexual conflict underlying paranoia has been shifted to the conflict

with the other, inasmuch as he escapes the sameness desired by the paranoid personality. Paranoia represents the extreme of the normal personality in search of cohesiveness coupled with the aggressive search for
space. Depression is also based on faulty cohesiveness, however, according to Lacan, "the depressive disruptions of the experienced reverses of
inferiority, . . . engender essentially the mortal negations that fix it [man's
ego] in its formalism. 'I am nothing of what happens to me. You are nothing of value'" (1966, p. 114; 1977, p. 20). Therefore depression provides
another instance of the ego's synthesizing function that does not correspond to experience. But whereas depression can lead to the disowning
of much that is good and desirable within the personality, in paranoia the
undesirable traits are disowned and projected. The ego attains unity at
the cost of its truncation.

The disowning taking place in psychosis led Lacan to introduce a new
term into the psychoanalytic vocabulary: foreclosure. It is based on the
assumption that repression, the defense in neurosis that allows the symptom to speak, does not abolish the function of language and the father in
the radical way psychosis is based on a lack, a gap, created in the unconscious by the foreclusure of the name of the father. The foreclosure of
the name of the father actually signifies the lack of a gap, the gap that exists between the enunciation of a word and the chain of signifiers. It is the
denial of the original castration taking place at the time of separation
from the mother and the assumption of the name of the father as the one
who forbids the child's becoming the desire of the mother or her phallus.

> the being [*l'être*] and the existent [*l'étant*] operate through the effects of the
> signifier, which I describe as metaphor and metonymy.
>
> It is in an accident in this register and in what takes place in it, namely
> the foreclosure of the Name-of-the-Father in the place of the Other, and in
> the failure of the paternal metaphor, that I designate the defect that gives
> psychosis its essential condition, and the structure that separates it from
> neurosis.   (Lacan, 1966, p. 575, 1977, p. 215)

> For the psychosis to be triggered off, the Name-of-the-Father, *verworfen*,
> foreclosed, that is to say, never having attained the place of the Other, must
> be called into symbolic opposition to the subject.
>
> It is the lack of the Name-of-the-Father in that place which, by the hole
> that it opens up in the signified, sets off the cascade of reshapings of the sig-
> nifier from which the increasing disaster of the imaginary proceeds, to the
> point at which the level is reached at which signifier and signified are sta-
> bilized in the delusional metaphor.

But how can the Name-of-the-Father be called by the subject to the only place in which it could have reached him and in which it has never been? Simply by a real father, not necessarily by the subject's own father, but by A-father.

Again, this A-father must attain that place to which the subject was unable to call him before. It is enough that this A-father should be situated in a third position in some relation based on the imaginary dyad o-o', that is to say, ego-object or reality-ideal, that interests the subject in the field of eroticized aggression that it induces.   (Lacan, 1966, pp. 577–78, 1977, p. 217)

As long as the real father is the third member of an imaginary dyad, he comes back from the outside, *le réel*, because the imaginary dyad has foreclosed in the unconscious his place and the place of the law that he embodies.

Lacan stresses that rather than going beyond Freud with this theory, he wants to differentiate himself from those who have gone back to an earlier stage. "At least what separates me from any other object is to restore access to the experience that Freud discovered." Applying this to the essential difference between the treatment of neurosis and psychosis, he says: "For to use the technique he established, outside the experience to which it was applied, is as stupid as to toil at the oars when the ship is on sand" (1966, p. 583, 1977, p. 221).

Despite Lacan's devotion to the practice of psychoanalysis and his warnings against applying it to problems that are unsuitable, Lacan's theoretical formulations basically focus on the issues of psychosis. This becomes apparent in his concentration on the issue of language used concretely, his focus on the problem of narcissism, his pervasive distrust of the ego, his emphasis on splitting, and the polemical attacks against those who have abandoned the essential dividedness of the subject. In his theory, there is no notion of compromise formation, derivatives, or the reality principle acting in the service of the pleasure principle. Such fusion between conscious and unconscious is unthinkable in the Lacanian system. In order to buttress his distrust of thinking, the Cartesian *cogito*, Lacan (1966, p. 56) chooses the example of the abbé de Choisy, who wrote in his memoirs, "I think when I am," which for him meant, according to Lacan, "I am when I am dressed in women's clothes." Lacan distrusts conscious thinking because of his opposition to notions such as derivatives, which would postulate that the unconscious finds expression even in conscious thought. To Lacan, the unconscious reveals itself only through the symbolic use of language, and he appeals to Freud once more in order to justify this exclusive concentration:

> the appeal made in passing to unknown intellectual mechanisms is no more in this case than his [Freud's] distressed excuse for the total confidence he placed in symbols, a confidence that wavers as a result of being justified beyond all limits.
>
> If for a symptom, whether neurotic or not, to be admitted in psychoanalytic psychopathology, Freud insists on the minimum overdetermination constituted by a double meaning (symbol of a conflict long dead over and above its function in a *no less symbolic* present conflict), and if he has taught us to follow the ascending ramification of the symbolic lineage in the text of the patient's free associations, in order to map it out at the points where its verbal forms intersect with the nodal points of its structure, then it is already quite clear that the symptom resolves itself entirely in an analysis of language, because the symptom is itself structured like a language, because it is from language that speech must be delivered.
>
> (1966, p. 269, 1977, 59)

> The symptom is here the signifier of a signified repressed from the consciousness of the subject. A symbol written in the sand of the flesh and on the veil of Maia, it participates in language by the semantic ambiguity that I have already emphasized in its constitution.
>
> But it is speech functioning to the full, for it includes the discourse of the other in the secret of its cipher.   (Lacan, 1966, p. 280-81; 1977, p. 69)

And Lacan believes that Freud has discovered the displacement of the signifier within the subject, outside his awareness. Its presence in the unconscious determines neurosis, whereas its foreclosure determines psychosis. In neurosis, the analyst attempts to give back to the symptom the speech that was lost due to repression and due to the action of the imaginary, whose search for wholeness counteracts the irruptions of the unconscious. Analysis restores the tripartite division of the subject: the symbolic, the imaginary, and the real, which Bowie (1991, p. 112) calls facetiously but not inaccurately, Absence, Fraud, and Impossibility.

Lacan did not explore any subject concerning psychopathology in any systematic way. Instead his observations are found in places where one might not necessarily expect them. There is a fascinating passage on his refusal to work by the clock, that is, time that is not in tune with the unconscious, in his well-known article "The Function and Field of Speech and Language in Psychoanalysis" (1966). Here he points to the transference of the obsessional patient, who is willing to work as long as the analyst cooperates in maintaining himself as the judge of the value of the patient's productions. Lacan suggests that the arbitrary interruption of the session stresses the futility of the patient's endeavor; he also points to the usefulness of some disdain for the patient's slavish devotion to work. The freedom of the analyst to determine time and not to submit to the exigencies of the clock expresses some of his disdain, and Lacan's unwillingness to subordinate himself to rules, which, in the case of the length of the hour, could be called arbitrary. In this context he describes the obsessional in the most delightful way:

> The keynote of forced labour that envelops everything for this subject, even the activities of his leisure time, is only too well known.
>
> This meaning is sustained by his subjective relation to the master in so far as it is the master's death for which he waits.
>
> In fact the obsessional subject manifests one of the attitudes that Hegel did not develop in his dialectic of the master and the slave. The slave has given way in the face of the risk of death in which mastery was being offered to him in a struggle of pure prestige. But since he knows that he is mortal, he also knows that the master can die. From this moment on he is able to accept his labouring for the master and his renunciation of pleasure in the meantime; and in the uncertainty of the moment when the master will die, he waits.
>
> Such is the intersubjective reason, as much for the doubt as for the procrastination that are character traits of the obsessional subject.
>
> In the meantime, all his labour falls under the heading of this intention, and becomes doubly alienating by this fact. For not only is the subject's handiwork taken from him by another—which is the constituting relation of all labour—but the subject's recognition of his own essence in his handiwork, in which this labour finds its justification, also eludes him, for he himself "*is*" not in "it." He *is* in the anticipated moment of the master's death, from which moment he will begin to live, but in the meantime he identifies himself with the master as dead, and as a result of this he is himself already dead.
>
> Nevertheless he makes an effort to deceive the master by the demonstration of the good intentions manifested in his labour.
>
> (1966, p. 314; 1977, pp. 99–100)

It is evident that Lacan does not want to support the patient's devotion by being willing to wait, not even for the conventional end of the session, and although he does not say so, he might consider the average analyst's willingness to wait as an acting out of the patient's death wishes against him. He believes apparently that a patient who is not supported in his psychopathology will return to his own desire and give up the transference that is predicated on the death of one of the participants.

The obsessional wants to cheat death, and his ego lends him the support for this ruse. However, in this cooperation between the death wishes and their evasion the subject is nothing but a shadow of himself "because he annuls gain as well as loss, by first of all abdicating desire which is at stake" (Lacan, 1966, p. 453). He describes the pleasure the obsessional permits himself by putting the other into the place of the spectator, only to identify with his pleasure and to wait until that other dies.

He objects to the notion that the ego in neurosis is weak. Its strength becomes apparent both by the way it reinforces the exclusion of the unconscious and by the cooperation neurotics obtain for themselves from those who are presumed normal.

Comparing the two major neuroses, Lacan says,

> Indeed, we will not be surprised to see that hysterical neurosis like obsessional neurosis supposes in its structure terms without which the subject cannot accede to the notion of the falsity with regard to his/her sex in one, his/her existence in the other. To which the one and the other of these structures constitute a kind of response.   (1966, p. 451)

Lacan is equally graphic in his description of the dilemma of the hysteric, especially in an article devoted to the questions left unanswered in Freud's treatment of Dora. The hysteric, described as a woman, is incapable of incorporating her own sex, therefore she attempts to identify with another woman in order to obtain pleasure from her own sexuality. She is quite unable to understand the pleasure of a man in a heterosexual relationship; instead she identifies with him in wanting to give pleasure to the woman through whom she expects to have access to her own desire. "It is in this way that the hysteric experiences herself in the devotion addressed to another, and offers the woman in whom she adores her own mystery to the man whose role she takes without being able to enjoy it" (Lacan, 1966, p. 452). Freud's mistake, according to Lacan, was that he was blind to Dora's identification with the men in her life, including him, and this mistake brought on the acting out that ended the analysis.

Just as Lacan used the ego in paranoia as a model for the ego in general, so too he appears to use hysteria in order to describe woman. Ultimately, as we have seen, not only is the female body a stranger to the hysteric woman, Lacan does not ever enunciate a theory of feminine sexuality except as the other to the male, and as the jouissance of which she is capable but which brings her outside the realm of language, an inarticulable ecstasy that is described without being inscribed into the symbolic or the imaginary realm. It is outside law. I believe that jouissance in Lacan's thinking is the descendant of the convulsive beauty of the surrealists, the woman who defies the law in search of the realization of her dream. She is not neurotic because the neurotic is the person who yields to reason, to his ego, to his narcissism, at the cost of his desire, his essence. Not so the ecstatic woman, who risks going beyond that which can be symbolized. The symbolic is split off from his awareness in a gesture that Lacan calls "his suicide."

> In the "emancipated" man of modern society, this splitting reveals, right down to the depths of his being, a neurosis of self-punishment, with the hysterico-hypochondriac symptoms of its functional inhibitions, with the psychasthenic forms of its derealizations of others and of the world, with its social consequences in failure and crime. It is this pitiful victim, this escaped, irresponsible outlaw, who is condemning modern man to the most formidable social hell, whom we meet when he comes to us; it is our daily task to open up to this being of nothingness the way of his meaning in a discreet fraternity—a task for which we are always too inadequate.
>
> (Lacan, 1966, p. 124; 1977, pp.28–29)

The Role of the Analyst as Seen by Lacan

Lacan regards the analyst as the Other in the sense that he represented the unconscious of the patient, and he considered his work to be that of restoring the speech of that unconscious in such a way that the patient once more gains access to his desire. In his attempt to distinguish between orders of motivation, he set up three categories. Desire, that which is in constant motion, excentric and insatiable, is differentiated from demand, the second category, expressed by speech to the other "whose very signifiers it takes over in its formulation" (Sheridan's translator's notes, Lacan, 1977, p. viii). The third category, need, is not a subject for analysis because it is derived from organic needs that are satisfied by specific objects. The analysand approaches the analyst with the intention of engaging him in the satisfaction of a demand addressed to him. The example given earlier is that of the obsessional neurotic who demands recognition for his submissiveness and his willingness to work. The job of the analyst is not to respond but to act as a dialectician who listens for gaps in the manifest statements that allow him to propose an antithesis that speaks for the unconscious. By all accounts, this involves in practice silences of greater duration than those of analysts belonging to other schools. According to Leavy (1983), "Lacan's doctrine of the inner relatedness of the signifiers and of their dominance over the discourse (Lacan, 1966, p. 30) liberates the analyst from strict adherence to the speech of the patient" (p. 52). This approach to the psychoanalytic dialogue sets in motion the beginning of the search for the meaning of the patient's symptoms. The meaning is structured by linguistic rules of metaphor and metonymy, which for Lacan replace the Freudian notions of condensation and displacement.[5] Nowhere is there mention of synthesis, the third term of the Hegelian dialectics: thesis, antithesis, and synthesis. Synthesis would be too static a concept for the Lacanian notion of a chain of meaning and also too reminiscent of ego psychology, which Lacan denounces tirelessly. Leavy (1980) suggests that "Lacan's real contribution here (to what is, after all, not exactly new to analysts) is that the 'otherness' of the unconscious is the counterpart of its revelation through the person of the external other, the analyst. The unconscious is by this very fact revealed to be dialectical in nature, not so much personal as transpersonal" (p. 528). The analyst essentially gives back what is already there, this is the significance of the overlap between the other as the unconscious, the other as the Nom-du-Père in the unconscious, and the other as the analyst.

Leavy (1977) suggests that

> Lacan is by no means the first analyst who calls on us to focus on the psychoanalytic situation, but he stands out among theorists in returning all psychoanalytic concepts to this setting. In a sense, even his interest in language is subordinate to his interest in the psychoanalytic dialogue—or rather, he teaches the radical unity between dialogue and language. We are able to make inferences about mind outside analysis—that is, compose our psychoanalytic psychology—because analysis serves as a model for all other forms of dialogue, real or imagined. From this point of view it is not an exaggeration to say that the theory of psychoanalytic technique is the only metapsychology—although I do not think Lacan would put it quite that way.   (P. 203)

Lacan draws an analogy between psychoanalytic technique and the practice of Zen, "which is applied as a means for the revelation of the subject in the traditional ascesis of certain Far-Eastern schools" (Lacan, 1966, p. 315; 1977, p. 100). The analyst is emphatically not an object in the sense that he would be the representation of the parents or other important people in the individual's memories, fantasies, or experiences. Lacan plays down the aspect of analysis that is a process in which repetition serves a function other than elucidating speech. It is the corollary to the de-emphasis in Lacanian analysis of the holding environment or containing aspects that represent the maternal realm.[6] Nor is there any notion of the working alliance or engaging the faculty of self-observation. These are ego functions that are not viewed favorably in this system: neither for the patient nor for the analyst.

Lacan equally strenuously opposes resistance analysis. He maintains that giving back to the patient the language of his unconscious is the only meaningful task of the analyst. It brings results that, he thinks, make analysts uncomfortable:

> No doubt the whole process that has culminated in this present tendency of psychoanalysis goes back, and from the very first, to the analyst's guilty conscience about the miracle operated by his speech. He interprets the symbol and, lo and behold, the symptom, which inscribes the symbol in letters of suffering in the subject's flesh, disappears. This unseemly thaumaturgy is unbecoming to us, for after all we are scientists, and magic is not a practice we can defend. So we disclaim responsibility by attributing magical thinking to the patient. (1966, p. 306; 1977, p. 92)

Resistance analysis depends on the ego as an ally and objectivates the analysand; it is not for Lacan a means toward subjectivity.

> if I call the person to whom I am speaking by whatever name I choose to give him, I intimate to him the subjective function that he will take on again in order to reply to me, even if it is to repudiate this function.
>
> Henceforth the decisive function of my own reply appears, and this function is not, as has been said, simply to be received by the subject as acceptance or rejection of his discourse, but really to recognize him or to abolish him as a subject. Such is the nature of the analyst's *responsibility* whenever he intervenes by means of speech.
> (Lacan, 1966, p. 300; 1977, pp. 86–87)

As the patient utters his truth, the analyst waits for nodes of meaning. The law of overdetermination applies to the salience of those nodes, and in this respect, Lacan's view is in agreement with the mainstream of psychoanalysis. However, his reply to the patient does not involve aspects of compromise formations between drive and defense, conscious and unconscious, surface and depth. There is one subject that concerns him:

speaking for desire within the unconscious. "In order to liberate the speech of the subject, we introduce him to the speech of his desire, that is to say to the primary language in which, beyond what he says about it,[7] he already speaks to us unknown to himself and, first of all, in the symbols of the symptom" (Lacan, 1966, p. 293; 1977, p. 81).

> It is . . . always in the relation between the subject's ego (*moi*) and the "I" (*je*) of his discourse that you must understand the meaning of the discourse if you are to achieve the dealienation of the subject.
>
> But you cannot possibly achieve this if you cling to the idea that the ego of the subject is identical with the presence that is speaking to you.
>
> This error is fostered by the terminology of the analytic topography,[8] which is all too tempting to an objectifying cast of mind, allowing it to make an almost imperceptible transition from the concept of the ego defined as the perception-consciousness system, that is, as the system of the objectification of the subject—to the concept of the ego as correlative with an absolute reality and thus, in a singular return of the repressed in psychologistic thought.   (Lacan, 1966, p. 304, 1977, p. 90)

The technique advocated by Lacan also aims to avoid a narcissistic transference in which the analyst incorporates the image of the double. Earlier I mentioned briefly that Lacan sees a strong connection between aggressivity and narcissism; therefore, were the analyst seen as the double, he would also be the object of terror because of the aggression projected on him.

Lacan has compared his technique to that of the dummy in a bridge game, the Zen master who is his question; most important, his technique has been described as consisting of very long periods of silence during which the patient is left on his own. During those periods, the analyst too must wait until it (id) speaks, the other speaks, for in this scheme the analyst must avoid contacting the patient by way of the imaginary. Commenting on this aspect, Etchegoyen (1991) says, "The analyst's art and science consists in reestablishing the symbolic order without allowing himself to be captured by the specular situation" (p. 124). Meaning is produced; it is not pregiven:

> The positive fruit of the revelation of ignorance is the not-knowing, that is, not a negation of knowledge, but its most elaborated form. The training of a candidate could not be completed without the action of the master or masters who educate him to the not-knowing, without which he will never be anything but a robot analyst. . . . "Indeed, the being of the analyst is in

action even during his silences, and it is at the lowest level of the truth that sustains him, that the subject will profer his speech.

(Lacan, 1996, pp. 358–59)

Schneiderman, an American analyzed by Lacan, says with considerable humor that "Lacan did not teach people how to get along with other people, interpersonally, but rather how to negotiate and to enter into commerce with the dead" (Schneiderman, 1983, p. 63). Transference does not have a privileged status in this view of the psychoanalytic process, and it is not clear whether Lacan assumes that if the analyst maintains his position of dialectician, transference can be avoided. He does say that transference appeared in Freud's treatment of Dora when the dialectical process got stuck. According to Etchegoyen, since transference is always an imaginary phenomenon and the analyst's job is to transform the relationship into a symbolic one, the concept of transference loses much of its preeminence and is possibly even not inevitable.

The ideas of antiauthoritarianism and insubordination are apparent in this return to Freud. The analyst, the subject who is supposed to know, is revealed in his ignorance, analytic training is made into something haphazard, and the sacred fifty-minute hour is interrupted by the analyst who does not know, except that he knows that nothing more productive can happen during the remaining time.

To demonstrate how the attitudes toward this practice vary, I turn to two accounts of Lacan's technique, illustrating Pontalis's contention cited earlier, that how Lacan is regarded is predicated on transference. Schneiderman has highlighted the advantages of this approach through the indifference of the analyst. He describes Lacan counting his banknotes during one of his sessions, which tells him that Lacan thereby conveys that he has enough money and does not need his. One might say Lacan conveys that the patient is on his own. This positive attitude is in sharp contrast to that of Anzieu (1986), a French analyst treated by Lacan (and coincidentally the son of the famous patient Aimée), who wrote a very critical account of the method.

> At the beginning of my analysis, he gave me sessions of normal length, forty to forty-five minutes, and he saw me at the prearranged times. After two years of work with him, the analytic framework developed a snag. The length of the sessions was reduced to thirty then to twenty minutes. The waiting room became filled with persons anxious to know if they would be received. Lacan opened the door, designated the chosen one, who would

retrace his steps ten or fifteen minutes later in order to leave. I read. Lacan tapped me on the shoulder: it was my turn to pass in front of everyone or to find myself sent away to come back another day. . . . The master, heaving a deep sigh, confided in me, as in a friend, that he was overloaded, that he had to make an unforeseen appointment, face a difficult case, giving me to understand that I was not one, that I could therefore come back, and that he was sure that I understood him. This reinforced my narcissism, which did not need this, and made it difficult for me to express my astonishment, my disagreement, that is, a negative transference, without which a psychoanalysis is not complete.

During the sessions, Lacan was intermittently attentive. Sometimes, instead of sitting in his analyst chair, he paced back and forth in the room in order to stretch his legs, to take a book; he sat at his work table and read, leafing through pages covered with Chinese letters, which, apparently, he was learning. . . . Sometimes, his maid knocked on the door, to bring tea, sandwiches, the mail, or to alert him that he was wanted on the telephone. Lacan gave instructions for the answers or even went to answer himself. "Don't let this prevent you from continuing your session during my absence" he told me once as he disappeared from the office.   (P .34)

It is difficult to know the degree to which this conduct was typical, but it is in keeping with Lacan's attitude toward those rules that are not of the unconscious, which he thought to represent.

It is evident that Lacan was consistent in his basic assumptions. He changed many details, such as the meaning of the other or the Other, over the years, but he did not waver in his fundamental approach to psychoanalysis. He saw the human condition as fated to become that which would satisfy the desire that must never be fulfilled, and in this respect, he differs fundamentally from other analysts, including, of course, Freud, who envisaged satisfaction in love and work to be within man's reach. Bowie (1991) believes that Lacan and Freud were "professional students of human conduct who expect their studies of mental structure to reveal a set of principles to live by" (p. 99). However, much as Lacan appeals to Freud's authority throughout his work, he insisted on psychoanalysis being modeled only on itself, the psychic sphere, whereas Freud attempted to position psychoanalysis at the frontier between the psyche and the soma. Whereas Freud thought that drive satisfaction is desirable and the result of synthesis, with Lacan we have what Whitebook (1994) calls "an essentialization of fragmentation." It "can be traced back to Lacan's a priori 'Heraclitean' predilection for deficiency, discord and fragmentation and a suspicion of all forms of finality, reconciliation and synthesis" (p. 15). Instead of being dualistic, it privileges decentering and the undoing of the work of Freud's eros. It is generally assumed that this approach was influenced by Lacan's adherence to modern philosophy, and while this is undoubtedly correct, it is equally noteworthy that as early as 1823 the German poet Heine deplored the French philosophy of the Enlightenment for lacking one essential element: love. The absence of love, eros, or its derivative, the synthetic function of the ego, is equally missing in Lacan's work except as an object of attack, reflecting this French tradition. He persisted in refusing to distinguish between the ego's tendency to delude itself and its capacity for approximating truth because he was opposed to attributing any merit to synthesis and harmony. In this, much as Lacan's thinking appears to be the product of modern philosophy, it is essentially French. Lacan provided the French with a psychoanalysis of their own.

However, Lacan's constant reminder of the true foundation of the psychoanalytic enterprise has the merit of counteracting any attempt to reify either the theory or its application in practice. He admonished psychoanalysts to remember that the analyst was meant not to create the holding environment, the empathic echo, or the temporary maternal womb to which the sick can retreat, but to engage in an enterprise in which two people have specific tasks, ultimately yielding for the patient the self-knowledge he or she needs to proceed with life. I firmly believe that Lacan was right in this respect, and while I have never been a Lacanian, I have shared his distrust of ego psychology as coming perilously close to a return to academic psychology. This is also true of the genetic approach favored by Mahler, which skirts reification of the separation process. Lacan's positions in this respect are a welcome antidote to these developments in psychoanalysis.

At present, his legacy is in disarray, caused by the ambiguity of his work and by his being a man of his time. That time has passed. Just as surrealism and structuralism have had their day, so has Lacan's psychoanalysis given way to more constructive ways of approaching the psychoanalytic situation.

NOTES

1. For a more detailed account of the relationship between Breton and Freud, see Oliner, 1988.

2. Both Roudinesco (1986, pp. 149–61) and Macey (1988, p. 97) stress that

Lacan was introduced to Hegel's work by Alexandre Kojeve, whose lectures he attended, and that his thinking comes closer to being Kojevian than Hegelian, especially since the Hegelian notion of synthesis is contrary to his thinking about the division within the subject.

3. These are the replacements for the Freudian mechanisms of condensation and displacement.

4. In Lacan's work, the meaning of the term "other" depends strictly on the context in which it is found. Here the sense is relatively straightforward in that it describes the other whose desire the infant wants to be.

5. Lacan suggests in effect that he is only reconceptualizing the unconscious that Freud described without the benefit of the discoveries of modern linguistics (Lacan, 1966, p. 799).

6. Recently, there was an article entitled "Tiresias and the Breast: Thinking of Lacan, Interpretation, and Caring," in the *International J. Psychoanalysis*, suggesting that there was something elusively maternal in Lacan's approach (Webb, Bushnell, and Widseth, 1993). I rather think that the analogy is as elusive as the breasts Tiresias appropriates for himself in order to be taken for a woman. In my opinion it is too far-fetched to be taken seriously.

7. This word *lui* in the original appears to me to refer to *désir*, and therefore I translated it as "it"; Sheridan translates it as "himself," referring back to the word "subject."

8. The French have never adopted the differentiation between the topographic and the structural hypothesis in psychoanalysis. They have retained topography as the name they give to both of Freud's maps of the mind. For Lacan, it was undoubtedly particularly important not to confuse structure as it is used in ego psychology with structure as he saw it applying to the unconscious. For him, therefore, there is only one structure, the one based on linguistics.

REFERENCES

Anzieu, D. 1975. *L'auto-analyse de Freud et la découverte de la psychanalyse*. Paris: Presses Universitaires de France.

Anzieu, D. 1986. *Une peau pour les pensées*. Paris: Clancier-Guernaud.

Bowie, M. 1991. *Lacan*. Cambridge: Harvard University Press.

Etchegoyen, R. H. 1991. *The Fundamentals of Psychoanalytic Technique*. London, NY: Karnac Books.

Freud, S. 1920. Beyond the Pleasure Principle. In *Standard Edition*, vol. 18. London: Hogarth Press.

Heine, H. 1968 [1823]. Über Polen. In *Heinrich Heine Werke Wolfgang Preisendanz*, pp. 63–88. Frankfurt: Insel Verlag.

Lacan, J. 1966. *Ecrits*. Paris: Editions du Seuil. Passages cited in the text are my translations.

————. 1975. *Le Séminaire*. Vol.20, *Encore*. Comp. Jacques-Alain Miller. Paris: Seuil. Passages cited in the text are my translations.

————. 1977. *Ecrits: A Selection*. Trans. Alan Sheridan. New York: Norton.

Laplanche, J. 1981. *L'inconscient et le ça*. Problématiques IV. Paris: Presses Universitaires de France.

Laplanche, J., and Pontalis, J.-B. 1973. *The Language of Psychoanalysis*. New York: Norton.

Leavy, S. A. 1977. The Significance of Jacques Lacan. *Psychoanalytic Quarterly* 46:201–19.

————. 1980. The Four Fundamental Concepts of Psychoanalysis by Jacques Lacan [Review]. *Psychoanalytic Quarterly* 49:526–29.

————. 1983. Some Linguistic Approaches to Psychoanalysis. *Psychoanalytic Quarterly* 52:34–55.

Macey, D. 1988. *Lacan in Contexts*. London: Verso.

Pontalis, J.-B. 1979. Le métier à tisser. *Nouvelle Revue de Psychanalyse* 20:5–12.

Roudinesco, E. 1986. *Histoire de la psychanalyse en France*. Vol. 2. Paris: Seuil.

Schneiderman, S. 1983. *Jacques Lacan*. Cambridge: Harvard University Press.

Webb, R. E., Bushnell, D. B., and Widseth, J. C. 1993. Tiresias and the Breast: Thinking of Lacan, Interpretation and Caring. *International Journal of Psychoanalysis* 74: 597–612.

Whitebook, J. 1994. *Perversion and Utopia: A Study in Psychoanalysis and Critical Theory*. Cambridge: M. I. T. Press.

Chapter Fifteen

Feminist Psychoanalysis
The Uneasy Intimacy of Feminism and Psychoanalysis

Cynthia Burack

EDITORS' INTRODUCTION

Feminists, including psychoanalytic feminists, have aggressively challenged Freud's view of women, particularly his essentialism and biologism as reflected, for example, in his concepts of penis envy and the castration complex. More generally, psychoanalytic feminists, from a variety of theoretical perspectives, have been centrally interested in sexual ideology, exploring the symbolic modes through which patriarchy and gender roles are encoded by women and men in our society. The discussion of the link between gender-differentiated subjectivity and the structures of the social world is psychoanalytic feminists' biggest contribution. That is, they have provided a more nuanced and compelling understanding of the connection between unconscious passions and gender identity, thus problematizing subjectivity and sexuality and making them crucial issues in need of deconstruction and political debate. A feminist-inspired psychoanalysis thus encourages vigilant attention to how sex and gender inform the theoretical models that in part shape our clinical work.

Cynthia Burack's essay is concerned with contextualizing psychoanalysis within the wider "feminist" political movement and understanding some of psychoanalysis's weaknesses and strengths in its conversation with feminism. As she sees it, feminists have focused on power, especially the unequal, naturalized, and institutionalized power relations between women and men. It is not surprising, then, that feminists have usually spoken in a political rather than a psychological idiom. Even so, many feminist scholars continue to be drawn to psychoanalytic modes of thought as tools for conceptualizing women's identities. Burack makes the important point that compared to the "mainstream" psychoanalytic establishment, which tends to put forth universalizing discourses about women, psychoanalytic feminists try to situate the behavior of women in their political, social, and historical context.

Psychoanalytic feminists, says Burack, have challenged psychoanalytic theory in a number of ways. For example, they have criticized normative psychoanalytic theories of identity and subjectivity that disparage or disregard women's feelings, thought, speech, and action, such as the notion of a genderless self; they have questioned versions of psychoanalytic theory that "privilege a teleology of separation and individuation. . . . that promotes stereotypically masculine character in the guise of maturity or psychic health"; they criticize the theoretical figure of "the mother," pointing out that "psychoanalytic theory has frequently made the mother the causal agent of psychopathology while casting the father in the role of the rescuer who delivers children, especially male children, into culture, civilization, or the Symbolic." "A more devastating criticism," says Burack, is that "psychoanalysis conflates 'woman' and 'mother' in a way that insinuates ideological prescriptions concerning femininity and child rearing into the very definition of femaleness." She also notes that feminists strive not to generate a narrative of women's psychopathology, but rather to shed light on the social and political genealogies that constitute women as damaged or mutilated.

Feminists who gravitate to psychoanalysis, Burack says, do so in the hope that more theoretically nuanced and "empirically sensitive" accounts of women's lives than those found in politics can arise. In her view, the goal of a psychoanalytic feminism is to integrate analysis of the political and social context in which individual development occurs. The implication of this perspective for psychoanalysis in general, and psychoanalytic feminism in particular, is a call for political sophistication and knowledge. Theorists and clinicians, says Burack, must acknowledge and confront the ways widely shared assumptions about sex and gender influence the construction of theory, and thus practice. For example, how do such frequently taken-for-granted categories as femininity, masculinity, intimacy, erotic desire, mothering, and maturity shape the building of theory itself? What are the ways distinctive experiences of violence and fear of violence affect the development of girls and women? How do members of marginal groups, like Black women and men and working class women and men, reconfigure aspects of their identities and social lives to take account of the demands of femininity and masculinity that are fashioned by their own communities? Feminist-inspired psychoanalysis thus encourages us to continuously question the many ways our understanding of sex and gender informs the theories that guide our clinical work. (P. M. and A. R.)

Feminism is first and foremost a social and political movement. Feminists have been concerned with power, especially the unequal, naturalized, and institutionalized relations of power between women and men. It is not surprising, then, that feminists have tended to speak in a political rather than a psychological language. It may not even be obvious why some feminists would use a discourse as ostensibly removed from social and political reality as psychoanalysis. Yet numbers of feminist scholars continue to be attracted to psychoanalytic modes of thought.

Why are some feminists attracted to psychoanalytic theories even as others deny their fruitfulness? It is impossible to understand the alliance between feminism and psychoanalysis without engaging this debate. The debate originates in the feminist search for a language with which to theorize identity that does not obstinately inscribe some real or imagined masculinity as the measure of the human. Feminists who turn to psychoanalysis do so in the hope that more theoretically subtle and empirically sensitive accounts of women's lives than those found in politics can emerge. On the other hand, many feminists who contest psychoanalysis express political reservations. The task for a psychoanalytic feminism is to use the resources provided by psychoanalytic theory while negotiating these many legitimate concerns. In so doing, psychoanalytic feminism poses a challenge to psychoanalysis itself; if political accounts of identity are psychologically incomplete when they fabricate their own visions of human nature, psychoanalytic accounts are incomplete when they ignore the political contexts in which individual development is situated. As psychoanalytic feminist theory demonstrates, a synthetic approach to political and psychological knowledge transforms theory and practice.

Feminism and the Languages of Identity

Feminists have long challenged normative accounts of identity and subjectivity that disparage or ignore women's feelings, thought, speech, and
action. In the Western political tradition two strategies emerge for conceptualizing the nature of the self. In the first, political theorists are not
explicit about the identities of those who populate the polis. This does
not preclude some degree of piecemeal integration of attributes that supports the theorists' arguments about social and political life. It does mean
that the presentation of any comprehensive vision of human nature, including gender, is avoided. In this strategy, the self (or "individual") is
often depicted as solitary, rational, principled, abstract, and genderless.

In the second strategy, "individuals" (or people or citizens) and
"women" constitute distinct, albeit unacknowledged, categories. "Men"
(a term that means "people," as we are often told) are identified unam-
biguously with the metaphysical qualities attached to autonomous individuals, while "women" (a term that it is understood refers *only* to biological females) can be simultaneously identified with maternity, biological need, passion, or "nature."

The fiction of the genderless self in political thought is significant. The
issue of gender is foreclosed, those who raise the issue are penalized, and
the stage is set for the theoretical and historical banishing of women to a
primordial and dimly imagined prepolitical realm. The identification of
the distinctively human with the masculine is also guaranteed. Although
feminists are often blamed for initiating accounts of gender that needlessly
dichotomize feminine and masculine, this story about gender as difference
is as old as philosophy itself. With few exceptions, versions of human nature in Western political thought are embedded in, and inextricable from,
assumptions about the different natures of women and men. These accounts have been (and continue to be) buttressed by arguments and assumptions about the "public" sphere as male and the "private" as female.
Long before the twentieth century, feminists challenged this dichotomy of
"public" and "private" spheres and the content ascribed to them in theory and practice. Yet this split continues to exert its influence. It ratifies
the interest of political theorists in men—their problems and interests, as
well as their development and capacities—and consigns women to a paradoxical position of alternating presence and absence.

Concern about gender is not merely academic. Whatever accounts of
selves are constructed by theorists provide foundations and rationales for

conceptions of politics that are consistent with such selves, within which persons so constituted would fit and function. They also obscure the fates of those who do not fit—those who are conceived of as marginal, whose unacknowledged labor sustains a desired form of social life, or whose very existence seems to threaten notions of virtue, or "the good." If political thinkers have often been reluctant to debate and examine their own assumptions about the nature of gendered selves, feminists have not been. Feminists have demonstrated that such common locutions as "man" and "men" not only fail to satisfy some political standard of equal linguistic treatment, but also mystify the positioning of women in theoretical discourse. It is feminists who have persistently pointed to the implications of the alternating, and always theoretically meaningful, appearance and disappearance of women in political thought.

The realization that existing models of the self in political thought are flawed—perhaps irreparably—has spurred many feminists to look outside politics for ways to theorize women's identity. Psychoanalytic paradigms have provided one set of sources. This is not only so for the obvious reason—that female and male psychoanalytic thinkers have shown varying degrees of explicit interest in women. Indeed, feminist critiques of philosophy have demonstrated incisively that systems of thought can easily incorporate women while maintaining maleness as a norm. Attention to sex and gender can result in no more than a reinscription of the idea of "woman" as flawed, defective, or diseased. Moreover, the regulatory potential of such idea systems may be every bit as great as those that obscure the existence of sex and gender.

Why is psychoanalytic theory attractive to feminists, if not merely because of its explicit attention to women? It is so for a number of reasons. Unlike political discourse, psychoanalysis does not privilege conscious, institutional, and public dimensions of identity over relational and private ones. This is particularly important to those whose own identities have been conceived exclusively in relation to a private, prepolitical, or antipolitical realm of existence. In addition, the aversion to intimacy, sexuality, and passion in political thought is reversed in psychoanalysis. The very shamelessness of psychoanalytic thought—its attention to the body, passion, fantasy—subverts the stories about identity that are told in political theory. This subversion creates a theoretical space in which alternative and threatening stories about the nature of selves, female and male, can be told.

There are persuasive theoretical and historical reasons for alliances to be forged between feminist and psychoanalytic theories. In spite of affinities, however, the history of the relationship between feminism and psychoanalysis is a complex one. Among feminists, the bond with psychoanalytic thought is fragile and contentious. Uneasiness marks the feminist appropriation of psychoanalytic ideas.

Joining Feminism and Psychoanalysis

Women have been drawn to psychoanalysis from its earliest days. Anna Freud, Melanie Klein, Karen Horney, and numerous others seized opportunities to build the young discipline, and left an indelible mark on it. Adam Phillips's anecdotal observation on the intellectual impact of women psychoanalysts on Donald Winnicott—that "wherever he went, he met a woman on her way back"—captures the significance of this presence.[1] Yet as with the interest in women among psychoanalytic theorists, the mere presence of women in the ranks is insufficient to account for the willingness of feminists to employ psychoanalysis. Neither does the presence of women as analysts account for the feminist wedding of political and social criticism with psychoanalytic theory.

Feminists have made eclectic and creative use of psychoanalytic perspectives. Loyalty to particular paradigms and pioneers has never been an issue for feminist theorists, who look to psychoanalytic theory for its possible contributions to their own enterprises more than they set out to defend and consolidate favored theories. It is this willingness to borrow, critique, and reconstruct psychoanalytic ideas that has been the greatest strength of a feminist appropriation of psychoanalysis. The relative absence of orthodoxy has set up a lively and protean environment for feminist work in psychoanalytic theory. As a result, the intersection of feminism and psychoanalysis is complicated in two major ways: first, feminists have borrowed from the full range of psychoanalytic paradigms. Some feminists have rejected Freud's ideas while others have used them. Self psychology and feminist modifications of Lacanian-inspired French psychoanalysis are attractive to a growing number of theorists working in the humanities and social sciences. Feminist clinicians of all descriptions mix and modify psychodynamic ideas to create woman-centered therapies. Among American feminist theorists, object relations theories remain the most widely used and reconfigured of all psychoanalytic paradigms. Indeed, the triumph of object relations theory is such that many theorists (feminist and nonfeminist) routinely use insights acquired from object relations via feminism, without fully realizing their intellectual origins.[2]

A second source of complexity in the relationship between feminism and psychoanalysis is the often contentious internecine debate within feminism over the usefulness of psychoanalysis. This debate should not be surprising to those acquainted with the internal diversity of feminism. Feminists have always been divided over goals, philosophies, and methods; it is more responsible and accurate to speak, as many do, of the plural, "feminisms." The category "feminism" itself is in significant respects a convenience. Some feminists have attempted to claim for women the promises of Enlightenment liberalism: reason, liberty, autonomy, equality. For these feminists psychoanalysis is an unnecessary ally; the liberal political accounts of identity serve the women who have been excluded from their enjoyment as well as they serve the men whose interests they have championed. Others have exposed these very claims and promises as incoherent, or as the residue of unexamined forms of domination. To them, psychoanalytic accounts of identity point up the vacuity of rationalistic and individualistic alternatives.

A variety of themes emerges in feminist critiques of psychoanalytic theory. The most frequent of these is that psychoanalytic theory privileges a teleology of separation and individuation. Some feminists argue that psychoanalysis creates a normative discourse that promotes stereotypically masculine character in the guise of maturity or psychic health. The ideal (male) individual of political theory is the autonomous and individuated self of psychoanalysis. One example of such a criticism is that of psychologist Carol Gilligan, who deplores the reliance of feminists on object relations theory. Gilligan suggests that object relations theory "ties the formation of the self to the experience of separation, joining separation with individuation and thus counterposing the experience of the self to the experience of connection with others."[3] In a similar vein, Gilligan begins *In a Different Voice* with a critique of Freud and Erik Erikson. The theme that Gilligan reads in the work of both analysts is that of separation: the masculine preoccupation with "separation, autonomy, individuation, and natural rights" that has been transformed into a "developmental litany."[4] It is important to note that this concern is not just with description—the way psychoanalysis symbolizes the psychic world—it is also with the normalizing capacity of a psychoanalytic discourse. Many feminists who reject psychotherapies of all sorts for women make two arguments: that psychodynamic therapies uphold standards of health and maturity that misconstrue the nature of women's affiliations, and that the definitions of health and maturity offered by these therapies easily become a normative standard. Women then measure themselves (and are measured) against standards by which they will be found wanting. An additional argument mounted specifically against the therapeutic process is that analysis privatizes, that it takes pain and distress whose causes are social and treats them as individual matters, to be understood in the light of an individual case history and solved in abstraction from common consciousness and action.[5]

A second critique involves the theoretical figure of "the mother." Feminist critics have pointed out that psychoanalytic theory has frequently made the mother the causal agent of psychopathology while casting the father in the role of the rescuer who delivers children, especially male children, into culture, civilization, or the Symbolic. Alternatively, the mother may be depicted as a (more or less successful) mirror of the child. Here the mother's project is neither care for herself nor comprehension of the larger social relations in which her life is embedded. Her purpose and performance are conceptualized in the absence of any consideration of the cultural meanings of motherhood, gender inequalities, and variations of material resources.

A more devastating criticism is simply that psychoanalysis conflates "woman" and "mother" in a way that insinuates ideological prescriptions concerning femininity and child rearing into the very definition of femaleness. Like the "woman" who emerges in political philosophy only when she is needed to serve a particular purpose, the "woman" of psychoanalysis serves a normalizing function. She is the "good enough mother" or the "phallic mother," the (in the infant's perception) "good" mother or the "bad" mother. One need only try to imagine the categories "man" and "father" being so conflated to understand the veracity of this claim. Many feminists have further argued that psychoanalytic theories have failed to give a nonideological account both of the mothering relation and of children's needs.[6] This is another way of saying that women are disciplined by the putative needs of "the infant," and that these "needs" are a function of the expert discourses of psychoanalysts.

And what of women who may or may not be mothers, and who are not heterosexual? A third criticism revolves around the assumption of "normal heterosexuality" that is commonplace in psychoanalysis. Freud's theorizing about a primary state of bisexuality notwithstanding, the assumption that human beings are by nature heterosexual is pervasive. Because heterosexuality is not problematized, bisexuals and lesbians can be understood as deviants from some (at least implicit) norm of human sexual expression. But heterosexual response is not merely the predictable relational manifestation of a natural biological desire; in fact, desire in human subjects is mediated through social institutions and practices and is shaped by relations of power.

Psychoanalysis does not acknowledge or account for the effects of sex/gender systems that require heterosexuality in women and that punish other sexualities as sinful, selfish, unfeminine, "phallic," regressive, or destructive to civilization. It does not attend to the legal, economic, social, and religious pressures that have historically existed for women to contract heterosexual marriage, bear children, and remain in heterosexual relationships. These pressures are not without profound psychological consequences. To assume as "natural" an orientation toward sexual and relational fulfillment that is coercively enforced by virtually all social and political institutions easily slides into an intellectual version of the fear and loathing of ordinary bigots.

A fourth criticism suggests that psychoanalysis is inherently constrained in its scope by its emphasis on infancy and early childhood. It needlessly assumes the hegemony of childhood psychic life over later development and mature experience. This is one argument made against the Kleinian-influenced theory of Dorothy Dinnerstein, who is criticized for her assumption of the dominant and malignant influence of infantile and childhood experience. This is not an unfair depiction. Dinnerstein does indeed focus on "the way in which adult feeling resonates with the emotional atmosphere of infancy."[7] Such conviction prompts many feminists to read in psychoanalysis a determinism that would militate against social and political improvement. Some respond by rejecting psychoanalytic stories of development altogether. Others prefer psychologies that are more sensitive to life-span and social issues than psychoanalytic theories tend to be. In this way, possibilities for transformation in lived reality and consciousness are preserved.

A fifth and related issue is the charge that psychoanalytic theory endows fantasy and intrapsychic life with more significance than social and political reality. In this view, a preoccupation with intrapsychic phenomena deflects attention from the world of women's economic exploitation, physical oppression, material want, and historical activity. Even feminist psychoanalysis focuses on the imputed intrapsychic dimension of women's experience, diminishing the importance of women's material existence. Psychoanalytic theory is a form of analysis in which women's needs, capacities, and experiences are privatized and reduced to a language of fantasy; the fact that women's identities are understood to be in some measure determined by psychic events amenable mainly to interpretation by experts means that women lose control of their own voices.

Finally, feminists have criticized psychoanalysis as a universalizing discourse. In this reading, psychoanalytic theory is a product of, and reproduces, a very particular historical situation. But psychoanalysis disclaims this social and historical particularity, preferring to read its own theoretical products as timeless and objective. Thus, it is unable to accommodate and address differences between women, particularly differences of race, class, and historical period. Gilligan charges that the unself-conscious use of singular categories, such as "the mother" and "the child," is a clue to the way psychoanalytic theory cloaks the real diversity behind the ostensibly neutral descriptions.[8] Mothering (and fathering) is a kind of relationship, one that differs across time, as well as by culture and class. Psychoanalysis betrays its middle-class, white, patriarchal origins and biases by, as one theorist has suggested, "suppos[ing] that the sex-gender system with which we are most familiar remains, at least in essentials, always and everywhere the same."[9]

Although a concern with a universalizing tendency of psychoanalytic theory is not exclusively associated with postmodern philosophy, postmodernism questions the legitimacy of all claims for transhistorical aspects of identity or subjectivity. If psychoanalytic theories posit, either explicitly or implicitly, the existence of fixed qualities in human beings as the objects of knowledge and discourse, they are vulnerable to postmodern skepticism and deconstruction. The intersection of postmodernism and feminism is itself a matter of debate. Yet for feminists who incline toward postmodernism, the concern would be, first, with the status of psychoanalysis as itself a discourse of power and mythic truth, and second, with any fixed representations of human or female "nature."

There are obviously many pitfalls for feminists in the alliance with psychoanalytic theory. Those whose first concern is with the social and political standing of women and with injustices against women fear that psychoanalysis courts solipsism and a dereliction of concern with real problems suffered by real women. This is always a seduction in psychoanalytic perspectives. It may be tempting for theorists frustrated by the vastness of worldwide discrimination and brutality against women to turn to a theoretical system that is relatively disengaged from the daily realm of political activism, danger, and despair. It may also be tempting to attribute psychological causes to social problems, especially if this makes problems seem more manageable. Even so, there are reasons for feminists to remain open to psychoanalytic theory and defend it as a useful source for feminism.

Psychoanalytic Feminism

Over the last twenty years, ideas drawn from the work of psychoanalytic feminists have had a profound impact on feminist thought. Many feminists have used psychoanalytic theory in a variety of disciplinary settings: sociology, political theory, literary criticism, history, anthropology, and philosophy, among others. Feminists have also borrowed freely from the range of psychoanalytic perspectives. Feminists who use psychoanalytic theory do not accept it as it is, but rewrite it with a specifically feminist attention to sex and gender. They also respond to criticisms, at times defending a psychoanalytic feminism, and at times concurring with critics.

It is undeniable that feminists who use object relations theories have been the most vocal about defending feminist psychoanalytic theory from its critics. Of these, Nancy Chodorow has been the most vehement apologist, but she has certainly not been alone. Jessica Benjamin, for instance, addresses the criticism that object relations theory perpetuates a masculine consciousness of separation and estrangement. She argues that, far from dictating a telos of radical individuality, object relations theory moves psychoanalysis in a new direction. Unlike orthodox Freudian theory, object relations theory is founded on "the assumption that we are fundamentally social beings."[10]

Nancy Chodorow argues, along the same line, that it is object relations theory, of all variants in the psychoanalytic paradigm, that best conceptualizes intersubjectivity, or the ways all infants (and, by extension, adults) accomplish myriad connections with others. "Object-relations theory develops its account of primary sociality by describing the relational construction of the self, both developmentally and in daily life."[11] "Object relations theory does not need to idealize a hyperindividualism; it assumes a fundamental internal as well as external relatedness to the other."[12]

Benjamin further notes that "separation," as it is used in the language of some psychologies, may be misunderstood, and thus connote an undesirable ideal. "Separation is not just a 'beating back' but a move *toward* the world, implying an ability to extend the love felt for primary others to the world at large."[13]

The most important reconceptualization of psychoanalytic theory by feminists concerns the treatment of motherhood and the female identity with which it is generally conflated. Even some feminist critics of psychoanalysis have in this one respect praised feminists who employ psychoanalysis. They suggest that psychoanalytic feminism shifts the perspective of the "mother-child relationship . . . [to] the mother's rather than the child's point of view," making women subjects, and not just objects of men's and children's needs.[14] Chodorow's contribution to the feminist reconceptualization of mothering attempts to do just this by questioning the processes of psychological development that predispose women toward nurturance of children and thereby help to reproduce the sex/gender system. This is true in spite of the fact that she has been criticized for falsely assuming that all women are so predisposed.

The conflation of "woman" and "mother" is not specific to psychoanalysis. Feminists have pointed out the peculiar consequences of arguments in political thought in which theorists assume as natural to humans a self-interestedness that would seem to preclude the nurturance of children, and then presume that women will provide just this kind of selfless care. Conclusions about "human nature" in psychoanalytic theory have rarely emerged in such caricature. Even so, psychoanalytic feminists have gradually called into question the assumptions about women that have seemed safest for psychoanalysts to hold, while being, coincidentally, those that most neatly construct the fit between womanhood and mothering. The history of psychoanalytic theory is filled with assertions of penis envy, women's natural masochism, women's inner space, and maternal identification. All these concepts, as well as many others, foreclose political questions about the relation of women to children, of men to women, and of men to children. In addition, such naturalizing strategies abet a larger cultural attempt to ignore political questions about collective social responsibilities to children and the structural economic disparities that separate men as a group from women and children as a group. By confronting these questions, feminists push psychoanalysis to embrace a broader and more complex vision of women's identities.

Feminist perspectives on the question of sexual orientation have ranged from replicating the psychoanalytic assumption of (at least the numerical prominence of) heterosexuality to interrogating all psychoanalytic claims about the translation of desire into a consistent "sexuality." Nancy Chodorow has actually pursued both of these strategies. In her 1978 book, she merely acknowledges that most women are heterosexual, then carries out her exegesis of female development with this assumption. In a recent essay, she criticizes the psychoanalytic unwillingness to commit the same intellectual resources to theorizing the sources of heterosexuality that are expended on inquiring into homosexuality.[15] Provocative work on sexuality also emerges from feminists, such as Luce Irigaray, who are influenced by French psychoanalytic theory.[16]

The debate between psychoanalytic feminists and their critics does appear to contain intractable issues. One of these is the claim that psychoanalytic theory misunderstands the nature of development, presuming deep and ineradicable continuities between infant and adult being. On the one hand are those who understand early experience and relations as constitutive of adult experience. On the other hand are those who attend more closely to life-span experiences and discontinuities between childhood and adulthood. Feminist thinkers and activists whose principal aims involve reconstructing institutions to facilitate voice, participation, and self-determination often object to the focus on early childhood on principle. Yet the emphasis on early life need not be apolitical. For example, although Dinnerstein's work focuses on infantile life, it does not sacrifice an analysis of the consequences of gender inequality for women; the results of "the emotional atmosphere of infancy" are not the same for women and men: "The hate, fear, loathing, contempt, and greed that men express toward women so pervade the human atmosphere that we breathe them as casually as the city child breathes smog."[17]

Another intractable issue between gender feminists and others concerns the importance of fantasy, or the intrapsychic. Ruth Perry paraphrases the concerns of these feminists when she rhetorically asks, "Why read about Freud and object relations theory when real problems stalk the earth?" Her own answer is that "By exploring the primal experience of growing up in a family, psychoanalytic theory can account for . . . how a culturally constructed sex/gender system takes hold in the unconscious, showing itself in intractable emotional responses or retrograde erotic fantasies that no amount of rational analysis can eradicate."[18] Perry's argument vindicates feminist interest in psychoanalysis by emphasizing the dialectic between the unconscious and the forms of social life in which it is embedded. Certainly the pursuit of this connection is not unique to feminism. Indeed, the following statement by Jessica Benjamin might have been made by virtually any psychoanalytic theorist: "The focus on differentiation in infancy does not mean that infancy determines later experiences, but that it establishes certain issues and patterns that reappear later, sometimes in other forms."[19] The cultural psychoanalysis of Erich Fromm and the radical psychoanalysis of Joel Kovel are well known efforts to situate individuals in groups, and groups in a larger social nexus of power relations.[20] What feminism brings to this debate is the insistence that power be understood not merely in Marxist terms. Instead power is a category of analysis that illuminates the usual, comfortable states of desire and feeling that help to construct, perpetuate, and enforce social and familial inequality.

In response to the specific claim that object relations theory cannot theorize diversity, Jane Flax argues that it is the very "logic" of object relations theory that accounts for changes in "human nature . . . as social relations change."[21] Many feminists argue that, although it has not often been used in this way, psychoanalytic theory is amenable to the construction of theories that explain the dialectic between psyches and changing social forms. Embedded in this argument is an understanding of psychoanalysis as explicating not a static human "nature," but psychic processes.

As social arrangements, relational experiences, and forms of nurturance differ, so too do the subjective consequences and their imprint on identity differ. Nancy Chodorow makes the strongest case for object relations theory as a way of conceptualizing not immutable sets of individual and group attributes, but psychic processes like "splitting, fantasy, [and] repression." These are, she argues, universally human operations, although their form and content (and, presumably, consequences) vary historically with "social experience."[22]

As feminist critics claim, psychoanalytic theory has not theorized meaningful class, racial, cultural, and historical differences between women (and between men). This does not imply, however, that psychoanalytic theory is inadequate to this task. In recent years, African American and other nonwhite feminists have written eloquently of the ways the category "women" obscures the distinctive qualities of many communities and familial arrangements and their effects on identity formation. White feminists have only just begun to respond to these criticisms by acknowledging the ways feminist social theory written by white women has assumed white and middle-class social positioning and relative privilege. If the effects of this dialogue have only begun to transform feminist thinking, surely psychoanalytic theory should not be prematurely disregarded.

Women and "Human Nature" in Psychoanalytic Theory

It is much more difficult to talk about *a* feminist psychoanalysis than may be supposed. What exists instead is a field of innovation and debate over psychoanalysis that maps onto the already vital field of feminist thought. Yet feminists who use psychoanalytic theory do share certain concepts: the idea of an unconscious, an account of women that is essentially relational rather than atomistic, an interest in defenses and the ways these are shaped by relations of power, and a focus on early—and thus in certain respects constitutive—emotional patterns. Feminists turn to psychoanalytic theory for help in understanding the ways in which women are constantly negotiating shifting and intersecting political and psychological realities.

On the other hand, there are ways the goals of psychoanalysis and even a psychoanalytically informed feminism diverge. Feminists share an interest in the lived realities of women and a concern with articulating the nature of women's struggles. The counterpart of the clinical dimension (and raison d'être) of psychoanalysis is the activist political dimension of feminism. This is to say that although both sets of practices attempt to diagnose and change a hurtful reality, they do so in quite different ways, with different tools, goals, assumptions, and ideas of what constitutes amelioration. As a form of therapeutic practice, psychoanalysis addresses itself to the individual, the person whose palpable distress must be accounted for. For feminists, the hurtful and oppressive reality is conceptualized as shared, by virtue of some combination of sex, race, ethnicity, and class.

For psychoanalysts, a central question may be the nature and causes of individual pain or pathology, even when it is acknowledged that individuals are inextricably related to social and intimate others. Feminists attempt not to create an account of women's psychopathology, but rather to expose the social and political genealogies that constitute women as harmed or maimed. The focus for psychoanalytic feminists is on how harm to women is constituted, and on how women survive, not on the harmed self as pathogenic.

This focus derives from the feminist political critique of institutions and practices whose operations are more usually either taken for granted or insulated from analysis, including interrelated critiques of gender, marriage, and family life. For most feminists, families are not "natural" (presocial or precivil) collectives; nor are they neutral crucibles of psychological development. They are, rather, groups whose membership, structure, and norms are shaped historically and politically. They are also sites of power relations that are understood in a liberal political framework as "private" at the same time that they are ineluctably connected with social sanctions and demands.

Within families, the meanings of femininity and masculinity are transmitted even while they are obfuscated through appeals to "nature." And these meanings continue to perpetuate disparities in rights, income, roles, aspirations, and treatment (social, legal, and familial) between women and men. Psychoanalytic feminist theorists have shown the many ways these disparities and differences in desires, fantasies, feelings, and representations of self and others mutually influence each other. This effort must be joined by the broader psychoanalytic community. Although both political and psychoanalytic thought have often presumed a neat split between spheres of life, there is no respite from the necessity to theorize the intersections between "public" and "private" selves.

Like many other spheres of thought, psychoanalysis has also been naive about the impact on women's lives of violence and the threat of violence. Girls and women of all ages suffer disproportionately from sexual violence perpetrated by men who are strangers, acquaintances, and family members. Violence against adult women by husbands and partners alone is so prevalent that over one third of all adult female murder victims are killed by a spouse or domestic partner.[23] Both for women who are victims of violence and for women who are not, the pervasive threat of sexual assault and other forms of violence helps to structure autonomy, self-esteem, and subjectivity. Women's rage and fear—including disclaimed rage and fear—are political issues, in the sense that they disempower women in their public roles as workers and citizens. To the extent that psychoanalytic theorists aspire to confront the psychological needs and dilemmas of women, these emotions and their consequences must be issues for psychoanalytic theory as well.

Feminists, like other kinds of theorists, create stories about women's lives. These stories are animated and informed by commitments to women—commitments to end physical brutality, social and political injustice, and interpretations of women's lives that empower others at women's expense. Feminists who choose to depend more on traditional political discourses may find it more difficult to conceptualize connections between emotional patterns, needs, and desires and economic, social, and political modes of life. Feminists who choose psychoanalytic theory are likely to be deflected from interpretations that integrate social and political inequality, the effects of poverty, and "ordinary" (and thus invisible) traumas that women experience. Either perspective sacrifices something that is crucial to theorizing the sources of women's pain. The tasks for feminist theorists and clinical practitioners are not the same. Even so, it is possible to imagine a discussion between political and psychological languages that diminishes the barriers between them and more adequately accounts for the lives of women *and* men.

From Theory to Practice

Psychoanalytic theorists have virtually always paid more explicit attention to sex and gender than have political thinkers. Psychoanalysts have acknowledged that sex and gender play a part in reality construction and the constitution of identity, even if disagreement over these issues abounds. In spite of the attention ostensibly given to gender in psychoanalytic theory, analysts—like political theorists—have often both neglected gender (assuming the genderlessness of psychic processes) and attended to gender in ways that reproduce oppressive features of social relations. These aspects of psychoanalytic theory remain deeply embedded in the working assumptions and clinical techniques of psychoanalysts.

In this respect psychoanalysts are not that different from political theorists: both begin to build theory on a foundation of assumptions about human nature, human experience, and valued ends. Such assumptions are not idiosyncratic; in spite of variations, they derive from the very set of contexts that are so indistinctly visible to those who come to maturity within them. Psychoanalysts are no more adept at ruthlessly separating themselves from these cultural conventions and "habits of the heart" than are political theorists. The consequence is that theories and clinical interpretations reproduce founding assumptions, often for audiences who find their own comfortable convictions encouraged.

Feminism challenges the interpretations of those who do not consistently inquire into their theoretical models or their own intuitive understandings of sex and gender. It is easy for feminists to root out the most glaring of political theorists' convictions about female "nature." Often a simple injunction to employ nonsexist or "inclusive" language is offered as the panacea for unreflective gender bias. It is much more difficult to acknowledge and confront the ways widely shared assumptions about femininity, masculinity, intimacy, erotic desire, mothering, and maturity influence the construction of theory itself. Psychoanalysts must constantly ask themselves if their premises are implicated either in the suppression of women's experiences or in the stubborn assertion of gender differences. They must consider the political and social context in which even the earliest individual development occurs. Finally, analysts must attend to the reality of harms to women that differ either in frequency or in kind from those suffered by men. This perspective does not come easily to anyone. Charlotte Kraus Prozan argues that even psychoanalytic feminist theorists can pay insufficient attention to the actual effects of trauma and abuse on girls and women.[24] This only underscores the necessity for theorists and clinicians to make the effort to integrate these issues into their work.

Women's lives are shaped by resistances to and accommodations to pain—the inevitable pain and frustration of life, but also the unnecessary pains of coercive femininity, disproportionate poverty, and social and domestic domination. Feminism enjoins theorists and clinicians to consider girls and women in two ways: as individuals with unique life histories and as members of groups whose distress is socially and politically meaningful. It is only by joining psychic interpretation to political awareness that the hope for *ordinary* unhappiness can be realized.

NOTES

1. Phillips, *Winnicott*, p. 45
2. Burack, *The problem of the passions.*
3. Gilligan, "Moral Orientation," p. 28.
4. Gilligan, *In a different voice*, p. 23.
5. Kitzinger and Perkins, *Changing our minds.*
6. Doane and Hodges, *From Klein to Kristeva.*
7. Dinnerstein, *The mermaid and the minotaur*, p. xiii.
8. Gilligan et al., "Psyche embedded," p. 91.
9. Fee, "Critiques of modern science," p. 49.
10. Benjamin, *The bonds of love*, p. 17.

11. Chodorow, *Feminism and psychoanalytic theory*, p. 149.
12. Chodorow, *Feminism and psychoanalytic theory*, p. 159.
13. Benjamin, *The bonds of love*, p. 269.
14. Kahn, "Excavating those dim Minoan regions," p. 33.
15. Chodorow, "Heterosexuality as a compromise formation."
16. See Irigaray, *This sex which is not one*.
17. Dinnerstein, *The mermaid and the minotaur*, p. 88.
18. Perry, "Book reviews," p. 599.
19. Benjamin, *The bonds of love*, p. 248.
20. See Fromm, *Escape from freedom* and Kovel, *The age of desire*.
21. Flax, "Political philosophy and the patriarchal unconscious," p. 250.
22. Chodorow, *The reproduction of mothering*, p. 53.
23. This figure compares with the nine percent of male murder victims who are killed by a spouse or partner. Colburn, "When violence begins at home," p. 7.
24. See, e.g., her criticism of Chodorow in Prozan, *Feminist psychoanalytic psychotherapy*, p. 132.

REFERENCES

Benjamin, Jessica. 1988. *The bonds of love: Psychoanalysis, feminism and the problem of domination*. New York: Pantheon.

Burack, Cynthia. 1994. *The problem of the passions: Feminism, psychoanalysis, and social theory*. New York: New York University Press.

Chodorow, Nancy J. 1978. *The reproduction of mothering: Psychoanalysis and the sociology of gender*. Berkeley: University of California Press.

———. 1989. *Feminism and psychoanalytic theory*. New Haven: Yale University Press.

———. 1992. "Heterosexuality as a compromise formation: Reflections on the psychoanalytic theory of sexual development." *Psychoanalysis and Contemporary Thought* 15 (3): 267–304.

Colburn, Don. 1994. "When violence begins at home: AMA conference addresses 'problem of shocking dimensions.'" *Washington Post*, March 15, p. 7.

Dinnerstein, Dorothy. 1976. *The mermaid and the minotaur: Sexual arrangements and human malaise*. New York: Harper and Row.

Doane, Janice, and Devon Hodges. 1992. *From Klein to Kristeva: Psychoanalytic feminism and the search for the "good enough" mother*. Ann Arbor: University of Michigan Press.

Fee, Elizabeth. 1986. "Critiques of modern science: The relationship of feminism to other radical epistemologies." In *Feminist approaches to science*, ed. Ruth Blier, pp. 42–56. New York: Pergamon.

Flax, Jane. 1983. "Political philosophy and the patriarchal unconscious: A psychoanalytic perspective on epistemology and metaphysics." In *Discovering reality: Feminist perspectives on epistemology, metaphysics, methodology, and philosophy of science*, ed. Sandra Harding and Merrill B. Hintikka, pp. 245–81. Boston: D. Reidel.

Fromm, Erich. 1965. *Escape from freedom*. New York: Avon.

Gilligan, Carol. 1982. *In a different voice: Psychological theory and women's development*. Cambridge: Harvard University Press.

———. 1987. "Moral orientation and moral development." In *Women and moral theory*, ed. Eva Feder Kittay and Diana T. Meyers, pp. 19–33. Savage, MD: Rowman and Littlefield.

Gilligan, Carol, Lyn Brown, and Annie Rogers. 1990. "Psyche embedded: A place for body, relationships, and culture in personality theory." In *Studying persons and lives*, ed. A. I. Rabin, Robert A. Zucker, Robert A. Emmons, and Susan Frank, pp. 86–147. New York: Springer.

Irigaray, Luce. 1985. *This sex which is not one*. Trans. Catherine Porter with Carolyn Burke. Ithaca: Cornell University Press.

Kahn, Coppelia. 1982. "Excavating those dim Minoan regions: Maternal subtexts in patriarchal literature." *Diacritics* 12:32–41.

Kitzinger, Celia, and Rachel Perkins. 1993. *Changing our minds: Lesbian feminism and psychology*. New York: New York University Press.

Kovel, Joel. 1981. *The age of desire*. New York: Pantheon.

Perry, Ruth. 1991. "Book reviews: *Feminism and psychoanalytic theory, Thinking fragments: Psychoanalysis, feminism, and postmodernism in the contemporary west, Refiguring the father: New feminist readings of patriarchy*." *Signs* 16:597–603.

Phillips, Adam. 1988. *Winnicott*. Cambridge: Harvard University Press.

Prozan, Charlotte Krause. 1992. *Feminist psychoanalytic psychotherapy*. Northvale, NJ: Jason Aronson.

Chapter Sixteen

Sigmund Freud
The Questions of a Weltanschauung and of Defense

Alan Bass

EDITORS' INTRODUCTION

It is an awesome task that Alan Bass took on when he agreed to write the Freud chapter. Bass notes that what he has tried to do is give the reader a sense of "his Freud," realizing that there is no one "authoritative" Freud, nor should there be. As we will intimate, Bass's reading of Freud is informed by a postmodern sensibility; it is deconstructive, anti-ideological, and ironic, not surprising for an analyst who has translated the work of Jacques Derrida into English.

Bass begins his provocative essay "disruptively": he questions the main assumption of this volume, namely, that implicitly or explicitly, each theory represented in the volume has a Weltanschauung embedded in it. Bass indicates that Freud was against the idea of a psychoanalytic weltanschauung in part because it was antipsychoanalytic, that is, it went against the basic thrust of psychoanalysis, which for Bass, following Freud, is that "it cannot be systematic." Philosophers, theologians, and psychotics, according to Freud, strive for systematicity, but psychoanalysis should not, in part, because it fundamentally concerns itself with "unconscious energic processes" that by definition are contradictory, paradoxical, and ambiguous, and therefore must challenge our habitual conscious patterns of organizing data. In other words, for Bass, like Freud, to seek out or create a Weltanschauung is to succumb to an "illusory wish fulfillment." A commitment to such systematization not only is a form of imprisonment, but also misses some of the "essential things about psychoanalysis" that suggest what Freud thought constituted aspects of the human condition: for example, that human consciousness is inescapably ambiguous and contradictory, that an "infinite polysemousness and uncategorizable, pulsating fluidity" constitute the human experience (Barnaby Barratt). It is thus impossible and perhaps misguided to attempt to systematize Freudian psychoanalysis (or any other perspective) whether as a theoretician or practitioner. Rather, Bass suggests, psychoanalysis must push against the tendency to mold itself into the habitual patterns of conscious perception; against Weltanschauungen, it should strive to be more like an endless movement that perpetually undoes itself. More specifically, as Freud and Bass indicate, psychoanalysis should be a science that is midway between positivistic science and speculative philosophy, that combines elements of both, without being confined to a simplistic choice between either. In this view, according to Bass, "sexuality, the drives, and libido can be for psychoanalysis what matter, force, and gravitation became for physics as relativity and atomic structure transformed it: the phenomena that cannot be treated according to the systematizing logic of conventional thought." In this sense, "the future of psychoanalysis belongs to its Freudian past."

Citing Freud, who wrote that repression is "the cornerstone on which the whole structure of psychoanalysis rests," Bass focuses on the significance of the concept of "defense" as Freud's fundamental tenet: "That all psychopathology is an attempt to rid oneself of a reality that one finds unbearable, and that any theory of mind must account for the tendency to defense." Defense against reality, defense against love are central problematics for Bass's Freud. He points out that a Weltanschauung, "to the extent that it is consistent and logical, can be so precisely in the interest of defending against something unbearable: defenses and system building go hand in hand. When Freud compared system formation to secondary revision in dreams, and then compared both to forms of psychopathology ranging from the psychotic to the neurotic in *Totem and Taboo*, he was building distance from all systematicity into psychoanalytic theory. Wherever one finds systematicity, one can, from a psychoanalytic point of view, ask the question of what unbearable piece of reality is being defended against by means of the system." Furthermore, says Bass, "to found a theory of psychopathology and then of mind on the idea of defense is to create the necessity for a permanent irony about one's own theory, because of its possible defensiveness."

In this context, Bass indicates that Freud viewed psychopathology (as well as religion and philosophy) as characterized by a "delusional systematicity in the interest of defense." These defensive operations are largely unconscious, they serve the primary process, they reduce tension by attempting to eliminate the reality of whatever is perceived. In a word, they work in the interest of Thanatos. As Bass points out, neurosis, psychosis, and perversion, for example, can be understood in terms of both ego and id being split in varying degrees between Eros and defense, tension increase and tension reduction. In general, then, this formulation implies that the person who is psychopathological is the one who cannot embrace contradiction and ambiguity. Similarly, says Bass, Freud throughout his life undermined his own theories "based on the difficulties and paradoxes of clinical practice—narcissism, the death drive, signal anxiety, and ego splitting are a few prominent examples—bear testimony to his embracing of contradictory positions as a condition of progress." As Bass points out, one can infer that "if defenses serve nondifferentiation, and if defenses go hand in hand with system building and Weltanschauungen, then the therapeutic stance in favor of life, differentiation, and Eros would have to take a critical stance toward any worldview."

In Bass's narrative, psychoanalytic treatment is centrally concerned with undermining systematicity. Its focus is on clarifying the ongoing defensive process in which wishes and fantasies repetitively replace whatever form of differentiation has become too anxiety provoking. As the "scientific cure by love" says Bass, it is oriented to changing the balance in favor of life, of Eros as tension increase and differentiation. It is also the "perverse science." "As a therapy of neurosis, psychoanalysis undoes defenses against perversion; metaphorically, as the theory of mind that pushes against the habitual organizing forms of consciousness and perception, it 'perverts' them, and is always ready to 'pervert' itself." "Like any science, . . . psychoanalysis must always become strange to itself if it is to be able to produce the therapeutic strangeness that modification of defensive systematicity always demands." It is this "spirit of Freud's work" that must "haunt" psychoanalysis if it is to be true to what is most subversive, creative, and life affirming in Freud. (P. M. and A. R.)

Does Freud Have a Worldview?

What is the role of Freud in a volume like this? One theorist among many? The founder who exists as an overt or covert reference for every other theorist? A part of psychoanalytic history or an overriding presence in the whole of it? Paul Marcus and Alan Rosenberg, the editors, outlined their views on such questions in a prospectus sent to all the contributors. They wrote that if there was once a time when "mainstream psycho-analysis could insist on the primacy of Freud's drive theory and the version of the world associated with it" as the major guiding theory of clinical work, that time is no more. Like any other theorist, Freud implicitly has a "story" about the human condition. Therapeutic work is always informed by the "explicit tenets" of this story about the human condition, which in turn contains a "less obvious and often unstated version of the world."

My task, then, is to tease out Freud's version of the world in order to delineate the more unstated principles that shaped his theory and practice. Since we are more than ever aware that every statement of a fact or a concept is embedded in a rhetoric or a narrative strategy, which itself is embedded in an "unstated version of the world," this task seems particularly important in the case of Freud. His theory *has* served as a master narrative for psychoanalysis. The more Freud's implicit narratives and their underlying worldview are made explicit, the more psychoanalysis knows about why it does what it does, and how it might be limited by unstated propositions. To undertake this task in relation to Freud is daunting not only for all the obvious reasons, but also because it has repercussions for the entire field of psychoanalysis.

In their prospectus, Marcus and Rosenberg cited one of Freud's strongest statements about a worldview for psychoanalysis in relation to their project: "Although Freud wrote that 'Psychoanalysis, in my opinion, is incapable of creating a Weltanschauung of its own'—an 'intellectual construction that solves all the problems of existence uniformly on the basis of one overriding hypothesis'—we believe that each theoretical position to be represented in this book has attempted to do just that and their clinical concepts reflect this goal." Here we face an immediate problem. In Freud's view the question of a *Weltanschauung* is important enough to warrant an entire chapter of the *New Introductory Lectures* (number 35). However, Freud's consistent position on this question is that psychoanalysis per se "is incapable of creating a *Weltanschauung* of its own." How intrinsic is this position to Freud's overall conception of psychoanalysis? I would like to argue that it is intrinsic indeed, and that it stems from Freud's most basic clinical and theoretical ideas. Thus, my approach here is somewhat disruptive. In a volume devoted to spelling out the Weltanschauungen of all the major theorists, I would like to show that Freud's contra-Weltanschauung position says essential things about psychoanalysis. As I outline Freud's position, I will also attempt to justify why this relatively neglected area of his thought must be taken into account in this context.

If it is true, as Marcus and Rosenberg state, that mainstream psychoanalysis for a long time insisted on the primacy of drive theory and the version of the world associated with it, Freud himself was explicit that his theories did not produce a worldview based on the primacy of the drives and the search for gratification. In *Inhibition, Symptom, and Anxiety* he took to task those analysts who were creating a psychoanalytic Weltanschauung in terms of the dominance of the id, the drives, over the ego. Such a view is one-sided, he said, and specifically ignores the ego's strengths—access to consciousness and the external world, and the capacity to repress (1926, p. 95). Analysts who believe they have a uniform explanation of mental life based on drive theory are in fact succumbing to the anti-analytic temptation to write a guidebook to the psyche. Freud mockingly refers to such a guidebook as a "Baedeker for life" or an all sufficient catechism, the kind of thing only philosophers seem to be unable to do without (1926, p. 96). And, he continues to joke, everyone knows that such guidebooks forever have to be brought up to date. But the joking tone contains an implicit warning: to be a psychoanalyst is to be confronted by the kind of phenomena that make one *wish* for a guidebook. As soon as one has succumbed to this wish, however, one functions philosophically, not analytically. If, even in his own day, Freud found it necessary to criticize the temptation to make drive theory into a Weltanschauung, what would he say about psychoanalysis being organized around competing Weltanschauungen? As his sarcasm makes clear, he would probably view it as a lapse into the kind of philosophizing he thought psychoanalysis should avoid.

In "The Question of a *Weltanschauung*," Freud (1933) spells out why he thinks that science and Weltanschauungen are mutually exclusive, in order to reassert his conviction that psychoanalysis has to be a science. Immediately after writing that psychoanalysis is unfit to create a Weltanschauung of its own, he states that it has to accept the scientific one. However, the scientific Weltanschauung is not really such. A worldview in general provides a current, uniform explanation of the phenomena it encompasses. Science, for Freud, assumes that any uniform explanations are a program for the future (1933, p. 159). In fact, as science progressively examines mental phenomena, it examines the ever renewed demand for a Weltanschauung, but *without* viewing the demand as justified. Freud clearly implies that to have a Weltanschauung is to be a philosopher, not to have one is to be a scientist. Thus, his opposition to the idea of a psychoanalytic Weltanschauung is intrinsic to his ongoing "narrative" of why psychoanalysis has to be a science, and cannot be philosophy. As the science of unconscious processes, psychoanalysis will have to explain why the wish for a Weltanschauung is perennial, and why the gratification of such a wish is inimical to psychoanalysis.

Within certain quarters, such an explanation by Freud would probably be viewed as sophistry. It is often held that Freud's conception of science belongs to the nineteenth century, and that his arguments for psychoanalysis as a science are themselves less scientific than scientistic. The usual conception of Freud as a nineteenth-century scientist is that his metapsychology is based on outdated conceptions of energic processes and a positivist view of phenomena as reducible to quantifiable relations of forces. Although it is possible to find many individual passages in Freud that seem to confirm this conception, at the very least it overlooks what Freud himself had to say about it. In a 1924 paper, "The Resistances to Psychoanalysis," Freud begins by arguing for a medical, scientific conception of psychoanalysis, only to show why scientific medicine will have to resist psychoanalysis. He writes:

> the contemporary generation of physicians . . . had been brought up to respect only anatomical, physical and chemical factors. . . . They obviously had doubts whether psychical events allowed of any exact scientific treatment whatever. . . . During this materialistic, or, rather, mechanistic period, medicine made tremendous advances, but it also showed a short-sighted misunderstanding of the most important and most difficult among the problems of life. (1924c, pp. 215–16)

Freud's position, then, is that science itself does not have to conform to the positivist or reductionist view that only "anatomical, physical and chemical factors" can enter its domain. Moreover, he is also opposed to the either-or view that any discipline that is not mechanistically scientific has to be speculative or philosophical. Philosophy resists psychoanalysis as much as positivist science:

> The overwhelming majority of philosophers regard as mental only the phenomena of consciousness. . . . What, then, can a philosopher say to a theory which, like psychoanalysis, asserts that on the contrary what is mental is itself unconscious and that being conscious is only a quality. . . ? He will naturally say that anything both unconscious and mental would be an impossibility. (1924c, p. 216)

As a discipline, then, or even as a science, psychoanalysis in Freud's view can be neither reductively mechanistic nor speculative. This is one of its intrinsic difficulties: "So it comes about that psychoanalysis derives nothing but disadvantages from its middle position between medicine and philosophy" (1924c, p. 217). It is my overall impression that most of the contemporary debates about whether psychoanalysis is a science in the way Freud always insisted lose sight of the fact that he clearly did not mean that psychoanalysis had to be a positivist science, or that the only alternative to positivist science was speculative thought. As a new discipline between medicine and philosophy, psychoanalysis will have to combine elements of both, without being confined to a simplistic choice between either. The contemporary debates about the disciplinary status of psychoanalysis often focus on what appear to be the models of truth within science or speculative thought, that is, correspondence or coherence. Once more, the oversimplification consists in saying that there has to be an either-or choice between science and correspondence or speculation and coherence. In "The Question of a *Weltanschauung*" Freud explicitly argues for both. Like any science, psychoanalysis "examines more strictly the trustworthiness of the sense-perceptions on which it bases its conclusions. . . . Its endeavor is to arrive at correspondence with reality" (1933, p. 170). How is such a correspondence with reality to be brought about in a discipline like psychoanalysis, which has "to do without the assistance afforded to research by experiment"? Freud states, "We bring expectations with us into the work, but they must forcibly be held back . . . to begin with the pieces do not fit together. . . .we renounce early convictions so as not to be led by them into overlooking unexpected factors, and in the end our whole expenditure of effort is rewarded, the scattered findings fit themselves together" (1933, p. 174). This is a clear statement of a coherence theory. The point, again, is that in Freud's conception, what is original and difficult about psychoanalysis is that it has to operate with both models of truth, just as it occupies a middle position between mechanistic science and philosophy. Thus, Freud's ongoing "narrative" about why psychoanalysis has to be a science does not mean that psychoanalysis is ipso facto a nineteenth century, mechanistic science. And the idea of a Weltanschauung belongs to the kind of speculative philosophy that accredited the opposition between itself and mechanistic science along idealist and materialist lines. The larger import of psychoanalysis is that it is part of the breaking down and rethinking of such oppositions. To attempt to delineate Freud's Weltanschauung as if his anti-Weltanschauung statements were not intrinsic to this thought would be to situate him, and implicitly psychoanalysis itself, back in a conceptual framework he explicitly questioned. A contemporary analyst who is keenly aware of such issues, Barratt, has written, "The history of post-Freudian theorizing comprises manifold attempts, implicit and explicit, to relocate a seminally innovational psychology within existing conceptual frameworks to which it is foreign, to make its practice conform to epistemological paradigms it transgresses" (1984, p. 55). It is my own conviction that if psychoanalysis itself is to have a future, it will only be as a result of the way it breaks down and rethinks—transgresses—existing conceptual frameworks. The debates between science and hermeneutics, materialism or idealism, correspondence or coherence models of truth are retrogressive and ignore the Freud who had already thought through such questions. Paradoxically, then, the future of psychoanalysis belongs to its past if it is not to be trapped in sterile debates. My own disruptive approach here is part of the general effort of reopening the future of psychoanalysis to the intrinsically disruptive narrative of why Freud considered psychoanalysis a science and why he insisted it could not have a Weltanschauung.

The basic contention, then, is that much of psychoanalytic theory, even when it considers itself Freudian, has not attended to the complexity of Freud's view of science. To argue that he did not view psychoanalysis as either mechanistic science or philosophy is by no means to ignore the mechanistic elements of his theory. If anything, Freud seems to resemble in his scientific outlook those physicists who were working at about the time he was. Starting from a traditional positivist view of science and a traditional mechanistic understanding of energy and matter, these physicists created the revolution in science that led to the end of the classical worldview of a mechanical universe. Their aim, however, was not revolution itself, and at first many of them attempted to understand their anomalous findings within the positivist framework from which they necessarily started. As one of the great fathers of quantum mechanics, Max Planck, wrote, "I tried . . . to weld the elementary quantum of action . . . somehow into the framework of classical theory. . . . My futile attempts to fit the elementary quantum of action into the classical theory continued for a number of years" (Pais, 1986, p. 133)."

There is ample evidence for a similar procedure in Freud. For many years, he attempted to integrate his revolutionary findings into the framework of classical science, only to find himself continually dissatisfied with the results. Thus, while it is inarguable that much of his initial metapsychology contains an energy theory based on mechanistic principles, it is also demonstrable that Freud viewed such explanations as always provisional. In fact, he continually stated that any attempt to view his metapsychology as a definitive statement was the result of the perennial wish to make theory into the kind of internally consistent logic that was open only to the builders of Weltanschauungen. In his *Autobiographical Study* (1925), Freud repeated an idea he had already outlined in "On Narcissism" (1914a) and "Instincts and Their Vicissitudes" (1915). Responding to both traditional scientific and philosophical criticisms that such concepts as drive and libido lacked sufficient precision, Freud wrote, "Clear and basic concepts and sharply drawn definitions are only possible in the mental sciences insofar as the latter seek to fit a region of facts into the frame of a *logical system*" (1925, p. 57; my emphasis). And, just as he did in "On Narcissism," Freud asserts here that physics itself would not have advanced if it had had to wait for systematic clarity in such basic concepts as matter, force, and gravitation. Significantly, Freud elsewhere stated that the drastic changes brought about by the theory of relativity and the discovery of radium had had the effect of making many people doubt science itself, precisely because such discoveries flew in the face of the Weltanschauung constructed around a certain idea of science (1921, p. 178). The implication is that sexuality, the drives, and libido can be for psychoanalysis what matter, force, and gravitation became for physics as relativity and atomic structure transformed it: the phenomena that cannot be treated according to the systematizing logic of traditional thought.

Precisely because he was aware of how progress in science, particularly physics, had to lead to rethinking science itself, Freud was perennially attentive to the problem of observation in psychoanalysis. Observations made by conscious perception always tend to be remolded into the general organizing patterns of consciousness and its worldview—the basic obstacle to all theoretical advance. In the *Outline of Psychoanalysis* he wrote,

> In our science as in the others the problem is the same: behind the attributes . . . of the object under examination which are presented *directly to our perception*, we have to discover something else which is more *independent* of the particular receptive capacity of our sense organs and which approximates more closely to what may be supposed to be the real state of affairs. We have no hope of being able to reach the latter itself, since it is evident that *everything new that we have inferred must nevertheless be translated back into the language of our perceptions, from which it is simply impossible for us to free ourselves*. But herein lies the *very nature and limitation* of our science. It is as though we were to say in physics: "If we could see clearly enough we should find that what appears to be a solid body is made up of particles of such and such a shape and size occupying such and such relative positions." (1940a, p. 196; my emphasis)

Freud was able to return again and again to basic metapsychological questions, and was even able to change his definition of such a basic energic concept as drive, as he grappled more and more extensively with the way his discoveries could not fit into a classical scientific framework. One needs to read Freud's metapsychology and his energic thinking just as one might read Planck's original attempts to make his findings fit into the framework from which he started. One wonders whether the perennial demands to rid psychoanalysis of its supposedly antiquated drive theory are not precisely expressions of the wish to construct the most up-to-date Weltanschauung, to make psychoanalysis a consistent system that conforms to "the language of our perceptions." The importance of energic concepts in Freud's thought is that they can never be directly confirmed by consciousness or perception. Because they are inferred, in order to explain clinical phenomena, they must be subject to constant correction, especially correction of the contextual assumptions in which the inferences are made. This is what happened in physics in Freud's day, and it is the only way to create a theory of unconscious processes that does not conform to the precepts of mechanistic science or philosophical system building. This is yet another reason I think that the future of psychoanalysis belongs to its Freudian past: much—most—psychoanalytic theory building since Freud has not understood why a theory of unconscious processes cannot do without energic thinking as part of the way such a theory has to challenge the contextual assumptions in which it is elaborated. It thus tries to make psychoanalysis conform to the conscious Weltanschauung in which thought is either mechanistic or philosophical.

This line of thought is consistent with Freud's most basic view of psychopathology. In "On Narcissism" he made the famous statement that "we must begin to love in order not to fall ill" (1914a, p. 85). This is not a sentimental or philosophical or religious precept about the redeeming power of love, but a specific consequence of the theory of unconscious energic processes. The complete sentence reads: "A strong egoism is a protection against falling ill, but in the last resort we must begin to love in order not to fall ill, and we are bound to fall ill if, in consequence of frustrations, we are unable to love." In the most general terms, love is understood by Freud as the opposite of the psychopathological processes that in their most extreme form produce philosophical systems with their Weltanschauungen—and psychosis.

The link between psychosis and system building stems from the familiar basics of Freud's energic theories. The psychic apparatus is "first and foremost a device designed for mastering excitations which would otherwise be felt as distressing or would have pathogenic effects" (1914a, p. 85). (This idea is probably the most important instance of Freud fitting his own findings into a mechanistic theory of energic processes. This is not to say that the idea is completely wrong, but the way it can conflict with the less mechanistic aspects of the theory of unconscious energic processes has to be spelled out. In the rich literature on this subject, the writings of Laplanche [1976] and Loewald [1980] stand out; I will return to this question below.) If a frustrating obstacle prevents the direct discharge of such excitations, then "working them over in the mind helps remarkably towards an internal draining away of excitations" (Freud, 1914a, p. 85). In energic terms, Freud understands psychosis as the withdrawal of libidinal investment in external reality and its consequent reinvestment in the ego, a narcissistic regression. In psychosis, then, the libido attached to objects is not repressed, as in neurosis. Rather, the reinvestment of libido in the ego produces the kind of megalomanic self-love that is *not* the "strong egoism" that serves as a protection against illness. It inevitably collapses in on itself, leading to the desperate attempts to reinvest libido in a delusional or hallucinatory reality that no longer contains the frustrating obstacle (1914a, p. 86). The point is that in psychosis megalomania is the beginning of a process in which a quantity of libido is withdrawn from objects and is dangerously reinvested in the ego. Although neurotic repression is also a dangerous attempt to forbid the discharge of libido in relation to a prohibited object, the major difference is that repression allows the libido to remain attached to unconscious fantasies. The more extreme pathology of psychosis is the result of a more extreme inability to love. This more extreme inability to love, manifested as too great a libidinal investment in the ego, is precisely the "origin" of philosophical systems for Freud.

The concept of narcissistic overinvestment in one's own thought had already led Freud to state in *Totem and Taboo* that "a paranoiac delusion is a caricature of a philosophical system" (1913, p. 73). Freud takes up the question of Weltanschauungen as psychopathology in *Totem and Taboo* when he links narcissistic overinvestment in thoughts to animism. Animism, he contends, is a "system of thought" that allows us "to grasp the whole universe as a single unity from a single point of view." Thus, it is both the "first" and "most consistent and exhaustive *Weltanschauung*" (1913, p. 77). Further on, Freud extends his linkage of psychopathology and systematicity in terms of basic psychoanalytic principles. The secondary revision of dreams, he tells us, is "an admirable example of the nature and pretensions of a system" (1913, p. 95).

> Conscious intellect in general demands unity, connection and intelligibility from any material, whether of perception or thought that comes within its grasp. . . Systems constructed in this way are known to us not only from dreams, but also from phobias, from obsessive thinking and from delusions. The construction of systems is seen most strikingly in delusional disorders . . . where it dominates the symptomatic picture; but its occurrence in other forms of neuropsychosis must not be overlooked.   (1913, p. 95)

In other words, and in terms of Freud's general theory of love and energic processes, wherever love is frustrated, we find the creation of systems, of uniform Weltanschauungen. Science, then, which analyzes the need for Weltanschauungen without lapsing into delusional consistency, is like love. Freud makes the comparison explicitly. Science, he alleges, has its "exact counterpart" in the state of maturity in which one has "renounced the pleasure principle, adjusted himself to reality and turned to the external world for the object of his desires" (1913, p. 90). All the more reason that psychoanalysis must be a science, and that, as Freud famously put it in a letter to Jung, "it is actually a cure by love" (McGuire, 1974, pp. 12–13; see also Nunberg and Federn, 1962, p. 101).

Love, in scientific, psychoanalytic terms, demands finding one's object of desire in the external world without using desire to impose illusory, systematic order on the world, that is, the object. And if it also demands renunciation of the pleasure principle, it necessarily implies an energics not governed exclusively by the idea of tension reduction (the psychic apparatus's purportedly original function of warding off stimulation), for the two are synonymous. Love, then, moves the psyche beyond both philosophy and mechanistic principles of energy regulation. This is the reason why the analyst cannot have a Weltanschauung, either clinically or theoretically. If the analyst has a consistent worldview, he will make the patient part of it, and then by definition will be narcissistically (or philosophically) involved with the patient. This would mean that the patient is not for the analyst an "external object," who in turn is suffering from an inability to love, and is therefore trapped by the mechanistic regulation of the pleasure principle. Without a scientific understanding of the relations between love and science, narcissism and Weltanschauungen, psychoanalysis could become one more philosophical system whose clinical effect would be to leave its patients within the mechanistic forms of energy regulation that are intrinsic to their psychopathology.

Freud was explicit about this potential danger to psychoanalysis, from both a clinical and an institutional point of view. In his lecture "The Question of a *Weltanschauung*" he repeated what we have seen in *Totem and Taboo*: the wishes that create the desire for a Weltanschauung are the same as those that create the "systems of religion and philosophy," and thus call for scientific study. But to allow such demands into the sphere of knowledge itself "would be to lay open the paths which lead to psychosis, whether to individual or group psychosis" (1933, p. 160). When he speaks of individual psychosis, Freud is referring to the possibility of a masked *folie à deux* in treatment, if the analyst makes the patient part of his Weltanschauung, as we have just outlined. When he speaks of group psychosis, the reference is to the creation of psychoanalytic "systems," a process that unfortunately has dominated the institutional history of psychoanalysis. A book like this one, from Freud's point of view, could serve to worsen an already crazy situation, by presenting psychoanalysis today as organized around competing systems, each one of which has to brand all the others insufficient. The challenge, also represented by a book like this one, is to integrate clinical and theoretical findings in a way that is psychoanalytically rigorous (or scientific or loving), precisely in a way that takes into account Freud's conception that Weltanschauungen are the antithesis of psychoanalysis. The "disruptive" approach I have chosen to begin with, then, is part of the attempt to refocus psychoanalysis on what is most challenging and disruptive in Freud's view of both clinical practice and theory building. For this reason too, I have chosen not to focus on the more expectable readings of Freud's cultural writings, in which he spells out many of the sociological implications of his thought. My emphasis is rather on the ways the clinical theory itself leads to a metapsychology that both requires reinterpretation and constantly pushes against the tendency to remold psychoanalysis into the habitual patterns of conscious perception.

The Centrality of Defense

If there is anything at all like a fundamental Freudian tenet, an organizing idea that remains consistent, that even produces Freud's opposition to worldviews, it is not wishes, drives, sexuality, the pleasure principle, or even the unconscious. It is defense. From first to last, Freud's originality, what makes Freud Freud and psychoanalysis psychoanalysis, is the concept of defense. In a recent article on the entire topic of defense, Vaillant (1992) made the same point, and cited Van der Leeuw (1971): "Defense had to be conceptualized before the concept of the unconscious could be introduced in psychoanalysis" (p. 51). Before the seduction theory, before the Oedipus complex and wish fulfillment, before any theory of psychic topography, Freud took the crucial step of differentiating himself from all other investigators of neurosis by reconceptualizing it in terms of defense in the 1894 paper "The Neuro-Psychoses of Defence." At the approximate midpoint of his psychoanalytic career, in 1914, Freud stated in "On the History of the Psychoanalytic Movement" that the theory of repression—i.e. defense—is "the cornerstone on which the whole structure of psychoanalysis rests" (1914b, p. 16). And his last, posthumous legacy to us, which he says might appear "long familiar and obvious," but is actually "entirely new and puzzling," is "The Splitting of the Ego in the Process of Defense" (1940b, p. 275). Defense is at the beginning, the middle, and the end. What does the central role of defense imply? That all psychopathology is an attempt to rid oneself of a reality that one finds unbearable, and that any theory of mind must account for the tendency to defense. This is yet another reason why Freud's hostility to Weltanschauungen is so intrinsic to his thought. A worldview, to the extent that it is consistent and logical, can be so precisely in the interest of defending against something unbearable: defenses and system building go hand in hand. When Freud compared system formation to secondary revision in dreams, and then compared both to forms of psychopathology ranging from the psychotic to the neurotic in *Totem and Taboo* , he was building distance from all systematicity into psychoanalytic theory. Wherever one finds systematicity, one can, from a psychoanalytic point of view, ask the question of what unbearable piece of reality is being defended against by means of the system.

Freud's broad perspective, that is, that dreams, psychopathology, religion, and philosophy all show a delusional systematicity in the interest of defense, demonstrates the larger import of all clinical work. The individual and social manifestations of defense must not be replicated by psychoanalytic theory and treatment. As a theory that postulates that defense and systematicity go hand in hand, psychoanalysis itself would have to be particularly attentive to this question. Again, one wonders whether this basic Freudian tenet is taken into account in the various psychoanalytic "systems." And if it is not, just as with the question of what kind of science Freud understood psychoanalysis to be, one has to wonder even more why this aspect of Freud's thought is eliminated from so many psychoanalytic debates. Perhaps this is the key to the phenomenon noted by Barratt, the ever renewed attempts to make psychoanalysis "conform to epistemological paradigms it transgresses." To found a theory of psychopathology and then of mind on the idea of defense is to create the necessity for a permanent irony about one's own theory, because of its possible defensiveness. The reintroduction of this irony into psychoanalytic theory would be another way its future belongs to its past.

The idea of defense also implies an ethical stance. If, in the broadest sense, all psychopathology is due to defense against an unbearable reality, then the reversal of psychopathology implies regaining contact with that reality. To keep to the formula about illness as the result of an inability to love, and to Freud's assertion that psychosis defends against an unbearable external reality, and neurosis against an unbearable internal reality (1924a, p. 149), both demand reconnection with the defended against reality in order to make love possible. In "The Loss of Reality in Neurosis and Psychosis" Freud modified his external/internal distinction between the reality defended against in each disorder, and emphasized that in *both* there is a fantasy-based substitution for it (1924b, p. 187). In terms of the linkage of secondary revision in dreams to system construction (*Totem and Taboo*), pathological substitute formation is just such an attempt to create an illusory order that replaces a disturbing and defended against reality. Such substitute formation always compromises the ability to love. Reversal of defensive, systematic substitutes always aims at love of reality—whether the reality of the external world or the reality of the internal world.

One could reconceptualize Freud's entire clinical and theoretical enterprise as a rethinking of three key terms—defense, love, reality. The theory of mind that results from the clinical practice revolving around these terms has to be an inferred energics if it is to account for them scientifically in terms of unconscious processes. This is the "knot" of Freud's work: its ethical stance in favor of reversing defense and embracing reality implies the scientific stance that always has an ironic distance from the data of conscious perception and from its own inferential theories of unconscious processes. This knot binds the clinician as much as it does the theoretician. It asks of the clinician that the patient become an object of scientific love. This means that the analyst always attempts to reverse those defensive processes that prevent the patient from embracing a piece of internal or external reality, while not engaging in the narcissistic gratifications of making this work confirm a system. Stated in such reduced fashion, this clinical-theoretical knot creates a double bind. It casts suspicion on every theoretical principle, while simultaneously advocating a theory of unconscious energic processes. It creates a clinical practice guided by the idea of defense while alleging that the same idea makes any overriding principle into the kind of "guidebook" Freud so consistently mocked.

Perhaps this double bind represents the kind of anxiety-producing reality that Freud asks us to embrace. Another reason to call psychoanalysis an impossible profession is that to embrace a double bind is to affirm apparently contradictory positions. But the embracing of double binds is exactly what both system building and conscious perception intrinsically screen out. Is it too fanciful to propose that what makes Freud still the most important psychoanalytic thinker is that more than anyone else, he has rigorously embraced such double binds as the very means to advance the theory and practice of psychoanalysis? The analogy to physics is tempting: such scientific advances as relativity and the discovery of radium led to the questioning of science itself. Certainly Freud wanted psychoanalysis to have a similar effect; thus his objections to the *uniform* explanations implicit in Weltanschauungen. Uniform explanations do not permit the embracing of contradictory positions. Of all the evidence that could be cited to support this view of Freud, I will offer a late epistolary exchange between him and Marie Bonaparte. It once more concerns physics, double binds, and the question of a Weltanschauung. On October 20, 1932, Bonaparte wrote to Freud that she had met Niels Bohr, another of the great fathers of quantum physics. Bonaparte was troubled by what Bohr told her, and wrote to Freud that she could not "accept one of the points of his theories which he explained to us: namely the 'free will' of the atom. The atom is now to be excluded from determinism" (Schur, 1965, p. 10). In other words, a double bind, like the kind induced by relativity and the discovery of radium: Bohr's physics put into question one of the underlying principles that had defined science, or at least classical science itself, namely, determinism. Freud wrote back to Bonaparte, "What you tell me about the great physicist is really very remarkable. It is here that the breakdown of today's *Weltanschauung* is actually taking place" (p. 11).

The general spirit of Freud's theory and clinical practice always implies the breakdown of a Weltanschauung, whether the Weltanschauung of individual psychopathology or the general Weltanschauung provided by consciousness and the data of perception. Freud's lifelong ability to subvert his own theories based on the difficulties and paradoxes of clinical practice—narcissism, the death drive, signal anxiety, and ego splitting are a few prominent examples—bear eloquent testimony to his embracing of contradictory positions as a condition of progress. Like any science, but particularly as the science of individual psychopathology, psychoanalysis must always become strange to itself if it is to be able to produce the therapeutic strangeness that modification of defensive systematicity always demands. Freud's stance was always to make reality strange as he revised our understanding of it by rethinking love and defense. One wonders whether psychoanalysis today can grasp Freud in this manner, such that what appears to be systematic dogma, particularly the theory of the drives, can be recaptured in its original strangeness.

Science and love, science and strangeness, defense against reality, expansion of the real through the reversal of defense: these are the coordinates of "my" Freud. (Another paper could be written about "the Freud" who is a shadow figure for each theorist in this volume.) In what follows I will attempt to "illustrate" these coordinates with some specific moments from Freud's work. "Illustrate" has to be put in quotation marks for the same reason that "clinical illustrations" always demand an ironic distance. Moreover, I will not "illustrate" in depth the systematic or even dogmatic Freud, who unfortunately is so often invoked in the debates over various systems and the therapeutic techniques that conform to and "confirm" them. As the scientific therapy that intervenes in defensive systematicity, psychoanalytic technique is optimally of a piece with the theory's antisystematic spirit, its push against the habitual forms of consciousness and perception in the direction of the strange and unfamiliar. My own conviction is that the future of the psychoanalytic enterprise depends on maintaining this general spirit of Freud's work.

Defense and "Posthumous Primary Processes"

The 1894 paper "The Neuro-Psychoses of Defence" is a remarkable document. Like so much of Freud's early work, it needs to be read not only for its specific concepts, but also for its adumbration of the general spirit of his theory and clinical practice. As already stated, the paper is significant because in it we see Freud differentiating himself from the other principal investigators of hysteria (including Breuer, the coauthor of *Studies on Hysteria*, which was still to be published) by the notion of defense. The characteristic "splitting of consciousness" and "formation of separate psychical groups" that most observers of hysteria already agreed on is due to "an occurrence of incompatibility . . . in their ideational life," Freud tells us. The hysteric is someone who has faced "an experience, an idea or a feeling which aroused such a distressing affect that the subject decided to forget about it, because he had no confidence in his power to resolve the contradiction between that incompatible idea and his ego by means of thought activity" (1894, p. 47). In this apparently simple description we find the germs of much that is to come. Neurosis is due to repression, to a forgetting motivated by the encounter with something that is traumatic because it is dissonant with the putatively normal state of consciousness. The double gesture that will direct the rest of Freud's thought is apparent here: to understand and treat neurosis one will have to stretch the limits of individual consciousness, which will in turn affect what we take to be mind in general. The entire theory will grow out of the idea that the encounter with whatever is incompatible, dissonant, or traumatic provokes defense.

The field of what is traumatic for the neurotic is quickly linked to sexuality. Freud cites first cases of hysteria, then of obsession, phobia, and even psychosis that show defense against incompatible experiences related to love and sexuality (1894, pp. 53–58). There is as yet no theory of why there might be an *intrinsic* link between sexuality and defense. But if this empirical observation is to hold, then the theory will have to explain how the basic tendency to defense is intrinsically linked to love and sexuality. The question becomes, what can make love and sexuality traumatic, incompatible with normal consciousness, subject to defense? And how can understanding what makes love and sexuality traumatic produce a theory of psychopathology and mind that is continuist, that sees common processes at work in neurosis *and* psychosis? For even at this early date, Freud views both neurosis and psychosis in terms of defenses against the internal or external realities of love and sexuality, and knows that such a continuist theory will teach us about the relations of mind and reality in general. The development of such a continuist theory will be Freud's focus for the rest of his life. By linking the question of love (the body) to the question of defense (the mind), Freud implicitly puts sexuality in the position of bridging any mind-body gap. Already, he says that defense against an incompatible sexual idea is a process that occurs "without consciousness," whose existence "can only be presumed" (1894, p. 53). Defensive maneuvers are comparable to "physical processes whose psychical consequences present themselves as if . . . the latter had really taken place" (p. 53). Thus, Freud lays the groundwork for a theory of automatic, nonconscious processes that have profound psychological effects, but that occur at the juncture of mind and body. The fact that such processes "can only be presumed" creates the necessarily inferential and ironic stance in theory building we have already discussed.

Freud concludes "The Neuro-Psychoses of Defence" with a statement that deserves to be quoted in full:

> I should like, finally, to dwell for a moment on the working hypothesis which I have made use of in this exposition of the neuroses of defence. I refer to the concept that in mental functions something is to be distinguished—a quota of affect or sum of excitation—which possesses all the characteristics of a quantity (though we have no means of measuring it), which is capable of increase, diminution, displacement and discharge, and which is spread over the memory-traces of ideas somewhat as an electric charge is spread over the surface of a body. This hypothesis, which incidentally, already underlies our theory of abreaction in our "Preliminary

Communication," can be applied in the same sense as physicists apply the hypothesis of a flow of electric fluid. It is provisionally justified by its utility in coordinating and explaining a great variety of psychical states.

(1894, pp. 60–61)

The reference is to the Breuer-Freud "Preliminary Communication" of 1893, which had outlined their joint theory of hysteria. The role of memory (hysterical symptoms as the symbols of memories so distressing that the subject cannot admit them into consciousness) and the therapeutic measure of full affective recall of these memories (abreaction) were the foci of that paper. The notion of defense was mentioned, but not given the specific etiological role it is given here. But Freud is reminding the reader that the basic hypotheses that hysterics possess a store of memories not available to consciousness and that treatment by recall reverses symptom formation already implied a theory of energic processes. Now he is telling us that even if the notion of defense was not intrinsic to the original Breuer-Freud theory, it will have to be integrated with the theory of memory and energic processes. Like the rest of Freud's metapsychology, this hypothesis is presented as "provisionally justified," because it "coordinates" and "explains" many psychic phenomena. It compares progress in physics with progress in what is not yet even called "psychoanalysis." Throughout the nineteenth century the study of electricity had been one of the great impetuses for theories of atomic structure, eventually yielding the strange results that led to the rethinking of science itself. This early metapsychological hypothesis pulls together the themes of love, defense, and reality in a theory of energic processes at the boundary of mind and body—the foundation of a strange psychological science.

Toward the end of 1895 Freud wrote what we today call the "Project for a Scientific Psychology," published posthumously. As Strachey says in his editor's introduction, "the *Project*, or rather its invisible ghost, haunts the whole series of Freud's theoretical writings to the very end" (1895, p. 290). It is an essential document for understanding the general "spirit" of Freud's work. And as Strachey's metaphor reminds us, to understand the "spirit" of a body of work is to compare that spirit to a "ghost" (in German the words are the same, *Geist*), a noncorporeal being that always comes back, that "haunts." In the "Project," one might say, Freud meets his own "ghost," comes to be haunted by new ways of thinking about love, defense, and reality that will come back throughout his work. Another way of putting the general question I am raising here is whether psychoanalysis, like Freud, still permits itself to be haunted by this "spirit."

The "ghost" enters the "Project" via the notions of primary and secondary process. Primary process is defined as the wishful, hallucinatory revival of the memory of a previous satisfaction (1895, pp. 319, 326–27). Hallucinatory recall of memories of previous satisfaction is a *perceptual* experience, and thus like the experience of dreams, which are wish fulfillments (1895, pp. 335–40.) (Note how early Freud understood the link between dreams, hallucinations, and wish fulfillment, well before the idea of even writing a book about dreams.) Without the ego's inhibition of this primary process, there is no way to distinguish between the perceptual experience of hallucinatory recall and the reality of the external world. The ego's secondary process is this inhibiting function (1895, p. 327). Thus, we already find here the bases for a theory of psychic "reality," *real* because it is *perceived* in dreams and hallucinations, and yet "unreal" because it seeks to eliminate the reality of painful experiences through the wishful revival of a previous satisfaction.

What is so important for the rest of the theory is that Freud conceives what he calls "primary wishful attraction" at the *origin of defense.* Just as wishes primarily replace pain with images of gratification, so defenses prevent energic investment in painful experience itself: "The wishful state results in a positive *attraction* towards the object wished for, or more precisely towards its mnemic image; the experience of pain leads to a repulsion, a disinclination to keeping the hostile mnemic image cathected. Here we have primary *wishful attraction* and primary *defence*" (1895, p. 322; Freud's emphasis). This theory shows clearly why Freud defined primary process in terms of the pleasure-unpleasure principle: wishes are the attempts to replace unpleasure with pleasure, defenses are the attempts to eliminate the registration of unpleasure per se. Thus, the basic conflict between the primary and secondary processes: the primary wishful-defensive process tends toward inertia (1895, p. 312), and uses discharge to eliminate whatever is dissonant, painful, or traumatic; the secondary process inhibits this functioning, allowing energic investment in the dissonant reality.

The way wish and defense complement each other to eliminate the traumatic makes it possible to understand why the theory of psychopathology yields a new theory of mind that has to explain resistance to whatever is construed as painful or dissonant. When Freud calls "primary defense" the "first biological rule" (1895, pp. 370–71), he situates the pathological processes at the juncture of mind and body in the larger context of mind's conservative tendencies. Certainly such processes are

framed in terms of a classical conception of energy: the tendency to inertia is given a "biological" cast. While there are many more questions
raised than answered by such a conception, one must not overlook that
it explains why the hallucinatory perception of wishes can substitute for
the perception of whatever is not in accord with wishes in the interests of
defense. Freud's later linkage of system building, wish fulfillment, and defense has its basis in this early assertion that the tendency toward inertia
leads to substitution of primary process for whatever is experienced as
dissonant or traumatic. Such processes are at work in all pathological
substitute formation.

How does all of this concern love and sexuality? There is not yet in
Freud's theory the juxtaposition of wish fulfillment with sexuality itself,
but rather the observation that hysterical symptoms are the result of an
attempted repression of memories of incompatible sexual experiences,
ideas, or feelings. Such symptoms are understood by Freud as *symbols* of
the repressed memories. These symptomatic symbols are formed by the
primary process in the same way dreams are: the complementary push
and pull of wish and defense create a hallucinatory substitution for the
incompatible sexual material (1895, pp. 353–55). Here, Freud puts a
crucial question to himself. Is there some particular characteristic that
would explain why in hysteria symptomatic symbol formation always
concerns sexuality? Using the example of his patient Emma's symptomatic inability to enter shops alone, Freud finds a chain of both conscious and repressed memories concerning adolescent sexual excitement
in shops and a childhood memory of a shopkeeper grabbing at her geni-
tals through her clothing (1895, pp. 353–54). Freud's contention is that
the earlier repressed memory *became* traumatic when the patient reached
puberty and could experience sexual excitement. The memory of the assault by the shopkeeper becomes incompatible and traumatic, calling for
repression and symbolic substitution after the fact: "Here we have the
case of a memory arousing an affect which it did not arouse as an experience, because in the meantime the change [brought about] in puberty
had made possible a different understanding of what was remembered.
. . . We invariably find that a memory is repressed which has only become
a trauma by *deferred action*" (1895, p. 356). Sexuality then, because of
the delay in its development, makes it possible for childhood memories
to become traumatic enough for the adult to produce a neurosis: "*The
retardation of puberty makes possible posthumous primary processes*"
(1895, p. 359; Freud's emphasis). Even before the theory of endogenous

infantile sexuality, sexuality itself makes possible those peculiar memory processes intrinsic to neurosis, particularly the complex interactions of present and past governed by the primary tendency to defense. Sexuality is the physiological process that specifically brings delayed, defensive reactions to memory into the heart of psychopathology and the new theory of mind.

The famous seduction theory advanced in the 1896 lecture "The Aetiology of Hysteria" in no way contradicts these basic premises. Freud reminds his audience that there is something "astonishing" in the fact that hysterical symptoms have to do with memory, and with the interaction of memories of present and past (1896, p. 197.) (Freud's astonishment here reminds us of what I call the "original strangeness" of his theory.) Again, it is sexuality that explains why such processes occur. Freud makes a point of emphasizing that the conscious sexual memories of puberty symbolically expressed in symptoms are themselves not usually traumatic, and yet have a traumatic impact (1896, pp. 200–201.) (This is one element of what is "astonishing.") Now the linkage of sexuality, memory, and defense takes Freud back to early childhood, to *repressed* memories of infantile seductions. Repression is as central to the theory as are the actual seductions: the infantile sexual material must be present in the form of *unconscious* memories (1896, p. 211). The trivial sexual experiences of puberty *become* traumatic because of their associative connection to the repressed infantile memories. Again, it is a question not so much of the original pathological effect of the seduction, but of how the *memory* of it may produce the adult symptom "posthumously" (1896, p. 213), as in the "Project." (That memories can posthumously have a greater traumatic impact than the event itself is what is most astonishing.) The actual content of the sexual memories has a particularly shocking form. Because of the child's sexual immaturity, the seductions "include all the abuses known to debauched and impotent persons, among whom the buccal cavity and the rectum are misused for sexual purposes" (1896, p. 214). This apparently empirical observation will become theoretically momentous. Psychopathology will also have to concern itself with perversion, with memories of oral and anal sexuality. What Freud calls here the "future psychology of the neuroses" will have to elaborate the intrinsic connections between perverse seductions, unconscious memory, and defense—"a psychology of a kind for which philosophers have done little to prepare the way for us" (1896, p. 219).

Freud's assertion that the reality of infantile seductions was *the* specific etiological precondition for future neurosis was dubbed by him "an important finding, the discovery of a *caput Nili* in neuropathology" (1896, p. 203). Here we have the positivist, if not dogmatic, Freud, the seeker of singular causes, grounding principles, facts that seem to produce systematic consistency. However, the theory as already developed, such that sexuality and memory are brought together in terms of primary wish fulfillment and defense in order to explain the "posthumous" effect of early experience, belies the positivistic logic of systematic consistency. Thus, it will not be the role of repressed memories of perverse seductions that will change when Freud "abandons" the seduction theory, but rather the "discovery" of infantile seductions as the psychopathological equivalent of the discovery of the source of the Nile. (This is why Freud is perfectly consistent in maintaining his lifelong interest in the role of infantile seductions in neurosogenesis. For a survey of most of the major passages that demonstrate that Freud never abandoned his interest in seduction per se, see Robinson, 1993.) But the tension between a simplistic positivism and complex science will remain in Freud's work until the end. For those who wish to discredit Freud's theories, this tension will always make it possible to find a strain of dogmatic "scientism" in them, while Freud himself continues to develop an extremely sophisticated theory that often far outstrips his most "up-to-date" critics. The extraordinary task Freud set himself—to explain the "energics" of mind such that "posthumous primary processes" become comprehensible—places him far beyond a positivistic framework.

Perversion and Science

Perversion plays an increasingly pivotal role in Freud's efforts to understand mind and psychopathology in terms of the energics of posthumous primary processes. In July 1897, more than a year after postulating the seduction theory, and a few months *before* its abandonment as the single etiological source of neurosis (in the well known letter of September 21, 1897), we find the following in the Fliess letters:

> the defense against memories does not prevent their giving rise to higher psychic structures, which persist for a while and then are themselves subjected to defense. This, however, is a most highly specific kind—precisely as in dreams, which contain . . . the psychology of the neuroses in general. What we are faced with are falsifications of memory and fantasies. . . . I know roughly . . . why they are stronger than genuine memories, and I have

learned new things about the characteristics of the processes in the Ucs. *Alongside these, perverse impulses arise*; and when as later becomes necessary, these *fantasies and impulses are repressed*, the higher determinations of the symptoms already following from the memories make their appearance.   (Masson, 1985, p. 255)

Paraphrased, these few dense sentences state that psychic structure formation includes defended against memories, and that structure itself may be defended against to the extent that it contains such material. This process is to be found in dreams. Because defense and memory are so intertwined in the formation of psychic structure, distorted memories and fantasies play a greater role in its formation than actual memory, as already established in the "Project" and "The Aetiology of Hysteria." While these processes occur, perverse impulses—that is, the entire range of sexual wishes not included under the rubric of "normality"—are active. Such impulses are conjoined to the fantasy material characteristic of unconscious processes. As structure formation proceeds, with renewed defensive efforts, the conjoined perverse and fantasy material is repressed, creating the possibility for the later neurotic symptom.

Thus, even before the official "abandonment" of the seduction theory, Freud adds the element of perverse *wishes* to the basic understanding of sexuality and memory, of "posthumous primary processes." It is but a short step from here to the idea that the infantile wishes in dreams and neurosis are themselves perverse. The theory of perversion, then, will have to be central to the psychoanalytic understanding of love, sexuality, defense, mind, and reality.

The word itself is difficult. Etymologically, "perversion" has an undeniable moral charge. Another of the double binds Freud asks us to embrace is to keep the word, and yet free it from its conventional moral overtones. The entire *Three Essays on the Theory of Sexuality* (1905) is devoted to demonstrating that what is conventionally considered the exception, perversion, is actually the norm. To the extent that we have all been children, and have gone through the long period of the development of our sexuality that the usual, "normal" adult picture masks, we are all perverse. Neurosis eventually reveals that adult conflicts in love and sexuality are due to the kind of defensive reactions to fantasy and perverse impulses already understood in 1897. Those who are manifestly perverse have less become so than remained so (1905, p. 172). (Eventually Freud was to expand his understanding of perversions themselves, and the complex psychodynamics that create and sustain them.) The overall point is that intrinsically perverse infantile sexuality pulls together the theory of neurosis based on defense, wish, fantasy, and memory. The Freudian theory of love and the inevitable defenses against it stands on the two ideas that sexuality can produce delayed effects and that it is universally perverse.

Freud was well aware of the problematic nature of the word. Reviewing the crucial role of perversion in his thinking much later, he wrote,

> The detaching of sexuality from the genitals has the advantage of allowing us to bring the sexual activities of children and of perverts into the same scope as those of the normal adult. . . . Looked at from the psychoanalytic standpoint, even the most eccentric and repellent perversions are explicable as manifestations of the component instincts of sexuality which have freed themselves from the primacy of the genitals and are now in pursuit of pleasure on their own account as they were in the very early days of the libido's development. The most important of these perversions, homosexuality, scarcely deserves the name. . . . If I have described children as "polymorphously perverse," I was only using a terminology that was generally current; no moral judgement was implied. . . . Psychoanalysis has no concern whatever with such judgements of value.   (1925, p. 38)

More emphatically, Freud's message is that the ethical stance in favor of reversing defense inevitably reveals the workings of the infantile, perverse past in the reality of everyone's love life. "Judgments of value" would be like "systems," that is, essentially animistic (narcissistic) constructions whose very consistency—like "normal, adult sexuality"—depends upon maintaining a defensive stance in relation to perversion and fantasy. As science, and particularly as a scientific therapy, psychoanalysis not only cannot be systematic, it also embraces the perverse. Here, I am deliberately extending the literal meaning of perversion in its sexual sense into the metaphoric sense of what might be called "perverse science." Literally, as a therapy of neurosis, psychoanalysis undoes defenses against perversion; metaphorically, as the theory of mind that pushes against the habitual organizing forms of consciousness and perception, it "perverts" them, and is always ready to "pervert" itself. The double bind of perversion, that the supposed abnormal exception is the universal, that a moral term understood psychoanalytically undermines systematic morality, is one of the most essential aspects of what I am calling the "spirit" of Freud's work.

To be haunted by this spirit always means coming back to the perverse, in its most specific and general senses. Most of the advances in

Freud's thought come about through returns to the conjoined issues of perversion and defense. An expansion of the theory of the ego comes about in just this way. In the initial period of his psychoanalytic work, Freud seemed to be fascinated by the fantasy and wishful *content* organized by the repression of perverse infantile sexuality, as "posthumously" revealed by adult neurosis. After the very detailed theory of the ego developed in the "Project," Freud did not pay much attention to defensive process and the ego per se. A turning point comes with "On Narcissism" (1914a). Freud characteristically begins by considering narcissism as a perversion (1914a, p. 73). It is the very possibility that one may treat one's own body as a sexual object, and then the integration of this specific perversion with the entire theory of infantile sexuality (in terms of a "phase" of narcissistic object choice) that bring the development of the ego back into fundamental theory. One of the first results of this expansion is the understanding of psychosis and animism as examples of libidinal overinvestment in the ego, as initially broached in *Totem and Taboo*. As this idea became a definitive part of the theory of psychopathology and of mind, the theory of defense also had to change.

Freud knew that the ideas of libidinal investment of the ego and of narcissistic object choice were also a perversion of his theory thus far: as the agent of repression, the ego was the "enemy" of libido. Now we learn that repression itself cannot be divorced from the ego's perverse self-love, its self-aggrandizement, the formation of its own ideal: "the formation of an ideal heightens the demands of the ego and is the most powerful factor favoring repression" (1914a, p. 95). Narcissism as the most powerful factor favoring repression plays a double role. On the one hand, it is the outcome of Freud's continuist theory of psychopathology, for the narcissism revealed by the study of psychosis gives greater insight into the foundation of the theory of the neuroses: "Just as the transference neuroses have enabled us to trace the libidinal instinctual impulses, so dementia praecox and paranoia will give us an insight into the psychology of the ego" (1914a, p. 82). The narcissism that leads to the defensive withdrawal from external reality in psychosis is then the precondition for the later defensive withdrawal from internal reality in neurosis, that is for repression. On the other hand, as the precondition for repression, the theory of narcissism itself begins to "pervert" the way repression organized the theory of mind, psychopathology, and treatment. Even if Freud distinguished between the transference neuroses and the narcissistic neuroses as those treatable by analysis and those not, he begins to elaborate a theory of the narcissism intrinsic to neurosis. Once one understands the narcissistic components of neurosis and repression, one has a deeper insight into the systematicity found in all pathological substitute formation. As we have seen, such considerations hold as much for the general theory of psychoanalysis as they do for the specific theory of psychopathology. By introducing narcissism as the key to the study of the ego, and as an essential factor in all psychopathology, Freud "perverts" the tendency to make repression—until now "the cornerstone on which the whole structure of psychoanalysis rests"—into another "*caput Nili* in neuropathology." Narcissism becomes the precondition of the cornerstone, a "source" before the "source." It is no accident that in the context of this perversion of his own theory, Freud makes one of his most forceful statements about psychoanalysis not having a "logically unassailable foundation." Psychoanalysis, he says, will have to progress in the same way as "is happening in our day in the science of physics, the basic notions of which . . . are scarcely less debatable than the corresponding notions in psychoanalysis" (1914a, p. 77).

There is a clinical problem embedded in this theoretical expansion. If the transference neuroses are the disorders treatable by analysis, and the narcissistic disorders those not, what about the narcissistic components of neurosis? If interpretation of repressed contents is the specific therapeutic modality in the transference neuroses, do the narcissistic components of neurosis take care of themselves as analysis resolves defenses against love? Or can one learn from psychosis, from whatever therapeutic measures might be effective in its treatment, more about what actually happens in the treatment of the neurosis via interpretation? There are no definitive answers to such questions in Freud's work, another source of the complicated reactions to it. Until the end, one finds both repeated statements that successful treatment demands the lifting of infantile repressions and an increasingly sophisticated elaboration of the continuist theory of defense and psychopathology, which would imply an equally sophisticated rethinking of analytic technique.

There are two "perversions" of his previous theories in Freud's late work that would be central to such a rethinking of psychoanalytic treatment. These are the theory of the death and life drives and the theory of disavowal and ego splitting. Each has major ramifications for the general theory of mind and the general conception of psychoanalytic technique, although Freud did not spell them out in detail. And both developments have the capacity to make psychoanalysis into an even stranger science, since both begin to account in new ways for how psychopathology reveals the inherently conservative processes that resist expanding what we think of as reality.

Beyond the Pleasure Principle is famous as one of Freud's most troublesome texts. However, the closest readers have pointed out that the introduction of the death drive is not as startling—or dismissible—as is sometimes thought. Strachey's editor's introduction makes the basic point that much of Freud's thinking in *Beyond* is based on the "Project" (1920, p. 6). In our terms here, then, in *Beyond* Freud continues in the spirit of his work, and encounters again the "ghost" that had haunted him since the writing of the "Project." As we have seen, in that work Freud understood primary process as tending toward inertia. The pleasure-unpleasure principle expressed this tendency as "primary wishful attraction and primary defense." The introduction of the death drive in 1920 is actually a reformulation of this basic idea. As the embodiment of mind's tendency toward tension reduction, toward repetition of a previous state of satisfaction, the death drive expresses the conservative side of the drives in general, "the urge inherent in organic life to restore an earlier state of things" (1920, p. 36). However, the paradox that had been implicit in this theory finally becomes evident: the very continuity between understanding the wish as the repetition of a previous satisfaction and the death drive as the force of repetition and tension reduction makes it look as though the death drive *is* the drive in general.

The way out of this paradox was indicated by Hans Loewald: "the death instinct is nothing startlingly new in Freud's theory. The constancy or unpleasure principle always regulated the psychic apparatus and in that sense was intrinsic to it. . . . What *is* new in Freud's new instinct theory and in the structural theory is the life instinct as an intrinsic motive force of the psyche paired with the death instinct" (1980, p. 79.) (Loewald's thinking here demands comparison with Laplanche's equally compelling discussion of the relations between the constancy principle, the tendency to tension reduction, and the death drive; see Laplanche, 1976, chap. 6.) Although Freud twists and turns in his late work when he speaks of the relation between the death drive and the pleasure principle, there is a clear line of thought that supports Loewald's contention. Eros, the life instinct, becomes the embodiment of change in the psychic apparatus, the nonconservative force that Freud had not considered up to this point. Sexuality is again the key to understanding the life drive: "union with the living substance of a *different* individual increases tensions, introducing what may be described as fresh '*vital differences*'" (1920, p. 55; my emphasis). The contrast is made more explicit in *The Ego and the Id*:

> If it is true that . . . [the] principle of constancy governs life, which thus consists of a continuous descent toward death, it is the claims of Eros, of the sexual instincts, which, in the form of instinctual needs, hold up the falling level and introduce fresh tensions. The id, guided by the pleasure principle—that is, by the *perception of unpleasure*—fends off these tensions in various ways.   (1923, p. 47; my emphasis)

The clearest statement about Eros as a source of change, of differentiation, and about the death drive as the conservative principle of return to a less differentiated state comes in the posthumous *Outline of Psychoanalysis* : "the death instinct fits in with the formula . . . that instincts tend towards a return to an earlier state. In the case of Eros (or the love instinct) we cannot apply this formula. To do so would presuppose that living substance was once a unity which had later been torn apart and was now striving towards reunion" (1940a, p. 149). What is new about Eros, to continue Loewald's train of thought, is that it introduces a principle of change, of "vital differences," of sexuality and love as something other than reunion in the service of tension reduction. The wish, precisely because it works as repetitive reunion with a previous experience, operates in opposition to Eros. Sexuality itself may serve either to reduce or to increase tension, to dedifferentiate or to differentiate. To the extent that all psychopathology is rooted in repetition of the past, and that perverse infantile sexuality is the somatopsychic pathway of unconscious, "posthumous" memory, psychopathology itself implies the "perversion" of differentiation, that is, varying degrees of replacing differentiation with wishful repetition. The theory of the life and death drives itself "increases the tension" of the double binds implicit in Freud's understanding of sexuality and perversion: sexuality now can intrinsically serve both life and death, differentiation and dedifferentiation. As psychopathology is rethought in terms of life and death, differentiation and dedifferentiation, the psychoanalytic process has to be rethought accordingly. The basic therapeutic task of reversing defensive substitute formation and expanding the real now implies that the analytic process aims to reverse the wishful tendency toward nondifferentiation, toward the dominance of tension reduction. One can view such a rethinking of therapy as an expansion of the idea discussed above that as a science, psychoanalysis is a cure by love, with love now reconceptualized as the capacity to increase the tension of differentiation.

The "perversion" of sexuality implied by the theory of the life and death drives, the understanding that it serves the ends of differentiation and nondifferentiation, tension increase and tension reduction, change and reunion, applies equally to the ego. Starting with *The Ego and the Id*, Freud places increasing emphasis on the unconscious aspects of the ego, meaning the ego's defensive operations (1923, pp. 17–18). The idea that anxiety functions as a signal of danger, of an impending and possibly traumatic increase of tension, also leads to a renewed emphasis on *defensive process*. Repression itself becomes one of a panoply of defenses carried out against whatever aspects of internal or external reality provoke the "perception of unpleasure." Thus, Freud again is actually reviving the basic theory of the "Project": defense as "the first biological rule." The ego's defensive operations are unconscious in the late theory for the same reason as they are in the earliest theory. They serve the primary process, the reduction of tension by attempting to eliminate the reality of whatever is perceived—rightly or wrongly—to increase tension traumatically. Once defensive process is unconscious and serves tension reduction, it too basically works in the interest of death. This is why Freud can finally say that the ego's self-preservative functions work in the interest of Eros (1940a, p. 148), inherently dividing the ego between life and death. To return to our initial problematic, one can infer that if defense serves nondifferentiation, and if defenses go hand in hand with system building and Weltanschauungen, then the therapeutic stance in favor of life, differentiation, and Eros would have to take a critical stance toward any worldview.

In line with the "perversion principle" in Freud's work, it is a new insight into a specific perversion that leads to his final statement about defensive process. The posthumous "Splitting of the Ego in the Process of Defense" generalizes a line of thought from "Fetishism" (1927). Freud's new insight is that the specific defense of disavowal explains the dynamics of fetishism. Disavowal describes the way the ego can first register something that would cause it unpleasure, and then replace the distressing reality with a perceived fantasy, as in the fetishist's demand that an actual object be there, present, *perceivable* in order to assuage castration anxiety. But the fetishist's anxiety about the distressing reality does not simply disappear. The fetishist has a "divided attitude": his ego is split between the distressing reality and the replacement for it (1927, p. 156). By the time Freud wrote the *Outline of Psychoanalysis*, he realized that the way disavowal explained fetishism was also the key to a continuist theory of psychopathology in terms of defensive process. Returning to the comparisons of neurosis and psychosis that had preoccupied him from the beginning, he began to rethink defense itself in terms of the dynamics of fetishism:

> The view which postulates that in all psychoses there is a *splitting of the ego* could not call for so much notice if it did not turn out to apply to other states more like the neuroses and finally, to the neuroses themselves. I first became convinced of this in cases of *fetishism*. . . . It must not be thought that fetishism presents an exceptional case as regards a splitting of the ego; it is merely a particularly favourable subject for studying the question. . . . Whatever the ego does in its efforts of defence, whether it seeks to disavow a portion of the real external world [psychosis] or whether it seeks to reject an instinctual demand from the internal world [neurosis], its success is never complete and unqualified. The outcome always lies in two contrary attitudes. (1940a, pp. 202–4)

That disavowal is intrinsic to defensive process, such that there is always a "splitting of the ego in the process of defense," is what Freud calls "new and puzzling" in the paper of the same name (1940b, p. 275). How can we understand what seemed new and puzzling in this modification of the theory of defense at the end of Freud's life? He is aware that it might also appear "old and familiar," as old as the idea of defense itself. Certainly a description of defensive process that shows how in both neurosis and psychosis, and now in perversion as well, fantasy replaces a distressing internal or external reality corresponds to the overall trend of Freud's entire corpus. What is new is that disavowal and ego splitting as intrinsic to defense itself go very far in replacing repression as the "cornerstone" of the theory of defense and of psychic structure. (Several authors, myself among them, recently have begun to analyze the way in which disavowal leads to a fundamental shift in Freud's conception of defense; see Bass, 1991, 1993; Brook, 1992; Morris, 1993). Just as the perversion of narcissism had led to understanding a precondition of repression, so the perversion of fetishism leads to another precondition: there is first disavowal and splitting of the ego, and then the defensive operations that lead to neurosis (repression) or psychosis. Moreover, as a description of the way fantasy replaces a distressing reality, disavowal unites the operation of wish and defense in the service of tension reduction and nondifferentiation. This implication of his theory is not spelled out by Freud, but is consistent with his late theorizing. Disavowal describes from the vantage of defense the way in which Eros, tension increase, or differentiation is the basic reality registered by the psychic apparatus, and potentially experienced as a threat that calls for replacement by "primary wishful attraction and primary defense." It is now disavowal that describes the workings of "primary defense."

The rethinking of the bases of psychopathology and the aims of treatment in terms of the conflict between differentiation and nondifferentiation is congruent with the rethinking of defense in terms of disavowal and ego splitting. Neurosis, psychosis, and perversion can be reinterpreted in terms of both ego and id being split in varying degrees between self-preservation and defense, tension increase and tension reduction. Narcissism, too, can be reinterpreted as a self-love which creates the systematic belief that tension reduction is self-preservation. In other words, defense itself is unthinkable without significant narcissistic and fetishistic components.

What does psychoanalytic technique look like in these terms? Generally, I think that an increased emphasis on process is the inevitable outcome of the shift away from understanding psychopathology and psychic structure in terms of repressed fantasy content. Fantasy itself, of course, has to be made conscious to the extent that it is defended against; interpretation of content remains the specific means for doing so. However, once one understands that disavowal and ego splitting contribute to the construction of wish and fantasy themselves, and that the use of fantasy to create belief in the possibility of systematic substitution for a distressing reality is one of the functions of narcissism, it can no longer be assumed that making defended against fantasy conscious is the sole therapeutic task. Rather, the ongoing *defensive process* in which wishes and fantasies repetitively replace whatever form of differentiation has become too anxiety-provoking becomes the focus of treatment. To a certain extent this is a modification of an ego psychological approach to psychoanalytic treatment, with the major difference that differentiating processes, and the defenses against them, are understood as being unconscious. All psychopathology in this conception represents a balance in favor of nondifferentiation and tension reduction, in other words, death. As the scientific cure by love, analytic technique then is geared toward changing the balance in favor of life, of Eros as tension increase and differentiation. Analytic love, then, remains the opposite of seduction, whether in the overt sense or in the more usual, and insidious seduction into narcissistic investment in a system and a worldview. Neutrality remains the basic stance of the analyst, particularly as the therapeutic task becomes one of changing the basic balance of psychic energy in favor of Eros without seduction into the illusions of narcissistic systematicity. However, as interventions become more precisely geared to defensive process, analysts can become more flexible about which technical approaches have the best chances of modifying the particular patterns of energic investment in the substitutions for a defended against reality.

The life of psychoanalysis, like any life in Freud's conception, is a constantly resisted encounter with a differentiating, tension-increasing reality, with internal division, and with double binds. And if there is no life that can avoid such encounters, then like Freud it has to embrace being "haunted" by them. Freud's opposition to the idea of a psychoanalytic Weltanschauung, I have been contending, needs to continue to haunt psychoanalysis if the understanding of defense, love, and the perversion of the real as the basic stance of science is also to remain alive in psychoanalysis. To be haunted by Freud, who himself was haunted by the ideas of "primary wishful attraction and primary defense," is essential to the *life* of psychoanalysis.

REFERENCES

Barratt, Barnaby. 1984. *Psychic Reality and Psychoanalytic Knowing.* Hillsdale, NJ: The Analytic Press.

Bass, Alan. 1991. Fetishism, reality and "The Snow Man." *American Imago* 48:295–328.

———. 1993. Psychopathology, metaphysics. *American Imago* 50:197–225.

Brook, J. A. 1992. Freud and splitting. *International Review of Psychoanalysis* 19:335–50.

Freud, S. 1894. The neuro-psychoses of defence. In S.E., vol. 3.

———. 1895. Project for a Scientific Psychology. In *Standard Edition of the Complete Works of Sigmund Freud.* London: Hogarth Press (hereafter cited as S.E.), vol. 1.

———. 1896. The aetiology of hysteria. In S.E., vol. 3.

———. 1905. *Three Essays on the Theory of Sexuality.* In S.E., vol. 7.

———. 1913. *Totem and Taboo* . In S.E., vol. 13.

———. 1914a. On narcissism: An introduction. In S.E., vol. 14.

———. 1914b. *On the history of the psychoanalytic movement.* In S.E., vol. 14.

———. 1920. *Beyond the Pleasure Principle.* In S.E., vol. 18.

———. 1921. Psychoanalysis and telepathy. In S.E., vol. 18.

———. 1923. *The Ego and the Id.* In S.E., vol. 19.

———. 1924a. Neurosis and psychosis. In S.E., vol. 19.

———. 1924b. The loss of reality in neurosis and psychosis. In S.E., vol. 19.

———. 1924c. The resistances to psychoanalysis. In S.E., vol. 19.

———. 1925. *An Autobiographical Study.* In S.E., vol. 20.

———. 1926. *Inhibition, Symptom, and Anxiety.* In S.E., vol. 20.

———. 1927. Fetishism. In S.E., vol. 21.

———. 1933. *New Introductory Lectures on Psychoanalysis.* In S.E., vol. 22.

———. 1940a. *An Outline of Psychoanalysis.* In S.E., vol. 23.

———. 1940b. The splitting of the ego in the process of defense. In S.E., vol. 23.

Laplanche, Jean. 1976. *Life and Death in Psychoanalysis.* Baltimore: Johns Hopkins University Press.

Loewald, Hans. 1980. *Papers on Psychoanalysis.* New Haven: Yale University Press.

Masson, Jeffrey, ed. 1985. *The Complete Letters of Sigmund Freud to Wilhelm Fliess.* Cambridge: Harvard University Press.

McGuire, William, ed. 1974. *The Freud/Jung Letters.* Princeton: Princeton University Press.

Morris, Humphrey. 1993. Narrative representation, narrative enactment, and the psychoanalytic construction of history. *International Journal of Psychoanalysis* 74:33–54.

Nunberg, H., and Federn, E., eds. 1962. *Minutes of the Vienna Psychoanalytic Society.* Vol. 1. New York: International Universities Press.

Pais, Abraham. 1986. *Inward Bound.* New York: Oxford University Press.

Robinson, Paul. 1993. *Freud and His Critics.* Berkeley: University of California Press.

Schur, Max, ed. 1965. *Drives, Affects, Behavior.* New York: International Universities Press.

Vaillant, George. 1992. The historical origins and future potential of Sigmund Freud's concept of the mechanisms of defense. *International Review of Psychoanalysis* 19:35–50.

Van Der Leeuw, P. J. 1971. On the development of the concept of defense. *International Journal of Psychoanalysis* 52:51–58.

Contributors

C. *Fred Alford*, Ph.D., is a professor of government at the University of Maryland, College Park. He is the author of dozens of articles and five books applying psychoanalysis to social theory, including *Melanie Klein and Critical Social Theory*, *The Psychoanalytic Theory of Greek Tragedy*, and *Group Psychology and Political Theory*. He is a member of the A. K. Rice Institute, and a frequent consultant to what are often called Tavistock groups.

Alan Bass, Ph.D., is a practicing psychoanalyst in New York City. A member of the International Psychoanalytic Association and the New York Freudian Society, he is on the faculties of the Institute for Psychoanalytic Training and Research, the National Psychological Association for Psychoanalysis, and the New York Center for Psychoanalytic Training. The author of many essays, he is also known for his translations of works by Jacques Derrida.

Cynthia Burack is an assistant professor of political science at the Center for Women's Studies and Gender Research at the University of Florida. She is the author of *The Problem of the Passions: Feminism, Psychoanalysis, and Social Theory* and articles in feminist theory and psychoanalysis.

Martha E. Edwards, Ph.D., is a faculty member at the Ackerman Institute for Family Therapy in New York and a classical Adlerian psychotherapist in private practice.

Michael Eigen, Ph.D., is a senior faculty member and a control/training analyst at the National Psychological Association for Psychoanalysis and faculty supervisor at the New York University Postdoctoral Program for Psychoanalysis and Psychotherapy. He is the author of *The Psychotic Core*, *Coming through the Whirlwind*, and *The Electrified Tightrope*.

Gerald J. Gargiulo, M.A., is associate editor of the *Psychoanalytic Review* and immediate past president of the National Psychological Association for Psychoanalysis Training Institute. He is currently president of the International Federation for Psychoanalytic Education as well as honorary research fellow in psychoanalysis at the University of Kent in England. A member and training analyst of the International Psychoanalytical Association, he has authored numerous articles on English object relations theory. He practices in Greenwich, Connecticut, and East Hampton, New York.

James S. Grotstein is a clinical professor of psychiatry at UCLA School of Medicine, and a training and supervising analyst at the Los Angeles Psychoanalytic Institute and the Psychoanalytic Center of California. He is the author of *Splitting and Projective Identification*, *The Borderline Patient*, and *Fairbairn and the Origin of Object Relations*.

Edith Kurzweil, Ph.D., is a university professor of social thought at Adelphi University. She is the editor of the *Partisan Review* and the author of a number of books, including *The Freudians: A Comparative Perspective* and *Freudians and Feminists*.

Paul Marcus, Ph.D., is a member of the National Psychological Association for Psychoanalysis and founder of its Center for the Psychoanalytic Study of Social Trauma. He is coeditor of *Psychoanalytic Reflections on the Holocaust: Selected Essays, Healing Their Wounds: Psychotherapy with Holocaust Survivors and Their Families*, "Bruno Bettelheim's Contribution to Psychoanalysis" (a special issue of the *Psychoanalytic Review*), and two psychoanalytically informed children's books, among other works.

Marion M. Oliner, Ph.D., is a practicing psychoanalyst in New York City. She is a supervising and training analyst at the New York Freudian Society, a member of both the National Psychological Association for Psychoanalysis and the International Psychoanalytic Association. She is the author of *Cultivating Freud's Garden in France* and numerous articles about a variety of clinical subjects.

Paul H. Ornstein, M.D., is a professor of psychoanalysis, department of psychiatry, University of Cincinnati, and codirector of the International Center for the Study of Psychoanalytic Self Psychology. He is a training and supervising analyst at the Cincinnati Psychoanalytic Institute and is in part-time private practice in psychoanalysis. He has edited and introduced four volumes of Heinz Kohut's *Search for the Self.*

Michelle Price, C.S.W., is a faculty member and supervisor at the American Institute for Psychoanalysis of the Karen Horney Psychoanalytical Center and a faculty member of the Mt. Sinai School of Medicine. She is the director of the Treatment Center for Incest and Abuse at the Karen Horney Clinic and has written a number of scholarly articles on childhood sexual abuse, postmodernism, and gender.

Paul A. Roth, Ph.D., is a professor of philosophy at the University of Missouri-St. Louis. He is the author of *Meaning and Method in the Social Sciences: A Case for Methodological Pluralism* and a number of scholarly papers aimed at developing an account of narrative as a form of explanation in history, anthropology, and psychoanalysis.

Alan Rosenberg is an assistant professor of philosophy at Queens College, City University of New York. He is the coeditor of *Echoes from the Holocaust: Philosophical Reflections from a Dark Time* and *Healing Their Wounds: Psychotherapy with Holocaust Survivors and Their Families.*

Louis A. Sass, Ph.D., is a professor of clinical psychology at Rutgers University. He is the author of *Madness and Modernism: Insanity in the Light of Modern Art, Literature, and Thought* and *The Paradoxes of Delusion: Wittgenstein, Schreber, and the Schizophrenic Mind.* He has also coedited *Hermeneutics and Psychological Theory.*

Henry T. Stein, Ph.D., is a classical Adlerian psychotherapist in private practice, and director of the Alfred Adler Institute of San Francisco. He was trained by Sophia de Vries and Anthony Bruck, both of whom studied with Alfred Adler. After twenty years of professional collaboration with de Vries, he published an audiocassette study-consultation program, *Classical Adlerian Psychotherapy: A Socratic Approach*, which is the first full-lenghth documentation of Adler's original style of psychotherapy. Since 1991 he has been spearheading the Adlerian translation project.

Murray Stein, Ph.D., is the editor of *Jungian Analysis* and of many volumes, including the *Chiron Clinical Series.* He is the author of *In Midlife, Jung's Treatment of Christianity*, and *Solar Conscience Lunar*

Conscience. He is a training analyst at the C. G. Jung Institute of Chicago.

M. Guy Thompson, Ph.D., received his analytic training from R. D. Laing and his associates at the Philadelphia Association in London. He is a faculty member of the California School of Professional Psychology and the Wright Institute and the founder and director of Free Association. He is the author of *The Death of Desire: A Study in Psychopathology* and *The Truth about Freud's Technique: The Encounter with the Real*.

Warren Wilner, Ph.D., is a faculty member and supervisor in the postdoctoral programs of Adelphi University and New York University and at the Manhattan Institute for Psychoanalysis. He is also the supervising analyst at the William Alanson White Institute.

Index

Made in the USA
Las Vegas, NV
08 April 2022

47101812R00277